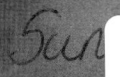

Economics
Student Workbook and Reader

FIFTH EDITION

John Sloman
Mark Sutcliffe
University of the West of England

FT Prentice Hall
FINANCIAL TIMES

An imprint of Pearson Education
Harlow, England · London · New York · Boston · San Francisco · Toronto · Sydney · Singapore · Hong Kong
Tokyo · Seoul · Taipei · New Delhi · Cape Town · Madrid · Mexico City · Amsterdam · Munich · Paris · Milan

Pearson Education Limited
Edinburgh Gate
Harlow
Essex CM20 2JE
England

and Associated Companies throughout the World.

Visit us on the World Wide Web at:
www.pearsoned.co.uk

First edition published 1991
Second edition published 1994
Third edition published 1997
Fourth edition published 2000
Fifth edition published 2003

© John Sloman and Mark Sutcliffe 1991, 2003

The rights of John Sloman and Mark Sutcliffe to be identified as authors of this work have been asserted by them in accordance with the Copyright, Designs and Patents Act 1988.

All rights reserved. No part of this publication may be reproduced, stored in a retrieval system, or transmitted in any form or by any means, electronic, mechanical, photocopying, recording or otherwise, without either the prior written permission of the publisher or a licence permitting restricted copying in the United Kingdom issued by the Copyright Licensing Agency Ltd, 90 Tottenham Court Road, London W1T 4LP.

ISBN 0-273-65864-6

British Library Cataloguing-in-Publication Data
A catalogue record for this book can be obtained from the British Library

10 9 8 7 6 5 4 3 2
08 07 06 05 04

Typeset by 35 in 8/12 pt Stone Serif
Printed and bound in Great Britain by Henry Ling Ltd., at the Dorset Press, Dorchester, Dorset

Contents

	Preface	iv
	Acknowledgements	vii
1	Introducing Economics	1
2	Supply and Demand	13
3	Government Intervention in the Market	31
4	Background to Demand	43
5	Background to Supply	58
6	Profit Maximising under Perfect Competition and Monopoly	79
7	Profit Maximising under Imperfect Competition	93
8	Alternative Theories of the Firm	104
9	The Theory of Distribution of Income	116
10	Inequality, Poverty and Policies to Redistribute Incomes	134
11	Markets, Efficiency and the Public Interest	147
12	Applied Microeconomics	165
13	The National Economy	186
14	Unemployment and Inflation	197
15	The Open Economy	208
16	The Roots of Modern Macroeconomics	220
17	Short-run Macroeconomic Equilibrium	229
18	Money and Interest Rates	243
19	The Relationship between the Money and Goods Markets	256
20	Fiscal and Monetary Policy	270
21	Aggregate Supply, Unemployment and Inflation	290
22	Long-term Economic Growth and Supply-side Policies	306
23	International Trade	321
24	The Balance of Payments and Exchange Rates	336
25	Global and Regional Interdependence	351
26	Economic Problems of Developing Countries	363

Preface

TO THE STUDENT

Welcome to this *Economics Workbook and Reader*. We hope that the book will help to make your study of the fascinating subject of economics both enjoyable and thought provoking and that it will improve your ability to analyse the economic problems faced by individuals and nations: problems that we hear about daily in the news or come across in our own lives.

Studying economics can be much more rewarding if it is not just seen as a body of knowledge to absorb. Applying the theories, working through problems, analysing data, examining and discussing case studies, gathering information, scouring newspapers, reports and official publications and debating with other students can all help to bring the subject alive. This *Workbook and Reader* will give you the opportunity to do all these things.

The book may be used with any introductory text, although it is specifically designed to be used with John Sloman, *Economics* (5th edition). Each chapter in the *Workbook and Reader* corresponds to a chapter in the main text.

Each chapter is divided into five sections: (A) Review, (B) Problems, exercises and projects, (C) Discussion topics and essays, (D) Articles, (E) Answers. Between them, these sections will help you prepare for all types of examination and assessment currently used at first-year degree level and A level, and on BTEC and professional courses.

Review

This section takes you step-by-step through the material covered in the respective chapter of *Economics* (5th edition), using a mixture of narrative and short questions.

The questions are of seven different types, six of which are signified by symbols.

Multiple choice

These are set out in the standard multiple-choice format. In virtually all cases there are five alternative answers and you are required to circle the correct one. The questions are typical of those used at first-year degree level and at A level.

Written answer

These require you to give one or two words or sentences. Sometimes there will be a list of points for you to give.

Delete wrong word

These are sometimes *true/false* questions, sometimes *yes/no* questions, or sometimes deleting one of two or more alternative answers.

Diagram/table manipulation

These involve you completing a diagram or table, or reading things off a diagram or table.

Calculation

These involve short mathematical calculations, usually just simple arithmetic, but in some of the optional, starred questions (see below) they involve simple differentiation.

Matching/ordering

These are of two types. The first involves matching a set of definitions to a set of descriptions, or a set of answers to a set of questions. The second involves putting a set of points or events into the correct order.

The final type of question is embedded in the narrative, and involves you deleting the wrong word, phrase or sentence from two or more alternatives given.

Some questions are starred. These are on additional topics and may be omitted if desired.

Problems, exercises and projects

This section consists of longer, multi-part questions, often involving simple calculations or the manipulation of graphs. There are also questions involving the gathering and analysis of data. These 'mini-project' questions can be set by your tutor as an assigned piece of work, to be done either individually or in groups. The information gathered can then be used for in-class discussions.

Discussion topics and essays

These questions, as the name suggests, can be used for practice in writing essays or making essay plans (which will help you prepare for exams), or for discussion with fellow students. Most of the questions in this section are designed to raise issues of policy or controversy, and thus should be more stimulating than the more purely descriptive, theoretical or analytical questions sometimes used for essays. The last question in this section is usually a motion for a debate.

Articles

This section consists of newspaper, magazine or journal articles (normally three per chapter). We have written a brief introduction to each article and a set of short questions at the end of each one. These articles help to relate the economic theories you have studied to topical issues and events.

Answers

Full answers *plus*, where appropriate, full explanations are given to all section A questions. These will help you check on your understanding as you work your way through the relevant chapter of the main text. They allow section A to be used as a comprehensive revision tool.

TEACHING AND LEARNING: A NOTE TO TUTORS

In devising this Workbook and Reader, we intended that it should be both an independent study tool for the student and also a useful teaching aid for tutors. Sections A to D can all be used in a classroom context, adding variety and spice to the delivery of economic principles and policy. Outlined below are some suggestions for ways in which you might use the various sections.

Review

The main purpose of this section is to help reinforce students' learning and understanding of key principles by putting them to use in answering simple questions. The questions are built up in a sequence that mirrors that in the main text.

In addition to being used as a learning tool by students and as a useful revision and practice aid for exams, these questions could also be used in class. Students might be asked, either prior to the class meeting, or in the first part of the class, to complete a set number of questions from this section. Then, preferably in small groups, they would attempt to identify the definitive answer. Groups would be expected to explain the reasoning behind the answers they had chosen.

Alternatively, at the end of a lesson (lecture, seminar or class), a short test based on questions in this section could be set. This would be quick to administer and mark, and give you feedback on the success of your lesson in meeting its objective(s). With the answers provided to all section A questions at the end of each chapter, students could mark each other's work.

Problems, exercises and projects

As the title of this section suggests, there are three types of question to be found here.

- Multi-part problems. These longer questions provide ideal material for use in very large workshops (of up to 200 students). We have been running workshops similar to these for a number of years and find them very popular with students and a good medium for learning and applying basic economic concepts. Students can work through these multi-part questions (or a portion of them), discussing them with their neighbours as they do so, and then the lecturer can go through the answers from the front. If you leave one row free in every three in the lecture theatre, tutors can go round giving help to students if they are stuck. This is a good way of using postgraduate teaching assistants. Answers to these questions are given on the CD.
- Exercises. Many of these questions require students to look up data or other information from books or electronic media. They are best set in advance of the lesson, unless information collection is one

of its main purposes. Once the information has been collected, however, students could work in small groups to devise answers to the questions. This is a very effective way of stimulating debate and discussion.
- Mini projects. These involve students gathering information, sometimes by field work, and then writing a small report or considering a question relating to the information obtained. Again, this work could be done in small groups.

These last two types of question also lend themselves well to group presentations, which help to develop useful communication skills. As part of their presentation, students could be required to consider the method(s) by which they solve problems and construct answers. Telling others how they approached such issues also helps to develop useful skills for themselves and their audience.

The questions in this section also lend themselves very well to being used as assigned pieces of work. They generally require of the student a greater depth of understanding than section A questions.

Discussion topics and essays

These questions can be set as essays, or they can be used as the basis of class discussion. Why not, mid-way through a lecture, or class, following a particular point of theory, pose one of the questions for students to discuss and to ascertain its relevance to what they have just been taught. For example, you have introduced your students to the idea of profit maximisation. You now want them to consider its relevance to real-world business decision making. Ask them the following discussion question:

Imagine you were the managing director of a fashion house producing expensive designer clothing. What achievements of you and your company would give you special satisfaction?

After a short period of time ask the supplementary question:

Are the achievements consistent with profit maximisation?

You can then proceed to discuss alternative theories of the firm and students can debate whether managerial utility maximisation might be more relevant as a goal of business rather than the maximisation of profit.

The last question in section C is usually a debate. We suggest that the debate is conducted as formally as possible, with two student proposing the motion and two opposing it. After the formal speeches we suggest that the debate is opened to question and/or contributions from the floor. Finally the proposer and opposer could give a concluding speech. By conducting the proceedings formally, you can develop an atmosphere of theatre, with students acting parts. This can make the learning environment fun.

Articles

The application of economic principles and theory to the world around us is often the most stimulating way to teach economics. Students not only come to understand economic principles better but can identify their relevance to events and issues.

The articles in this section have been carefully selected for their relevance to material covered in the chapter. Many are case studies which illustrate theory or discuss particular economic problems or policies. They are particularly suitable for using in class-based work. The articles tend to be short, and the questions at the end address both points of comprehension regarding the article, and the relevance of the article to economic concepts and theory. Small-group work is particularly successful when using such material. For example, students could be assigned to read one or more articles before the class and have some preliminary thoughts about the questions, and then, in groups of three or four, they could come up with agreed answers. The class as a whole could then debate the answers of the different groups.

ACKNOWLEDGEMENTS

The whole team at Pearson Education has been very helpful and we have really appreciated everyone's hard work. A particular thanks to Catherine Newman, the book's editor, for her encouragement and good humour, and to Karen Mclaren for meticulously guiding the book through production. Most of all, we owe the book to the unfailing support of Alison and Sheila and the rest of our families.

John Sloman and Mark Sutcliffe
UWE Bristol, January 2002

Acknowledgements

We are grateful to the following for permission to reproduce copyright material:

National Statistics for Table 8.2 from *Financial Statistics*, Table 10.2 from *Family Spending*, Table 14.1 from *Labour Market Trends* and Table 15.3 from *Monthly Digest of Statistics*, Crown copyright material is reproduced with the permission of the Controller of Her Majesty's Stationery Office and the Queen's Printer for Scotland; Office of European Publications for the European Communities for Tables 17.7 and 17.8 from *Statistical Annex of the European Economy*, Spring 2002; Organisation for Economic Co-operation and Development for Tables 21.2 and 21.3 from *Economic Outlook*.

Guardian Newspapers Ltd for the articles 'Blair to launch "fairer" student finance system' by Nicholas Watt from *The Guardian* 14.2.02, 'EU ready for battle over fish policy' by Andrew Osborn from *The Guardian* 19.4.02, 'British Gas feels the heat after 10% price rise' by Felicity Lawrence from *The Guardian* 9.1.02, '100m more must survive on $1 a day' by Charlotte Denny and Larry Elliott from *The Guardian* 19.6.02 and 'Why the poor are picking up the tab' by Larry Elliott from *The Guardian* 1.6.98, © The Guardian; Philip Allan Updates for the article 'Why study economics?' by Alan Hamlin from *Economic Review* Vol. 14, No. 1, September 1996; The Economist Newspaper Limited for the articles 'Lurching ahead' from *The Economist* 29.11.01, 'The London effect' from *The Economist* Web site July 2001, 'Biology meets the dismal science' from *The Economist* 25.12.93, 'An insurer's worst nightmare' from *The Economist* 29.7.95, 'Untangling e-conomics' from *The Economist* 21.9.00, 'Dedicated followers of fashion' from *The Economist* 23.12.95, 'An unsettling settlement' from *The Economist* 8.11.01, 'Race, sex and the dismal science' from *The Economist* 6.6.98, 'Investing in people' from *The Economist* 26.3.94, 'Is Santa a deadweight loss?' from *The Economist* 20.12.01, 'Fixing for a fight' from *The Economist* 18.4.02, 'The end of privatisation?' from *The Economist* 13.6.98, 'A blunt tool' from *The Economist* 28.1.01, 'Great expectations, and rational too' from *The Economist* 14.10.95 and 'Making aid work' from *The Economist* 14.11.98, © The Economist Newspaper Limited, London; Financial Times for the articles 'Chip overload puts sector under pressure' by Paul Abrahams and Alexander Harney from *Financial Times* 2.9.01, 'Crisis call to coffee growers' by Mark Mulligan and Andrew Bounds from *Financial Times* 16.4.02, 'Users focus sharply on cost cuts and flexibility' by Penelope Ody from *Financial Times* Web site 5.12.01, 'Grasping the nettle' by Alan Pike from *Financial Times* Web site 28.11.01, 'Policy seen as complex and failing its target audience' from *Financial Times* 14.3.02, 'Taxation road to nowhere' by Richard Tomkins from *Financial Times* 2.9.99, 'Alternatives to inflation targets' by Samuel Brittan from *Financial Times* 1.3.01, 'Voices in the air' by Samuel Brittan from *Financial Times* 2.9.99, 'In praise of the international monetary non-system' from *Financial Times* 28.3.94 and 'The heart of the new world economy' by Martin Woolf from *Financial Times* 1.10.97, © *Financial Times*; OFGEM for the article 'OFGEM sets out future of regulation in gas and electricity supply' from the OFGEM Web site; News International for the articles 'Battle lines are drawn for EU farm reforms' by Rory Watson from *The Times* 28.6.02 and 'Should the Tories claim credit for Labour's economic success?' by Anatole Kaletsky from *The Times* 3.4.01, © Times Newspapers Limited; Reuters Reprint Management Services for the article 'Microsoft slashes European Xbox prices. US next?' by Ben Berkowitz and Scott Hillis from Reuters Web site 18.4.02; Institute for Public Policy Research for the articles 'Governance and stakeholding' by Rajiv Prabhaker from *New Economy* Vol. 5, No. 2, June 1998, 'Is NAIRU worth a can of beans?' by Geoffrey Dicks and John O'Sullivan from *New Economy* August 1999 and 'Social exclusion and urban policy' by Peter Lee from *New Economy* August 1999; Haymarket Publishing Services Limited for the articles 'The business of fast growth: the secrets of hypergrowth' by David Smith from *Management Today* February 1996, 'The low-inflation challenge' by David Smith from *Management Today* March 1995, 'Nirvana is not so unattainable' by David Smith from *Management Today* August 1999 and 'The balance of trade' by Robin Niblett from *Management Today* December 1995; Confederation of British Industry for the articles 'Different combinations' from *CBI News* March 1998 and 'The critical difference' from *CBI News* July/August 1999; Her Majesty's Stationery Office for the article 'The Low Pay Commissions 2000 Report on the UK National Minimum Wage'; Independent Newspapers (UK) Limited for the articles 'Successive generations of children may be "learning to be poor"' by Cherry Norton from *The Independent* 29.3.99, 'Toasters, PCs, radios: everything must go in the EU recycling bin. But who foots the bill?' by Stephen Castle from

The Independent 9.4.02, 'Currency bomb is still ticking' by Lea Patterson from *The Independent* 30.6.98, 'The City: a British success or a study in failure?' by Jeremy Warner from *The Independent* 27.10.01, 'Free-trade supporters must speak frankly' by Diane Coyle from *The Independent* 13.9.99 and 'The real cost of IMF rescue deals' by Gavyn Davies from *The Independent* 16.11.98; Organisation for Economic Co-operation and Development for the articles 'Who pays the highest income tax?' from *OECD Observer* Summer 1999 and 'Poland: privatisation as the key to efficiency' from *OECD Observer* August/September 1998; the author, Oliver Tickell for the article 'Stream of abuse' by Oliver Tickell from *The Guardian* 4.3.98; Institute for Economic Affairs for the article 'The case for road pricing' by Alan Day from the *Journal of the Institute of Economic Affairs* Vol. 18, No. 4, December 1998, first published by the Institute of Economic Affairs, London, 1998; the author, Marc Lopatin for the article 'The crisis – a crash course in globalisation' by Marc Lopatin from *Independent on Sunday* 13.11.98; Investors Chronicle for the articles 'Minding the output gap mythology' by Dan Oakley from *Investors Chronicle* 5.4.96, 'Wall Street's Faustian pact' by Dan Oakley from *Investors Chronicle* 31.5.02, and Merrill Lynch, Pierce, Fenner & Smith Incorporated for the figure "Merrill Lynch survey of eurozone fund managers May 2002; quality of earnings in terms of transparency, predictability and volatility" published in *Investors Chronicle* May 2002, and 'No silver lining' by Dan Oakley from *Investors Chronicle* 15.3.02; Macmillan Magazines Limited for the article 'Progress and pitfalls along the path towards a "greener" method of calculating national productivity' from *Nature* Vol. 395, pp. 428–9, October 1998, © 1998 Macmillan Publishers Ltd; Social Market Foundation for the article 'The death of work has been greatly exaggerated' by Mauricio Rojas from *Millennium Doom – Fallacies about the End of Work*; the author, Tony Thirlwall for the articles 'Inflation is no devil in monetary policy detail' by Tony Thirlwall from *The Guardian* 24.12.01, © Tony Thirlwall 2001, 'Free lunch as Keynes makes a comeback' from *The Guardian* 7.4.94, 'Why the government needs to get real on economic policy' from *The Guardian* 5.10.98; Business Week for the articles 'There's a cloud inside that silver lining' from *Business Week* 11.3.02, 'The twin deficits are back – and as dangerous as ever' from *Business Week* 8.7.02, 'So much for discipline' by John Rossant and David Fairlamb from *Business Week* 3.6.02 and 'When everything is made in China' by Jeffrey E. Garten from *Business Week* 17.6.02; the author, Stephen Timewell for the article 'How the internet redefines banking' by Stephen Timewell and Kung Young from *The Banker* June 1999; Bank of England for the articles 'Understanding broad money' by Ryland Thomas from *Bank of England Quarterly Bulletin* May 1996 and 'Money, aggregate demand and prices' by Mervyn King from *Bank of England Quarterly Bulletin* August 1994; the author, Edmond Warner for the article 'The danger of growing up quickly' from *The Guardian* 4.9.99; the author, Wynne Godley for the article 'Kick-start strategy fails to fire spluttering US economic motor' by Wynne Godley from *The Guardian* 21.1.02, © Wynne Godley 2002; the authors Juli Collins-Thompson, Simon Rubinsohn, Ian McCafferty and Michael Hume for the article 'Four economists have a say on Brown's measures' from *Financial Times* 18.4.02, © Juli Collins-Thompson, Simon Rubinsohn, Ian McCafferty and Michael Hume; Oxford University Press and the British Computer Society for the article 'Skills shortage or productivity gap?' by John McDermid from *Computer Bulletin* March 2001; United Press International for the article 'US steel protectionism angers' by Shihoko Goto from *The Washington Times* 27.3.02; Oxfam Publishing for the articles 'Time for a Tobin Tax? Some practical and political arguments' from *Oxfam Discussion Paper*, May 1999 and 'Farmers, food and the WTO' from Oxfam Web site 23.6.98.

Every effort has been made by the publisher to obtain permission from the appropriate source to reproduce material which appears in this book. In some instances we have been unable to trace the owners of copyright material, and we would appreciate any information that would enable us to do so.

Chapter One

1

Introducing Economics

A REVIEW

In this first chapter we start by looking at the subject matter of economics. What is it that economists study? How is the subject divided up? What makes a problem an *economic* one?

Although all countries face economic problems, they nevertheless tackle them in different ways. In some countries the government plays a major role in economic decision making. In others decisions are left much more to individuals. Section 1.2 examines how these different types of economy operate.

We then turn to examine types of reasoning employed by economists. Do economists proceed like natural scientists, or does being a *social* science make economics different from subjects like physics and chemistry? We also examine the extent to which economists can contribute to policy making. Can economists tell governments what they *ought* to do?

1.1 What do economists study?

(Page 4) Economists study many issues, but all of them stem from the central economic problem of *scarcity*. Scarcity occurs because there are not enough resources (labour, land and capital) to produce everything that people would like.

Q1. The problem of scarcity is *directly* relevant:
A. only to those times when rationing has been enforced.
B. only to developing countries low in resources.
C. only to those on low incomes.
D. only to those periods of history before mass production.
E. to all countries and all individuals.

Q2. The problem of scarcity will eventually disappear with the development of new technology and resulting higher levels of production. *True/False*

(Page 4) In order to tackle the problem of scarcity, societies produce goods and services for people to consume. This production involves using various resources or *factors of production*.

Q3. It is normal to group factors of production into three broad categories. These are:

1. ....

2. ....

3. ....

Q4. Which one of the following would *not* be classified as a factor of production?
A. Jim Bodget, a bricklayer for a local construction firm.
B. The cement mixer Jim uses.
C. The cement Jim puts in the mixer.
D. The building site Jim works on.
E. The wage Jim gets paid at the end of the week.

Multiple choice | Written answer | Delete wrong word | Diagram/table manipulation | Calculation | Matching/ordering

2 CHAPTER 1 INTRODUCING ECONOMICS

(Page 5) One way of understanding the problem of scarcity is in terms of *potential demand and supply*. Potential *demand* relates to the **Q5.** *wants/needs* of individuals, whereas potential *supply* is determined by **Q6.** *the level of resources available/the amount that consumers demand*.

(Pages 5–7) Because of scarcity, people are concerned that society should produce *more* goods and that the resources should be used as *fully* as possible. This is the subject of **Q7.** *microeconomics/macroeconomics*. But given that enough can never be produced to satisfy *potential demands*, choices have to be made: *what* items to produce and in what quantities, *how* to produce them and *for whom*. These choices between alternatives are the subject of **Q8.** *microeconomics/macroeconomics*.

Q9. Which of the following are macroeconomic issues and which are microeconomic ones?
(a) The level of government spending. *micro/macro*
(b) A grant given by the government to the UK film industry. *micro/macro*
(c) The level of investment in the UK by overseas firms. *micro/macro*
(d) The price of cotton cloth. *micro/macro*
(e) The rate of inflation. *micro/macro*
(f) The average wage rate paid to textile workers. *micro/macro*
(g) The total amount spent by UK consumers on clothing and footwear. *micro/macro*
(h) The amount saved last year by households. *micro/macro*

(Page 7) Choices involve sacrifices or *costs*. If as a society we consume more of one good or service then, unless there are idle resources, we will be able to consume less of other goods and services.

Q10. The cost of one good measured in terms of what we must sacrifice is called the:
A. real cost.
B. opportunity cost.
C. average cost.
D. potential cost.
E. social cost.

Q11. Economists assume that economic decisions are made *rationally*. In the case of consumers, rational decision making means:
(a) That consumers will not buy goods which increase their satisfaction by just a small amount. *True/False*
(b) That consumers will attempt to maximise their individual satisfaction for the income they earn. *True/False*
(c) That consumers buy the sorts of goods that the average person buys. *True/False*
(d) That consumers seek to get the best value for money from the goods they buy. *True/False*
(e) That consumers compare (maybe very casually) the cost of an item they are purchasing with the benefit they expect to gain from it. *True/False*

(Pages 8–9) When we make rational choices, what we are in fact doing is weighing up the marginal benefit of each activity against its marginal (opportunity) cost. If the marginal benefit (i.e. the *extra* benefit of doing a *bit more* of the activity) exceeds its marginal cost (i.e. the extra cost of doing a bit more), it is rational to choose to do that bit more.

Even though we may not be conscious of doing so, we apply this marginal analysis on a regular basis in our day-to-day decision making.

Q12. Which one of the following statements is *not* an example of marginal analysis?
A. If I eat another chocolate bar, I might be sick.
B. If mortgage rates rise by another 1 per cent, some people will no longer be able to afford the repayments.
C. If a firm earns more from selling its products than they cost to produce, it will make a profit.
D. If J. Bloggs (Warehousing) Ltd buys a new forklift truck of the latest design, it should be able to stack another 500 pallets per day.
E. Fitting flue gas desulphurisation equipment to a coal-fired power station in Britain producing x kilowatts will reduce the costs of acid rain pollution in Scandinavia by £y.

(Pages 10–13) One way in which scarcity, choice and opportunity cost can all be illustrated is via a *production possibility curve*. This depicts a simplified world in which a country produces just two goods. The curve shows all the possible combinations of the two goods that the country can produce in a given period of time.

Figure 1.1 shows the production possibility curve for a country that can produce various combinations of two goods X and Y.

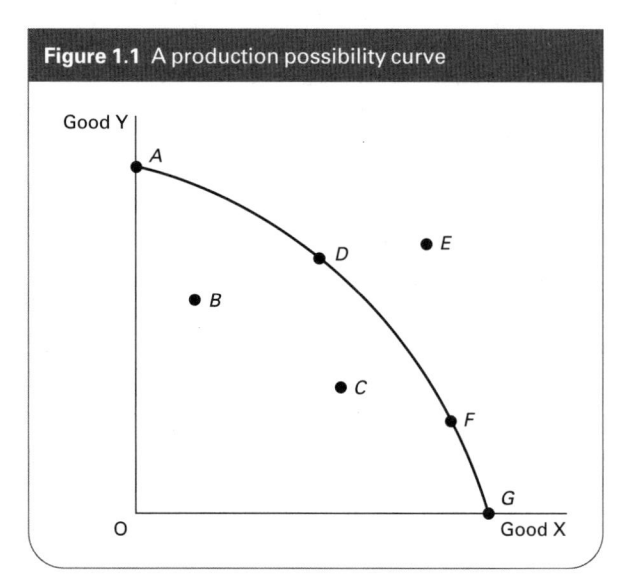

Figure 1.1 A production possibility curve

⊖ **Q13.** Which point or points illustrate a situation:

(a) Which is efficient? ....

(b) Which is inefficient? ....

(c) Of complete specialisation? ....

(d) Which is unobtainable? ....

Moving from one point to another round a production possibility curve illustrates the concept of opportunity cost.

▤ **Q14.** Figure 1.2 shows a production possibility curve. Production is currently at point A. The opportunity cost of producing one more unit of good X is:
- *A.* 10 units of X.
- *B.* 1 unit of X.
- *C.* 8 units of Y.
- *D.* 6 units of Y.
- *E.* 2 units of Y.

Figure 1.2 Production possibility curve

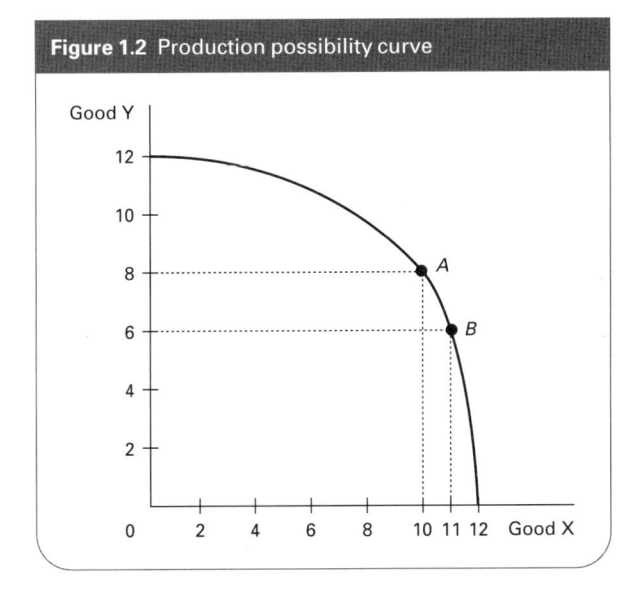

(?) **Q15.** A production possibility curve is typically drawn bowed outward from the origin. This illustrates

....

▤ **Q16.** Figure 1.3 shows a country's production possibility curves for two years, 2000 and 2003. The production point shifts outward from point A in 2000 to point B in 2003. The following are possible things that might have happened:
 (i) Potential output has increased.
 (ii) Actual output has increased.
 (iii) A fuller use has been made of resources.
Which is correct?

Figure 1.3 Production possibility curves for two years

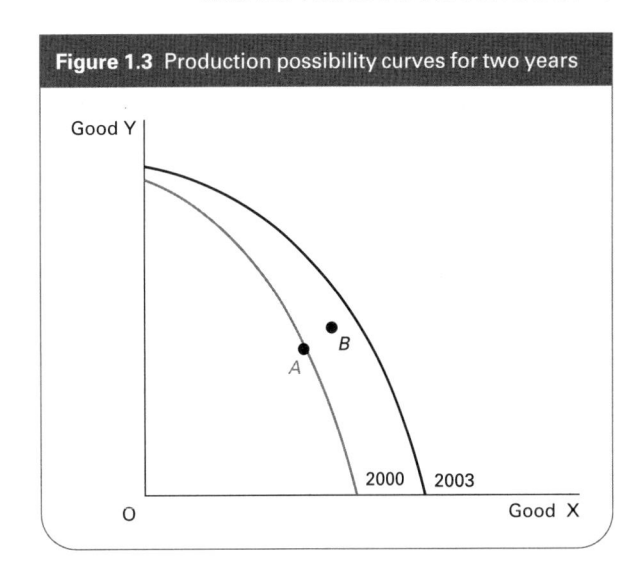

- *A.* (i), (ii) and (iii).
- *B.* (i) and (ii), but not (iii).
- *C.* (ii) and (iii), but not (i).
- *D.* (ii), but not (i) or (iii).
- *E.* It is impossible to say from the information given.

▤ **Q17.** Which one of the following would directly lead to an outward shift of a country's production possibility curve?
- *A.* An increase in the population of working age.
- *B.* A reduction in the level of unemployment in the economy.
- *C.* A reduction in value added tax and duties on petrol and alcohol.
- *D.* An increase in the general level of prices.
- *E.* A reduction in government expenditure on education.

A production possibility diagram can illustrate the distinction between microeconomics and macroeconomics.

◐ **Q18.** Which of the following are microeconomic and which are macroeconomic issues?
(a) Whether the production possibility curve shifts outwards over time. *micro/macro*
(b) Whether the economy is operating on the production possibility curve or inside it. *micro/macro*
(c) The choice whether to produce more X and less Y, or more Y and less X (i.e. where to produce on the production possibility curve). *micro/macro*

(Pages 13–14) Another diagram that can be used to illustrate the distinction between micro- and macroeconomics and the process of satisfying consumer wants is the *circular flow of income diagram*. It shows the inter-relationships between firms and households in a money economy. A simplified circular flow diagram is illustrated in Figure 1.4.

4 CHAPTER 1 INTRODUCING ECONOMICS

Figure 1.4 The circular flow of incomes and of goods and services

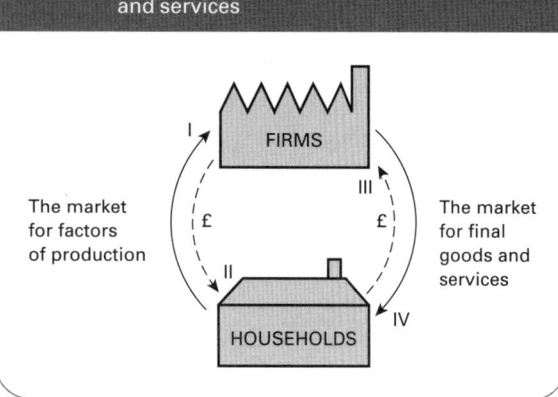

Q19. Which flow (I, II, III or IV) illustrates each of the following?
(a) Goods and services. *I/II/III/IV*
(b) Wages, rent, profit and interest. *I/II/III/IV*
(c) Factor services. *I/II/III/IV*
(d) Consumer expenditure. *I/II/III/IV*

1.2 Different economic systems

(Pages 15–16) Different countries tackle the problem of scarcity in different ways. One major way in which the economic systems of countries differ is in the extent to which they rely on the market or the government to allocate resources.

Q20. At the one extreme is the *full command economy*. Here all decisions concerning *what* should be produced, *how* it should be produced, and *for whom* are made by

....

Q21. At the other extreme is the completely free-market economy. Here all economic decisions are made by

....

(Pages 16–17) There are a number of potential advantages of a command economy.

Q22. Which one of the following is *not* a potential advantage of a command economy?
A. The planning authority can obtain an overall view of the whole economy and ensure a *balanced* expansion of its various parts.
B. Resources can be distributed according to need.
C. The system of planning can ensure that producers respond automatically to consumer wishes.
D. Resources can be diverted from consumption to investment if it is desired to increase the rate of economic growth.
E. Unemployment can be avoided.

Q23. Name two potential *disadvantages* of a pure command economy.

1. ....

2. ....

(Pages 17–20) In a totally free-market economy the questions of *what*, *how* and *for whom* to produce are determined by the decisions of individual households and firms through the interaction of demand and supply. In goods markets households are **Q24.** *suppliers/demanders/price setters*, whereas in factor markets households are **Q25.** *suppliers/demanders/neither suppliers nor demanders* of factor services.

Demand and supply are brought into balance by the effects of changes in price. If supply exceeds demand in any market (a surplus), the price will **Q26.** *rise/fall/stay the same*. This will lead to **Q27.** *a rise in the quantity both demanded and supplied/a fall in the quantity demanded and supplied/a rise in the quantity demanded but a fall in the quantity supplied/a rise in the quantity supplied but a fall in the quantity demanded*. If, however, demand exceeds supply in any market (a shortage), the price will **Q28.** *fall/rise/stay the same*. This will lead to a **Q29.** *fall/rise* in the quantity demanded and a **Q30.** *fall/rise* in the quantity supplied. In either case the adjustment of price will ensure that demand and supply are brought into equilibrium, with any shortage or surplus being eliminated.

Goods and factor markets are linked. A change in demand or supply in one market will stimulate changes in other markets.

Q31. If the demand for houses rises, how will this affect the wages of bricklayers?

....

Provided there are many firms competing in each market, the free-market economy can be claimed to lead to a number of advantages.

Q32. These include:
(a) A lack of bureaucracy in economic decision making.
True/False
(b) Producers respond to changes in demand and consumers respond to changes in supply. *True/False*
(c) The competition provides an incentive for producers to be efficient. *True/False*
(d) The interaction of demand and supply ensures that resources are equally distributed. *True/False*
(e) Firms will produce goods that are desirable for society, since only such goods can be sold profitably.
True/False

(Pages 20–2) In reality no economy is a completely planned or completely free market. All economies are *mixed*. The

mixture of government and the market varies, however, from one economy to another. It is thus the degree and form of government intervention that distinguishes one type of economy from another.

Q33. List three different ways in which the government can intervene.

1. ....
2. ....
3. ....

1.3 The nature of economic reasoning

(Pages 22–3) The methodology used by economists has much in common with that used by natural scientists. Like natural scientists, economists construct *models*.

Q34. Which one of the following is *not* true of economic models?
A. They simplify reality.
B. They provide an explanation of the cause of certain economic phenomena.
C. They enable predictions of the 'if . . . then . . .' variety to be made.
D. They are constructed by conducting experiments under controlled conditions.
E. They can be tested by appealing to the facts.

Building models involves a process known as **Q35.** *deduction/induction*, whereas using a model to make a prediction involves a process known as **Q36.** *deduction/induction*.

Let us assume that an economist was attempting to establish the relationship between the rate of growth in the supply of money in the economy and the rate of inflation (i.e. the annual percentage increase in retail prices) the following year. In the process a number of steps are followed.

Q37. Rearrange the following steps in the correct order:
(a) Predict the rate of inflation next year.
(b) Collect data on the current rate of growth in the money supply.
(c) Collect data on the rate of growth in the money supply and the rate of inflation over a number of past years.
(d) If the prediction is wrong, amend the theory or abandon it.
(e) Establish a hypothesis about the relationship between the two variables.
(f) Continue collecting more evidence.
(g) Conduct observations to establish whether the prediction is correct.

Correct order: ....

(Pages 23–4) Despite using similar models to the natural sciences, economists tend to be less accurate in their predictions.

Q38. Give two reasons for this.

1. ....
2. ....

(Page 24) Economists have an important role in helping governments to formulate and assess economic policy. In doing this it is important to separate *positive* questions about what the effects of the policies are, from *normative* ones as to what the goals of policy should be. Economists in their role as economists have no superior right to make normative judgements on the ideological/moral/political basis of the policy. They can and do, however, play a major role in assessing whether a policy meets the political objectives of government (or opposition).

Q39. Which one of the following is a normative statement?
A. The privatisation of the railways has reduced the level of traffic congestion.
B. The privatisation of the railways has led to an increase in fares.
C. Many on the political left believe that the privatisation of the railways is wrong.
D. It is fairer that rail commuters should pay the full costs of the journeys rather than having them subsidised by the government.
E. Rail privatisation has attracted private investment the industry.

Q40. Which of the following statem and which are normative?
(a) The best policy is one that of economic growth for t
(b) Government pol inflation tha
(c) The g ing une
(d) If the govern unemployment, electorate.

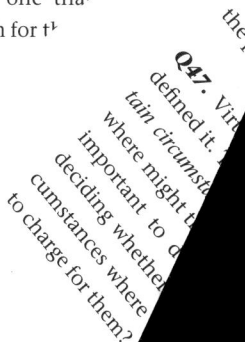

6 CHAPTER 1 INTRODUCING ECONOMICS

B PROBLEMS, EXERCISES AND PROJECTS

Q41. Make a list of 5 things you did yesterday and any items you purchased. What was the opportunity cost of each? If your fellow students are doing this question, have a look at some of their lists and see if you agree with their estimates of their opportunity costs.

Q42. Imagine that country X could produce just two goods: food and clothing. Assume that over a given time period it could produce any of the following combinations:

Units of clothing	0	1	2	3	4	5	6
Units of food	24	23	21	18	14	8	0

(a) Draw the production possibility curve for country X on Figure 1.5.
(b) What is the opportunity cost of producing one more unit of clothing if the current level of production is (i) 2 units, (ii) 3 units, (iii) 4 units?
(c) Assume that technical innovation in agriculture allows a greater food output per unit of resources devoted to agriculture. What effect will this have on the opportunity cost of producing clothes?
(d) Now assume that there is a drought that halves the amount of food that can be produced per unit of resources. Draw the new production possibility curve.

Q43. Conduct a survey to establish what your fellow non-economics students believe economics to be about. To what extent is their perception of the contents of economics the same as yours (a) was before you started your current course (b) is now?

Q44. Choose two current economics news items reported in the newspapers. Choose two newspapers of opposing political views which report this item. Give examples from these reports of *positive* statements and *normative* statements. Are there any statements that are not clearly one or the other?

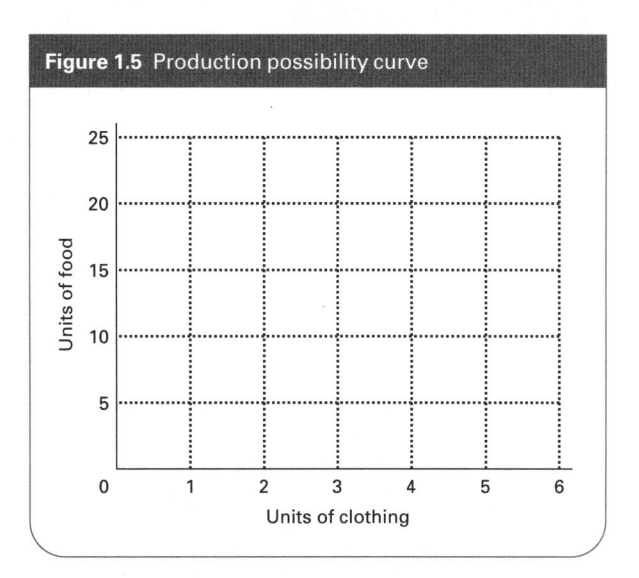

Figure 1.5 Production possibility curve

Q45. East European economies have undergone considerable changes since 1989. Using data from the Internet or from your institution's library:
(a) Plot annual economic growth, unemployment and inflation figures since 1989 for three 'transitional' economies.
(b) Describe the patterns.
(c) How might greater reliance on market forces have (i) improved and (ii) worsened the performance of your chosen three economies?
(d) Using the data and other relevant articles, discuss the adverse consequences caused by shifting from a command economy to a market economy.

C DISCUSSION TOPICS AND ESSAYS

Q46. Make a list of some current problems that are the concern of economists. Are they microeconomic or macroeconomic problems, or a bit of both? How do they relate to the problem of scarcity?

Q47. Virtually every good is scarce in the sense we have defined. There are, however, a few exceptions. Under certain circumstances water and air are not scarce. When and where might this be true for (a) water and (b) air? Why is it necessary to define water and air very carefully before deciding if they are scarce or abundant? Under circumstances they are *not* scarce, would it be possible

Q48. How can scarcity be a problem when the shops are well stocked, there are well over one million people unemployed (a *surplus* of labour), and there are butter and grain 'mountains' in many countries?

Q49. Using relevant examples, explain what is meant by 'technological progress'. What would cause the rate of technological progress to increase? Will technological progress eventually overcome the economic problem?

Q50. In the past 15 years, many countries have experienced an increase in the proportion of goods and services provided by the private sector.

(a) Why has this occurred?
(b) What are the economic implications of an increase in the proportions of health care and education that are provided by the private sector?

Q51. 'Economists can advise on economic policy and still avoid value judgements.' Explain how this could be so. Is it desirable that economists should avoid value judgements?

Q52. Debate
Each side should prepare a case in support of one of the following two statements (you may wish to use current economics news items).

1. The distinction between positive and normative economics is a very important distinction, since it clearly delineates the boundary between the legitimate areas of enquiry, analysis and pronouncements by economists and those areas where the economist has no superior right of pronouncement to the layperson.
2. The distinction between positive and normative economics is a dangerous and often bogus one. It tends to confer a legitimacy on economists' pronouncements which, while seeming to be 'positive', are in reality highly normative in their implications.

D ARTICLES

The scrapping of student maintenance grants, the introduction of tuition fees and the drive to increase higher education participation rates have all been politically sensitive issues in the UK. The following article, which appeared on *The Guardian* Web site of 14 February 2002, suggests that the government of the day accepted that the system was failing students from low-income families and that action was required to redress the balance.

Blair to launch 'fairer' student finance system

Nicholas Watt, political correspondent

Tony Blair came close to admitting yesterday that ministers have made a mess of the student finance system when he said the government needs to do more to help poorer students.

Speaking in the wake of the restoration of means-tested student grants in Wales, the prime minister said that he was determined to introduce a fairer system in England.

'We are looking at how we get a fairer balance between the contribution the state makes and the contribution students make,' Mr Blair told MPs at the weekly session of prime minister's questions. 'We are looking at how we can help poorer students particularly.'

The remarks were Mr Blair's frankest admission yet that the government's controversial scrapping of the maintenance grant and the introduction of tuition fees has penalised poor students. The government announced last year that a new system of grants would be introduced to help poor students.

Mr Blair underlined the depth of the change of thinking in government circles when he congratulated the Welsh assembly for reintroducing means-tested grants. In response to the Liberal Democrat leader, Charles Kennedy, whose party forced a similar change of policy in Scotland, Mr Blair said: 'We are looking at the moment at how we improve access for students in our country.'

But Mr Blair said there could be no return to the system in which the state paid the entire cost of tuition fees and funded full maintenance grants for less well-off students.

'If we are to get higher education participation rates above 50% there is no way we can do that under the old system,' he said. 'There is no way we are going to get more students and still get resources to the frontline of universities unless we change the system of student finance.'

Mr Blair also said the current system, which proved to be one of the least popular government policies during last June's general election, does help poorer students. He said that 50% of students do not pay tuition fees.

Details of the new student finance system are still being worked out. But a means-tested maintenance grant will be brought back and there will be more loans. These will be funded by a graduate tax which all students will have to pay.

(a) Explain why the abolition of maintenance grants and the introduction of tuition fees has reduced participation of students from low-income families.
(b) What are the likely long-term consequences of the such policies with respect to the type of student entering college and the courses on which they enrol?
(c) In deciding not to attend university because the costs are perceived to outweigh the benefits, the individual is assumed to be making a rational choice. Why may such a 'rational' choice for the individual not be optimal for society as a whole?
(d) Analyse the likely beneficial and adverse effects of three policies that the government could use to encourage greater entry to higher education.

Students are frequently asked to distinguish between *positive* and *normative* statements. We are told that positive statements are factual (correct or incorrect), whereas normative ones involve moral (or aesthetic) judgements. That seems a simple distinction. However, when it comes to specific examples, distinguishing between them is far from easy. In the reading below, taken from the *Economic Review*, volume 14, number 1 of September 1996, Alan Hamlin shows how positive and normative economics statements might be disentangled, and why making economic policy recommendations involves the use of both.

Why study economics?

Why do we study economics? What is economics for?

What sorts of questions can a study of economics equip us to answer?

I want to distinguish between two broad types of questions which economists address, and to emphasise that each type of question involves a rather different approach to economics.

The first type of question can be labelled 'positive' or 'scientific'. These questions are primarily concerned with explaining and understanding various economic phenomena. How do markets of a particular type work and what factors influence market prices? What would be the impact of the imposition of a tax on beer? How can we explain the wage differential between nurses and surgeons? All of these are essentially 'positive' questions.

The second type of question can be labelled 'normative' or 'moral'. These questions are primarily concerned with evaluating and judging various economic phenomena. Should we regulate a particular market to control prices? Should we raise or lower the tax on beer? Should we attempt to redistribute income? All of these are essentially 'normative' questions.

It should be clear from these examples that there are often very close links between positive and normative questions. It would surely be impossible for an economist to give a full discussion of the *normative* question of whether we should raise or lower the tax on beer without tackling the *positive* question concerning the impact of a tax on beer. But there is still an important distinction between the two types of question, and the closeness of the relationship between the positive and the normative can be dangerous since it can sometimes lead economists to think that they are engaged in positive analysis when they are actually engaged in normative analysis. This in turn can lead economists to ignore the moral dimension of economic analysis.

Positive economics

One way of thinking of the content of positive economics is illustrated in the top section of Figure 1. We begin with the simple idea of description. If we are to make any progress as economists we must be able to describe the economic world around us in a clear and recognisable way. So the first task of positive economics is to develop the terms and ideas which allow of such description.

Describing the economy is a complex task. There may be no single description which is useful for all purposes, and we need to be sensitive to the variety of functions that may be served by any part of the economic structure.

A next step is to *explain* or *understand* the workings of an economy. Explanation in positive economics emphasises the logical analysis of economic activity. The basic building blocks of positive explanation are models which attempt to capture important elements of the real world, but also to simplify it to allow a clear focus on just one or two issues. One hallmark of economic models is the assumption that individuals are rational. Indeed much economic modelling can be thought of as trying to work out the implications of rational decision-making in a variety of circumstances, thereby offering an explanation of economic phenomena as the outcomes of rational action by individuals.

Another possibility within positive economics is to shift attention from understanding some aspect of the economy to *predicting* or *forecasting* its behaviour.

So, purely positive economics can allow us to describe, explain, understand and (sometimes) forecast aspects of the economy.

It may be interesting and intellectually exciting to understand or even forecast the economy, but unless that

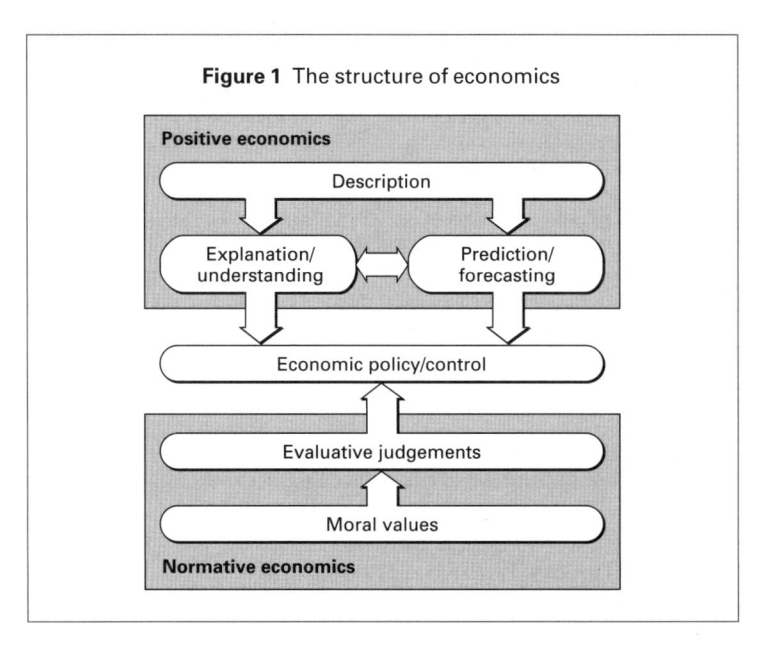

Figure 1 The structure of economics

Positive economics
- Description
- Explanation/understanding ↔ Prediction/forecasting
- Economic policy/control
- Evaluative judgements
- Moral values

Normative economics

understanding can help us to *do* something, many people would think that economics was rather pointless. In short, most people do not simply want us to understand the economy but to make it perform better.

Normative economics

So the next step is to attempt some degree of influence or control over the economy – to think about policies that might improve economic performance in one way or another. But this is where positive economics runs out. As soon as we enter the realms of judgements about whether this or that economic arrangement is better, or whether this or that policy should be enacted, we enter the realm of normative economics.

The basic idea here is sketched in the lower panel of Figure 1. Normative or moral ideas usually begin with the identification of moral values. We might think of a range of potential moral values including human well-being, respect for human rights, equality of opportunity, and so on. There is no easy answer to the basic question of what we should value – but the question cannot be avoided. Equally, we cannot avoid the question of the extent to which these values may conflict with each other in some circumstances.

In standard economics we typically focus on two types of values as providing the normative basis for economic policy debate. On the one hand is the concern for improving each individual's own perception of his or her welfare.

On the other hand is the concern for equity or fairness across individuals. Economic policies are then defended on the grounds that they offer means of improving efficiency or improving distributional equity or fairness.

The point here is not to defend these particular values, or to offer alternatives, but simply to stress that all economics that sets out to contribute to the policy debate – and that is virtually all economics – must be based on some specific moral stance. Economics cannot be reduced to a purely positive science and still retain policy relevance. There can be no policy conclusion without a normative input.

(a) Pick out an article in the press on some current economic issue. Identify positive and normative statements. In each case, state why they are positive or normative.
(b) How would you respond to the following argument? 'Economists should just describe, explain and predict. Moral and evaluative judgements should be left to the politicians.'
(c) If 'all economics that sets out to contribute to a policy debate must be based on some specific moral stance', what problems does this create when we attempt to judge the findings of economists' research?

Russia has continued to reform its economy and rely more and more on market forces. The following article appeared on *The Economist* Web site in November 2001. The article suggests that the economic reforms are delivering improved economic performance, but that unless more reforms are adopted, the longer-term situation still looks bleak.

Lurching ahead

While President Vladimir Putin wows the West, Russia is changing, slowly

Foreign policy: splendid but fragile. Economic reform: cautiously encouraging. Democracy: still wobbly. The stirrings of public spirit: small but detectable. That would crudely sum up the remarkable but contradictory changes in Russia, some of them apparent since September 11th.

The best news is that, for whatever reason, President Vladimir Putin is plotting a course that broadly suits the West and would have seemed barely imaginable only three months ago. There is little talk these days of a 'strategic partnership' with China or of North Korea's dictator, Kim Jong Il, as a 'thoroughly modern man', or even of that old Soviet tactic of trying to wean Europe away from its alliance with America. Instead, Russia is itself fast cosying up to the United States.

Mr Putin has learned to woo foreign politicians and journalists alike. Harangues and bluster have given way to a relaxed, articulate, convincing manner, backed by a formidable command of detail, and even salted with the occasional dry joke. He is winning some new friends at home, too. At a state-sponsored 'civil forum' last week for voluntary outfits, even some die-hard human-rights campaigners were impressed by the authorities' willingness at least to listen to them.

Recruiting foreign opinion is not just a matter of patter. After September 11th Mr Putin acted speedily and decisively to portray Russia as a trustworthy partner. He gave unstinting support, both diplomatic and practical, to America's war in Afghanistan; during past American interventions, in Yugoslavia and the Gulf, Russia's stance was querulous or outright hostile. Mr Putin has also moved quickly to tidy up other loose ends, from closing military bases abroad to opening negotiations to end the war in Chechnya.

One big reason for the change is that Mr Putin genuinely loathes what he calls 'Islamic terrorism'. Whatever Russia's differences with the West – over missiles or Yugoslavia – they are mere nuances compared with what he sees as a shared threat from Russia's south. In the previous era of grumpy indecision, Russia sat impotently on the global sidelines, flirting with countries poorer and nastier than itself, while its western neighbours once under Russia's sway,

The Putin performance sheet

Policy/reform	Importance	Resistance	Progress so far
Justice system	•••••	•••••	Goodish new laws, bad old habits
Bureaucracy	•••••	•••••	No big changes yet
Tax	••••	•••	Flat rates introduced, fearsome bureaucracy remains
Customs system	••••	••••	Crooked officials and their friends yielding very slowly
Banking	••••	••••	Reform blocked by Central Bank
Armed forces	•••	••••	Putin's pal is minister but soldiery still ill-paid and useless
Household charges*	•••	•••••	Painful price rises promised soon
Land	•••	••	Only urban market freed, open sale of farmland promised
Centralisation	•••	•••	Disintegration checked but regions no better run
Tycoons	••	•••	Stroppy old guard out, docile new guard in
Foreign affairs	••	••	Shiny new image, broadly pro-western

Source: *The Economist*. *Heating, utilities, rent and maintenance costs.

such as Poland and Estonia, raced away to rejoin the modern world.

Now Mr Putin has placed his chips. He wants a strong, modern Russia, and that means money and know-how from the West, whatever the short-term cost in political concessions. Generals and other hawks are uneasy or outright angry but their protests get nowhere. The press and opposition parties are docile.

Mr Putin's other main achievement is that Russia no longer feels like a disintegrating country. The Kremlin is plainly in charge, both at the centre and in the provinces. The president has humbled most of the tycoon-politicians who infested public life in the Yeltsin era. There is a steady government, a growing economy, a balanced budget and low inflation. Some big reforms, to simplify taxes and free the market in urban land, should soon reap at least some benefits. Mr Putin is popular.

And yet the really difficult reforms – of the bureaucracy, of the military and security empires, of state-run heating and housing – still lie ahead. Even where good laws have been passed, most of them have yet to bite. And economic growth, fuelled by the high oil price and the effects of the 1998 devaluation, is tailing off again. Last year it was more than 8%; this year it may be less than 5%.

The good news is that the past two years have created a cushion, of both cash and credibility. That should make borrowing money from abroad cheaper and easier. The country can survive a year or so of lower oil prices with only modest belt-tightening. Only if oil falls below $12 for some time will the economy stop growing.

Many steppes still to go

In the medium run, though, things still look pretty bleak. Around 40% of Russian businesses make a loss, even after the two best years in the country's economic history. Imports are shooting up, exports (raw materials aside) are still pitifully few. Most factories are direly managed. Their machinery on average is 16 years old, roughly three times the figure in the West. Government interferes very widely. The crony-ridden, state-dominated banking system keeps old businesses going but chokes off capital from new ones. Small firms, the backbone of most strong economies, in Russia are becoming fewer.

The bureaucracy and the corrupt overlap between politics and business are still the country's biggest problems. The most encouraging signs here lie in the work of the Audit Chamber, a government watchdog run by a former prime minister, Sergei Stepashin. Despite government resistance, he has been poking around some of the country's most lucrative state bodies: those dealing with fisheries, customs, railways, natural resources, the press and civil emergencies. All in all, billions of dollars have gone adrift, he says. A clutch of bigwigs are under investigation.

Another bit of the government is slowly trying to get rid of the red tape that fosters corruption and incompetence. The number of licences and other bits of paper that businesses need has shrunk. After next summer it should become easier to register a new company.

Reform of the justice system is the single biggest condition for real change. Despite a bunch of new laws passed last week, it will be very slow. Judges will be better paid and easier to sack, but finding and training good ones will take years. The prosecutor's office remains notably unreformed, as are other powerful agencies, including the FSB (the domestic security service), the tax police, the interior ministry and the armed forces. For all the talk of legality, state authorities still do pretty much as they want, including using the law against political opponents and the independent media. This week TV6, the last big opposition television station left, looked set to succumb to a state-backed squeeze.

More helpful nudges are coming from elsewhere. A new code on corporate governance may make big business a little more open and law-abiding. Some liberal politicians are planning to introduce a law on freedom of information next year.

But two big things are still missing. One is a commitment to clean government at the top. The suspicion remains that, as the old team gets whacked, a new lot takes over. Many of Mr Putin's old St Petersburg chums seem to be doing very well for themselves; so do a bunch of other well-connected tycoons.

The other big shortage is of public spirit. Most Russians would still rather pay up or shut up than kick up a fuss. Few think that the latest kerfuffle over corruption or working for pressure groups will improve their own lives. Still, Elena Panfilova, who runs Russia's branch of Transparency International, an anti-corruption lobby, thinks that time is on the side of good government. 'It is the logic of history,' she says. 'But it will take a generation.'

© *The Economist*, London (29.11.01)

(a) With reference to the article, what economic advantage does the free-market economy have over the command economy?

(b) Explain why the longer-term economic outlook is still bleak for Russia.

(c) What obstacles are likely to lie in the way of further reforms?

E ANSWERS

Q1. E. We define scarcity as the excess of human wants over the means of fulfilling those wants. Virtually everyone would like more than they have. Even very rich people would normally like a higher income, and even if money was no object at all for them, they would still have a shortage of *time* to do everything they would like to do.

Q2. False. Human desires are virtually boundless. For example, in 100 years people will want things that have not been invented yet.

Q3. Labour, land (and raw materials), and capital.

Q4. E. All the others contribute towards production. The wages are the *reward* for Jim's labour: they do not add to production.

Q5. *wants*. Potential demand refers to what people would *like* to have and not merely to those items that are thought of as being necessities.

Q6. *the level of resources available*. What society can produce depends on what labour, land and capital are available.

Q7. *macroeconomics*.

Q8. *microeconomics*.

Q9. *(a)* macro.
(b) micro.
(c) macro. (It would be micro if we were looking at overseas investment in a *specific* industry.)
(d) micro.
(e) macro.
(f) micro. (We are only referring to wages in a *specific* industry.)
(g) micro.
(h) macro. (We are referring to total household saving in the economy, not to the saving of specific households or to saving in specific financial institutions.)

Q10. B. The opportunity cost is the cost measured in terms of next best alternative forgone.

Q11. (b), (d), (e) *true*; (a) and (c) *false*. Rational behaviour involves weighing up the costs and benefits of any activity. For consumers this involves comparing the price of a good with the benefit the consumer expects to receive. The consumer will think (however briefly), 'Is this item worth purchasing?' The answer will vary from person to person according to their tastes (i.e. not (c)).

Q12. C. All the other statements consider the effects of a bit *more* of something (eating another chocolate bar, mortgage rates rising by another 1 per cent, purchasing another forklift truck, installing anti-pollution equipment on one more power station). In the case of C, however, we are considering the effect of *total* revenues for the firm exceeding its *total* production costs.

Q13. *(a)* A, D, F and G. All these points lie *on* the production possibility curve and thus show that the country is fully utilising its potential.
(b) B and C. These points lie *inside* the curve and thus illustrate that not as many goods are being produced as could be.
(c) A and G. Point A shows complete specialisation in good Y and point G shows complete specialisation in good X.
(d) E. Point E lies outside the production possibility curve and is thus unobtainable.

Q14. E. When production is initially at point A, producing one more unit of good X (i.e. the eleventh unit) will involve reducing production of good Y by 2 units (from 8 to 6 units).

Q15. The phenomenon of *increasing opportunity costs*. As more and more of one good is produced, increasingly larger and larger amounts of the other have to be sacrificed.

Q16. B. The outward shift of the curve illustrates an increase in potential output (i). The movement outward of the production point from A to B illustrates an increase in actual output (ii). But the fact that point A is *on* the earlier curve whereas point B is *inside* the later curve means that resources are being used less fully (or efficiently) than previously.

Q17. A. An increase in the population of working age represents an increase in (human) resources and hence an increase in production potential. Note: B represents a movement outward of the production point towards the production possibility curve; C may encourage increased *consumption* and may as a result stimulate a greater level of production (a movement outward of the production *point*) but does not directly increase *production* potential; D means that the *money* value of output potential has risen, but there is no change in *physical* output potential; E is likely to lead to an *inward* shift of the curve as the quality of the labour force declines.

Q18. (a) and (b) *macro*, (c) *micro*. In the case of (a) and (b) the whole economy is being considered: whether it is growing (a), or whether there is a full use of resources (b). In the case of (c), however, the question is one of the *composition* of production: how much of *each* good is being produced.

Q19. *(a)* IV.
(b) II.
(c) I.
(d) III.

Q20. The state or some central or local planning agency.

Q21. Individuals: households and firms.

Q22. C. In a pure command economy, firms do not have the discretion to respond to changes in consumer demand.

Q23. Costly in terms of administration; difficulty in devising incentives to ensure that the plan is carried out as the planners would like; loss of individual liberty; planners may not act in the interests of the people.

Q24. demanders.

Q25. suppliers.

Q26. fall.

Q27. a rise in the quantity demanded but a fall in the quantity supplied.

Q28. rise.

Q29. fall.

Q30. rise.

Q31. The rise in demand for houses will cause a shortage of houses. This will cause the price of houses to rise. This will increase the profitability of house construction. This in turn will increase the demand for bricklayers. The resulting shortage of bricklayers will lead to a rise in their wages (the 'price' of bricklayers).

Q32. *(a)* True.
(b) True.
(c) True. Competition will help to keep prices down and thus encourage firms to reduce their costs in order to make a satisfactory level of profit.
(d) False. While competition between firms may prevent very high profits in any industry and the competition between workers may prevent very high wages in any type of job, the *ownership* of resources is not equal. Some people own a lot of property; others own none; some workers are skilled and can command high wages; others are unskilled.
(e) False. Goods that are profitable for a firm may not necessarily be socially desirable. For example, the production of certain industrial goods may damage the environment. On the other hand, some things that *are* socially desirable (such as pavements) may not be profitable for private enterprise to supply.

Q33. Examples include: state ownership of various industries (nationalisation); legislation to affect production or consumption (e.g. to control pollution); taxation (e.g. high rates on tobacco and spirits); subsidies and benefits (e.g. pensions and other benefits to help the poor); direct provision (e.g. of education and policing); price controls and controls over interest rates and exchange rates.

Q34. D. It is usually not possible to conduct controlled experiments in economics since, unlike certain of the natural sciences, it is not a *laboratory* science. It is not possible to hold other things constant. Instead, we simply have to *assume* that other things are constant (*ceteris paribus*). Note: although economic models can usually be tested by appealing to the facts (answer E), there will be a delay if a prediction of the future is being tested.

Q35. induction.

Q36. deduction.

Q37. (c), (e), (b), (a), (g), (d), (f).

Q38. Reasons include: it is impossible to conduct controlled experiments in economics; economics deals with human behaviour (it is a *social* science) and humans are not totally predictable; economic data tend to be incomplete and often inaccurate.

Q39. D. This statement is a question of *value*. Some people may regard it as fair, some may not: it depends on what they believe to be right or wrong. The other statements in principle can all be tested by an appeal to facts. They may be correct or incorrect, but they are statements about what is or is not the case. Note that statement C is positive because it is not a statement about whether privatisation is desirable or not, but about what those on the left believe.

Q40. (b) and (d) are *positive*. The person making the statements is not saying whether government policies are good or bad, or what the government ought to do. In both cases the statements can be assessed by an appeal to the facts (albeit in the case of (d) you would have to wait to see how the electorate responded). (a) and (c), on the other hand are *normative*. The person making the statements is saying what the government *ought* to do or what the *goals* of government policy *should* be. Note: in the case of (d), there *is* the implication that if the government wants to be popular with the electorate, it would be wise to give a higher priority to curing unemployment, but that does not make it a normative statement. The statement as it stands is only about means to ends, not whether those ends are desirable. Only if the person making the statement is *implying* that the government *ought* to do what is popular with the electorate does the statement have normative overtones.

Chapter Two
2
Supply and Demand

A REVIEW

In this chapter we examine the workings of the *free market*. The *market* simply refers to the coming together of buyers (demanders) and sellers (suppliers).

We look first at *demand*, then at *supply* and then put the two together to show how price is determined. We then turn to examine just how responsive demand and supply are to their various determinants and particularly to changes in price; in doing this we will examine the important concept of *elasticity*.

The response of demand, supply and price to changing market conditions is unlikely to be instantaneous. In the final section, therefore, we examine the *time dimension* of markets. We look at the process of adjustment after the elapse of different periods of time.

2.1 Demand

(Page 30) There are several determinants of consumer demand for a product. The relationship between demand and one of these determinants is expressed in the *law of demand*.

Q1. The law of demand states that:
A. quantity demanded increases as price decreases.
B. demand rises as income rises.
C. producers respond to an increase in demand by producing more.
D. an increase in demand causes an increase in price.
E. the amount purchased depends on the amount demanded.

(Page 30) The effect of a change in price on the quantity demanded can be divided into an *income* effect and a *substitution* effect.

Q2. The income effect refers to the effect on price and quantity demanded of a change in consumer income.
True/False

Q3. The substitution effect refers to the effect on the quantity demanded of a change in the price of a substitute good.
True/False

(Pages 31–2) The relationship between price and the quantity demanded can be shown graphically on a *demand* curve. A demand curve can be an individual's demand curve, or that of a group of individuals (a *section* of the market) or that of the whole market.

Q4. Consider the (imaginary) data in Table 2.1. This shows the annual demand for tennis shoes in three sections of the market.

Multiple choice   *Written answer*   *Delete wrong word*   *Diagram/table manipulation*   *Calculation*   *Matching/ordering*

14 CHAPTER 2 SUPPLY AND DEMAND

Table 2.1 The demand for tennis shoes

Price	Tennis club members (annual) (000s)	Players but not club members (annual) (000s)	Non-tennis players (annual) (000s)	Total market (annual) (000s)
£100	6	1	0	...
£80	7	3	0	...
£60	8	6	2	...
£40	9	10	8	...
£20	10	18	20	...

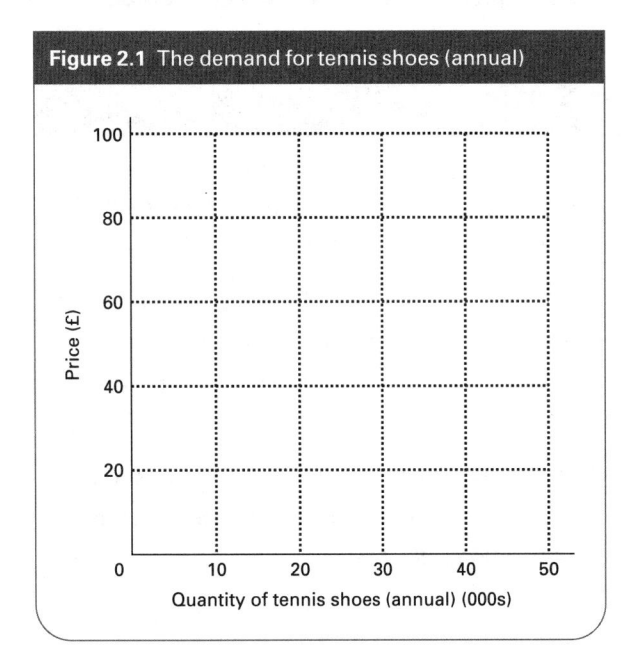

Figure 2.1 The demand for tennis shoes (annual)

[Graph: Price (£) on y-axis from 0 to 100; Quantity of tennis shoes (annual) (000s) on x-axis from 0 to 50]

(a) Fill in the column for annual market demand.
(b) Draw the annual demand curve for each of the three groups and the annual market demand on Figure 2.1.

(Pages 32–3) But price is not the only factor that determines how much of a good people will demand. Let us take the case of a particular product:

🏁 **Q5.** It is normal to group the various determinants of demand into categories. The categories include:
 (i) The price of the good.
 (ii) The price of substitute goods.
 (iii) The price of complementary goods.
 (iv) Tastes.
 (v) Income.
 (vi) Expectations of future price changes.

Into which of the above categories would you put the following determinants of the demand for tennis shoes?
(a) The price of tennis rackets.

....

(b) The amount shops charge for tennis shoes.

....

(c) The earnings of people who might possibly buy tennis shoes.

....

(d) The price of running shoes.

....

(e) The likelihood that the government will impose a tax on imported sportswear in order to protect the domestic sportswear industry.

....

(f) The amount of coverage to tennis given on the television.

....

(Page 33) When the price of a good changes, we say that this causes the **Q6.** *demand/quantity demanded* to change. This is shown by **Q7.** *a shift in the demand curve/a movement along the demand curve*. When one of the other determinants changes, however, we say that this causes the **Q8.** *demand/quantity demanded* to change. This is shown by **Q9.** *a shift in the demand curve/a movement along the demand curve*.

◗ **Q10.** Consider the demand curve for petrol. What effect will the following have?
(a) An increase in the price of cars. *Rightward shift/leftward shift/movement up along/movement down along/need more information to say.*
(b) An increase in the proportion of the population owning cars. *Rightward shift/leftward shift/movement up along/movement down along/need more information to say.*
(c) A rise in transport costs of shipping oil. *Rightward shift/leftward shift/movement up along/movement down along/need more information to say.*
(d) A growing concern for environmental issues by the general public. *Rightward shift/leftward shift/movement up along/movement down along/need more information to say.*
(e) An increase in duty on diesel. *Rightward shift/leftward shift/movement up along/movement down along/need more information to say.*
(f) A reduction in duty on petrol. *Rightward shift/leftward shift/movement up along/movement down along/need more information to say.*

One of the most important determinants of demand is the level of consumer income. When considering the effect of a change in income on demand, we distinguish between *normal* goods and *inferior* goods.

Q11. We define a normal good as one

....

Q12. On the other hand, we define an inferior good as one

....

2.2 Supply

(Page 36) The relationship between supply and *price* is **Q13.** *a direct/an inverse* relationship.

Q14. Which of the following are explanations of this relationship between price and market supply (there are more than one)?
(a) Costs tend to rise over time. *Yes/No*
(b) As price rises, producers find that it is worth incurring the higher costs per unit associated with producing more. *Yes/No*
(c) At higher prices it is worth using additional, less productive factors of production. *Yes/No*
(d) The lower the price, the more firms will switch to producing other products which are thus now relatively more profitable. *Yes/No*
(e) Technological improvements mean that more can be produced and this in turn will affect prices. *Yes/No*

(Pages 36–7) Given that the quantity supplied is likely to rise as price rises, the supply curve is likely to be upward sloping.

(Pages 37–8) As with demand, price is not the only thing that affects supply.

Q15. Other determinants of supply include:

1. ....
2. ....
3. ....
4. ....
5. ....

(Pages 38–9) If price changes, the effect is shown by **Q16.** *a shift in/a movement along* the supply curve. We call this effect a change in **Q17.** *supply/the quantity supplied*. If any other determinant of supply changes, the effect is shown by **Q18.** *a shift in/a movement along* the supply curve. We call this effect *a change in* **Q19.** *supply/the quantity supplied*.

Q20. Consider the case of the supply curve of organically grown wheat. What effect would the following have?
(a) A reduction in the cost of organic fertilisers. *Rightward shift/leftward shift/movement up along/movement down along.*
(b) An increase in the demand for organic bread. *Rightward shift/leftward shift/movement up along/movement down along.*
(c) An increase in the price of organic oats and barley. *Rightward shift/leftward shift/movement up along/movement down along.*
(d) The belief that the price of organic wheat will rise substantially in the future. *Rightward shift/leftward shift/movement up along/movement down along.*
(e) A drought. *Rightward shift/leftward shift/movement up along/movement down along.*
(f) A government subsidy granted to farmers using organic methods. *Rightward shift/leftward shift/movement up along/movement down along.*

2.3 Price and output determination

(Page 40) If the demand for a good exceeds the supply, there will be a **Q21.** *shortage/surplus*. This will lead to a **Q22.** *fall/rise* in the price of the good. If the supply of a good exceeds the demand, there will be a **Q23.** *shortage/surplus*. This will lead to a **Q24.** *fall/rise* in the price.

Price will settle at the equilibrium. The equilibrium price is the one that clears the market.

Q25. This is the price where

....

(Pages 41–2) If the demand or the supply curve *shifts*, this will lead either to a shortage or to a surplus. Price will therefore either rise or fall, **Q26.** *causing a shift in/movement along* the other curve, until a new equilibrium is reached at the position where the supply and demand curves *now* intersect.

Q27. The demand and supply schedules for organically grown wheat in a free market are shown in Table 2.2.
(a) Draw the demand and supply curves on Figure 2.2.
(b) What would be the size of the shortage or surplus at a price of €180 per tonne?

Shortage/surplus of ....

(c) What would be the size of the shortage or surplus at a price of €340 per tonne?

Shortage/surplus of ....

(d) What is the equilibrium price and quantity?

P = ...; *Q* = ...

16 CHAPTER 2 SUPPLY AND DEMAND

Table 2.2 The market for organically grown wheat (imaginary figures)

Price per tonne (€)	100	140	180	220	260	300	340	380
Tonnes supplied per week	220	260	320	400	500	640	880	1400
Tonnes demanded per week	770	680	610	550	500	460	400	320

Figure 2.2 The market for organically grown wheat (weekly figures)

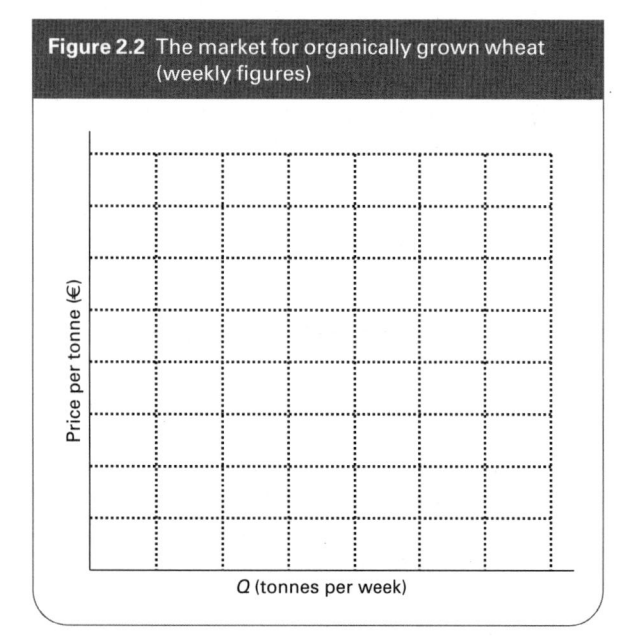

[Empty graph: Price per tonne (€) on y-axis, Q (tonnes per week) on x-axis]

(e) Now assume that the demand for organic wheat increases by 180 tonnes per week at all prices. Draw the new demand curve.

(f) What is the size of the shortage or surplus at the original equilibrium price?

Shortage/surplus of ....

(g) What is the new equilibrium price? ....

(h) Has the equilibrium quantity increased by more or less than the 180 tonnes per week increase in demand?
More/Less

Assume that supply now changes by an equal amount at all prices.

(i) What would this change have to be to restore the original equilibrium price?

Increase/Decrease of ....

(j) What would this change have to be to restore the original equilibrium quantity?

Increase/Decrease of ....

(k) Is there any shift in the supply curve that could restore both the original equilibrium price and the original quantity?
Yes/No

Explain ....
....

Q28. If income increases, then for an inferior good, the quantity sold will decrease and the price will increase.
True/False

Q29. Figure 2.3 shows the demand for and supply of new purpose-built flats.

The supply and demand curves are initially given by S_0 and D_0. The market is in equilibrium at point x. Various factors then change which have the effect of shifting the demand curve to D_1 or D_2 and/or the supply curve to S_1 or S_2. What is the new equilibrium point in each of the following cases? (Remember that in each case the market is initially in equilibrium at point x.)

(a) A rise in the price of building materials.
Point ....

(b) Flat living becomes more fashionable.
Point ....

(c) A fall in the price of new houses.
Point ....

(d) A rise in the price of old houses and flats.
Point ....

(e) The imposition of a new construction tax on houses (but not flats).
Point ....

(f) The belief that the price of flats will soon rise substantially.
Point ....

Figure 2.3 The market for new flats

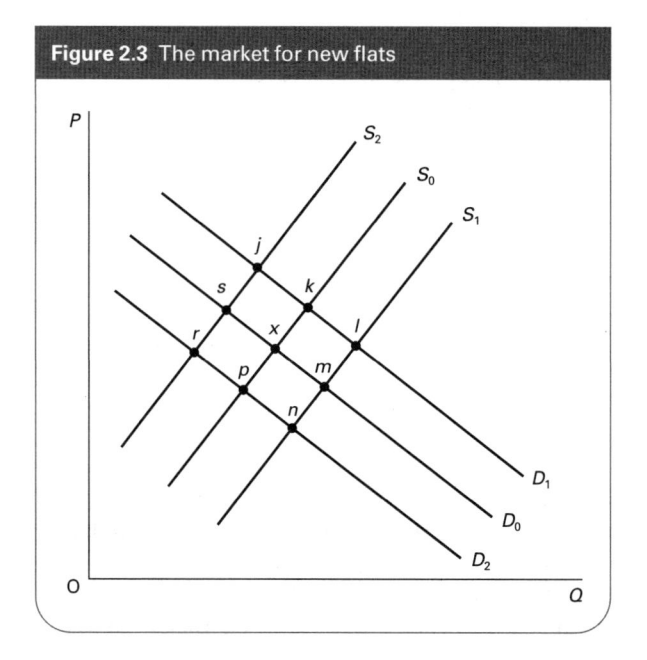

[Graph showing supply curves S_2, S_0, S_1 and demand curves D_1, D_0, D_2, with intersection points labelled j, s, k, r, x, l, p, m, n]

(g) An increase in mortgage interest rates.
Point ....

Q30. Suppose that it is observed that the price of butter falls but that the quantity sold rises. From this we can deduce:
A. That the demand curve has shifted to the right, but we cannot deduce whether or not the supply curve has shifted.
B. That the demand curve has shifted to the left, but we cannot deduce whether or not the supply curve has shifted.
C. That the supply curve has shifted to the right, but we cannot deduce whether or not the demand curve has shifted.
D. That the supply curve has shifted to the left, but we cannot deduce whether or not the demand curve has shifted.
E. Nothing. Either curve could have shifted either way depending on which way the other shifted.

*(Pages 33–5, 39) Demand and supply curves can be represented by equations.

***Q31.** The supply and demand curves for commodity X are given by the following equations:

$Q_s = 2 + 3P$
$Q_d = 50 - 5P$

(a) Without drawing a diagram or completing a table, find the equilibrium price and quantity.
(You will need to use simultaneous equations.)

....

(b) Using the two equations above, fill in the figures in Table 2.3.
(c) Draw a graph of the two curves on Figure 2.4.
(d) Assume that the demand equation now becomes: $Q_d = 66 - 5P$. Draw the new demand curve on Figure 2.4 and find the equilibrium. How is the shape of the demand curve affected?
(e) Assume that the demand equation now becomes: $Q_d = 50 - 9P$. Draw the new demand curve and find the equilibrium. How is the shape of the demand curve affected this time?

Table 2.3 $Q_s = 2 + 3P$; $Q_d = 50 - 5P$

P	0	1	2	3	4	5	6	7	8	9	10
Q_s	.	.	.	11	.	.	.	.	.	.	.
Q_d	.	.	40	.	.	.	.	.	.	.	.

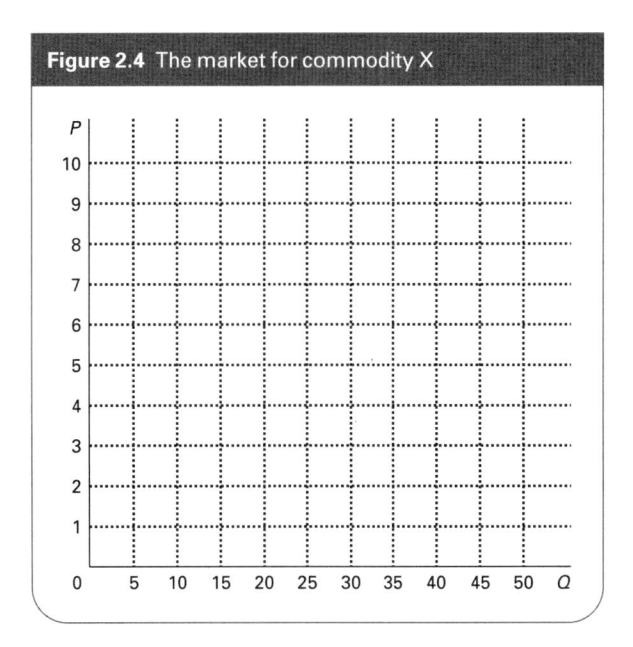

Figure 2.4 The market for commodity X

2.4 Elasticity

Elasticity (ϵ) is a measure of the responsiveness of demand (or supply) to a change in one of the determinants, and is one of the most important concepts we shall come across in the whole of economics. It is defined as the proportionate (or percentage) change in quantity demanded (or supplied) (Q) divided by the proportionate (or percentage) change in the determinant (X).

$$\epsilon = \Delta Q/Q \div \Delta X/X$$

(Pages 44–6) The *price elasticity of demand* measures the responsiveness of **Q32.** *the quantity demanded/price* to a change in **Q33.** *the quantity demanded/the quantity supplied/ price*.

Q34. The formula for the price elasticity of demand ($P\epsilon_d$) is

....

If the quantity demanded changes proportionately more than the price, we say that demand is **Q35.** *elastic/inelastic*. If the quantity demanded changes proportionately less than the price, we say that demand is **Q36.** *elastic/inelastic*. Assuming that a demand curve is downward sloping, the price elasticity of demand will have **Q37.** *a positive value ($\epsilon > 0$)/a negative value ($\epsilon < 0$)*.

Let us now ignore the sign (positive or negative) and consider just the value for elasticity: for example $\epsilon = 1.8$ or $\epsilon = 0.43$.

Q38. Match each of the following figures for elasticity to definitions (a)–(e) below.

CHAPTER 2 SUPPLY AND DEMAND

(i) $\epsilon = 1$
(ii) $1 > \epsilon > 0$ (This means that the figure for elasticity is greater than 0 but less than 1.)
(iii) $\epsilon = 0$
(iv) $\epsilon = \infty$
(v) $\infty > \epsilon > 1$

(a) Elastic.
(b) Unit elastic.
(c) Totally inelastic.
(d) Inelastic.
(e) Totally elastic.

(Page 46) Demand will be more elastic **Q39**. *the greater/the less* the number and closeness of substitute goods, **Q40**. *the higher/the lower* the proportion of income spent on the good and **Q41**. *the longer/the shorter* the time period that elapses after the change in price.

Q42. Rank the following in ascending order of price elasticity of demand (i.e. least elastic first):

(a) Margarine ....
(b) 'Scrummy' low-fat margarine ....
(c) Spreads for bread ....
(d) Low-fat margarine ....
(e) 'Scrummy' low-fat margarine with a token for the current competition

....

Q43. The price elasticity of demand for holidays abroad (in general) is likely to be high because
A. people tend to book up a long time in advance.
B. there are plenty of different foreign holidays to choose from.
C. foreign holidays are an expensive luxury.
D. holidays at home provide no real alternative.
E. people need a holiday if they are to cope with the year ahead.

We must be careful when drawing inferences about price elasticity from demand curves.

Q44. Referring to the two demand curves in Figure 2.5, which of the following statements are correct?
(a) Curve D_2 is elastic. *True/False*
(b) Curve D_1 has a price elasticity of –1. *True/False*
(c) At point x, curve D_1 has an elasticity of zero. *True/False*
(d) At point y, curve D_2 has an elasticity of infinity. *True/False*
(e) Curve D_2 is more elastic than curve D_1. *True/False*

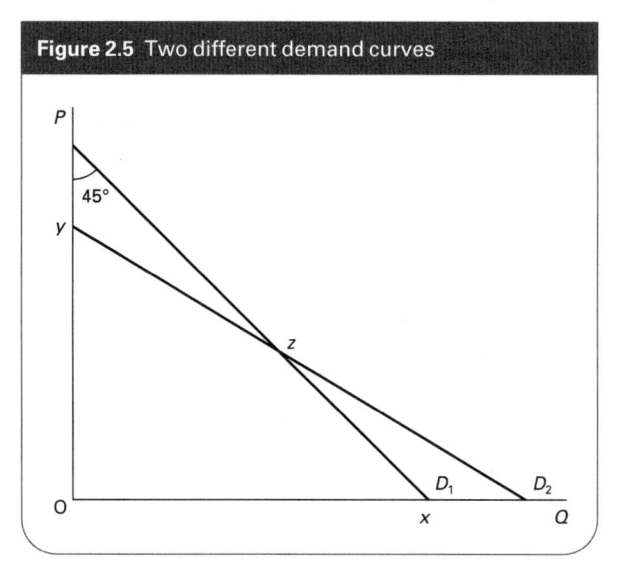

Figure 2.5 Two different demand curves

(f) At point z, the two curves have the same price elasticity. *True/False*
(g) Curve D_2 is more elastic than curve D_1 over any given price range. *True/False*

(Pages 48–50) Given that demand curves normally have different elasticities along their length, we can normally only refer to the specific value for elasticity between two points on the curve or at a single point.

Q45. Elasticity measured between two points is known as

....

When applied to price elasticity of demand its formula is:

$$\frac{\Delta Q_d}{\text{average } Q_d} \div \frac{\Delta P}{\text{average } P}$$

where average Q_d is the average value of Q_d at the two points between which we are measuring elasticity. Thus if at one point $Q_d = 6$ and at the other $Q_d = 4$, then average $Q_d = 5$: i.e. average $Q_d = (Q_{d_1} + Q_{d_2})/2$.

Q46. Similarly average $P = $ ....

Q47. Given the following equation: $Q_d = 20 - 2P$:
(a) Fill in the figures for quantity demanded in Table 2.4.
(b) Estimate the price elasticity of demand between:
  (i) $P = 2$ and $P = 0$
  (ii) $P = 6$ and $P = 4$
  (iii) $P = 9$ and $P = 7$
  In each case state whether demand is elastic or inelastic.
(c) Using this arc method, how would you estimate price elasticity at a single point?

....

Table 2.4 Demand schedule: $Q_d = 20 - 2P$

P(£)	10	9	8	7	6	5	4	3	2	1	0
Q_d	.	.	.	.	8	.	.	.	.	.	.

(d) Using this method, estimate the price elasticity of demand at:
  (i) $P = 2$
  (ii) $P = 6$
  (iii) $P = 5$
  (iv) $P = 0$
  (v) $P = 10$

(Pages 47–8) One of the most important applications of price elasticity of demand concerns the relationship between the *price* of a good and the total amount of *expenditure* by consumers (and hence the *revenue* earned by firms). We define *total expenditure* as price times quantity sold: $TE = P \times Q$.

⊖ **Q48.** Fill in a new row in Table 2.4 showing the level of total expenditure at each price.

◐ **Q49.** Referring again to Table 2.4:
(a) What will be the effect on total expenditure of reducing price (and hence increasing the quantity demanded) when demand is price *elastic*?   rise/fall
(b) What will be the effect when demand is price inelastic?   rise/fall
(c) What will be the elasticity at the price where total expenditure is the maximum?

....

◐ **Q50.** When the price elasticity of demand for a good is –1.4, then a rise in the price will result in fewer goods being sold but greater consumer expenditure.   True/False

◐ **Q51.** When demand is price inelastic, total expenditure will vary directly with price but inversely with quantity demanded.   True/False

◐ **Q52.** The elasticity of a straight-line demand curve will fall as you move down the curve, from infinity at the point where it intersects the vertical axis to zero at the point where it intersects the horizontal axis.   True/False

(Pages 51–3) Another way of measuring elasticity is to use the point method. Remember that the arc formula for price elasticity is:

$$\frac{\Delta Q_d}{\text{average } Q_d} \div \frac{\Delta P}{\text{average } P}$$

If we want to measure elasticity at a point, then average P and Q_d simply become P and Q_d, and the 'change' (Δ) in price and quantity becomes infinitesimally small. An infinitesimally small change is written d. The formula thus becomes:

$$dQ_d/Q_d \div dP/P$$

(?) *****Q53.** Rearranged this formula becomes:

$dQ_d/dP \times$ ....

where dQ_d/dP is the *****Q54.** *slope/inverse of the slope* of the tangent to the demand curve at the point in question.

⊖ *****Q55.** Given the following equation for a demand curve:

$$Q_d = 50 - 20P + 2P^2$$

(a) Fill in the figures in Table 2.5.
(b) Draw the demand curve on Figure 2.6.
(c) Draw the tangent to the curve where $P = 3$, $Q = 8$. What is its slope?

....

(d) What is the price elasticity of demand where $P = 3$?

....

Table 2.5 Demand schedule: $Q_d = 50 - 20P + 2P^2$

P	5	4	3	2	1	0
Q_d						

Figure 2.6 Demand curve: $Q_d = 50 - 20P + 2P^2$

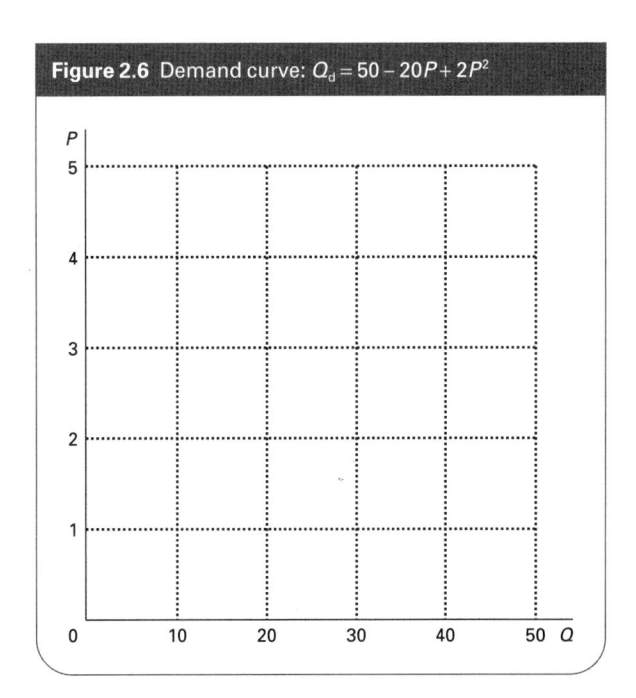

CHAPTER 2 SUPPLY AND DEMAND

(Pages 53–4) We turn now to other types of elasticity and start with *price elasticity of supply*.

Q56. There are two goods A and B. Which is likely to have the more price-elastic supply in each of the following cases?
(a) It is less costly to shift from producing A to another product than it is to shift from B to another product. *A/B/cannot say*
(b) The supply of A is considered over a longer period of time than B. *A/B/cannot say*
(c) The cost of producing extra units increases more rapidly in the case of A than in the case of B. *A/B/cannot say*
(d) Consumers find it easier to find alternatives to A than to B. *A/B/cannot say*
(e) A is a minor by-product of B. *A/B/cannot say*
(f) A higher proportion of national income is spent on A than on B. *A/B/cannot say*

Q57. Consider the three supply curves in Figure 2.7. Which of the following statements are correct?
(a) Curve S_1 has an elasticity equal to 1 throughout its length. *True/False*
(b) The elasticity of all three curves is the same at point x. *True/False*
(c) Curve S_2 has an elasticity greater than 1 throughout its length. *True/False*
(d) Curve S_3 has an elasticity equal to zero at point z. *True/False*
(e) Curve S_2 has an elasticity equal to infinity at point y. *True/False*
(f) Curve S_3 has a constant elasticity less than 1 throughout its length. *True/False*

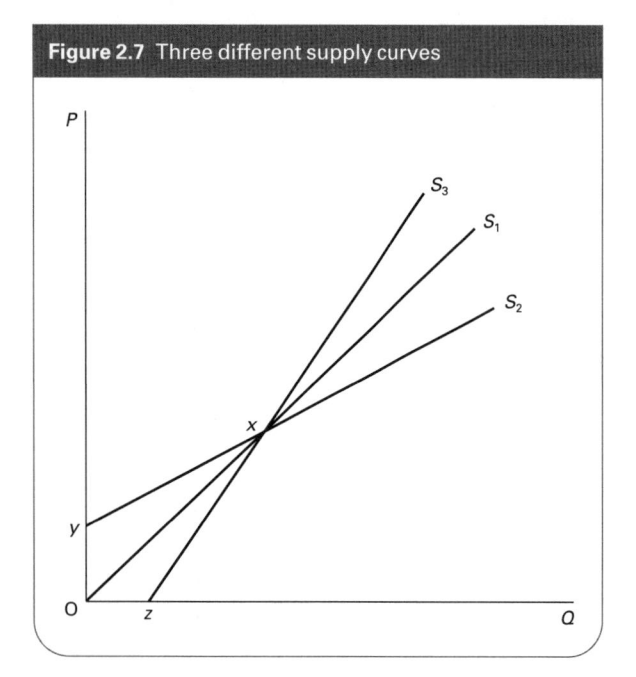

Figure 2.7 Three different supply curves

(Pages 54–5) Income elasticity of demand measures the responsiveness of demand to a change in income. For normal goods it has a **Q58.** *positive/negative* value.

Q59. Table 2.6 shows the quantity of three goods (A, B and C) purchased in two years (year 1 and year 2). The only factor affecting demand that changes between these two years is consumer incomes.

Table 2.6 Demand for goods A, B and C in years 1 and 2

	Quantity demanded Good A (000s)	Quantity demanded Good B (000s)	Quantity demanded Good C (000s)	Consumer income (Y) (£bn)
Year 1	30	52	190	45 000
Year 2	50	48	210	55 000

(a) What is the income elasticity of demand for the three goods between Y = £45 billion and £55 billion? (Use the arc method.)

Good A ....

Good B ....

Good C ....

(b) Which of the three goods has an income-*elastic* demand over the given income range? *A/B/C*
(c) Which of the goods is an inferior good over the given income range? *A/B/C*

Q60. The share of income devoted to a good will increase with income if the good has an income elasticity of demand greater than 1. *True/False*

(Page 55) Cross-price elasticity of demand measures the responsiveness of the demand for one good to a change in the price of another and thus is a means of judging the degree of substitutability or complementarity of two goods.

Q61. Match each of the following five values for cross-price elasticity (i)–(v), to the pairs of products (a)–(e).
(i) Considerably greater than zero
(ii) Slightly greater than zero
(iii) Zero
(iv) Slightly less than zero
(v) Considerably less than zero

(a) Petrol and cars ....

(b) Salt and petrol ....

(c) Cars and bicycles ....

(d) Escorts and Astras ....

(e) Petrol and cross-Channel ferry crossings ....

2.5 The time dimension

(Page 56) To get a fuller picture of how markets work we must take into account the time dimension. Given that producers and consumers take a time to respond fully to price changes, we can identify different equilibria after the elapse of different lengths of time. Generally, short-run supply and demand tend to be **Q62.** *more/less* price-elastic than long-run supply and demand. As a result, any shifts in demand or supply curves tend to have a relatively bigger effect on **Q63.** *price/quantity* in the short run and a relatively bigger effect on **Q64.** *price/quantity* in the long run.

Q65. The short-run (retail) supply of freshly cut flowers is much less elastic than that of pot plants because
A. households generally keep pot plants much longer before throwing them away (and often never throw them away).
B. fresh flowers are more likely to be purchased for special occasions.
C. the price of freshly cut flowers fluctuates much more than that of pot plants.
D. supplies of fresh flowers fluctuate much more with the weather and the season.
E. florists cannot keep freshly cut flowers as long as pot plants.

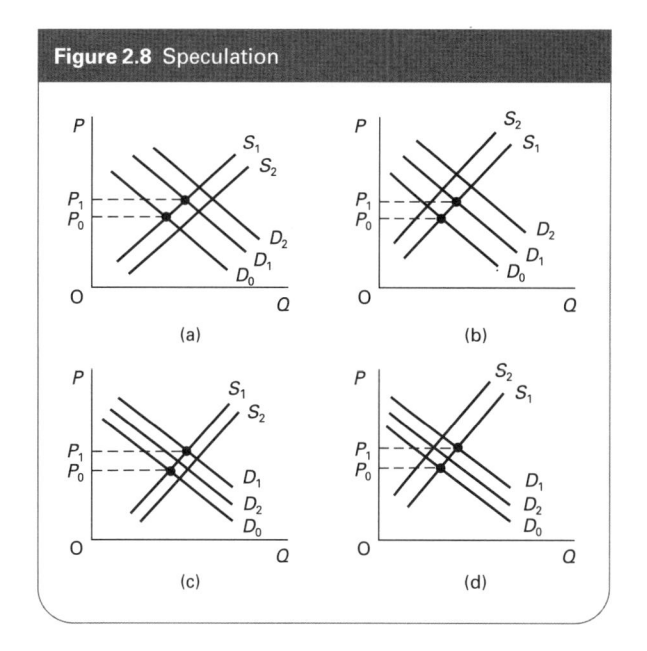

(Pages 56–61) Realising that prices can fluctuate, buyers and sellers are likely to try to anticipate what will happen to prices if they are in a position to wait before buying or selling. In such cases, if people believe that prices are likely to rise, current supply will shift to the **Q66.** *left/right* and current demand will shift to the **Q67.** *left/right*. This will have the effect of causing the price to **Q68.** *rise/fall*.

This activity where buyers or sellers predict price changes and then act on these predictions is called *speculation*. It can be of two types, *stabilising* and *destabilising*.

Q69. Figure 2.8 shows a market where demand has just increased from D_0 to D_1 with a resulting price rise from P_0 to P_1. People then make a judgement from this about future price changes. Which one of the four diagrams represents stabilising speculation and which destabilising?
Stabilising *(a)/(b)/(c)/(d)*
Destabilising *(a)/(b)/(c)/(d)*

Figure 2.8 Speculation

B PROBLEMS, EXERCISES AND PROJECTS

Q70. Clearly defining the market may be crucial in explaining the effect of a price change on the quantity of a good demanded.

The market for petrol is a good example. The demand for all petrol is relatively inelastic to changes in price: there are few substitutes and it takes time for consumers to change their consumption patterns. Yet if you consider the demand for a single brand of petrol, it becomes far more elastic, as there are several substitute brands available.

Consider the two diagrams in Figure 2.9.

If the price of *all* petrol rises from 50p per litre to 70p as in diagram (a), total revenue increases from area *abc* 0 to area *def* 0: from (£0.50 × 50m) = £25m to (£0.70 × 45m) = £31.5m.

Alternatively, if a *particular company* raises its price *independently* of its competitors, the demand for its particular

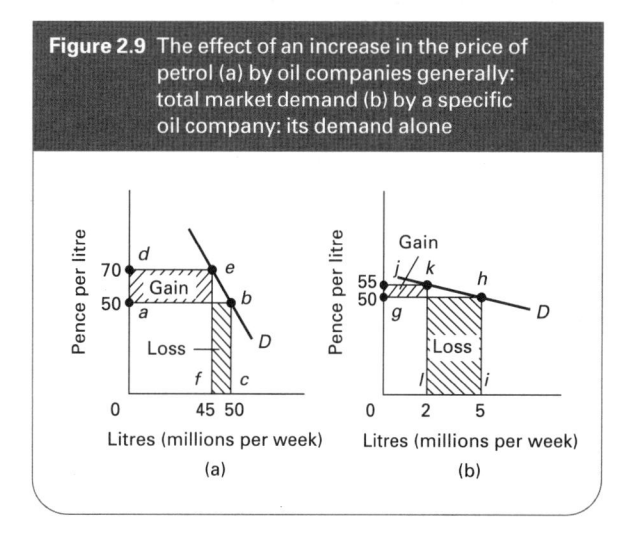

Figure 2.9 The effect of an increase in the price of petrol (a) by oil companies generally: total market demand (b) by a specific oil company: its demand alone

brand will fall dramatically. In diagram (b), when the company raises its price to 55p its total revenue falls from area *ghi*0 to area *jkl*0: from (£0.50 × 5m) = £2.5m to (£0.55 × 2m) = £1.1m.

Generally, the more narrowly we define a market, the more substitutes there will be outside that market and therefore the more elastic the demand will be.

(a) Using the arc method of calculating elasticity, what is the price elasticity of demand between the two points on each of the two curves in Figure 2.9?

(b) Which would you expect to have the higher price elasticity: the demand for a particular brand of petrol or the demand for petrol from a particular filling station? Explain your assumptions.

Q71. Collect annual data for the annual percentage changes in house prices and GDP (gross domestic product: the value of national output) and for the average annual level of interest rates for the UK from 1990. You should use data from the ONS Web site and in the Treasury Pocket Databank on the Treasury site (see the hotlinks section on the book's Web site).

(a) Plot a time-series graph for the three indicators. Plot the years on the horizontal axis, the percentage changes in house prices and GDP on one vertical axis and the percentage interest rate on the other vertical axis.

(b) Describe the pattern of house price changes over the period.

(c) What is the likely relationship between the rate of house price inflation and (i) the rate of interest; (ii) the rate of growth in GDP? Use diagrams to support your answer.

(d) Discuss two other factors that might have caused the change in house prices. Draw diagrams to illustrate your analysis.

(e) Forecast what will happen to house prices over the next two years, identifying the factors that are likely to influence demand and/or supply.

Q72. Imagine that you were given a rise in grant/pay/allowance of £10 per week.

(a) Make a list of the things on which you would spend this extra income and work out your income elasticity of demand for each.

(b) Are there any items of which you would now buy less? Explain.

Now imagine you had an increase in income of £100 per week.

(c) Answer questions (a) and (b).

(d) Are your answers different this time? Explain.

Q73. Select an item that is purchased by all or most of your class or seminar group. Conduct interviews with everyone to establish the amounts they would buy at six different prices. Now divide the class into two groups (by sex or age or any other feature that you may feel relevant in determining demand).

(a) From the replies given at your interviews, construct a demand curve for each group and a demand curve for the class as a whole.

(b) What is the total expenditure of each group at each price? Explain any differences between the two groups. (You will need to consider both the elasticity and the magnitude of demand.)

C   DISCUSSION TOPICS AND ESSAYS

Q74. Using supply and demand diagrams, illustrate the effects of a substantial fall in the world output of oil and gas on the prices of (a) oil, (b) coal, (c) cars, and on (d) bus fares.

Q75. Is the following statement true? 'An increase in demand will cause an increase in price. This increase in price will then cause a reduction in demand, until demand is reduced back to its original level.' Explain your answer.

Q76. It is observed that over time the price and the quantity demanded of a product both rise. Does this mean that the demand curve is upward sloping? What does this tell us about the difficulty of determining the shape of demand and supply curves?

Q77. The demand for pears is more price elastic than the demand for bread and yet the price of pears fluctuates more than that of bread. Why should this be so? If pears could be stored as long and as cheaply as flour, would this affect the relative price fluctuations?

Q78. A fish and chip shop finds that on Friday early evening, Saturday lunch time and between 10.30 and 11.00 every evening it has queues out of the door, whereas at other times it is empty. Would it be a good idea to charge different prices at different times?

Q79. When share prices move upwards on the stock market, people tend to start buying, whereas when they move downward people often sell. Does this mean that the demand curves for shares slope upwards and the supply curves slope downwards?

Q80. Debate
The price of manufactured goods will always be more stable than that of agricultural goods in the short term, but will be less stable in the long term.

D ARTICLES

After falling in the early 1990s, house prices have risen every year since 1996. But the rate of increase has not been steady or uniform across the UK. House prices in London have increased by more than that in the north of England or Scotland. The following article appeared on *The Economist* Web site in July 2001. The article argues that the house price gap between London and elsewhere is unlikely to shrink

The London effect

The gap between prices in London and elsewhere is not likely to shrink

That favourite dinner-party topic is back. London house prices, which were subdued for much of last year, are now marching up again. In the year to the second quarter they rose by 17%, over double the national increase. By contrast, house prices rose by just 4% in Scotland and the north, according to the Halifax price index.

The resurgence in London house prices has reawakened fears that the housing market may once again be heading for boom-and-bust. The last episode in that unhappy cycle occurred in the late 1980s and early 1990s. Then, the London market led the way to soaring house prices across the country. As borrowers stretched themselves to get into the market, price-to-income ratios rose way above their long-run averages. They were restored only by the housing-market slump of the early 1990s.

Some doomsayers are already warning that this will happen again. Even before the latest jump in London house prices, Cambridge Econometrics, an economic consultancy, warned that house prices had risen to unsustainable levels.

But there are important differences between today's housing market and that of the late 1980s. Then there was an upsurge in the number of first-time buyers as the baby-boomers born in the late 1950s and early 1960s scrambled into the market. However, the size of the 25–35 age-group is now falling sharply as a result of the baby-bust of the 1970s.

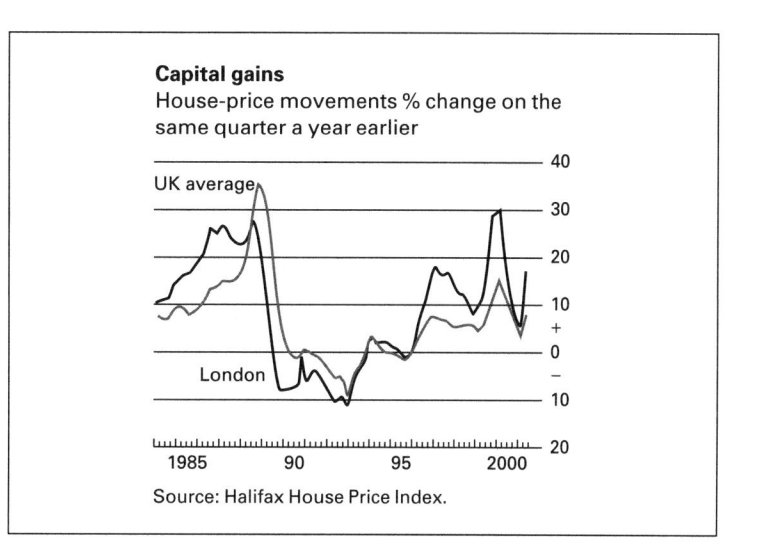

Capital gains
House-price movements % change on the same quarter a year earlier

[Chart showing UK average and London house-price movements from 1985 to 2000, with percentage change ranging from -20 to +40]

Source: Halifax House Price Index.

Furthermore, the incentives to invest in housing have weakened since the late 1980s. The tax system no longer subsidises mortgage borrowing, tax shelters are now widely available for equity investments and low overall inflation reduces the incentive to protect wealth by acquiring real assets.

This suggests that the surge in London house prices is largely specific to the capital and the surrounding commuter-belt. London's population is burgeoning, in large measure because it receives most international migration. Its population is younger than the rest of the country. More people are in the key house-buying age-groups. The City's role as a world financial centre has driven incomes for many professions up to international levels.

Since these are relatively new developments, long-run price-to-earnings ratios may no longer apply to the capital. If this is the case, three conclusions follow, two favourable and one awkward. London house prices may not be as over-stretched as they appear, although they remain vulnerable to a downturn in the City's fortunes. The country will not follow London in a runaway property-price boom. Which means that the economic chasm between the capital and the country will remain wide, creating all sorts of difficulties, not least for the government's attempts to improve public services without banishing national pay scales.

© *The Economist*, London (July 2001)

(a) Using a supply and demand diagram, explain why house prices in London have increased at such a rapid rate.
(b) Why is this trend likely to continue in the future?
(c) What are the likely economic consequences of the widening gap between London house prices and rest of the country?
(d) What policies could the government pursue to reduce the widening gap in house prices? Illustrate the effects of these through a supply and demand diagram.

The semiconductor (computer chip) industry traditionally follows a cyclical pattern of booms and 'pauses'. The following article, however, from the *Financial Times* of 2 September 2001, argues that adverse supply and demand conditions have resulted in a very severe downturn that may cause considerable restructuring in the industry.

Chip overload puts sector under pressure

Overproduction and a slump in demand makes restructuring in the industry, say Paul Abrahams and Alexander Harney

Californian chardonnay was flowing last month in San Jose's Technology Museum at the southern tip of Silicon Valley in celebration of the 20th anniversary of the International Business Machines personal computer and the birth of the $140bn PC industry. On hand for the festivities were the elite of the digerati: Bill Gates, chairman of Microsoft; Carly Fiorina, Hewlett-Packard's chief executive; and lesser-known figures such as Dave Bradley, the man who invented the Control–Alt–Delete key combination, used to unfreeze and reboot computers.

Also present was Andrew Grove, chairman of Intel, the world's largest chip company. But Mr Grove had less reason to celebrate. For the semiconductor industry, which supplies the microprocessors that power PCs, as well as servers, telecommunications equipment, mobile phones, handheld computers and countless other electronics devices, is in deep trouble.

Semiconductor companies are used to cyclical fluctuations in their fortunes but the speed, depth and duration of the downturn of the past year are unprecedented. The industry, accustomed to compound annual growth rates of between 15 and 17 per cent, has been convulsed by a collapse in revenues. From their peak just last year, quarterly revenues have fallen between 25 and 75 per cent. Margins have been crushed and most companies have fallen into loss.

From Taipei to Tokyo, from Seoul to Silicon Valley, chip makers are struggling to survive. In South Korea, Hynix, formerly known as Hyundai Electronics, the world's third largest maker of D-ram memory chips, has defaulted on some of its debts.

Manufacturers are asking how it got this bad and how long they will have to wait before their fortunes recover. If the chip depression continues much longer, the sector is set for a fundamental restructuring that will transform the industry.

'Normally, the down-cycles are caused by supply,' says Seth Dickson, semiconductor analyst at Lehman Brothers in San Francisco. 'The semiconductor makers overinvest in capacity, which drives down prices. But this time, the excess supply coincided with a downturn in demand. That is why it has been so damaging.'

Demand has suffered for two reasons. First, there is still a hangover from 1999 and early 2000, when a combination of Y2K preparations, virtually free capital for dotcoms and the initial euphoria of building the internet created unsustainable sales growth. The second blow to demand has been the unexpectedly sharp downturn in the global economy.

The unhappy coincidence of excess supply and anaemic demand has been particularly painful because it has occurred in almost every customer segment. In the second quarter of this year, Gartner Dataquest reported that global PC sales dropped for the first time in 15 years. Gateway, the US's fourth largest PC maker, is pulling back most of its international operations. Even Dell, currently the most successful PC manufacturer, has warned that its sales this quarter could fall 5 per cent.

Personal computer chipmakers' revenues could fall from $50bn in 2000 to just $38bn in 2001, estimates International Data Corporation, the market research company.

The once fast-growing wireless industry has also disappointed. At the beginning of last year, the big debate was whether handset sales would reach 600m units. In the event, 400m were sold. In the second quarter of this year, sales of mobile phones fell year on year for the first time, according to Gartner Dataquest.

As for the telecommunications infrastructure market, most companies are so indebted that they seem incapable of investing. 'Communications is in the sick bay. It could take a year for overinvestment to wear off,' says Craig Barrett, president and chief executive of Intel.

With supply and demand so far out of balance, prices for most semiconductors have tumbled. In May, D-ram shipments were down 62 per cent year on year. Demand has been so bad that volumes have fallen. 'The industry is used to dollar shipments going down sometimes – but not volumes,' says Mr Dickson at Lehman Brothers.

The hope is that next quarter will be a turning-point. The three months to September will see revenues fall for the fourth consecutive quarter, a record. But Morgan Stanley Dean Witter and Goldman Sachs both predict sequential growth next quarter. They say that inventories are beginning to return to normal and that the promotion of Windows XP, Microsoft's new operating system, and Intel's Pentium 4 microprocessor, should drive some sort of uptick in PC demand.

Even so, most analysts think recovery is less likely to be 'V-shaped' than 'L-shaped'. The reason is that while demand may pick up, prices may not. 'As first new orders come through for commodity products such as flash memory and logic chips, there will be such competition that customers will be able to drive hard bargains,' says Mr Dickson at Lehman Brothers.

The biggest concern is that the semiconductor industry's problems could be compounded by a lull in demand for ever-faster chips. 'PCs are functionally OK for most users. They do not need faster processors,' argues Clayton Christensen, a professor of business administration at Harvard Business School. 'The semiconductor industry has overshot the needs of most of its customers.'

Nonetheless, the industry seems incapable of slowing its rate of innovation. Last month, Intel launched its 2 gigahertz Pentium 4 chip, capable of 2bn cycles per second. The company also slashed the prices of its 1.8 gigahertz chip by more than 50 per cent. 'Almost every application available today runs fine at 1 gigahertz,' says Mr Dickson at Lehman Brothers. 'Why upgrade? The limiting factor for most PCs is slow access to the internet, not processing speed.'

Louis Burns, vice-president and general manager of desktop platforms at Intel, disagrees: 'Every time we introduce a new chip, we get told that we are overproviding,' he says. 'Innovation is sometimes predictable and sometimes not but the applications will be built that take advantage of the extra power.'

Even if there is a recovery later this year, the industry is likely to emerge from this downturn fundamentally restructured.

During the past month, Toshiba, Hitachi and NEC, the only Japanese companies still making D-rams, have axed 37,500 jobs. NEC, which has a joint venture with Hitachi for D-rams but still makes some chips on its own, has signalled its intention to withdraw from the sector entirely. Toshiba has shut down a production line in Japan and is negotiating with Infineon of Germany and Samsung of South Korea about combining its D-ram and flash memory operations. Questions are also being asked about Motorola's commitment to its semiconductor business.

In Taiwan, Robert Tsao, chairman of United Microelectronics, last year cheerfully described the downturn as a 'blessing in disguise' that would show the power of Taiwan's 'foundry' model of making chips to customers' order. In recent months, UMC laid off hundreds of staff and suffered quarterly losses and low utilisation rates that have been galling to a company that was struggling to meet demand for much of 2000.

For the moment, a semiconductor maker's capital structure appears to be its most important source of competitive advantage. 'At this point, it is a balance sheet war. It is how long you can keep your balance sheet in shape,' says Don Floyd, technology analyst at Lehman Brothers in Taipei. Cash-strapped Hynix is unlikely to be able to invest in the latest generation of chip-making equipment and could well be squeezed out of the market.

The semiconductor sector has prided itself on being high-growth and at the forefront of technological innovation. So, too, did the plastics industry in the 1960s. For the moment, much of the semiconductor industry looks increasingly like other capital-intensive industries such as petrochemicals, steel and paper: plagued by low growth and low returns and highly cyclical.

(a) Why are both the price elasticity of demand for and the price elasticity of supply of semiconductors likely to be elastic?

(b) Using a supply and demand diagram, explain why the price of semiconductors has fallen so dramatically.

(c) 'The problem of the semiconductor industry is simply one of over-capacity. As the restructuring and closures continue, the price will eventually rise.' With reference to the article, do you agree with this statement?

The coffee market has a history of fluctuating prices. However, the long-run price trend is downwards. The following article, which appeared in the *Financial Times* of 16 April 2002, argues that the structure of the coffee market is likely to cause this downward trend to continue.

Crisis call to coffee growers

Development agencies are warning that changes in market structure are permanent

Mark Mulligan and Andrew Bounds

The collapse in coffee prices is not only having devastating effects on Latin America's peasant farmers. It has also hit related business sectors and forced governments to rein in public spending.

This crisis is set to intensify over the next few years, according to two reports from development agencies.

Adjusted for inflation, in recent years coffee prices have fallen to their lowest in a century. The collapse has thrown as many as 540,000 people out of work and cost at least $713m in foreign exchange receipts for some of the world's poorest countries, the reports say.

'It appears that the changes in the structure of the world coffee market are not transitional,' says a survey of that region by the World Bank, the Inter-American Development Bank and the US Agency for International Development.

'Accordingly, the impact of the crisis in Central America could be long-lasting, if proper actions are not taken,' it says.

The United Nations' Economic Commission for Latin America and the Caribbean (Eclac) report says the global price slump has also hit related sectors such as transport and finance, and forced some governments to cut social spending because of declining tax revenues.

The coffee glut is one of several in the agriculture and mining sectors that are forcing Latin American governments to rethink long-term growth forecasts and rein in spending plans.

The low prices have come on top of a general decline in profitability among Central American producers – Nicaragua, Guatemala, Honduras, El Salvador and Costa Rica – blamed on outdated technologies and a proliferation of diseases because of climatic conditions and ageing plantations.

The crisis has forced cashstrapped governments to pay out or lend hundreds of millions of dollars to save growers from financial ruin – a measure that 'has not prospered', according to Eclac.

It calls for subsidised credits to finance more efficient farming methods, and the diversification into specialist 'boutique' and organic beans to capitalise on global consumption trends.

USAID is to spend $6m in Central America to encourage such methods. Its report says much of the region produces

26 CHAPTER 2 SUPPLY AND DEMAND

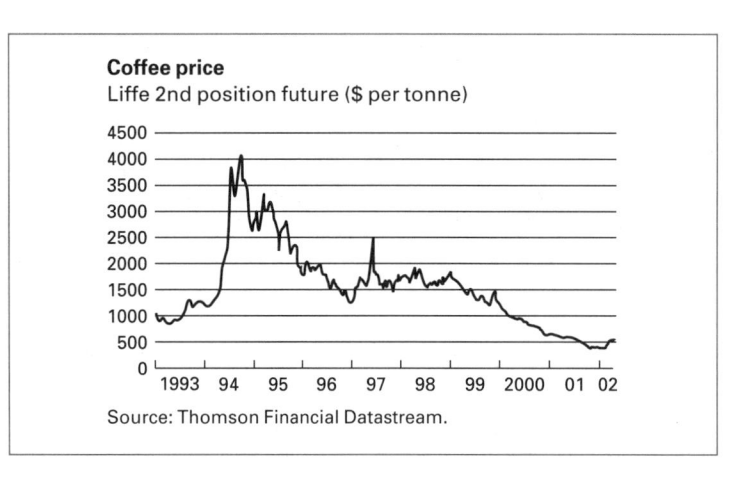

Coffee price
Liffe 2nd position future ($ per tonne)

Source: Thomson Financial Datastream.

high-quality coffee thanks to the use of trees to shade bushes, the high altitude and volcanic soil. It could be sold at a premium with correct marketing.

That requires incentives for producers, improved transport links to highland farms and independent quality certification.

The report says that producers should forge direct links with retailers, cutting out traders and the New York bulk market, and brand their coffee to distinguish it, as a few have already done.

It says those farming in areas that do not produce high-quality coffee should be helped to switch to other crops.

Eclac says domestic consumption – which is curiously low in most producer countries – needs to be encouraged through industry or government-sponsored campaigns such as the one in Brazil, which accounts for about 25 per cent of global production.

Still, Mr Giovannucci of the World Bank says that while changing the market structure offers long-term hope, 'it is too late for many. The crisis is already upon us.'

(a) Using a supply and demand diagram and the concept of elasticity, explain the factors that are causing the long-run price of coffee to decline.

(b) Would subsidies to coffee producers benefit them in the longer term? Explain your answer.

(c) Why would diversification into high-quality coffee and the destruction of low-quality plantations improve the long-term prospects for coffee producers?

(d) Would the encouragement of greater domestic consumption in coffee-growing countries provide the best long-term solution to the plight of coffee growers?

E ANSWERS

Q1. A. There is an inverse relationship between price and quantity demanded. The higher the price, the less the quantity demanded; the lower the price, the greater the quantity demanded.

Q2. *False.* It refers to the effect of a change in the *price* of the good on quantity demanded as a result of the consumer becoming better or worse off as a result of the price change: in other words, because of the effect of the price change on the purchasing power of the consumer's income.

Q3. *False.* It refers to the effect of a change in the price of the *good itself*, not to a change in the price of a substitute. The point is that if a good comes down in price, it will now be cheaper relative to the substitute than it was before, and thus people are likely to switch to it from the substitute.

Q4. *(a)* See table below.

Price (£)	Annual market demand (000s)
100	7
80	10
60	16
40	27
20	48

(b) See Figure A2.1.

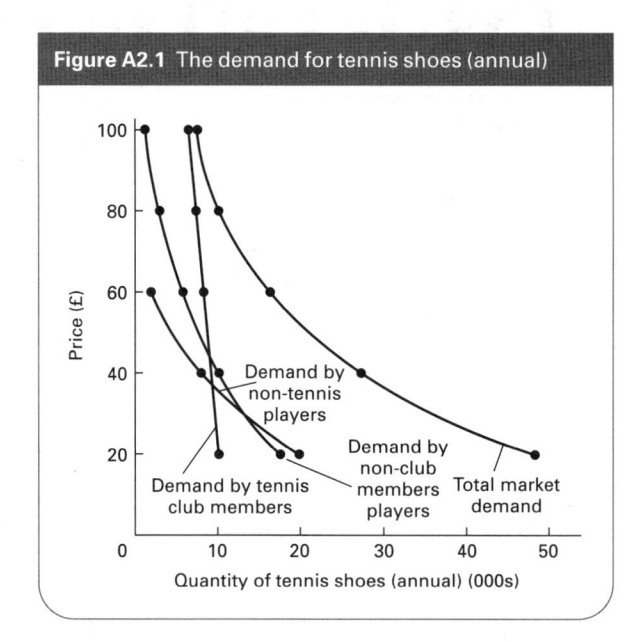

Figure A2.1 The demand for tennis shoes (annual)

Q5. (a) (iii), (b) (i), (c) (v), (d) (ii), (e) (vi), (f) (iv)
Q6. *quantity demanded.*

Q7. *a movement along the demand curve.*

Q8. *demand.*

Q9. *a shift in the demand curve.*

Q10. *(a) Leftward shift.* There will be a reduction in the demand for cars and hence for petrol. (Petrol and cars are complements.)

(b) Rightward shift. With more car owners the demand for petrol will be higher.

(c) Movement up along. This pushes up price (a shift in the supply curve). A change in price causes a movement along the demand curve.

(d) Need more information to say. An increased concern for the health hazards from diesel (e.g. asthma from diesel fumes) would cause people to switch from diesel to petrol (a *rightward* shift in the demand for petrol). On the other hand, an increased concern for the problems of traffic congestion, global warming, etc. will cause people to use cars less and thus use less petrol (a *leftward* shift in the demand curve).

(e) Rightward shift. People will switch to petrol (a substitute for diesel).

(f) Movement down along. This will reduce the price of petrol.

Q11. *whose demand increases as income increases.*

Q12. *whose demand decreases as income increases.*

Q13. *direct.*

Q14. What we are looking for is explanations of why a higher price will lead to a greater quantity being supplied (or why a lower price will lead to a smaller quantity). (b), (c), (d) are correct because they all explain this direct relationship. (a) does not provide an explanation because these cost increases are not associated with extra output. (e) is not an explanation because changes in technology are independent of price changes. They may cause price to change, but they are not a reason why a price change affects output.

Q15. The *costs* of production; the profitability of *alternative products*; the profitability of goods in *joint supply*; *random shocks*; and *expectations* of future price changes.

Q16. *a movement along* the supply curve.

Q17. *a change in the quantity supplied.*

Q18. *a shift in* in the supply curve.

Q19. *a change in supply.*

Q20. *(a) Rightward shift.* A reduction in the cost of producing organic wheat.

(b) Movement up along. The demand for organic wheat has increased and hence also its price.

(c) Leftward shift. These goods are in *alternative supply*.

(d) Immediate effect: leftward shift. Anticipating higher prices, farmers put more organic wheat into store, hoping to sell later when the price has gone up. This reduces current supplies on the market. Subsequent effect: *rightward shift.* Farmers switch to organic methods in anticipation that they will be more profitable. Supply increases.

(e) Leftward shift. The supply of wheat (of all types) decreases.

(f) Rightward shift. (As (a) above.)

Q21. *shortage.*

Q22. *rise.*

Q23. *surplus.*

Q24. *fall.*

Q25. *Demand equals supply.*

Q26. *movement along.*

Q27. *(a)* See Figure A2.2.

(b) Shortage of 290 tonnes per week.

(c) Surplus of 480 tonnes per week.

(d) P = €260; Q = 500 tonnes per week.

(e) See Figure A2.2.

(f) Shortage of 180 tonnes per week.

(g) P = €300.

(h) Less. It has only increased by 140 tonnes per week.

(i) Increase (rightward shift) of 180 tonnes per week. This would mean that at the old price of €260, 680 tonnes per week would now be both demanded and supplied.

(j) Decrease (leftward shift) of 900 tonnes per week. This would mean that at a new equilibrium price of €380, 500 tonnes per week would once again be both demanded and supplied.

(k) No. Given that the demand curve slopes downwards, a rightward shift in supply is essential to restore the old equilibrium price, and a leftward shift is essential to restore the old equilibrium quantity. (Only a leftward shift in *demand* could restore both simultaneously.)

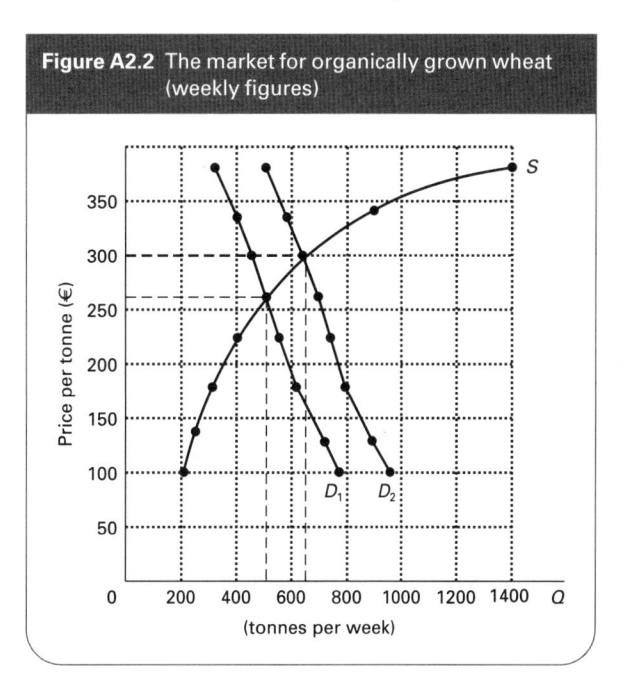

Figure A2.2 The market for organically grown wheat (weekly figures)

Q28. *False.* The demand curve will shift to the left. This will cause a decrease in the quantity sold *and also* a decrease in the price.

Q29. *(a) Point s.* Increased costs shift the supply curve to the left. No shift in the demand curve.

(b) Point k. A shift in tastes towards flats shifts the demand curve to the right. No shift in the supply curve.

(c) Point n. The fall in house prices reduces the demand for flats (a substitute). The demand curve shifts to the left. The fall in house prices makes their construction less profitable relative to flats (which are in alternative supply). The supply curve of new flats therefore shifts to the right.

(d) Point k. This will increase the demand for *new* houses and flats. The demand curve for new flats shifts to the right. No shift in the supply curve. (Builders cannot switch to building *old* houses and flats!)

(e) Point l. The construction tax on houses will make building flats more profitable. The supply curve will shift to the right. The higher price of houses resulting from the tax will increase the demand for flats. The demand curve shifts to the right.

(f) Point j. People will rush to buy flats now before prices rise. Demand shifts to the right. Builders will wait to sell their new flats until the price has risen. Supply will shift to the left.

(g) There are two possible answers here:
  (i) *Point p.* If higher mortgage interest rates reduce the demand for *all* types of property, the demand curve for flats will shift to the left.
  (ii) *Point k.* If flats are seen as an inferior good (to houses), the demand may *rise* as purchasers switch from houses to flats.

Q30. C. A shift in the demand curve alone must cause price and quantity to change in the *same* direction. Thus if price and quantity change in opposite directions, the *supply* curve must have shifted, causing a movement along the demand curve. In this case there must be a rightward shift in the supply curve causing a movement down along the demand curve. There may have been a less significant shift in the demand curve too, but we cannot tell.

*Q31. *(a)* Set the two equations equal (given that in equilibrium supply equals demand).
$2 + 3P = 50 - 5P$
$\therefore 8P = 48$
$\therefore P = 6$
Substituting $P = 6$ in either of the two equations (since demand *equals* supply) gives:
$Q = 20$

(b) See table below.

P	0	1	2	3	4	5	6	7	8	9	10
Q_s	2	5	8	11	14	17	20	23	26	29	32
Q_d	50	45	40	35	30	25	20	15	10	5	0

(c) See Figure A2.3.

(d) Parallel shift to the right by 16 units. The interception point with the horizontal axis (given by the constant term) increases from $Q = 50$ to $Q = 66$. The equilibrium point now becomes $P = 8, Q = 26$.

(e) The curve flattens. The interception point with the horizontal axis remains at $Q = 50$, but the slope (given by the inverse of the P term) flattens from $-1/5$ to $-1/9$. The equilibrium point is now $P = 4, Q = 14$.

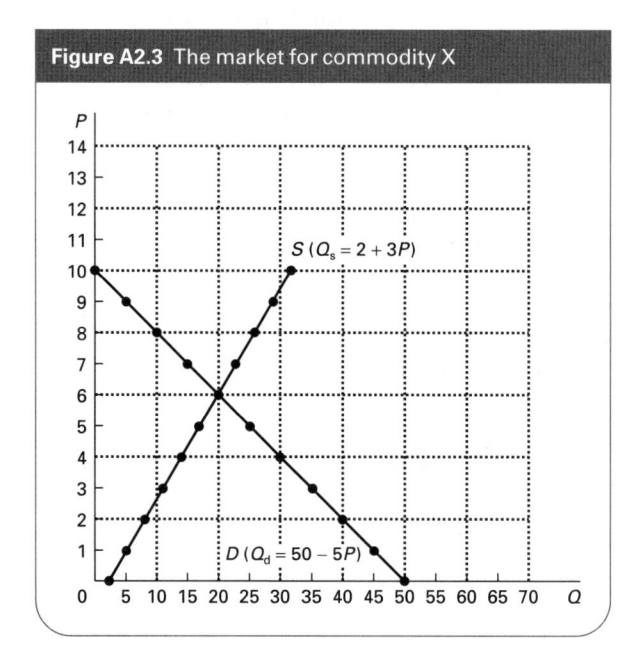

Figure A2.3 The market for commodity X

Q32. *the quantity demanded.*
Q33. *price.*
Q34. $\Delta Q_d / Q_d \div \Delta P / P$.
Q35. *elastic.*
Q36. *inelastic.*
Q37. *a negative value* ($\epsilon < 0$).
Q38. (a) (v), (b) (i), (c) (iii), (d) (ii), (e) (iv).
Q39. *the greater.* The more substitutes there are and the closer they are, the more willing consumers will be to switch from one product to the other as the price of one of them changes.
Q40. *the higher.* The higher the proportion of people's income spent on a good, the more they will be forced to cut back on its consumption as its price rises.
Q41. *the longer.* People will have more time to find alternative products and to change their consumption patterns.

Q42. (c), (a), (d), (b), (e). As we move from (c) to (e) in this order, so the number of substitutes becomes greater. Thus 'Scrummy' low-fat margarine with the current competition token has many substitutes, including: 'Scrummy' low-fat margarine without a token, other brands of low-fat margarine, other brands of margarine, dairy low-fat spreads and butter.

Q43. C. There are two reasons contained in this answer. The first is that foreign holidays are a luxury. This means that people do not regard them as vital, and will thus be prepared to substitute other items (e.g. holidays in their own country or day trips out) if the price of foreign holidays rises. What we are talking about here is a big substitution effect. The second is that, being a large item of people's expenditure, many people may not feel able to afford them if their price rises. What we are talking about here is a big income effect. Note that B would only be an answer if we were talking about a *specific* foreign holiday rather than foreign holidays in general.

Q44. *(a)* *False*. Except in the case of vertical and horizontal demand curves, the elasticity of straight-line demand curves will vary along their length.

(b) *False*. Again, downward-sloping straight-line demand curves have varying elasticities along their length. A curve with elasticity = –1 is a rectangular hyperbola (i.e. a curve bowed in toward the origin that approaches but never reaches the two axes).

(c) *True*. In *proportionate* terms any change in price from zero is an *infinite* change, and thus dividing a proportionate change in quantity by infinity will give a zero elasticity.

(d) *True*. In proportionate terms any change in quantity from zero is an *infinite* change, and thus elasticity must also be infinity.

(e) *False*. The elasticities of the two curves differ along their length (getting greater as you move down each curve). There are points high up on curve D_2 which are less elastic than points low down on curve D_1. Only if we specify that we are referring to the *same price range* in each case does the statement necessarily become true (see (g) below).

(f) *False*. At point z, curve D_2 is more elastic than curve D_1.

(g) *True*. See answer to (e) above.

Q45. *Arc elasticity*.

Q46. $(P_1 + P_2)/2$.

Q47. *(a)* See table below.

P(£)	10	9	8	7	6	5	4	3	2	1	0
Q_d	0	2	4	6	8	10	12	14	16	18	20

(b) $\Delta Q_d/(Q_{d_1} + Q_{d_2})/2 \div \Delta P/(P_1 + P_2)/2$

(i) $4/18 \div -2/1 = -1/9$ *inelastic*
(ii) $4/10 \div -2/5 = -1$ *unit elastic*
(iii) $4/4 \div -2/8 = -4$ *elastic*

(c) Take two points an equal distance either side of the point in question, and calculate arc elasticity between these two points.

(d) (i) $4/16 \div -2/2 = -1/4$
(ii) $4/8 \div -2/6 = -1\tfrac{1}{2}$
(iii) $4/10 \div -2/5 = -1$
(iv) $4(?)/20 \div -2(?)/0 = 0$
(v) $4(?)/0 \div -2(?)/20 = \infty$

Q48. See table below.

P(£)	10	9	8	7	6	5	4	3	2	1	0
Q_d	0	2	4	6	8	10	12	14	16	18	20
TR(£)	0	18	32	42	48	50	48	42	32	18	0

Q49. *(a)* Total expenditure will *rise* (as it does from £10 down to £5).

(b) Total expenditure will *fall* (as it does from £5 downwards).

(c) –1.

Q50. *False*.

Q51. *True*.

Q52. *True* (assuming that both axes start from zero).

*Q53. P/Q.

*Q54. *inverse of the slope*.

*Q55. *(a)* See table below.

P	5	4	3	2	1	0
Q_d	0	2	8	18	32	50

(b) See Figure A2.4.

(c) See Figure A2.4. The slope of the tangent is $-4/32 = -1/8$.

(d) $-8 \times 3/8 = -3$.

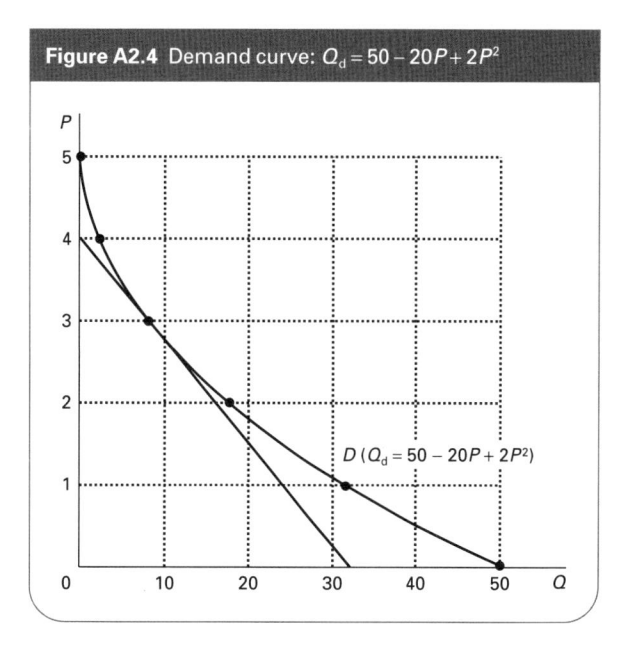

Figure A2.4 Demand curve: $Q_d = 50 - 20P + 2P^2$

Q56. *(a)* A. This means that for any given percentage fall in price, there will be a greater shift away from producing A than B.

(b) A. There is more time for supply to adjust to changing prices and hence profitability.

(c) B. For any given percentage increase in price, there will be a bigger percentage increase in resources attracted into B than into A before cost increases make it unprofitable to expand further.

(d) *Cannot say.* (A will have a more elastic *demand* than B.)

(e) B. The supply of A is unlikely to be affected much by its price if it is going to be produced anyway as a by-product.

(f) *Cannot say.* This affects elasticity of demand not elasticity of supply.

Q57. *(a)* *True.* All straight-line supply curves passing through the origin have an elasticity equal to 1 *irrespective of their slope.* (Try drawing some on graph paper and working out their elasticity over various sections.)

(b) *False.* See (c) and (d) below.

(c) *True.* The elasticity equals infinity at point y (see (e) below) and then diminishes as you move up the curve, but nevertheless stays above 1. (Again, try drawing it on graph paper and working out its elasticity over various sections.)

(d) *True.* At the point where it crosses the horizontal axis the proportionate change in price is infinite, and thus the elasticity is zero (a number divided by infinity is zero).

(e) *True.* At the point where it crosses the vertical axis, the proportionate change in quantity is infinite.

(f) *False.* It has an elasticity less than 1 throughout its length, but this nevertheless rises towards 1 as you move up the curve.

(g) *False.* See (a), (c), (d) and (e).

Q58. *Positive.* A *rise* in income causes a *rise* in demand.

Q59. *(a)* Good A: $Y\epsilon_d = 20/40 \div 10\,000/50\,000 = 2.5$.
Good B: $Y\epsilon_d = -4/50 \div 10\,000/50\,000 = -0.4$.
Good C: $Y\epsilon_d = 20/200 \div 10\,000/50\,000 = 0.5$.

(b) Good A. ($Y\epsilon_d > 1$.)

(c) Good B. ($Y\epsilon_d$ negative: a rise in income leads to *less* being purchased as people switch to superior goods.)

Q60. *True.* Expenditure on the good increases by a larger proportion than does income.

Q61. *(a)* (v) (strong complements).
(b) (iii) (unrelated).
(c) (ii) (moderate substitutes).
(d) (i) (close substitutes).
(e) (iv) (mildly complementary).

Q62. *less* price elastic.

Q63. *price.*

Q64. *quantity.*

Q65. E. Once they are cut, the supply is virtually fixed. The florist cannot choose to sell a given bunch of flowers next week or next month instead of today if today's demand is low. Note: A and B refer to *demand.* C is an *effect* of supply inelasticity, not a *cause.* D refers to *shifts* in the supply curve.

Q66. *left.*

Q67. *right.*

Q68. *rise.* The speculation is thus self-fulfilling.

Q69. Stabilising: (c).
Destabilising: (b).

Chapter Three

3

Government Intervention in the Market

A REVIEW

Chapter 2 examined the working of the free market. In the real world, the government often intervenes in the market. This intervention can take various forms. Examples include: price fixing, taxes or subsidies on various goods and services, directly taking over production, and rules and regulations governing the supply of certain goods.

In the first section we look at the effects of controlling prices, and in particular at the effects of setting either minimum or maximum prices. In the second section we examine the 'incidence' of taxes and subsidies on goods and services: who ends up paying the tax or receiving the subsidy – the producer or the consumer? To do this we must see what happens to price and this will depend on the price elasticities of demand and supply. In the third section we look at the extreme case of where the government rejects allocation by the market and either prohibits the production of certain goods or takes over production directly. Finally, we look at agriculture as a case study of different types of government intervention.

3.1 The control of prices

(Pages 64–6) The commonest form of price control is the setting of minimum or maximum prices.

If a minimum price (a price floor) is set above the equilibrium price, a **Q1.** *shortage/surplus* will result. If a maximum price (a price ceiling) is set below the equilibrium price, a **Q2.** *shortage/surplus* will result.

⊖ **Q3.** Figure 3.1 shows the demand and supply for petrol. The market is initially in equilibrium with a price of 50p per litre and sales of 40 million litres per day.

(a) Assume that the government is worried about inflation and decides to set a maximum price for petrol. What will be the effect if it sets this price at:

(i) 60p?..

(ii) 40p?..

(iii) Is a black market in petrol likely to emerge in either case?

60p: Yes/No

40p: Yes/No

(iv) Explain your answer to (iii).

....

....

Multiple choice   *Written answer*   *Delete wrong word*   *Diagram/table manipulation*   *Calculation*   *Matching/ordering*

32 CHAPTER 3 GOVERNMENT INTERVENTION IN THE MARKET

Figure 3.1 Intervention in the market for petrol

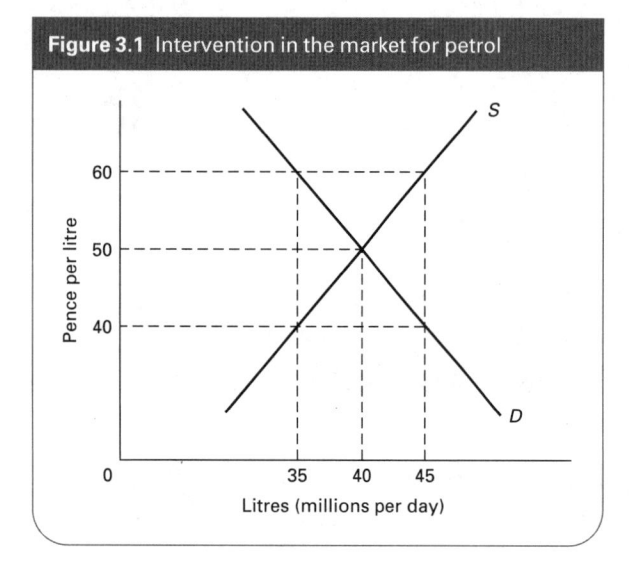

(b) Assume now that, worried about the effect of excessive fossil fuel consumption on global warming, the government passes a law forcing companies to sell petrol at 60p per litre, but agrees to buy (at 60p) any surplus and put it into store.
  (i) What will be the effect on consumer expenditure?

  ....

  (ii) How much will the government have to buy from the petrol companies?

  ....

  (iii) How much revenue will the petrol companies earn?

  ....

Q4. Which one of the following controls would involve setting a minimum price rather than a maximum price (where 'price' can include the price of the services of a factor of production)?
A. Controls on rents to protect tenants on low incomes.
B. Controls on wages to protect workers on low incomes.
C. Controls on basic food prices to protect consumers on low incomes.
D. Controls on transport fares to protect passengers on low incomes.
E. None of the above.

Q5. Give three problems that can occur when the government imposes maximum prices.

1. ....

2. ....

3. ....

Q6. Give three problems that can occur when the government imposes minimum prices.

1. ....

2. ....

3. ....

3.2 Indirect taxes

(Pages 67–8) Another form of government intervention in markets is the imposition of taxes on goods (indirect taxes). Such taxes include VAT and excise duties (on items such as cigarettes, alcohol and petrol). The taxes will have the effect of raising prices and thus could be used as a means not only of raising revenue for the government, but also of reducing the consumption of potentially harmful products.

A tax imposed on a good will have the effect of shifting the supply curve **Q7.** *upward/downward*. A specific tax will **Q8.** *make the supply curve steeper/make the supply curve shallower/leave the slope of the supply curve unaffected*. An *ad valorem* tax will **Q9.** *make the supply curve steeper/make the supply curve shallower/leave the slope of the supply curve unaffected*.

Q10. Figure 3.2 shows the effects of imposing taxes or giving subsidies on a good.
   Match each of the following to one of the four diagrams.
(a) An *ad valorem* subsidy   (i)/(ii)/(iii)/(iv)
(b) A specific tax   (i)/(ii)/(iii)/(iv)
(c) An *ad valorem* tax   (i)/(ii)/(iii)/(iv)
(d) A specific (per-unit) subsidy   (i)/(ii)/(iii)/(iv)

Figure 3.2 The effects of indirect taxes and subsidies

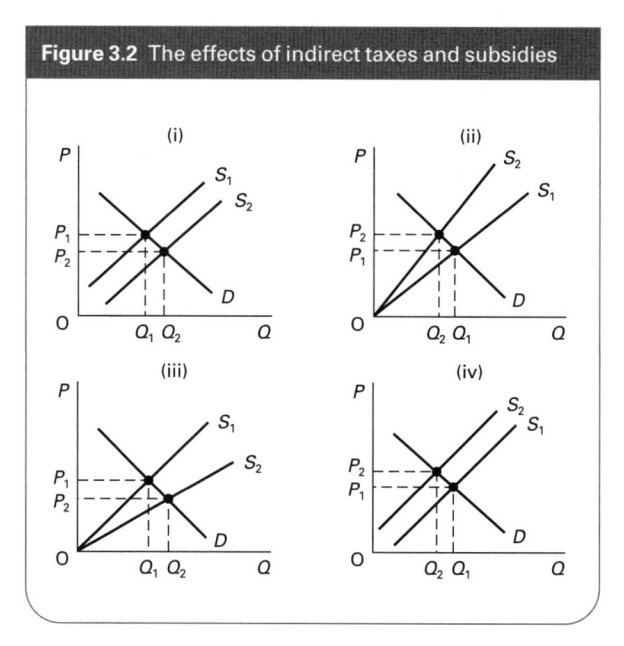

Q11. If the imposition of a tax (t) on a good has the effect of increasing the price from P_1 to P_2 and reducing the quantity sold from Q_1 to Q_2 then the consumers' share of the total tax paid is:
A. $P_2 \times Q_2$
B. $t \times (Q_1 - Q_2)$
C. $(P_2 - P_1) \times Q_2$
D. $(t - (P_2 - P_1)) \times Q_2$
E. $(P_2 - t) \times (Q_1 - Q_2)$
(Try sketching a diagram and attaching the appropriate labels.)

Q12. Referring to the information in Q11, the producers' share of the tax is:
A. B. C. D. E.

Q13. In which of the following situations would the imposition of a tax on a good involve the highest producers' share of the tax?
A. An elastic demand and an elastic supply.
B. An inelastic demand and an inelastic supply.
C. A unit-elastic demand and a unit-elastic supply.
D. An elastic demand and an inelastic supply.
E. An inelastic demand and an elastic supply.
(In each case 'elasticity' is referring to 'price elasticity'.)

3.3 Government rejection of market allocation

(Pages 69–70) With some goods and services, the government may feel that it is best to reject allocation through the market altogether. At one extreme, it may feel that certain products are so important to people that they ought to be provided free at the point of use. This is the equivalent of setting **Q14.** *a maximum price/a minimum price* of zero. The result is that there is likely to be a shortage of provision. This shortage is likely to be greater, the **Q15.** *greater/lower* is the price elasticity of demand for the product.

Q16. In the case of the provision of health care, shortages result in:
(a) Some people taking out private health insurance
   True/False
(b) Waiting lists   *True/False*
(c) Fewer people being treated than if the price were allowed to rise to the equilibrium   *True/False*
(d) Rationing   *True/False*
(e) Non-urgent cases not being treated   *True/False*
(f) Some non-serious cases not being treated   *True/False*
(g) Resources being diverted from education and social security   *True/False*

(Pages 70–1) At the other extreme, the government may feel that some products are so harmful, they ought to be banned.

Q17. Assume that a product (such as a drug) is made illegal. This will have the effect of:

(a) shifting the demand curve to the   *left/right*
(b) shifting the supply curve to the   *left/right*
(c) making the price in the illegal market (compared with the previous legal market)
   higher/lower/either higher or lower (depending on the relative shifts in the demand and supply curves)

Q18. Assuming that making a product illegal has the effect of making the illegal market price higher than the previous legal market price, under which one of the following circumstances would the price rise be the greatest?
A. A small shift in the supply curve and a large shift in the demand curve.
B. A small shift in the supply curve and a price-elastic demand.
C. A small shift in the supply curve and a price-inelastic demand.
D. A large shift in the supply curve and a price-elastic demand.
E. A large shift in the supply curve and a price-inelastic demand.

Q19. Assume that the government wishes to reduce consumption of a certain product. To achieve the same level of reduction by using a tax as by banning the product:
(a) A bigger shift in the supply curve will be required.
   True/False
(b) A smaller rise in price will be required.   *True/False*

3.4 Agriculture and agricultural policy

(Pages 71–3) Governments have intervened massively in agricultural markets throughout the world.

Short-term fluctuations in agricultural prices are due to problems on both the demand and supply sides.

Q20. Price fluctuations are likely to be greater,
(a) the more price elastic the supply.   *True/False*
(b) the greater the fluctuations in the harvest.   *True/False*
(c) the more price elastic the demand.   *True/False*

Q21. The following are possible features of the market for wheat.
 (i) There is substantial technical progress leading to increased production over the years.
 (ii) There is an income-inelastic demand for wheat.
(iii) There is a price-inelastic demand for wheat.
(iv) Wheat harvests fluctuate substantially with the weather.

Which of the above help to explain why incomes (i.e. revenues) of wheat farmers are likely to grow more slowly than incomes of producers of non-foodstuffs?
A. (ii) and (iii).
B. (i) and (iv).
C. (i), (iii) and (iv).
D. (i), (ii) and (iii).
E. (ii), (iii) and (iv).

34 CHAPTER 3 GOVERNMENT INTERVENTION IN THE MARKET

(Pages 73–81) There are several different ways a government can intervene to stabilise prices and/or to support farmers' incomes.

Q22. With each of the following schemes decide whether they will stabilise prices, support incomes or both.
(a) Buffer stocks (whose size fluctuates but is not allowed to grow bigger and bigger over the years).
Stabilise prices/Support incomes/Both
(b) Output subsidies (of a fixed amount per unit of output). *Stabilise prices/Support incomes/Both*
(c) Minimum prices with the government buying any resulting surpluses.
Stabilise prices/Support incomes/Both
(d) 'Set-aside' schemes (whereby farmers are paid to let land lie fallow). *Stabilise prices/Support incomes/Both*
(e) Variable import levies (to bring imported foodstuffs up to an agreed price level).
Stabilise prices/Support incomes/Both
(f) Investment grants to farmers.
Stabilise prices/Support incomes/Both
(g) A tariff of 10 per cent on imported food.
Stabilise prices/Support incomes/Both
(h) Quotas on the numbers of cattle that farmers are allowed to keep. *Stabilise prices/Support incomes/Both*
(i) 'Lump-sum' subsidies unrelated to output.
Stabilise prices/Support incomes/Both

Q23. Which of the schemes in Q22 will:

1. increase output of domestic producers? ....

2. decrease output of domestic producers? ....

3. either increase or decrease output of domestic producers depending on the circumstances?

   ....

4. have no effect on the output of domestic producers?

   ....

5. increase consumption? ....

6. decrease consumption? ....

7. either increase or decrease consumption depending on the circumstances?

   ....

8. have no effect on consumption? ....

If the government wants to support farmers' incomes, rather than merely stabilise prices, then two of the most widely used policies worldwide have been output subsidies and high minimum prices.

Q24. Figure 3.3 shows the market for a foodstuff in which a country is self-sufficient. The market price of P_1 is regarded as too low and the government wants farmers to receive a price of P_2.

Assume first that farmers are paid a guaranteed minimum price of P_2.
(a) How much will the government have to buy from producers?

....

(b) How much will it cost the taxpayer? ....

Assume now that the government, instead of paying a minimum price, gives an output subsidy.
(c) What must be the size of the subsidy per unit of output to have the same effect on farmers' incomes as the minimum price of P_2?

....

(d) How much will it cost the taxpayer? ....

In some cases the country may be a net importer of food, in which case the diagram for such a foodstuff will look like Figure 3.4.

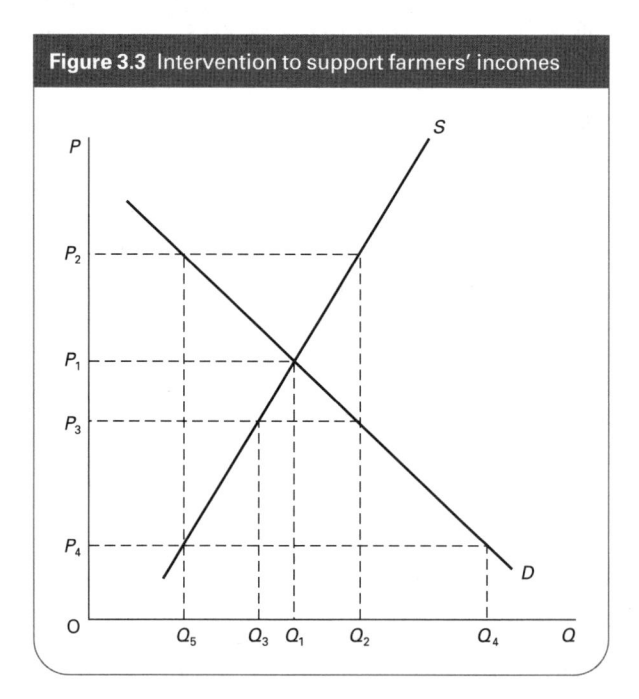

Figure 3.3 Intervention to support farmers' incomes

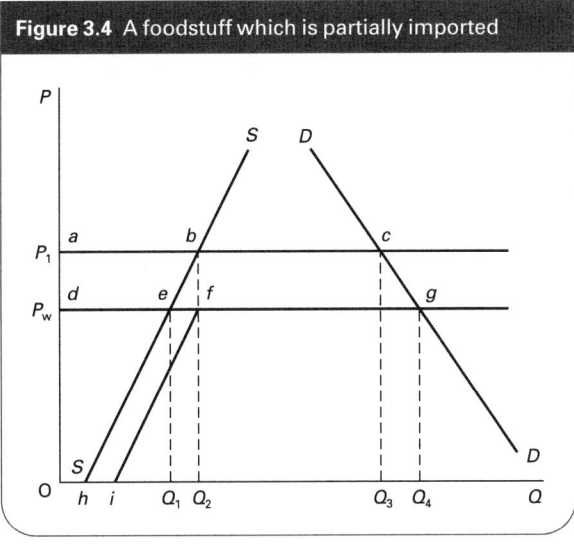

Figure 3.4 A foodstuff which is partially imported

Q25. Assume in Figure 3.4 that the world price is P_w and that initially there is no government intervention. The domestic supply and demand curves are given by SS and DD respectively.

(a) What is the total supply curve (domestic plus world)?

....

(b) What is the level of domestic production? ....

(c) What is the level of domestic consumption?

....

(d) What is the level of imports? ....

Now assume that the government imposes an import duty in order to raise the domestic price to P_1.

(e) What will the total supply curve be now?

....

(f) What will be the level of domestic production?

....

(g) What will be the level of domestic consumption?

....

(h) What will be the level of imports? ....

Q26. Continuing from the last question, now assume that instead of import duties, the government gives farmers a *subsidy* to bring their revenue per unit to a level of P_1.

(a) What will the supply curve be now? ....

(b) What will be the market price? ....

(c) What will be the level of domestic production?

....

(d) What will be the level of domestic consumption?

....

(e) What will be the level of imports? ....

Q27. Comparing the EU system of high minimum prices (and import levies) with a system of subsidies and free-market prices, the EU system
A. benefits consumers.
B. leads to less waste.
C. leads to less imports.
D. is less damaging to agriculture in developing countries.
E. leads to lower food prices.

Q28. Which of the following benefits could be argued to have resulted from the EU system of high minimum prices for agricultural produce?
(a) It has helped to lead to greater European self-sufficiency in food. *Yes/No*
(b) It has led to lower food prices in the short run. *Yes/No*
(c) It has led to lower food prices in the long run. *Yes/No*
(d) It has led to increased agricultural investment. *Yes/No*
(e) It has redistributed income more equally than would a system of subsidies. *Yes/No*
(f) It has benefited developing countries' agriculture. *Yes/No*
(g) It has led to more stable prices. *Yes/No*
(h) It has given a roughly equal level of agricultural support (per head of the agricultural population) to all the member countries. *Yes/No*

Q29. Give two ways in which the Common Agricultural Policy has harmed the agricultural sector in developing countries.

1. ....

2. ....

Compared with the free-market position, direct income support for farmers has the advantage of leading (in the short run) to **Q30.** *lower/higher/the same* prices and **Q31.** *lower/higher/the same* output.

B PROBLEMS, EXERCISES AND PROJECTS

Table 3.1 Demand and supply of solar panels

Price (per sq. metre) (£)	Quantity demanded (sq. metres per year) (000s)	Quantity supplied (sq. metres per year) (000s)
100	5	40
90	10	30
80	15	25
70	20	20
60	25	15
50	32	9
40	40	2
30	58	0

Q32. Table 3.1 gives (imaginary) information about the market for solar panels.
(a) What is the equilibrium price?
(b) Over what price range(s) is the demand curve a straight line?
(c) What is the price elasticity of demand (using the arc method) at the equilibrium price?
(d) Assume that the government wants to promote the purchase of solar panels by householders in order to save energy. As a result it decides to impose a maximum price. What will be the effect if the maximum price is: (i) £90, (ii) £60?
(e) Will a maximum price of £50 lead to a higher or lower level of panels being sold than if the price was left free to be determined by the market?
(f) Assume that the government abandons the use of maximum prices and instead decides to grant a subsidy to producers. What size subsidy must be granted in order to reduce the price to £60?
(g) How much will this subsidy cost the taxpayer?
(h) What will be the incidence of this subsidy between consumers and producers?

Q33. Refer back to the last two Budget speeches by the Chancellor of the Exchequer. (The Budget is given in March each year.) The speech is reported in full in *The Times* and in *Hansard*. See also the Treasury website at http://www.hm-treasury.gov.uk.

Examine the Chancellor's justification for any changes in the rate of duty on alcohol, petrol, tobacco or betting. What assumptions are being made about the price and income elasticities of demand for these items? Are the arguments consistent and are there any conflicts of objectives in government policy towards taxing these items?

Q34. Do a library or web search to find articles discussing problems and reform of the CAP. Your search could include web addresses A_1 to A_9, E_{14}, G_3 and G_9 in the websites appendix in Sloman 5th edition (see also the hotlinks section on the Sloman Web site at http://www.booksites.net/sloman).

Summarise the alternative agreements or proposals and consider their relative merits and any problems they are likely to cause.

C DISCUSSION TOPICS AND ESSAYS

Q35. Under what circumstances are black markets likely to develop? What will determine the level of the black market price?

Q36. Compare the relative merits of alternative means of reducing waiting lists for operations in National Health Service hospitals.

Q37. Give three examples of price controls. In each case identify the reasons for these controls and whether any other form of intervention could have achieved the same objectives.

Q38. Identify some measures the government could take to encourage energy conservation. Would any of these measures prevent a market equilibrium being achieved?

What effects would there be in other markets from the various measures?

Q39. How do the price elasticities of demand and supply affect the incidence of an indirect tax?

Q40. Assume that the government wishes to reduce smoking. Compare the relative advantages and disadvantages of (a) increased taxes on cigarettes, (b) making smoking illegal and (c) increased advertising of the health effects of smoking as means of achieving the government's objective.

Q41. Why are free-market agricultural prices and incomes subject to large fluctuations? What measures could a government adopt (a) to stabilise prices, (b) to stabilise incomes, (c) to stabilise both prices and incomes?

Q42. What would be the likely economic implications for consumers, farmers and the government, in both the short and long run, of totally removing the system of agricultural price support in the EU and replacing it with a system of subsidies unrelated to output?

Q43. Consider the relative advantages and disadvantages of alternative means of reforming the CAP.

Q44. Debate
The UK government was correct to abolish rent control in the 1980s.

D ARTICLES

The European Union has long intervened in the fishing industry through the use of subsidies and quotas. The following article, which appeared on *The Guardian* Web site on 19 April 2002, argues that the EU is finally facing the need for reform within the sector as fish stocks continue to decline.

EU ready for battle over fish policy

The EU's 'nightmarish' common fisheries policy is up for renewal and not before time but opponents of change are lying in wait, warns Andrew Osborn.

Fish hate it, fishermen either love it or loathe it and politicians curse the day they first heard of the EU's Common Fisheries Policy (CFP). It is, in the words of one EU official, 'a total nightmare' and has brought much of Europe's fish stocks to the brink of extinction.

Along with the EU's Common Agricultural Policy (CAP) it is denigrated and ripped apart on a regular basis by all and sundry. It is, in short, one of those indefensible, deeply flawed EU policies that give Brussels a bad name.

It has been around in its current form since the 1970s and is in desperate need of reform if Europe's depleted waters are to host any fish at all. People have been talking about shaking it up since its inception and now, after much lobbying and years of misery, the moment of truth has finally come – at least in theory.

On Wednesday of next week the European Commission will unveil its masterplan for change and tell the world's press that a new policy must be in place by 1 January 2003.

The precise details of the commission's plan remain a mystery but the broad outline is no secret. The EU's aptly named fisheries supremo Franz Fischler will say that Europe's fishing fleet is far too large and needs to be cut back – perhaps by as much as 50%. There are, he will say for the umpteenth time, simply too many boats chasing too few fish.

He is also likely to announce that some waters will have to be closed to fishing altogether if endangered stocks are to have any chance of recovery. The free-for-all is over, he will declare, and it is time to tweak the CFP in order to give the fish a fighting chance, something they simply don't have at the moment.

Fishermen will not be allowed to use any old net in future. In crude terms nets with smaller holes are in, Mr Fischler will say, while nets with larger holes are out.

The rationale behind this is simple. More tightly meshed nets will allow fishermen to catch only the fish they are chasing, and end the outrageous state of affairs where all kinds of other species are hoovered up inadvertently at the same time. These are usually thrown back into the sea, of no use to man or beast, by which time they are dead.

An age-old Brussels tradition – the annual setting of catch quotas – is also likely to be targeted for abolition. Each December EU fisheries ministers haggle with one another until they are blue in the face, which is usually by about three or four in the morning. The event always generates dramatic headlines such as 'cod quotas cut to 40-year low' and fishermen are usually quoted as saying, with some justification, that the new deal will put many of their number out of work.

The current system may provide predictable theatre but it is hideously short-termist. Ministers routinely ignore or dismiss scientific evidence of collapsing stocks and instead engage in an undignified bout of horse-trading motivated by domestic politics.

These annual circuses must be scrapped, the commission will insist, and replaced with bumper meetings every four or five years which can address long-term strategy and the sustainability of stocks.

EU subsidies – which have helped build up one of the world's most sophisticated fishing fleets – are also likely to be in the firing line.

No more money for new vessels or the modernisation of existing trawlers but plenty of EU funds for the definitive scrapping of boats.

Nor are fishermen likely to be left to their own devices. A new EU inspection agency with the power to police Europe's territorial waters to ensure that quotas are being respected is likely to be proposed.

All of this is highly progressive but whether any of it actually happens is up to the member states and things don't look good. A group of six countries is lining up to oppose much of what the commission will propose.

Laughably named 'the friends of fishing', the group – made up of France, Italy, Spain, Portugal, Greece and Ireland – is determined to frustrate many of the commission's ideas.

These countries are reluctant to cut their fleets or lose precious EU subsidies and argue (quite rightly) that many fishermen will lose their jobs if the commission gets its way. The fact that these same fishermen will not have any fish to catch if radical changes are not pushed through does not seem to have dawned on them.

Ironically the final shape of a new improved common fisheries policy is likely to be hammered out at another marathon session of horse-trading in Brussels – driven by domestic politics. The fish, it would seem, haven't got a chance.

(a) Explain how the EU fisheries policy has led to overfishing.
(b) How will the proposed reforms protect fish stocks and what are the likely consequences for consumers?
(c) What possible strategies could the EU use to reduce the severity of the impact of the reforms on local fishing communities?

The UK's privatised utilities have had regulators to control price rises and protect consumers' interests. The following press release by the Gas and Electricity Regulator (OFGEM) on 26 November 2001 suggests that there is a great enough degree of competition within these sectors to remove the use of price controls. It does, however, raise concerns about the interests of certain consumers.

Ofgem sets out future of regulation in gas and electricity supply

- MORI survey shows competition to be well established
- 38 per cent of all electricity and 37 per cent of all gas customers have switched supplier
- Less well off customers switching at same rate as the better off
- All remaining price controls on domestic electricity and gas supply to be lifted

Findings from the latest research into the state of competition in the domestic gas and electricity markets have supported energy regulator Ofgem's view that now is the time to remove all remaining price controls on gas and electricity suppliers.

Ofgem announced today (Monday) that, as predicted, competition has developed to such an extent that it is possible to lift price controls while still ensuring that customers are protected and continue to receive real benefits.

Today 38 per cent of all electricity customers and 37 per cent of all gas customers have switched supplier and they continue to do so at a rate of 100,000 electricity customers and 67,000 gas customers a week. This is a higher rate than for any other deregulated utility. More than 70 per cent of all gas customers and half of all electricity customers are now on tariffs which are not price controlled.

Ofgem Chief Executive, Callum McCarthy, said: 'This decision heralds the future of regulation for these markets. As the markets have become more and more competitive, there has been less justification for price controls.

'The focus of Ofgem's work going forward will increasingly be on monitoring competition and using competition law to tackle market abuse, pursuing a range of measures aimed at helping vulnerable customers and continuing work with other organisations to make it easier for customers to choose and change supplier.

'I would urge all customers to shop around for the best deals as there will be continuing pressure on prices thanks to the introduction of new wholesale trading arrangements.'

Each year, Ofgem commissions comprehensive research into the state of competition in these markets to inform its decisions. Highlights from this year's findings by MORI include:

- Customers are switching supplier across all income groups, with low income groups switching at a higher rate than the national average
- Around 100,000 electricity customers switch each week, with about 67,000 customers changing their gas supplier each week
- Companies are increasingly targeting customers on prepayment meters, and these customers are switching at as high a rate as other quarterly credit customers.

Under today's proposals, Ofgem will continue to protect customers by monitoring the domestic market to ensure competition is working effectively. Ofgem will take action against any company abusing its position using powers under the Competition Act.

Ofgem also continues to pursue a range of measures under the Social Action Plan to help customers in fuel poverty, and is working with energywatch and the industry to ensure that choosing and changing supplier is a simple experience.

Older people is one group which has not switched as much as other age groups – around 30 per cent compared to about 38 per cent on average. Ofgem will be working with Age Concern to raise awareness among older people of the savings that can be made by switching.

Gordon Lishman, Director General, Age Concern England, said: 'Older people are among the most reluctant to switch utility suppliers, yet many on low incomes could benefit from a better value deal by doing so. We look forward to explaining with Ofgem how we can encourage more older people to shop around for the best deal for them.'

(a) Why might a government wish to set a maximum (low) price?
(b) What are the likely economic consequences of the lifting of price controls in the gas and electricity markets?
(c) Are competition and market forces likely to maintain low prices in the future?
(d) What possible strategies could the government adopt to protect those most at risk from the removal of the price controls?

For many years, the EU has been attempting to reform the Common Agricultural Policy. The McSharry reforms (1992) and reforms under the Agenda 2000 programme (1999) are examples (see section 3.4 of *Economics* (5th edition)). These reforms have tried to do two main things: reduce the total amount of support and shift support away from keeping prices high to giving farmers grants unrelated to output. In 2002, the European Commission proposed more radical reforms. These are considered in the following article, which appeared in *The Times* of 28 June 2002.

Battle lines are drawn for EU farm reforms

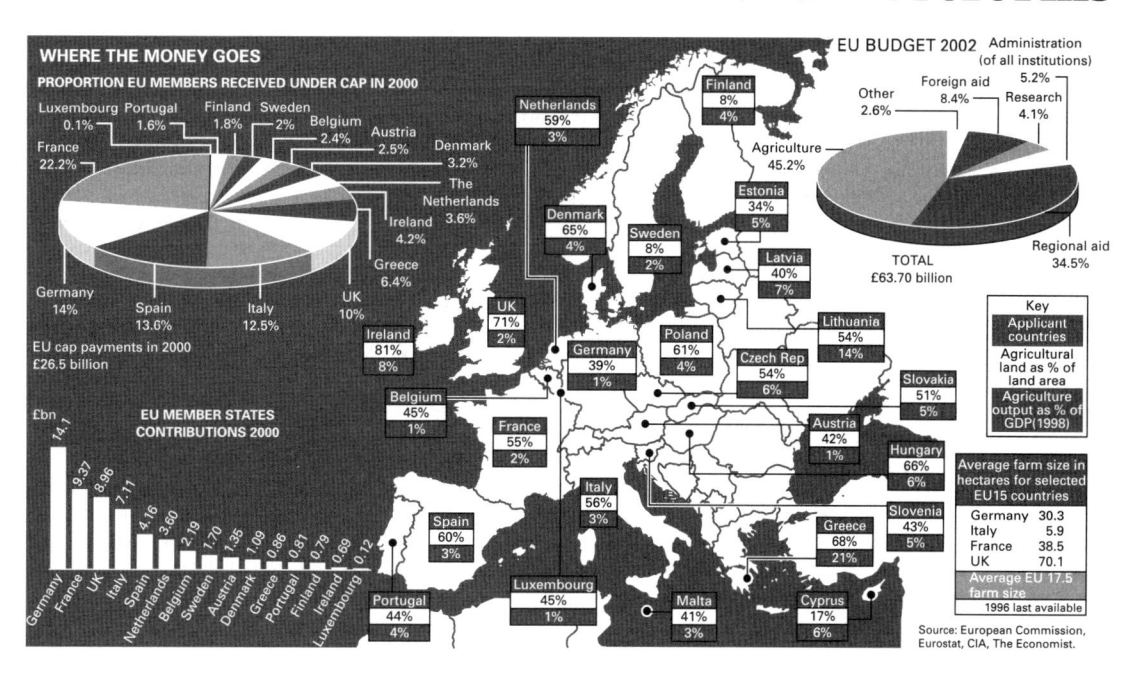

Source: European Commission, Eurostat, CIA, The Economist.

Big farmers will lose cash as subsidies shift to aid rural revival

Rory Watson

The European Commission is about to unveil far-reaching reforms of its £27 billion-a-year farm policy that aim to end food mountains, curb factory farming and restore the rural environment.

Describing the common agricultural policy (CAP) as 'no longer acceptable or sustainable', a 33-page draft strategy paper seen by *The Times* contains proposals that will change the face of European farming. The reforms – the most radical in the CAP's 40-year history – would cut the cash handouts that encourage relentless increases in production to the detriment of food safety, animal welfare and the countryside.

The paper proposes to shift funds away from the sort of intensive farming that contributed to the foot-and-mouth and BSE epidemics. Instead EU money will be redirected towards programmes to improve the environment and revive rural economies.

Main points

The planned reforms would:
- Sever the link between subsidies and production levels
- Promote rural economies and the environment
- Cap EU subsidies to the largest farms
- Simplify payments to farmers and reduce red tape
- Promote animal welfare and encourage food quality

It would also cap the huge subsidies paid to large farmers, most of whom are in Britain and eastern Germany. The National Farmers' Union said 580 farms in England would lose around £62 million.

The general thrust will be welcomed by the Government which has long championed reform of a policy that is widely discredited but accounts for nearly half the EU's budget.

However, the paper's publication on 10 July will set the scene for a bitter fight between the 15 member states that looks likely to culminate at December's Copenhagen summit. On one side will be the reformers – northern states led by Britain and the CAP's biggest financier, Germany. On the other will be defenders of the status quo championed by France, whose farmers are the CAP's biggest beneficiaries.

Franz Fischler, the Agriculture Commissioner who has drawn up the blueprint, argues that fundamental change is essential to respond to growing public concern about the way food is produced and agriculture supported. 'A common agricultural policy that encourages surpluses which then have to be disposed of – at considerable costs – is no longer acceptable or sustainable,' he says in the document.

The paper proposes to uncouple EU payments from production, removing farmers' incentive to produce ever more. Instead of being paid for every animal they keep or acres they harvest, farmers would receive a single income payment. This would be based on the subsidy received in previous years.

But the payments would be conditional on good farming practices.

Farmers would have to respect statutory environmental, animal welfare, food safety and occupational safety standards and could receive subsidies to help to meet them.

Herr Fischler is also looking to strike a better balance between agricultural production and rural policy by reducing direct payment subsidies to large farmers by 3 per cent annually for six years from 2004. The savings, estimated to be between £330 million and £400 million a year, would be channelled into schemes to improve rural development.

However, smaller farms, which make up 75 per cent of all farms in Europe, would be exempt from the annual subsidy cuts because they are more labour intensive, less prosperous and receive less support.

Particularly controversial for large British and German farms is the proposed introduction of a maximum annual subsidy per farm of £200,000.

British farmers complained of discrimination. 'They have just assumed that the 20 per cent of farmers who get 80 per cent of the CAP payments are the big boys with the most land,' Oliver Walston, an arable farmer, said. 'This will penalise us quite badly.'

One farmer with more than 5000 acres in Essex, who did not wish to be identified, said that he was following rumours with concern. He said that there would be a 'huge hole' in his accounts if these reforms went through.

'People will have to get round it and a lot will divide up the holdings for their children,' he said.

The main outcome, however, is likely to be an increase in contract farming, in which holdings of less than 2000 acres are let to tenant farmers.

Farmers' leaders are also 'extremely worried' about the rumours for reform. One senior figure in the National Farmers' Union said: 'We console ourselves that it is a negotiating position after all, and it may not be as grim.'

The union is anxious to know the finer details of the plan before being seen to disparage it publicly. There is no quarrel with Brussels' aim to protect small farmers, because this would help a number of hill farmers. They are also unclear whether some livestock farmers may be able to recoup lost subsidies by submitting claims for rural development projects, especially if it were seen as a kinder form of farming. Farmers who keep cattle in fields instead of rearing them by intensive farming production methods (for example, by keeping them indoors) are being named as potential winners. The union is concerned that Brussels may be ready to start cutting subsidies by 3 per cent a year for seven years from 2007.

Even though most Labour MPs consider farmers almost 'Luddite' in their opposition to reform, one of the first surprises which greeted Margaret Beckett, the Rural Affairs Secretary, when she took office last year was the goodwill towards CAP reform from individual farmers and farmers' leaders. This mood has grown since last year's foot-and-mouth epidemic and was best distilled in the blueprint for food and farming by Sir Don Curry and his team. His vision depended on a 20 per cent switch from wasteful handouts for food production towards more environmentally friendly farm practices by 2007, and is being hailed by all the leading green campaign groups.

Even organisations such as the Royal Society for the Protection of Birds and the National Trust now say that they have more to dread from the will of the Treasury in achieving their priorities for greener farming than from the attitude of farmers and landowners. They fear that Gordon Brown, the Chancellor, will not provide the £500 million in next month's comprehensive spending review to press for reform.

Even though Ben Gill, president of the National Farmers' Union, initially resisted this switch from handouts for food to environmental schemes, known as modulation, it was not because he was intrinsically against reform. His motivation was based on fear that current rules on modulation were too bureaucratic and would penalise farmers. He is now trying to work with the Government to develop a fair means of achieving modulation which reduces bureaucracy but which would still give farmers a basic income for managing the land.

(a) Why does the CAP system of price support encourage the production of 'mountains' and 'lakes'?

(b) What are the proposals for reform that are considered in the article?

(c) Who in the farming community would be the likely gainers and losers if these reforms were implemented?

(d) Would (i) consumers and (ii) taxpayers gain or lose from these reforms?

(e) Why were different countries within the EU likely to react differently to these proposals?

ANSWERS

Q1. *surplus.* If the minimum price is set at any point above the equilibrium, supply will exceed demand.

Q2. *shortage.* If the maximum price is set at any point below the equilibrium, demand will exceed supply.

Q3. *(a)* (i) *No effect.* Maximum price is above existing price.
  (ii) *Shortage of 10 million litres per day* (i.e. 45 − 35).
  (iii)/(iv) 60p: *No.* Price remains at the equilibrium of 50p.
  40p: *Possibly.* There will remain unsatisfied demand of 10 million litres, with, no doubt, some people being prepared to pay considerably more than 40p. Whether black marketeers can operate depends on whether there are any sources of supply that can avoid detection. This would clearly be difficult in the case of petrol.

  (b) (i) *Increase from £20 million per day* (40m × £0.50) *to £21 million* (35m × £0.60).

(ii) *10 million litres per day.*

(iii) *£27 million per day (45m × £0.60).*

Q4. B. Wage control to help those on low incomes will involve setting a minimum wage *above* the equilibrium wage in low-paid occupations. In the other three cases, the purpose of price controls would be to keep prices *below* the equilibrium if the aim was to help those on low incomes afford the particular type of good or service. In such cases, therefore, a *maximum* price (or rent) would be appropriate.

Q5. If the maximum price is set below the equilibrium, the following problems could occur: producers' income will be cut and thus supplies of an already scarce product (e.g. food supplies in a drought) are likely to be reduced further (a movement down the supply curve); firms will also be discouraged from investing and thus *future* supplies are likely to be less; unless a system of rationing is in place, some consumers may be unable to obtain the product (given that there will be a shortage at the maximum price), and this clearly could be unfair; a black market may develop; queues may develop and this is time consuming.

Q6. If the minimum price is set above the equilibrium, the following problems could occur: surpluses will be produced, which is wasteful (in the case of minimum wages, levels of unemployment in such occupations could rise); the government may have to spend taxpayers' money on purchasing the surpluses; high prices may cushion inefficiency, with firms feeling less need to find more efficient methods of production and to cut costs; firms may be discouraged from producing alternative goods which they could produce more efficiently or which are in higher demand, but which nevertheless have a lower (free-market) price; firms may find ways of evading the price controls and dumping the surpluses onto the market.

Q7. *upward.*

Q8. *leave the slope of the supply curve unaffected.*

Q9. *make the supply curve steeper.*

Q10. (a) (iii), (b) (iv), (c) (ii), (d) (i).

Q11. C. $(P_2 - P_1) \times Q_2$. See Figure A3.1.

Q12. D. $(t - (P_2 - P_1)) \times Q_2$. See Figure A3.1.

Q13. D. Price will rise less, and hence the producers' share will be larger, the more elastic is demand and the less elastic is supply (see cases (2) and (3) in Figure 3.5 on page 68 of Sloman 5th edition).

Q14. *maximum price.*

Q15. *greater.*

Q16. (a) *True.*
  (b) *True.*
  (c) The answer here depends on the assumptions made. The statement would be *true* if the supply curve were upward sloping (which would occur if money earned from selling health care were ploughed back into a greater level of provision). The statement would be *false* if (i) supply were totally inelastic or (ii) the government responded to the shortage by increasing the level of provision.
  (d) *True.* Some sort of rationing will normally occur. For example, specialists may decide which patients will be given expensive treatment and which will have to go without and have a cheaper (but less effective) treatment.
  (e) *False.* People would probably have to wait for non-urgent treatment, but most (if not all) serious non-urgent cases would still be treated.
  (f) *True.* Some people might be refused treatment. Others may not bother with treatment (or pay for private treatment) rather than wait.
  (g) *True* or *false* depending on the government's response to shortages.

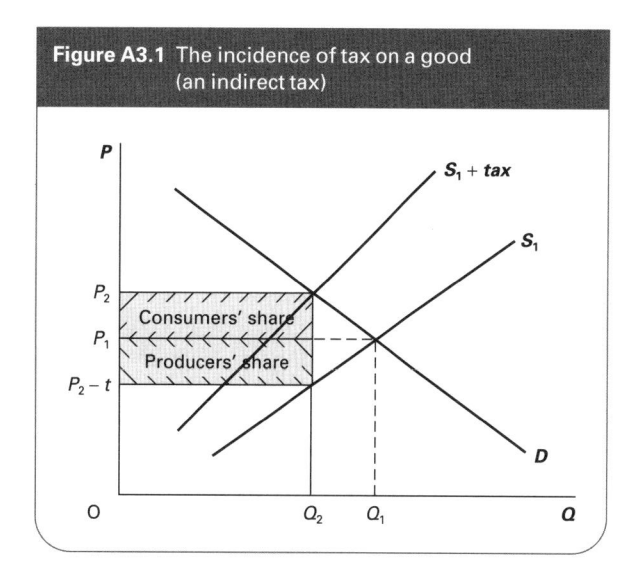

Q17. (a) *left.*
  (b) *left.*
  (c) *either higher or lower* (*depending on the relative shifts in the demand and supply curves*). Normally, it would be expected that the price would rise. The reason is that the penalties for supplying illegal products are usually higher than those for buying/possessing them. Thus the supply curve would shift to the left more than the demand curve.

Q18. E.

Q19. (a) *True.* The reason is that a tax (unlike making a product illegal) will not shift the demand curve.
  (b) *False.*

Q20. (a) *False.* The more elastic the supply, the less will price fluctuate for any given (horizontal) shift in either the demand or the supply curve.
  (b) *True.* The greater the fluctuations in the harvest, the bigger the shifts in the actual supply curve, and hence the bigger the fluctuations in price.
  (c) *False.* The more elastic the demand, the less will price fluctuate for any given (horizontal) shift in either the demand or the supply curve.

Figure A3.1 The incidence of tax on a good (an indirect tax)

42 CHAPTER 3 GOVERNMENT INTERVENTION IN THE MARKET

Q21. D. A larger increase over time in supply (i) than demand (ii), combined with a price inelastic demand (iii) will push prices down and hence lead to a relatively small growth in revenue. Fluctuations in the harvest (iv), on the other hand, will have little effect on *long-term* supply, and may even cause revenues to grow *more* rapidly over time if the fluctuations cause uncertainty and hence a fall in investment and a resultant smaller growth in supply.

Q22. *(a) Stabilise prices*. Prices will be kept up by buying into the stocks in years of good harvest, and selling from stocks in years of poor harvest. If the stocks are not allowed to grow over the years, the average price to the farmer will be no higher, just more stable.

(b) Support incomes. Output and hence prices will still fluctuate with the harvest, however.

(c) Both. If the minimum price is above the market price, this will both support farmers' incomes and stabilise the price (at the minimum level).

(d) Support incomes. Output will be reduced and, with a price-inelastic demand for food, farmers' revenue will thereby increase. Output will still fluctuate with the harvest, however.

(e) Both. If the agreed price is above the market level, this will both support farmers' incomes and stabilise the price (at the agreed level).

(f) Support incomes. Incomes will be supported in the short run, but in the long run, to the extent that the investment increases output, farmers' incomes will *fall*.

(g) Support incomes. This raises price to the farmer, but prices will still fluctuate with supply.

(h) Support incomes (slight stabilising effect on prices). To the extent that supply is reduced, price will rise. Prices will still fluctuate with demand and also with milk yields, even though the number of cattle will be more stable.

(i) Support incomes. Output will be largely unaffected, except for those farmers who would not have survived without the subsidy, and thus prices will continue to fluctuate.

Q23. 1. (b), (c), (e), (f) and (g).
2. (d) and (h).
3. (a). In years of good harvest, the government will buy into the buffer stock to keep prices up. This will increase domestic supply above the free-market level (unless supply is totally inelastic). In years of poor harvest, the government will release stocks on to the market to keep prices down. This will reduce domestic supply below the free-market level (unless, again, supply is totally inelastic).
4. (i). A lump-sum subsidy, by definition, does not depend on output. The profitability of producing extra output, therefore, is not affected by the subsidy. Thus the subsidy will have no effect on supply. (The one exception is those farmers who would not have survived without the subsidy.)
5. (b) and (f).
6. (c), (d), (e), (g) and (h).
7. (a). Consumption will be kept below the free-market level in years of good harvests because the government keeps the price up by buying into the buffer stocks. Consumption will be kept above the free-market level in years of bad harvest because the government releases supplies from the stocks to keep prices down.
8. (i).

Q24. *(a)* $Q_2 - Q_5$.
(b) $(Q_2 - Q_5) \times OP_2$.
(c) $P_2 - P_3$. This would shift the supply curve downwards by an amount $P_2 - P_3$ and thus reduce the price to P_3. Sales would increase to Q_2. Farmers would thus earn $(P_3 + \text{subsidy}) \times OQ_2$: the same as with the high minimum price of P_2.
(d) $(P_2 - P_3) \times OQ_2$.

Q25. (a) *heg*, (b) Q_1, (c) Q_4, (d) $Q_4 - Q_1$, (e) *hebc*, (f) Q_2, (g) Q_3, (h) $Q_3 - Q_2$.

Q26. (a) *ifg*, (b) P_w, (c) Q_2, (d) Q_4, (e) $Q_4 - Q_2$.

Q27. C. For any given price to the producer, and hence given domestic supply, the EU system of high minimum prices will lead to a higher price to the consumer and thus a lower level of consumption, and hence a lower level of imports. Note that in the case of A consumers pay a *higher* price under the EU system; in the case of B there are surpluses under the EU system and no surpluses under a system of subsidies; in the case of D the EU system leads to dumped foodstuffs on world markets and involves tariffs on imports of food (including from developing countries); in the case of E the EU system is specifically designed to lead to higher prices.

Q28. Yes: (a), (d), (g).
No: (b), (e), (f), (h).
In the case of (c) the answer could be either *yes* or *no*. It depends on whether the additional agricultural investment resulting from the CAP (and hence a lower *free*-market price) has been sufficient to offset maintaining the price above the equilibrium.

Q29. It has been more difficult for these countries to export to the EU; cheap EU food exports into these countries have made their domestic food production less profitable.

Q30. *the same*.

Q31. *the same*. Since direct income support (as opposed to output subsidies) is unrelated to output, it should have no effect on output, and hence no effect on prices – except that, by enabling farmers to invest more and marginal farmers to survive, it could increase output (and hence reduce prices) in the *long* run.

Chapter Four

4

Background to Demand

A REVIEW

In Chapter 2 we were concerned with the *total market* demand and supply. In this chapter and the next we go behind the demand and supply curves to examine the behaviour of individuals: individual consumers and individual producers.

In this chapter we consider the behaviour of consumers. We see what determines the quantity of various goods that people will demand at various prices and incomes. By building up a picture of individuals' demand we will then be in a better position to understand total market demand.

There are two major approaches to analysing consumer demand: the marginal utility approach and the indifference approach. We examine both of them in this chapter. We also look at the problem of making rational choices when we only have limited information.

4.1 Marginal utility theory

(Pages 88–9) People generally buy goods and services because they expect to gain satisfaction from them. We call this satisfaction *utility*. An important distinction we make is between *total* and *marginal* utility.

Q1. Total utility (*TU*) can be defined as

....

Q2. Marginal utility (*MU*) can be defined as

....

Q3. If I gain 20 units of satisfaction from consuming 4 toffees and 23 units of satisfaction from consuming 5 toffees, then my marginal utility from the 5th toffee is
A. 43 units.
B. 23 units.
C. 20 units.
D. 3 units.
E. −3 units.

Q4. Total utility will *fall* whenever
A. marginal utility is falling.
B. marginal utility is rising.
C. marginal utility has reached a maximum.
D. marginal utility is zero.
E. marginal utility is negative.

A problem with the utility approach to analysing consumer demand is that utility cannot be measured.

Nevertheless in order to understand how utility relates to consumer choice it is convenient to assume that it can be measured. We thus use an imaginary unit of satisfaction called 'utils'.

Q5. Table 4.1 shows the total utility that Katie derives from visits to the cinema per week.

Multiple choice | Written answer | Delete wrong word | Diagram/table manipulation | Calculation | Matching/ordering

44 CHAPTER 4 BACKGROUND TO DEMAND

Table 4.1 Katie's total and marginal utility from cinema visits

Visits	1	2	3	4	5	6	7	8
TU (utils)	12	20	25	28	30	31	31	29
MU (utils)	.	.	.	.	.	.	.	.

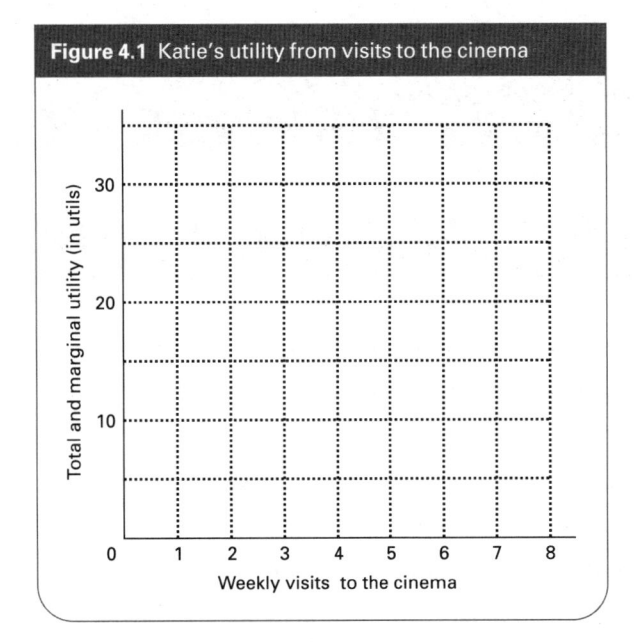

Figure 4.1 Katie's utility from visits to the cinema

(graph with y-axis "Total and marginal utility (in utils)" from 0 to 30+, x-axis "Weekly visits to the cinema" from 0 to 8)

(a) Fill in the figures for marginal utility. (Note that the *MU* figures are entered mid-way between the *TU* figures. This is because marginal utility is the extra utility of going from one level of consumption to the next.)
(b) Draw a graph of the figures for total and marginal utility on Figure 4.1.
(c) Assume that Katie now falls for a guy who also likes going to the cinema. As a result her marginal utility for each visit doubles. What is her total utility now for:
  (i) 3 visits?
  (ii) 6 visits?
  (iii) 7 visits?

You will notice from Figure 4.1 that the marginal utility curve slopes downwards. This is in accordance with the *principle of diminishing marginal utility*.

Q6. Which of the following are directly related to the principle of diminishing marginal utility?
(a) Rather than eating one large savoury course at dinner, I prefer to have less first course so as to leave room for a pudding. Yes/No
(b) I prefer to spend my time playing sport rather than watching television. Yes/No
(c) I like to watch a little television in the evenings. Yes/No
(d) I like watching comedy programmes more than documentaries. Yes/No
(e) I get bored easily. Yes/No

Q7. Diminishing marginal utility implies that total utility:
A. decreases at a decreasing rate.
B. decreases at a constant rate.
C. increases at a constant rate.
D. increases at an increasing rate.
E. increases at a decreasing rate.

(Page 90) When we draw up a utility schedule (like that in Table 4.1) we have to assume *ceteris paribus*. In other words, we assume that other factors which affect the utility gained from the product remain constant.

Q8. Make a list of four things that affect your marginal utility from a glass of orange juice (other than the number of glasses of orange juice you have already had). Will they increase or decrease your marginal utility?

1. .... Increase/Decrease
2. .... Increase/Decrease
3. .... Increase/Decrease
4. .... Increase/Decrease

(Pages 90–3) How much of a good will people buy? If they wish to maximise their self-interest (what is known as 'rational' behaviour), they will compare the marginal utility they expect to get from consuming the good with the price they have to pay. This will involve perceiving marginal utility in *money* terms (i.e. how much an extra unit of the good is worth to them). If the marginal utility exceeds the price, rational consumers will **Q9.** *buy more/buy less/not change their level of consumption*. If, however, price exceeds marginal utility, rational consumers will **Q10.** *buy more/buy less/not change their level of consumption*.

What we are saying is that the rational consumer will seek to maximise his or her *total consumer surplus (TCS)* from the good.

Q11. Table 4.2 shows the marginal utility a person gets from consuming different quantities of a good. Assume that the good sells for £10.
(a) What is the person's total utility from consuming 4 units?

....

(b) What is the person's total expenditure from consuming 6 units?

....

Table 4.2 Marginal utility for person Y from good X

Quantity consumed	0	1	2	3	4	5	6
Marginal utility (£s)		25	20	16	12	8	4

(c) What is the person's marginal consumer surplus from consuming a second unit?

....

(d) What is the person's marginal consumer surplus from consuming a fifth unit?

....

(e) What is the person's total consumer surplus from consuming 2 units?

....

(f) At what level of consumption is the person's total consumer surplus maximised?

....

(g) What is the marginal consumer surplus at this level?

....

(h) What is the relationship between price and marginal utility at this level?

....

Q12. In Figure 4.2 which area(s) represent total utility at a level of consumption of Q?

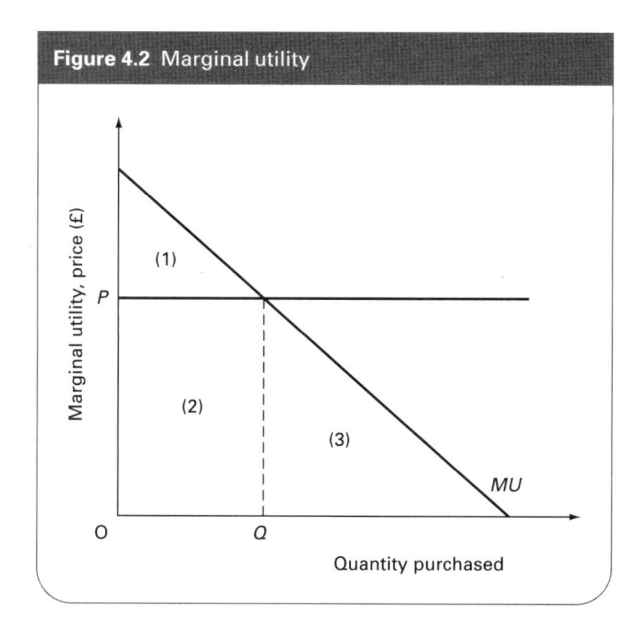

Figure 4.2 Marginal utility

A. 1
B. 2
C. 1 + 2
D. 2 + 3
E. 1 + 2 + 3

Q13. In Figure 4.2 which area(s) represent total consumer surplus at a level of consumption of Q?
A. 1
B. 2
C. 3
D. 1 + 2
E. 2 + 3

If we assume that an individual's income remains constant, his or her demand curve for a good will be directly related to **Q14.** *total utility/marginal utility*.

(Pages 93–6) Rather than focusing on how much of a *single* good people will buy, it is more satisfactory to examine how people will allocate their incomes *between* alternative goods. *Rational choice* involves comparing the marginal utility of each good relative to its price.

Take the simple case where a consumer buys just two goods, X and Y. If at the current level of consumption $MU_X/P_X > MU_Y/P_Y$, to maximise total utility the consumer should **Q15.** *buy more X relative to Y/buy more Y relative to X/buy whichever item is the cheaper*.

Q16. The consumer will continue switching until

....

Q17. Alison loves cheese. She particularly likes Dolcelatte, but also quite likes Cheddar. Her marginal utility from her last gram of Dolcelatte is double that from her last gram of Cheddar. Assuming that she consumes cheese 'rationally', and that Cheddar costs £4.00 per kilo, what is the price per kilo of Dolcelatte?
A. £1.00
B. £2.00
C. £4.00
D. £8.00
E. £16.00

Q18. Andrea spends all her income on just three goods X, Y and Z. If at her present level of consumption $MU_X/P_X > MU_Y/P_Y > MU_Z/P_Z$, which one of the following can we conclude?
A. She will buy more X and Y, and less Z.
B. She will buy more X, and less Y and Z.
C. She will buy more X, less Z, and the same amount of Y.
D. She will buy more X and less Z, but we cannot say whether she will buy more, less or the same amount of Y.
E. She will buy more X, but we cannot say whether she will buy more, less or the same amount of Y and Z.

4.2 Demand under conditions of risk and uncertainty

(Pages 97–100) When people buy consumer durables they may be uncertain of their benefits and any additional repair and maintenance costs. When they buy financial assets they may be uncertain of what will happen to their price in the future. Buying under these conditions of imperfect knowledge is therefore a form of gamble.

When we take such gambles, if we know the odds, then we are said to be operating under conditions of **Q19.** *probability/possibility/risk/uncertainty/certainty*. If we do not know the odds we are said to be operating under conditions of **Q20.** *probability/possibility/risk/uncertainty/ignorance*.

Q21. If you are prepared to accept odds of 10:1 on drawing an ace from a pack of cards (i.e. you win £10 for a £1 bet if you draw an ace), then how would your risk attitude be described? *Risk neutral/risk loving/risk averse*

Q22. Figure 4.3 shows the total utility that Clive, a first-year degree student, would get from different levels of annual income. Assume at the moment that his annual income (from an allowance from his parents and some part-time work in a burger bar) is £4000. Spending this rationally gives him a total utility of 500 'utils'.

Assume that he is offered the chance to gamble the whole £4000 on the toss of a coin at odds of 2:1 (i.e. if he wins, he doubles his money; if he loses, he loses the lot).

(a) If he takes the gamble, what will be his utility this year if he wins?

.... utils.

(b) If he takes the gamble, what will be his utility this year if he loses?

.... utils.

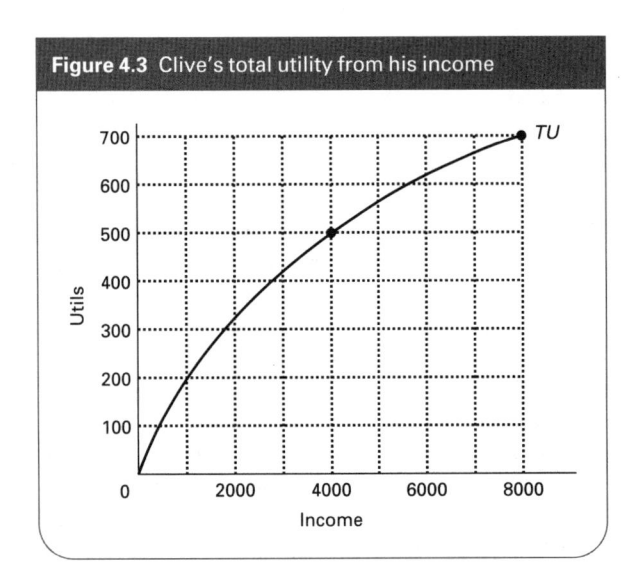

Figure 4.3 Clive's total utility from his income

(c) What would be his average expected utility from the gamble?

.... utils.

(d) Why is it likely that he will not take the gamble, and thus be risk averse?

.... utils.

Q23. People will be prepared to pay insurance premiums only if the insurance gives them 'fair odds'.
True/False

Q24. Of the following:
 (i) the law of large numbers
 (ii) the ability to spread risks
 (iii) the independence of risks
 (iv) the fact that insurance companies are technically 'risk lovers'
which help to explain why insurance companies are prepared to take on risks that individuals are not?
A. (i).
B. (i) and (ii).
C. (i), (ii) and (iii).
D. (ii), (iii) and (iv).
E. (i), (ii), (iii) and (iv).

Q25. In which of the following cases are the risks independent?
(a) Accident insurance for members of a football team travelling abroad.
Independent/Not independent
(b) Insurance against loss of income from redundancy (for people working for different companies all over the country).
Independent/Not independent
(c) Insurance against loss of income from accidents at work (for people working for different companies all over the country).
Independent/Not independent
(d) House contents insurance for houses in a particular neighbourhood.
Independent/Not independent
(e) Life assurance for people over 65.
Independent/Not independent
(f) Life assurance for soldiers.
Independent/Not independent

*4.3 Indifference analysis

(Pages 101–2) A problem with marginal utility analysis is that utility cannot be measured. An alternative approach is to use *indifference analysis*. This merely examines a consumer's preferences between different bundles of goods. It does not involve measuring utility.

Table 4.3 Sally's preferences between books and CDs (per year)

Set 1	Books	40	30	23	16	12	10	6	4	
	CDs	3	5	8	14	19	22	30	37	46
Set 2	Books	33	22	16	13	7	4			
	CDs	7	14	20	25	37	45			
Set 3	Books	40	30	22	20	17	14	11	6	2	1
	CDs	1	2	4	5	7	10	13	20	30	37
Set 4	Books	27	20	11	5					
	CDs	6	10	20	33					
Set 5	Books	30	20	16	12	6	3	1		
	CDs	1	3	4	6	10	14	20		

Figure 4.4 Sally's indifference curves between books and compact discs

(Number of books vs Number of compact discs — empty grid)

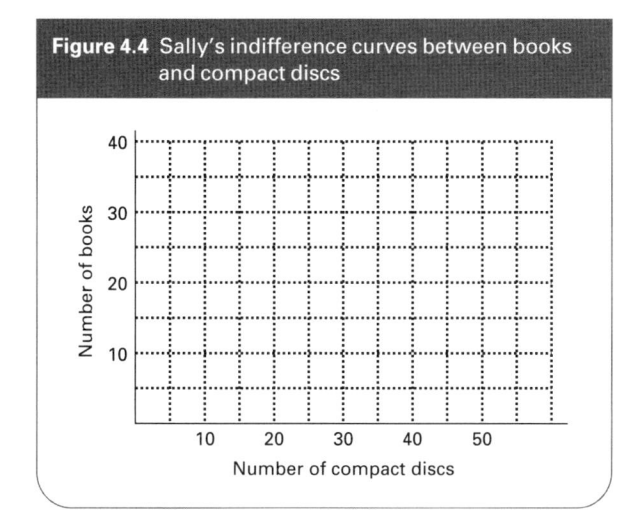

Q26. Sally, a first-year degree student, lives in a hall of residence and pays a fixed amount for food and accommodation. The money she has left over she spends on books and compact discs. Her preferences between various combinations of books and CDs are shown in Table 4.3. She is indifferent between the combinations in each of the five sets shown, but has preferences between sets.

(a) Plot indifference curves on Figure 4.4 corresponding to each of the sets in Table 4.3.
(b) Which set would Sally like best?
   set 1/set 2/set 3/set 4/set 5
(c) Between which two sets is Sally indifferent?
   set 1/set 2/set 3/set 4/set 5
(d) Which set does Sally like the least?
   set 1/set 2/set 3/set 4/set 5
(e) Given the information in Table 4.3, why would Sally *not* be indifferent between the combinations in the following set: 36 books and 5 CDs, 23 books and 8 CDs, 12 books and 13 CDs, 3 books and 20 CDs?

....

(Pages 102–3) The slope of the indifference curve is given by $\Delta Y / \Delta X$, where Y is the good measured on the vertical axis and X is the good measured on the horizontal axis. The slope gives the *marginal rate of substitution (MRS)*.

Q27. This can be defined as the amount of one good (Y) that a consumer is prepared to give up for

....

Q28. Referring again to Table 4.3, what is Sally's marginal rate of substitution of books for CDs in set 5 for

(a) the fourth CD? ....
(b) the sixth CD? ....
(c) the tenth CD? ....

Q29. Why are indifference curves drawn convex (bowed in) to the origin? Explain this in terms of the marginal rate of substitution.

....

....

Q30. The slope of an indifference curve (the *MRS*) also gives:
A. MU_X/MU_Y
B. MU_Y/MU_X
C. MU_X/P_X
D. MU_Y/P_Y
E. P_Y/P_X

(Pages 103–4)

Q31. Figure 4.5 shows a person's budget to spend on two goods X and Y.

Figure 4.5 A budget line

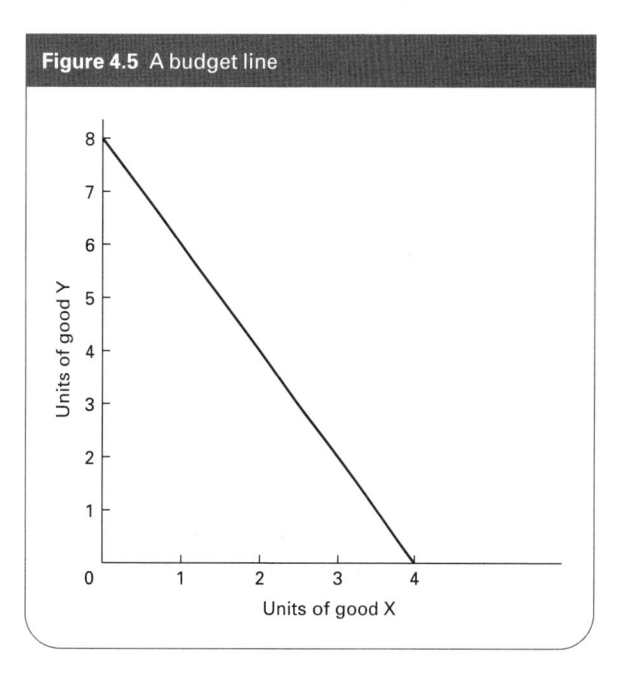

(Budget line from (0, 8) to (4, 0); Units of good Y vs Units of good X)

48 CHAPTER 4 BACKGROUND TO DEMAND

(a) If the size of the budget was £20, what would be the price of X and Y?

$P_X = $ ...., $P_Y = $ ....

(b) Assume that the price of Y rises to £4 (but that the price of X and the level of money income stay the same). Draw the new budget line.

(c) If the budget line does not shift again, but the price of X is now £10, what must be the size of the total budget now?

....

(d) What will be the price of Y now? $P_Y = $ ....

(e) If the prices of X and Y both double, but the consumer's money income also doubles, what will happen to the budget line?

....

Q32. Which of the following gives the slope of the budget line?
A. MU_X/MU_Y
B. MU_Y/MU_X
C. P_X/P_Y
D. P_Y/P_X
E. MRS

(Pages 104–6)
Q33. Referring back to Q26, assume that Sally has £300 per year to spend on a combination of books and CDs, and assume that all the books and CDs she wants cost £10 each.
(a) Draw in her budget line on Figure 4.4.
(b) What is the optimum amount of books and CDs for her to buy with this £300?

.... books, ... CDs

(c) Assume now that the price of CDs rises to £20. Draw in her new budget line.
(d) What is the optimum amount of books and CDs per year for her to buy now?

.... books, ... CDs

Q34. Match each of the following changes in an indifference diagram to the causes (a)–(h) of those changes. (In each case assume *ceteris paribus* and that units of Y are measured on the vertical axis and units of X on the horizontal axis.)
 (i) A parallel shift outwards of the budget line.
 (ii) The budget line becomes steeper.
 (iii) The indifference curves become flatter.
 (iv) A parallel shift inwards of the budget line.
 (v) A movement along the budget line to a higher indifference curve.
 (vi) A pivoting inwards of the budget line round the point where the budget line crosses the X axis.
 (vii) The indifference curves become steeper.
 (viii) A movement along the budget line from an old tangency point to a new one.

(a) An increase in the price of Y ....

(b) A shift in tastes towards Y and away from X.

....

(c) A rise in income ....

(d) A change in the optimum level of consumption resulting from a change in tastes

....

(e) A shift in tastes towards X and away from Y.

....

(f) An increase in utility resulting from a change in consumption.

....

(g) A decrease in the relative price of Y ....

(h) A fall in income ....

(Pages 106–7) We can use indifference analysis to show the effects of changes in price of one of the two goods on the quantity demanded of the good. This then enables us to derive an individual's demand curve for that good.

Q35. Tom has an income of £160 to spend on two goods X and Y. Assume that the price of Y is constant at £16.
(a) On Figure 4.6 plot the budget lines corresponding to $P_X = £10$, $P_X = £16$, $P_X = £20$, $P_X = £32$ and $P_X = £40$.
(b) Now show how much X will be consumed at each price. From this construct a *price–consumption curve*.
(c) Use this information to construct Tom's demand curve for good X.

The demand curve you have just derived is for the simple case where the consumer is only buying two goods (X and Y). In the real world people buy many goods.

Q36. How can we derive the demand for good X under these circumstances? The answer is to measure good X on the horizontal axis and

.... on the vertical axis.

Figure 4.6 The effect of change in the price of good X on Tom's consumption

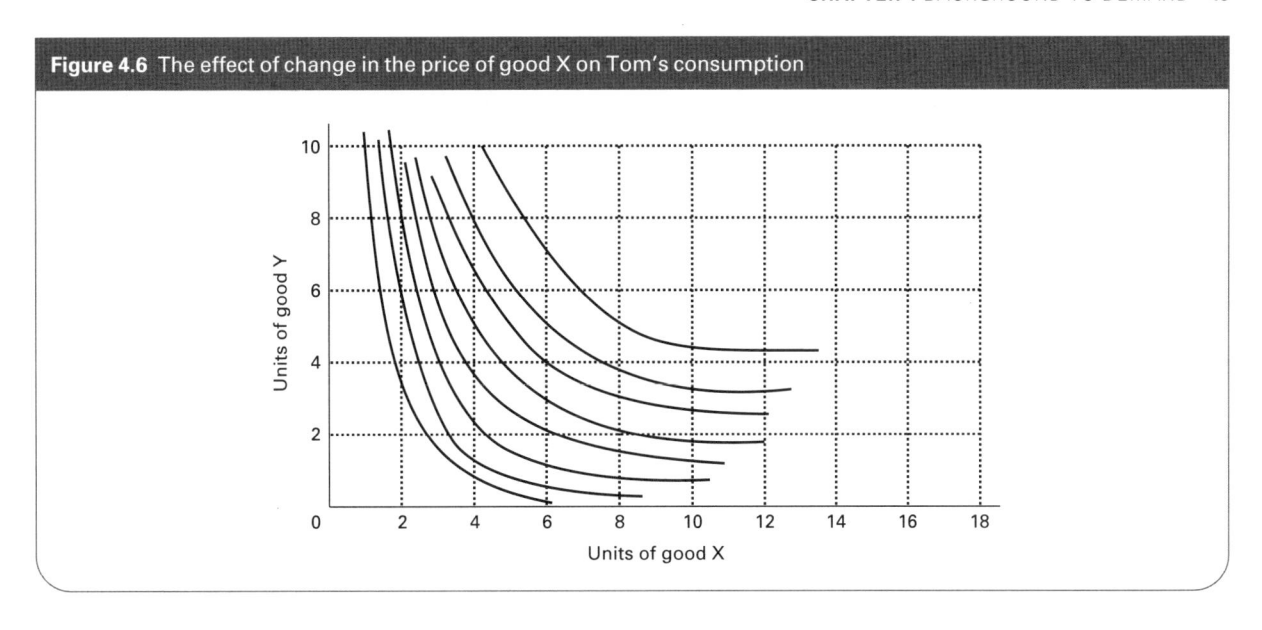

Figure 4.7 The income and substitution effects of a reduction in the price of good X

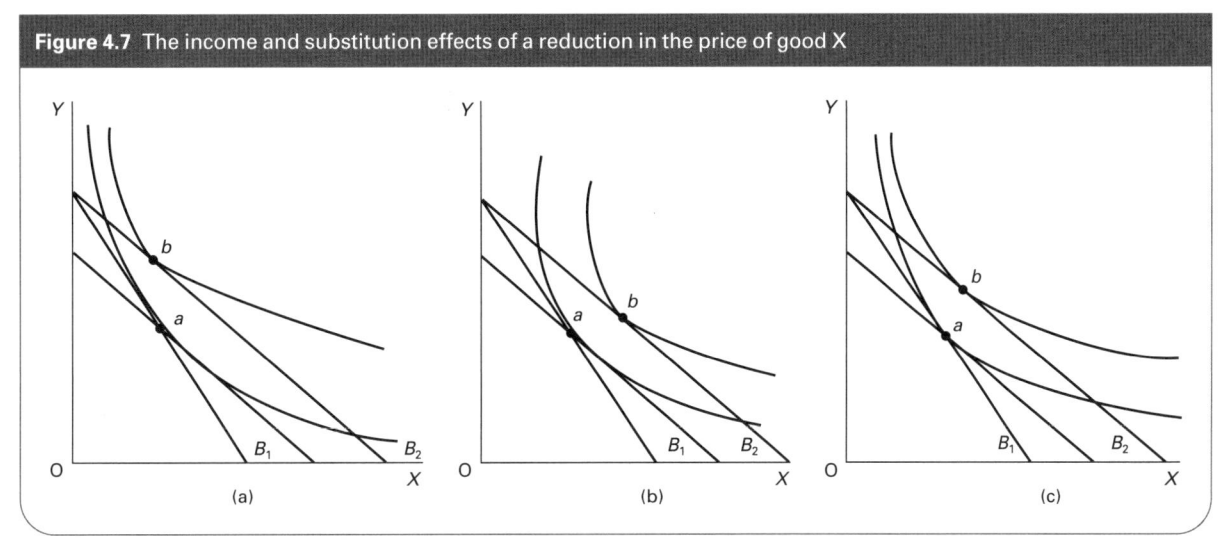

(Pages 107–11) As we saw in Chapter 2, the effect of a change in price can be divided into an income effect and a substitution effect. In examining these effects we can distinguish three types of good: a *normal good*, an *inferior (non-Giffen) good* and a *Giffen good*.

⊖ **Q37.** Figure 4.7 illustrates each of these three types of good measured on the X axis) and the effect in each case of a reduction in the price of good X and a consequent shift in the budget line from B_1 to B_2.
(*a*) Mark the income and substitution effects in each diagram.
(*b*) In which diagram is X

　　(i) a normal good? ....

　　(ii) an inferior, but non-Giffen good? ....

　　(iii) a Giffen good? ....

Table 4.4 Income and substitution effects of a price change

Type of good	Substitution effect	Income effect	Which is the bigger effect?
Normal	positive/ negative	positive/ negative	income/substitution/ either
Inferior (non-Giffen)	positive/ negative	positive/ negative	income/substitution/ either
Giffen	positive/ negative	positive/ negative	income/substitution/ either

◐ **Q38.** Table 4.4 is used to summarise the direction and relative size of the income and substitution effects. Cross out the incorrect information.

◐ **Q39.** When the price of an inferior (but non-Giffen) good rises, people will consume more of it. *True/False*

B PROBLEMS, EXERCISES AND PROJECTS

Q40. Select three items of foodstuff that you purchase regularly (e.g. bread, eggs, potatoes).
(a) In each case estimate how much per week you would purchase at different prices.
(b) In each case work out the amount of consumer surplus you receive per week.
(c) Now ask yourself how much money you would need to be given in each case in order to persuade you not to buy any of the good at all.
(d) Are the answers to (b) and (c) similar? Should they be?
(e) Now choose one of the three goods and select a substitute good for it. How will (i) a 10 per cent rise, (ii) a 20 per cent fall and (iii) a 50 per cent rise in the price of the substitute affect the consumer surplus you gain from the original good?
(f) How will your consumer surplus for each of the three goods be affected by a change in your income?

Q41. Imagine that you have £30 to spend on three goods, A, B and C. The marginal utility you gain from each good is independent of the amount you consume of the other two goods. Your marginal utility from successive units of each of the three goods is shown in Table 4.5.

Table 4.5 Marginal utilities (in utils) from the consumption of three goods A, B and C

Units of good A	1	2	3	4	5	6	7	8	9	10
Marginal utility	45	40	25	20	16	12	9	6	4	2
Units of good B	1	2	3	4	5	6	7	8	9	10
Marginal utility	80	70	60	50	40	30	20	10	0	0
Units of good C	1	2	3	4	5	6	7	8	9	10
Marginal utility	22	20	18	16	14	12	10	8	6	4

(a) Imagine that good A costs £4, good B costs £3 and good C costs £2. How much will you consume of each?
(b) Assume now that the price of A rises to £10, that the price of B falls to £2 and the price of C remains unchanged at £2. How much of each will be consumed now, assuming the budget remains unchanged at £30?
(c) In which situation (a) or (b) is total utility higher?

***Q42.** Harry gains equal satisfaction from the following combinations of annual visits to the theatre and visits to football matches:
 14 theatre and 3 football
 11 theatre and 4 football
 8 theatre and 6 football
 6 theatre and 9 football
 4 theatre and 16 football

(a) Using graph paper, plot Harry's indifference curve corresponding to these figures. Plot theatre visits on the vertical axis.
(b) If Harry actually visited the theatre 5 times, how many football matches would he have to attend in order to obtain the same satisfaction as in the other 5 combinations?
(c) What is the marginal rate of substitution of theatre visits for football matches between 4 and 6 football matches?
(d) What is the marginal rate of substitution of theatre visits for football matches at the 8 theatre, 6 football point on the indifference curve?
(e) Assume that Harry decides to allocate a total of £280 per year to these two activities. Assume also that both football matches and theatre visits cost £20. How many visits to the theatre could he make if he attended 9 football matches?
(f) Draw Harry's budget line on your diagram.
(g) How many theatre performances and football matches will he attend?
Why will he not attend an equal number of each?
(h) Assume now that the price of theatre tickets increases to £40, but that Harry unfortunately cannot afford to budget for any more than the £280. Draw Harry's new budget line.
(i) Poor Harry is now going to have to economise on the number of visits to either or both types of event. So he sits down and thinks about alternative combinations that would give him equal satisfaction to each other (but less than before). He comes up with the following combinations:
 12 theatre and 2 football
 9 theatre and 3 football
 6 theatre and 5 football
 3 theatre and 8 football
 2 theatre and 11 football
 1 theatre and 15 football
Draw this indifference curve on the diagram.
(j) How many theatre performances and football matches will he now attend?
(k) Assume that Harry now wonders whether to try to maintain his previous level of satisfaction by allocating a bigger budget to compensate for the higher price of theatre tickets. If he did do this, what would his new budget line look like? (Draw it.)
(l) How many theatre performances and football matches would he attend under these circumstances?
(m) How much would this cost him?
(n) Had he maintained his original combination of visits, how much would this now have cost him?
(o) On second thoughts he reluctantly decides he will have to restrict himself to the original £280 and thus the answer to (j) above holds. What will be the size of the income and substitution effects

of the rise in the price of theatre tickets from £20 to £40?
(p) Are theatre visits a normal or an inferior 'good' for Harry? Explain.
(q) If Harry meets Sally and she likes going to the cinema with Harry rather than to the theatre, how will this affect Harry's indifference curves between visits to the theatre and visits to football matches?

C DISCUSSION TOPICS AND ESSAYS

Q43. If people buy things out of habit, does this conflict with the assumption of rational behaviour?

Q44. In the UK most domestic consumers pay for water through a system of water rates which are based on the value of the person's property. This is a flat sum and does not vary with the amount of water consumed. What would you expect a person's marginal utility for water to be? Make out a case for and against having water meters and charging for water on a per litre basis.

Q45. What are the drawbacks in attempting to measure utility in money terms?

Q46. Explain how goods with little total utility to the consumer can sell for a high price.

Q47. Explain the difference between the terms 'risk loving', 'risk neutral' and 'risk averse'. Would a risk-loving person ever be prepared to take out insurance?

Q48. How can insurance companies protect themselves against the problems of adverse selection and moral hazard?

*Q49. Could indifference curves ever intersect (i) over the same time period, (ii) over different time periods?

*Q50. Imagine that the price–consumption curve for good X was downward sloping. Are goods X and Y substitutes or complements? Explain.

*Q51. What are the limitations of indifference analysis for (a) explaining and (b) predicting consumption patterns for a given consumer?

Q52. Debate
It is wrong for the state to provide services such as health and libraries free at the point of use. With a zero price, people consume a wasteful amount. They consume to the point where marginal utility is zero.

D ARTICLES

When economists build models they are required to make a series of simplifying assumptions, none more so than that concerning human behaviour. Individuals are assumed to be 'rational utility maximisers', who are motivated by self-gain. Such an assumption is, in many cases, clearly unrealistic and a major limitation on the economist attempting to explain so-called 'irrational' economic behaviour. The article below, taken from *The Economist* of 25 December 1993, shows how such a perception of human nature is being questioned and how an understanding of biology might be the key to constructing a more realistic view of human economic behaviour.

Biology meets the dismal science

In the past few years a curious flirtation has developed in the halls of academe between economists and Darwinian biologists. They talk the same language, borrow each other's techniques and come to similar conclusions. A recent issue of the *American Economic Review* contained a series of papers on altruistic behaviour. In June, at the London School of Economics, a conference explored the common ground between economics and evolution. A new discipline of evolutionary economics is being born.

To thine own self be true
The common ground between economics and evolution is a focus on the individual. In the 1960s, both economists and students of the evolution of social behaviour in animals lurched towards individualism. They became convinced that you can understand what happens to groups, populations, nations or species only by understanding what motivates individual people and animals. Societies are the sums of individuals. According to economists, individuals maximise their 'utility functions' (roughly equivalent to

consumption); according to evolutionists, they maximise their 'fitness functions' (roughly, successful offspring). But the process is much the same.

Paul Romer, an economist at the University of California at Berkeley, insists that it is not just an analogy to see fitness and utility as similar concepts. When he talks to people who study the evolution of behaviour, he finds that they, like him, are concerned with the individual organism. None of them assumes that classes and groups have distinct properties of their own. In this respect, economics is closer to biology than it is to sociology – which talks about the actions of groups.

Biologists return the compliment. Helena Cronin, an evolutionary theorist at the London School of Economics, says economists are more aware of the problems of emergent properties than other scientists – that is, of how collective effects flow from individual behaviour.

So both evolutionists and economists found themselves arguing that individuals do things for the good of the larger group only if it is also for the good of the individual. Animals rarely do selfless things for their species. And people rarely do selfless things for the good of society. (If it were otherwise, communism might have stood a better chance.)

At first, such emphasis on individualism seems to leave both disciplines committed to a ruthless and opportunistic view of human nature: man as Robinson Crusoe, alone and self-centred. Such a view of mankind is patently wrong.

Never fear. Even desiccated economists had noticed the 'voter paradox': people vote in elections, despite the fact that no individual can expect to influence the outcome. Many other examples are much more obvious. People give to charity. Executives work long hours on behalf of their firms. Travellers tip waiters they will never see again. Soldiers willingly risk their lives for their country. Trust, co-operation and altruism are all part of human life.

But guess what. They are also part of animal life. Monkeys groom each other. Birds give alarm calls to warn each other of danger. Bees feed their queen and her daughters and defend their hives to the death. Animal altruism abounds. The question is: how do you reconcile altruism with the invisible hand and survival of the fittest?

Economists, observant folk, have always recognised that people are nicer to their children than to strangers. But they have had difficulty making sense of this in terms of their theories, because it seems to be merely an irrational whim. But as the theory of 'kin-selection' gained ground within evolutionary biology – a theory in which the survival not of the individual but of its genes (in descendants and close relatives) became the criterion of fitness – so economists have learnt to adjust their utility functions to include not just people's own consumption, but also their children's.

Any theory of how people save and spend needs to take this into account. To put it starkly, economists used to be puzzled by the way people continue saving right up to the ends of their lives. Now they recognise that 'utility' includes leaving something to your children.

A theory of preferences

Economists believe in a typical human being, whose actions they can predict based on an assumption of what motivates him or her. Evolutionary psychologists find evidence that they are right.

Utah's Alan Rogers describes economics as an elaborate theory that takes human preferences as its premise. Evolution, he says, can be construed as a theory of those preferences. In other words, economists may assume that people generally love their children; evolutionists can explain why they love their children.

Take the issue of 'concern for fairness'. Economists have noticed that a concern for fairness seems to be a strong motive in human decisions. The desire to see fair play drives much political debate. People are not the ruthless opportunists that naive economic theory assumes.

Parallels in the business world are immediately apparent. Few businessmen would think of themselves and the others they come across as ruthless or impatient self-seekers. Instead, they see people who seek co-operation, do deals on trust, share secrets with confidants, and get ahead by building friendships and alliances. Robert Maxwells, who betray their employees and confederates, and do not care what people think of them, are the exceptions, not the rule. Lord Vinson, a successful British entrepreneur, cites as one of his ten commandments of entrepreneurship: 'Trust everyone unless you have a reason not to.'

Naive economics and naive sociobiology still teach that people are ruthlessly self-interested. But where the two disciplines have come together, a much sunnier side of mankind's nature has emerged. People are opportunistic seekers of co-operation. Nice guys, far from finishing last, may in fact attract the kind of co-operation that enables them to come out ahead.

© *The Economist*, London (25.12.93)

(a) Explain what is meant by the 'voter paradox'. Give some examples from your own experience of altruistic behaviour (i.e. doing things for others with no gain to yourself).

(b) If people are not always motivated by self-interest, does this make marginal utility theory redundant?

(c) Assuming that people take the interests of others into account when making economic decisions, how would this affect the nature of demand curves? Would people still respond in the same way to price changes as under traditional assumptions of self-interested behaviour?

*(d) Would the assumptions of altruism and co-operation make indifference curve analysis irrelevant?

(e) Does the article in any way challenge the economist's definition of the central 'economic problem'?

Economists assume that individuals make rational economic decisions. They do so by weighing up the associated costs and benefits of any given purchase or decision: in other words, they estimate the total utility they might gain from such an activity. But how certain can they be about their decision? Can they guarantee that costs will not change? Once uncertainty is considered, individuals may seek ways of reducing such unpredictability: for example, by taking out insurance. The article below, taken from *The Economist* of 29 July 1995, looks at the role of insurance and the problems facing insurance companies.

An insurer's worst nightmare

Aeroplane crashes, oil spills and product failures are generally unpredictable events. But they are not totally random: their occurrence can sometimes be influenced by human actions. And although insurance can help to protect people from the financial impact of accidental misfortune, it may also inadvertently make them more accident-prone.

Insurance works on the principle of pooling risks and charging each customer a premium based only on the average risk of the pool. This approach has much appeal: as the chart shows, worldwide spending on insurance premiums continues to rise. But it also presents two problems, which economists call 'adverse selection' and 'moral hazard'.

Customers who have the greatest incentive to buy insurance are likely to be those who pose the worst risk for insurers, hence adverse selection. A person will be keener to buy health insurance, for example, if he is already ill. This increases the odds that insurers will have to pay claims and so may drive up premiums for healthier people. It should not, however, increase society's total risk.

Moral hazard does. This describes the temptation for a customer, once he has bought insurance, to take greater risks than he otherwise might have done.

Moral hazard can take different forms. A customer might, for instance, increase the chances that he will incur a loss; somebody with car insurance may drive more recklessly than he would if he were uninsured. And even though an insured person may try to reduce the odds of a mishap, he may do so in a way that increases the size of the potential loss. A firm that discovers it has a defective product, for example, may withhold its finding to avoid early lawsuits it has to settle itself, while raising the risk of a huge later payout that falls on its insurance company.

Insurers have long looked for ways to cope with these problems. To counter adverse selection, they may practise a bit of their own: setting lower health-insurance rates for young people, for instance, or having their offices on the fourth floor without a lift. And to fend off moral hazard, they tend not to offer full insurance, but to pass some risk back to customers. The best technique for this depends on the kind of moral hazard an insurer faces.

When confronted with moral hazard that increases risk, insurers often resort to a 'deductible'. This requires the customer to pay in full the first portion of any claim. When someone crashes a car, for example, he often has to pay the first few hundred dollars of expenses before collecting the rest from his insurer. This not only encourages customers to drive more safely, but also cuts the insurer's administrative costs, since customers have no incentive to file small claims.

To cope with moral hazard that might increase the size of potential losses, insurers demand 'co-payments'. Rather than making customers pay the cost of a claim in full up to a certain limit, insurers require them to pay a fraction of the entire cost. Since bigger losses will mean bigger co-payments for the insured, it will remain in customers' interests to keep losses as low as possible.

Yet although insurers seem to have individual mechanisms that can cope with moral hazard, they run into trouble when they try to combine them. Many insurers, for instance, ask customers to pay an initial deductible and a small portion of all other costs above this. But this approach has a serious flaw, for deductibles can increase the moral hazard that raises the size of potential losses.

Consider, for example, a car maker that discovers a possible defect in a batch of cars that it has sold. There is a small chance that many of the cars have been built with a defective part, which would cause a string of fatal accidents. For a cost of, say, $20m, the firm can recall all of these cars and repair them. If it does nothing, it risks having to pay out several hundred million dollars if people are killed. The firm's insurer faces two kinds of moral hazard: if it insures the company against all recalls, the firm may often use them for trivial reasons; if it insures it only against large losses, the firm may avoid recalls altogether.

Mixing deductibles with small co-payments can make this worse. In some cases, the deductible will discourage a recall by more than the co-payment encourages one, even if the right decision is to recall the cars. But combining big deductibles with big co-payments might deter people from buying insurance altogether.

© *The Economist*, London (29.7.95)

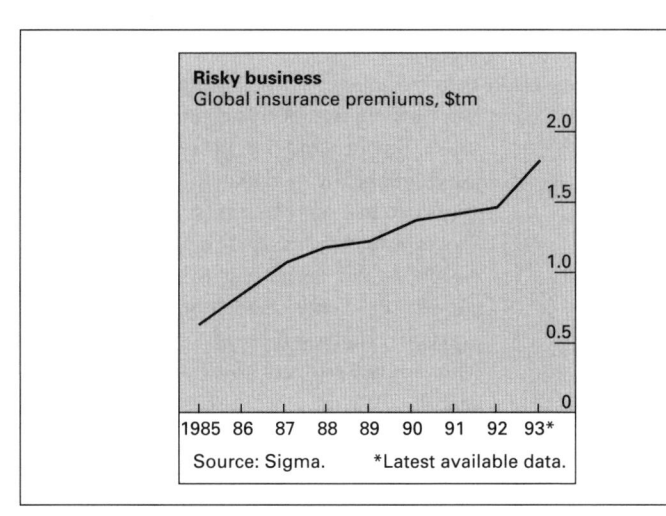

Risky business
Global insurance premiums, $tm

Source: Sigma. *Latest available data.

54 CHAPTER 4 BACKGROUND TO DEMAND

(a) What is the function of insurance and the role of the insurance company?
(b) What is meant by the terms 'adverse selection' and 'moral hazard'?
(c) How have insurance companies attempted to overcome the problems of (i) adverse selection and (ii) moral hazard?

E) ANSWERS

Q1. The total amount of satisfaction a consumer gains by consuming a given quantity of a good or service over a given time period.

Q2. The additional satisfaction a consumer gains by consuming one more unit of a good or service within the same time period.

Q3. D. By consuming the fifth toffee, my total utility has gone up from 20 units to 23 units: a rise of 3 units.

Q4. E. If total utility is falling then the last unit must *reduce* total utility: its marginal utility must be negative.

Q5. (a) See table below.

Visits	1	2	3	4	5	6	7	8
TU (utils)	12	20	25	28	30	31	31	29
MU (utils)	12	8	5	3	2	1	0	-2

(b) See Figure A4.1.

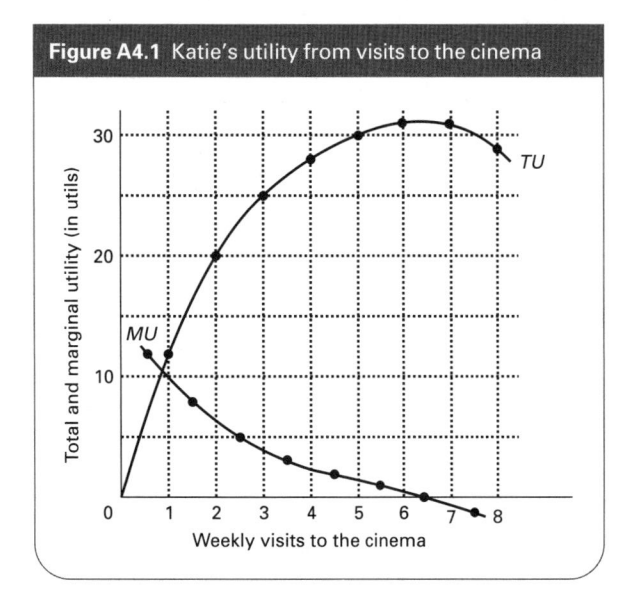

Figure A4.1 Katie's utility from visits to the cinema

(c) (i) 50; (ii) 62; (iii) 62. A doubling of marginal utility leads to a doubling of total utility.

Q6. (a), (c), (e). In each of these cases I only consume/do a certain amount and then do something else. The implication is that as the marginal utility declines, so it becomes preferable to switch to an alternative. (Note that (b) and (d) simply state a preference without saying how the preference *changes* according to the level of consumption.)

Q7. E. Marginal utility is the extra utility gained from one more unit consumed. If it falls then total utility will still rise (provided that MU does not become negative), but will rise *less* than for the previous unit.

Q8. The list could include increased consumption of other drinks (MU decreases), the weather (on a hot day the MU will increase), increased consumption of dry food (MU increases), fashion, etc.

Q9. Buy more. They are gaining more from extra consumption than it is costing them.

Q10. Buy less. The last unit being consumed is costing them more than it is benefiting them.

Q11. (a) £73 (= £25 + £20 + £16 + £12).
(b) £60 (6 units @ £10 each).
(c) £10 (= £20 (MU) − £10 (P)).
(d) −£2 (= £8 (MU) − £10 (P)).
(e) £25 (= £45 (TU) − £20 (TE)).
(f) 4 units (TCS = £33).
(g) (i.e. between +2 (between 3 and 4 units), and −2 (between 4 and 5 units)).
(h) P = MU = £10.

Q12. C. It is given by the area under the MU curve at the output (Q) in question.

Q13. A. It is given by the area between the MU curve and the price.

Q14. marginal utility. With a constant income and when the consumption of this good is too insignificant to affect the demand for other goods, the demand curve will be the marginal utility curve (where MU is measured in money terms).

Q15. Buy more of X relative to Y. If $MU_X/P_X > MU_Y/P_Y$, then people would be getting a better value (MU) for money (P) from X than from Y. They would thus consume relatively more of X and relatively less of Y. This would cause MU_X to fall (and MU_Y to rise) until $MU_X/P_X = MU_Y/P_Y$.

Q16. $MU_X/P_X = MU_Y/P_Y$.

Q17. D. If Dolcelatte gives her twice as much marginal utility as Cheddar, it must be costing her twice as much, in order for the equi-marginal principle to be satisfied.

Q18. D. We can say for certain that if she is 'rational' she will switch away from Z and towards X, but whether she alters her consumption of Y and in which direction will depend on how rapidly the marginal utilities of X and Z change.

Q19. risk.

Q20. uncertainty.

Q21. *Risk loving.* The chances of drawing an ace are 1:13. If for a £1 bet you only won £10 each time you drew an ace, then on average you would lose money. If, therefore you were prepared to accept odds of 10:1, you would be risk loving.

Q22. *(a)* 700 utils (with a total income of £8000).
(b) 0 utils (with a total income of £0).
(c) (700 + 0) ÷ 2 = 350 utils.
(d) because, with a diminishing marginal utility of income, by taking the gamble his average expected utility (350 utils) is less than by not taking the gamble (500 utils).

Q23. *False.* The total amount paid to insurance companies in premiums will exceed the amount received back in claims: that is how the companies make a profit. Thus the odds are inevitably unfair for the client. It is still worthwhile, however, to take out insurance because people are risk averters (given the diminishing marginal utility of income).

Q24. C. A company can spread its risks over a large number of policies (ii). The more people the insurance company insures, the more predictable the total outcome (i), provided that the risks are independent (iii). Insurance companies are not risk lovers, because on average they will make a profit.

Q25. *(a) Not independent.* They may all meet with an accident in the coach or on the plane.
(b) Not independent. In a recession, people in many otherwise unconnected parts of the economy will be under greater threat of redundancy.
(c) Independent. One person having an accident will not affect the risks of others having an accident.
(d) Not independent. A particular neighbourhood may be more subject to burglaries. (Insurance companies charge house contents premiums based on your postcode. People living in high-risk areas pay higher premiums.)
(e) Independent. If a person over 65 dies, this will not affect the chances of other people over 65 dying. Under certain circumstances, however, the risks would *not* be independent. These circumstances would include an epidemic or an exceptionally severe winter.
(f) Not independent. In a war, soldiers' lives will generally be at greater risk.

Q26. *(a)* See Figure A4.2.
(b) Set 2. It gives an indifference curve furthest out from the origin.
(c) Sets 1 and 4. They lie along the same indifference curve.
(d) Set 5. It gives an indifference curve furthest in toward the origin.
(e) Because a curve drawn through these combinations would cross other indifference curves, and indifference curves cannot cross. 36 books and 5 CDs are preferable to 30 books and 5 CDs (set 1) and yet 3 books and 20 CDs are inferior to 6 books and 20 CDs (set 3) and yet set 1 is preferable to set 3! Thus, given the other sets, 36 books and 5 CDs cannot lie along the same indifference curve as 3 books and 20 CDs.

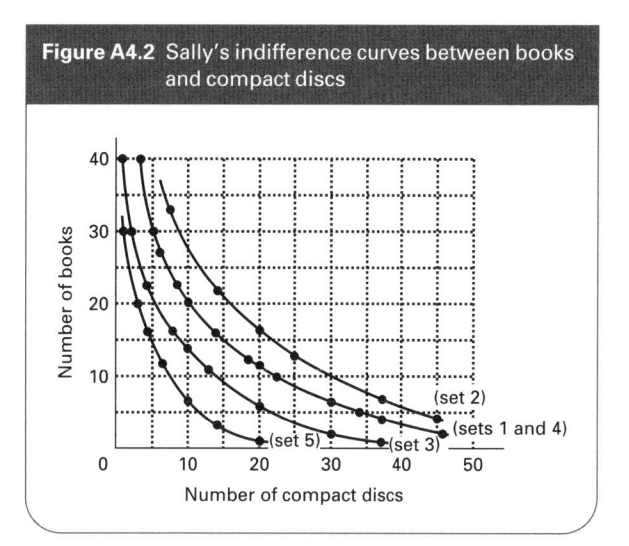

Figure A4.2 Sally's indifference curves between books and compact discs

Q27. The marginal rate of substitution of Y for X is the amount of Y that a consumer is prepared to give up *for a one unit increase in the consumption of X*.

Q28. *(a)* $\Delta B/\Delta CD = 4/1 = 4$.
(b) $\Delta B/\Delta CD = 4/2 = 2$.
(c) $\Delta B/\Delta CD = 6/4 = 1.5$.

Q29. The *MRS* diminishes (e.g. see answer to Q28). The reason is that as more of one good is consumed relative to the other, so its marginal utility will decrease relative to that of the other. Thus the consumer would be prepared to give up less and less of the other good for each additional unit of the first good.

Q30. A. If the slope ($\Delta Y/\Delta X$) were 2/1, this would mean that the person would be prepared to give up 2 units of Y for 1 unit of X. This would mean that X has twice the marginal utility of Y, i.e. $MU_X/MU_Y = 2$.

Q31. *(a)* P_X = £5 (i.e. 4 could be purchased if the whole budget were spent on X).
P_Y = £2.50 (i.e. 8 could be purchased if the whole budget were spent on Y).
(b) The new budget line will join 5 on the Y axis with 4 on the X axis. The reason is that, with a new price for Y of £4, if all £20 were spent on Y, 5 units could now be purchased.
(c) £40 (i.e. 4X could be purchased at a price of £10 each).
(d) £8 (i.e. if 5Y can be purchased for £40, the price must be £8).
(e) Nothing. The consumer will be able to buy exactly the same quantities as before. Although money income has doubled, *real* income has not changed.

56 CHAPTER 4 BACKGROUND TO DEMAND

Figure A4.3 Sally's indifference curves between books and compact discs

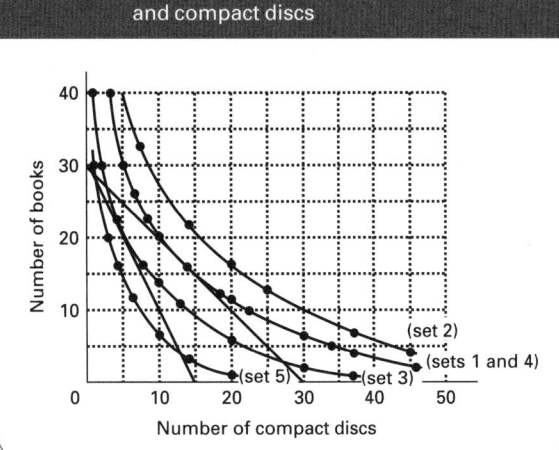

Figure A4.4 The effect of a change in the price of good X on Tom's consumption

Q32. C. If the slope were 2/1, this would mean that 2 units of Y could be purchased for each 1 unit of X sacrificed. Thus X must be twice the price of Y: $P_X/P_Y = 2$ = slope of budget line.

Q33. *(a)* See Figure A4.3.
(b) 16 books and 14 CDs.
(c) See Figure A4.3.
(d) 20 books and 5 CDs.

Q34. *(a)* (vi).
(b) (iii). (As tastes shift towards Y and away from X so MU_X/MU_Y will fall, and thus the curve will become flatter.)
(c) (i).
(d) (viii).
(e) (vii). (MU_X/MU_Y will rise.)
(f) (v).
(g) (ii).
(h) (iv).

Q35. *(a)* See Figure A4.4.

(b)

P	Q_d
10	8.0
16	5.6
20	5.0
32	3.6
40	3.0

See Figure A4.4 for the price–consumption curve.

(c) The five sets of figures (plus any others you choose to read off from the price–consumption curve) can then be plotted with P on the vertical axis and Q_d on the horizontal axis. The points can then be connected to give a demand curve.

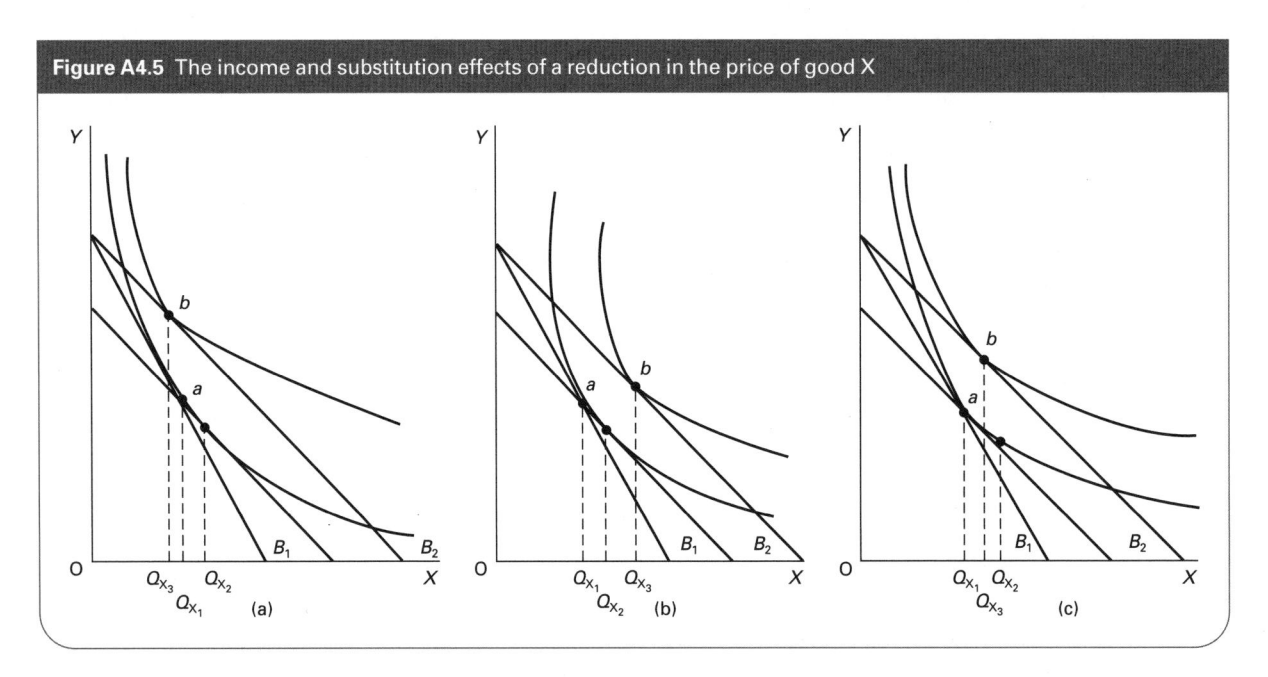

Figure A4.5 The income and substitution effects of a reduction in the price of good X

Q36. *expenditure on all other goods.*

Q37. *(a)* See Figure A4.5. In each diagram the substitution effect is represented by the movement from Q_{X_1} to Q_{X_2} and the income effect by the movement from Q_{X_2} to Q_{X_3}.

   (b) (i) diagram (b) (negative income (and substitution) effect), (ii) diagram (c) (positive income effect, but smaller than the negative substitution effect), (iii) diagram (a) (positive income effect which outweights the negative substitution effect).

Q38. See table below.

Type of good	Substitution effect	Income effect	Which is the bigger effect?
Normal	*negative*	*negative*	*either*
Inferior (non-Giffen)	*negative*	*positive*	*substitution*
Giffen	*negative*	*positive*	*income*

Q39. *False.* People would only consume more if the positive income effect (because the good was inferior) outweighed the (usual) negative substitution effect. This is the case only with a Giffen good.

Chapter Five

5

Background to Supply

A REVIEW

We now turn to the theory of supply. We will examine what determines the quantity that firms will produce at various prices and various costs.

In this chapter (and the next two) we will be making the traditional assumption that firms are profit maximisers: that they wish to produce the level of output that will maximise the total level of their profit (TΠ). We define total profit as total revenue (*TR*) minus total costs (*TC*).

In order then to discover how a firm can maximise its profit, we must first consider what determines costs and revenue. We start by examining costs in both the short run and the long run. We then examine revenue. Finally we put the two together to examine profit.

5.1 The short-run theory of production

(Pages 115–18) The cost of producing any level of output will depend on the amount of inputs used. The relationship between output and inputs is shown in a *production function*.

Q1. In the following production function for good A, a good is produced by using two factors labour (*L*) and capital (*K*). How much will be produced if 6 units of labour and 3 units of capital are used?

$TPP = 10L + 4K$ ....
(where *TPP* is total physical product: i.e. total output).

Extra output involves using extra input. But increasing the amount of certain inputs may take time: it takes time, for example, to build a new factory or to install new machines. We thus make a distinction between *short-run* production and *long-run* production.

Q2. The short run is defined as

A. a period of time less than one year.
B. the shortest time period in which a firm will consider producing.
C. the period of time in which at least one factor of production is fixed in supply.
D. the period of time it takes for raw materials to be converted into finished goods.
E. the length of time taken for a minimum-sized production run.

In the short run, production will be subject to the *law of diminishing (marginal) returns*.

Q3. The law of diminishing marginal returns states that

....

....

Q4. Imagine that a firm produces good X with just two factors: capital which is fixed in supply, and labour which

Multiple choice   *Written answer*   *Delete wrong word*   *Diagram/table manipulation*   *Calculation*   *Matching/ordering*

Table 5.1 The relationship between the output (total physical product) of good X and the number of workers employed

(1) Number of workers	(2) TPP	(3)	(4)
0	0		
1	10	.	.
2	26	.	.
3	41	.	.
4	52	.	.
5	60	.	.
6	65	.	.
7	67	.	.
8	67	.	.
9	63	.	.

Figure 5.1 The total physical product of labour for good X

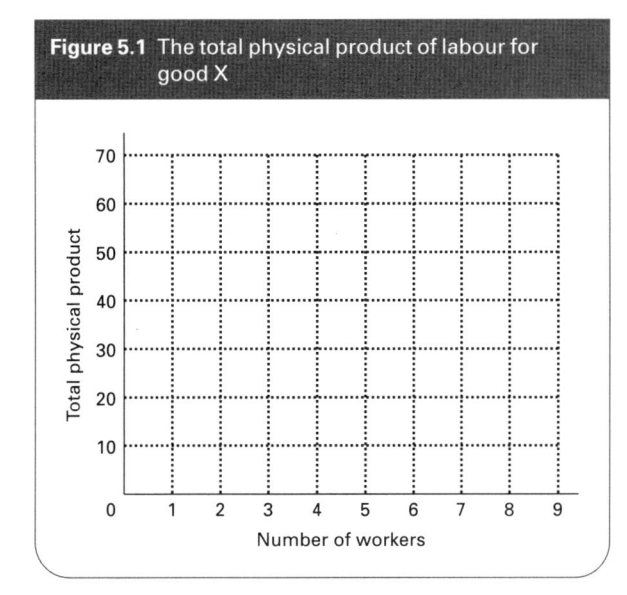

is variable. The effect on total output (*TPP*) of increasing the number of workers is shown in column (2) of Table 5.1. (We will fill in columns (3) and (4) later.)

(a) Draw the total physical product curve on Figure 5.1.
(b) Beyond what number of workers do diminishing returns set in?

(Pages 118–20) We can use total physical product data to derive *average* and *marginal physical product* data. We define marginal physical product (*MPP*) as **Q5.** *the number of units of the variable factor required to produce one more unit of output/the amount of extra output gained from the use of one more unit of the variable factor.*

Q6. If *L* is the quantity of labour, then of the following:
(i) *TPP/L*
(ii) $\Delta L/\Delta TPP$
(iii) $\Delta TPP/\Delta L$
(iv) $\Delta L/TPP$

(a) Which is the formula for the marginal physical product (*MPP*) of labour? *(i)/(ii)/(iii)/(iv)*
(b) Which is the formula for the average physical product (*APP*) of labour? *(i)/(ii)/(iii)/(iv)*

Q7. Referring back to Table 5.1, fill in the figures for *APP* and *MPP* in columns (3) and (4) respectively. (Note that the figures for *MPP* are entered between the lines. The reason is that the marginal physical product is the extra output gained from *moving* from one level of input to one more unit of input.)

Q8. Draw the *APP* and *MPP* curves on Figure 5.2.

Figure 5.2 The average and marginal physical product of labour of good X

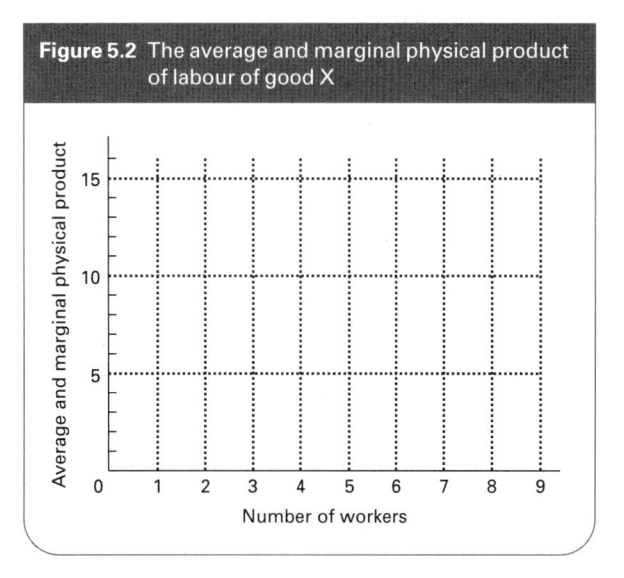

Q9. Why does the marginal product curve pass through the top of the average physical product curve?

....

....

Q10. The total physical product for any given amount of the variable factor is the sum of all the marginal physical products up to that point. *True/False*

Q11. Assume that the following two pieces of information are obtained from a production function for good X. (1) 1000 units of good X can be produced with a combination of 20 units of input A, 30 units of input B and 40 units of input C. (2) 1005 units of good X can be produced with 20 units of input A, 30 units of input B and 41 units of input C. From these two pieces of information it can be deduced that at this point on the production function:

A. the *MPP* of good X is 5 units.
B. the *MPP* of input C is 5 units.
C. the *MPP* of good X is 1005/1000 units.
D. the *MPP* of input C is 1005/40 units.
E. the *MPP* of input C is 1005/41 units.

5.2 Costs in the short run

(Pages 121–2) We now examine how a firm's costs are related to its output. When measuring cost we should be careful to use the concept of *opportunity* cost. In the case of factors not already owned by the firm, the opportunity cost is simply **Q12.** *the implicit/explicit* cost of purchasing or hiring them. In the case of factors that *are* already owned by the firm, we have to impute an opportunity cost when they are used.

Q13. Assume that a firm already owns a machine that has a total life of 10 years. The cost of using the machine for one year to produce good X is:
A. a tenth of what the firm paid for the machine in the first place.
B. a tenth of what it would cost to replace the machine.
C. the value of one year's output of X.
D. the scrap value of the machine at the end of its life.
E. the maximum the machine could have earned for the firm in some alternative use during the year in question.

Q14. The opportunity cost of using a factor owned by the firm that has no other use and whose second-hand or scrap value is not affected by its use is zero. *True/False*

(Page 122) In the short run, by definition, at least one factor is fixed in supply. The total cost to the firm of these factors is thus fixed with respect to **Q15.** *time/the firm's output.*

Q16. Which of the following are likely to be fixed costs and which variable costs for a chocolate factory over the course of a month?
(a) The cost of cocoa. *Fixed/Variable*
(b) Business rates (local taxes). *Fixed/Variable*
(c) An advertising campaign for a new chocolate bar. *Fixed/Variable*
(d) The cost of electricity (paid quarterly) for running the mixing machines. *Fixed/Variable*
(e) Overtime pay. *Fixed/Variable*
(f) The basic minimum wage agreed with the union (workers must be given at least one month's notice if they are to be laid off). *Fixed/Variable*
(g) Wear and tear on wrapping machines. *Fixed/Variable*
(h) Depreciation of machines due simply to their age. *Fixed/Variable*
(i) Interest on a mortgage for the factory: the rate of interest rises over the course of the month. *Fixed/Variable*

(Pages 122–5) We use a number of different measures of cost: fixed and variable; and average and marginal.

Q17. Which of the measures of cost – total fixed cost (*TFC*), total variable cost (*TVC*), total cost (*TC*), average fixed cost (*AFC*), average variable cost (*AVC*), average (total) cost (*AC*), marginal cost (*MC*) – are described by each of the following?

(a) TC/Q ....

(b) $AC - AFC$ ....

(c) $\Delta TC/\Delta Q$ ....

(d) $\Delta TVC/\Delta Q$ ....

(e) $(TC - TVC) \div Q$ ....

(f) $(AFC + AVC) \times Q$ ....

(g) ΣMC ....

(h) $\Sigma MC + TFC$ ....
(Note: Σ means 'the sum of'.)

Q18. Table 5.2 gives the short-run costs for an imaginary firm.

Table 5.2 Short-run costs for firm X

Output	TFC	TVC	TC	AFC	AVC	AC	MC
0	.	.	.				
1	.	8	.	10.0	.	.	.
2	.	12	.	.	.	.	4
3	10	.	25	.	.	.	.
4	.	.	27	.	.	.	.
5	.	.	.	.	4.0	.	.
6	.	.	.	.	4.0	.	.
7	.	.	.	.	.	.	5
8	.	.	.	.	.	5.75	.
9	.	48	.	.	.	6.44	.
10	.	70	.	.	.	.	.

(a) Fill in the figures for each of the columns.
(b) At what output do diminishing marginal returns set in (assuming constant factor prices)?

....

(c) Draw *TFC*, *TVC* and *TC* on Figure 5.3. Mark the point on the *TVC* curve where (i) *MC* is at a minimum, (ii) *AVC* is at a minimum.
(d) Draw *AFC*, *AVC*, *AC* and *MC* on Figure 5.4. Be careful to plot the *MC* figures mid-way between the figures for quantity (i.e. at 0.5, 1.5, 2.5, etc.).

Q19. If the marginal cost is below the average cost, then:
A. the marginal cost must be falling.
B. the marginal cost must be rising.
C. the average cost must be falling.

Figure 5.3 Total costs for firm X

Figure 5.4 Average and marginal costs for firm X

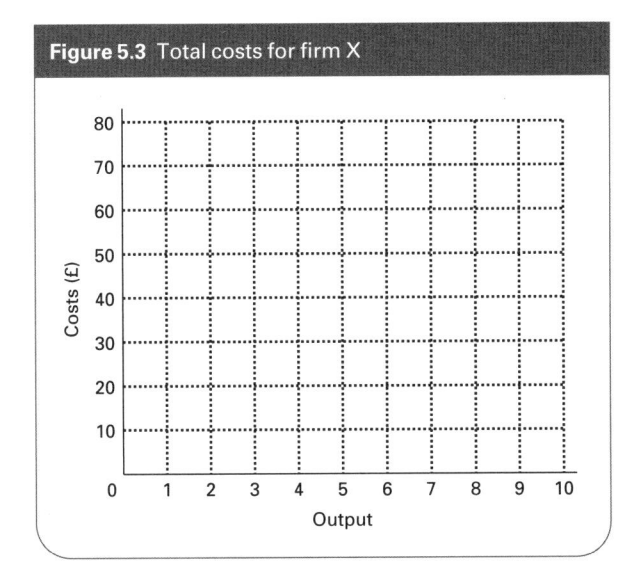

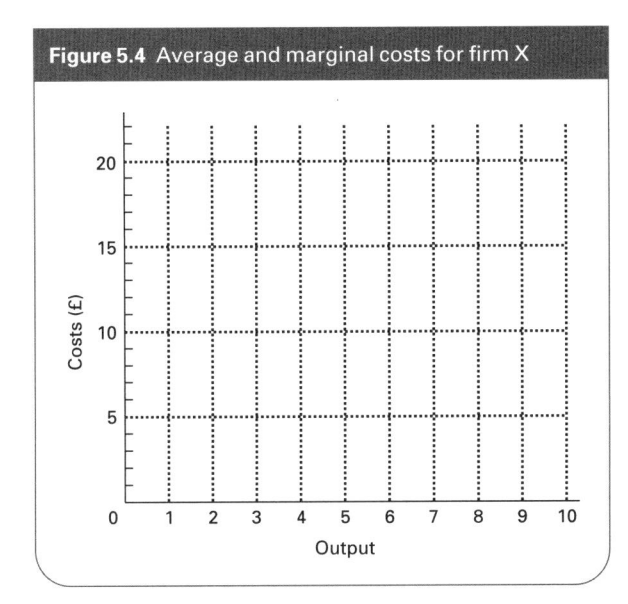

D. the average cost must be rising.
E. the average cost could be either rising or falling depending on whether the marginal cost is rising or falling.

5.3 The long-run theory of production

(Pages 126–8) In the long run, all factors become variable. Given time, more capital equipment can be installed, new techniques of production can be used, additional land can be acquired and another factory can be built.

If a doubling of inputs leads to a more than doubling of output, the firm is said to experience **Q20.** *decreasing returns to scale/increasing returns to the variable factor/increasing returns to scale*.

⊖ **Q21.** Assume that a firm uses just two factors of production. Table 5.3 shows what happens to output as the firm increases one or both of these inputs.

Table 5.3 The effects of increasing the amounts of both inputs

	Situation (i)			Situation (ii)	
Input 1	Input 2	Output	Input 1	Input 2	Output
1	1	12	1	2	14
2	2	24	2	2	24
3	3	36	3	2	32
4	4	48	4	2	38
5	5	60	5	2	42

(a) Which situation represents the long run? *(i)/(ii)*
(b) Does the firm experience increasing returns to scale? *Yes/No*

Explain ....

(c) Are the figures consistent with the law of diminishing marginal returns? *Yes/No*

Explain ....

If a firm experiences increasing returns to scale, it is also likely to experience *economies of scale*.

▤ **Q22.** Economies of scale can be defined as:
A. large-scale production leading to bigger profits.
B. large-scale production leading to lower costs per unit of production.
C. large-scale production leading to greater marginal productivity of factors.
D. large-scale production leading to greater output per unit of input.
E. large-scale production leading to a better organisation of the factors of production.

♟ **Q23.** The following is a list of various types of economy of scale:
 (i) The firm can benefit from the specialisation and division of labour.
 (ii) It can overcome the problem of indivisibilities.
 (iii) It can obtain inputs at a lower price.
 (iv) Large containers/machines have a greater capacity relative to their surface area.
 (v) The firm may be able to obtain finance at lower cost.
 (vi) It becomes economical to sell by-products.
 (vii) Production can take place in integrated plants.
 (viii) Risks can be spread with a larger number of products or plants.

Match each of the following examples for a particular firm to one of these types of economy of scale.
(a) Delivery vans can carry full loads to single destinations.

....

(b) It can more easily make a public issue of shares.

....

(c) It can diversify into other markets.

....

(d) Workers spend less time having to train for a wide variety of different tasks, and less time moving from task to task.

....

(e) It negotiates bulk discount with a supplier of raw materials.

....

(f) It uses large warehouses to store its raw materials and finished goods.

....

(g) A clothing manufacturer does a deal to supply a soft toy manufacturer with offcuts for stuffing toys.

....

(h) Conveyor belts transfer the product through several stages of the manufacturing process.

....

Q24. Referring to the list (i)–(viii) of economies of scale in Q23, which arise from increasing (physical) returns to scale?

....

Q25. Which of the following are *internal* and which are *external* economies of scale for firm A?
(a) Firm A benefits from a pool of trained labour in the area. *Internal/External*
(b) Firm A benefits from lower administration costs per unit as a result of opening a second factory. *Internal/External*
(c) Firm A is able to sell by-products to other firms. *Internal/External*
(d) Firm A benefits from research and development conducted by other firms in the industry. *Internal/External*
(e) Other firms benefit from firm A's discovery of a new technique of mass production. *Internal/External*

(Pages 128–9) Given that all factors of production are variable in the long run, a firm will want to choose the least-cost combination of inputs for any given level of output.

Q26. Assuming that a firm uses three factors A, B and C, whose prices are respectively P_A, P_B and P_C, which of the following represents the least-cost combination of these factors?
A. $P_A = P_B = P_C$
B. $MPP_A = MPP_B = MPP_C$
C. $MPP_A \times P_A = MPP_B \times P_B = MPP_C \times P_C$
D. $MPP_A/MPP_B = MPP_B/MPP_C = MPP_C/MPP_A$
E. $MPP_A/P_A = MPP_B/P_B = MPP_C/P_C$

Q27. Table 5.4 gives details of the output of good X obtained from different combinations of the three factors A, B and C.

Table 5.4 Output of good X from various factor combinations

Quantity of input A	Quantity of input B	Quantity of input C	Output of X
100	50	30	1000
100	50	31	1005
100	51	30	1010
101	50	30	1003

Assume that the price of factor A is £6. What must the prices of factors B and C be if the least-cost factor combination to produce 1000 units of X is the one shown in the top row of Table 5.4?

Price of B ....

Price of C ....

(Pages 129–33) The least-cost combination of factors to produce various levels of output can be shown graphically by drawing isoquants and isocosts. This analysis assumes that there are just two factors.

*Q28. Table 5.5 shows the output of good X obtained from different inputs of factors A and B.
(a) Draw the 100, 200, 300 and 400 unit isoquants on Figure 5.5.
(b) If factor A and factor B both cost £200 each, what is the least-cost combination of A and B to produce 300 units of good X? (You will need to draw the appropriate isocost.)

....

(c) How much will this cost the firm? ....

Table 5.5 Various factor combinations to produce different levels of output of good X

100 units of X	
	70A, 1B; 52A, 3B; 40A, 8B; 31A, 15B; 22A, 25B; 17A, 33B; 14A, 40B; 10A, 50B; 4A, 70B
200 units of X	
	70A, 3B; 58A, 5B; 45A, 10B; 33A, 20B; 26A, 30B; 18A, 45B; 10A, 63B; 5A, 80B
300 units of X	
	70A, 7B; 55A, 11B; 46A, 16B; 40A, 20B; 32A, 30B; 26A, 40B; 21A, 50B; 13A, 70B; 8A, 86B
400 units of X	
	70A, 11B; 58A, 15B; 50A, 19B; 39A, 28B; 32A, 38B; 26A, 50B; 20A, 63B; 12A, 83B

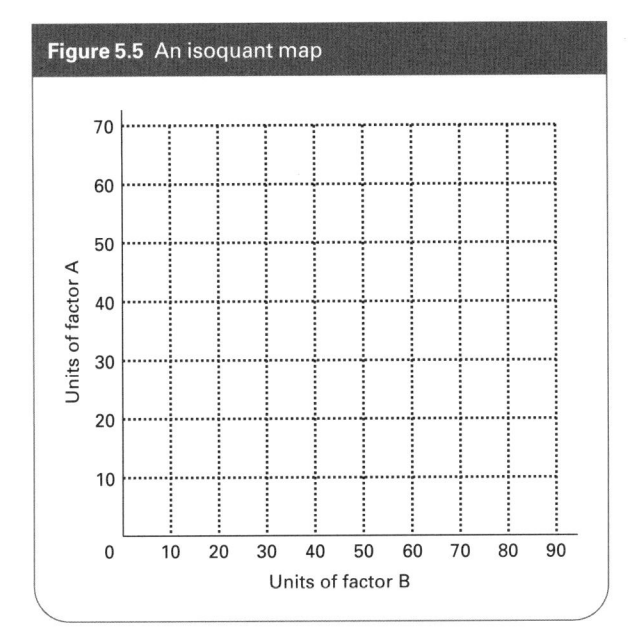

Figure 5.5 An isoquant map

(d) Suppose now that the price of factor B rises to £300 but that the firm's total cost remains the same as in (b). What is the maximum output the firm can now produce for this cost?

....

(e) How many units of A and B will it now use?

....

At the point where an isocost is tangential to an isoquant, the firm is producing the highest possible output for a given cost and at the lowest possible cost for a given output.

Q29. With the quantity of factor A measured on the vertical axis and the quantity of factor B measured on the horizontal axis, the slope of an isoquant gives (for that output):

A. P_A/P_B
B. P_B/P_A
C. MPP_A/MPP_B
D. MPP_B/MPP_A
E. $MPP_A/P_A = MPP_B/P_B$

Q30. With the quantity of factor A measured on the vertical axis and the quantity of factor B measured on the horizontal axis, the slope of an isocost gives:

A. P_A/P_B
B. P_B/P_A
C. MPP_A/MPP_B
D. MPP_B/MPP_A
E. $MPP_A/P_A = MPP_B/P_B$

5.4 Costs in the long run
(Pages 134–8)

Q31. Which of the following assumptions do we make when constructing long-run cost curves? (There may be more than one.)

(a)	Factor prices are given.	Yes/No
(b)	The state of technology is given.	Yes/No
(c)	All factors are variable.	Yes/No
(d)	Firms will choose the least-cost factor combination.	Yes/No
(e)	The firm experiences economies of scale.	Yes/No
(f)	There are no fixed factors of production.	Yes/No
(g)	The MPP/P ratios for all factors are equal.	Yes/No

Q32. Assume that a firm experiences economies of scale up to a certain level of output, then constant (average) costs, and then diseconomies of scale. Sketch its long-run average and marginal cost curves on Figure 5.6.

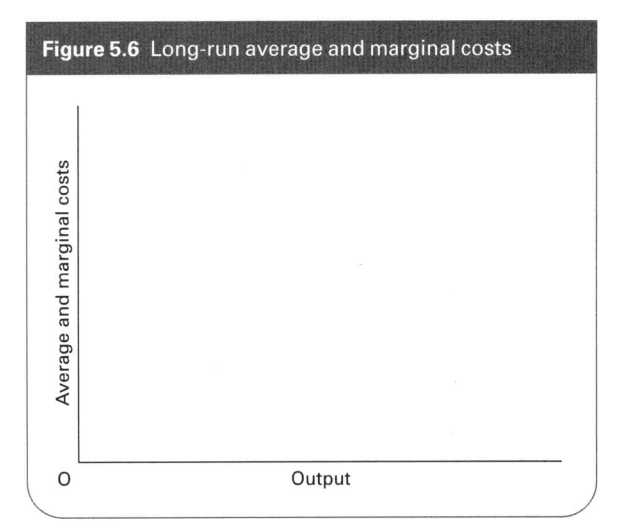

Figure 5.6 Long-run average and marginal costs

Q33. The long-run average cost curve will be tangential with the bottom points of the short-run average cost curves. *True/False*

Q34. If a firm is achieving maximum economies of scale then its $LRAC = SRAC = LRMC = SRMC$. *True/False*

Q35. Figure 5.7 shows a (weekly) isoquant map for a firm which uses two factors of production, labour (L) and

64 CHAPTER 5 BACKGROUND TO SUPPLY

Figure 5.7 A firm's isoquant map for good X

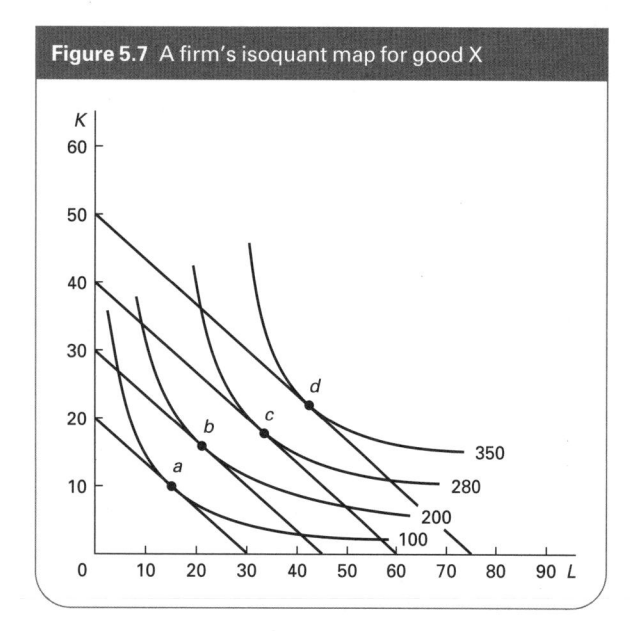

capital (*K*), to produce good X. The optimum factor combinations to produce four levels of output are shown by points *a*, *b*, *c* and *d*. These represent the following factor combinations: *a* = 10*K*, 15*L*; *b* = 16*K*, 21*L*; *c* = 18*K*, 33*L*; *d* = 22*K*, 42*L*. The cost of capital is £240 per unit per week. The cost of labour (the wage rate) is £160 per week.

(a) What is the (minimum) total cost of producing:

  (i) 100 units?..

  (ii) 200 units?..

  (iii) 280 units?..

  (iv) 350 units?..

(b) What is the (minimum) average cost of producing these four levels of output?

  (i) ...., (ii) ...., (iii) ...., (iv) ....

(c) Over what output range does the firm experience economies of scale?

  ....

5.5 Revenue

(Pages 139–42) Remember we said that profit equals revenue minus cost. We have looked at costs. We now turn to revenue.

Let us assume that firm S is a price taker. In other words it faces a **Q36.** *downward-sloping/horizontal* **Q37.** *demand curve/supply curve.*

⊗ **Q38.** Let us assume that it faces a market price of £2 per unit for its product.

(a) What is its total revenue from selling:

  (i) 5 units?..

  (ii) 8 units?..

(b) What shape is its total revenue curve?

  ....

(c) What will be its marginal revenue from selling:

  (i) the fifth unit?..

  (ii) the eighth unit?...................................

(d) What shape is its marginal revenue curve?

  ....

Now assume that firm T faces a downward-sloping (straight-line) demand curve. This is shown in Table 5.6.

Table 5.6 The demand curve for the product of firm T

Price (Average revenue) (£)	Quantity (units)	Total revenue (£)	Marginal revenue (£)
20	0	.	.
18	1	.	.
16	2	.	.
14	3	.	.
12	4	.	.
10	5	.	.
8	6	.	.
6	7	.	.

(e) Fill in the columns for *TR* and *MR*. (Note that the figures for *MR* are entered between 0 and 1, 1 and 2, 2 and 3, etc.)

(f) What is the price elasticity of demand at *P* = £10?

  ....

(g) Over what price range is demand price elastic?

  ....

(h) Over what price range is demand price inelastic?

  ....

⊗ **Q39.** If a reduction in the price of good X from £20 to £15 leads to a rise in the amount sold from 100 to 130 units, what would be the *MR*?

  ....

⊖ **Q40.** A wine merchant will supply bottles of Champagne to a wedding at £10 per bottle, but is willing to offer a 10 per cent discount on the total bill if 50 bottles or more are purchased. What would be the firm's marginal revenue for the 50th bottle?
A. £450
B. £9
C. £1
D. −£40
E. −£45

5.6 Profit maximisation

(Pages 142–3) There are two methods of showing the profit-maximising position for a firm. The first uses total revenue and total cost curves.

⊖ **Q41.** Figure 5.8 shows the total cost and revenue curves for a firm on the same diagram.
(a) At what output is the firm's profit maximised?

....

(b) How much profit is made at this output? ....

(c) Draw the *TΠ* curve over the range of output where positive profit is made.
(d) How much is total fixed cost? ....

(e) At what output is the price elasticity of demand equal to −1?

....

(f) At what outputs does the firm break even? ....

(Pages 143–6) The second method of showing the profit-maximising position is to use *AR*, *MR*, *AC* and *MC* curves.

Figure 5.8 A firm's total cost and total revenue

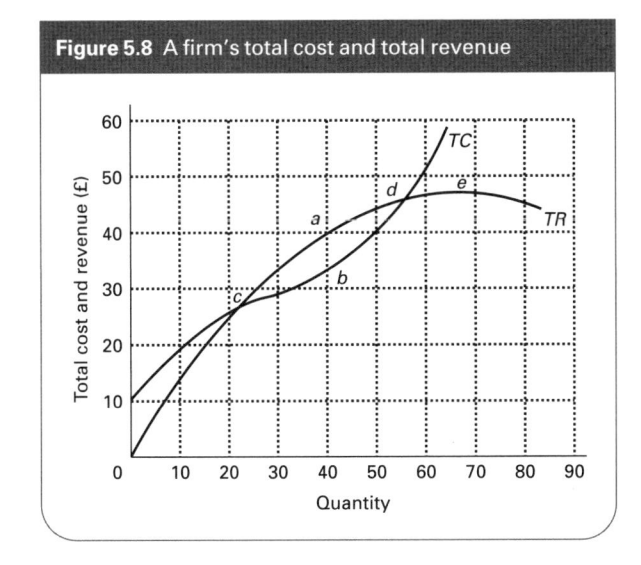

Table 5.7 Costs and revenues for the production of good X

Quantity (units)	Average costs (£)	Marginal costs (£)	Average revenue (£)	Marginal revenue (£)
100	4.80	1.40	3.20	3.20
200	3.60	0.80	3.20	3.20
300	2.90	0.85	3.20	3.20
400	2.45	1.30	3.20	3.20
500	2.30	2.30	3.20	3.20
600	2.55	4.00	3.20	3.20
700	3.05	6.30	3.20	3.20
800	3.80	(above 7.00)	3.20	3.20
900	5.10	(above 7.00)	3.20	3.20

Figure 5.9 Average and marginal costs and revenue for the production of good X

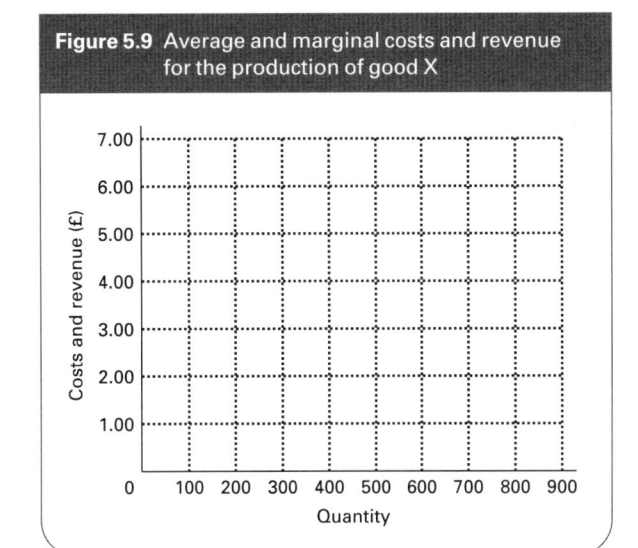

⊖ **Q42.** Table 5.7 gives a firm's average and marginal cost and revenue schedules for the production of good X.
(a) Draw the *AC*, *MC*, *AR* and *MR* curves on Figure 5.9.
(b) Explain the shape of the *AR* curve ....
(c) At what output is profit maximised? ....
(d) How much is average cost at this output?

....

(e) How much is average profit at this output?

....

(f) Shade in the area representing maximum total profit in Figure 5.9.
(g) How much is the maximum total profit? ....

(h) What is the lowest price the firm could receive if it were not to make a loss?

....

CHAPTER 5 BACKGROUND TO SUPPLY

Q43. If at the current level of output a firm's price exceeds its marginal revenue and its marginal revenue exceeds its marginal cost, then to maximise profits it should:
A. reduce price and output.
B. raise price and output.
C. reduce price and raise output.
D. keep price the same and reduce output.
E. keep price the same and increase output.

Q44. The optimum point for a profit-maximising firm to produce will be at the bottom of the *AC* curve.   *True/False*

Q45. A firm will always maximise profits by charging a price equal to both marginal cost and marginal revenue.
True/False

Q46. A firm will choose to shut down rather than continue to produce in the *short run* whenever:
A. *AR* is less than *AC*.
B. *TR* is less than *TC*.
C. *MR* is less than *MC*.
D. *TR* is less than *TFC*.
E. *AR* is less than *AVC*.

Q47. Figure 5.10 shows a firm's cost and revenue curves. It is currently producing at an output of *OX*. In order to maximise profits it should:
A. continue to produce at *OX* in the short run and expand production in the long run.
B. continue to produce at *OX* in the short run and close down in the long run.
C. reduce output in the short run and expand output in the long run.
D. reduce output in the short run and close down in the long run.
E. close down straight away.

*Q48. A firm faces the following total cost and total revenue schedules:

$TC = 100 - 20Q + 3Q^2$
$TR = 60Q - 2Q^2$

Figure 5.10 Average and marginal costs and revenues

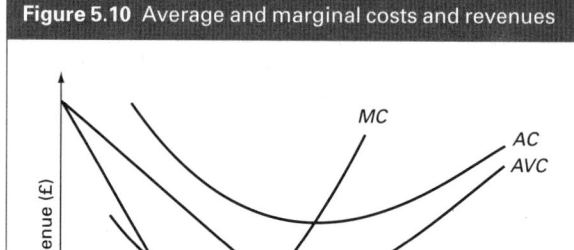

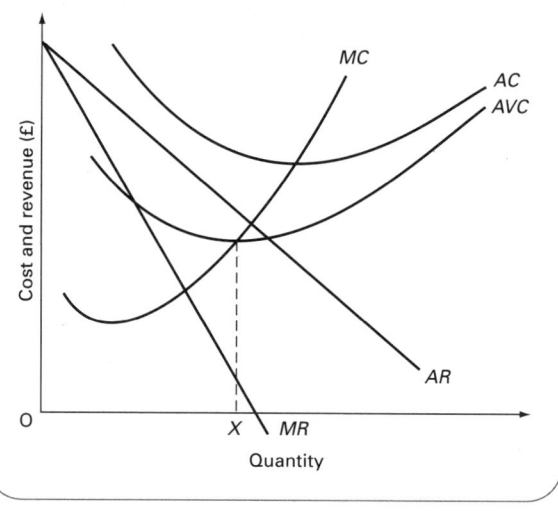

(a) What is the equation for average cost? ....
(b) What is the equation for marginal cost? ....
(c) What is the equation for average revenue? ....
(d) What is the equation for marginal revenue? ....
(e) At what output is profit maximised? ....
(f) What is average profit at this output? ....
(g) How much is total profit at this output?.......................
(h) What is the equation for total profit? ....
(i) Using this equation, find the output at which profit is maximised (thereby confirming the answer given in (e) above).

....

B PROBLEMS, EXERCISES AND PROJECTS

Q49. Table 5.8 shows the short-run total cost curves of three alternative plants producing luxury cars. The three plants are of different sizes: one small, one medium and one large.
(a) Calculate the (short-run) average cost for each level of output given in the table for each of the three plants.
(b) Plot the (short-run) *AC* curve for each of the three plants (on the same diagram).
(c) From these three short-run *AC* curves sketch the long-run *AC* curve.
(d) Are there increasing, decreasing or constant returns to scale?
(e) Assuming that a firm could choose with what size plants to operate in the long run, which of the three size plants would it choose to produce an output of 10 cars per day?
(f) Assume that a firm is producing 10 cars per day with the optimum-sized plant, and now wishes to increase output to 30 cars per day in response to a temporary

Table 5.8 Costs of car production

Output (daily)	TC small plant (£000)	TC medium plant (£000)	TC large plant (£000)
0	35	70	90
5	90	120	200
10	140	170	300
15	180	195	345
20	220	210	360
25	300	225	375
30	420	255	405
35	595	315	455
40	880	400	540
45	1260	585	675
50	1900	950	900
55	2750	1430	1265
60	3900	2400	1800

increase in demand. What will its average cost of production now be?

(g) Now assume that the rise in demand to 30 cars per day is perceived by the firm to be a permanent increase. After its long-run adjustment, what will its average cost be now?

(h) Now assume that demand increases to 45 cars per day in the long run. Would the firm alter its plant size? Would it alter its plant size if output increased to 50 cars per day? Explain.

Q50. Table 5.9 gives details of a firm's total costs and total revenue.

(a) Fill in the columns for AR, MR, AC and MC – but ignore columns for AR_1, TR_1 and MR_1 until you get to (e) below. Remember that MC and MR are the extra cost and revenue of producing *one* more unit (not ten).

(b) At what output and price is profit maximised?

(c) How much is total profit at this output?

Table 5.9 Costs and revenue for firm X

Q	AR	(AR_1)	TR	(TR_1)	MR	(MR_1)	TC	AC	MC
0	30	–	0	–		–	300	–	
10	…	–	280	–	…	…	350	…	…
20	…	…	520	…	…	…	380	…	…
30	…	…	720	…	…	…	420	…	…
40	…	…	880	…	…	…	480	…	…
50	…	…	1000	…	…	…	600	…	…
60	…	…	1080	…	…	…	780	…	…
70	…	…	1120	…	…	…	980	…	…
80	…	…	1120	…	…	…	1280	…	…
90	…	…	1080	…	…	…	1710	…	…
100	…	…	1000	…	…	…	2300	…	…

(d) Assume that total fixed cost rises by £200. What effect will this have on the profit-maximising price and output?

(e) What effect will it have on profit?

(f) Now assume that TFC returns to its original level and that demand increases by 20 units at each price. Fill in the columns for AR_1, TR_1, and MR_1. (Do not fill in the spaces with a dash.)

(g) What will be the new profit-maximising price and output? (Note: It may help if you draw the AR, MR, AC and MC curves on graph paper and then show the effects of shifting the AR and MR curves.)

The remaining parts of the question continue with the assumption that demand has increased by 20 units at each price.

(h) Now let us assume that the government imposes a *lump-sum* tax of £100 on producers (i.e. a total tax that does not vary with output). What will be the profit-maximising price and output now?

(i) Now assume instead that the government imposes a *specific* tax of £12 per unit. What will be the profit-maximising price and output now? (See if you can spot the answer from the table without entering new cost columns.)

Q51. Should your educational establishment take on more students? The answer given to this question by the administrators of many universities, colleges and schools since the early 1990s has been a resounding 'Yes', as they have avidly competed for students. At the same time the amount of resources they have available per student has declined: and yet many of the administrators have claimed that the quality of education that students have received has not declined and some claim that it has even increased. The arguments they use have partly to do with the marginal cost per student being lower than the average cost and the possibility of achieving economies of scale.

Many of the academic and administrative staff, on the other hand, claim that it is only their harder work that prevents a decline in standards and that a further reduction in moneys earned per student would lead to an inevitable erosion of the service they could provide for students.

Assess these arguments in the context of your own establishment, and in particular consider the following:

(a) What are the fixed and what are the variable costs associated with your particular course? Would the marginal cost be significantly different from the average cost? How will the answer differ in the short run and the long run?

(b) Are there any significant economies of scale associated with (i) courses with large numbers of students; (ii) large educational establishments?

(c) Should your establishment take on extra students at present?

(d) Should there be an expansion of some courses relative to others?

(e) If there were a further decline in the 'unit of resource' (i.e. the money earned per student), should your establishment take on more or fewer students?

(f) Should inefficient educational establishments close down?

Try interviewing teaching staff and administrative staff to help you answer these questions. Explain any differences in the replies they give.

C DISCUSSION TOPICS AND ESSAYS

Q52. Imagine that you are a small business person employing five people, and are pleased to find that business is expanding. As a result you take on extra labour: a sixth worker this month, a seventh next month and an eighth the month after. The seventh worker discovers that when she is taken on, output increases more than when either the sixth or eighth worker was taken on. Not surprisingly, she claims that she is a more efficient worker than her colleagues. Do the facts necessarily support her case?

*Q53. Use isoquant analysis to illustrate the effect on the factor proportions used by a firm of the granting of an employment subsidy (per worker) to the firm.

Q54. What are the likely effects on firms' costs of more people participating in higher education?

Q55. A firm observes that both its short-run and its long-run average cost curves are ⌣ shaped. Explain why the reasons for this are quite different in the two cases.

Q56. Using relevant examples, explain why an increase in the minimum wage is likely to have a greater impact on the price of services than that of manufactured goods.

Q57. Would there ever be any point in a firm attempting to continue in production if it could not cover its long-run average (total) costs?

Q58. The price of personal computers has fallen significantly in recent years, while demand has been increasing. Use cost and revenue diagrams to illustrate these events.

Q59. Debate
It is better to have manufacturing concentrated in just a few large plants in each industry and in just a few parts of the country. That way production will take place at minimum costs.

D ARTICLES

In the article below, taken from the *Financial Times* Web site in December 2001, the discussion focuses on how improved supply chain management by firms is essential for business survival during economic downturns.

Users focus sharply on cost cuts and flexibility

Penelope Ody

Building supply chains to cope with growth or forging collaborative alliances to improve responsiveness and visibility are all very well when the economy is buoyant. But when much of industry worldwide is facing harder times, it is rather different: cutting costs, focusing on agility and damage limitation are now the priorities.

Today, companies are opting for adaptable supply webs and a flexible manufacturing base with collaborative initiatives that aim to share risk and find opportunities for all participants to cut costs.

'When demand outstripped supply, having rapid access to an extensive supply planning network was essential,' says Adrian Edwards, European lead partner for supply chain planning at PwC Consulting. 'In a downturn, it is more important to have a very flexible network so that you can switch out of supply without damaging the brand.'

Branded goods suppliers – notably in the telecoms and high-tech sectors – are reinventing themselves as marketing operations. They are using a network of sub-contracted manufacturing facilities to fuel a highly visible supply chain, giving new meaning to the 'extended enterprise' concept.

This move to outsourced manufacturing is also driving greater use of supplier relationship management (SRM) tools. 'It needs a more collaborative and complex approach,' says Terry Austin, president of European operations at Manugistics. 'It needs an emphasis on collaborative product design and configurable products tailored to markets and individuals'.

In addition, 'you add price and revenue optimisation, looking at demand elasticity and each customer's unique willingness to pay,' he says. 'With this sort of optimisation we believe that an increase in revenue of just 1 per cent will have a five-fold impact on profit performance,' he says.

Optimisation techniques can also offer the 'quick wins' demanded by many companies in today's environment for IT investment, he adds.

Systems specialists are also focusing on building closer links between supply chain planning and execution attributes to increase adaptability. 'In a downturn there is less emphasis on blue sky long-term plans and more on flexible execution and adaptability,' says Ray Hood, founder and chief executive of Dallas-based Exe Technologies.

Mysteries

'Visibility is essential: it is amazing how little people actually know of what happens as goods cross barriers through the supply chain from manufacturer to consolidator to shipper – there are too many black holes,' he says.

Exe believes that many supply chains still contain up to 15 per cent excess inventory and better visibility and monitoring can add this sum to working capital. 'In the CPG sector, planning can be facetious,' adds Mr Hood. 'You can't plan a fashion – the reality is to react quickly to demand with visibility from producer through to end-consumer.'

Austin Bendall, a consultant at Strategy Partners Group, believes the emphasis should be on 'demand chain optimisation': the total supply chain needs to be much more responsive to consumer demand at a store level, he says. 'It needs a flexible supply chain and internal change so that buyers work more closely with store managers – and the space allocation needs within the store are reflected right through the supply chain to the producer.'

QRS, a California-based software specialist which operates largely in the soft goods sector, is adding an assortment planning tool to its Tradeweave sourcing suite to do just this. 'Local consumer demand for different sizes, for example, needs to go right back down the pipeline so that the producer in China or wherever is actually packing and shipping those goods in that assortment for that store,' suggests John Simon, executive vice president for strategy and business development.

With good supplier relationships and a truly visible supply chain, a packed carton could then travel unopened and unchecked to its final destination with electronic payment triggered on arrival.

This 'purchase to pay' integration is seen by many as one of the next key supply chain developments, integrating financial as well as product information into the model. PwC Consulting suggests that the total figure for processing a purchase order – including the tracking, staff costs and invoice matching – can be around $150.

'Given the need to cut costs, there is a lot of mileage to be gained here,' says Charlie Hawker, European lead partner for supply chain, 'and these types of self-billing or payment-on-consumption or delivery models are starting to proliferate.'

This growth in seamless, extended enterprise models and greater trust between trading partners, is also leading the main software specialists such as Manugistics and i2 Technologies, to spread their product range from design to delivery: from supplier relationship tools to streamline collaborative product development right through to customer facing products more usually associated with CRM (customer relationship management) specialists.

'The supply chain is taking a bigger footprint within the enterprise,' says Simon Pollard, vice president for European research with AMR Research. 'It is an area where we are still seeing IT investment. Even before September 11, most senior executives were looking at ways to manage the downturn and we were seeing a shift to more tactical collaborative process support, and away from the sort of strategic supply chain communities that had been dominating developments. There is much more emphasis now on sharing problems and processes with shared performance metrics between trading partners.'

Value networks

These communities are variously seen as supply webs or value networks with links between all parties through a central co-ordinating hub. At Scio – a joint venture development between Transport Development Group and Cap Gemini Ernst & Young – managing director Mike Branigan sees the traditional linear supply model as creating 'silos' of information.

In contrast, he says, the web structure can provide total visibility throughout the extended enterprise, using adaptable XML-based interfaces.

Scio's central hub model, which includes applications from Yantra, IBM, and Websphere, is easily extendible, allowing new members to be added to the supply web as need be to meet specific requirements in just a few minutes.

'With this model we believe you can very easily see a 10 per cent improvement in performance,' says Mr Branigan, 'although it could be more than 25 per cent in some cases.'

Within these complex supply webs, with their high levels of activity and information exchange, automated monitoring and tracking systems are also appearing to improve supply chain event management (SCEM).

'Systems are starting to identify supply chain problems before they go too badly wrong in a management by exception approach,' says Mr Pollard at AMR Research. 'The next stage is for trading partners mutually to agree the key performance indicators and establish business rules to automate the decision-taking and create a self-adaptive operation.'

Applying this approach to a grocery promotion, for example, the system could identify consumer response levels and automate a course of action – such as increase production or initiate markdown – as defined in the rules.

Human limitations and pressure on executive time usually mean that this sort of item-level event monitoring within the supply chain is virtually impossible, but automated systems could press the alarm bells more quickly to cut losses and optimise profit.

'We've really seen a major increase in interest over the past three months,' says Neil Anderson, European senior vice president and managing director at Viewlocity, an SCEM specialist. 'The driver is undoubtedly the need to cut costs and that was happening well before September 11. Europe is probably about six months behind the US on SCEM, but interest is starting here now.'

But while better information flows and event management can help control costs and improve performance, in the post-September 11 world, there have been many suggestions that leaner supply chains and a 'just-in-time' approach will give way to a more cautious 'just-in-case'.

'The answer lies somewhere in the middle,' suggests Mr Hood at Exe Technologies. 'No-one wants the risk of a single source of supply and no-one wants to risk stock-outs and that was as true before September 11 as now. You need systems in place that can enable a quick reaction to demand and identify emerging problems – and that is where supply chain developments are moving.'

(a) Why might fluctuations in demand encourage firms to hold large stocks of supplies, and what effect will this have on the total and average cost?

(b) Explain the effects on the firm of technological advancements in supply chain management during periods of high or low demand.

(c) Why might developing a supply web for a company be superior to relying on few suppliers through a supply chain?

The article below, taken from *The Economist* of 21 September 2000, discusses whether the economic benefits of innovations in information technology will match those of earlier technological revolutions, such as steam power or electricity.

Untangling e-conomics

Will the economic benefits of information technology match those of earlier technological revolutions? Quite probably, says Pam Woodall, our economics editor; but the laws of economics will still apply.

'Everything that can be invented has been invented.' With these sweeping words, the Commissioner of the United States Office of Patents recommended in 1899 that his office be abolished, so spectacular had been the wave of innovation in the late 19th century. History is littered with such foolish predictions about technology. The lesson is that any analysis of the economic consequences of the current burst of innovation in information technology (IT – computers, software, telecoms and the Internet) should proceed with care. At one end, the Internet's boosters have boldly proclaimed it as the greatest invention since the wheel, transforming the world so radically that the old economics textbooks need ripping up. At the other extreme, sceptics say that computers and the Internet are not remotely as important as steam power, the telegraph or electricity. In their view, IT stands for 'insignificant toys', and when the technology bubble bursts, its economic benefit will turn out to be no greater than that of the 17th-century tulip bubble.

The first programmable electronic computer, with a memory of 20 words, was built in 1946, but the IT revolution did not really start until the spread of mainframe computers in the late 1960s and the invention of the microprocessor in 1971. The pace of technological advance since then has been popularly summed up by Moore's Law. Gordon Moore, the co-founder of Intel, forecast in 1965 that the processing power of a silicon chip would double every 18 months. And so it has, resulting in an enormous increase in computer processing capacity and a sharp decline in costs (see Chart 1). Scientists reckon that Moore's Law still has at least another decade to run. By 2010 a typical computer is likely to have 10m times the processing power of a computer in 1975, at a lower real cost.

Over the past 40 years global computing power has increased a billionfold. Number-crunching tasks that once took a week can now be done in seconds. Today a Ford Taurus car contains more computing power than the multimillion-dollar mainframe computers used in the Apollo space programme. Cheaper processing power allows computers to be used for more and more purposes. In 1985, it cost Ford $60,000 each time it crashed a car into a wall to find out what would happen in an accident. Now a collision can be simulated by computer for around $100. BP Amoco uses 3D seismic-exploration technology to prospect for oil, cutting the cost of finding oil from nearly $10 a barrel in 1991 to only $1 today.

The capacity and speed of communications networks has also increased massively. In 1970 it would have cost $187 to transmit *Encyclopaedia Britannica* as an electronic data file coast to coast in America, because transmission speeds were slow and long-distance calls

Chart 1 Moore power, less cost

Moore's Law
Millions of transistors per microprocessor

- Pentium III — 100
- Pentium II — 10
- Pentium
- 80486 — 1
- 80386
- 80286 — 0.1
- 8086
- 8080 — 0.01
- 8008 — 0.001

1970 75 80 85 90 95 2000

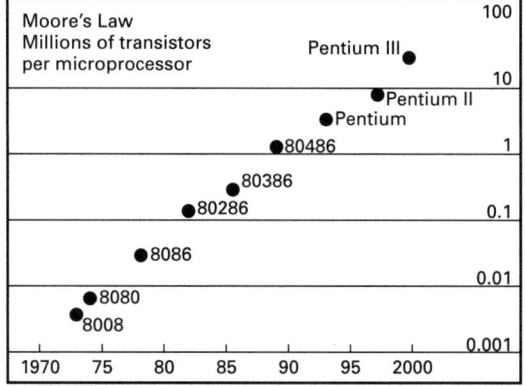

Price of power and speed, $	1970	1999
Cost of 1 MHz processing power	7,601	0.17
Cost of 1 megabit storage	5,257	0.17
Cost of sending 1 trillion bits	150,000	0.12

Sources: The Bank Credit Analyst, Federal Reserve Bank of Dallas.

expensive. Today the entire content of the Library of Congress could be sent across America for just $40. As bandwidth expands, costs will fall further. Within ten years, international phone calls could, in effect, be free, with telecoms firms charging a monthly fee for unlimited calls.

As communications costs plunge, more and more computers are being linked together. The benefit of being online increases exponentially with the number of connections. According to Metcalfe's Law, attributed to Robert Metcalfe, a pioneer of computer networking, the value of a network grows roughly in line with the square of the number of users. The Internet got going properly only with the invention of the World Wide Web in 1990 and the browser in 1993, but the number of users worldwide has already climbed to more than 350m, and may reach 1 billion within four years.

Between the extremes

IT is revolutionising the way we communicate, work, shop and play. But is it really changing the economy? The ultra-optimists argue that IT helps economies to grow much faster, and that it has also eliminated both inflation and the business cycle. As a result, the old rules of economics and traditional ways of valuing shares no longer apply. Cybersceptics retort that sending e-mail, downloading photos of friends or booking holidays online may be fun, yet the Internet does not begin to compare with innovations such as the printing press, the steam engine or electricity. Some even say that America's current prosperity is little more than a bubble.

Whom to believe? The trouble is that IT commentators go over the top at both extremes. Either they deny that anything has changed, or they insist that everything has changed. This survey will argue that both are wrong, and that the truth – as so often – lies somewhere in the middle. The economic benefits of the IT revolution could well be big, perhaps as big as those from electricity. But the gains will be nowhere near enough to justify current share prices on Wall Street. America is experiencing a speculative bubble – as it has done during most technological revolutions in the past two centuries.

The Internet is far from unique in human history. It has much in common with the telegraph, invented in the 1830s, as Tom Standage, a journalist on this newspaper, explains in his book *The Victorian Internet*. The telegraph, too, brought a big fall in communications costs and increased the flow of information through the economy. But it hardly turned conventional economic wisdom on its head.

Extra brain-power

The value of IT and the Internet lies in their capacity to store, analyse and communicate information instantly, anywhere, at negligible cost. As Brad DeLong, an economist at the University of California at Berkeley, puts it: 'IT and the Internet amplify brain power in the same way that the technologies of the industrial revolution amplified muscle power.' But is IT really in the same league as previous technological revolutions? There are several tests.

First, how radically does it change day-to-day life? Arguably, the railways, the telegraph and electricity brought about much more dramatic changes than the Internet. For instance, electric light extended the working day, and railways allowed goods and people to be moved much more quickly and easily across the country. Yet the inventions that have the biggest scientific or social impact do not necessarily yield the biggest economic gains. The printing press, seen by some as the most important invention of the past millennium, had little measurable effect on growth in output per head. In scientific terms, the Internet may not be as significant as the printing press, the telegraph or electricity, but it may yet turn out to have a bigger economic impact. One reason is that the cost of communications has plummeted far more steeply than that of any previous technology, allowing it to be used more widely and deeply throughout the economy. An invention that remains expensive, as the electric telegraph did, is bound to have a lesser effect.

A second test of a new technology is how far it allows businesses to reorganise their production processes, and so become more efficient. The steam age moved production from the household to the factory; the railways allowed the development of mass markets; and with electricity, the assembly line became possible. Now computers and the Internet are offering the means for a sweeping reorganisation of business, from online procurement of inputs to more decentralisation and outsourcing.

The ultimate test, however, is the impact of a new technology on productivity across the economy as a whole, either by allowing existing products to be made more efficiently or by creating entirely new products. Faster productivity growth is the key to higher living standards. After years when people puzzled over the apparent failure of computers to boost productivity, there are signs at last that productivity growth in America is accelerating. The question is whether that faster growth is sustainable. Undeniably, though, America's economy has had a fabulous decade in which it achieved both faster growth and lower inflation, and some part of that is due to IT.

And whatever the impact of IT so far, there is more to come. Paul Saffo, who heads the Institute for the Future, in California, believes that the IT revolution has only just begun, both in terms of innovation and the adoption of new technologies. Corporate America's R & D has increased by an annual average of 11% over the past five years, which suggests that innovation will go on. As yet, only 6% of the world's population is online; even in the rich world, the figure is only 35%. Only a third of American manufacturing firms are using the Internet for procurement or sales. All technologies follow an S-shaped path (see Chart 2). They are slow to get going, but once they reach critical mass the technology spreads fast. The world may already be half-way up the curve for computers, but for the Internet it is only at the bottom of the steep part, from where it is likely to take off rapidly. Moreover, IT is only one of three technological revolutions currently under way. Together with fuel-cell technology, and genetics and biotechnology, it could create a much more powerful 'long wave' than some of its predecessors.

Even so, predictions about future growth must be kept in perspective. Those who claim that technology has created a new growth paradigm that will allow America's GDP to keep expanding at well over 4% a year do not realise just how bold their forecasts are. That sort of annual rate implies growth in GDP per head of more than 3%. For that to materialise, computers and the Internet would need to be a far more important engine of growth than steam, railways or electricity. Through most of the 19th century America's GDP per head grew by less than 1.5% a year, and in the 20th century by an average of just under 2%. In truth, many current

Chart 2 The S-curve

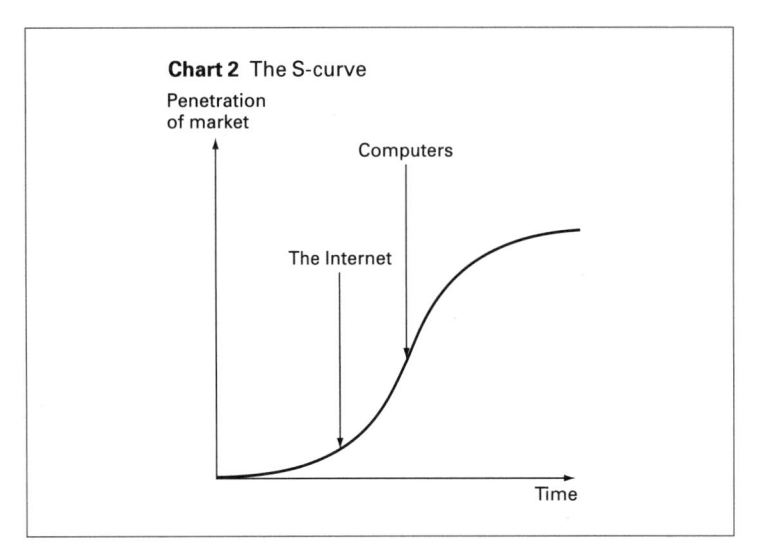

[Graph showing Penetration of market (y-axis) vs Time (x-axis), with an S-curve. Arrows point to the curve labelled "Computers" (near top) and "The Internet" (near bottom).]

expectations for American growth are probably unrealistic.

On the other hand, global growth may well turn out to be faster than in the past. America has been the first to embrace the IT revolution and the new economy, which is why so much of the evidence in this survey is concentrated in that country. But it is no longer alone. A later section of the survey will argue that if the rewards from IT are significant in America, the gains in Europe, Japan and many emerging economies could be even bigger. If so, this could yet prove to be the biggest technological revolution ever for the world as a whole.

So is it true that the 'new economy' is making a nonsense of the laws of economics? It is argued that rules for, say, monetary and antitrust policy that worked in the age of steel and cars no longer apply now that computers and networks hold sway. But as Carl Shapiro and Hal Varian neatly put it in their book *Information Rules*: 'Technology changes, economic laws do not.' The business cycle has not really been eliminated; if economies grow too fast, inflation will still rise; share prices still depend on profits; and governments still need to remain on their guard against the abuse of monopoly power.

Don't burn the textbooks

But perhaps the most important economic rule of all is that new technology is not a panacea that cures every economic ill. To reap the full benefits from IT, governments still need to pursue sound policies. America's recent economic success is not due to new technology alone, but also to more stable fiscal and monetary policies, deregulation and free trade. A period of pervasive structural change lies ahead. Economies will enjoy big gains overall, but these will not be evenly spread. Many existing jobs and firms will disappear. In this environment, the risks of policy errors are high.

To see how governments can choke the economic benefits of innovation, look back 600 years to China, which at that time was the most technologically advanced country in the world. Centuries before the West, it had invented moveable-type printing, the blast furnace and the water-powered spinning machine. By 1400 it had in place many of the innovations that triggered the industrial revolution in Britain in the 18th century. But then its technological progress went into reverse, because its rulers kept such tight control on the new technology that it could not spread. It is a warning that the fruits of the IT revolution should not be taken for granted.

© *The Economist*, London (21.9.00)

(a) Why has the cost of information technology (in terms of processing power) been falling over time? Do you think that this is likely to continue in the future?

(b) What effect will technological innovations have on a manufacturing firm's productivity and costs, and the price it charges?

(c) Why shouldn't we burn our economics textbooks?!

For many products, style is a key component to their success. Two such products are clothing and cars. Both markets exhibit 'fashion price cycles'. However, in recent times, whereas clothing seasonal price variations have become more pronounced, the seasonal pricing variation in the market for cars has diminished. The article below, taken from *The Economist* of 23 December 1995, explores the factors affecting the price of fashion products, and in particular looks at the role of *costs*.

Dedicated followers of fashion

According to standard economic theory, Giorgio Armani, a world-famous Italian fashion designer, runs a simple business. His company combines inputs of labour (seamstresses), capital (dyeing and weaving machines) and raw material (cloth) to make clothes with the best possible trade-off between cost and quality. He then calculates what the demand is for his designs, and estimates how many units he can make without marginal costs exceeding marginal revenues. He sells these at the market-clearing price, and earns just enough profit to compensate him for his investment of time and money.

The flaw of this stylised view is that it ignores the most important thing that designers such as Mr Armani sell: fashion itself. In industries as diverse as clothing, cars and music, the key to making money is to work out (or, better still, invent) what is going to be 'in' by the time a new product comes to market.

At first glance, economists would seem to have little to say about this phenomenon. For example, they have no special means of telling which styles of clothing are fashionable (if you doubt this, take a look at what the next economist you meet is wearing), let alone what is likely to be hip in future. So when fashions wax and wane, people tend to give simplistic explanations: they say that people's tastes have changed, or that they have become more (or less) fashion-conscious.

Can economics offer more revealing insights than these? A recent study by three economists – Peter Pashigian and Eric Gould from the University of Chicago's Graduate School of Business, and Brian Bowen from the Chicago Mercantile Exchange – argues that it can. They start by looking at the pattern of prices for fashion-sensitive goods, which tends to follow well-established cycles. Prices are high at the start of the buying season, they fall gradually as the season progresses, and then they rise again as new styles are introduced for the next period.

The main reason for this is uncertainty. When producers introduce a new line of, say, cars or dresses, they do not know how successful it will be. To avoid selling it for less than is necessary, they initially set a high price, then lower it for lines that do not sell well. A good way to measure the importance of fashion, therefore, is to look at the variation in seasonal prices. The first chart, for example, compares prices for men's and women's clothing during the autumn–winter season. As you would expect, fashion seems to play a more important role in women's clothing than in men's.

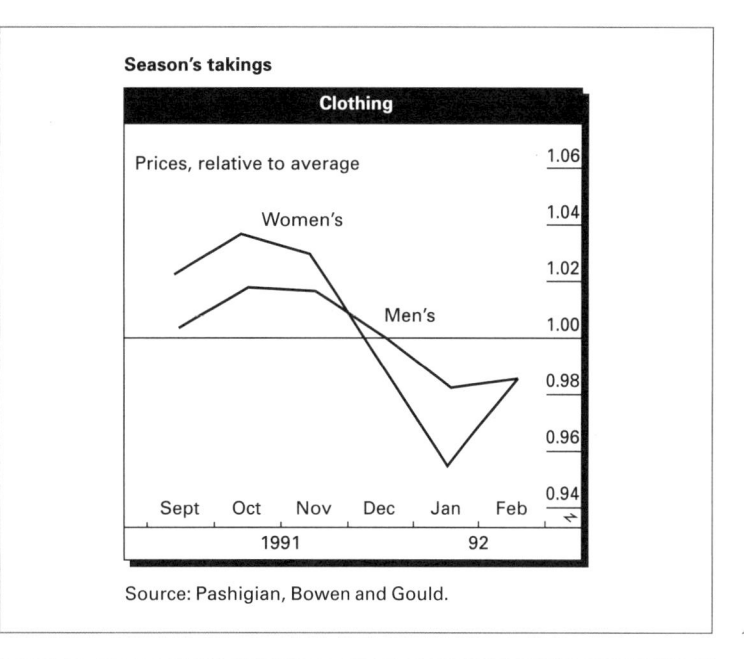

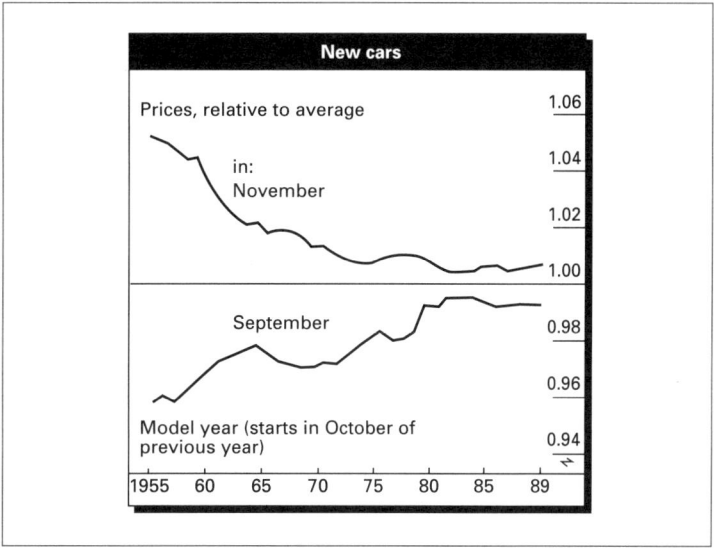

The strength of this pattern, however, can change over time. Over the past few decades, seasonal price variations for women's clothing have become more pronounced. However, prices in the American car market, which also tend to follow a 'fashion' cycle, have displayed the opposite trend. As the second chart shows, prices in November, at the beginning of the new model year, are higher than they are the following September. Since the mid-1950s, however, this seasonal gap has been narrowing steadily.

Explaining this is harder than it looks. It is no use, for example, simply to say that people's tastes are changing. If so, why are people caring more about fashion when buying clothing, but less when choosing cars? Or perhaps rising incomes are what matter? But these should not have opposing effects in the two markets.

Fashion cents

The three economists claim to have solved the puzzle. The answer, they say, is to focus on supply rather than demand. They argue that the different trends for cars and clothes are due less to shifts in the tastes of consumers than to changes in the technology of producers.

Advances in the textile industry, such as the development of sophisticated electronic weaving and knitting machines, have made it cheaper for designers to revamp their lines each season. But in the car industry, say the authors, it has become more costly to make radical style changes every year. Although new technology has made it easier to change the size and shape of a car's body, they show that the cost of doing so as a share of the total production costs has actually risen.

As a result, they say, most car makers have been forced to make more modest changes each year. They have focused on those that improve a car's quality, such as better engines and new gadgets, rather than its look.

© *The Economist*, London (23.12.95)

74 CHAPTER 5 BACKGROUND TO SUPPLY

(a) Why might it be very difficult to estimate the likely demand for a given fashion product? Why might Armani have fewer problems in setting price than, say, a common high-street retailer?

(b) If consumers are aware that unsuccessful lines of clothing will fall in price as the season progresses, why do they buy when prices are set high at the start of the season? What does this tell us about the shape of the demand curve for a given fashion product (i) at the start, and (ii) at the end of the season?

(c) How might we account for the differing fashion price cycles of clothing and new cars?

(d) What has happened to fixed costs as a proportion of total costs in the production of cars? How has this affected car design strategy?

E ANSWERS

Q1. $(6 \times 10) + (3 \times 4) = 72$ units of output.

Q2. C. The actual length of time of the short run will vary from industry to industry depending on how long it takes to vary the amount used of all factors.

Q3. when one or more factors are held constant, then, as the variable factor is increased, there will come a point when additional units of the variable factor will produce less extra output than previous units.

Q4. (a) See Figure A5.1.
(b) Diminishing returns set in beyond point *a* (beyond 2 workers): i.e. the *TPP* curve rises less rapidly after point *a*.

Figure A5.1 The total physical product of labour for good X

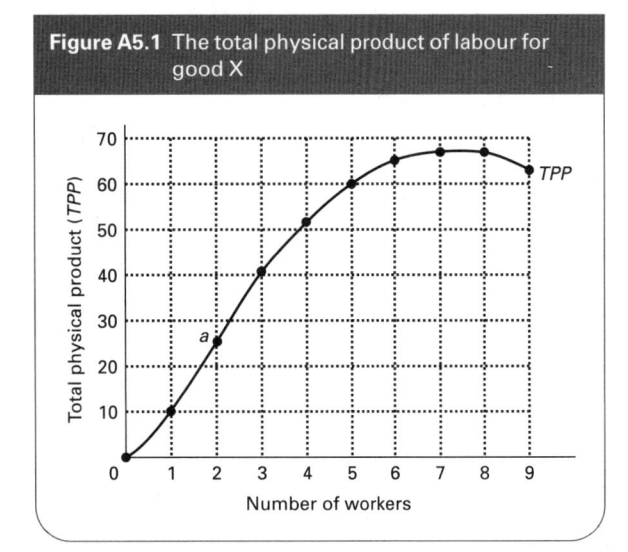

Q5. the amount of extra output gained from the use of one more unit of the variable factor.

Q6. (a) (iii) Thus if an extra two workers were taken on ($\Delta L = 2$) and between them they produced an extra 100 units of output per period of time ($\Delta TPP = 100$), then the extra output from *one* more unit of the variable factor (i.e. labour) would be $100/2 = 50$.

(b) (i) Thus if 200 workers are employed ($L = 200$) and between them they produce a total output of 30 000 units per period of time ($TPP = 30\,000$), the average output per worker would be $30\,000/200 = 150$.

Q7. See table below.

(1) Number of workers	(2) TPP	(3) APP	(4) MPP
0	0	—	
			10
1	10	10	
			16
2	26	13	
			15
3	41	13.67	
			11
4	52	13	
			8
5	60	12	
			5
6	65	10.83	
			2
7	67	9.57	
			0
8	67	8.38	
			−4
9	63	7	

Q8. See Figure A5.2.

Figure A5.2 The average and marginal physical product of labour for good X

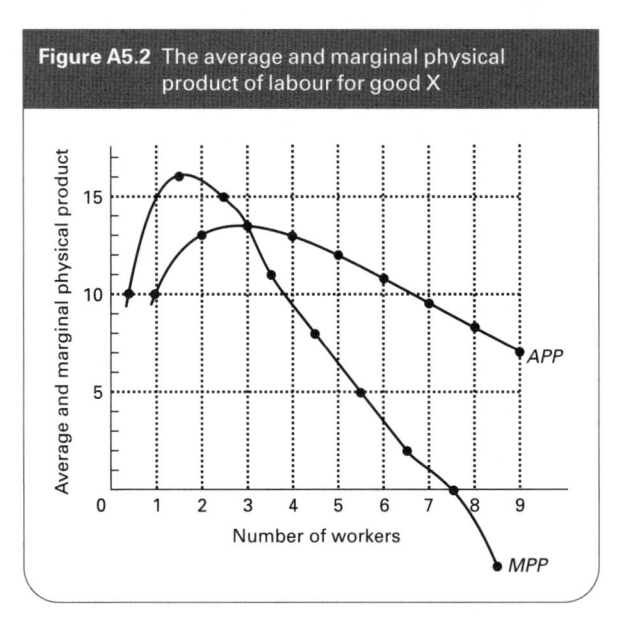

Q9. To the left of this point the *MPP* is above the *APP*. Thus extra workers are producing more than the average. They have the effect of pulling the average up. The *APP* curve must therefore be rising. To the

right of this point the *MPP* is below the *APP*. Extra workers produce less than the average and thus pull the average down. The *APP* must be falling.

Q10. *True.* (Try adding the figures in the *MPP* column in Q7.)

Q11. B. $MPP = \Delta TPP/\Delta F = (1005 - 1000)/(41 - 40) = 5$.

Q12. *explicit.*

Q13. E. This is what the firm is having to forgo by using the machine. The alternative forgone may be the production of some other good, or it may be the additional second-hand value from selling it at the beginning of the year rather than after producing X for a year.

Q14. *True.*

Q15. *the firm's output.*

Q16. (a) *variable*, (b) *fixed* (c) *fixed* (unless the firm deliberately chooses to spend more on advertising the more it produces), (d) *variable* (even though the bill may not be paid this month, the total cost of the electricity will nevertheless vary with the amount of chocolate produced), (e) *variable*, (f) *variable* (even though the basic wage is fixed per worker, the amount spent on basic wages will increase if extra workers are taken on to produce extra output, and will fall if workers quitting are not replaced because of falling output), (g) *variable*, (h) *fixed*, (i) *fixed* (the rise in interest rates is not the result of increased *output*: i.e. the cost is still fixed with respect to output).

Q17. **(a)** *AC.*
 (b) *AVC.*
 (c) *MC.*
 (d) *MC.* (Given that fixed costs, by definition, do not vary with output, marginal costs will consist of variable costs.)
 (e) *AFC.*
 (f) *TC.*
 (g) *TVC.*
 (h) *TC.*

Q18. **(a)** See table below.

Output	TFC	TVC	TC	AFC	AVC	AC	MC
0	10	0	10	–	–	–	
1	10	8	18	10.0	8.0	18.0	8
2	10	12	22	5.0	6.0	11.0	4
3	10	15	25	3.33	5.0	8.33	3
4	10	17	27	2.5	4.25	6.75	2
5	10	20	30	2.0	4.0	6.0	3
6	10	24	34	1.67	4.0	5.67	4
7	10	29	39	1.43	4.14	5.57	5
8	10	36	46	1.25	4.5	5.75	7
9	10	48	58	1.11	5.33	6.44	12
10	10	70	80	1.0	7.0	8.0	22

 (b) 4. After this level of output *MC* begins to rise.
 (c) See Figure A5.3.
 (d) See Figure A5.4.

Figure A5.3 Total costs for firm X

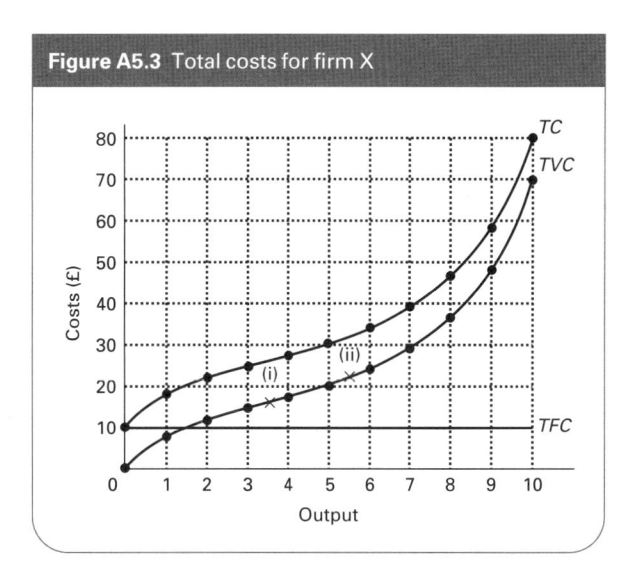

Figure A5.4 Average and marginal costs for firm X

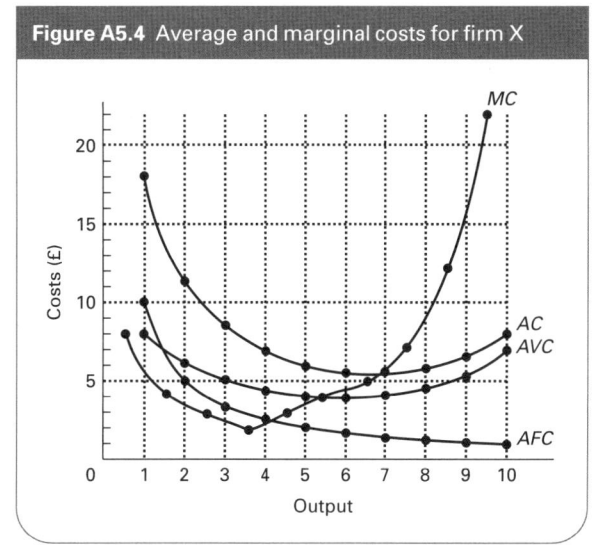

Q19. C. If the marginal cost is below the average cost, then additional units will cost less to produce than the average and will thus pull the average down. You can see that this is the case by looking at Figure A5.4.

Q20. *Increasing returns to scale.* Notice the terminology here. The 'to scale' refers to the fact that *all* the factors have increased in the same proportion: that the whole scale of the operation has increased.

Q21. **(a)** *Situation (i)*: both factors are being varied.
 (b) *No.* Output increases proportionately. A doubling of inputs leads to a doubling of output. The firm is experiencing *constant returns to scale*.
 (c) *Yes.* The marginal physical product of input 1 diminishes. In other words, when input 2 is held constant, each additional unit of input 1 produces less and less additional output (10, 8, 6, 4).

Q22. B. Economies of scale are defined as lower *costs* per unit of output as the scale of production increases. These lower costs will probably be in part due to

76 CHAPTER 5 BACKGROUND TO SUPPLY

increasing returns to scale (answer D), but they may also be the result of lower input prices that large firms can negotiate.

Q23. (a) (ii); (b) (v); (c) (viii); (d) (i); (e) (iii); (f) (iv); (g) (vi); (h) (vii).

Q24. (i), (ii), (iv), (vii).

Q25. External economies of scale occur when a firm experiences lower costs as a result of the *industry* being large. Thus (a) and (d) are external economies of scale for firm A, whereas (b), (c) and (e) are internal economies of scale. Note that (e) is an external economy of scale for *other* firms, but not for firm A.

Q26. E. If the *MPP/P* ratio for any factor were greater than that for another, costs would be reduced by using more of the first factor relative to the second. But as this happened, diminishing marginal returns to the first factor would cause its *MPP* to fall (and the *MPP* of the second to rise) until their *MPP/P* ratios became equal. At that point there would be no further savings possible by substituting one factor for another.

Q27. The *MPP* of A is 3 (i.e. output rises from 1000 to 1003 when one more unit of A is used); the *MPP* of B is 10; the *MPP* of C is 5. If the price of A is £6, then $MPP_A/P_A = 3/6 = 1/2$. If the least-cost combination of factors to produce 1000 units is shown in the top row of Table 5.4 then $MPP_A/P_A = MPP_B/P_B = MPP_C/P_C = 1/2$. Thus:
$P_B = MPP_B/1/2 = 10 \div 1/2 = £20$
$P_C = MPP_C/1/2 = 5 \div 1/2 = £10$

*****Q28.** (a) See the four curves in Figure A5.5.
 (b) 40*A* and 20*B*. Production will be at point *s*, where the isocost of the slope $(-)P_B/P_A = (-)1$, is tangential to the 300 unit isoquant. This will involve using 40 units of factor A and 20 units of factor B.
 (c) £12 000 (i.e. 40*A* @ £200 + 20*B* @ £200).
 (d) 200 units of X. If the price of A rises to £300, the £12 000 isocost will pivot inwards on point *u*, so that its slope becomes 300/200. The maximum output that can now be produced is where the isocost touches the highest isoquant: namely at point *t* on the 200 unit isoquant.
 (e) 45*A* and 10*B* (point *t*).

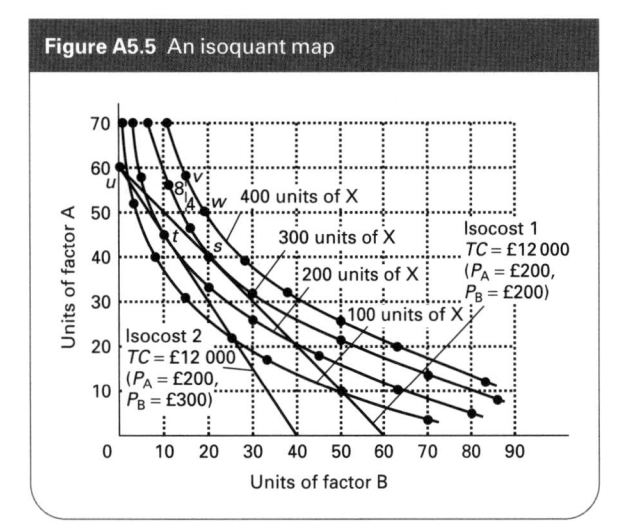

Q29. D. For example, if we move from point *v* to point *w* in Figure A5.5, an extra 4 units of B can replace 8 units of B and output will stay at 400 units. Thus the *MPP* of B must be twice that of A (8/4). Thus the (average) slope of the curve (8/4) must equal MPP_B/MPP_A.

Q30. B. For example, isocost 2 in Figure A5.5 has a slope of 60/40 = 3/2. But the price of B is £300 and the price of A is £200 and thus $P_B/P_A = 3/2$.

Q31. All except (e) are assumed. (In the case of (a) and (b), if factor prices or the state of technology change, the long-run costs curves will shift. In the case of (e) firms may or may not experience economies of scale. Note that (d) and (g) are the same.)

Q32. See Figure A5.6.

Figure A5.6 Long-run average and marginal costs

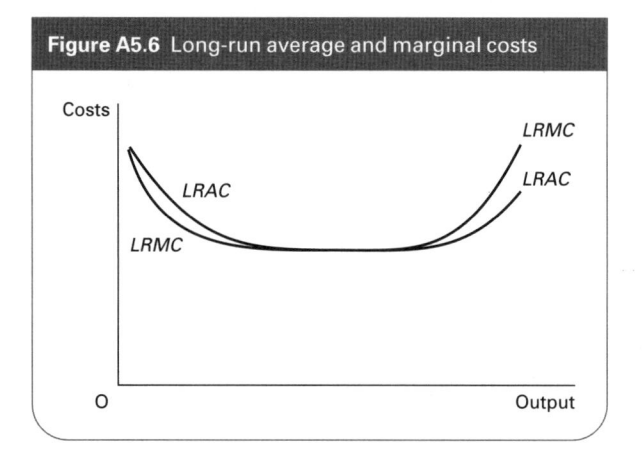

Q33. *False*. This is the so-called 'envelope curve'. It *will* be tangential with the short-run average cost curves, but only with the bottom points where the *LRAC* is horizontal. (Try drawing it.)

Q34. *True*. Maximum economies of scale will be achieved at the bottom of the *LRAC* curve. The *LRMC* must equal *LRAC* at this point – when *LRAC* is neither rising nor falling. The *LRAC* curve is tangential with the *SRAC* curves. At the *bottom* of the respective *SRAC* curve, through which point the *SRMC* curve passes.

*****Q35.** (a) (i) 10*K* + 15*L* = £4800.
  (ii) 16*K* + 21*L* = £7200.
  (iii) 18*K* + 33*L* = £9600.
  (iv) 22*K* + 42*L* = £12 000.
 (b) (i) £4800 ÷ 100 = £48.00.
  (ii) £7200 ÷ 200 = £36.00.
  (iii) £9600 ÷ 280 = £34.29.
  (iv) £12 000 ÷ 350 = £34.29.
 (c) Economies of scale are experienced up until 280 units of output. Thereafter the firm experiences constant costs.

Figure A5.5 An isoquant map

Q36. horizontal.
Q37. demand curve.
Q38. (a) (i) 5 × £2 = £10; (ii) 8 × £2 = £16.
(b) A straight line out from the origin.
(c) (i) When sales rise from 4 units to 5 units, total revenue rises from £8 to £10. Thus MR = 2. (ii) When sales rise from 7 units to 8 units, total revenue rises from £14 to £16. Thus MR = 2. MR is thus constant and equal to price. The reason is that price is constant. The marginal revenue from selling one more unit, therefore, is simply its price.
(d) A horizontal straight line and equal to the firm's demand 'curve'.
(e) See table below.

P(AR) (£)	Q (units)	TR (£)	MR (£)
20	0	0	
18	1	18	18
16	2	32	14
14	3	42	10
12	4	48	6
10	5	50	2
8	6	48	−2
6	7	42	−6

(f) −1. (Where MR = 0 and TR is at a maximum, demand is unit elastic.)
(g) Over £10. (A fall in price leads to a proportionately larger rise in quantity demanded and thus a rise in total revenue.)
(h) Under £10. (A fall in price leads to a proportionately smaller rise in quantity demanded and thus a fall in total revenue.)

Q39. MR = ΔTR/ΔQ = ((15 × 130) − (20 × 100)) ÷ (130 − 100) = −50/30 = −£1.67.

Q40. D. The total revenue for 49 bottles would be 49 × £10 = £490. The total revenue for 50 bottles would be 50 × £9 = £450. Total revenue thus falls by £40 for the 50th bottle sold.

Q41. (a) 40 (where the two curves are furthest apart).
(b) £7 (the size of the gap).
(c) The curve should plot the size of the gap, crossing the horizontal axis at outputs of 21 and 56 and reaching a peak of £7 at an output of 40.
(d) £10 (the point where the TC curve crosses the vertical axis).
(e) 65 (the peak of the TR curve: where MR = 0).
(f) 21 and 56 (where TP = 0).

Q42. (a) See Figure A5.7.
(b) The firm is a price taker. It has to accept the price as given by the market, a price that is not affected by the amount the firm supplies. The AR curve is thus a horizontal straight line, and

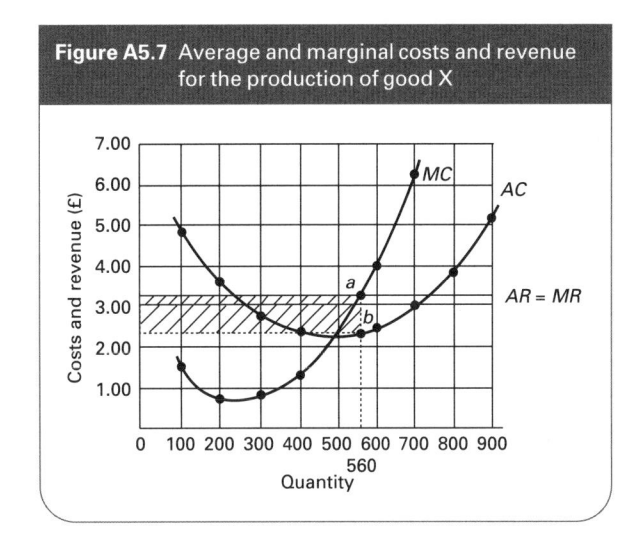

Figure A5.7 Average and marginal costs and revenue for the production of good X

the AR also equals the MR, given that each *additional* unit sold will simply earn the market price (AR) as additional revenue (MR) for the firm.
(c) 560 units, where MC = MR (point a).
(d) £2.40 (point b).
(e) £3.20 − £2.40 = £0.80 (a − b).
(f) See Figure A5.7.
(g) 560 × £0.80 = £448.00.
(h) £2.30 at an output of 500 (the minimum point on the AC curve).

Q43. C. With MR > MC, the firm should increase output. With price > MR the firm must face a downward-sloping demand (AR) curve. In order to increase output, therefore, the firm must reduce price.

Q44. False. The optimum (profit-maximising) output for the firm will be where MC = MR. The profit-maximising firm will thus choose to produce at the bottom of the AC curve *only* if MR and MC happen to intersect at this point. (As we shall see in the next chapter, this *will* be the case in the long run under perfect competition.)

Q45. False. It should produce at an *output* where MR = MC, but unless it is a price taker whose MR thus equals price, it will sell at a price *above* MR and MC.

Q46. E. If AR is greater than AVC, it will be able to cover the costs arising directly from remaining in production, and will be able to make some contribution to paying its fixed costs which, in the short run, it will have to pay anyway whether it remains in production or not. If it cannot even cover its variable costs, it will lose less by closing down.

Q47. D. In the short run it is covering its average variable cost and therefore it should continue in operation; but it will minimise its losses (i.e. maximise the contribution towards paying off its fixed costs) by producing where MR = MC. It should therefore reduce output. In the long run, since it is not covering its average (total) cost (AC) it should close down.

Q48. *(a)* $AC = TC/Q = 100/Q - 20 + 3Q$.
(b) $MC = dTC/dQ = -20 + 6Q$.
(c) $AR = TR/Q = 60 - 2Q$.
(d) $MR = dTR/dQ = 60 - 4Q$.
(e) Profit is maximised where $MR = MC$
 i.e. where $60 - 4Q = -20 + 6Q$
  where $10Q = 80$
  where $Q = 8$.
(f) $A\Pi = AR - AC = (60 - (2 \times 8)) - ((100/8) - 20 + (3 \times 8)) = 60 - 16 - 12.5 + 20 - 24 = 27.5$.
(g) $T\Pi = A\Pi \times Q = 27.5 \times 8 = 220$.
(h) $T\Pi = TR - TC = (60Q - 2Q^2) - (100 - 20Q + 3Q^2)$
 $= -100 + 80Q - 5Q^2$.
(i) Profit is maximised where $dT\Pi/dQ = 0$
 where $80 - 10Q = 0$
 where $Q = 8$.

Chapter Six
6
Profit Maximising under Perfect Competition and Monopoly

A REVIEW

The amount firms will supply and at what price will depend on the amount of competition they face – on the market structure. In this chapter we look at the two extreme types of market structure.

At one extreme is perfect competition. This is where there are so many firms competing that no one firm has any market power whatsoever. Firms are too small to influence market price or have any significant effect on market output. At the other extreme is monopoly, where there is only one firm in the industry which thus faces no competition at all from inside the industry (although it may well face competition from firms in related industries).

6.1 Alternative market structures
(Pages 149–50) It is usual to divide markets into four categories.

Q1. In ascending order of competitiveness, these are (fill in the missing two):
1. monopoly
2. ....
3. ....
4. perfect competition.

Q2. To which of the four categories do the following apply? (There can be more than one market category in each case.)

(a) Firms face a downward-sloping demand curve.
....

(b) New firms can freely enter the industry.
....

(c) Firms produce a homogeneous product.
....

(d) Firms are price takers.
....

(e) These is perfect knowledge on the part of consumers of price and product quality.
....

Q3. In which of the four categories would you place each of the following? (It is possible in some cases that part

80 CHAPTER 6 PROFIT MAXIMISING UNDER PERFECT COMPETITION AND MONOPOLY

of the industry could be in one category and part in another: if so, name both.)

(a) A village post office ....

(b) Restaurants in a large town...

(c) Banks..

(d) Hi-fi manufacturers..

(e) Growers of potatoes ....

(f) Water supply...

(g) Local buses ....

(h) Local builders...

(i) The market for foreign currency ....

We can get an indication of the degree of competition within an industry by observing *concentration ratios*.

Q4. A 5-firm concentration ratio shows:
A. the proportion of industries in the economy that have just five firms.
B. the share of industry profits earned by the five largest firms.
C. the sales of the five largest firms as a proportion of the total industry's sales.
D. the size of the largest firm relative to the total size of the five largest firms.
E. the output of good X produced by the five largest firms as a proportion of their total output of all types of good.

6.2 Perfect competition

(Pages 150–2) The theory of perfect competition is based on very strict assumptions.

Q5. These include the following (delete the incorrect one in each case):
(a) Firms are *price makers/price takers* and thus face a *horizontal/downward-sloping* demand curve.
(b) Firms in the industry produce a *homogeneous/differentiated* product.
(c) Producers and consumers have *complete/limited* knowledge of the market.
(d) Entry of new firms is *free/restricted*.

Q6. Before examining what price, output and profits will be, we must distinguish between the short run and the long run as they apply to perfect competition.
(a) The short run is defined as that period which

....

(b) The long run is defined as that period which

....

Q7. Which one of the following is true for the marginal firm under perfect competition?
A. It can earn only normal profits in both the short run and the long run.
B. It can earn supernormal profits in both the short and long run.
C. It can earn supernormal profits in the long run but only normal profits in the short run.
D. It can earn supernormal profits in the short run but only normal profits in the long run.
E. Whether it earns normal or supernormal profits in the short and long run will depend on the conditions in that particular industry.

(Pages 152–3) Short-run price and output under perfect competition can be found by applying the general rules for profit maximisation that we examined in the last chapter.

Q8. Under perfect competition a firm will increase output if:
A. marginal cost is less than price.
B. price exceeds marginal revenue.
C. marginal revenue equals average revenue.
D. marginal cost exceeds marginal revenue.
E. marginal cost equals marginal revenue.

Q9. Figure 6.1 shows the cost and revenue curves faced by a perfectly competitive firm.
(a) What is the maximum profit the firm can earn?

....

(b) What is the maximum output the firm can produce and still earn normal profits?

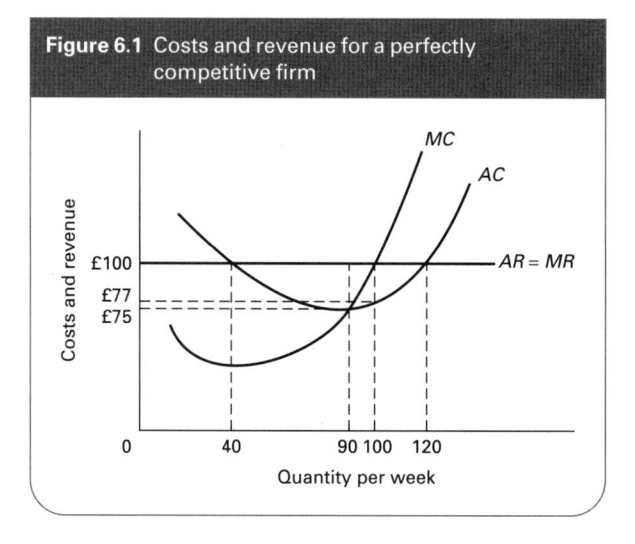

....

Figure 6.1 Costs and revenue for a perfectly competitive firm

(c) Assuming that there are no internal or external economies or diseconomies of scale, what will be the long-run price and output?

....

Q10. A perfectly competitive firm is currently earning £130 total profit per week from selling 100 units per week. Its total cost schedule is given in Table 6.1.
(a) Fill in its marginal cost schedule in Table 6.1. (Remember that marginal cost is the cost of producing *one* more unit.)
(b) What is the market price? (Clue: find its total revenue from selling 100 units.)
(c) Should the firm alter its level of production if it wishes to maximise its profit? If so, to what? If not, why not?

Table 6.1 Total and marginal costs

Output (Q)	0	20	40	60	80	100	120	140	160	180
TC (£)	100	190	270	340	420	520	640	780	940	1140
MC (£)		...	...	...	...	...	...	...	...	...

(Pages 153–4) The profit-maximising rule tells us how much a firm will produce at any given price. From this we can derive the firm's short-run supply curve.

Q11. A firm's supply curve under perfect competition in the short run will be equal to:
A. the upward-sloping portion of its *AC* curve.
B. the upward-sloping portion of its *MC* curve above its *AC* curve.
C. the upward-sloping portion of its *AVC* curve.
D. the upward-sloping portion of its *MC* curve.
E. the upward-sloping portion of its *MC* curve above its *AVC* curve.

The *industry* supply curve under perfect competition can be derived from the supply curves of the member firms. All we do is simply add up the amounts supplied by each firm at each price to give the total industry supply at each price.

Q12. A perfectly competitive industry consists of 1000 firms. Because of their location, 400 of the firms (type A firms) have higher costs. The cost schedules of the two types of firm are given in Table 6.2.
Assume that minimum *AVC* = £4.50 for type A firms and £3.50 for type B firms.

Table 6.2 Costs for two types of firm in a perfectly competitive industry

Output: weekly (Q)	1	2	3	4	5	6	7	8	9
MC: Type A firm (£)	4	3	4	5	7	10	15	23	40
MC: Type B firm (£)	3	2	3	4	5	7	10	15	23

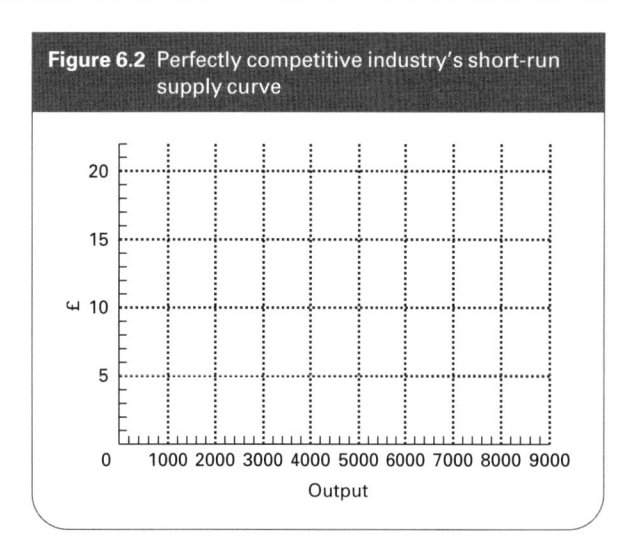

Figure 6.2 Perfectly competitive industry's short-run supply curve

(a) What will short-run industry supply be at each of the following prices?

(i) £15 ....per week

(ii) £7 ....per week

(iii) £4 ....per week

(iv) £3 ....per week

(b) Draw the industry's short-run supply curve on Figure 6.2.

(Pages 154–5) We now turn to the long-run equilibrium under perfect competition.

Q13. If the firm is in long-run equilibrium, the market price is equal to its:
(a) long-run average costs.   True/False
(b) long-run marginal costs.   True/False
(c) short-run average costs.   True/False
(d) short-run average variable costs. True/False
(e) short-run marginal costs.   True/False
(f) average revenue.   True/False
(g) marginal revenue.   True/False

Q14. A perfectly competitive firm is producing 1000 tins of toffees per week, which it sells for £1.50 per tin. This output on 1000 tins per week incurs the following costs:
Total fixed cost   £1000
Total variable cost   £1200
Marginal cost   £1.00

What should the firm do in the short run?
A. Raise its price.
B. Decrease output.

C. Increase output.
D. Maintain output at its present level.
E. Cease production altogether.

Q15. Referring to the firm in the previous question, assuming that its long-run total cost is £1600, its long-run marginal cost is £1.50 and the price has remained unchanged, what should it do in the long run?
A. Raise its price.
B. Decrease output.
C. Increase output.
D. Maintain output at its present level.
E. Cease production altogether.

The long-run industry supply curve will reflect the changing number of firms as higher prices attract new firms into the industry and lower prices encourage firms to leave the industry.

Q16. If all firms (existing and potential entrants) face the same *LRAC* curves, then the long-run industry supply curve will:
A. necessarily be horizontal.
B. slope upwards if there are external economies of scale.
C. only be horizontal if there are constant external costs with respect to industry size.
D. slope downwards if there are external diseconomies of scale.
E. slope upwards if there are internal diseconomies of scale.

Q17. Why would it be impossible for industries which experience substantial internal economies of scale to be perfectly competitive?

....

....

....

(Page 156) Perfect competition is argued to be more in the public interest than other types of market structure.

Q18. Which of the following are claimed to be advantages of perfect competition?
(a) It leads to allocative efficiency. Yes/No
(b) It leads to production at minimum short-run *AC*. Yes/No
(c) It leads to production at minimum long-run *AC*. Yes/No
(d) It leads to the lowest very long-run *AC* curve. Yes/No
(e) It leads to high levels of investment. Yes/No
(f) It leads to intense non-price competition. Yes/No
(g) The competition acts as a spur to X efficiency. Yes/No
(h) It leads to firms combining their factors in the least-cost way. Yes/No
(i) It leads to consumer sovereignty. Yes/No

6.3 Monopoly

(Page 158) A monopoly may be defined as an industry that consists of one firm only. In practice it is difficult to determine whether firms are monopolies or not, because it depends on how narrowly 'the industry' is defined.

Q19. Each of the following firms could be claimed to be *either* a monopoly *or* imperfectly competitive (monopolistic competition or oligopoly) depending on how we define the market (industry) in which it is operating. In each case identify two markets in which the firm operates: (1) where it is a monopoly; (2) where it competes in imperfect competition with other suppliers. Here is an example:

British Telecom (1) Supply of telephone lines to those customers not having access to a competitor (monopoly).
(2) Sale of telephones (imperfectly competitive).

The Post Office (1) ....
(2) ....

Your refectory (1) ....
(2) ....

Car spares manufacturer (1) ....
(2) ....

Local water company (1) ....
(2) ....

Local ice skating rink (1) ....
(2) ....

An ice cream van (1) ....
(2) ....

Q20. A firm would have a 'natural' monopoly if:
A. its average revenue curve were vertical.
B. it controlled the supply of a natural resource essential to the production of the good in question.
C. there were *total* barriers to the entry of new firms.
D. it had gained significant experience of producing the good in question.
E. its long-run average cost curve were downward sloping at the profit-maximising level of output.

CHAPTER 6 PROFIT MAXIMISING UNDER PERFECT COMPETITION AND MONOPOLY

(Pages 158–9) In order for a firm to maintain its monopoly position there must be barriers to the entry of new firms.

Q21. Which one of the following would not be a barrier to firms entering an industry?
A. An upward-sloping long-run average cost curve.
B. Patents on key processes.
C. Substantial economies of scale.
D. Large initial capital costs.
E. The threat of takeover by the existing firm(s).

(Pages 159–60) Given its market power, a monopolist will face a downward-sloping demand curve that **Q22.** *is elastic throughout its length/is inelastic throughout its length/must be elastic for some of its length but may be inelastic for part of it.* This downward-sloping demand curve will mean that the monopolist will charge a price **Q23.** *above/below/equal to* its marginal cost of production.

Q24. Because of its market power, a monopolist can choose how much to sell and what price to sell it at.
True/False

Q25. In Figure 6.3 which letter gives the profit-maximising price: A, B, C, D or E?

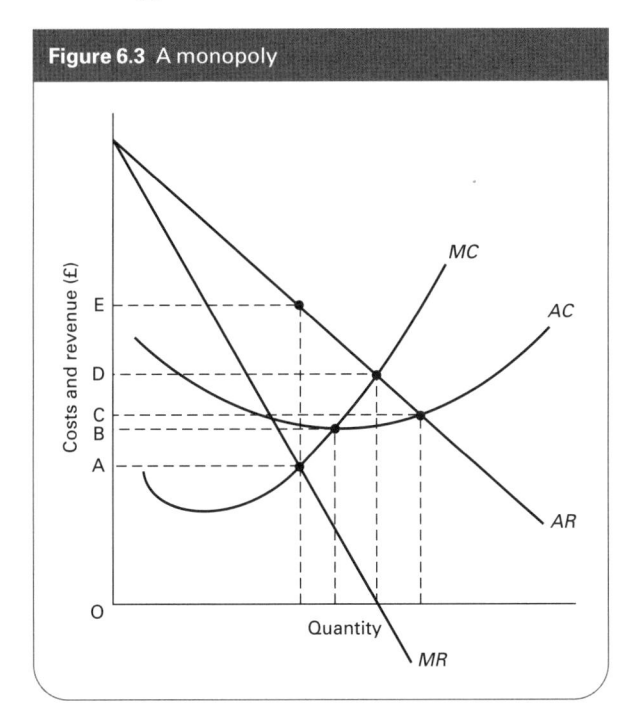

Figure 6.3 A monopoly

Q26. Table 6.3 shows the costs and revenues of a monopolist producer of specialist luxury rough terrain cars.
(a) Fill in the figures for TR, MR, TC and MC.
(b) At what daily output of cars will the monopolist maximise profits?

....

(c) How much profit will be made? ....

Table 6.3 A monopoly car producer

Quantity (cars per day)	AR (£000s)	TR (£000s)	MR (£000s)	AC (£000s)	TC (£000s)	MC (£000s)
1	100	...		110	...	
2	95	...	...	90	...	...
3	90	...	...	80	...	...
4	85	...	...	75	...	...
5	80	...	...	74	...	...
6	75	...	...	76	...	...
7	70	...	...	81	...	...

Q27. The profit-maximising monopolist will never produce where MR is negative. *True/False*

Q28. At the profit-maximising output, the monopolist's demand will be price inelastic. *True/False*

Q29. Referring to Table 6.3, what is the price elasticity of demand at the profit-maximising point? (Use the mid-point arc method over the price range either side of the profit-maximising price.)

....

Q30. In the long run, a perfectly competitive firm will produce at the bottom of its AC curve. Why will a monopolist probably not do so?

....

....

(Pages 160–3) There are several reasons why monopoly may be against the public interest, but several reasons also why the consumer may gain.

Q31. Figure 6.4 shows a perfectly competitive industry for eggs. The egg producers then get together and set up a marketing agency which becomes the monopoly seller of eggs. The agency sets the profit-maximising price and gives each producer an output quota to ensure that total output is kept to the profit-maximising level. Assuming that industry costs are not affected, the consumer will:
A. gain because price falls from P_2 to P_1.
B. gain because price falls from P_3 to P_2.
C. gain because price falls from P_3 to P_1.
D. lose because price rises from P_1 to P_2.
E. lose because price rises from P_2 to P_3.

Q32. A monopoly will always produce a lower output and at a higher price than if the industry were under perfect competition. *True/False*

84 CHAPTER 6 PROFIT MAXIMISING UNDER PERFECT COMPETITION AND MONOPOLY

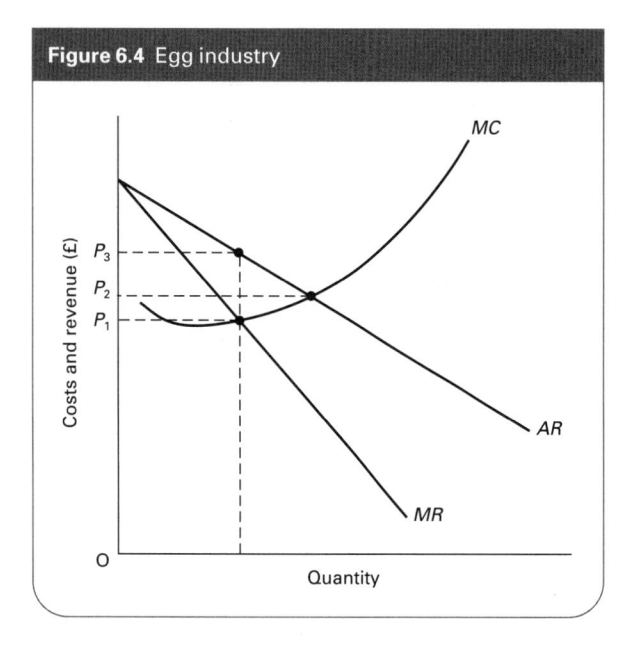

Figure 6.4 Egg industry

Referring again to Figure 6.4, assume now that the egg producers' marketing agency sets up a research laboratory into new efficient methods of egg production and as a result is able to shift the industry MC curve downwards. This could result in the profit-maximising industry price being lower than before the agency was set up.

Q33. On Figure 6.4 draw two new MC curves below the original curve. Draw them so that one of them results in a lower price than before the agency was set up and the other still results in a higher price.

*Q34. A monopolist's average revenue and average cost functions are given by:

$$AR = 1200 - 4Q$$
$$AC = 400/Q + 300 - 4Q + 3Q^2$$

where AR and AC are in £s.

(a) What is the equation for the monopolist's demand curve?

....

(b) What is the equation for total revenue?

....

(c) What is the equation for marginal revenue?

....

(d) What is the equation for total costs?

....

(e) How much are total fixed costs?

....

(f) What is the equation for marginal cost?

....

(g) At what output is profit maximised?

....

(h) What is the price at this output?

....

(i) What is average cost at this output?

....

(j) How much is average profit at this output?

....

(k) How much is total profit at this output?

....

6.4 The theory of contestable markets

(Pages 164–8) Even if a firm is currently a monopoly, it may be forced to behave as if it were in a competitive market if there is potential competition: i.e. if the market is contestable. The threat of this competition will be greater
Q35. *the higher/the lower* the entry costs to the industry and
Q36. *the higher/the lower* the exit costs from the industry.

Q37. A perfectly contestable market is defined as one where

....

....

Q38. Classify each of the following markets as highly contestable, moderately contestable, slightly contestable or non-contestable. If it depends on the circumstances, explain in what way.
(a) satellite broadcasting   highly/moderately/slightly/non
(b) hospital cleaning services
     highly/moderately/slightly/non
(c) banking on a university/college campus
     highly/moderately/slightly/non
(d) piped gas supply   highly/moderately/slightly/non
(e) parcels delivery   highly/moderately/slightly/non
(f) siting for the Olympic games
     highly/moderately/slightly/non
(g) bus service to the area where you live
     highly/moderately/slightly/non

B PROBLEMS, EXERCISES AND PROJECTS

Q39. A perfectly competitive industry consists of 100 equal-sized firms. The firms fall into three categories according to their cost structures. Their short-run marginal costs are shown in Table 6.4.

Table 6.4 Marginal costs for firms in a perfectly competitive industry

Output per day	40 firms (type A) MC per firm (£)	30 firms (type B) MC per firm (£)	30 firms (type C) MC per firm (£)
1	20	40	20
2	25	45	30
3	30	50	40
4	35	55	50
5	40	60	60
6	45	65	70
7	50	70	80
8	60	75	90
9	70	80	100
10	80	85	110
11	90	90	120

(a) How much will a type A firm supply at a price of £40?
(b) How much will total supply of type B firms be at a price of £80?
(c) What will total industry supply be at a price of £50?
(d) Assuming that marginal cost is above average variable cost for all firms at all levels of output, construct the total industry supply schedule at £10 intervals between £20 and £90 on the following table.

P	20	30	40	50	60	70	80	90
Q_S	…	…	…	…	…	…	…	…

(e) What is the industry price elasticity of supply between £50 and £60?
(f) Assume that the demand schedule facing the industry is given by

$$Q_D = 1100 - 5P$$

Construct the industry demand schedule at £10 intervals between £20 and £90 on the following table.

P	20	30	40	50	60	70	80	90
Q_D	…	…	…	…	…	…	…	…

(g) What is the equilibrium industry price and output?
(h) If a tax of £10 per unit is levied on type A firms and a subsidy of £10 is paid to type B firms, how much will each type A and each type B firm supply at a price of £50?

Q40. Look up double glazing, builders, solicitors and taxis in the *Yellow Pages* telephone directory. Approximately how many firms are there in each category? Do any of these industries come fairly close to being perfectly competitive? Look at the advertisements appearing with the telephone numbers.

In what ways are the firms attempting to make their position less like that of firms under perfect competition?

Q41. Figure 6.5 shows cost and revenue curves for a monopolist.
(a) At what output will the firm maximise profits?
(b) What price will it charge to maximise profits?
(c) How much profit will it make?
(d) Assume that a potential rival had a minimum average cost of £3.70. How much can the monopolist sell if it does not want to attract that firm into the industry?
(e) How much profit will the monopolist now make?
(f) What would have to be the position of the monopolist's revenue curves if its maximum profit output were to be at minimum average cost?
(g) Is there any position of the revenue curves which would give a profit-maximising output at minimum average cost *and* a price equal to minimum average cost?
(h) At what price and output would this industry produce if it were a perfectly competitive industry (but with the same cost curves and demand curve)?
(i) Does this represent a long-run equilibrium position for the (perfectly competitive) industry?
(j) In the long run would *individual* perfectly competitive firms produce more or less than they did in (h)?

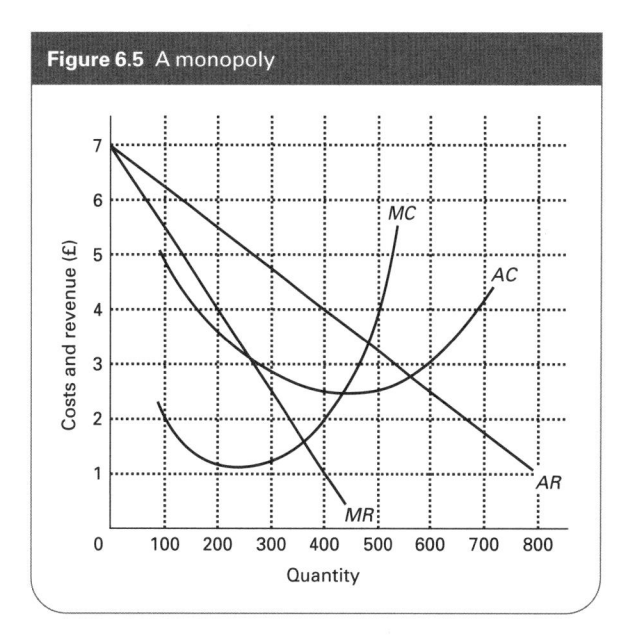

Figure 6.5 A monopoly

Q42. Look through the business sections of the 'quality' newspapers of two or three days and identify those companies that have substantial monopoly power. What are the barriers to entry in their respective industries? Is there anything in the reports that suggests that these firms act either in or against the public interest? Can this behaviour be explained by their market power?

C DISCUSSION TOPICS AND ESSAYS

Q43. What is the point of studying perfect competition if it does not exist, or only very rarely exists, in the real world?

Q44. Give some examples of markets where the suppliers are price takers. In each case consider whether they are operating under perfect competition.

Q45. Under perfect competition a firm's supply is entirely dependent on its cost of production. In what sense, then, is total industry output the result of the interaction of supply *and* demand?

Q46. Is it possible for a perfectly competitive industry to have falling long-run average costs? Explain.

Q47. Is perfect competition always in the consumer's best interest?

Q48. Using examples, discuss the proposition that whether a firm is regarded as a monopoly or not depends on how narrowly the industry is defined.

Q49. With reference to examples, explain why it is more difficult for firms to enter some markets than others.

Q50. 'A monopolist's demand will always be elastic at the profit-maximising output.' 'The greater a monopolist's power, the less elastic its demand curve.' 'The monopolist will try wherever possible to increase its monopoly power.' Reconcile these three statements.

Q51. Assume that an art gallery displaying a unique collection of paintings by old masters finds that all its costs (staffing, heating, lighting, rent, security, etc.) are fixed costs. What price should it charge if it wants to maximise profits?

Q52. How does the level of exit costs from an industry in which there is currently only one firm affect the level of prices the firm will charge?

Q53. Debate
Using relevant examples, argue the case for and against the following proposition. *A monopoly that makes supernormal profits is acting against the public interest.*

D ARTICLES

In the article below, taken from *The Guardian* of 9 January 2002, the correspondent argues that many individuals are switching away from British Gas in favour of other suppliers. However, as a result of certain practices, British Gas is still a monopoly supplier for some sections of society.

British Gas feels the heat after 10% price rise

Poll shows that 2.7m of the supplier's users want to switch

Felicity Lawrence, consumer affairs correspondent

British Gas is facing a mass desertion by its customers, with nearly 20% preparing to switch to cheaper suppliers in response to the company's announcement that it is raising prices by 10% in less than 10 months.

An ICM poll for energywatch, the gas and electricity watchdog, has found that 2.7m of the 13.5m British Gas users are ready to change supplier.

The research, published last night, also found that 84% of customers of other energy companies had been put off switching to British Gas, despite its advertising campaign suggesting it has won back 2m customers since deregulation.

The revolt comes after a Consumers' Association campaign, Switch with Which? launched last week, to encourage people to look for better deals elsewhere. The CA set up a website to enable customers to find clear information on which company would be cheapest for their particular circumstances.

British Gas said that its price increases were the result of rising wholesale costs which it had no choice but to pass on to domestic customers. 'The margins on gas are very tight, and wholesale gas prices are linked to oil prices,' a spokesman said.

Ann Robinson, chairman of energywatch, disputed whether the scale of the rise was justified and was critical of the timing of the increases during the winter months when poorer customers struggle to pay their heating bills. 'British Gas has lost the argument about how necessary these price increases were and lost its reputation for fairness, now it's set to lose its customers,' she said. 'Their greed is beginning to dog them.' The CA said the survey showed that only informed consumer action could make competitive markets work. 'If you have a massively dominant incumbent such as British Gas, the regulator cannot make competition work. It takes people to switch to do that,' a spokesman, Adam Scorer, said.

The action comes at a time when the regulator, Ofgem, has been arguing that the market no longer needs price controls. The deadline for consultations on lifting controls is January 18. But pressure groups said that there are still major regulatory issues to sort out.

'They have to crack down on doorstep selling and they need to end debt blocking,' Mr Scorer said.

Complaints to energywatch suggest that one of the deterrents to switching is malpractice over doorstep selling. Complaints about problems transferring accounts are rising at a time when the market should be settling. 'Around 7000–10,000 people a week are unhappy with the way they are treated when switching. That level of complaints is a sign the market is not working well,' said energywatch spokesman, Karl Brookes.

Debt blocking is a practice which stops those who still owe money on their bills, often the poorest customers, from switching to a cheaper supplier. Many poorer customers are also supplied on prepayment meters, but there is no effective competition in this sector of the market. The market 'is not working for the most vulnerable energy customers', according to Ms Robinson.

She also warned other companies which had announced punitive rises to take note of the findings. 'Powergen and London Electricity are equally guilty in taking British Gas's lead to justify their own greedy price rises.'

The European commission announced a year ago that it would investigate claims that wholesale gas prices in the UK have been kept artificially high by manipulation of the interconnector pipe between Britain and the continent. The new pipe from Norfolk to Zeebrugge in Belgium connects the UK to the European gas network. Mergers of major producers have created a concentration of power offshore, and companies using the pipe vote on the day which way gas should flow. In January last year, although demand in the UK was high, they voted to export to Europe. UK prices rose by 42%.

The Energy Intensive Users Group has estimated that price rises last year cost schools, local authorities, the NHS and commercial users £1bn. The European competition commission has still not produced its report.

(a) With reference to the article, what are the practices that are maintaining British Gas as a monopoly supplier?
(b) What is the aim of the regulator (OFGEM)? How can OFGEM increase the degree of competition within the market?
(c) What sort of changes need to be introduced for the market 'to work for the most vulnerable energy customers'?
(d) Using supply and demand analysis, explain why UK wholesale gas prices rose by 42%.

In the article below, taken from *The Economist* of 8 November 2001, the discussion focuses on important developments in the US Department of Justice's case against Microsoft. The correspondent argues that, in essence, the changes have meant that Microsoft can maintain its monopoly power.

An unsettling settlement

Although nine states have rebuffed Microsoft's deal with the Justice Department, the company is unlikely to get more than a slap on the wrist.

Antitrust experts had a strong feeling of déjà vu after the Justice Department and Microsoft announced on November 2nd that they had reached a settlement. The dominant reaction was that Charles James, head of the department's antitrust division, had cut a bad deal under time pressure – just as had Anne Bingaman, the trustbuster who negotiated the first 'consent decree' with the software giant back in July 1994.

If the settlement goes into effect in its current form, Microsoft will once again get away with a slap on the wrist – even after last-minute 'clarifications' negotiated by the 18 state attorneys-general who are, along with the Justice Department, the plaintiffs in the case. The agreement would, in effect, turn the company's defeat in court into victory – an astounding turn of events after even the conservative Washington, DC, appeals court unanimously found that Microsoft had repeatedly abused its monopoly power. Although half of the attorneys-general decided this week not to sign the settlement, opting instead to pursue litigation, they are unlikely to succeed in greatly toughening the penalties on Microsoft.

To understand the settlement, it helps to read from the end. 'The software code that comprises a Windows Operating System Product shall be determined by Microsoft in its sole discretion,' says one of the document's last sentences. This means that the question underlying the

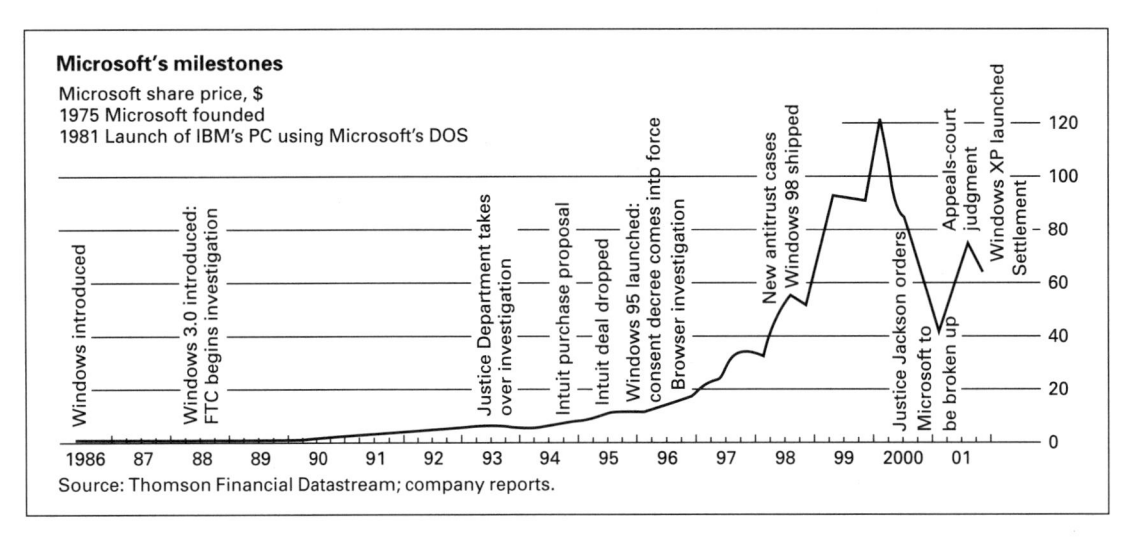

Microsoft's milestones
Microsoft share price, $
1975 Microsoft founded
1981 Launch of IBM's PC using Microsoft's DOS

Timeline annotations:
- Windows introduced
- Windows 3.0 introduced: FTC begins investigation
- Justice Department takes over investigation
- Intuit purchase proposal
- Intuit deal dropped
- Windows 95 launched: consent decree comes into force
- Browser investigation
- New antitrust cases
- Windows 98 shipped
- Justice Jackson orders Microsoft to be broken up
- Appeals-court judgment
- Windows XP launched
- Settlement

1986 87 88 89 90 91 92 93 94 95 96 97 98 99 2000 01
Source: Thomson Financial Datastream; company reports.

entire case has been clearly answered in Microsoft's favour: it can freely add other software elements to its flagship program, even if this expands its monopoly.

Even better for Microsoft, the agreement fails to administer any penalty for its past misdeeds. A 'remedies decree' in an antitrust case is supposed, among other things, to 'deny to the defendant the fruits of its statutory violation', according to the Supreme Court. For instance, Microsoft could have been required to place its browser technology in the public domain. But in the proposed settlement, the firm does not even have to admit that it behaved illegally.

Given its fundamental bias in favour of Microsoft, the settlement's actual provisions are almost secondary. They attempt to restrict Microsoft's conduct and to increase competition in two main ways. The first is to give PC makers more freedom to hide Microsoft 'middleware' (mainly its Internet-related programs, such as a web browser and an online music player) and to install competing software. Microsoft will not be allowed to stop the Dells and Compaqs of this world from installing icons or links to competing middleware. The firm must also make it possible for PC makers to remove access to Microsoft middleware and to designate other programs as default options. And Microsoft will be required to offer the same licensing terms to all its big customers.

The agreement's second main goal is to put Microsoft and competing software vendors on to a more level playing-field. The firm must now publish the specifications for how its middleware and server software work together with Windows. Unless they have these specifications, rivals cannot develop products that stand a chance against Microsoft's offerings.

All this sounds quite reasonable and will restrain Microsoft somewhat. But the devil is in the details, and the settlement is peppered with exceptions. PC makers may hide Microsoft's middleware, but they are not allowed to remove the code that makes it easy to reactivate the software. And the agreement lets Microsoft do just that, under certain circumstances. Two weeks after users have first turned on their PCs, for instance, Windows may ask them whether they want to reconfigure their machine.

The requirement to publish programming interfaces and 'communication protocols' also has limits. Microsoft can keep them secret for middleware which it does not distribute separately from Windows and is not trademarked. And the company will not have to disclose specifications to parties which, in its view, do not have a viable business – a potential problem for open-source software, the free programs that compete with Microsoft products.

The nine dissenting attorneys-general are also unhappy with the enforcement provisions. A three-member panel will oversee compliance. However, these three will not be lawyers, but software experts (the Justice Department and Microsoft will each select one member; together, those members will pick the third). They will not be allowed to inform the public about their work. Nor will they be able to impose fines for non-compliance. Instead, they can merely notify the department, which in turn may file another lawsuit.

The opposition of half the 18 states means that the trial is now entering uncharted territory. If all the states had gone along, the next step would have been a superficial court review under the Tunney Act, which is supposed to ensure that antitrust settlements are not the result of political wheeling and dealing. In a hearing, the trial judge, Colleen Kollar-Kotelly, would have simply determined whether the agreement was in the 'public interest'.

The judge has now decided to let the trial continue on two parallel tracks – a Tunney Act review and proceedings to hear the arguments of those states that want tougher remedies. In the first track, supporters and critics of the settlement have 60 days to file their comments with the judge, after which the Justice Department has 30 days to respond. The dissenting states, for their part, have to file their suggested list of remedies by early December, with hearings planned for March.

It does not bode well for the states that their coalition broke apart over the settlement. More of them may yet endorse the deal if Microsoft makes minor adjustments. Much will depend on Judge Kollar-Kotelly. Whatever she does, she will proceed cautiously. Her predecessor, Thomas Penfield Jackson, was removed from the case for talking to the press. His predecessor, Stanley Sporkin, suffered the same fate after stubbornly refusing to approve the July 1994 settlement. Subsequent events, however, have shown that he was right: it was the deficiencies of that deal that led to the latest antitrust trial. Might history repeat itself yet again?

© *The Economist*, London (8.11.01)

(a) Does the settlement imply that Microsoft is still a monopoly?
(b) 'Continual innovations by Microsoft are improving the quality of the product for the customers. Therefore, consumers and governments shouldn't be concerned about Microsoft's monopoly.' Discuss this statement.
(c) What sort of signal does the settlement send to Microsoft and other companies in a similar situation about their future strategies?

ANSWERS

Q1. Monopoly; oligopoly; monopolistic competition; perfect competition.

Q2. (a) All except perfect competition.
(b) Perfect competition and monopolistic competition.
(c) Perfect competition and certain oligopolies (e.g. sugar, regular unleaded petrol, cement).
(d) Perfect competition only.
(e) Perfect competition only.

Q3. (a) Monopoly for certain items and for certain people. Oligopoly or monopolistic competition for other items where alternative suppliers exist locally, and for people who are mobile.
(b) Monopolistic competition.
(c) Oligopoly.
(d) Oligopoly.
(e) Perfect competition (approximately), assuming no marketing agency.
(f) Monopoly. Although there are several water companies in the UK and in some other countries, there is usually only one company able to supply each customer.
(g) Monopoly if there is only one; oligopoly if there are more than one.
(h) Monopolistic competition.
(i) Perfect competition. (There are many foreign currency dealers; the product is homogeneous; dealers are virtually price takers according to demand and supply from their various customers.)

Q4. C. This measures the market share of the five largest firms in the industry. It is also common to measure the 3-firm or 4-firm concentration ratios.

Q5. (a) price takers: horizontal.
(b) homogeneous.
(c) complete.
(d) free.

Q6. (a) there is too little time for new firms to enter the industry.
(b) is long enough for new firms to enter the industry.

Q7. D. Given that in the short run there is not enough time for firms to enter the industry, supernormal profits could be earned by the firm. In the long run, however, supernormal profits would attract new firms to enter, thus driving down the market price until the marginal firm was just earning normal profits.

Q8. A. If marginal cost is less than price ($= MR$), the firm will make additional profits if it produces extra output. Note: price (AR) equals marginal revenue and thus B will never occur under perfect competition. C, on the other hand, will always occur, but thus gives no guidance as to whether a firm should expand or contract production. In the case of D the firm should reduce output. In the case of E this is the profit-maximising position and hence the firm should not change its output.

Q9. (a) £2300 per week. (Profits are maximised where $P = MC$, at an output of 100 units per week. Profit per unit equals £100 − £77 = £23. Total profit thus equals 100 × £23 = £2300.)
(b) 120 units. (Above that $AC > P$.)
(c) P = £75; Q = 90 (i.e. at the bottom of the AC curve: where just normal profits remain).

Q10. (a) $MC = \Delta TC/\Delta Q$ (in this case $\Delta Q = 20$).

Q	0	20	40	60	80	100	120	140	160	180
TC(£)	100	190	270	340	420	520	640	780	940	1140
MC(£)		4.50	4.00	3.50	4.00	5.00	6.00	7.00	8.00	10.00

(b) P = £6.50. (100 units are costing £520 to produce and earning £130 profit. The total revenue from these 100 units must therefore be £520 + £130 = £650. Therefore price = TR/Q = £650/100 = £6.50.)
(c) *Yes.* At the current output (100), MR = £6.50 and MC is between £5.00 and £6.00, i.e. $MR > MC$. Thus the firm should produce *more*. Profit will be maximised where $MC = MR$ = £6.50. This will be at an output of approximately 120. At this output, total profit = $TR − TC$ = (120 × £6.50) − 640 = £140.

Q11. E. The firm, by equating marginal cost and price, will always produce that output for each price that is given by its MC curve, but only so long as price, and hence MC, is above AVC. If price, and hence MC, were below AVC, the firm would shut down.

Q12. (a) (i) 7600 (i.e. 400 firms producing 7 units each plus 600 firms producing 8 units each).
(ii) 5600 (i.e. 400 firms producing 5 units each plus 600 firms producing 6 units each).
(iii) 2400 (i.e. 600 firms producing 4 units each; type A firms will not produce as price is below AVC).
(iv) 0 (i.e. price is below AVC for all firms).

Figure A6.1 Perfectly competitive industry's short-run supply curve

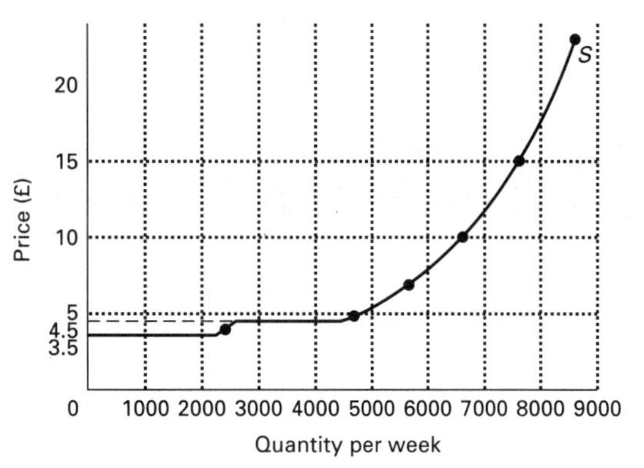

(b) See Figure A6.1.

Note the horizontal sections of the supply curve. These correspond to the prices where the two types of firm leave the industry in the short run because they cannot cover average variable costs.

Q13. All *true* except (d).

Q14. C. The firm is currently making a loss because its AC (= £2200/1000 = £2.20) is greater than the price (£1.50). It is nevertheless covering its AVC (= £1.20) and should therefore continue in production. It should increase output because MR (£1.50) is greater than MC (£1.00). This will help to reduce its loss.

Q15. E. The firm's LRMC is £1.50, which is also equal to the price. The firm is thus producing at the long-run profit-maximising/loss-minimising point. But with a long-run total cost of £1600, its LRAC is £1.60. It is thus making a loss and should therefore cease production.

Q16. C. If there are constant external costs, firms' LRAC curves will not shift as the size of the industry changes. If all firms have the same LRAC curves, then any increase in demand, and hence any rise in price above the bottom of firms' LRAC, will attract new firms. This will simply push price back down to the bottom of the LRAC curve. This means that in the long run supply will increase without any increase (or decrease) in price. (Note that E is wrong because higher prices attract *new* firms which can come in at the minimum point of the LRAC curve.)

Q17. Because the first firms to take advantage of large-scale production would drive the other firms out of the industry until there were too few firms left for them to remain price takers. Markets are not big enough for a large number of large firms.

Q18. (a), (c), (g), (h) and (i), *yes*.

(b), (d), (e) and (f), *no*. In the case of (b), firms can make supernormal profits or a loss in the short run. In the case of (d) and (e), firms may not be able to afford extensive research and development and investment. As a result their very long-run average costs may not be as low as if they were able to obtain long-run supernormal profits that could be ploughed back into the firm. In the case of (f), there is no non-price competition because, by definition, the firms produce homogeneous products.

Q19. The Post Office: (1) letter mail; (2) stationery.

Your refectory: (1) meals served on site; (2) food retailing.

Car spares manufacturer: (1) for particular makes of car where only one manufacturer produces them; (2) spare parts generally (i.e. general motor accessories) and spare parts for specific cars which are made by more than one manufacturer.

Water company: (1) water supply to a particular area; (2) water supply where the consumer has a choice of location (e.g. a firm setting up in business).

Ice skating rink: (1) ice skating in that area; (2) ice skating nationally; sports facilities.

Ice cream van: (1) ice cream supply at certain events or public places; (2) ice cream supply in the general area or when there is a shop or another van nearby.

Q20. E. If the long-run average cost curve is downward sloping, one firm supplying the whole market would be able to produce at a lower average cost than two firms sharing the market. The established firm would thus be able to undercut the price charged by any new entrant. (Although a downward-sloping LRAC curve would be a *sufficient* condition for a firm to have a natural monopoly, it is not a *necessary* condition. A firm could still have a natural monopoly if it was operating at the bottom, or even just beyond the bottom, of its LRAC curve, provided that two firms sharing the market would entail moving back up along the LRAC curve to a significantly higher level of long-run average cost.)

Q21. A. With an upward-sloping LRAC curve, two firms could produce at a lower AC than one. A new firm could thus 'steal' some of the monopoly's market by producing at a lower cost.

Q22. *must be elastic for some of its length but may be inelastic for part of it.* Although a monopolist is likely to face a less elastic demand at any given price than an imperfectly competitive firm, its demand curve *must* be elastic along part of its length. The reason is that profits are maximised where MR is to equal MC. Now MC will be positive and thus MR must also be positive. But where MR is positive, demand is elastic.

Q23. *above.* With a downward-sloping demand curve, price is above MR. Thus if MR = MC, price must also be above MC.

Q24. *False.* The monopolist can choose *either* price *or* quantity but not both. Given its demand curve, there is only one price corresponding to each level of sales and only one level of sales corresponding to each price.

Q25. E. The price given by the demand curve at the output where $MR = MC$.

Q26. *(a)* See table below.

Quantity (cars per day)	AR (£000s)	TR (£000s)	MR (£000s)	AC (£000s)	TC (£000s)	MC (£000s)
1	100	100		110	110	
			90			70
2	95	190		90	180	
			80			60
3	90	270		80	240	
			70			60
4	85	340		75	300	
			60			70
5	80	400		74	370	
			50			86
6	75	450		76	456	
			40			111
7	70	490		81	567	

(b) 4 cars per day (where $MC = MR$).
(c) £40 000 (i.e. $TR - TC$).

Q27. *True.* MC cannot be negative: it cannot cost less (in total) to produce more. Therefore if $MC = MR$, MR cannot be negative.

Q28. *False.* Demand is elastic over the output range where MR is positive: a rise in output causes a rise in total revenue (quantity rises proportionately more than price falls). Demand is inelastic over the output range where MR is negative: a rise in output causes a fall in total revenue (quantity rises proportionately less than price falls). But since MC cannot be negative and thus MR cannot be negative where it equals MC, demand must be elastic at the output where the monopolist maximises profit.

Q29. $P\epsilon_d = \Delta Q/\text{mid}Q \div \Delta P/\text{mid}P = 2/4 \div -10/85 = -4.25$ (which is elastic).

Q30. Given the barriers to the entry of new firms, supernormal profits will not be eliminated by competition. Price will remain above AC. It will only be chance if MR and MC happen to intersect at the bottom of the AC curve. For example, Figure 6.3 (on page 80) could represent a long-run situation as well as a short-run one. Here MR and MC intersect to the left of the minimum point of the AC curve.

Q31. E. Before the agency was formed, the price was determined by the simple interaction of demand (given by the AR curve) and supply (given by the MC curve). Price was therefore P_2. Once the agency has been formed, it will sell that quantity where $MC = MR$, at a price of P_3.

Q32. *False.* If a monopolist operates with a significantly lower MC curve (e.g. because its size allows it to operate more efficiently), this could be sufficient to offset the fact that the monopolist's price will be above the MC whereas the perfectly competitive price will equal MC.

Q33. See Figure A6.2. Before the agency was set up, the price was P_0, where MC_0 crosses the demand curve.

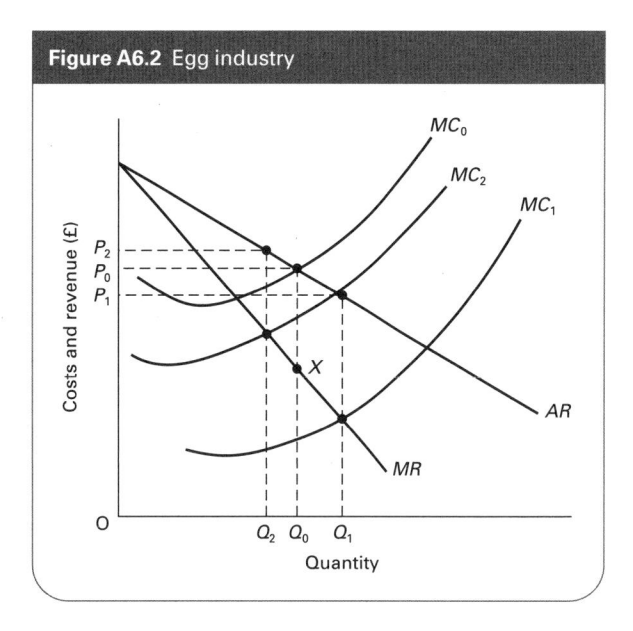

Figure A6.2 Egg industry

If the agency reduces costs to MC_1, price will fall to P_1. If it only reduces costs to MC_2, however, price will be P_2, which is still higher than the original level.

Q34. *(a)* $300 - P/4$.
(b) $TR = 1200Q - 4Q^2$.
(c) $MR = 1200 - 8Q$.
(d) $TC = 400 + 300Q - 4Q^2 + 3Q^3$.
(e) $TFC = 400$.
(f) $MC = 300 - 8Q + 9Q^2$.
(g) $MR = MC$
$\therefore 1200 - 8Q = 300 - 8Q + 9Q^2$
$\therefore 9Q^2 = 900$
$\therefore Q = 10$.
(h) $P = AR = 1200 - (4 \times 10) = £1160$.
(i) $AC = 400/10 + 300 - (4 \times 10) + (3 \times 10^2) = £600$.
(j) $A\Pi = £1160 - £600 = £560$.
(k) $T\Pi = £560 \times 10 = £5600$.

Q35. *lower.*

Q36. *lower.* The lower the exit costs, the less risky it will be for new firms to enter the industry: the more easily they can move to some other industry if they fail in their challenge.

Q37. *entry and exit costs are zero.*

Q38. *(a)* *slightly.*
(b) *highly* if the cleaning is put out to periodic tender.
non if the hospital employs its own cleaners or if an outside firm has a permanent contract.
(c) *moderately* if the banks are invited to tender periodically for a site licence.
non if a single bank is given a permanent site licence.
(d) *non* if the gas pipe grid is owned by a single company and if other companies are not permitted to use it or to establish a rival grid.

slightly (in densely populated areas) if companies are permitted to construct a rival grid. *moderately* if rival companies are permitted to use the existing grid.

(e) *highly* unless prohibited by law or unless an existing service is heavily subsidised.

(f) *moderately* (at the bidding stage). The failure costs may be high if a city invests a lot on facilities – as several unsuccessful cities can testify (but, of course, the facilities can still be enjoyed by the inhabitants).

(g) as (e).

Chapter Seven

7

Profit Maximising under Imperfect Competition

A REVIEW

Imperfect competition is the general term we use to refer to all market structures lying between the two extremes of monopoly and perfect competition. We examine the two broad categories of imperfect competition: *monopolistic competition* and *oligopoly*. We also look at a common practice of firms under imperfect competition (and monopoly too): *price discrimination*.

In this chapter we continue with the assumption that firms want to maximise profits. In the next chapter we will drop this assumption and consider the effects of firms pursuing other goals.

7.1 Monopolistic competition
(Pages 170–2) Monopolistic competition is nearer the perfectly competitive end of the spectrum.

Q1. From the list of points below, select those which distinguish a monopolistically competitive industry from a perfectly competitive industry.
(a) There are no barriers to the entry of new firms into the market. Yes/No
(b) Firms in the industry produce differentiated products. Yes/No
(c) The industry is characterised by a mass of sellers, each with a small market share. Yes/No
(d) A downward-sloping demand curve means the firm has some control over the product's price. Yes/No
(e) In the long run only normal profits will be earned. Yes/No
(f) Advertising plays a key role in bringing the product to the attention of the consumer. Yes/No

Q2. At which of the following outputs would a monopolistically competitive seller maximise profits?
A. Where marginal revenue equals average cost.
B. Where price equals marginal revenue.
C. Where marginal revenue equals marginal cost.
D. Where average cost is at a minimum.
E. Where price equals average cost.

Q3. Following a rapid growth in the demand for home-delivered fast foods, Pukka Pizza is now earning substantial supernormal profits on its dial-a-pizza business. As a result of this success, a number of other local restaurants and fast-food diners are diversifying into the home-delivery market.
(a) What will be the likely effect on the position and elasticity of Pukka Pizza's demand curve from this increased competition?

....

(b) How will this depend on the type of food that the new competitors are supplying?

....

(c) At what point will firms stop entering the market?

....

Multiple choice | *Written answer* | *Delete wrong word* | *Diagram/table manipulation* | *Calculation* | *Matching/ordering*

94 CHAPTER 7 PROFIT MAXIMISING UNDER IMPERFECT COMPETITION

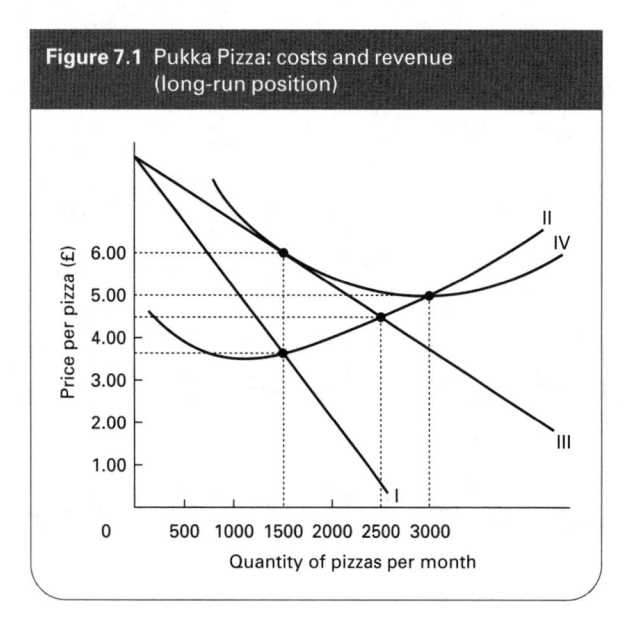

Figure 7.1 Pukka Pizza: costs and revenue (long-run position)

⊖ **Q4.** Figure 7.1 represents Pukka Pizza's long-run equilibrium position.

(a) Label the curves.

Curve I: ....

Curve II: ....

Curve III: ....

Curve IV: ....

(b) What is the long-run equilibrium price? (Tick)

£3.50 ... £4.50 ... £5.00 ... £6.00 ...

(c) What is the long-run equilibrium quantity? (Tick)

1500 ... 2500 ... 3000 ...

(Pages 172–3) Firms under imperfect competition are likely to engage in advertising and other forms of non-price competition. The aim of this is to **Q5.** *shift the demand curve to the right and make it less elastic/shift the demand curve to the right and make it more elastic.*

Q6. For a profit-maximising firm, the amount it should spend on advertising should be:
A. as little as possible because advertising costs money.
B. as much as possible because advertising increases demand.
C. that where the average cost of the advertising equals the average revenue earned from it.
D. that where the average revenue from the advertising minus the average cost of it is at a maximum.
E. that where the marginal revenue from the advertising equals the marginal cost of it.

Q7. Which of the following are reasons why a monopolistically competitive firm is inefficient in the long run?
(a) It is only making normal profits. Yes/No
(b) It is producing at a price above the minimum average cost. Yes/No
(c) It is producing an output below that at minimum average cost. Yes/No
(d) It faces a downward-sloping *AR* curve. Yes/No
(e) It is producing where marginal cost is below average cost. Yes/No
(f) It faces an upward-sloping *MC* curve. Yes/No

Q8. The monopolistically competitive firm in the long run will produce less than a firm in perfect competition (given the same *LRAC* curve) but will charge a lower price due to the threat of rival firms. *True/False*

Q9. A monopolistically competitive industry in the long run will experience excess capacity. To which one of the following is this due?
A. Firms will only make normal profit.
B. Firms will enter the industry if supernormal profits can be made.
C. Firms will produce along the upward-sloping portion of their marginal cost curve.
D. The tangency point of the firm's *AR* and *LRAC* curves is to the left of the minimum *LRAC*.
E. The point where *AR* equals *LRAC* is vertically above the point where *MR* equals *LRMC*.

Q10. The monopolistically competitive firm in the long run will always produce at a lower price than a monopoly because it only makes normal profits. *True/False*

7.2 Oligopoly

(Page 174) Oligopoly is the most frequently occurring of the four market structures. Oligopolies, however, differ significantly one from another. Nevertheless they do have various features in common.

Q11. Which of the following are characteristics of oligopoly?
(a) There are just a few firms that dominate the industry. Yes/No
(b) There are few if any barriers to the entry of new firms into the industry. Yes/No
(c) The firms face downward-sloping demand curves. Yes/No
(d) There is little point in advertising because there are so few firms. Yes/No
(e) Oligopolists tend to take into account the actions and reactions of other firms. Yes/No

Q12. Under oligopoly the price charged by one firm is likely to affect the price charged by other firms in the industry. *True/False*

◐ **Q13.** Because oligopolists are interdependent this makes it easier to predict an oligopolist's price and output. *True/False*

(Pages 174–5) Sometimes oligopolists openly compete with each other; sometimes they collude. When they collude they will attempt to act as if they were a monopoly and make monopoly profits which they then must decide how to divide between them.

When oligopolists formally collude this is known as a *cartel*. One way of dividing up the market is to assign each cartel member a quota.

(?) **Q14.** Assume that a member of a cartel faces the situation shown in Figure 7.2. Assuming that P_c is the price set by the cartel and Q_1 is the firm's allotted quota, why would the firm have an incentive to cheat?

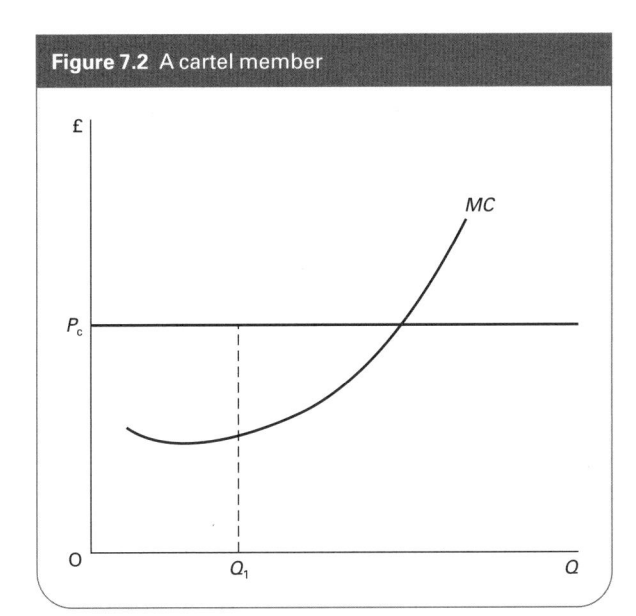

....

....

Figure 7.2 A cartel member

◐ **Q15.** There will be little point in non-price competition by cartel members if a strict quota system is enforced. *True/False*

In most countries there are laws that restrict either the formation of cartels or their activities. When formal or open collusion is against the law, firms may collude tacitly.

◐ **Q16.** Which of the following are examples of tacit collusion?
(a) Price leadership by a *dominant* firm. Yes/No
(b) Agreements 'behind closed doors'. Yes/No
(c) Discounts to retailers. Yes/No
(d) Setting prices at a well-known benchmark. Yes/No
(e) Increased product differentiation within the industry. Yes/No

(Pages 175–9) One form of tacit collusion is for firms to follow the prices set by the *price leader* in the industry.

⊗ **Q17.** Consider the model of price leadership shown in Figure 7.3.
(a) Which curve represents the market demand curve? *ABC/DBC/DE*
(b) Which curve represents the leader's demand curve? *ABC/DBC/DE*
(c) Which curve represents the leader's *MR* curve? *ABC/DBC/DE*
(d) What price will be set by the price leader if it wishes to maximise profits? $P_1/P_2/P_3/P_4$
(e) Q_1 is the output produced by *the leader/all other firms together*
(f) Mark total industry output on Figure 7.3.

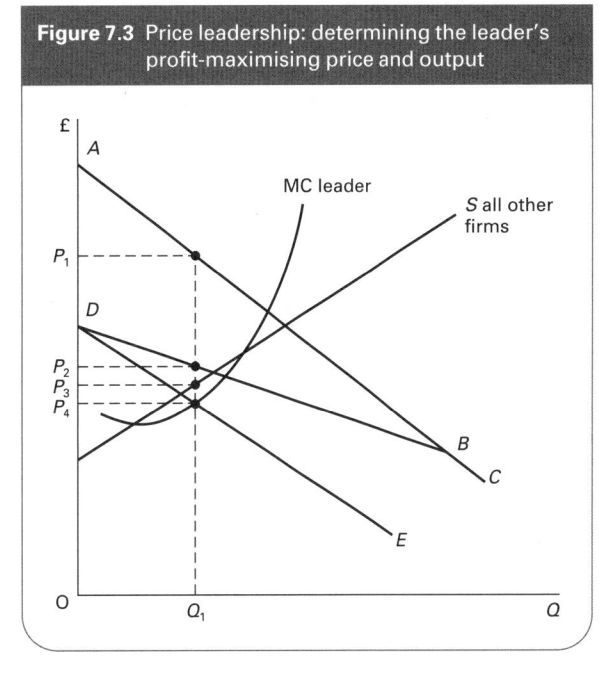

Figure 7.3 Price leadership: determining the leader's profit-maximising price and output

◐ **Q18.** In the *barometric price leader* model, the price leader is always the largest firm in the industry. *True/False*

(Pages 179–80) An alternative form of tacit collusion is for firms to follow simple 'rules of thumb'. An example is that of *average cost pricing*.

◐ **Q19.** Average cost pricing involves setting price equal to average cost. *True/False*

(Page 180) Sometimes, however, there will be no collusion of any sort between oligopolists, or, if there has been, it may break down.

96 CHAPTER 7 PROFIT MAXIMISING UNDER IMPERFECT COMPETITION

Q20. Under which of the following circumstances is collusion likely to break down?
(a) There is a reduction in barriers to international trade. Yes/No
(b) The market becomes more stable. Yes/No
(c) One of the firms develops a new cost-saving technique. Yes/No
(d) One of the firms becomes dominant in the industry. Yes/No
(e) The number of firms in the industry decreases. Yes/No

(Pages 181–5) The behaviour of firms under non-collusive oligopoly depends on (a) how they think their rivals will react, and (b) their attitudes towards taking a risk. The theory of games studies the alternative strategies a firm can adopt. Two possible strategies are *maximax* and *maximin*.

Q21. Which *one* of the following is the *maximax* strategy?
A. Choosing the policy whose best outcome is better than the worst outcomes of all alternative policies.
B. Choosing the policy whose best outcome is better than the best outcome of any alternative policy.
C. Choosing the policy whose worst outcome is better than the best outcome of any alternative policy.
D. Choosing the policy whose worst outcome is better than the worst outcomes of all alternative policies.
E. Choosing the policy whose worst outcome is worse than the best outcome of any alternative policy.

Q22. Which *one* of the strategies in Q21 is the *maximin* strategy?
A. B. C. D. E.

Table 7.1

Durashine's price

Supasheen's price	£5.00	£4.50
£5.00	A £6m each	B £2m for Supasheen £8m for Durashine
£4.50	C £9m for Supasheen £3m for Durashine	D £4m each

Table 7.1 shows the annual profits of two paint manufacturers. At present they both charge £5.00 per litre for gloss paint. Their annual profits are shown in box A. The other boxes show the effects on their profits of one or the other firm or both firms reducing their price per litre to £4.50.

Q23. Which of the two prices should Durashine charge if it is pursuing
(a) a maximax strategy? £5.00/£4.50
(b) a maximin strategy? £5.00/£4.50

Q24. Which of the two prices should Supasheen charge if it is pursuing
(a) a maximax strategy? £5.00/£4.50
(b) a maximin strategy? £5.00/£4.50

Q25. Why is this known as a *dominant strategy* game?

....

....

Q26. Assume now that the 'game' between Durashine and Supasheen has been played for some time with the result that they both learn a 'lesson' from it. They thus form a new agreement to fix the price at £5.00. It is now likely that:
A. both firms will cheat on the agreement.
B. both firms will stick to the agreement permanently.
C. both firms will stick to the agreement so long as costs of production remain constant.
D. Durashine alone will cheat.
E. Supasheen alone will cheat.

(Pages 185–6) One of the most famous of the non-collusive theories of oligopoly is that of the *kinked demand curve*. According to this theory, the firm under oligopoly perceives that its demand curve is steeper below the current price than it is above it: that it is kinked at the current price.

Q27. This kink is due to the firm's belief that its competitors:
A. will set a price at the kink of the demand curve.
B. will match any price increase it makes, but will not match a price reduction.
C. will not match a price increase but will match any price reduction.
D. will match all price increases and reductions.
E. will match neither price increases nor reductions.

The kinked demand curve theory suggests that a firm is likely to keep its price unchanged unless there are substantial shifts in revenue or cost curves.

Q28. Figure 7.4 shows a kinked demand curve. Which of the following represents the *MR* curve?
A. *fghi*
B. *jgkl*
C. *jghi*
D. *fgkl*
E. *jgk,hi*

(Pages 186–7) It is not possible to draw firm conclusions as to whether oligopolists act in the public interest given that there are many factors that influence their behaviour and given that circumstances differ from one oligopoly to another.

Figure 7.4 Kinked demand curve

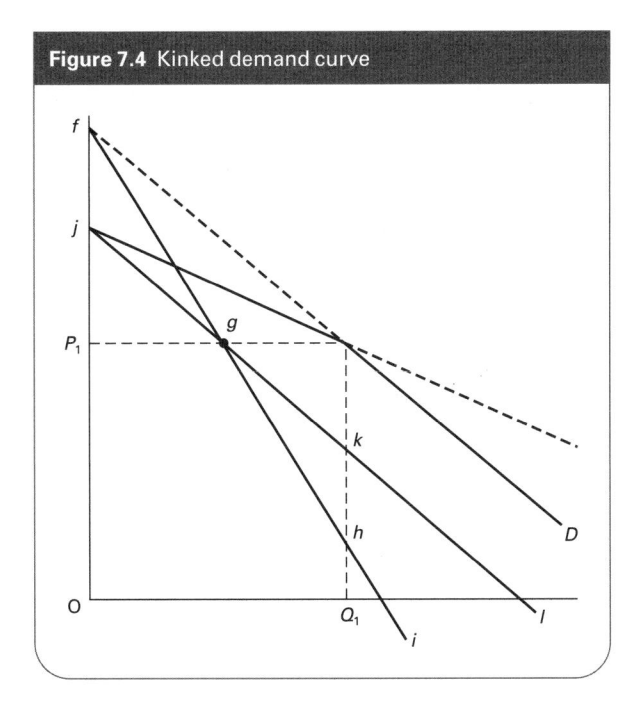

Q29. Which of the following aspects of oligopoly can be seen to be in the public interest?
(a) Prices are set collusively. Yes/No/Possibly
(b) Suppliers have countervailing power. Yes/No/Possibly
(c) Customers have countervailing power. Yes/No/Possibly
(d) There is non-price competition in the industry.
  Yes/No/Possibly
(e) There is substantial advertising. Yes/No/Possibly
(f) The market is contestable. Yes/No/Possibly
(g) The firms' products are highly differentiated from each other. Yes/No/Possibly
(h) There are substantial barriers to entry.
  Yes/No/Possibly

7.3 Price discrimination

(Pages 188–92) A firm may practise price discrimination. This is where it sells the same product (costing the same to produce) at different prices in different markets or to different customers.

In order for a firm to practise price discrimination it must be **Q30.** *a price setter/a price taker*. It must be able to distinguish between markets such that the good cannot be resold from the **Q31.** *low-/high*-priced market to the **Q32.** *low-/high*-priced market. In each market, price elasticity of demand will differ. In the low-priced market, demand will be **Q33.** *more elastic/less elastic* than in the high-priced market.

Q34. There are three types of price discrimination:
(i) First-degree price discrimination.
(ii) Second-degree price discrimination.
(iii) Third-degree price discrimination.
Match each of the three types to the following definitions:

(a) When a firm charges a consumer so much for the first so many units purchased, a different price for the next so many units purchased and so on.

....

(b) When a firm divides consumers into different groups and charges a different price to consumers in different groups, but the same price to all the consumers within a group.

....

(c) When a firm charges each consumer for each unit the maximum price which that consumer is willing to pay for that unit.

....

Q35. In Figure 7.5 if the firm is able to earn the revenue shown by the shaded area, which of the following must it be practising?
A. First-degree price discrimination.
B. Second-degree price discrimination.
C. Third-degree price discrimination.
D. No price discrimination at all.
E. It is impossible to say without knowing details about its costs of production.

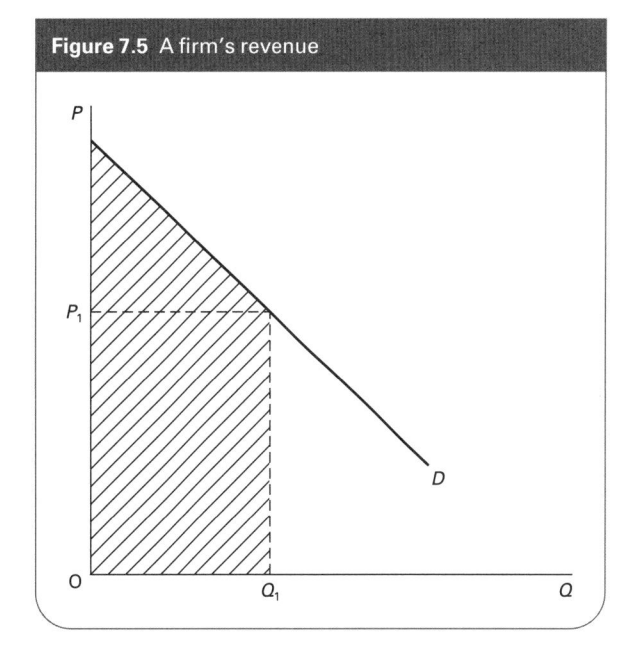

Figure 7.5 A firm's revenue

Q36. Which of the following are advantages to the firm from practising price discrimination?
(a) Higher total revenue. Yes/No/Possibly
(b) Lower costs. Yes/No/Possibly
(c) Less advertising. Yes/No/Possibly
(d) Helps to drive competitors out of business.
  Yes/No/Possibly
(e) Increases sales. Yes/No/Possibly

B PROBLEMS, EXERCISES AND PROJECTS

Q37. In recent years it has become fashionable for governments around the world to break up monopolies (sometimes nationalised and sometimes private but protected by licences or other regulations). The argument has been that the introduction of competition will stimulate firms to find ways of reducing costs and of providing a better service or product.

Take the case of buses and coaches. Many routes that were previously guaranteed to a single operator have now been opened up to competition. The immediate advantage is that on the routes used by a lot of passengers, the competition has often driven down the prices.

(a) Demonstrate this diagrammatically for an individual coach operator now finding itself under monopolistic competition.

On the other hand, on many routes facing cut-throat competition, coaches are running with empty seats.

(b) Does the theory of monopolistic competition predict this?

Also there is the danger that companies may cut corners (e.g. in terms of safety) in order to keep their costs as low as possible.

Then there is the problem that the less used routes may no longer be operated at all. A bus or coach company with a monopoly may be prepared to operate such routes even though it makes a loss on them. It 'cross-subsidises' them with the monopoly profits it gains on the popular routes. When the monopoly is broken up, however, the competitive firms may not be willing or able to carry on operating these routes. Thus country bus services may close down, as may also services early in the morning or late at night on the otherwise well-used routes.

(c) Is it desirable that a monopoly bus company *should* cross-subsidise loss-making routes?
(d) Would a profit-maximising monopoly bus company *choose* to cross-subsidise such routes? How may a local authority ensure that the company does so?
(e) How could a local authority ensure that loss-making routes continued to operate after the industry had become monopolistically competitive?
(f) Use the arguments contained in this case study to compare the relative benefits and costs to the consumer of monopoly and monopolistic competition.

Q38. Find out the prices of a range of foodstuffs and household items sold in two or three different supermarkets and two or three different small foodstores. Which items are sold at similar prices in all the different shops and which are sold at significantly different prices? Account for these similarities or differences.

Q39. Durashine paint company is considering what strategy it should adopt in order to maximise its profits. It is currently considering four options. The first is to introduce a 10 per cent price cut. The second is to introduce a new brand of high-gloss durable emulsion paint. The third is to launch a new marketing campaign. The fourth is to introduce no change other than increasing its prices in line with inflation.

It estimates how much profit each strategy (1–4) will bring depending on how its rivals react. It considers the effects of six possible reactions (a–f).

		Other firms' responses					
		a	b	c	d	e	f
Strategies	1	−25	50	−20	30	40	60
for	2	−20	20	−15	0	15	80
Durashine	3	0	15	30	0	20	30
	4	20	35	−10	40	30	70

(£000s)

(a) Which of the four policies should it adopt if it is pursuing:
 (i) A maximax strategy?
 (ii) A maximum strategy?
(b) Which of the four policies might be the best compromise?

Q40. A firm operating under conditions of oligopoly is currently selling 4 units per day at a price of £30. By conducting extensive market research its chief economist estimates that, if it raises its price, its rivals will not follow suit and that as a result it will face an average revenue curve given by

$$P = 40 - 5Q/2 \text{ (where } P = AR\text{)}$$

On the other hand, if it reduces its price, its rivals will be forced to reduce theirs too. Under these circumstances its average revenue curve will be given by

$$P = 50 - 5Q \text{ (where } P = AR\text{)}$$

(a) What will be the equation for the firm's *demand* curve if the firm raises its price?
(b) What will be the equation for the firm's demand curve if the firm reduces its price?
(c) How much will be demanded at the following prices?

 £40 ....

 £35 ....

 £30 ....

£20 ....

£10 ....

(d) Plot the two demand curves on Figure 7.6, marking in bold pen the portion of each that is relevant to the firm.
(e) Plot two marginal revenue curves corresponding to each of the demand curves. (Remember that the *MR* curve lies midway between the *AR* curve and the vertical axis). Mark in bold pen the portion of each *MR* curve that is relevant to the firm.
(f) Over what range of values can marginal cost vary without affecting the profit-maximising price of £30?

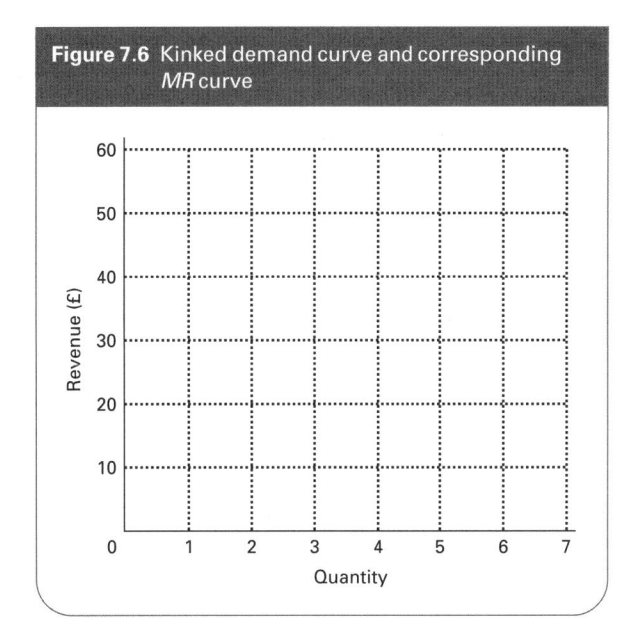

....

Figure 7.6 Kinked demand curve and corresponding *MR* curve

C DISCUSSION TOPICS AND ESSAYS

Q41. Why does monopolistic competition lead to a less than optimal allocation of resources? Does this inevitably mean that the consumer benefits more from perfect competition than monopolistic competition?

Q42. In what ways might the relative ease of firms to enter or exit a market affect the pricing, marketing strategy and productivity of the existing firm(s) in the market?

Q43. How would a firm set about determining the optimum type and amount of advertising? Why is the optimum amount of advertising difficult for a firm to determine?

Q44. Imagine that a group of wall tile manufacturers decide to form a cartel. What factors will determine whether the cartel is likely to be successful in raising prices?

Q45. Assume that an international airline cartel has been operating for a number of years. Imagine various circumstances that could lead to the breakdown of this cartel. What could the members of the cartel do to prevent its breakdown? Under what circumstances is the cartel likely to re-form in the future?

Q46. Describe what is meant by the *prisoners' dilemma* game. How will the outcome be affected by (a) the number of participants in the game and (b) the degree of similarity between the participants?

Q47. What are the main strengths and weaknesses of game theory as (a) a theory of oligopoly behaviour and (b) an aid to a real-world oligopolist in deciding its price and output?

Q48. Using relevant examples, show how the kinked demand curve can be used to demonstrate price stability under oligopoly. According to the kinked demand curve model, what would cause the price to change? Use a diagram to illustrate this.

Q49. In what ways may the consumer (a) gain and (b) lose from the behaviour of oligopolists?

Q50. Debate
Advertising confers no benefits on society. It merely increases costs, eliminates competition and as a consequence pushes up prices.

D ARTICLES

In the article below, taken from the Reuters Web site of 18 April 2002, the discussion highlights the causes and consequences of the ongoing price competition within the oligopolistic games console market.

Microsoft slashes European Xbox prices. US next?

Ben Berkowitz and Scott Hillis

Microsoft Corp. on Thursday slashed the price of its Xbox video game console in Europe and Australia and sharply pared its forecast for early sales of the machine, conceding it has struggled after a high-voltage launch.

US game publishers cheered the European price cut, and analysts said it was evidence that Microsoft would likely cut the price of the Xbox in the United States later this year in order to gain ground on archrival and market-leader Sony Corp.

Microsoft Chief Financial Officer John Connors said Microsoft expected to ship 3.5 million to 4 million units by the end of June, down as much as 40 percent lower than its prior forecast of 4.5 million to 6 million units.

By the end of fiscal 2003, the company expects the console's total worldwide installed base to be about 9 million to 11 million units, he said.

'This reflects the ongoing weakness in Japan and accounts for many weeks of sales opportunities lost in Europe while we were at the higher price,' Connors said.

Earlier in the day, Microsoft cut the Xbox's price tag for continental Europe by 38 percent to 299 euros ($266) and cut the price for Great Britain by 34 percent to 199 pounds ($288), and said it would offer a gift bundle for people who bought the console at the old price.

It also announced a price cut of almost 39 percent in Australia to A$399 ($215), with a gift pack for earlier buyers.

The new European prices, which Microsoft said were coming in sooner than it originally planned, will now match those of Sony Corp's best-selling PlayStation 2 console in Europe and will be closer to Nintendo's forthcoming GameCube console, which is still a bit cheaper.

It is the first price cut for Xbox, which launched in the US on November 15, in Japan on February 22 and in Europe and Australia on March 14. The company has given no further details of planned price cuts outside Europe.

US cut seen likely, Euro cut cheered

However, analysts and observers said they expected at least one Xbox price cut in the US this year, if not two, saying Microsoft may end up cutting its US price before Sony, which has sold for $299 in the US since PS2's November 2000 launch.

Wedbush Morgan Securities analyst Michael Pachter told Reuters he expects a cut from $299 to $249 in May and another to $199 in September.

'If there is [a price war] it won't be started by Sony,' said John Davison, editorial director of the Ziff Davis Media Game Group, which publishes a number of video game magazines.

But the head of the Xbox project gave no indication that price cuts were anything close to imminent in Japan or the United States.

'We're comfortable where we are in those markets,' Robbie Bach, Microsoft's 'Chief Xbox Officer,' told Reuters.

Retailers and analysts cheered the European cut, saying it should stoke sales for the console just as demand appeared to be on the wane. The suddenness of the move, industry observers said, indicates that Microsoft miscalculated the launch price dearly.

According to various retail data estimates, Xbox sales in the UK, its best-performing European market, have fallen off considerably since launch. Microsoft refused on Thursday to give European sales figures.

Lisa Morgan, commercial director of video game retailer Games Group Plc, said she was pleased with Xbox sales, but said the launch timing and price had slowed demand.

She said launching Xbox in March, when sales are relatively tepid compared with the Christmas season, had had an impact on European sales. She added Xbox has trailed PlayStation 2 in sales since launch because it was priced £100 higher.

The new price was also praised in the US, where game publishers have said the price was clearly too high for Microsoft to gain market share.

'We couldn't be happier,' said Jeff Lapin, vice chairman of THQ Inc., which was the first game publisher to publicly urge Microsoft to cut prices. 'Hopefully, this'll give the Xbox a shot in the arm and they'll sell more boxes.'

Microsoft's European representatives conceded the move was made for the sake of competitiveness.

'We want to make it very clear to the industry that we're here to compete,' Sandy Duncan, vice president of Xbox Europe, told Reuters.

He added a series of factors were considered in making the decision, including the strength of Xbox video games sales and the launch of Game Cube, which hits stores May 3 at a price of £169 in Britain and £249 in Europe.

Quickest price drop

Microsoft has made a huge bet on Xbox. It has invested billions of dollars in its development and committed $500 million to promote it to grab a stake of the $20 billion global game industry and cement Microsoft's place as a dominant consumer brand.

Stuart Dinsey, managing editor of *Games Trade Weekly MCV*, a UK-based trade publication covering the video game industry, said the publication estimates Xbox has performed well in the UK, selling an estimated 60,000 to 70,000 units.

The problem markets are France and Germany, he said, which he estimated sold 20,000 and 'as low as 12,000,' respectively.

(a) What would the short- and long-term consequences of the price war between games console makers be for consumers, console producers and game developers?

(b) How would the business model of selling games consoles at a loss promote the sales of games and lead to higher profits for Microsoft?

(c) What factors could cause the price cutting in the console market to stop?

In the article below, taken from the *BBC News Online* Web site of 18 December 2001, the discussion focuses on investigations into a proposed alliance between British Airways and American Airways in the highly competitive, but oligopolistic market of transatlantic flights.

BA-American deal faces obstacles

The US Justice Department has called for restrictions to be placed on a proposed alliance between British Airways and American Airlines.

'The alliance threatens a substantial loss of competition, which would likely result in higher airfares and reduced service,' the department said in a statement.

In August, the two airlines formally sought US antitrust immunity from the US Transportation Department for a new marketing alliance.

This was their second attempt at cementing a relationship in three years.

Misgivings

But on Monday the Justice Department said the US government should reject the proposed alliance unless certain conditions were put in place.

These include granting rival American carriers at least nine daily round trips to London's Heathrow Airport from New York and Boston.

The statement from the Justice Department said the alliance would give BA and AA more than 50% of the flights in many markets and an even higher share of the business travel market.

'If the Department of Transportation can secure meaningful access to Heathrow for new entrants, consumers will enjoy more choices for trans-Atlantic travel from more US cities at lower prices,' the statement said.

Alliance details

Unsurprisingly, the two airlines saw things differently.

Forcing the them to give up flights would be 'inappropriate,' they said in a joint statement.

The DoJ 'underestimated the commercial availability of slots at [London's] Heathrow [Airport] and the competitive advantages already being enjoyed by other global alliance networks,' the statement said.

Under the alliance, American Airlines and BA are hoping to coordinate their schedules and jointly set ticket prices on flights between the US and the UK.

But the partnership between the two airlines is wrapped up in complex negotiations for an 'open skies' agreement to liberalize trans-Atlantic aviation.

AA has argued for the new alliance by saying that the airline industry has changed greatly in five years.

In particular, AA said trans-Atlantic travel is less concentrated at Heathrow, where BA's operations are centred.

Decision due

The Transportation Department is expected to make a final decision on the alliance by early next year.

The issue of giving up take-off and landing slots at London's Heathrow airport was the stumbling block for previous attempts at an alliance in 1999.

The Justice Department also blocked a similar alliance request that AA made in 1996.

(a) Why would the US Justice Department view the alliance as a potential for higher airfares and a reduction in service?

(b) What arguments would BA and AA put forward to justify the benefits of the alliance to consumers?

(c) What strategy might other firms in the market adopt if the alliance was to proceed?

Watchdogs probe soccer kit market

Trade watchdogs have reopened an investigation into price fixing in the market for replica football shirts.

The Office of Fair Trading has confirmed to BBC News Online that investigators have raided the offices of a number of firms involved in the multi-million pound sector.

The probe follows continued complaints from retailers wanting to sell replica shirts at a heavy discount, who said manufacturers have refused to supply them.

And it comes two years after the OFT ended a two-year probe into the industry, amid mounting complaints from fans that they were paying over-the-odds for club shirts.

The inquiry has been ordered under strengthened trade laws which allow the OFT to impose penalties of up to 10% of turnover on firms found guilty of uncompetitive behaviour.

But while confirming that the raids followed initial research into the market, the OFT said it was too early to decide if competition rules had been broken.

'We will not be in a position to decide that until we have the facts,' an OFT spokesman told BBC News Online.

JJB denial

Although the OFT has declined to reveal the names of firms raided, sports retail giant JJB Sports has admitted its offices were among those targeted.

JJB, founded by former Blackburn Rovers player David Whelan, said its staff fully co-operated with OFT investigators during last week's raid.

'The directors of JJB advised the OFT that JJB has never been involved in price fixing, of either replica, or indeed any other product, that is sold by JJB,' the 420-store chain added in a statement to shareholders.

News of the probe failed to concern investors in the City, where JJB shares ended 1p lower at 409.5p on Wednesday.

'Flood of complaints'

The OFT first targeted the sector four years ago, amid a 'flood of complaints' over business practices in the market.

'Retailers told us that manufacturers had threatened to withhold supplies of replica kits if resale prices dropped below a set minimum,' former OFT head John Bridgeman said.

'We also have conclusive evidence that some premier league clubs have encouraged manufacturers to prevent discounting.

'I have no doubt that both supporters and parents have been paying artificially high prices.'

The OFT closed the probe two years ago, after receiving pledges from clubs and manufacturers that they would not prevent stores from selling shirts at a discount.

Continental imports

Yet even today, shirts typically priced in shops at £40 can cost £7 to make, some industry experts claim.

And retailers such as Tesco, which have sold shirts at a discount, claim they have continued to be denied kit supplies.

Tesco has resorted to buying replica shirts on the Continent, a company spokesman told BBC News Online.

'But we have not able to get enough to meet demand,' the spokesman said.

'In the spring we got hold of some Manchester United shirts which we sold for £19.99, compared with £39.99 in most sports shops. As you can imagine, stocks did not last very long.'

The firm denied it had made an official complaint to the OFT.

(a) How can the manufacturers influence the pricing decisions of the retailers?

(b) If the Office of Fair Trading finds that competition rules have been broken, what are its options?

(c) What would be the consequences for manufactures, retailers and consumers if the retailers started to discount the price of replica shirts?

ANSWERS

Q1. Yes: (b), (d) and (f). The rest ((a), (c) and (e)) apply to both perfect competition *and* monopolistic competition.

Q2. C. This is the universal law for profit maximisation no matter what the type of market structure.

Q3. (a) The demand curve will shift to the left as the market will now be divided between a larger number of firms. The curve will probably also become more elastic as there will be a larger number of suppliers to choose from, and hence the demand for Pukka Pizzas will be more price sensitive.

(b) The more similar the product and the service provided by the competitors, the more elastic will be the demand.

(c) Firms will stop entering the market when all supernormal profits have been eroded.

Q4. (a) Curve I: *marginal revenue (MR)*. Curve II: *marginal cost (MC)*. Curve III: *average revenue (AR)*. Curve IV: *average cost (AC)*.

(b) £6.00. The price where *MC* = *MR* and where *AC* = *AR*.

(c) 1500. The quantity where *MC* = *MR* and where *AC* = *AR*.

Q5. *Shift the demand curve to the right and make it less elastic.*

Q6. E.

Q7. Yes: (b), (c), (d) and (e). The long-run equilibrium is where *AR* = *AC*: i.e. where the *AR* curve is tangential to the *AC* curve. But since the *AR* curve is downward sloping (d), this point of tangency must be to the left of the minimum point of the *AC* curve (c), at a point where *AC* is falling and where therefore *MC* is below *AC* (e). Thus costs are not as low as they could be and therefore the price is higher (b) and output is lower than it would be (c) if production was at minimum *AC*.

Q8. *False.* The monopolistically competitive firm will produce less than the perfectly competitive firm if they both face the same *LRAC* curve, *but* it will charge a *higher* price because it is not producing at the bottom of the *LRAC* curve.

Q9. D. Normal profits will be made where the *AR* curve is tangential to the *LRAC* curve. But because the *AR* curve is downward sloping (unlike under perfect competition), its tangency point with the *LRAC* curve must be to the left of the minimum *LRAC* curve. In other words the firm is producing at less than minimum average cost. It is in this sense that we say the firm and industry experience excess capacity: if industry output were to be expanded, production would take place at lower cost.

Q10. *False.* The monopoly may achieve economies of scale giving it a lower *LRAC* curve. Also the monopoly may produce further down its *LRAC* curve, depending on where *LRMC* = *LRMR*.

Q11. Yes: (a), (c) and (e). No: (b) and (d). One of the features that allows oligopolists to maintain their position of power in the market is their ability to restrict the entry of new firms. Advertising is one of the major ways in which oligopolists compete with their rivals in their attempt to gain a bigger market share and bigger profits.

Q12. *True.* As one firm changes its price this will affect the demand for its rivals' products and hence their prices.

Q13. *False.* It is very difficult to predict price and output without knowing what degree of competition or collusion there is between the rival firms.

Q14. By producing more than Q_1, it will earn more profit provided price remains at P_c. At P_c it will maximise its profits where *MR* (= P_c) equals *MC*.

Q15. *True.* The firm *could* sell more at existing prices if it produced above its quota. There is thus little point in advertising or other types of non-price competition.

Q16. Yes: (a), (b) and (d).

Q17. *(a)* ABC; *(b)* DBC; *(c)* DE.

(d) P_2: i.e. the price given by the leader's demand curve at the output (Q_1) where the leader's *MC* = *MR*.

(e) Q_1 is the output produced by the leader.

(f) Total industry output is found by reading across from P_2 to the market demand curve.

Q18. *False.* The barometric firm is simply the one whose prices the other firms are prepared to follow: the one whose price setting is taken as a barometer of market conditions.

Q19. *False.* Price is equal to average cost *plus* a mark-up for profit.

Q20. Yes: (a) and (c). (a) is likely to increase competition from imports. (c) is likely to encourage the firm with reduced costs to undercut its rivals' prices in order to gain a bigger market share.

Q21. B.

Q22. D.

Q23. *(a)* Cut price to £4.50.

(b) Cut price to £4.50.

Q24. *(a)* Cut price to £4.50.

(b) Cut price to £4.50.

Q25. Because both maximax and maximin strategies lead to the same decision.

Q26. C. After a period of 'tit-for-tat' price cutting, both firms will come to realise that they are both worse off for having played this 'game' (profits in box D are lower for both firms than in box A). They are thus likely to be willing to reach an agreement to fix price which *they will both stick to*. If, however, costs of production change, they may have to negotiate a new price agreement between them, or follow some rule of thumb, such as raising prices by the same percentage that costs have risen.

Q27. C. Competitors will be quite happy to see the firm raise its price and lose market share. They will feel obliged to match price reductions, however, for fear of losing market share themselves.

Q28. E. The *MR* curve corresponds to the shallower *AR* curve at levels of output lower than that at the kink and to the steeper *AR* curve at levels of output higher than that at the kink.

Q29. (a) *No*; (b) *Yes*; (c) *Yes*; (d) *Possibly*; (e) *No*; (f) *Yes*; (g) *Possibly*; (h) *No*.

Q30. a *price setter*.

Q31. low.

Q32. high.

Q33. *more elastic*.

Q34. (a) (ii); (b) (iii); (c) (i).

Q35. A. It can charge each consumer the maximum price (above P_1) that he or she is prepared to pay.

Q36. (a) *Yes*; (b) *Possibly*; (c) *No*; (d) *Yes*; (e) *Possibly*.

Chapter Eight
8

Alternative Theories of the Firm

A REVIEW

In this chapter we drop the assumption that firms are always profit maximisers. Firms may not have the information to maximise profits. But even if they did, they may choose to pursue some alternative aim.

We first examine the reasons why firms may not be able to maximise profits or may have some alternative aim. Then we look at the effects of pursuing some alternative aim: either a single aim, such as growth or sales, or several aims simultaneously.

8.1 Problems with traditional theory

(Page 195) Firms may *want* to maximise profits, but lack the information to do so.

◐ **Q1.** If firms do not use *marginal* cost and marginal *revenue* concepts, they will not be able to arrive at their profit maximising output. *True/False*

◐ **Q2.** If a firm uses accountants' cost concepts that are not based on opportunity cost, then it will only be by chance if it ends up maximising profits. *True/False*

Given the problems in estimating the profit-maximising price and output, the firm may resort to simple rules of thumb. One such rule is the *cost-plus* method of pricing. Under this system a firm merely adds a *mark-up* for profit to its average cost of production. Thus if its average cost were 50p and it wanted to make a 20p profit, it would set a price of

⊗ **Q3.** ....

By a process of trial and error, adjusting the mark-up and adjusting output, the firm can move towards the profit-maximising position.

(Pages 195–8) An even more fundamental criticism of the traditional theory of the firm is that the decision makers in the firm may not even aim to maximise profits in the first place.

▤ **Q4.** On which of the following is this criticism based?
A. Many shareholders do not want to maximise profits.
B. Owners of firms are not 'rational'.
C. Shareholders are not the decision makers and have different interests from them.
D. Managers prefer to maximise profits because this is usually in their own interest.
E. Shareholders are really utility maximisers.

The divorce between the ownership and control of a firm is likely to be greater if **Q5.** *there are a few large shareholders/ there are many small shareholders*. It is also likely to be greater in **Q6.** *partnerships/private limited companies/public limited companies*.

? **Q7.** Firms must still make enough profits to survive. But this does not make them profit maximisers.

Instead they are 'profit ....'.

▤ *Multiple choice*   ? *Written answer*   ◐ *Delete wrong word*   ⊖ *Diagram/table manipulation*   ⊗ *Calculation*   ◆ *Matching/ordering*

Q8. If a firm under *perfect competition* had an aim other than profit maximisation, would this make any difference to the output it would choose to produce?
(a) In the short run? Yes/No
(b) In the long run? Yes/No

(Pages 198–9) The problem of managers not pursing the same goals as shareholders is an example of the *principal–agent problem*. Because of asymmetric information and different goals, agents may not always carry out the wishes of their principals. Asymmetric information, in this case, refers to the fact that **Q9.** *principals/agents* have superior knowledge and can, therefore, act against the interests of the other party.

Q10. In the following cases, which are the principals and which are the agents?
(a) Estate agents and house buyers:

   estate agents ....; house buyers ....
(b) Shareholders and managers:

   shareholders ....; managers ....
(c) House builders and architects:

   house builders ....; architects ....
(d) Employers and workers:

   employers......................; workers ....
(e) Shops and their customers:

   shops ....; customers ....

8.2 Alternative maximising theories

(Page 200) Long-run profit maximisation
The traditional theory of the firm assumes that firms are *short-run* profit maximisers. An alternative assumption is that firms seek to maximise *long-run* profits.

Q11. In what way might each of the following lead to smaller short-run profits but larger long-run profits?

(a) A large-scale advertising campaign ....

   ....

(b) Opening up a new production line ....

   ....

(c) Investing in research and development ....

   ....

(d) Launching a takeover bid for a rival company ....

   ....

(e) Installing expensive filter equipment to reduce atmospheric pollution from the factory's chimneys

   ....

A major problem with the theory of long-run profit maximisation is that it is virtually impossible to test.

Q12. Explain why.

   ....

   ....

Q13. It is also virtually impossible in advance to identify a long-run profit-maximising price and output. Which of the following are reasons for this?
(a) Cost and revenue curves are likely to shift unpredictably as a result of the policy pursued. Yes/No
(b) Cost and revenue curves are likely to shift as a result of unpredictable external factors. Yes/No
(c) The firm is likely to experience economies of scale. Yes/No
(d) Some policies may affect both demand *and* costs. Yes/No
(e) Different managers are likely to make different judgements about the best way of achieving long-run maximum profits. Yes/No

(Pages 200–2) Sales revenue maximisation (short run)
The success of many managers may be judged according to the level of the firm's sales. For this reason, sales or sales revenue maximisation may be the dominant aim in a firm. Nevertheless, firms will still have to make sufficient profits to survive. Thus sales or sales revenue maximising firms will also be profit-'satisficing' firms.

Q14. Figure 8.1 shows a firm's short-run cost and revenue curves. (It operates under monopoly or imperfect competition.) The level of output it produces will depend on its aims. For each of the following four aims, identify the firm's output.
(a) Profit maximisation

   ....
(b) Sales maximisation (must earn at least normal profits)

   ....
(c) Sales maximisation (must cover all variable costs)

   ....
(d) Sales revenue maximisation (must earn at least normal profits)

   ....
(e) Assume now that the diagram represents a perfectly competitive industry (also in the short run). What will the equilibrium level of output be?

   ....

106 CHAPTER 8 ALTERNATIVE THEORIES OF THE FIRM

Figure 8.1 A firm's short-run cost and revenue curves

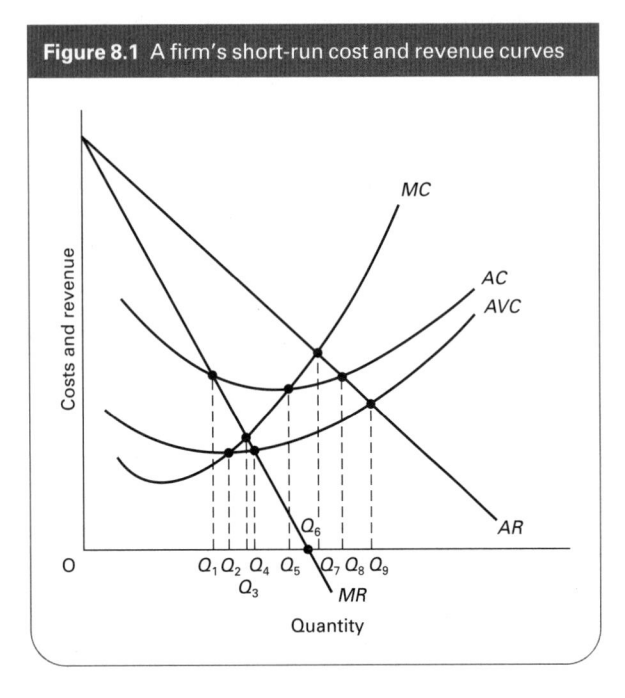

(f) Returning to the assumption that the diagram represents a firm under monopoly or imperfect competition, redraw the *AC* (and *AVC*) curves so that (b) and (d) produce the same output.

Q15. The profit-maximising output will never be greater than the (profit-satisficing) sales revenue maximising output. *True/False*

Q16. The (profit-satisficing) sales revenue maximising output will always be greater than the profit-maximising output. *True/False*

Q17. If in the short run the firm could maximise sales revenue and make more than the satisfactory level of profit, this situation would be unlikely to persist in the long run even if other firms were prevented from entering the industry. Why?

....

....

(Pages 202–7) Growth maximisation
Rather than aiming to maximise *short-run* sales revenue, managers may take a longer-term perspective and aim to maximise the rate of growth of their firm. Growth can be by internal expansion or by merger.

If growth is to be by internal expansion, the firm will need to increase both its productive capacity (by investment) and the demand for its product (by advertising). Both will require finance.

Q18. Name three ways in which a firm can finance such expansion.

1. ....

2. ....

3. ....

Firms may be prevented from growing too rapidly by the 'takeover constraint'.

Q19. Why does a takeover become more likely when a firm expands rapidly?

....

....

A firm can grow by merging with or taking over another firm. (We will use the term 'mergers' for both mergers and takeovers.) Mergers can be of three types: horizontal, vertical and conglomerate.

Q20. Match each of the three types of merger to the following examples.
(a) A soft drinks manufacturer merges with a pharmaceutical company.

....

(b) A car manufacturer merges with a car distribution company.

....

(c) A large supermarket chain takes over a number of independent grocers.

....

Q21. Various motives have been suggested for mergers other than the simple desire to grow. Name four of them.

1. ....

2. ....

3. ....

4. ....

Q22. Look at the answers to Q21. Which of the motives are consistent with the prime motive of:

(a) long-run profit maximisation? ....

....

(b) growth maximisation? ....

....

Q23. When comparing a growth-maximising firm with a short-run profit-maximising firm, which one of the following (in the short run) is likely for the growth-maximising firm?
A. A lower level of advertising.
B. A lower equilibrium output.
C. A lower price relative to average cost.
D. A lower level of investment.
E. A higher price elasticity of demand at the price charged by the firm.

8.3 Multiple aims
(Page 208)

Q24. Is it possible for a firm to *maximise* two objectives simultaneously? *Yes/No*

Explain ....

....

Sometimes firms may attempt not to maximise any one objective but merely to achieve a target level of several.

Q25. The setting of multiple targets (with no one objective to be maximised) is most likely:
A. when the firm has a complex multi-department organisation.
B. when there is a limited number of large institutional shareholders.
C. when one of the managers in the company is dominant.
D. when firms operate in highly competitive markets.
E. when firms produce a single product.

(Pages 208–11) A major development in the theory of the firm has been in *behavioural theories*. Rather than identifying various equilibrium positions for price, output, etc., behavioural theories examine how firms **Q26.** *should behave/ actually behave/could behave*.

Behavioural theories examine the conflicts that arise between different interest groups within a firm in setting and achieving targets. If targets cannot all be achieved, then a **Q27.** .... procedure will be adopted to find ways of rectifying the problem. This may involve revising the targets to make them less ambitious.

To avoid constant revision of targets, managers may allow *organisational slack* to develop.

Q28. Define organisational slack...

....

Q29. Which of the following will tend to lead to a higher level of organisational slack?
(a) A greater degree of uncertainty about future demand. *Yes/No*
(b) A more complex organisational structure in the firm. *Yes/No*
(c) The firm does better than planned (in terms of its various targets). *Yes/No*
(d) Managers become more cautious. *Yes/No*
(e) The number of rival firms decreases. *Yes/No*
(f) Industrial relations deteriorate. *Yes/No*

Q30. A frequent complaint of junior managers is that they are often faced with new targets from above and that this makes their life difficult. If their complaint is true, does this conflict with the hypothesis that managers will try to build in slack? *Yes/No*

Explain ....

....

....

Q31. When firms adopt a satisficing approach with multiple targets, their production is likely to be less responsive to changing market conditions. *True/False*

8.4 Pricing in practice
(Pages 212–14) Whether firms are profit maximisers or are pursuing some alternative objective(s), many set prices, not by referring to marginal cost and marginal revenue, but by adding a profit mark-up to average cost.

Q32. If a firm would like to maximise profits, it will be pure chance if it succeeds in doing so if it uses a mark-up system of pricing. *True/False*

Q33. A firm that is a profit maximiser is likely to adjust its mark-up more frequently than a firm that is a profit satisficer. *True/False*

Q34. For a firm which uses mark-up pricing and aims to achieve a particular level of total profit, its supply curve will be:
A. parallel to its average (total) cost curve.
B. parallel to its average variable cost curve.
C. parallel to its demand curve.
D. above its average (total) cost curve, but getting closer to it as output increases.
E. impossible to determine as long as the firm has market power.

CHAPTER 8 ALTERNATIVE THEORIES OF THE FIRM

B PROBLEMS, EXERCISES AND PROJECTS

Table 8.1 Total costs, revenue and profit

Quantity (units)	Total revenue (£)	Total cost (£)	Total profit (£)
0	0	20	−20
1	...	...	...
2	...	...	...
3	78	...	...
4	...	52	...
5	...	...	45
6	120	...	...
7	...	...	...
8	128	116	...
9	...	137	...
10	...	...	−40

Q35. A firm has the following total revenue and total cost functions:

$$TR = 32Q - 2Q^2$$
$$TC = 20 + 4Q + Q^2$$

(a) Fill in the figures in Table 8.1.

(b) At what output is profit maximised? ....

(c) At what output is sales revenue maximised? ....

(d) Assume that the firm regarded £15 as the minimum satisfactory level of profit. How much would it produce now if it were concerned to maximise sales revenue?

....

Assume now that fixed costs increase by £30.

(e) What will be the profit-maximising output now? How much profit would be made at this output?

....

(f) What would be the sales revenue maximising output assuming that the minimum profit constraint of £15 still applied?

....

Q36. Given the *TR* and *TC* functions of Q35:

(a) What is the function for *TΠ*?

(b) At what output, to the nearest whole number, is this function maximised? (You will need to use differentiation.)

(c) At what output is the *TR* function maximised?

Check that your answers for (b) and (c) are the same as for Q35 (b) and (c).

Table 8.2 Sources of capital funds of UK industrial and commercial companies

Year	Total from all sources (£ million)	Internal funds[1] (%)	Borrowing from banks etc. (%)	Shares and debentures (%)	Overseas sources (%)
1970	6 336	60.7	22.4	3.2	13.7
1980	28 913	66.1	22.3	4.9	6.7
1986	48 715	58.5	21.6	12.5	7.4
1987	79 475	49.6	21.1	25.3	4.0
1988	99 874	40.8	39.6	11.5	8.1
1989	108 025	32.7	41.7	14.9	10.7
1990	88 058	37.5	33.2	16.2	13.1
1992	53 452	68.3	−5.3	26.8	10.2
1994	82 469	72.9	−2.3	26.9	2.5
1996	114 501	53.0	20.0	19.0	8.0
1997	136 443	41.8	8.6	30.4	19.2

[1] Includes grants and tax relief.
Source: *Financial Statistics* (National Statistics, 1998).

Q37. Table 8.2 shows the sources of capital of UK industrial and commercial firms.

(a) How did the proportions of investment financed from the different sources change between 1970 and 1997?

(b) Explain any major changes in these proportions over the period. To what extent have they varied with the course of the business cycle? (see Figure 13.5 on page 389 of Sloman *Economics* (5th edition)).

Q38. Look through the business pages of two or three quality newspapers for a few days to find reports of companies that are merging, attempting to take over other firms, diversifying or simply expanding fast.

(a) Try to identify the objectives of the companies and whether there are any apparent conflicts in these objectives.

(b) Assess whether the stated aims are 'final' aims or merely the means to achieving other aims (stated or not stated).

(c) In each case try to assess what type of information you would need to have in order to judge (i) whether the companies really were pursuing the objectives stated and (ii) how successful they were in achieving them.

(d) In each case assess the extent to which the company's performance and objectives are in the public interest.

C DISCUSSION TOPICS AND ESSAYS

Q39. Under what circumstances is it likely that there will be a divorce between the ownership and control of a company?

Q40. Imagine you were the managing director of a fashion house producing expensive designer clothing. What achievements of you or your company would give you special satisfaction? Are these achievements consistent with profit maximisation?

Q41. Are sales revenue maximising firms likely to achieve more than normal profits in the long run (assuming that they have the market power to do so)?

Q42. Make up three seemingly outrageous business decisions and then attempt to justify each as being consistent with a policy of long-run profit maximisation.

Q43. Using a diagram, explain whether a consumer would be better off if a monopoly were a profit maximiser or a sales revenue maximiser.

Q44. To what extent will consumers gain or lose from the three different types of merger?

Q45. Consider the proposition that satisficing is irrational since it implies that people prefer less of an objective to more.

Q46. 'Ultimately it is not the goals that a firm pursues that determine its price and output but the nature of the competition it faces.' Discuss.

Q47. 'If a firm uses a cost-plus system of pricing, then it is unlikely to be aiming to maximise profits, either in the short run or the long run.' Discuss this proposition and consider what evidence you would need to have in order to establish what the aims are of a particular firm which uses cost-plus pricing.

Q48. Debate
Mergers are inevitably against the public interest as they increase monopoly power and reduce the incentive to innovate.

D ARTICLES

In whose interests should business be run? Just shareholders, or all the stakeholders – customers, employees, creditors, suppliers, local residents, the wider community? In the article below, taken from *New Economy*, volume 5, number 2 of June 1998, Rajiv Prabhaker analyses the issue of corporate governance and stakeholding.

Governance and stakeholding

Corporate governance has been a key issue of controversy over recent times. This concern has been academic, political and public. Aside from public concern over issues such as executive pay, there have been a series of reports (Cadbury, Greenbury and Hampel) on corporate governance and the new Secretary of State for Trade and Industry Margaret Beckett is taking a proactive stance on the issue. The academic debate has often been polarised between supporters of stakeholding and supporters of shareholding models of the firm. The key question is whether UK corporate governance would improve if it moved from a shareholding to a stakeholding approach.

Corporate governance concerns how a firm's assets are managed. In the modern firm, the management or control of those assets has become separated from their ownership. Hart (1995) outlines how that separation works in the shareholder model (also called the *principal–agent* model). Here the firm's owners (*principal*) are its shareholders. They seek to maximise shareholder value in the form of profits. Control is delegated to a set of managers (*agent*), however, who naturally seek to pursue their own interests. The so-called agency problem then arises: how can shareholders motivate managers to act in the shareholder's best interests?

Hart examines large UK and US public corporations. He notes the prevalence of a large number of small owners and argues that, since monitoring is costly, there is an incentive for shareholders to free-ride. Most shareholders may benefit from effective monitoring, whilst others undertake its costs. This makes it easy for managers to pursue their own interests, up to a point, limited by the threat of takeovers and the like.

The principal–agent model rests on a number of assumptions. I focus on two core ones: firstly that all parties – employers, employees or shareholders – are rational self-interested utility maximisers; and secondly that the objective of the firm is to maximise profits.

Keasey, Thompson and Wright (1997) note that the main challenge to this paradigm arises from stakeholding theorists. They argue that 'the central proposition at the heart of the stakeholder approach is that the purpose – the objective function – of the firm should be defined more widely than the maximisation of shareholder welfare alone'. Welfare is extended to cover other persons or groups such as workers, consumers, other firms and community groups. In one sense the shareholder–stakeholder dichotomy is somewhat stylised. All models may be seen as stakeholding. The principal–agent model is simply one in which shareholders are the only stakeholders that matter.

Social institutions

An influential stakeholding model has been proposed by Kay (Gamble *et al.* 1997). Kay argues that in continental Europe and Japan corporations are viewed as social institutions, with public responsibilities responsive to a variety of stakeholder groups. Kay argues that this view of the corporation is more accurate and he puts forward a model of trusteeship. Shareholders elect a managerial team, entrusted with ensuring that the firm continues to meet various obligations. Along with shareholder value, sensitivity to other stakeholders and the history of the firm are also important. The key is managerial freedom with accountability. He argues against greater involvement of shareholders in major decisions because of the free-rider problem already mentioned. Instead, he proposes a new Companies Act with policy instruments such as 'stakeholding statutes' for suitably defined companies (above a certain size).

Most stakeholding theorists, like Kay, have focused their attention on challenging the second core assumption that the only objective of the firm is to maximise profits but have not taken the argument much further. Often they suggest that a stakeholding approach would tend to improve the performance of firms. Kay argues that it would enable firms to gain a 'competitive edge'. But this has conventionally been taken to mean corporate profitability so is stakeholding then not so much about ends, but about means? If stakeholding did reduce profitability would the stakeholding theorists remain wedded to it? Are there other ethical justifications for stakeholding?

I argue that the driving force behind stakeholding comes instead from challenging the first core assumption – that of rational self-interest. In an uncertain world, we have to rely on and trust others to achieve common goals. If individuals act purely on self-interest such relationships will be hard to sustain. In fact, individuals may act according to non-instrumental reasons, for example by simply observing a social norm. Furthermore, they may not always act in a self-interested way. Both of these behaviours depart from rational self-interest, and may combine in different ways.

It might be claimed that even if this is the case, within economics the assumption of rational self-interest holds. Kay's model is essentially wedded to the conventional view of the self. It might be thought that part of the strength of his approach is that he succeeds in showing how, even on such an assumption, it is possible to favour stakeholding. However I would argue against this. The 'social capital' often seen as integral to a firm's success trades on a wider view of human motivation than used in orthodox modelling. I believe that the power behind Kay's model in fact derives from widening the view of the self. In any case, his focus on profit maximisation is different from mine.

(a) Distinguish between shareholding and stakeholding.

(b) What implications does the distinction between shareholding and stakeholding have for the aims of the firm and the strategies it is likely to adopt in their pursuit?

(c) Why is the nature of the 'principal–agent problem' in (i) the shareholder model; (ii) the stakeholder model?

(d) Is the concept of 'rational self-interested utility maximisation' the only form of self-interest? Could adherence to various social norms be a form of longer-term self-interested behaviour?

On very rare occasions there appears a company in the marketplace that grows at a phenomenal rate. What special ingredient(s) do such businesses have which enables them to perform so well? In the article below, taken from *Management Today* of February 1996, an attempt is made to identify the key ingredients and assess their importance.

The secrets of hypergrowth

Of all the beasts in the corporate jungle, the most fascinating is the one that emerges from nowhere, grows at a phenomenal rate and, before too long, is challenging some of the bigger animals. Hypergrowth companies are known in America as fast-growth tigers or threshold companies, and sometimes in Britain as baby sharks.

What are the lessons that firms with more prosaic performance records can learn from the management strategy and techniques of the hypergrowth companies? And is it the case that there is a 'tortoise and the hare' element to the experience of hypergrowth companies *vis-à-vis* the rest? In other words, do such companies, after a period of rapid expansion, either burn themselves out, bump up against financial or market ceilings, or come to the attention of larger firms as takeover targets?

Coopers & Lybrand, in a recent study of hypergrowth companies in Britain, defined them as firms which had achieved an increase in both turnover and employment of 100 per cent over the latest three years. From a sample of 501 successful medium-sized, or 'middle market' companies, 26 fell into the hypergrowth category, although there were 78 companies in all which met a less demanding 'supergrowth' definition (turnover up by 60 per cent or more over the latest three years), and 39 in all which were defined as supergrowth on the basis of a 60 per cent-plus rise in employment over three years.

The 26 hypergrowth companies tended to be young, with half under 10 years old. Most, around 70 per cent, were private, with current turnover typically ranging from £13 million to £50 million a year (although by their nature, some could be expected to expand rapidly out of this range). The vast majority served a single market, or supplied one type of product or service. In four-fifths of cases, this market was identified by the companies themselves as a niche market, either ignored by or underexploited by larger players. Although there were hypergrowth companies in manufacturing (fast-moving consumer goods, textiles and clothing, computers and electronics), they were proportionately more likely to be in service industries, notably transport, professional services and financial services.

Ann Todd and Professor Bernard Taylor of the Henley Management College, who looked at rapidly growing companies over a longer time-frame, 1980–90, found that the 'baby sharks' in their sample recorded profit and turnover growth of over 20 per cent a year, with the majority recording growth of over 40 per cent annually.

Todd and Taylor's baby sharks, like the Coopers & Lybrand companies, were often niche players, taking advantage of recently established technologies. But relatively few were in what could be described as pure high-technology markets; in other words, products or processes at the forefront of technology. Such markets often had prohibitively high entry barriers, particularly relating to the level of investment required and, in the case of untried technologies, substantial risks of failure.

They give two examples. Owners Abroad, now renamed First Choice, developed a chain of niche travel agents selling holidays on relatively high margins, by taking advantage of computer technology and proprietary software which enabled economies of scale to be achieved of a kind previously only available to the travel industry heavyweights. Indeed, it is a measure of its growth – away from its original timeshare business – that it had to change its name. Another successful niche market player was Iceland Frozen Foods, which set up a nationwide chain of low-overhead specialist food retailers.

Specialist Computer Holdings (SCH), under the chairmanship of Peter Rigby, is an example of a current hypergrowth company. Founded in 1975 by Rigby, who at the time was working for Honeywell, and based in Tyseley, Birmingham, it is a computer sales and service group involved in the integration and distribution of personal computer systems, mainframe computer bureau services and computer training. Its shift into very rapid growth has come with a move into mail order computer sales and the Byte chain of computer superstores – a network of seven such stores expanded to 17 during 1995.

SCH's turnover rose from £95 million in the 1993 financial year to £229 million in 1995. It is on target for a turnover of more than £350 million in the current financial year, ending on 31 March 1996. At the same time, group employment has risen from 500 to more than 850. Most of the company's expansion has been organic, although it has also made acquisitions, at a rate of roughly one a year. 'There is only one way to take the business – forward,' says Rigby. 'You can't stand still, or be half-hearted or complacent. You have to be forward-thinking.'

Both the Todd & Taylor and Coopers & Lybrand studies distil a number of common factors which typify the strategies followed by successful hypergrowth companies. According to Simon Greenstreet of Coopers & Lybrand, Specialist Computer Holdings is an embodiment of most of these factors. Thus, the company has improved the time to market for new products and services, vital in the rapidly-changing computer market. At the same time, it has kept tight control over stocks. SCH has reduced its risk by maintaining a close relationship and collaborating on marketing with its suppliers, which include IBM, Microsoft, Novell and the other industry giants who regard the company as an important source of information on developments in the UK market.

Thus, it has avoided confrontation with larger players, which can mean death for the hypergrowth company. SCH uses available technology effectively in its own distribution operations and benchmarks its performance against a range of yardsticks for the industry.

SCH has deliberately recruited managers with expertise outside the computer industry, notably with its expansion into the retail market. It operates an active employee incentive programme, with both share option and employee share ownership schemes. The company's borrowings are low, most of its growth having been funded by the reinvestment of profits.

But can hypergrowth ever be a realistic long-run proposition? One year on from the point at which they were identified as hypergrowth, Coopers & Lybrand's 26 companies are still going strong, and most expect to achieve performance at or near the hypergrowth level for the foreseeable future, although this could be dismissed as predictable optimism.

A study by McKinsey & Co. of fast-growth 'tiger' companies, however, found that rapid growth was sustainable. Indeed, it concluded: 'For the tigers, fast growth fuels itself. Multiple reinforcing feedback loops conspire to create a "virtuous circle", unleashing a momentum that competitors are powerless to stop.'

But research by both 3i and the Cranfield European Enterprise Centre suggests that the population of companies achieving hypergrowth is unstable between two time periods. In other words, companies are always moving in and out of the hypergrowth performance league, and relatively few are likely to sustain such performance over prolonged periods. This fits the popular image of hypergrowth companies – that their success is in exploiting a particular market niche or product advantage. Once the competition arrives, or the niche is fully exploited, the scope for continued rapid growth becomes that much more difficult. If this coincides with the typical problems of fast-growth businesses – loss of control of the finances, perhaps a falling-out between the original partners, or just a loss of impetus – the chances of sustained hypergrowth begin to look slim.

Taylor offers a middle ground between the two competing views on the sustainability of what is, on any definition, extraordinary business performance. He and Todd established a data-base of 176 high-growth, medium-sized companies, on the basis of their performance over the period 1980–85.

In the following five years, 52 per cent of the sample continued to record rapid growth in profitability and turnover, of at least 20 per cent and in most cases more than 40 per cent, annually. A further 9 per cent of the sample continued to grow, but at more modest rates, while

13 per cent experienced 'stagnation and decline' and 26 per cent were no longer in existence (as a result of poor performance, and not because their good records had led to their acquisition).

'When we started we were looking very much at the problems of growth and the strategies needed to secure rapid growth in terms of products, markets, finance and so on,' Taylor says. 'But we found that the problem of growth comes down to the people. If you're growing at 40 per cent or so every year, you are effectively creating a new business every three years. The management problems that this creates for the original entrepreneurs are enormous. Either they make their mind up to adapt to a much larger operation by taking on new management. Or, in many cases, they decide to be taken over.' This is the point, adds Taylor, when hypergrowth is likely to come to an end. 'Large companies find it difficult to innovate, so they pick up smaller innovative companies,' he says. 'This process of concentration is going on all the time.'

The problem is that the smaller, innovative company often ceases to be innovative once part of a larger organisation. It is a familiar story. The spur that drove on the original creators of the business is often lost once they have sold out, however powerful the contracts binding them to the business. Acquisition is often more effective as a means of snuffing out a younger, aggressive and more innovative competitor than of giving the larger firm an infusion of innovative sparkle.

It is from their relationship with large companies that medium-sized hypergrowth companies derive both their strength but also, ultimately, their vulnerability. The Coopers & Lybrand research found that hypergrowth companies tended to have a higher proportion of large company customers than their middle-market peers, and that this could be a source of problems, for example, in slow payment. At the same time, they had a proportionately bigger number of big company suppliers. The danger for hypergrowth middle-sized businesses is that they will be squeezed when they begin to become a serious threat. Either that or they get taken over by one of their bigger customers, suppliers or competitors and lose the edge that made them special in the first place.

(a) How might we define a 'hypergrowth' firm?
(b) What key characteristics do such firms have which enable them to grow so quickly?
(c) Do hypergrowth companies remain hypergrowth companies? What threats are they likely to experience?

In the following article, taken from the *Financial Times* Web site in November 2001, the correspondent discusses the principle that private businesses need to promote more social responsibility within their decision making.

Grasping the nettle

Alan Pike

Business in the Community, set up to promote corporate social responsibility in the private sector, is preparing to celebrate its 20th anniversary next year. Twenty years is a brief association with the subject compared with many of BITC's member companies, some of which can trace their involvement in earlier, philanthropic forms of corporate social responsibility back to the industrial revolution.

But the two decades since BITC was formed against a background of high unemployment, collapsing traditional industries and inner city riots can be seen as a turning point for the private sector. Contemporary businesses have to justify their actions, handle their relationships with wider society, protect their reputations and police their methods of operating to a greater extent than ever before.

That has not driven all companies to seize the corporate social responsibility agenda, but many have. The subject is becoming more professional, with company executives determined to identify and pursue the business justification for social engagement and manage programmes as efficiently as any other aspect of commercial life.

In an enhancement of this more rigorous approach, a group of 20 leading companies are about to begin measuring their impact on society against common criteria, making the results publicly available on a BITC website.

The indicators, covering market-place issues, the environment, the workplace, the community and human rights, are not intended to produce a league table of the best performing companies. But they will, like the UN-inspired Global Reporting Initiative due to be launched early next year, provide a firmer basis for comparing and verifying individual companies' social impact.

These developments come at a time when corporate social responsibility is receiving increased recognition as a core public policy issue. The European Union published a green paper aimed at promoting a European framework for corporate social responsibility this year.

It is wide-ranging in content, addressing both workplace issues, such as lifelong learning, health and safety and work–life balance, and companies' relationships with other stakeholders 'beyond their premises'. The green paper calls for greater consensus on the information companies should be prepared to disclose, and for an expansion of the reporting of businesses' social and environmental activities to include such subjects as staff consultation, child labour and human rights.

'A successful commitment to corporate social responsibility means instilling it in business culture from planning, implementation and staff policy to day-to-day decision-making, and being seen to do so,' says the green paper.

Consultation on the document closes at the end of December. BITC member-companies have welcomed its publication as recognition of corporate social responsibility's mainstream relevance.

But while supporting the case for broad global standards, most companies are opposed to trying to advance corporate social responsibility through detailed government or EU intervention and legislation. The EU should, they argue, encourage wider adoption of the UK's experience of the private sector forming partnerships with local authorities and voluntary organisations to build healthier and more competitive local communities.

Many of the government's current regeneration programmes, and forthcoming initiatives, such as business improvement districts and local strategic partnerships, provide ample opportunity for such activity. And the government's drive to extend private sector involvement in delivering public services should stimulate corporate social responsibility, by encouraging companies that bid for public contracts to demonstrate their ethical credentials.

But, in spite of excellent examples of business involvement in local level partnerships, there is still considerable room for improvement in the private sector's relationship with the wider community.

In October, a report by the National Council for Voluntary Organisations and the London School of Economics' centre for civil society took a gloomy view of business's involvement with the voluntary sector, describing it as 'patchy and a cause for concern'. The report was a follow-up to the influential Deakin study of the voluntary sector five years ago.

This led to the establishment of a BITC–NCVO taskforce but, in the view of the new research, the taskforce has had 'few concrete outcomes'. It says businesses's £315m financial contribution to charity is "a mere 5 per cent" of the voluntary sector's total donated income, with 97 per cent of the £315m coming from only 400 companies, and almost half from the most generous 25 corporate donors.

The private sector can justifiably respond that corporate social responsibility involves much more than charitable donations. But with financial support already at a relatively low level, the research raises legitimate questions about the prospects for corporate charitable support during an economic downturn.

A study of the IT industry by academics at De Montfort and Loughborough universities, supported by Microsoft, shows that companies in the sector expect charitable donations to be one of the first targets for spending cuts even though many of those questioned were unhappy with the current low level of contributions by industry as a whole, and IT companies in particular.

Expectations of what the private sector should be contributing to wider society are growing, sometimes to unrealistic proportions. But, particularly in the light of the intensification of the debate over the ethics of globalisation following the events of September 11 in the US, that is not about to change.

(a) With reference to the article, define corporate social responsibility and explain how it might be beneficial for the firm.

(b) Who are the stakeholders 'beyond their premises'? How will corporate social responsibility be beneficial for them?

(c) Would corporate social responsibility conflict with other theories/objectives of the firm? Could the pursuit of 'private' objectives be socially beneficial?

ANSWERS

Q1. *False.* Provided a firm measures cost in terms of opportunity cost, it could arrive at the profit-maximising position by a system of trial and error. It does this by sticking with policies that turn out to have increased profits and abandoning policies that turn out to have reduced profits.

Q2. *True.* If the firm does not use opportunity cost concepts, it cannot establish how much profit it is making, and whether profit is therefore at a maximum.

Q3. 70p.

Q4. C. Shareholders may well wish to maximise profits, but if they are separated from managers whose own personal interests may be better served by aiming for some other goal, such as power or prestige, profits will not be maximised. The managers may simply aim to make *enough* profits to keep shareholders quiet.

Q5. *there are many small shareholders*. If there are many of them, individual shareholders will have virtually no say in the firm's decisions.

Q6. *public limited companies*. These are companies where shares are traded publicly. Shareholders (unless they own a large percentage) are unlikely to have any influence on day-to-day decisions. They merely have a vote when broad issues of policy are put at shareholders' meetings.

Q7. *satisficers.*

Q8. *(a)* *Yes.* Provided it *could* earn supernormal profits, it may choose to sacrifice some or all of these in

order to achieve some other aim (e.g. increasing output).
- **(b)** No. It could only make normal profits anyway, which it must make to survive, whether it is a profit maximiser or merely a profit satisficer.

Q9. Agents.

Q10. **(a)** estate agents, *agents*; house buyers, *principals*.
- **(b)** shareholders, *principals*; managers, *agents*.
- **(c)** house builders, *principals*; architects, *agents*.
- **(d)** employers, *principals*; workers, *agents*.
- **(e)** shops, *agents*; customers, *principals*.

Q11. **(a)** Marginal advertising costs exceeding marginal revenue from advertising in the short run; but marginal revenue increasing in the long run as demand steadily grows with the product becoming more established.
- **(b)** Initial high set-up costs and initial 'teething' costs, costs that would fall in the long run. Also if demand is growing and it takes time to open a new production line, the opening of the line may lead to excess capacity in the short run, but not in the long run.
- **(c)** Revenue from new or improved products only occurs in the future *after* the research and development has taken place. Costs occur from the outset.
- **(d)** There may be high administrative and public relations costs associated with the bid. If successful, the acquisition of the new company is likely to lead to bigger profits (sheer size of output; economies of scale; increased monopoly power).
- **(e)** Costs of the filter equipment with little immediate return. In the long run consumers may prefer the firm's 'greener' image and the firm may avoid government-imposed restrictions that might turn out to be more expensive in the long run.

Q12. Because a firm could always, in hindsight, use it to justify virtually *any* decisions, no matter how unprofitable they eventually turn out to be.

Q13. Yes: (a), (b) and (e). Note that (c) and (d) will not in principle make price and output impossible to predict; they are merely factors that would need to be taken into account.

Q14. **(a)** Q_3; where $MC = MR$.
- **(b)** Q_8; the maximum level of sales consistent with AR being not less than AC.
- **(c)** Q_9; the maximum level of sales consistent with AR being not less than AVC.
- **(d)** Q_6; the point where $MR = 0$ and where, therefore, TR is at a maximum. (Note that in this diagram, the sales revenue maximising point more than satisfies the requirement that at least normal profits should be made. In this case supernormal profits will be made because the AR curve is above the AC curve at Q_6.)
- **(e)** Q_7; the point where MC (the industry supply curve) equals demand (AR).
- **(f)** The AC curve should now interest the AR curve at, or to the left of, Q_6.

Q15. *True*. At the profit-maximising point, $MC = MR$. Since MC will be positive, MR must also be positive, and thus revenue could be increased by producing *more*. The revenue-maximising firm will thus produce more than the profit-maximising firm (provided profits are above the satisfactory level and thus allow the firm to increase production).

Q16. *False*. Although the (profit-satisficing) sales revenue maximising output cannot be less than the profit-maximising output, it could be the same. This will occur when the maximum profits are no greater than the satisfactory level (e.g. under perfect competition in the long run).

Q17. Because the firm would be likely to spend the excess profits on advertising or product improvements in order to increase sales. It would continue doing this, even when the MC from advertising exceeded MR, as long as MR was positive and as long as profits were sill above the minimum level.

Q18. 1. from borrowing.
2. from a new issue of shares.
3. from retained profits.

Q19. Because dividends are likely to fall if the firm borrows too much, retains too much profit or issues new shares. Unless shareholders are convinced that dividends and the share price will increase in the long run, they may sell their shares. The resulting fall in share prices will make the firm vulnerable to a takeover bid.

Q20. **(a)** conglomerate.
- **(b)** vertical.
- **(c)** horizontal.

Q21. Answers could include: to achieve economies of scale; to gain greater market power; to obtain an increased share price; to reduce uncertainty; to take advantage of an opportunity that arises; to reduce the likelihood of being taken over; to defend another firm from a hostile takeover bid; asset stripping (i.e. selling off the profitable bits of the newly acquired company); empire building; broadening the geographical base of the company.

Q22. **(a)** All could be argued to be! This is an example of the problem with the theory of long-run profit maximisation: virtually any action could be justified as potentially leading to increased profits.
- **(b)** To achieve economies of scale; (to take advantage of an opportunity that arises); to reduce the likelihood of being taken over; empire building; broadening the geographical base of the company. These could be argued to lead directly to a faster growth in the size of the firm. Some of the

others could be argued to be consistent under certain circumstances.

Q23. C. The growth-maximising firm will be prepared to sacrifice profit in order to achieve higher output and sales. Note: in the case of E, the growth-maximising firm will be operating at a lower point on its *AR* curve. This will correspond to a lower level of *MR* and hence a *lower* price elasticity of demand.

Q24. *No*: if there is any trade-off between the objectives. For example, in order to sell more, a firm may have to accept lower profits. In such cases only one of the objectives can be maximised. Alternatively one of the objectives could be maximised *subject* to achieving a target level of another objective. For example, the firm could maximise sales revenue subject to achieving a *satisfactory* level of profits.

Q25. A. In a multi-department firm there may be many different potentially conflicting interests of different managers. In such cases, unless one manager is dominant, it is likely that managers will have to be prepared to be 'satisficers' rather than 'maximisers'.

Q26. *actually behave*.

Q27. *search*.

Q28. *Where managers allow spare capacity to exist in their department, thereby enabling them to respond more easily to changed circumstances.*

Q29. All of them. Organisational slack is likely to increase when firms face uncertain times and when they are not forced by competition to cut their slack.

Q30. *No*. The changes in targets may result from the fact the senior managers have built slack into their departments and can afford the 'luxury' of changing targets: perhaps experimentally. At the same time, the junior managers, fearing changed targets, may well be trying to increase the amount of organisational slack in their domain (but hoping not to let their bosses know for fear of being given tougher targets).

Q31. *True*. The greater the number of goals, and hence the greater the chance of conflict, the more likely firms are to build in organisational slack, and therefore the less they will need to change their level of production as market conditions change.

Q32. *False*. The choice of the level of mark-up may reflect the firm's assessment of what price the 'market will bear': what price will maximise profits. By not using marginal cost and marginal revenue, the firm may well not arrive at the profit-maximising price and output immediately (and in this sense the statement is true), but if the firm is willing to adjust its mark-up in the light of the perceived strength of demand, then it may, by an 'iterative' approach (i.e. a step-by-step approach), arrive at the profit-maximising mark-up. Note that even if a firm does try to equate marginal cost and marginal revenue, a lack of information, especially about the shape of the demand curve for its product, and hence its marginal revenue, may prevent it from arriving directly at the profit-maximising price. It may still, therefore, have to use an iterative approach.

Q33. *True*. A firm that is a profit maximiser will need to adjust its price (i.e. its mark-up) as revenue and cost curves shift. A profit satisficer, given the probability of a degree of organisational slack, will not need to be so responsive to changes in demand and costs.

Q34. D. As its output increases, it will need a smaller (average) profit mark-up on top of average cost in order to achieve a given level of *total* profit.

Chapter Nine

9

The Theory of Distribution of Income

A REVIEW

In this chapter we consider what determines the incomes earned by different factors of production.

We start by having a look at the income earned by labour. This takes the form of wages. We will look at wage determination in both perfect and imperfect markets. In doing so we will attempt to establish why wage rates can differ substantially from one occupation to another: why there can be substantial inequality in wages.

We then look at the rewards to non-human factors of production. We first look at the determination of the return to capital: at the *price of capital* that is either hired or sold and at the incomes – *profit* and *interest* – earned from the use of capital by its owners (capitalists).

Finally we look at the rewards to owners of land (landlords). This consists of the *rent* earned from hiring out land or using it to produce goods.

9.1 Wage determination under perfect competition

(Pages 216–17) In a *perfect* market the rewards to factors are determined by the interaction of demand and supply.

Figure 9.1 shows a local market for plasterers. It is assumed that it is a perfect market. This assumption means that **Q1.** *the price of plaster/the wage rate of plasterers/the profitability of employers of plasterers* cannot be affected by individual **Q2.** *employers/workers/employers or workers*. This means that **Q3.** *the supply curve of labour to/the demand curve for labour by* an individual employer is perfectly elastic, and that **Q4.** *the supply curve of labour by/the demand curve for labour from* an individual worker is perfectly elastic too.

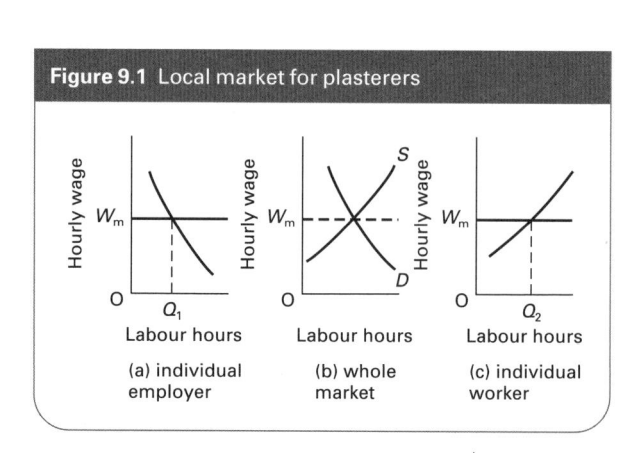

Figure 9.1 Local market for plasterers

(a) individual employer
(b) whole market
(c) individual worker

Q5. In Figure 9.1(b), which of the two curves would shift and in which direction as a result of each of the following changes?
(a) A deterioration in the working conditions for plasterers.
demand/supply; left/right
(b) A decrease in the price of plaster.
demand/supply; left/right
(c) A decrease in the demand for new houses.
demand/supply; left/right
(d) An increased demand for plasterers in other parts of the country. *demand/supply; left/right*
(e) Increased wages in other parts of the building trade (as a result of union activity).
demand/supply; left/right
(f) Increased costs associated with employing plasterers (e.g. employers having to pay higher insurance premiums for accidents to plasterers).
demand/supply; left/right

Q6. From Q5(c) it can be seen that the demand for a factor of production is:
A. a substitute demand.
B. a direct demand.
C. an elastic demand.
D. an inelastic demand.
E. a derived demand.

(Pages 217–19) The supply of labour
We can look at the supply of labour at three levels: the supply of hours by an individual worker, the supply of workers to an individual employer and the total market supply of a given category of labour.

When an individual worker works longer hours, each extra hour worked will involve additional sacrifice.

Q7. This additional sacrifice is known as

....

This sacrifice consists of two elements: the sacrifice of leisure and the extra effort/unpleasantness incurred from the extra work. As people work extra hours, these two sacrifices are likely to increase. As a result the supply curve will normally be **Q8.** *upward sloping/downward sloping*.

Under certain circumstances, however, the supply curve can bend backwards at higher wages. To understand why, we must distinguish between the *income* and *substitution* effects of a wage increase.

Q9. Which of the following is the income effect and which is the substitution effect?
(a) As wage rates rise, people will tend to work more hours, since taking leisure would now involve a greater sacrifice of income and hence consumption.
income effect/substitution effect
(b) At higher wage rates, people do not need to work such long hours. *income effect/substitution effect*

Thus the income effect is **Q10.** *positive/negative* and the substitution effect is **Q11.** *positive/negative*. The supply curve will thus become backward bending at high wage rates if the **Q12.** *income effect/substitution effect* becomes dominant.

Q13. The supply curve of labour to an *individual employer* in perfect competition will be perfectly elastic.
True/False

Q14. The *market* supply curve of labour will tend to be upward sloping. The position of this curve will depend on three main determinants. Of the following:
(i) the number of qualified people,
(ii) the wage rate,
(iii) the productivity of labour,
(iv) the pleasantness/unpleasantness of the job,
(v) the wages and non-wage benefits of alternative jobs,

which three determine the position of the supply curve?
A. (i), (ii) and (iii).
B. (i), (iii) and (iv).
C. (iii), (iv) and (v).
D. (i), (iv) and (v).
E. (ii), (iii) and (iv).

(Pages 219–20 and Web case 9.1) Elasticity of supply
The elasticity of the market supply of labour will depend on how readily workers are willing and able to move into jobs as their wage rate increases relative to other jobs. What we are referring to here is the mobility of labour. The less the mobility (the greater the immobility), the less elastic the supply.

Q15. There are several causes of immobility. In each one of the following cases, identify whether it is a cause of geographical immobility, occupational immobility or both.
(a) Social and family ties. *geographical/occupational/both*
(b) Ignorance of available jobs.
geographical/occupational/both
(c) Difficulty in acquiring new qualifications.
geographical/occupational/both
(d) Inconvenience of moving house.
geographical/occupational/both
(e) Fear of the unknown. *geographical/occupational/both*
(f) Less desirable working conditions in alternative jobs.
geographical/occupational/both

(Web case 9.1) The elasticity of supply of labour will determine what proportion of wages consists of *transfer earnings* and what proportion consists of *economic rent*. The definition of a person's **Q16.** *transfer earnings/economic rent* is 'anything over and above what that person must be paid to prevent him or her moving to another job'.

118 CHAPTER 9 THE THEORY OF DISTRIBUTION OF INCOME

Q17. A fashion model could earn £80 per week as a gardener, £160 per week working on a building site or £240 as a lorry driver. As a model, however, he earns £320. Assuming he likes all four jobs equally and that there are no costs associated with changing jobs, what is his economic rent from being a fashion model?
A. £80
B. £160
C. £240
D. £320
E. £480

Q18. In Figure 9.2, which area represents transfer earnings?
A. (i)
B. (ii)
C. (iii)
D. (i) + (ii)
E. (ii) + (iii)

Figure 9.2 A labour market

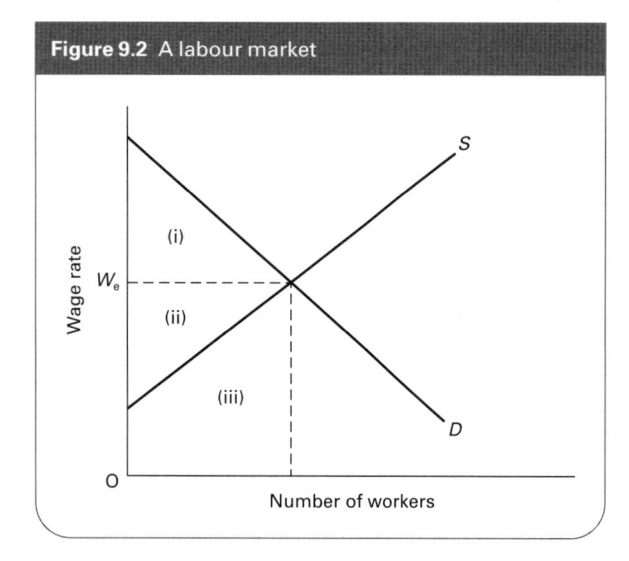

Q19. In Figure 9.2, which area represents economic rent?
A. (i)
B. (ii)
C. (iii)
D. (i) + (ii)
E. (ii) + (iii)

(Pages 221–2) The demand for labour: the marginal productivity theory

We turn now to the *demand* for labour. How many workers will a profit-maximising firm want to employ? What will be its demand for labour?

There are a number of concepts you will need to be clear about here.

Q20. Match the concepts (i)–(vii) to the definitions (a)–(g).

(i) Marginal cost (MC)
(ii) Marginal cost of labour (MC_L)
(iii) Average cost of labour (AC_L)
(iv) Marginal revenue (MR)
(v) Average revenue (AR)
(vi) Marginal physical product of labour (MPP_L)
(vii) Marginal revenue product of labour (MRP_L)

(a) The extra revenue a firm earns from the employment of one more worker. ....

(b) The wage rate. ....

(c) The price of the good. ....

(d) The extra cost of producing one more unit of output. ....

(e) The extra output gained from the employment of one more worker. ....

(f) The extra revenue from producing one more unit of output. ....

(g) The extra cost of employing one more worker. ....

The most important of these concepts in understanding the demand for labour is the marginal revenue product (MRP_L). This can be derived by multiplying **Q21.** MPP_L by MR/AR by MC_L/MR by AC_L.

The rule for profit maximising can thus be stated as 'whenever MC_L exceeds MRP_L the firm should employ **Q22.** *more/fewer* workers, and whenever MRP_L exceeds MC_L the firm should employ **Q23.** *more/fewer*.

Q24. The firm's demand curve for labour under perfect competition is given by the MRP_L curve.   *True/False*

(Page 222) We can conclude that under perfect competition, there are three main determinants of the amount of labour that a firm will demand: the productivity of labour (MPP_L), the wage rate (W) and the price of the good (P = MR).

Q25. Will a change in each of the following determinants lead to a shift in or a movement along the demand curve for labour?
(a) A change in the productivity of labour (MPP_L). *shift/movement along*
(b) A change in the wage rate (W). *shift/movement along*
(c) A change in the price of the good (P = MR). *shift/movement along*

(Pages 222–3) The demand curve for labour by the *whole industry* will not simply be the horizontal sum of the demand curves by individual firms.

◐ **Q26.** The (wage) elasticity of demand for labour will depend on a number of factors. Elasticity will be greater:
(a) the greater the price elasticity of demand for the good. *True/False*
(b) the harder it is to substitute labour for other factors and vice versa. *True/False*
(c) the greater the elasticity of supply of complementary factors. *True/False*
(d) the lower the elasticity of supply of substitute factors. *True/False*
(e) the smaller the wage cost as a proportion of total costs. *True/False*
(f) the longer the time period. *True/False*

(Pages 223–4) Even in a perfect market, inequality will exist between the earnings of different factors.

▤ **Q27.** Which one of the following would be a cause of inequality of wages between different occupations in the long run even if all labour markets were perfect?
A. There is short-run geographical immobility of labour.
B. Different jobs require people with different skills.
C. There is perfect knowledge of wages throughout the economy.
D. Everyone has to accept wages as given by the market.
E. Labour is homogeneous within any one particular labour market.

(Page 224) In practice, of course, factor markets are not perfect and this will provide a further reason for inequality in factor earnings.

❓ **Q28.** Name three types of market imperfection in factor markets.

1. ....
2. ....
3. ....

9.2 Wage determination in imperfect markets

(Page 224) In this section we shall consider the effect of economic power on wages.

✪ **Q29.** There are a number of types of economic power. These include:
(i) monopoly in goods markets
(ii) monopoly in labour markets
(iii) monopsony in goods markets
(iv) monopsony in labour markets
(v) bilateral monopoly

Match each of the following examples of economic power to the above five types.

(a) A group of local authorities get together as a purchasing consortium in order to be able to buy cheaper easy-empty dustbins from the manufacturers (dustbins that will be provided free to residents). ....
(b) A trade union operates a closed shop. ....
(c) A firm is the only domestic coal merchant supplying the area. ....
(d) The wages of postal workers are determined by a process of collective bargaining between the Post Office and the Union of Postal Workers. ....
(e) A factory is the only employer of certain types of skilled labour in the area. ....

(Page 225) Let us examine the situation where firms have power in the labour market. This is the case of *monopsony*, where a firm is the sole employer in a particular labour market (or *oligopsony*, where the firm is one of only a few employers). A monopsonist, unlike a perfectly competitive employer, will face **Q30.** *a downward-sloping/an upward-sloping/a horizontal* **Q31.** *supply curve of/demand curve for* labour.

⊖ **Q32.** Assume that a monopsonist faces the supply-of-labour schedule given in Table 9.1.
(a) Fill in the figures for TC_L and MC_L.
(b) Plot the figures for AC_L and MC_L on Figure 9.3, which also shows the firm's MRP_L curve.
(c) How many workers will the firm choose to employ in order to maximise profits?
(d) What wage rate will it pay?
(e) If Figure 9.3 were to illustrate a perfectly competitive market for labour (i.e. the sum of all firms), how many workers would now be employed and at what wage rate?

(Pages 225–7) What happens when labour also has economic power? Let us assume that a union is formed and that it has sole negotiating rights with a monopsony employer. What we have here is a case of *bilateral monopoly*. Wages are set by a process of collective bargaining, and

Table 9.1 A monopsonist's supply-of-labour schedule

Wage rate (AC_L)	£50	£60	£70	£80	£90	£100	£110	£120
Number of workers	1	2	3	4	5	6	7	8
Total wage bill (TC_L)	...	...	...	...	...	...	...	...
Marginal cost of labour (MC_L)	...	...	...	...	...	...	...	...

120 CHAPTER 9 THE THEORY OF DISTRIBUTION OF INCOME

Figure 9.3 A monopsonist

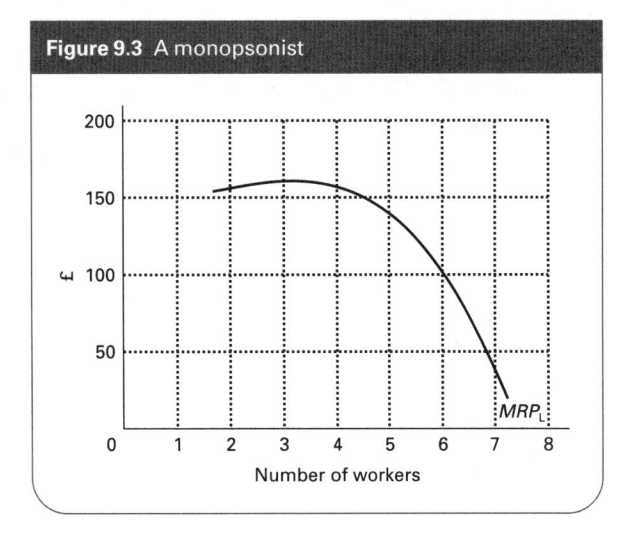

[Graph showing MRP_L curve, y-axis £ from 0 to 200, x-axis Number of workers from 0 to 8]

once the wage rate has been agreed, the firm has to accept that wage. It cannot therefore then drive the wage rate down by employing fewer workers. The firm thus now faces **Q33.** *an upward-sloping/a downward-sloping/a horizontal* supply-of-labour curve which is therefore **Q34.** *below/above/equal* to the new MC_L curve.

⊖ **Q35.** Referring still to Figure 9.3, assume that a union now represents labour and that wage rates are set by a process of collective bargaining.
(a) Draw the AC_L and MC_L if the agreed wage rate is £100 per week.
(b) How many workers will the firm now choose to employ?

....

(c) Explain briefly why the firm is willing to take on *more* workers than before despite now having to pay a higher wage rate.

....

....

(d) What is the highest negotiated wage rate at which the firm would still wish to employ the same number of workers as before the union was formed?

£ ....

(e) What is the equilibrium wage rate under bilateral monopoly?

£ ....

(Pages 227–30) Let us now look at the process of collective bargaining.

The outcome of the negotiations will depend on the attitudes of both sides, their skills in negotiating, the information they possess about the other side and the amount they are prepared to give ground. In particular, the outcome will depend on the relative power of both sides to pursue their objectives.

◐ **Q36.** How will each of the following affect the *power of a union* to cause the employer to give ground at the negotiating table?
(a) New figures showing that the firm's profits for the last year were less than anticipated.
Increase/Decrease the union's power.
(b) A rise in unemployment.
Increase/Decrease the union's power.
(c) New figures showing that inflation has risen.
Increase/Decrease the union's power.
(d) A successful recruiting drive for union membership.
Increase/Decrease the union's power.
(e) Increased competition for the firm's product from imports. *Increase/Decrease* the union's power.
(f) A rapidly growing demand for the firm's product.
Increase/Decrease the union's power.
(g) A closed shop agreement.
Increase/Decrease the union's power.
(h) The firm has substantial monopoly power in the goods market. *Increase/Decrease* the union's power.

(Pages 230–8) Power is not the only factor that makes actual wage determination different from the perfectly competitive model. There are various other imperfections that cause labour markets to be distorted.

? **Q37.** Give three different types of labour market imperfection.

1. ....

2. ....

3. ....

⊖ **Q38.** Figure 9.4 shows the effect of imperfect information on a particular labour market. Workers looking for a job are likely to spend a period of time searching for a

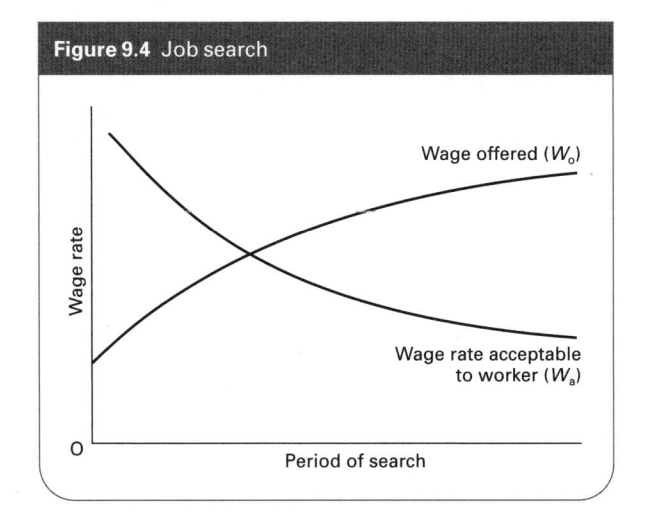

Figure 9.4 Job search

[Graph showing two curves: Wage offered (W_o) rising and Wage rate acceptable to worker (W_a) falling; y-axis Wage rate, x-axis Period of search]

suitable one. Likewise firms wanting to recruit more labour are likely to spend time searching for suitably qualified workers.

The 'wage offered' (W_o) curve shows that as the period of search increases, the average worker will discover better-paid jobs (with the curve flattening off as the information becomes complete). The acceptable wage (W_a) curve shows the minimum wage the average worker would be prepared to accept.

(a) Why is the W_a curve downward sloping?

....

(b) How long will the average worker in the diagram go on searching for a job?

....

(c) Which of the two curves will shift and in which direction in each of the following cases?
   (i) Workers become more optimistic about finding a high-paid job. W_o/W_a; *up/down*
   (ii) Firms become more optimistic that there is plenty of suitably qualified labour. W_o/W_a; *up/down*
   (iii) Unemployment benefit decreases, so that the costs to workers of searching becomes greater. W_o/W_a; *up/down*
   (iv) Demand in the goods market increases. W_o/W_a; *up/down*

Q39. Which of the following could explain why the average wage of women tends to be lower than that of men?
(a) Some employers are prejudiced against women. *Yes/No*
(b) Women are less strong physically. *Yes/No*
(c) Women tend to be less geographically mobile than men. *Yes/No*
(d) A lower proportion of female workers are in unions than male workers. *Yes/No*
(e) Women tend to work in more labour-intensive industries. *Yes/No*
(f) A lower proportion of the female population seeks employment than that of the male population. *Yes/No*
(g) A lower proportion of women have higher education qualifications. *Yes/No*

Q40. A particular industry (which operates in a competitive labour market) discriminates against black workers. Which one of the following effects is likely? (Assume no discrimination in other industries.)
A. White workers will be paid a lower wage rate in that industry than they would have been otherwise.
B. Black workers in other industries will be paid a higher wage rate than they would otherwise.
C. White workers in other industries will be paid a lower wage rate than they would otherwise.
D. The discriminating industry will employ more black workers than it would if it did not discriminate, because it will pay black workers lower wage rates than white workers.
E. The profits of the industry that discriminates will fall.

Q41. The marginal productivity theory states that firms will employ workers up to the point where their MRP_L is equal to their MC_L. Some labour market imperfections are consistent with this theory; some contradict it. From the following list of imperfections, which ones are consistent with the marginal productivity theory?
   (i) Firms discriminate against certain groups of workers.
   (ii) Firms have monopsony power.
   (iii) An industry has nationally negotiated wage rates.
   (iv) When reducing its labour force, a firm adopts a 'last in, first out' policy.
   (v) Firms are growth maximisers and profit satisficers.
   (vi) Wage rates (but not employment) are set by a process of collective bargaining.

A. (iv) only.
B. (iii) and (vi).
C. (ii), (iii) and (vi).
D. (i), (iv) and (v).
E. all six.

9.3 Capital and profit

(Page 239) As with wages, the incomes accruing to the owners of capital and land are the outcome of the forces of demand and supply: forces affected to varying degrees by market distortions.

At the outset it is necessary to make an important distinction. This is between the money received from selling capital and land outright, and the income from the *services* of capital and land (i.e. income or interest from using or hiring out capital, and rent from land). The first is the price of the factor. The second is the price of the services of the factor.

Q42. Wage rates are the price of labour. *True/False*

Q43. As with labour, the profit-maximising employment of land and capital *services* will be where the factor's *MRP* is equal to its *MC* (= price under perfect competition). *True/False*

(Page 240) Capital for hire

If firm A owns capital equipment, what determines the rate at which the firm can rent it out? The answer is that it will be determined by demand and supply.

The demand for capital services by firm B is given by the *MRP* of capital curve.

Q44. Draw the MRP_K, AC_K and MC_K curves for a firm that has monopsony power when hiring capital equipment. Mark the amount of capital equipment it will choose to hire and show what hire charge it will pay.

(Pages 240–2) The supply of capital services is determined in much the same way as the supply of goods. A firm will supply capital services up to the point where their marginal cost equals their marginal revenue. For a small firm supplying capital services (e.g. a tool hire company) the rental is given by the market and thus is the same as the **Q45.** *marginal revenue/marginal cost/average cost* from renting out equipment. The marginal cost will be the marginal *opportunity cost*.

Q46. Assume that a tool hire company already has a stock of tools. Which of the following are opportunity costs of hiring out the tools?
(a) The cost of replacing the equipment. Yes/No
(b) The depreciation of the equipment due to wear and tear. Yes/No
(c) The depreciation of the equipment due to ageing. Yes/No
(d) Maintenance costs of the equipment. Yes/No
(e) Handling costs associated with hiring out the equipment. Yes/No

(Page 242) The price of capital services in a perfect market will be determined by market demand and supply.

Q47. The price of capital services will be higher:
A. the lower the marginal physical productivity of capital.
B. the lower the price of the goods produced with the capital equipment.
C. the lower the opportunity costs of supplying the capital services.
D. the lower the demand for the goods produced with the capital equipment.
E. the lower the price of complementary factors.

(Pages 242–5) Capital for purchase: investment
The demand for capital for purchase (investment) will depend on the income it earns for the firm. To calculate the value of this income we need to use *discounted cash flow* (DCF) techniques.

These techniques allow us to reduce the future value of an investment back to a *present value* which we can then compare with the cost of the investment. If the present value exceeds the cost of the investment, the investment is worth while.

To find the present value we *discount* (i.e. reduce) the future values using an appropriate *rate of discount*.

*Q48. What is the present value of an investment in a project lasting one year that yields £110 at the end, assuming that the rate of discount is 10 per cent?

....

To work out the present value we use the following formula:

$$PV = \frac{X_1}{(1+r)} + \frac{X_2}{(1+r)^2} + \frac{X_3}{(1+r)^3} \cdots + \frac{X_n}{(1+r)^n}$$

where:
PV is the discounted present value of the investment, X_1 is the revenue from the investment earned in year 1, X_2 in year 2 and so on;
r is the rate of discount expressed as a decimal (e.g. 10% = 0.1).

*Q49. Suppose an investment costs £12 000 and yields £5000 per year for three years. At the end of the three years, the equipment has no value. Work out whether the investment will be profitable if the rate of discount is:

(a) 5%...

....

....

(b) 10%...

....

....

(c) 20%...

....

....

(Page 245) The rate of interest
The rate of interest is the price of loanable funds. This depends on the supply of savings and the demand for finance (which includes investment demand).

Q50. Would the following changes cause the rate of interest to rise or fall?
(a) People become more thrifty. Rise/Fall
(b) The productivity of investments generally increases. Rise/Fall
(c) The demand for goods increases. Rise/Fall
(d) The cost of machinery rises. Rise/Fall

Financing investment
(Pages 245–8) A firm can raise finance for investment in various ways.

Q51. Which of the following are categorised as internal sources and which as external sources of finance?
(a) Borrowing from the UK banking sector. *Internal/External*
(b) Retained profits. *Internal/External*
(c) Borrowing from abroad. *Internal/External*
(d) Issuing new shares. *Internal/External*

The stock market operates as both a primary and a secondary market in capital. As a primary market, it is where public limited companies can raise finance by issuing new shares or debentures. As a secondary market, it enables the buying and selling of existing shares and debentures.

Q52. Give two advantages and two disadvantages of using the stock market for raising new capital.

Advantages ....
....

Disadvantages ....
....

Q53. Stock markets can lead to an efficient pricing of shares. This efficiency of pricing can be of three different levels.
(i) Weak form of efficiency.
(ii) Semi-strong form of efficiency.
(iii) Strong form of efficiency.

Match each of the above to the following definitions.
(a) Where share prices adjust quickly, fully and accurately to all available information, both public and that only available to insiders.
....
(b) Where share dealing prevents cyclical movements in shares.
....
(c) Where share prices adjust quickly, fully and accurately to publicly available information.
....

9.4 Land and rent
(Pages 249–50) Rent on land, like the price of other factor services, will be determined by the interaction of demand and supply.

Q54. What effect would the following have on the rent on arable farmland?
(a) A rise in the demand for wheat. *rise/fall*
(b) A substantial rise in the demand for beef (but no fall in the demand for cereals). *rise/fall*
(c) A major coastal land reclamation scheme is completed. *rise/fall*
(d) The ending of the EU system of setting an artificially high price for grains. *rise/fall*
(e) The introduction of a government scheme to 'set aside' 20 per cent of all farm land. Farmers would be prohibited from growing crops on such land. (What would happen to the rent on land remaining in use?) *rise/fall*

Q55. In what sense has the supply of land an elasticity:

(a) equal to zero? ....

(b) greater than zero? ....

Q56. The following are possible explanations of why rents are higher in city centres than in rural areas:
(i) Land in city centres is of more use to commerce.
(ii) Transport costs are lower for people living in city centres.
(iii) The supply of agricultural land is elastic.
(iv) The marginal productivity of land is higher for shop and office use than for agricultural use.
(v) City centres are more congested than out-of-town areas.
(vi) Costs of living (other than rents) are higher in towns than in the countryside.

Which are valid explanations?
A. (i), (ii) and (iv).
B. (i), (iv) and (v).
C. (iii), (iv) and (vi).
D. (i), (iii), (iv) and (vi).
E. (i), (ii), (iii), (iv), (v) and (vi).

Q57. If land is totally fixed in supply, then
A. all rent is economic rent.
B. all rent is transfer earnings.
C. the proportions of total rent that are economic rent and transfer earnings will depend entirely on demand.
D. the size of transfer earnings will depend on the *position* of the demand curve.
E. the amount of economic rent depends entirely on the position of the supply curve.

(Page 250) Not all land is rented. Much of it is bought and sold outright. Nevertheless the price of land will depend on its potential annual rental value (R) and on the market rate of interest (i). The formula for working out the equilibrium price of land is R/i.

Q58. How much would a piece of land be worth that produces £2000 in rent each year if the market rate of interest were:

(a) 10 per cent per annum? ....

(b) 20 per cent per annum? ....

PROBLEMS, EXERCISES AND PROJECTS

Q59. Assume that you are offered some part-time evening work serving in a bar. You need this to supplement your meagre income/allowance. How many hours would you work if you were offered 50p per hour, £1, £2, £5, £20, £100, £1000? Is your behaviour rational? Do you have a backward-bending supply curve of labour and if so over what range? How would your behaviour differ if you were offered the job for 1 day, 1 week, 1 year, 40 years?

To what extent does your supply of labour per week depend on the number of weeks you *anticipate* being able to work at those rates? How would your behaviour differ if you were not allowed to save your wages or to invest it in shares, property, etc?

Try discussing this question with other students. Note down their answers and tabulate the information. Does a common pattern emerge?

Q60. Access the UK National Statistics Web site (www.statistics.gov.uk) and in the 'Bookshelf' section, download the latest version of the *New Earnings Survey (NES): Analyses by occupation*. In Tables D1 and D2 (Average gross weekly earnings, hourly earnings and weekly hours) identify six occupations, each from a separate major group. Provide an explanation of the following:
(a) Differences in average gross hourly earnings between the six occupations for full-time males.
(b) Differences in average gross hourly earnings between the six occupations for full-time females.
(c) Differences in average weekly hours for males between the six occupations.
(d) Differences between female and male average gross hourly earnings between the six occupations.
(e) Compare your answers with other students to arrive at a set of conclusions about the differences in earnings between occupations and between women and men.

Q61. Table 9.2 shows how a firm's output of a good increases as it employs more workers. It is assumed that all other factors of production are fixed. The firm operates under perfect competition in both the goods and labour markets. The market price of the good is £2.
(a) Fill in the missing figures in Table 9.2.
(b) How many workers will the firm employ (to maximise profits) if the wage rate is (i) £50 per week, (ii) £110 per week, (iii) £100 per week?

Q62. A profit-maximising firm has monopsony power in the labour market but its employees are not initially members of a trade union. Labour is the only variable factor and its supply schedule to the firm and the firm's total physical product of labour are shown in Table 9.3. The firm's product sells for £2.

Table 9.2 Total physical product of labour (weekly)

Number of workers	Total physical product (units)	Marginal physical product (units)	Marginal revenue product (£)
1	50		
2	110	60	...
3	170	...	...
4	220	...	...
5	260	...	...
6	...	30	...
7	...	...	40
8	...	15	...

Table 9.3 A monopsonist's labour supply and output (hourly data)

Workers (number)	Wage rate (AC_L) (£)	Total wages (TC_L) (£)	MC_L (£)	TPP_L (units)	TRP_L (£)	MRP_L (£)
10	4	...	...	500	...	...
20	5	...	...	575	...	...
30	6	...	...	645	...	...
40	7	...	...	705	...	...
50	8	...	...	755	...	...
60	9	...	...	800	...	...
70	10	...	...	840	...	...

(a) Fill in the columns for the total wage bill, MC_L, TRP_L and MRP_L. (Remember that the MC_L is the extra cost of employing *one* more worker not ten; similarly the MRP_L is the extra revenue earned from employing *one* more worker.)
(b) How many workers will the firm employ in order to maximise profits?
....
(c) What wage will the firm pay? ....
(d) Assuming that the fixed costs of production are £600 per hour, what will be the firm's hourly profit?
....
(e) If the fixed costs increase to £1200 per hour, what will be the effect on the firm's output?
....
(f) Assume now that the price of the good rises to £4. How many workers will the firm now employ to maximise profits?
....

(g) Returning to the original price of £2, assume now that the workers form a trade union and that a situation of bilateral monopoly is the result. What is the maximum wage the trade union could negotiate without causing the firm to try to reduce the size of the labour force below that in (b) above?

....

(h) How much profit will the firm make, assuming that fixed costs were at the original £600 per hour level?

....

(i) What has happened to the level of profits and the wage bill compared with (c) and (d) above?

....

(j) If the union only succeeds in pushing the wage up to £9 per hour, what will happen to the level of employment?

....

(k) If, as a result of industrial action, the union succeeds in achieving a wage rate of £12 per hour with no reduction in the workforce below the level of that in (b) above, what will the firm's level of profit be now?

....

Q63. Collect data on office rental prices in different locations throughout your town/city (or nearest one). To collect your data, try visiting local estate agents which deal in business letting or look at advertisements in local papers.
(a) Explain the differences in rents.
(b) How would a profit-maximising firm decide whether to locate its offices in high-rent accommodation in a city centre or in low-rent accommodation in a less central location?

C DISCUSSION TOPICS AND ESSAYS

Q64. What is the relationship between the mobility of labour and the proportion of wages that consists of economic rent? (See Web case 9.1.)

Q65. To what extent will a perfect market economy lead to equality of wage rates (a) within any given labour market and (b) between labour markets?

Q66. If, unlike a perfectly competitive employer, a monopsonist has to pay a higher wage to attract more workers, why, other things being equal, will a monopsonist pay a lower wage than a perfectly competitive employer?

Q67. Why do the most pleasant jobs often pay the highest wages? Why does a Premiership football player get paid more than a National Health Service nurse?

Q68. Use the bilateral monopoly model to explain why a statutory minimum wage does not necessarily lead to a lower level of employment in a firm which would otherwise pay a lower wage rate.

Q69. Why is it impossible to identify an 'equilibrium wage' under bilateral monopoly?

Q70. Would a higher national average wage for men than women in a country be evidence of sexual discrimination in the labour market? Consider the impact on the labour market of equal pay legislation.

*****Q71.** Should a profit-maximising firm always go ahead with a project that has a present value greater than the cost of the investment?

*****Q72.** If a project's costs occur throughout the life of the project, how will this affect the appraisal of whether the project is profitable?

Q73. How can the concept of marginal revenue product be used to explain why rents are higher in city centres than in out-of-town areas?

Q74. Mary Giles, a farmer, earns £100 000 from her farm where she owns all the land. After paying the wage bills of the two workers employed on the farm, and the bills for seeds, fertiliser, equipment, maintenance, fuel, etc. she has £20 000 left over. How should this £20 000 be classified: as her wages, her profit, her rent, or a combination of all three?

Q75. To what extent can marginal productivity theory explain inequality of income?

Q76. Debate
A society where wages are based on productivity will be an unfair and unjust society.

ARTICLES

Issues surrounding discrimination and its practice have been at the forefront of political debate for many years. How has economics contributed to this discussion? Can it add something to the debate? The article below, taken from *The Economist* of 6 June 1998, evaluates the contribution of economics and reviews some of the findings economics has made.

Race, sex and the dismal science

More than 30 years after the passage of America's landmark civil-rights legislation, discrimination is still an explosive social issue. Although it is illegal to treat female job applicants differently from males or to refuse to rent flats to Hispanic families, many Americans believe that unfair treatment persists in many parts of their economy.

There is no question that there are economic inequalities in America. Women earn less than men; Hispanics earn less than non-Hispanics; blacks are less likely to have mortgages than Caucasians. But are these inequalities due to deliberate discrimination, or are other factors at work? Economic analysis should be able to reveal the answer. But as a symposium in the *Journal of Economic Perspectives* makes clear, discrimination is devilishly difficult to pin down.

The legal definition of discrimination is disparate treatment of an individual on the basis of race, gender, age, religion or ethnic origin. The first economic attempt to understand such behaviour, developed by Gary Becker of the University of Chicago, suggested that prejudiced individuals with a 'taste for discrimination' must face additional costs if their prejudice is unfounded. A bigoted factory owner, for instance, will have to pay higher wages if he insists on hiring only white employees, and this will make his business less profitable than that of an unprejudiced competitor.

Since a price must be paid for prejudice, many economists have suggested (though Mr Becker's own model does not necessarily imply this) that in fully competitive markets discrimination should eventually disappear, because prejudiced firms will fail. Discrimination could persist only if entrepreneurs are willing to sacrifice part of their returns or if customers share – and are prepared to pay for – the employer's prejudice.

This taste-based analysis may well explain discrimination in settings where individuals interact and so tastes matter. But it is less successful at explaining prejudice in one-off or impersonal transactions. For instance, it does not clarify why blacks might find it harder than whites to get mortgage loans. In these situations, a second theory, offered by Kenneth Arrow and Edmund Phelps in the early 1970s, is more useful. Their approach, called 'statistical discrimination', suggests that people use an individual's race or sex as a proxy for individual characteristics. Thus a mortgage company might be reluctant to lend to a black client because it believes blacks, in general, have higher default rates. Using a racial 'proxy' is cheaper for the mortgage company than examining the individual's own credit history.

Unfortunately, this theory also is hard to square with persistent discrimination. The reason is that even if such a proxy is generally correct for a large group, it will not be true for all individuals within the group. Those firms able to distinguish among, say, high-risk and low-risk borrowers on an individual basis will eventually win out over those who use crude – and discriminatory – proxies.

Discrimination might be easier for economists to understand if they were able to measure it. There are two main techniques for doing this. The first is regression analysis, which seeks to measure whether an outcome, such as wage differentials between blacks and whites, is correlated with race once all other relevant factors, such as education and experience, are taken into account. Regression analysis has provided important evidence: a famous study of mortgage applications by the Federal Reserve Bank of Boston, for instance, showed that loan denial rates for blacks were eight percentage points higher than those for whites, once a large number of factors that affected the risk of default were included.

But, as John Yinger, of Syracuse University, points out in the *JEP* symposium, regression analysis has drawbacks as a tool for measuring discrimination. In particular, it is hard to measure certain variables, such as the quality of an individual's 'human capital', which may explain employer decisions that superficially appear discriminatory. Excluding such factors overstates discrimination in the labour market; including them may understate it, since the quality of human capital may be related to discrimination in other areas, such as education.

Take a test

An alternative technique for studying discrimination involves audits. In an audit, two individuals or couples, equal in all respects save one (such as race or sex) sequentially visit an employer, banker or rental agent to look for evidence of forms of disparate treatment that would otherwise be difficult to capture statistically. A 1991 employment audit in Washington, DC, for instance, showed that white testers were almost 10 per cent more likely to be invited for job interviews than black testers. A 1989 study involving 2000 audits of American estate agents found only 13 per cent of black testers posing as house buyers were offered assistance in mortgage financing, compared with 24 per cent of white testers.

Audits, however, have their problems as well, as James Heckman, of the University of Chicago, points out in a penetrating commentary. Audit studies assume that pairs of testers are alike in every relevant way save one. This may well not be the case. Employers may react differently to different auditors for reasons that have nothing to do with race or sex, meaning that audits may detect discriminatory behaviour when there is none. Fundamentally, audits and regressions suffer the same problem: it is hard to identify the characteristics that matter.

So how well has America dealt with discrimination against the various groups its lawmakers have sought to protect? Anecdotally, there is ample evidence that discrimination is far less rampant than it used to be, but that it is still all too common. Very few studies, however, have sought to look at changes in discrimination over time. Demonstrating incontrovertibly that it even exists is still beyond the ability of the dismal science.

© *The Economist*, London (6.6.98)

(a) Why, given Gary Becker's theory of discrimination, might discrimination disappear over the longer term? Why might this seem an unlikely outcome?

(b) What problems might be encountered in attempting to measure discrimination?

The link between labour market flexibility and economic competitiveness has been at the centre of many of the economic reforms of the last 20 years, both in the UK and elsewhere in the world economy. The article below, taken from *CBI News* of March 1998, explores the various forms that labour market flexibility might take and the differing strategies adopted by countries in Europe to achieve it.

Different combinations

The debate about labour-market flexibility has never been more important or contentious, but unfortunately it is often characterised by stereotypes, misconceptions and confusion over definitions. The European labour market is typically portrayed as rigid and inflexible, whereas the US and UK are seen as possessing dynamic and flexible labour markets leading to low unemployment. While there is some truth in this generalisation, we must recognise that there are strengths and weaknesses to all labour markets and that the European picture is not uniform but varied.

Dimensions

There are six different dimensions of flexibility. All are important, but in different ways for productivity growth and employment creation:

- Geographical mobility is clearly important to avoid regional unemployment as far as possible. Some high national levels of unemployment around Europe are essentially regional problems in each country.
- Flexible working patterns, such as part-time work and fixed-term contracts, can be important sources of improved company performance and productivity growth and are popular with employees.
- Wage flexibility is important for maintaining competitiveness and employment, and will become more so in EMU, when countries can no longer devalue their currencies to remain competitive.
- Numerical flexibility – the ability to adjust the size of the workforce – is perhaps the most controversial dimension of flexibility. But limited numerical flexibility can distort the labour market and cause unemployment by discouraging hiring.
- The last two dimensions of flexibility – skills and functional flexibility – are the least controversial and yet, in many ways, the most important. A workforce with good and transferable skills, which can be moved easily between jobs, is essential for rapid productivity growth. Functional flexibility goes further than that and relates to the involvement of people in their work tasks, to devolving responsibility and to the willingness of both managers and employees to change their working practices – often vital to competitive success.

In order for a country to be flexible it does not need maximum flexibility in each of these areas but rather to have sufficient flexibility overall. Different countries have developed different responses and each state draws strengths from its own combination. Weaknesses in one area are often compensated for by strengths in another. Some states are strong in areas which call for active flexibility (for instance, skills and function). Others gain flexibility through a more passive use – where it is the absence of rigidity that gives the freedom to use flexibility (for instance, numerical flexibility or flexibility in working patterns). Countries need to find a combination of flexibility which delivers growth and high, sustainable levels of employment.

When examining EU states, what we find is a picture of great national variability far removed from the simplistic slogans of: UK flexible . . . Europe inflexible.

The Italian economy has seen rapid growth in productivity, accompanied by moderate wage increases. But there are large regional differences. Northern Italy has most of the manufacturing and forms part of the 'core' of Europe, sharing a similar industrial structure to France and Germany. Southern Italy has higher unemployment, a greater share of people employed in agriculture and poor skill levels. Italian unemployment is high owing to high levels of social security contributions and stringent employment protection that discourage employment creation, though the *cassa integrazione* and on-the-job training contracts provide companies with some flexibility in adjusting the size of their workforce. There is little flexibility in working patterns as the use of fixed-term contracts is restricted and part-timers cannot work overtime.

Germany's absolute productivity levels are very high and result from a skilled workforce, able to make full use of multiskilling and teamworking. Collective bargaining is primarily conducted at the sectoral level and characterised by a high degree of informal co-ordination. As automatic indexation is forbidden and wages do not appear to be influenced by inflation expectations, pay settlements are generally sensitive to the macroeconomic situation. But they do not provide for differentiation at company level. Wage dispersion is also low. This has meant the service sector is relatively underdeveloped. Numerical flexibility is limited; the General Dismissal Protection Act applies to all employees after six months' service and requires that all ordinary dismissals are qualified as socially justified. There are restrictions on the use of fixed-term contracts.

In the UK, there are few restrictions on the use of flexible patterns of work and numerical flexibility is high. Skills flexibility has been historically limited and company training has been used to remedy the lack of basic skills of the workforce. The development of functional flexibility is hindered by the weak skills base but is improving, especially in the service sector. The long-term record on wage restraint is weak, with a tendency to inflationary settlements. But a major recent shift to decentralised wage setting and improved links between company/individual performance and pay has increased flexibility.

The Netherlands has interesting lessons to offer about how labour markets can be reformed within a consensual model. Its economy is doing well, unemployment is low, and GDP growth is strong. There has been considerable reform since the 80s when both unemployment and inflation were high and growth low. Co-operation between the social partners – the government, business and unions – helped reform rigid labour market policies such as working pattern restrictions and a high minimum wage, while wage restraint has improved competitiveness. The workforce is skilled and there is significant flexibility in working patterns. However, numerical flexibility is limited; employers need authorisation before dismissing workers. Dutch labour-force participation is also low by international standards.

In France, skills flexibility is high: 77 per cent of the population are qualified to level two (five GCSEs equivalent) or above. Unit labour costs have fallen throughout most of the 90s but a high minimum wage continues to be a barrier to employment growth, especially among young people. Benefit replacement levels are also high. As in Spain, numerical flexibility is limited. Redundancies are permitted for serious and genuine failures in performance of individual employees or because of financial difficulties experienced by the firm but not to improve profitability. The number of temporary work contracts is growing rapidly as an alternative to flexibility in permanent employment. Whether this is desirable or not remains to be seen.

Spain is now among the fastest-growing countries of the European Union. It has a higher than EU average share employed in manufacturing and has made continual 'catch-up' productivity improvements, particularly helped by the devaluation of the peseta in 1992 by 20 per cent. Spain has made considerable efforts to improve its skills base over the past two decades, but gaps still remain in its education and training provision, especially with regard to vocational training and lifelong learning. Flexibility in working patterns was facilitated by a set of reforms in 1994. Functional flexibility has also improved since the abolition of the *ordenanzas laborales* – regulations that limited the responsibilities which different trades are allowed to perform. Spain has high unemployment (currently around 20 per cent), owing to deep structural problems. Wages are the most inflexible in the OECD, preventing the low skilled and young pricing themselves into the market. Numerical flexibility is severely limited. Severance payments are among the highest in the world and 30 per cent of the workforce are on temporary contracts to avoid these restrictions.

(a) Attempt a definition of a 'flexible labour market'.
(b) In what ways has the UK approach to flexibility differed from those in other European countries?
(c) Which of the countries considered in the article do you consider to have the strongest approach to flexibility? Explain your answer and identify the criteria on which you made your judgement.

The following extract, taken from the Low Pay Commission's 2000 *Report on the UK National Minimum Wage*, considers the impact of the minimum wage nine months after its introduction. It seemed to be bringing substantial benefits to large numbers of people at minimum cost to business.

Competitiveness

The National Minimum Wage was set cautiously so as not to undermine competitiveness. Nevertheless, we are conscious that its impact on economic performance will depend on a number of critical factors.

Business costs

The impact of the minimum wage appears to be widespread among businesses. Secondary analysis we commissioned on the 1998 Workplace Employee Relations Survey suggests that around one-third of establishments had employees who would have been entitled to higher pay by the National Minimum Wage (McNabb and Whitfield, 1999). We are aware that the legislation has been a particular challenge for firms where profitability is low or the scope for innovation is limited, but the absence of general pressures to restore wage differentials, and the way in which firms have managed the change, mean that the costs have been manageable for most of them.

Various special surveys quantify the costs incurred by low-paying firms. A survey we conducted in September–October 1999 covered over 350, mainly small firms in retail and hospitality, whose pay bill costs had risen because of the minimum wage. Among the firms whose pay bill had risen, 87 per cent reported that the rise had been under 10 per cent; half the firms in retail stated that their pay bill costs had risen by 5–10 per cent, while the corresponding figure for hospitality was a third. A national survey by the British Chambers of Commerce estimated that employment costs had risen by an average of 6 per cent among those firms directly affected by the National Minimum Wage. They concluded that 'most firms have been able to afford to lower their profits to cope with the NMW'.

While official data can be examined in order to assess the overall costs to business, interpreting the figures is not straightforward. We do not know what wage growth would have been in the absence of the policy, nor are official data sufficiently accurate to assess very small effects.

In our first report, assuming the maximum of two million beneficiaries, we estimated the first-round direct cost of the National Minimum Wage on the UK wage bill to be 0.6 per cent. We know that many firms have taken measures to control pressures on their wage costs, and our own survey shows that two-thirds of affected firms had done so. We have already explained that the potential number of beneficiaries is slightly lower than the original estimate, and compliance is building up. These developments lead us to conclude that the overall direct impact on the wage bill has so far been around 0.3 per cent, a figure which is likely to increase as compliance levels improve.

The indirect impact of the National Minimum Wage has similarly not been large. Based on evidence from official data and our consultation, our judgment is that the impact of the National Minimum Wage on the overall UK wage bill, covering both the direct and knock-on effects, has so far been around 0.5 per cent.

Productivity

While many of the UK's best companies match the performance of their overseas counterparts, productivity lags behind other major economies in a number of low-paying sectors (O'Mahony et al., 1996). Hence the overall impact of the National Minimum Wage on productivity is likely to be small, and extremely difficult to measure. The Federation of Small Businesses in Northern Ireland told us that the minimum wage had damaged incentives for some firms using piece rates. In contrast, we have evidence of companies which have made a virtue of necessity and taken steps to improve productivity. Other employers have also noted the protection given by the legislation from low-wage competitors. Large firms in security, for example, have favoured a National Minimum Wage because it reduces low-paying operators' ability to pitch for business based on unfair employment practices.

We commissioned the Economic and Social Research Council (ESRC) Centre for Business Research to examine the impact of the National Minimum Wage on employer responses among small and medium-sized enterprises (Hughes et al., 1999). From a survey of over 1500 enterprises between June and October 1999, they found that a sizeable minority of firms had attempted to improve their competitive performance, and a significant minority had invested in capital equipment to raise productivity. In general, there was more emphasis on cost advantage than product and service design. In cleaning and security, however, firms with a high proportion of low-paid workers were placing a stronger emphasis on improving product and service quality. The research concluded that this may be because there were fewer opportunities for non-wage competition in sectors where low wages were endemic.

In our own post-implementation survey of firms directly affected by the minimum wage, we found evidence of firms responding positively. Of these, three-fifths said they had made some changes to the way work was organised, one-third had increased their use of new technology, and one-third had improved the quality of service they provide. For many firms the changes were slight, though half of the firms had taken significant action to improve efficiency.

Prices

In our first report we concluded that the National Minimum Wage was likely to cause a small, temporary effect on prices, but that it was 'unlikely to cause a lasting increase in inflationary expectations'. From our evaluation, it is clear that, faced with pressures on their pay bill, employers in low-paying sectors have found a wide range of ways to adapt. So far, the effect on prices appears to have been extremely small, even when focusing on the products of low-paying sectors.

External factors, such as the strength of sterling and global economic weakness, have helped subdue inflation during the period when the National Minimum Wage was introduced. Moreover, we would expect its impact on prices to be spread over time because of employer anticipation, the time taken for compliance to develop, and time lags between rises in labour costs and adjustment in prices. We cannot, however, detect any impact on the aggregate Retail Prices Index in the first few months of the National Minimum Wage. In the six months following its introduction, underlying inflation has remained below its target of 2.5 per cent. Last year, the Bank of England estimated that the minimum wage would have a small, temporary effect on inflation, adding 0.4 per cent to prices over two years. In its November 1999 *Inflation Report*, it lowered the estimate of the impact on earnings growth by one-third, which would also indicate a weaker-than-expected impact on the price level.

The impact of the National Minimum Wage on prices has been concentrated on particular employers, and has been spread over time. More time is needed for the full effects to appear. For these reasons it is difficult to detect an effect in monthly economic data, even when looking at indices for low-paid products. We consider that factors other than the minimum wage will continue to dominate the general inflation outlook.

(a) In any discussion of a national minimum wage, why is it important to distinguish its impact on a competitive labour market from that on a labour market dominated by a monopsonistic employer?

(b) Why are certain industries likely to be more affected by the adoption of a minimum wage than others? How relevant might your answer to (a) be in answering this question?

(c) Given the evidence in the article, what conclusions can be drawn about the impact of the minimum wage on business?

(d) In the light of the evidence, discuss the case for and against increasing the national minimum wage.

ANSWERS

Q1. *the wage rate of plasterers*. We are referring to a perfect factor market: i.e. the market for plasterers, *not* the market for plaster or plastered walls. (These may or may not be perfect.)

Q2. *employers or workers*. Both demanders (employers) and suppliers (workers) are 'wage takers', under perfect competition.

Q3. *the supply curve of labour to*.

Q4. *the demand curve for labour from*.

Q5. (a) *supply; left*. Plasterers will be prepared to work fewer hours at any given wage rate.
(b) *demand; right*. Plaster is a complementary good. Thus as its price comes down, more of it will be demanded *and* hence also more plasterers will be demanded to use it.
(c) *demand; left*. As fewer houses are demanded so fewer plasterers will be needed.
(d) *supply; left*. This will push up plasterers' wages in other parts of the country and hence encourage plasterers to leave this part of the country to get jobs elsewhere.
(e) *demand; left*. This will push up the price of new buildings and hence lead to a lower quantity of them being demanded and hence a lower demand for plasterers.
Also: *supply; left*. Plasterers will be encouraged to move into other parts of the building trade.
(f) *demand; left*. Employers will try to economise on the number of plasterers they employ. Many small builders may do the plastering themselves instead.

Q6. E. The demand for a factor of production is derived from the demand for the good it is used to produce: the more of the good that is demanded, the more of the factor that will be demanded to produce it.

Q7. *marginal disutility* (the opportunity cost of work).

Q8. *upward sloping*. A higher wage rate will be necessary to persuade a person to work extra hours.

Q9. (a) *substitution effect*. People substitute income for leisure (leisure has a higher opportunity cost).
(b) *income effect*. People can afford to take more leisure.

Q10. *negative*. Here higher wage rates will encourage people to work *less*.

Q11. *positive*. Here higher wage rates encourage people to work *more*.

Q12. *income effect*. If this becomes dominant above a certain wage, the number of hours offered by the worker will get *less* as the wage rate rises.

Q13. *True*. The firm is a 'wage taker': i.e. it has to pay the market wage, but at that wage can employ as many workers as it likes.

Q14. D. (ii) is not correct because a change in the wage rate is shown by a movement *along* the supply curve. (iii) is not correct because it determines the *demand* for labour not the supply.

Q15. (a) *geographical*.
(b) *both*.
(c) *occupational*.
(d) *geographical*.
(e) *both*.
(f) *occupational*.

Q16. *economic rent*.

Q17. A. He earns £80 more than he could in the next best paid job (as a lorry driver). Thus he earns £80 more than is necessary to prevent him giving up being a model and becoming a lorry driver instead.

Q18. C. The vertical distance below the supply curve shows the wage the marginal worker must receive to persuade him or her to move to this job: it shows the marginal worker's transfer earnings. When all these transfer earnings are added together we get the total area under the supply curve.

Q19. B. The area between the supply curve and the wage rate (W_e) shows the excess of actual wages over the minimum needed to persuade workers to stay in this job.

Q20. (a) (vii); (b) (iii); (c) (v); (d) (i); (e) (vi); (f) (iv); (g) (ii).

Q21. MPP_L by MR.

Q22. *fewer*.

Q23. *more*.

Q24. *True*. Under perfect competition the firm will always demand that quantity of workers where $MRP_L = W$. Thus, like the demand-for-labour curve, the MRP_L curve shows for each wage the number of workers the firm will employ.

Q25. (a) *shift*.
(b) *movement along* (given that the wage rate is measured on the vertical axis).
(c) *shift*.

Q26. (a) *True*. A fall in W will lead to higher employment and more output. This will drive P down. If the demand for the good is elastic, this fall in P will lead to a lot more being sold and hence a lot more people being employed.
(b) *False*. If labour can be *readily* substituted for other factors, then a reduction in W will lead to a large increase in labour used to replace these other factors.
(c) *True*. If wage rates fall, a lot more labour will be demanded if plenty of complementary factors can be obtained at little increase in their price.
(d) *False*. If wage rates fall and more labour is used, less substitute factors will be demanded and

their price will fall. If their supply is *elastic*, a lot less will be supplied and therefore a lot more labour will be used instead.

  (e) *False*. If wages are a *large* proportion of total costs and wage rates fall, total costs will fall significantly; therefore production will increase significantly, and so, therefore, will the demand for labour.
  (f) *True*. Given sufficient time, firms can respond to a fall in wage rates by reorganising their production processes to make use of the now relatively cheap labour.

Q27. B. The perfect labour market will cause people with the *same* skills to be paid the same in the long run, but it will not cause people with a high level of skills to be paid the same as those with a low level of skills.

Q28. Market power; barriers to entry into various markets; imperfect knowledge.

Q29. (a) (iii); (b) (ii); (c) (i); (d) (v); (e) (iv).

Q30. *upward sloping*.

Q31. *supply curve of* labour. If the firm wants to employ extra workers, it will have to offer higher wages to attract the necessary labour into the market. Conversely, by cutting back on the number of workers it can force down the wage rate.

Q32. (a) See following table.

Wage rate (AC_L) (£)	50	60	70	80	90	100	110	120
Number of workers	1	2	3	4	5	6	7	8
Total wage bill (TC_L) (£)	50	120	210	320	450	600	770	960
Marginal cost of labour (MC_L) (£)		70	90	110	130	150	170	190

  (b) See Figure A9.1.
  (c) 5 workers (where $MRP_L = MC_L$).
  (d) £90 (as given by the supply curve).
  (e) 6 workers at £100 (where MRP_L = supply of labour).

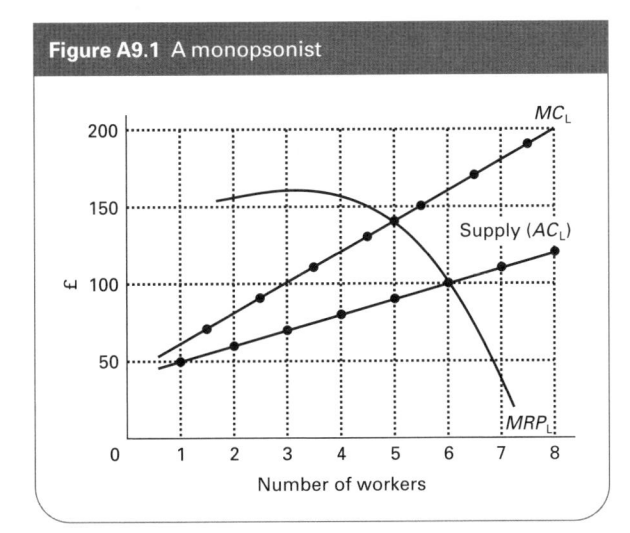

Figure A9.1 A monopsonist

Q33. *horizontal* (along to the point where it reaches the old supply curve: if it wants to employ beyond *that* point, it will have to pay *above* the negotiated rate in order to attract sufficient workers).

Q34. *equal to* (along to the point where it reaches the old supply curve: then it jumps up to the old MC_L curve).

Q35. (a) They are the same horizontal straight line at £100 up to 6 workers. Above that number of workers they are the same as the original curves.
  (b) 6 workers (where $MC_L = MRP_L$).
  (c) Because it is no longer in the position to be able to drive down the wage rate by cutting down on the number of employees. The MC_L has now become the same as the AC_L (a horizontal straight line).
  (d) £140. If this is the negotiated wage rate, it will now be the MC_L as well as the AC_L. Thus the firm will choose to employ 5 workers (the pre-union number) since this is where $MC_L = MRP_L$.
  (e) There is none! The actual wage will depend on the outcome of the bargain, but that cannot be predicted with any accuracy. It depends on how successful each side is in the negotiations.

Q36. (a) *Decrease* the union's power. The union will have less scope to press its claim.
  (b) *Decrease* the union's power. The firm can threaten to employ non-union labour; it can threaten redundancies (a greater threat when unemployment is high).
  (c) *Increase* the union's power. The firm will be more able to pass on any wage increases in higher prices (given that it expects inflation to cause competitor firms to raise their prices).
  (d) *Increase* the union's power. This will make it easier for the union to finance industrial action. It will also create more solidarity among workers and make it more difficult for the firm to recruit non-union labour.
  (e) *Decrease* the union's power. It will make the firm more resolved to resist high wage claims so that it can keep its prices competitive.
  (f) *Increase* the union's power. The firm will be more anxious to avoid a dispute so as not to allow other firms to capture this market. The firm may be anxious to take on extra labour. Also if the firm's profits have increased, it may be in a better position to pay higher wages.
  (g) *Increase* the union's power. The firm will not be able to use non-union labour or to divide the workforce by making separate (lower) offers to less militant groups of workers.
  (h) *Increase* the union's power. The firm will find it easier to pass on wage increases to the consumer in higher prices.

Q37. *Discrimination* (by race, sex, age, class, etc., i.e. not based on differences in productivity), *imperfect*

132 CHAPTER 9 THE THEORY OF DISTRIBUTION OF INCOME

knowledge of labour market conditions (by workers and/or employers), *non-maximising behaviour*.

Q38. *(a)* As time elapses, the costs to the worker of searching will increase. Thus the longer the typical worker is unsuccessful in getting a job, the lower the wage he or she would be prepared to settle for.

(b) The point on the horizontal axis corresponding to the intersection of the two curves.

(c) (i) W_a; *up*.
  (ii) W_o; *down*.
  (iii) W_a; *down*.
  (iv) W_o; *up*.

Q39. Yes: all except (f).

Q40. E. If it is discriminating, it is preferring to employ white workers to black even when black workers are more able. It is thus sacrificing profit. (Note that D is wrong because the lower wages are the *result* of lower demand for black workers by the employers in the industry in question.)

Q41. C. These imperfections, although they affect wages, will not affect a firm's choosing to employ people up to the point where $MRP_L = MC_L$.

Q42. *False*. Wage rates are the price of labour *services*. When a firm pays a person a week's wages, the wages are for the person's labour. The firm has not purchased the actual person.

Q43. *True*. The principle is the same.

Q44. The diagram will be similar to Figure A9.1, but with the amount of capital measured on the horizontal axis. The amount of capital equipment the firm will hire is given by the intersection of the MC_K and MRP_K curves. The hire charge is given by the AC_K curve (i.e. the supply of capital curve).

Q45. *marginal revenue*.

Q46. Yes: (b), (d) and (e). These are all opportunity costs since they vary with the amount that the equipment is hired out.

Q47. E. The lower the price of complementary factors, the more of them will be demanded and hence the more capital equipment will be demanded. This will push up its market price.

Q48. £100 (i.e. £100 invested at 10 per cent will be worth £110 after one year).

Q49. Using the discounting formula gives:

(a) $PV = £5000/1.05 + £5000/1.05^2 + £5000/1.05^3$
    $= £4761.90 + £4535.15 + £4319.19$
    $= £13\,616.24$

Therefore the investment is profitable at a 5 per cent discount rate.

(b) $PV = £5000/1.1 + £5000/1.1^2 + £5000/1.1^3$
    $= £4545.45 + £4132.23 + £3756.57$
    $= £12\,434.25$

Therefore the investment is also profitable at a 10 per cent discount rate.

(c) $PV = £5000/1.2 + £5000/1.2^2 + £5000/1.2^3$
    $= £4166.67 + £3472.22 + £2893.52$
    $= £10\,532.41$

Therefore the investment is not profitable at a 20 per cent discount rate.

Q50. *(a)* *Fall*. Caused by an increase in the supply of loanable funds.

(b) *Rise*. Caused by firms wanting to invest more and thus demanding more loans.

(c) *Rise*. Caused by a rise in investment demand as firms respond to the rise in consumer demand; also by a decrease in savings as a result of the increased spending.

(d) *Rise*: if the demand for machinery is inelastic. More will now be spent on machinery and thus more funds will be required. *Fall*: if the demand for machinery is elastic and thus less funds will be demanded.

Q51. (a) *External*; (b) *Internal*; (c) *External*; (d) *External*. 'Internal' means financed from within the firm.

Q52. *Advantages*: (a) It enables savings to be mobilised to generate output. (b) Firms listed on the stock exchange are subject to regulations. This is likely to stimulate investor confidence, making it easier for business to raise finance. (c) It makes mergers and takeovers easier, thereby increasing competition for corporate control.

Disadvantages: (a) The cost to a business of getting listed can be immense; (b) Directors' and senior managers' decisions will often be driven by how the market is likely to react, rather by what they perceive to be in the business's best interests. (c) It can encourage short-termism.

Q53. (a) (iii); (b) (i); (c) (ii).

Q54. *(a)* *rise*. Being a derived demand, the *demand* for arable land would *rise* and hence the rent would *rise*.

(b) *rise*. The rise in the demand for beef would encourage farmers to move from cereals to beef production. This would cause a shortage of cereals and hence a rise in the price of cereals. This would cause the *demand* for arable land to *rise*. Also the switching of land to beef production would cause a *fall* in the *supply* of land for cereal production. Both effects will lead to a *rise* in rent on arable land.

(c) *fall*. The reclamation scheme would *increase* the *supply* of land.

(d) *fall*. The quantity of grain supplied would fall and hence the *demand* for arable land would *fall*.

(e) *rise*. The set-aside scheme would *reduce* the *supply* of arable land.

Q55. *(a)* *Land in total*: i.e. for all uses (assuming that land cannot be reclaimed from the sea or from deserts).

(b) *Land for specific uses*. The higher the rent or price of land for a specific use (e.g. building houses), the more land will be offered for sale for that purpose and thus transferred from other uses (e.g. agriculture).

Q56. A. All these cause a higher demand for land in city centres.

Q57. A. If the supply curve is totally inelastic, there are no transfer earnings: all rent is economic rent. The *size* of the economic rent will depend on the position of the demand curve relative to the supply curve.

Q58. (a) £2000/0.1 = £20 000.
(b) £2000/0.2 = £10 000.

Chapter Ten
10
Inequality, Poverty and Policies to Redistribute Incomes

A REVIEW

In this chapter we examine the distribution of income in practice and ask why incomes are unequally distributed. We start by looking at different ways of measuring inequality and poverty, and then examine their causes.

We then turn to look at what can be done. In particular we look at the role of taxes and benefits as means of redistributing incomes.

10.1 Inequality and poverty

(Pages 254–6) There are a number of different ways of looking at the distribution of income and wealth. Each way highlights a different aspect of inequality.

Q1. Match the following measures of inequality (i)–(x) to the examples (a)–(j).
  (i) Size distribution of income.
  (ii) Functional distribution of income: broad factor categories.
  (iii) Functional distribution of income: narrow factor categories.
  (iv) Functional distribution of income: occupational.
  (v) Distribution of income by recipient: class of person.
  (vi) Distribution of income by recipient: geographical.
  (vii) Size distribution of wealth.
  (viii) Distribution of wealth by class of holder.
  (ix) Absolute poverty.
  (x) Relative poverty.

(a) The average income of manual workers compared with non-manual.

....

(b) The percentage of people with an income below what is considered to be a minimum acceptable level.

....

(c) The average level of income in the south-east compared with that in the north-west.

....

(d) Profits as a proportion of national income.

....

(e) The proportion of total savings held by people over retirement age.

....

(f) The ratio of the income of the richest 20 per cent to that of the poorest 40 per cent.

....

Multiple choice — *Written answer* — *Delete wrong word* — *Diagram/table manipulation* — *Calculation* — *Matching/ordering*

(g) The average income of doctors compared with that of nurses.

....

(h) The number of people without adequate food and shelter.

....

(i) The proportion of the nation's assets held by the richest 1 per cent of the population.

....

(j) The average income of one-parent families as a proportion of the national average income.

....

(Pages 256–7) The size distribution of income can be measured by the use of *Lorenz curves* and *Gini coefficients*.

⊖ **Q2.** Assume that the economy is grouped into five equal-sized groups of households according to income. The figures (imaginary) are shown in Table 10.1.

Draw two Lorenz curves corresponding to these two sets of figures on Figure 10.1.

Table 10.1 Percentage size distribution of income by quintile groups of households

	Quintile groups			
Lowest 20%	Next 20%	Middle 20%	Next 20%	Highest 20%
Income before taxes and benefits				
1.0	6.0	15.0	25.0	53.0
Income after taxes and benefits				
6.0	10.0	17.0	22.0	45.0

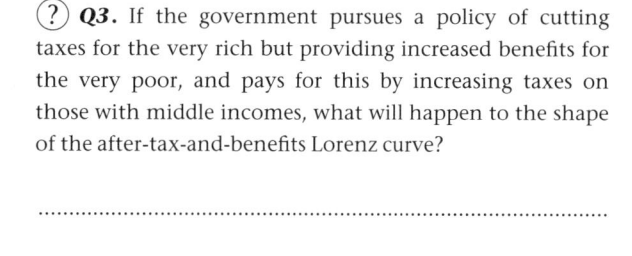

Figure 10.1 Lorenz curves corresponding to Table 10.1

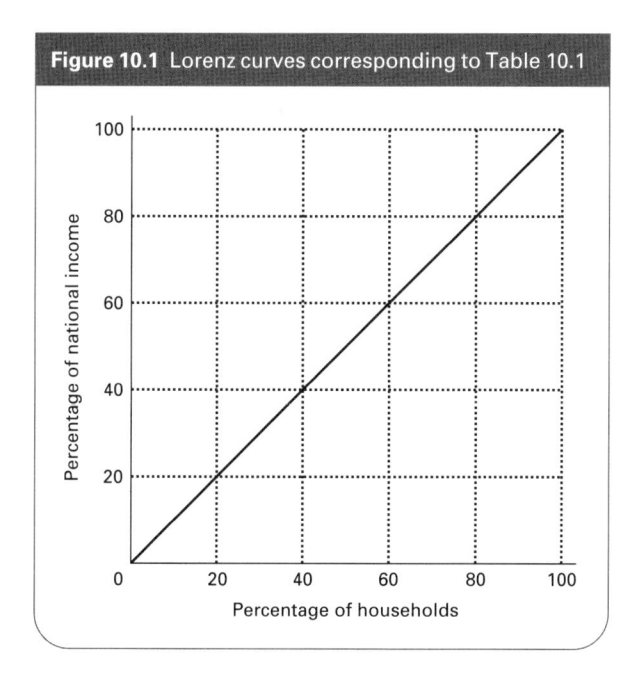

(?) **Q3.** If the government pursues a policy of cutting taxes for the very rich but providing increased benefits for the very poor, and pays for this by increasing taxes on those with middle incomes, what will happen to the shape of the after-tax-and-benefits Lorenz curve?

....

....

The Gini coefficient is a way of measuring in a single figure the information contained in the Lorenz curve.

Q4. In Figure 10.2 the Gini coefficient is the ratio of areas:
A. Y to Z
B. Z to $(X + Y + Z)$
C. Z to $(Y + Z)$
D. Y to $(Y + Z)$
E. Y to $(X + Y + Z)$

Figure 10.2 A Lorenz curve

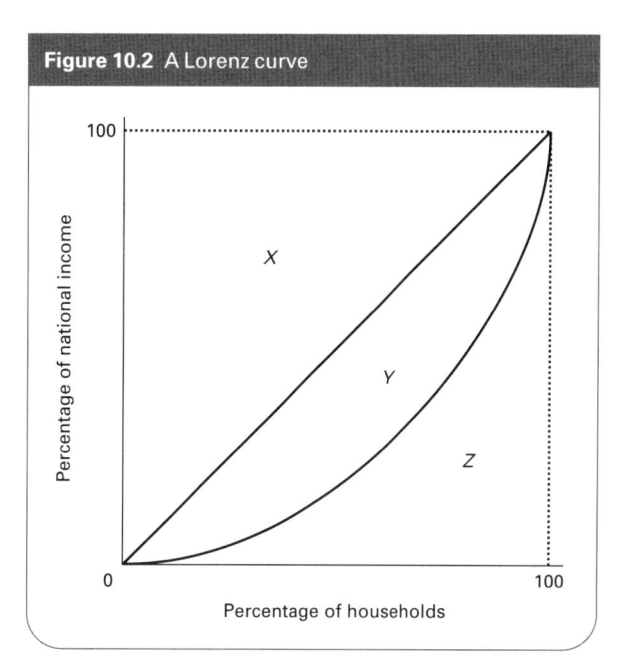

Q5. If the Gini coefficient rises, this means that income distribution has become more equal. *True/False*

(Pages 257–65) A common way of representing the degree of inequality in a country is to look at the functional distribution of income by source.

⊖ **Q6.** Table 10.2 shows the sources of UK household income by quintile groups. What do the figures suggest are the major causes of inequality in incomes?

....

....

CHAPTER 10 INEQUALITY, POVERTY AND POLICIES TO REDISTRIBUTE INCOMES

Table 10.2 Sources of UK household income as a percentage of total household income: 2000/1

Gross household weekly incomes (quintiles)	Wages and salaries (1)	Income from self-employment (2)	Income from investments (3)	Pensions and annuities (4)	Social security benefits (5)	Other (6)	Total (7)
Lowest 20%	6	1	3	8	80	2	100
Next 20%	31	5	4	15	43	2	100
Middle 20%	62	6	4	11	15	1	100
Next 20%	75	7	3	8	6	2	100
Highest 20%	77	12	4	3	2	1	100
All households	67	9	4	7	12	1	100

Source: *Family Spending* (National Statistics, 2002).

There is marked inequality of income between females and males. The average gross hourly earnings of full-time adult female workers is only 80 per cent of those of full-time adult male workers.

Q7. Although the average wage of women is less than that of men, the average wage of women is approximately the same as that for men *in the same occupation*. True/False

Q8. The distribution of wealth in the UK is less equal than the distribution of income. True/False

Q9. Give four different causes of the inequality of wealth.

1. ....

2. ....

3. ....

4. ....

Q10. The following are possible causes of inequality:
(i) Differences in wealth.
(ii) Differences in attitudes.
(iii) Differences in power.
(iv) Differences in household composition.
(v) The proportion of the population over retirement age.
(vi) The proportion of the population below working age.

Which can help to explain inequality in wage rates?
A. (iii) only.
B. (ii) and (iii).
C. (i), (ii) and (iii).
D. (i), (ii), (iii) and (iv).
E. (i)–(vi).

Q11. Referring to the same list of possible causes of inequality as in Q10, which can help to explain inequality between households?

A. (iv) only.
B. (i) and (iv).
C. (iv), (v) and (vi).
D. (i), (iv), (v), and (vi).
E. (i)–(vi).

10.2 Taxes, benefits and the redistribution of income

(Pages 266–70) We turn now to the role of the government in redistributing incomes more equally. The two means of redistributing income that we shall consider are taxes and benefits. We first examine taxation.

Principles of taxation

Q12. The following is a list of requirements that people have argued should be met by a good tax system:
(i) Equitable between recipients of benefits (the benefits principle).
(ii) Convenient to the government.
(iii) Horizontally equitable.
(iv) Minimal disincentive effects.
(v) Non-distortionary.
(vi) Vertically equitable.
(vii) Difficult to avoid.
(viii) Difficult to evade.
(ix) Convenient to the taxpayer.
(x) Cheap to collect.

Match the following descriptions to each of the above requirements.

(a) Taxes whose amount paid is the same for people in the same economic circumstances.

....

(b) Taxes whose rates can be quickly and simply adjusted.

....

(c) Taxes where the authorities can easily prevent illegal non-payment.

....

CHAPTER 10 INEQUALITY, POVERTY AND POLICIES TO REDISTRIBUTE INCOMES   137

(d) Taxes with minimal administrative costs.

....

(e) Taxes where people pay in proportion to the amount of public services they use.

....

(f) Taxes that do not alter market signals in an undesirable direction.

....

(g) Taxes that people cannot escape paying by finding legal loopholes.

....

(h) Taxes that do not discourage initiative or effort.

....

(i) Taxes whose method of payment is easily understood and straightforward.

....

(j) Taxes whose rates depend on people's ability to pay.

....

Q13. Why may there be a conflict between the principle of vertical equity and the benefits principle?

....

....

Q14. How well do the following two taxes meet (i) the vertical equity principle and (ii) the benefits principle?

(a) Income tax:

(i) ....

....

(ii) ....

....

(b) A flat charge on all individuals, such as the community charge (poll tax), used in the UK in the early 1990s:

(i) ....

....

(ii) ....

....

(Pages 270–1) Taxes as a means of redistributing incomes
The degree of redistribution will depend on the degree of progressiveness of the tax.

Taxes can be categorised as *progressive, regressive, proportional* or *lump sum* (where lump-sum taxes are an extreme form of regressive tax).

Q15. Figure 10.3 shows how these four different categories of tax vary with income. Diagram (a) shows the total amount of tax paid. Diagram (b) shows the average tax rate. On each diagram which of the four curves correspond to which category of tax?

(a) Progressive   Curve ....

Regressive   Curve ....

Proportional   Curve ....

Lump sum   Curve ....

(b) Progressive   Curve ....

Regressive   Curve ....

Proportional   Curve ....

Lump sum   Curve ....

Figure 10.3 The variation of different taxes with income

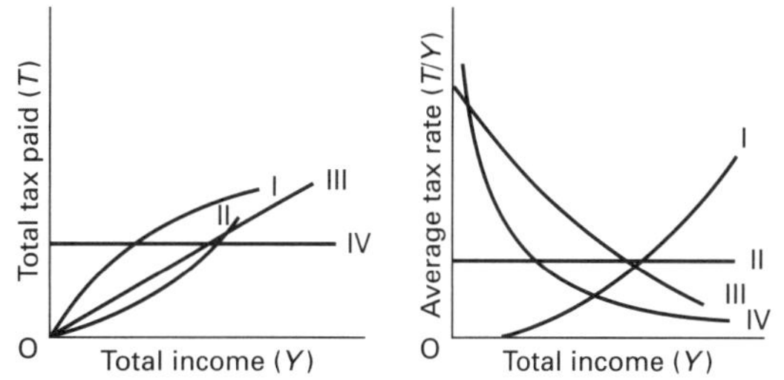

(a) Total tax paid

(b) Average tax rates

Q16. If Clyde's income tax goes up from £1000 to £1100 as a result of a rise in his income from £10 000 to £10 400:

(a) What was his original average rate of tax? ....

(b) What is his new average rate of tax? ....

(c) What is his marginal rate of tax? ....

Q17. An income tax levied at a constant marginal rate with a tax-free allowance of £5000 will be a proportional tax. *True/False*

Q18. Indirect taxes levied at the same rate on all goods would be:
A. progressive.
B. regressive.
C. proportional.
D. lump sum.
E. progressive at low levels of national income and regressive at high levels.

(Pages 271–3) There are various problems in using taxes to redistribute incomes. For example, there are difficulties in helping the very poor.

Q19. Since taxes *take away* incomes, changing taxes alone cannot benefit the poor. To give additional help to the poor will require additional *benefits*. *True/False*

Q20. Which of the following will provide most help to the very poorest people in society? (In each case assume the total reduction in tax revenue for the government is the same.)
A. Cutting the rate of income tax.
B. Increasing tax thresholds on income tax.
C. Reducing excise duties.
D. Reducing the main rate for national insurance contributions.
E. Reducing VAT on basic goods.

Q21. Which of the following will provide most help to those on low incomes but who nevertheless are still liable to income tax? (As before, in each case assume the total reduction in tax revenue for the government is the same.)
A. Cutting the rate of income tax.
B. Increasing tax thresholds on income tax.
C. Reducing excise duties.
D. Reducing the main rate for national insurance contributions.
E. Reducing VAT on basic goods.

The effectiveness of a rise in income tax in redistributing incomes away from high-paid workers will depend on the elasticity of supply of labour.

Q22. The more elastic the supply of high-paid workers, the more effective will be an income tax in redistributing income away from this group. *True/False*

(Pages 273–5) Taxes and incentives
Perhaps the biggest drawback of using taxes to redistribute incomes is that they create *disincentives*.

Q23. The effects of imposing an income tax can be divided into an *income effect* and a *substitution effect*. Which of these two effects will be to:
(a) *increase* the amount people work?
Income effect/Substitution effect
(b) *decrease* the amount people work?
Income effect/Substitution effect

Whether people thus work more or less after a rise in income tax will depend on which of the two effects is the larger.

Q24. Which of the two effects of a rise in the rates of income tax is likely to be the larger in each of the following cases?
(a) For people with large long-term commitments (e.g. mortgages). *Income effect/Substitution effect*
(b) For second income earners in a family where the second income is not relied upon for 'essential' consumption. *Income effect/Substitution effect*
(c) For those on very high incomes.
Income effect/Substitution effect
(d) For people with large families.
Income effect/Substitution effect
(e) For those just above the tax threshold.
Income effect/Substitution effect

Q25. The Laffer curve shows that:
A. At very high levels of income tax, the government can expect to earn very high levels of revenue.
B. The government's tax revenue will be highest when the marginal rate of income tax is 50 per cent.
C. A rise in income tax beyond a certain level will reduce the government's tax revenue.
D. The government's tax revenue is at a maximum when the substitution effect begins to outweigh the income effect.
E. Tax revenues will be at a maximum when the marginal rate of tax is equal to the average rate.

Q26. Raising the higher rate(s) of income tax (but leaving the basic rate unchanged) will have a relatively small income effect and a relatively large substitution effect. *True/False*

Q27. For all those above the old tax threshold, reducing tax allowances will have no disincentive effect at all. *True/False*

CHAPTER 10 INEQUALITY, POVERTY AND POLICIES TO REDISTRIBUTE INCOMES

The relationship between income taxes and incentives can be examined in the context of tax *cuts* as well as that of tax increases. If income tax rates are cut, people will choose to work *more* if the income effect **Q28.** *outweighs/is outweighed by* the substitution effect. For people already above the tax threshold, this will only be likely if tax cuts come in the form of **Q29.** *cuts in the basic rate of income tax/increases in tax allowances*.

(Pages 275–6) State benefits
Some benefits are *means tested* and some are *universal*.

Q30. Which of the following are universal benefits and which are means-tested benefits?
(a) State pensions — universal/means tested
(b) Child benefit — universal/means tested
(c) Contribution-based jobseeker's allowance — universal/means tested
(d) Income-based jobseeker's allowance — universal/means tested
(e) Working families tax credit — universal/means tested
(f) Housing benefit — universal/means tested
(g) Income support — universal/means tested
(see: http://www.dwp.gov.uk)

Q31. Four of the following are possible problems with means-tested benefits. Which one is *not* a problem?
A. They tend to have a lower take-up rate than universal benefits.
B. They cost the taxpayer more to provide a given amount of help to the poor than do universal benefits.
C. The application procedure may deter some potential claimants.
D. If based solely on income, they may ignore the special needs of certain people.
E. They may act as a disincentive to getting a job.

(Pages 276–9) When means-tested benefits are combined with a progressive tax system there can be a serious problem with disincentives. A situation known as the 'poverty trap' can arise.

Q32. What is meant by the *poverty trap*?

....
....
....

Q33. If the marginal tax rate is 25 per cent and if for each extra £10 of take-home pay a person loses benefits of £6, what is the marginal tax-plus-lost-benefit rate?

....

One simple combined system of taxes and benefits which avoids the poverty trap is that of the *negative income tax*.

Q34. If everyone were entitled to a tax-free benefit of £1000 per annum (a 'negative income tax') paid by the tax authorities, and if the tax rate were 20 per cent, what would your net tax liability be if your income were:
(a) zero? ....
(b) £1000? ....
(c) £5000? ....
(d) £10 000? ....
(e) What is the marginal rate of tax-plus-lost-benefit?
....

Q35. What is the major drawback of a negative income tax system?

....
....

B PROBLEMS, EXERCISES AND PROJECTS

Q36. Refer to the latest edition of *Social Trends* (published annually by National Statistics). This should be taken by all university, college and reference libraries. It can also be downloaded from the 'Bookshelf' section of the National Statistics site: http://www.statistics.gov.uk. Turn to the chapter on income and wealth.
(a) Provide a summary of income distribution in the UK as described in this chapter.
(b) To what extent does the tax and benefit system redistribute incomes more equally?
(c) How has income distribution and redistribution changed between the years illustrated in the various tables? (You could also look at earlier editions of *Social Trends* for a more complete analysis, but be careful that the methods of calculating the statistics have not changed.)
(d) Identify any measures of inequality for which you think figures ought to be given if a more comprehensive analysis is to be provided.

Another, more complete, source is *Family Spending*, again published by National Statistics. Like *Social Trends*, it can be downloaded from the 'Bookshelf' section of the National Statistics Web site.

140 CHAPTER 10 INEQUALITY, POVERTY AND POLICIES TO REDISTRIBUTE INCOMES

Q37. In groups of two or three, write a report on the changing pattern of poverty in the UK since 1980. This report should include the use of five different indicators of poverty, a clear description of the pattern and an explanation of why changes in the pattern may have occurred. Conduct your own search for sources of information. To help in this, try using a search engine, such as http://www.google.co.uk. You should also find the Joseph Rowntree Foundation site useful at http://www.jrf.org.uk.

Q38. To which of the four categories in Q15 do each of the following types of tax belong?
(a) Income £10 000, tax £1000; income £20 000, tax £2000

....

(b) Income £10 000, tax £5000; income £20 000, tax £9000

....

(c) Income £10 000, tax £2000; income £20 000, tax £5000

....

(d) Income £10 000, tax £0; income £20 000, tax £400

....

(e) Income £10 000, tax £400; income £20 000, tax £400

....

(f) Income £10 000, tax £400; income £20 000, tax £4000

....

(g) Income £10 000, tax £8000; income £20 000, tax £12 000

....

Q39. Figure 10.4 shows the effect of imposing an indirect tax on a good produced under conditions of perfect competition. It can be used to illustrate the resource costs of the tax. The tax has the effect of raising the equilibrium price from P_1 to P_2 and reducing the equilibrium quantity from Q_1 to Q_2.
(a) Which area(s) represent(s) the original level of consumer surplus?

....

(b) Which area(s) represent(s) the loss in consumer surplus after the imposition of the tax?

....

(c) Which area(s) represent(s) the original level of profits for the producers?

....

Figure 10.4 The effect of imposing an indirect tax on a good

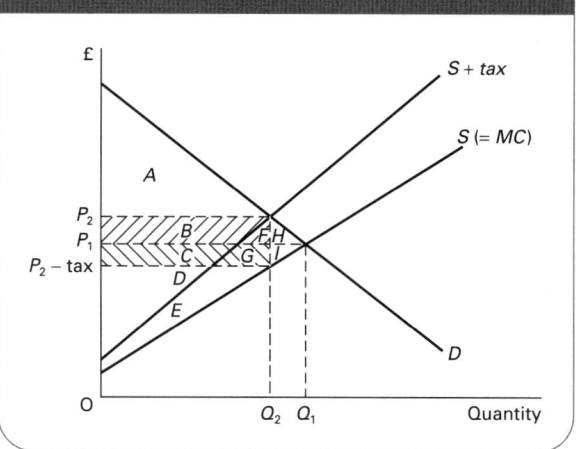

(d) Which area(s) represent(s) the loss in profits after the imposition of the tax?

....

(e) Which area(s) represent(s) the total loss to consumers and producers after the imposition of the tax?

....

(f) Which area(s) represent(s) the gain in tax revenue to the government after the imposition of the tax?

....

(g) Which area(s), therefore, represent the net loss to society as a whole after the imposition of the tax?

....

(h) Name two weaknesses in using this type of analysis to criticise the imposition of taxes.

1. ....

2. ....

*Q40. Figure 10.5 uses indifference analysis to show the effect of a tax cut on a person's choice between income and leisure. Assume that the person has 14 hours per day to distribute between work and leisure.
(a) Which of the two budget lines show the person's available choices *after* the tax cut? B_1/B_2
(b) How many hours will the person work before the tax cut?

....

Figure 10.5 A person's choice between income and leisure

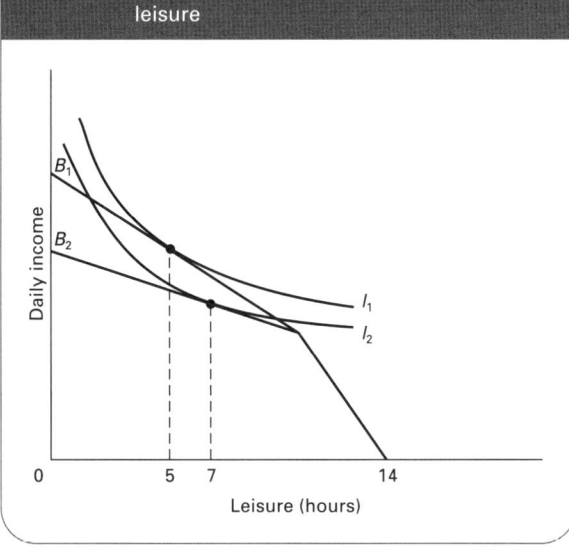

(c) How many hours will the person work after the tax cut?

....

(d) What is the size of the income effect? ....

(e) What is the size of the substitution effect? ....

(f) Draw new indifference curves to illustrate the situation where the income effect outweighs the substitution effect.

(g) How would you illustrate an increase in tax allowances on this type of diagram?

....

....

C) DISCUSSION TOPICS AND ESSAYS

Q41. What limitations are there in using Gini coefficients to compare the degree of inequality in different countries?

Q42. How well do the following taxes meet the requirements of a good tax system: (a) highly progressive income taxes; (b) VAT at a single rate on all goods and services; (c) excise duty on cigarettes?

Q43. What are the (UK) working tax credit and the child tax credit? (Details can be found on the Treasury site at www.hm-treasury.gov.uk.) Why might these be a better means of reducing poverty than a universal welfare benefit, such as child benefit?

Q44. 'The economic costs of an indirect tax will exceed the benefits.' Discuss with reference to its effect on producer and consumer surplus.

Q45. What effects will (a) cuts in basic rates of income tax and (b) increases in income tax allowances have on the labour supply of (i) high income earners, (ii) low income earners and (iii) those currently choosing not to work?

Q46. Discuss whether it is possible to reduce income inequality without creating disincentives to effort.

Q47. What is meant by the *poverty trap*? Will the targeting of benefits to those in greatest need necessarily increase the problem of the poverty trap?

Q48. Debate
Government intervention through tax-and-spend policies is the only solution to the problem of income inequality.

D) ARTICLES

Poverty breeds poverty. That seems to be the message of two reports published by the Joseph Rowntree Foundation. What are the economic consequences of this, both for the poor themselves, and for the wider community? The following review of the report is by Cherry Norton. It appeared in *The Independent* of 29 March 1999.

Successive generations of children may be 'learning to be poor'

Children growing up in low-income families may be 'learning to be poor' from an early age as diminished expectations of what their parents can afford lead them to scale down their hopes and aspirations for the future.

The ways that children's experiences of poverty affect their future welfare are examined in two research reports published by the Joseph Rowntree Foundation. They consider how children respond to growing up in a low income family, and analyse the risks that high levels of relative poverty among today's children may carry for future generations.

Taken together, they highlight many of the pressing problems that must be tackled if the Government's 20-year goal of overcoming child poverty – set earlier this month by the Prime Minister – is to be reached.

Poor children's attitudes to money

A study based on interviews with more than 400 children shows that those who live with a lone parent or in families claiming Income Support are more likely than other children to be frequently told that things they want are unaffordable. It found that:

- Children living in households claiming Income Support (42 per cent) were five times more likely to think that their family income was inadequate than other children (8 per cent). Children in lone-parent families (39 per cent) were four times more likely to believe it than children in two-parent families (9 per cent).
- Children living in lone-parent and Income Support families were more likely to have been involved in family discussions about money and spending. Two-thirds said they were often told that their family could not afford what they wanted, compared with less than half other children.
- Asked which presents they would like if it was their birthday next week, the children in lone-parent and Income Support families listed items that were significantly less expensive on average than those identified by other children.
- Children in lone-parent and Income Support families were less likely to receive regular pocket money than others. Although children in low income families were less likely to have part-time jobs, those who did worked for longer hours and lower rates of pay than other children.

Children in lone-parent or Income Support families had much lower expectations about their future careers than their peers. They were more likely than other youngsters to want jobs that required few qualifications and little training. And they were less likely to aspire to attaining professional qualifications or occupations.

Sue Middleton of the Centre for Research in Social Policy at Loughborough University, the study's co-author, said: 'As children learn about their family's financial situation, so they form views of where they stand in relation to other families. Our research suggests that children from low income families are learning to expect and accept less from an early age and to find ways of covering up their disappointment.'

She added: 'It seems entirely possible that for some children it is early learning of this sort that reduces both their immediate expectations and their future aspirations. There is a real sense in which they are learning to be poor.'

Child poverty and its consequences

A study by researchers at the Centre for Economic Performance at the London School of Economics shows how the number of children living in homes that are relatively poor is dramatically higher than 30 years ago. As many as one in three children (over 4.3 million) were living in households with less than half average income in 1995/96 compared with one in ten in 1968.

It also finds that spending by the poorest fifth of the population on toys, children's clothing, shoes and fresh fruit was no higher in real terms in 1995/96 than it was almost 30 years earlier. This evidence suggests that increasing inequality in expenditure has had a direct impact on the well-being of children and served to exclude them from the rising living standards of the prosperous majority.

Data from large-scale national surveys enable the researchers to calculate that a fifth of the rise in child poverty is attributable to an increase in the number of children living in lone-parent families. However, they find that a more important factor has been unemployment and the increasing chances that children find themselves in 'work poor' families where no adult has a paid job.

Using results from a long-term survey that has traced the development of children born in 1958 through to adulthood, the researchers demonstrate how social disadvantage during childhood has been linked to an increased risk of low earnings, unemployment and other adversity by the age of 33. Among family-based measures, poverty has been by far the most important force linking childhood development with later social and economic problems. Growing up in a lone-parent family has only been a significant factor when associated with family poverty.

Pursuing the links between poverty affecting one generation and the next, the study also finds that 33-year old parents in the survey who were themselves disadvantaged as children are more likely than other parents to have children who were performing poorly in school at an early age.

Stephen Machin, co-author of the report, said: 'Our study shows how the economic position of families strongly affects the present and future welfare of children. It suggests that today's high level of child poverty is likely to have continuing negative effects as the present generation of children in low income families grows up. Conversely, any measures that successfully address child poverty, especially by giving more households access to jobs, are likely to have wide-ranging, positive effects that go beyond improving the immediate welfare of children.'

(a) How does the article suggest that children 'learn to be poor', and how is this perpetuated between generations?

(b) What factors are argued to be responsible for the rise in child poverty?

(c) Given the findings of the report, what policies would you recommend to reverse the rise in child poverty?

(d) In April 2003, the government introduced the child tax credit (CTC). Find out what the CTC is and how it might help alleviate child poverty. Visit the Low Pay Unit (www.lowpay.gov.uk) to find information.

The UK, like most other European countries, is facing a pensions crisis – how to pay for them. As people live longer and demands on state pension funds grow, governments are increasingly looking for individuals to take more responsibility for their own pension arrangements. In this article, taken from the *Financial Times* of 14 March 2002, the UK government's pensions policy is evaluated.

Policy seen as complex and failing its target audience

Three years ago the government's pension policy was widely praised – by the pensions industry, by academic analysts and even, up to a point, by the opposition and charities for the elderly.

But now it is increasingly under fire from all sides. Changed stock market conditions, new accounting rules and greater longevity are causing big problems for final salary schemes, the traditional bedrock of private sector provision.

The planned pension credit – extra help that the government has introduced for people with small pension savings – is criticised for reducing the incentive to save. And the rebates intended to encourage people to opt out of the state second pension are being attacked for being too small, making it likely that hundreds of thousands will opt back into state provision.

Government policy has in essence four aims: to provide a better deal for today's poorer pensioners; to make private pension saving easier and safer; to ensure it is rewarded; and to reverse over time the balance of retirement income so that 60 per cent comes from private saving and only 40 per cent from the state.

To do that it has massively boosted means-tested income for today's poorest pensioners – to £100 a week from this April. At the same time the existing second state pension – Serps – is being re-cast into the new State Second Pension, which will be more generous to the low-paid: those on roughly £10,000 a year or less.

To make such private saving easier and safer, the government last April introduced stakeholder pensions – low-charge, flexible products that can be stopped, started and transferred without penalty.

To ensure that saving is worthwhile, it is introducing the pension credit. From October 2003, this will ensure that those with small savings see some benefit – rather than losing out compared to people who have never saved but qualify for means-tested help.

The policy is under fire on a number of fronts. First, final salary schemes are fracturing. More and more are closing to new members, and some have started closing to existing members. In general, employers tend to contribute less to money purchase pensions than final salary schemes – cutting total saving unless employees contribute more.

Some 700,000 stakeholder pensions have been sold. But the early evidence is that few have been used to opt out of the state system. Nor is it clear how many have been sold to the target group of low-to-moderate earners. And the pension credit is said to make it difficult to advise low-earners on what they should do.

The Institute for Public Policy Research, the left-of-centre think-tank, says pensions are now far too complex, and that the policy does not help to boost private saving.

Its view is shared by some in the pensions industry. The institute has argued that it should all be simplified dramatically by abolishing the second state pension and significantly increasing the basic state pension. That, it argues, would cut out much means-testing while providing clear incentives to save. It also says the state retirement age should be raised to 67 to help pay for it all.

(a) What is the main criticism that the article makes of government policy? In what way is the government not helping to solve the problems facing the pensions industry?

(b) Why does the government want people to opt out of the state pensions system?

(c) The government is reluctant to raise the retirement age to 67 (as suggested by the Institute of Public Policy Research). Why do you think this might be?

Why is it that the highest earners in a society are not necessarily those who pay the highest rates of tax? The article below, taken from the *OECD Observer* of Summer 1999, tells you why and identifies some of the implications.

Who pays the highest income tax?

It is not always high earners who pay the highest marginal rates of taxes on income. This assertion may appear to contradict what one would expect of progressive tax systems. Yet, in most OECD countries many individuals in low- to middle-income brackets find themselves exposed to higher marginal rates – that is the rate applied to the last additional dollar, yen or franc earned – than even the very rich. The question is why? Part of the answer lies in 'bubbles', which are humps in the structure of taxes on income. Bubbles can develop in cases where income is subject to both

144 CHAPTER 10 INEQUALITY, POVERTY AND POLICIES TO REDISTRIBUTE INCOMES

personal income tax and social security contributions. The tax base of those contributions may be identical or similar to that used for personal income tax. But unlike for income tax, a ceiling or cap often applies; earnings above that ceiling are not subject to social security contributions. A bubble appears if the combined marginal rate of income tax and 'capped' social security contributions exceeds the marginal income tax rate applicable to income earned above that contributions ceiling. For example, take a country that imposes social security contributions at a flat rate of 15 per cent on the first 50 000 units of income. Also, suppose the first 25 000 units earned are subject to 10 per cent personal income tax, the second 25 000 units is taxed at 20 per cent, and all income over 50 000 is taxed at the top rate of 30 per cent. To judge by the headline rate alone, the latter rate of 30 per cent would seem like the highest of the lot. But in practice it is those with taxable income in the middle bracket who pay the highest marginal rate, since the marginal income tax and social security add up to 35 per cent of their additional earnings. But taxpayers in the highest bracket are not required to pay the 15 per cent social security contribution and so only pay 30 per cent on their highest earnings.

But bubbles do not just show up in 'all-in' rates of the combined taxes on income. Occasionally, they appear in standard personal income tax schedules as well. In the second half of the 1980s the US federal income tax had such a rate structure. At the time, income in the first bracket was taxed at 15 per cent and income in the top bracket at 28 per cent. It follows that tax relief for high-income earners, which is determined by the marginal tax rate, was almost twice the tax relief for low-income earners. To recoup the higher tax relief for well-off taxpayers, lawmakers introduced a new 33 per cent bracket which they sandwiched between the low and high brackets. The new middle rate worked like this. Suppose for the sake of illustration that the personal exemption on income tax was $4000 across the board. Under the old structure before the 33 per cent band was created the tax bill of low-income earners would have been reduced by $600, since with the exemption they would not have had to pay the 15 per cent tax on that $4000. The tax bill for those in the highest taxed bracket would have been slashed by $1120, because they would have been exempt from paying 28 per cent on their highest $4000 of income. The difference of $520 in favour of higher earners was clawed back by inserting a middle bracket of $10 400 taxed at 33 per cent, that means 5 per cent more tax to pay than before, or $520. So, although the tax relief for the highest earners remained at 28 per cent, or $1120, by taxing middle earnings more, the new bracket effectively balanced the tax relief for those in the low and the top brackets at $600. The rates of the federal income tax in Switzerland show a similar 'bubble' today.

A job can make you poorer

Another rather curious situation which does not show up when studying headline rates is that low earners can find themselves confronted with very high marginal tax rates, in some rare cases exceeding 100 per cent. The reason for this is that lower earners not only pay more tax when their income goes up, but in many cases they lose part of their means-tested tax relief, subsidies and benefits as well. The loss of this income acts as an 'implicit' tax at the margin. The rational response of workers who find themselves in this situation is to reduce the number of hours they work. Their gross wage would of course be lower if they did, but in return they would pay less tax and receive more means-tested subsidies and benefits. As a result, their net disposable income would increase despite putting in fewer hours.

This type of situation occurs to varying degrees in different OECD countries, depending on the peculiarities of various social protection programmes. Take the example of an unemployed couple with two young children. Suppose that after five years' unemployment, one of them takes up a lowly paid job. In Finland or Sweden net income in and out of work would be the same in that case, since each unit of income earned is cancelled out by a unit of benefits forgone once employment is taken up. In other words, there is an implicit tax rate of 100 per cent. In the case of Denmark and the Czech Republic, the implicit rate in a similar case would be almost 100 per cent, and in Germany and the United Kingdom it would be around 80 per cent. In France and the United States the implicit rate would be about 50 per cent, since half the increase in earnings is wiped out by a loss of benefits. In Japan, the implicit tax actually exceeds 140 per cent, meaning our one-earner couple would be worse off with the new job than without it. What's more, they may have to be wary when it comes to staying in the job itself, since small wage increases can expose low-wage earners to high implicit tax rates as their means-tested benefits get cut further.

(a) What is meant by 'the marginal tax rate'?
(b) Explain what is meant by the term 'a bubble' in the structure of taxation.
(c) How can it be that marginal tax rates can exceed 100 per cent?
(d) How are workers and non-workers likely to respond to high marginal tax rates?

E ANSWERS

Q1. (a) (iii), (b) (x), (c) (vi), (d) (ii), (e) (viii), (f) (i), (g) (iv), (h) (ix), (i) (vii), (j) (v).
Q2. See Figure A10.1.
Q3. Moving up the curve, the new curve would initially be above the original one. It would then cross the original one and thereafter be below it up to the top right-hand corner.
Q4. D.
Q5. *False.* In Figure 10.2, as income distribution becomes more equal, the Lorenz curve will move closer to the

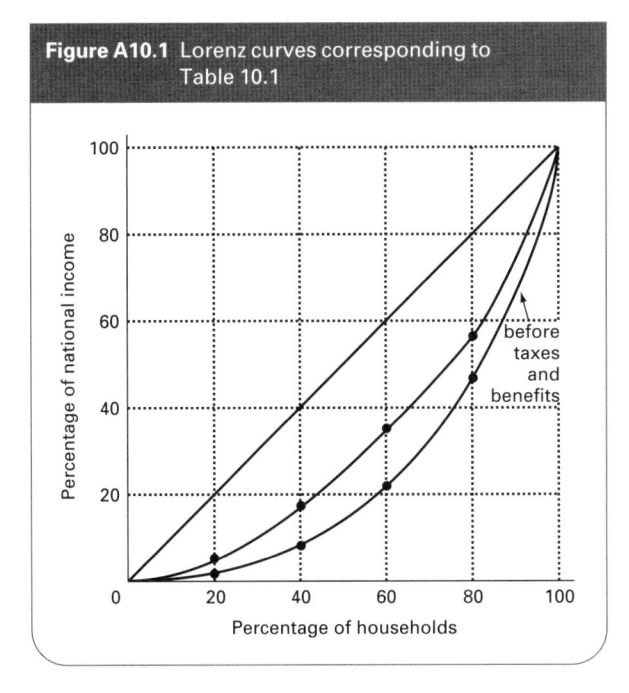

CHAPTER 10 INEQUALITY, POVERTY AND POLICIES TO REDISTRIBUTE INCOMES 145

Figure A10.1 Lorenz curves corresponding to Table 10.1

[Graph showing Lorenz curves: x-axis "Percentage of households" 0–100, y-axis "Percentage of national income" 0–100. The 45° line of equality and two curves labelled "before taxes and benefits" are shown.]

45° line and thus area *Y* will get smaller and hence the Gini coefficient will *fall* not rise.

Q6. (i) Differences in wages and salaries between different occupations, (ii) differences between incomes from self-employment and employment and (iii) differences between incomes from employment and self-employment on the one hand and social security benefits on the other.

Q7. *False*. Women are paid less even in the same occupation. The causes include: men promoted to more senior positions; the average age of full-time female workers is lower; women do less overtime; discrimination.

Q8. *True*. The wealthiest 10 per cent owned 50 per cent of UK wealth in 1995.

Q9. 1. *Inheritance*: this allows income inequality to be perpetuated and deepened from one generation to another.
2. *Income inequality*: people with higher incomes can save more.
3. *Different propensities to save*: people who save more will build up a bigger stock of wealth.
4. *Entrepreneurial and investment talent/luck*: some people are more successful than others in investing their wealth and making it grow.

Q10. B (possibly C). Wage rates will reflect workers' and employers' attitudes and their power in the labour market. The distribution of wealth will affect wages to the extent that it affects the distribution of economic power.

Q11. E. Household income is affected by wage rates (i.e. (ii) and (iii)), by income from assets (i.e. (i)) and by household composition (i.e. (iv), (v) and (vi)).

Q12. (a) (iii), (b) (ii), (c) (viii), (d) (x), (e) (i), (f) (v), (g) (vii), (h) (iv), (i) (ix), (j) (vi).

Q13. Because those who use a service the most (e.g. the sick using the health service) may be the least able to pay.

Q14. (a) (i) *relatively well*, if the rate of tax increases as people's incomes increase. Note, however, that income tax in the UK is not very progressive. Most people on the basic rate of income tax pay a marginal rate of 32% (i.e. 22% income tax and 10% national insurance). People on very high incomes pay a marginal rate of 40% (i.e. 40% income tax and 0% national insurance). Thus the difference in marginal rate between the moderately poor and the very rich is only 8%. (ii) *badly*, given that poor people (who pay less income taxes) will be in receipt of larger amounts of state benefit.
(b) (i) *very badly*, given that all except the very poor paid exactly the same amount per head within any given local authority area.
(ii) *well*, for services which were consumed relatively equally (e.g. refuse services and street lighting), but *moderately badly* for services which were consumed unequally (e.g. education).

Q15. (a) Progressive – curve II; regressive – curve I; proportional – curve III; lump sum – curve IV.
(b) Progressive – curve I; regressive – curve III; proportional – curve II; lump sum – curve IV.

Q16. (a) *10%* (i.e. (£1000/£10 000) × 100)
(b) *10.58%* (i.e. (£1100/£10 400) × 100)
(c) *25%* (i.e. $\Delta T/\Delta Y$ = (£100/£400) × 100)

Q17. *False*. It will be progressive. Although the marginal rate is constant, the average rate will rise as income rises because the tax-free allowance will account for a smaller and smaller proportion of total income.

Q18. B. The rich tend to save proportionately more than the poor and hence spend proportionately less. This means that they would pay proportionately less of this type of tax.

Q19. *False*. Provided the poor pay some taxes, *cutting* taxes for the poor *will* provide additional help. The problem comes for the very poor, who do not pay income taxes in the first place.

Q20. E. This will target the tax cuts to the poorest people, who spend a large portion of their meagre incomes on basic goods. (Note, in the case of B, that increasing tax thresholds will not help the very poor who are too poor to pay income tax in the first place.)

Q21. B. Everyone paying income tax will have the same *absolute* reduction in taxes. This will represent a larger *percentage* the lower a person's income (provided that they were paying at least as much in the first place as the size of the total tax cut).

Q22. *False*. In this case the main tax burden falls on employers: a significantly higher (pre-tax) wage will have to be offered in order to attacting enough workers. The employers' share of the tax is thus high.

Q23. *(a) Income effect.* Higher taxes reduce people's disposable income. They thus feel it necessary to work more or harder in order to try to recoup some of this lost income.

(b) Substitution effect. As an hour's work now brings in less income (and hence enables less consumption), people are likely to substitute leisure for income.

Q24. *(a) Income effect.* People will feel a greater need to maintain their level of disposable income and will thus work harder.

(b) Substitution effect. The second income earner will now be more inclined to stay at home or at least to work fewer hours.

(c) Income effect. A rise in income tax will cause them to have a *substantial* fall in income and may thus cause them to work harder to compensate.

(d) Income effect. These people will find it difficult to sustain a fall in income and will thus probably work harder.

(e) Substitution effect. For these people the rise in income tax will have virtually *no* effect on disposable income. The income effect will be negligible. Each *additional* pound earned, however, will be at the higher tax rate and thus the disincentive effect will still exist. Thus the substitution effect is likely to outweigh the income effect even though the marginal utility of money is greater for poor people.

Q25. C. Note that B is wrong because that there is no reason why the curve should peak at a 50 per cent marginal (or average) tax rate. D is wrong because the point where the substitution effect begins to outweigh the income effect will be to the *left* of the peak of the curve; even when the substitution effect is bigger than the income effect and thus people work fewer hours, they could still pay more tax if the percentage reduction in hours is less than the percentage rise in tax.

Q26. *True.* The total income of higher tax payers will only be moderately affected if the basic rate is unchanged and thus the income effect is relatively small (except for extremely well-paid people). The substitution effect, however, could be quite large given that the rich tend to have a lower marginal utility of income than the poor.

Q27. *True.* The rate of tax has not changed and thus there is no substitution effect. There is an income effect, however. People will suddenly have been made poorer and are thus likely to work harder to compensate for the lost income. Thus reducing tax allowances will act as an incentive.

Q28. *is outweighed by.* The income effect (people can now afford to take more leisure) will cause people to work less. The substitution effect (the opportunity cost of leisure has now increased) will cause people to work more.

Q29. *cuts in the basic rate of income tax.* With increases in tax thresholds, there will be *no* substitution effect because the marginal rate of tax has not changed. There will only be an income effect. Thus with increases in tax allowances, people will be encouraged to work less.

Q30. (a), (b), (c) and (e) are *universal*. (d), (f) and (g) are *means tested*.

Q31. B. *Universal* benefits cost more to provide a given amount of help to the poor. The reason is that some will go to those who are not poor. For example, child benefit is an expensive way of relieving child poverty because rich parents as well as poor are entitled to child benefit.

Q32. Where poor people are discouraged from working or getting a better job because any extra income they earn will be largely or wholly taken away in taxes and lost benefits.

Q33. *70%* (i.e. 25% + (60% × 75%)). In other words, if a person earned an extra £10, £2.50 would be taken off as taxes. Take-home pay would thus be £7.50, of which 6/10 (i.e. £4.50) would go in lost benefits, leaving a mere £3. Thus 70 per cent of the increase in pay has been lost.

Q34. *(a) −£1000.* The tax authorities would *pay you* a cash benefit (a negative tax) of £1000.

(b) −£800. The tax authorities would *pay you* £1000 benefit minus £200 tax.

(c) zero. You would be liable to a tax of £1000 which exactly offsets the benefit.

(d) +£1000. You would be liable to a net tax of £2000 minus the £1000 benefit.

(e) 20%. There is *no* lost benefit. Everyone is entitled to the benefit, which is offset against their tax liability. Thus the marginal tax-plus-lost-benefit rate is the same as the marginal tax rate.

Q35. If the marginal rate of tax is to be kept reasonably low (so as to avoid creating a disincentive to work), the benefit (i.e. the negative element) will have to be small, which reduces its effectiveness in providing help to the poor. If, on the contrary, the benefit were large but still only declined slowly (a low marginal rate of tax), the tax would only start to yield revenues from people with very high incomes and thus the tax would yield very little, if any, net revenue for the government!

Chapter Eleven

11

Markets, Efficiency and the Public Interest

A REVIEW

In this chapter we examine the question of *social efficiency* in the allocation of resources. It is the failure of markets to achieve social efficiency that provides much of the argument for government intervention in the economy. But likewise it is the failure of governments to achieve social efficiency in the allocation of resources that provides much of the argument for *laissez-faire*.

We start by seeing how, under certain conditions, a perfect market economy will lead to social efficiency. We then see how in the real world the market will fail to do so and we examine the causes and types of market failure. We see how a government can intervene to correct these failures and then look at *cost–benefit analysis* – a means of establishing whether a particular public project is desirable or not. We turn finally to the other side of the argument and consider the case against government intervention.

11.1 Efficiency under perfect competition

(Pages 283–4) Simple analysis: MB = MC
A socially efficient economy is defined as one that is *Pareto optimal* (named after Vilfredo Pareto (1848–1923)).

Q1. A situation of Pareto optimality is one where:
A. resources are allocated in the fairest possible way.
B. people can be made better off with no one being made worse off.
C. losses to the rich will be more than offset by gains to the poor.
D. there is no X inefficiency.
E. it is not possible to make anyone better off without making at least one other person worse off.

Q2. In any economy there will be many different possible Pareto-optimal situations, some of which will involve greater equality than others. *True/False*

Q3. Bill and Ben both like apples and currently have 8 apples each in their respective fruit bowls. This is shown in Figure 11.1 as point X. Various other alternative quantities of apples are also shown (points A–H).
(a) Which points would represent a Pareto improvement compared with point X?

....

(b) Is point X a Pareto improvement on any other points? If so, which?

....

(c) With the information given, can we say anything about the relative efficiency of point B compared with point X?

....

....

148 CHAPTER 11 MARKETS, EFFICIENCY AND THE PUBLIC INTEREST

Figure 11.1 Apples for Bill and Ben

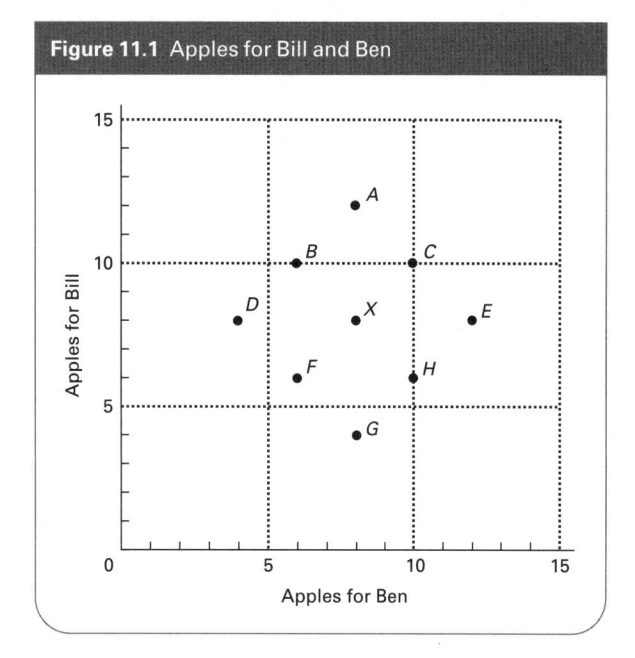

(Pages 284–6) Will a free-market economy lead to Pareto optimality, to social efficiency? The answer is that it will only do so under very strict conditions.

Q4. What two conditions must be fulfilled for the free market to be socially efficient?

1. ....

2. ....

Under perfect competition we assume that individuals behave *rationally*. Rational behaviour involves doing more of any activity whose **Q5.** *total cost/marginal cost/average cost* is **Q6.** *greater than/less than* its **Q7.** *total benefit/marginal benefit/average benefit*. Such behaviour will lead to *private efficiency*.

(Pages 286–7) In the absence of externalities and with perfect competition in all markets, the achievement of private efficiency in each individual market will lead to a *general equilibrium* throughout the whole economy which is *socially efficient*: i.e. Pareto optimal.

Q8. In a perfect market, social efficiency in any activity will be maximised where the activity's:
A. marginal benefit equals marginal cost.
B. total benefit equals total cost.
C. marginal social benefit exceeds marginal social cost.
D. marginal social benefit equals marginal social cost.
E. total social benefit exceeds total social cost.

In a perfectly competitive goods market, the consumer will achieve private efficiency where **Q9.** *marginal utility/marginal cost/marginal revenue* equals the price of the good.

The producer will achieve private efficiency where the price of the good equals the firm's **Q10.** *marginal revenue/marginal revenue product/marginal cost*.

Q11. Describe the process whereby social efficiency would be restored in all markets if the marginal social benefit of good X were to rise, causing initial disequilibrium. (Assume perfect competition and an absence of externalities.)

(a) Effects on the market for good X ....

....

(b) Effects on the market for factors used in producing good X.

....

....

(c) Effects on other goods markets ....

....

....

(d) Effects on other factor markets ....

....

(e) The final equilibrium state ....

....

(Pages 287–90) Intermediate analysis: MB ratios equal MC ratios

*Q12. If for two goods X and Y, MU_X/MU_Y (MRS) were greater than P_X/P_Y, what would a rational consumer do?

....

*Q13. A firm produces two goods X and Y. If it finds that MC_X/MC_Y (MRT) is greater than P_X/P_Y what should it do to maximise profits?

....

*Q14. If MU_X/MU_Y for person A exceeded MU_X/MU_Y for person B (i.e. $MRS_A > MRS_B$):
(a) How could a Pareto improvement be achieved?

....

(b) What would the Pareto optimum be?

....

CHAPTER 11 MARKETS, EFFICIENCY AND THE PUBLIC INTEREST

◐ *Q15.* Assuming no externalities, social efficiency will be achieved where *MRS* = *MRT* for all goods.   *True/False*

⊖ *Q16.* Figure 11.2 shows social indifference curves (I_1 to I_4) and a social transformation curve (production possibility curve) (*TT*) between two goods X and Y. It is assumed that there are no externalities.

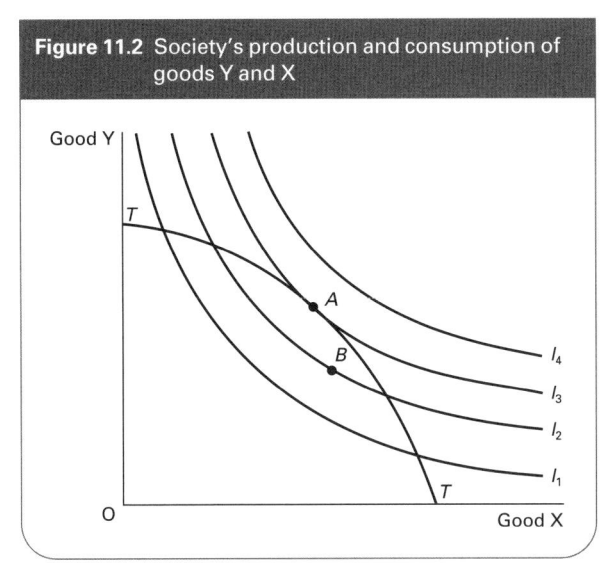

Figure 11.2 Society's production and consumption of goods Y and X

(a) What does the slope of the social indifference curves give?

....

(b) What does the slope of the production possibility curve give?

....

(c) Draw a line showing the *equilibrium* price ratio P_X/P_Y.

(d) Why are all points other than point *A* socially inefficient?

....

....

(e) If production were at point *B*, how could a Pareto improvement be achieved?

....

....

11.2 The case for government intervention

(Page 290) Real-world markets will fail to achieve social efficiency. What is more, efficiency is not the only economic objective, and real-world markets may fail to achieve these other objectives too.

(?) **Q17.** Give three other economic objectives.

1. ....

2. ....

3. ....

There are several reasons why real-world markets will fail to achieve a socially efficient allocation of resources.

⬣ **Q18.** The following are problems that cause market failings:
  (i) Externalities.
  (ii) Monopoly/oligopoly power.
  (iii) Monopsony/oligopsony power.
  (iv) Ignorance and uncertainty.
  (v) Public goods and services.
  (vi) Persistent disequilibria.
  (vii) Dependants.
  (viii) Merit goods.

Match each of the above problems to the following examples of failures of the free market. In each case assume that everything has to be provided by private enterprise: that there is no government provision or intervention whatsoever. Note that there may be more than one example of each problem. Also each case may be an example of more than one market problem.

(a) There is an inadequate provision of street lighting because it is impossible for companies to charge all people benefiting from it.

....

(b) Advertising allows firms to sell people goods that they do not really want.

....

(c) A firm tips toxic waste into a river because it can do so at no cost to itself.

....

(d) Firms pay workers less than their marginal revenue product.

....

(e) Prices take a time to adjust to changes in consumer demand.

....

(f) People may not know what is in their best interests and thus may underconsume certain goods or services (such as education).

....

150 CHAPTER 11 MARKETS, EFFICIENCY AND THE PUBLIC INTEREST

(g) Firms' marginal revenue is not equal to the price of the good and thus they do not equate *MC* and price.

....

(h) Firms provide an inadequate amount of training because they are afraid that other firms will simply come along and 'poach' the labour they have trained.

....

(i) In families one person may do the shopping for everyone and may buy things that other family members do not like.

....

(j) Farmers cannot predict the weather.

....

(Pages 290–2) As we saw in the last section, externalities are spillover costs or benefits.

Q19. Figure 11.3 shows the production of fertiliser by a perfectly competitive profit-maximising firm. Production of the good leads to pollution of the environment, however. This pollution is an external cost to the firm.

(a) Which of the two curves, *I* or *II*, represents the marginal social cost curve?   *I/II*

(b) What output will the firm produce if it takes no account of the pollution?

....

(c) What is the level of the marginal external cost at this output?

....

(d) What is the socially efficient level of output?

....

Figure 11.3 Fertiliser production by a perfectly competitive firm

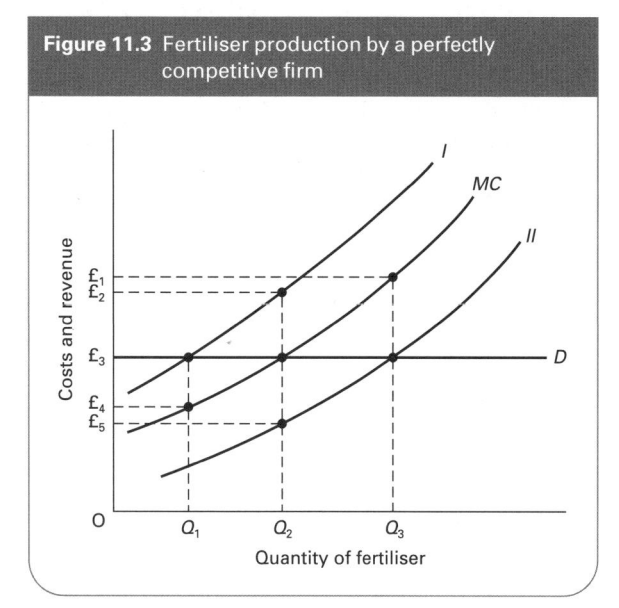

Q20. Give two examples of each of the following:

(a) External benefits of production ....

(b) External benefits of consumption ....

(c) External costs of consumption ....

Q21. In the absence of externalities, a monopoly will charge a price above the level where *MSC = MSB* and produce an output below the level where *MSC = MSB*.
True/False

(Pages 292–4) There is a category of goods that the free market, whether perfect or imperfect, will underproduce or fail to produce at all. These are *public goods*.

Q22. Which two of the following features distinguish public goods from other types of good?
  (i) Large external benefits relative to private benefits.
  (ii) Large external costs relative to private costs.
  (iii) A price elasticity of demand only slightly greater than zero.
  (iv) The impossibility of excluding free riders.
  (v) Ignorance by consumers of the benefits of the good.
  (vi) Goods where the government feels it knows better than consumers what people ought to consume.

A. (i) and (iv).
B. (ii) and (iii).
C. (v) and (vi).
D. (ii) and (v).
E. (iv) and (v).

Q23. Which of the following are examples of public goods (or services)? (Note that we are not merely referring to goods or services that just happen to be provided by the public sector.)
(a) Museums   *Yes/No*
(b) Roads in town   *Yes/No*
(c) Motorways   *Yes/No*
(d) National defence   *Yes/No*
(e) Health care   *Yes/No*
(f) Community policing   *Yes/No*
(g) Street drains   *Yes/No*
(h) Secondary education   *Yes/No*

Q24. The equilibrium price for a pure public good is zero.   *True/False*

(Pages 293–4) Some resources are not privately owned: they are available free of charge to anyone. Examples include fishing grounds and common land. These common resources are likely to be **Q25.** *overused/underused*. This is because, despite being publicly available, there is **Q26.**

rivalry/no rivalry in their use. Also their use involves **Q27.** *positive externalities/negative externalities/no externalities*.

⊖ **Q28.** Figure 11.4 shows the number of privately owned cattle grazing an area of common land. There are many cattle owners. As more cattle graze the land, so grass intake per cow declines, and so milk yields fall. This is shown by a falling *MRP* and *ARP* (it is assumed that the price of milk is constant). These costs of purchasing a cow, milking it and storing, processing and selling the milk are assumed to be constant and are shown by the horizontal *AC* and *MC* curves. As long as the revenue from an additional cow exceeds the costs, it will be worth owners purchasing more cows and grazing them on the land.

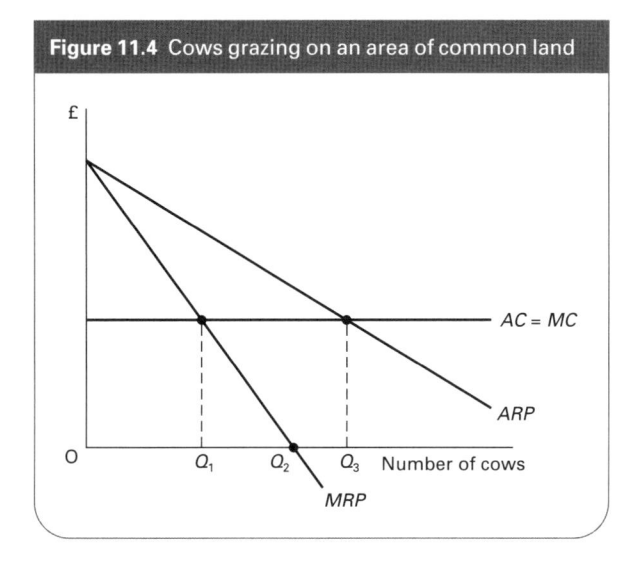

Figure 11.4 Cows grazing on an area of common land

Assuming owners are concerned to maximise profits:

(a) How many cows will be put to graze the land? ....
(b) What will be the *MRP* at this output? *Positive/Negative*
(c) How many cows will maximise the collective profits of all owners?

....

(d) Explain whether there will be more or less total expenditure on fertilising and maintaining the land than if it had been privately owned.

....

(Pages 294–5) A monopoly will be socially inefficient because it will result in *deadweight welfare loss*.

▤ **Q29.** Which one of the following is a definition of *deadweight welfare loss* under monopoly?
A. The loss in output compared with perfect competition.
B. The increase in price compared with perfect competition.
C. The loss of total consumer surplus compared with perfect competition.
D. The increase in total profit compared with perfect competition.
E. The loss of total consumer-plus-producer surplus compared with perfect competition.

(Pages 296–8)
(?) **Q30.** If the provision of health care were left to the free market, there would be a number of reasons why the market would fail to provide an optimum allocation of health-care resources. Give an example from health care of each of the following categories of market failure:
(a) Externalities

....

(b) Market power

....

(c) Ignorance

....

(d) Uncertainty about the future

....

(e) Dependants

....

(f) Inequality

....

(g) Poor economic decision making by people on their own behalf

....

11.3 Forms of government intervention

(Pages 299–300) If there were a market distortion in just one part of the economy and elsewhere there were perfect competition and an absence of externalities, then the *first-best* solution to the distortion would be possible.

(?) **Q31.** Define the first-best solution.

....

....

In the real world, where there are countless distortions, the first-best solution of correcting all these distortions simultaneously will be totally impossible. In this case the

152 CHAPTER 11 MARKETS, EFFICIENCY AND THE PUBLIC INTEREST

answer to a specific distortion is to adopt the *second-best* solution.

Q32. Which of the following represents the second-best solution to a market distortion?
A. Concentrating on making *MSB* equal *MSC* solely in the industry in question.
B. Correcting all the distortions in other parts of the economy that can be *identified*.
C. Concentrating on questions of equity and ignoring questions of efficiency.
D. Minimising the distortion relative to other distortions in the economy.
E. Tackling distortions one at a time.

(Pages 300–2) The use of taxes and subsidies
A policy instrument particularly favoured by many economists is that of taxes and subsidies.

Q33. In the first-best world, where there are no other market distortions, the problem of externalities can be corrected by imposing a tax equal to marginal social cost (at the optimum level of output) and a subsidy equal to marginal social benefit (at the optimum level of output).
True/False

Q34. Referring to Figure 11.3 (see Q19):
(a) Assume that the government imposes a 'pollution tax' on the firm at a constant rate per unit of output. What must the size of the tax per unit be in order to persuade the firm to produce the socially efficient level of output?

....

(b) Assuming that this firm is the only polluter in the industry, what effect will the tax have on the market price?

....

Q35. Give two advantages and two disadvantages of using taxes and subsidies to correct market imperfections.

Advantage 1 ....

Advantage 2 ....

Disadvantage 1 ....

Disadvantage 2 ....

(Pages 302–3) Extending property rights
An alternative to taxes and subsidies is to extend individuals' private property rights. That way individuals may be able to prevent others from imposing costs on them. For example, people living by a river may be granted ownership rights which allow them to decide whether a firm can dump waste into it and if so whether to charge it for so doing. Such a solution will be impractical, however, when **Q36.** *many/few* people are **Q37.** *highly/slightly* inconvenienced and when there are **Q38.** *many/few* culprits imposing the costs.

(Pages 303–4) Legal controls
Another alternative is to use laws. Laws can be used to prohibit or regulate activities that impose external costs; to prevent or control monopolies and oligopolies; and to provide consumer protection.

Q39. From each of the following pairs of problems select the one where legal controls would be more appropriate. (Tick.)
(a) (i) preventing accidents from worn car tyres

....

   (ii) encouraging people to use public transport

....

(b) (i) preventing monopolists from charging excessive prices

....

   (ii) preventing manufacturers from setting the *retail* price

....

(c) (i) preventing false claims by tobacco companies about the 'benefits' of smoking

....

   (ii) preventing ignorance about the spread of infectious diseases

....

(Pages 304–5) Other policies
In addition to taxes and subsidies, extending property rights, and legal controls, there are other ways that a government can offset market failures. These include regulatory bodies, price controls, the provision of information, the direct provision of goods and services and public ownership.

Q40. Match the methods of intervention (i)–(viii) to the examples (a)–(h).
   (i) Taxes and subsidies.
   (ii) Extending property rights.
   (iii) Legal controls.
   (iv) Regulatory bodies.
   (v) Price controls.
   (vi) The provision of information.
   (vii) The direct provision of goods and services.
   (viii) Public ownership.

(a) Government job centres. ....
(b) Nationalising an industry. ....
(c) OFGEM, OFWAT, OFTEL. ....
(d) Driving tests. ....
(e) State education. ....
(f) Grants for fitting loft insulation. ....
(g) Tightening the laws on trespass. ....
(h) Setting maximum rents that can be charged for private rented accommodation.
....

*11.4 Cost–benefit analysis

(Pages 306–10) If the government decides to replace or modify the market, it will need a means of assessing whether particular goods or services should be produced and, if so, in what quantities. *Cost–benefit analysis (CBA)* can help a government decide whether or not to go ahead with a public project.

Q41. All costs and benefits associated with the project should be identified. These include:
  (i) direct private monetary costs,
  (ii) external monetary costs,
  (iii) external non-monetary costs,
  (iv) direct private monetary benefits,
  (v) private non-monetary benefits,
  (vi) external monetary benefits,
  (vii) external non-monetary benefits.

Assume that a cost–benefit study is conducted to decide whether to build a road bridge across an estuary. At present the only way across is by ferry. Assume that building the bridge will drive the ferry operators out of business. Into which of the above seven categories should each of the following costs and benefits of the bridge be placed?

(a) Loss in profits to ferry operators. ....
(b) Tolls paid by the users of the bridge. ....
(c) Damage to local wildlife from constructing the bridge.
....
(d) The difference between what people would be prepared to pay in tolls and what they will actually be charged.
....
(e) Removal of the nuisance to local residents of people queuing for the ferry.
....
(f) Wages of the toll collectors. ....
(g) Increased profits from fishing in the estuary now that the ferry boats no longer disturb the fish.
....

One way of estimating both private and external non-monetary costs and benefits is to make inferences from people's behaviour.

Q42. Which of the following might be used to estimate the non-monetary benefits of a new by-pass round a village?
(a) The costs of its construction. *Yes/No*
(b) The difference in house prices in villages with a by-pass and villages with a main road running through them. *Yes/No*
(c) The amount that people are prepared to pay for a quicker mode of transport. *Yes/No*
(d) The loss in profits to local traders. *Yes/No*
(e) The savings on future road maintenance in the village. *Yes/No*

Another approach is to use questionnaires: to ask people how much they will suffer or gain from a project.

Q43. Give two problems with using questionnaires to assess cost and benefits.

1. ....

2. ....

Q44. Figures can be adjusted for *risk* by multiplying the value of the benefit or cost by the probability of its occurrence. *True/False*

But what if the costs and benefits are *uncertain*? One answer to this problem is to use *sensitivity analysis*.

Q45. A project has a number of costs whose magnitudes are uncertain. Estimates for these costs range from a total of £4m to £10m. Is the project's desirability sensitive to this possible variation in costs, if the project's projected surplus of revenue over all *other* costs is:
(a) £20m? *Yes/No*
(b) £6m? *Yes/No*
(c) £1m? *Yes/No*

Assume all costs and benefits are in present values.

(Pages 310–11) In a public project, the benefits and some of the costs can be expected to occur over many years. Thus to get an accurate assessment of benefits and costs, *discounting procedures* must be used.

154 CHAPTER 11 MARKETS, EFFICIENCY AND THE PUBLIC INTEREST

♦ **Q46.** Put the following steps in the discounting procedure in the correct sequence. (Number them.)

(a) Discount each year's net benefit to give it a present value. ....

(b) Recommend accepting the project if the net present value is greater than zero. ....

(c) Estimate the costs and benefits for each year of the life of the project. ....

(d) Add up the present values of each year's net benefit to give a total net present value of the project. ....

(e) Subtract the costs from the benefits for each year, to give a net benefit for each year. ....

It is argued that the rate of discount chosen should be a *social* rate of discount: i.e. one that reflects society's preferences for the present over the future. Just what this rate should be, however, is controversial.

(?) **Q47.** How may sensitivity analysis be used to ease the difficulty in choosing a social discount rate?

....

....

(Page 311) How may the *distribution* of costs and benefits be taken into account?

≡ **Q48.** One alternative is to use the Hicks–Kaldor version of the Pareto criterion. This states that a project will be desirable if:
A. the gainers fully compensate the losers and still have a net gain.
B. the government fully compensates the losers and there is still a net gain.
C. if it is impossible for people to make any further gains from the project without others losing.
D. if the gainers could in principle fully compensate the losers and still have a net gain, even though in practice no compensation is paid.
E. there are no losers.

(?) **Q49.** What is the problem with the Hicks–Kaldor criterion?

....

11.5 *The case for* laissez-faire
(Pages 314–18)

(?) **Q50.** Give six possible drawbacks of government intervention: i.e. reasons why the government may fail to ensure an optimum allocation of resources.

1. ....

2. ....

3. ....

4. ....

5. ....

6. ....

♦ **Q51.** Match the following words to the blanks in the statement about the *neo-Austrian* support for free-market capitalism.

dynamic; longer-term; risk taking; monopoly; growth; oligopolies; efficiency; free-market; innovation.

The neo-Austrian school of economics argues that, rather than focusing on questions of (a).......................... in the allocation of resources, we ought to judge (b)...................... capitalism in its (c)...................... context. The chances of (d).......................... profits encourage (e).........................., (f)...................... and (g)...................... Thus governments ought to take a (h)......................... view and not attempt excessive (or indeed *any*) regulation of monopolies and (i)......................

≡ **Q52.** Even if a firm is currently a monopoly producer in the country, there are various reasons why in practice its market power may be limited. Four of these reasons are given below. One, however, is not a reason. Which one?
A. It faces a continuously falling *LRAC* curve.
B. The market may be contestable.
C. There may be competition from closely related industries.
D. The firm may face countervailing power from its customers.
E. It may face competition from imports.

B PROBLEMS, EXERCISES AND PROJECTS

Q53. Conduct an audit of your activities during the course of a day.
(a) What external costs and benefits resulted from your activities? Make sure you try to identify *all* externalities you created. You may need to think very carefully.
(b) Were you aware of the externalities at the time? If so, did the existence of them make any difference to your actions?
(c) Were there any pressures on you to avoid generating external costs? If so, were these pressures social, moral or what?
(d) How could you best be encouraged/persuaded/forced to take the externalities fully into account? Are there any costs in such methods?
(e) Present your findings in groups and discuss each other's assessments of the externalities you create. Do your findings differ substantially one to another?

Q54. Assume that a firm produces organic waste that has the effect of increasing the fertility of neighbouring farmland and thus reducing the farmers' costs. It is impractical, however, to sell the waste to the farmers. Table 11.1 shows the firm's private marginal costs and these external benefits to farmers from the firm's production.

Table 11.1 A firm's costs and revenue (daily figures)

Output (units)	Price (£)	Marginal (private) cost (£)	Marginal external benefit (£)
1	20	16	6
2	20	15	5
3	20	15	4
4	20	16	3
5	20	17	2
6	20	18	2
7	20	20	2
8	20	22	2
9	20	24	2
10	20	27	1

(a) How much will the firm produce to maximise profits?

(b) What is the marginal social cost of producing 3 units of output per day?

(c) What is the socially optimum level of output?

(d) What subsidy per unit would the government have to pay the firm to encourage it to produce this level of output?

(e) What would it cost the government?

(f) If new farming technology doubled the benefit of the waste to the farmer, what would be the socially optimum level of the firm's output?

Q55. Figure 11.5 shows an industry which was previously perfectly competitive but is now organised as a monopoly. Cost and revenue curves are assumed to be the same in both situations. (Assume that there are no fixed costs of production.)
(a) What is the perfectly competitive price and output?

(b) What is the monopoly price and output?

(c) What areas represent consumer surplus in the perfectly competitive situation?

Figure 11.5 Industry under perfect competition and monopoly

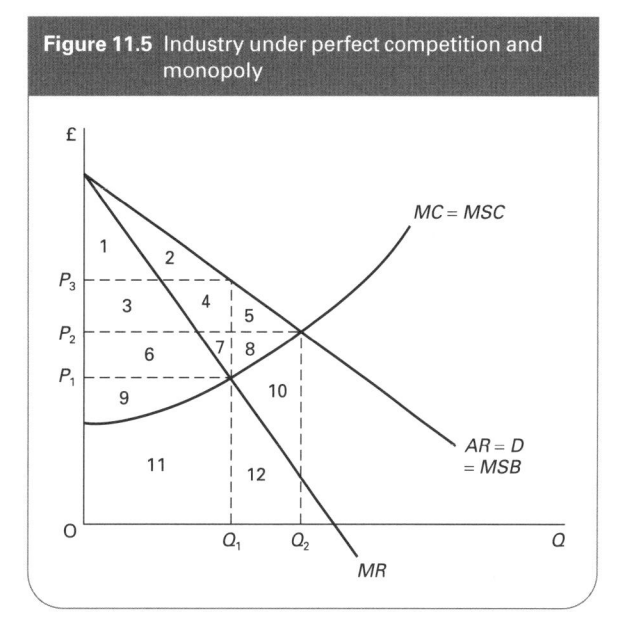

156 CHAPTER 11 MARKETS, EFFICIENCY AND THE PUBLIC INTEREST

(d) What areas represent consumer surplus after the industry has become a monopoly?

....

(e) What areas represent the loss in consumer surplus after the industry has become a monopoly?

....

(f) What areas represent producer surplus in the perfectly competitive situation?

....

(g) What areas represent producer surplus after the industry has become a monopoly?

....

(h) What areas represent the gain in producer surplus after the industry has become a monopoly?

....

(i) What areas represent total deadweight welfare loss under monopoly?

....

Q56. Figure 11.6 illustrates the situation where a firm produces *two* market distortions. It creates a marginal external cost in the form of pollution, and it also has monopoly power. (Assume that it is possible for the firm to make a profit.)

(a) What is its profit-maximising price and output?

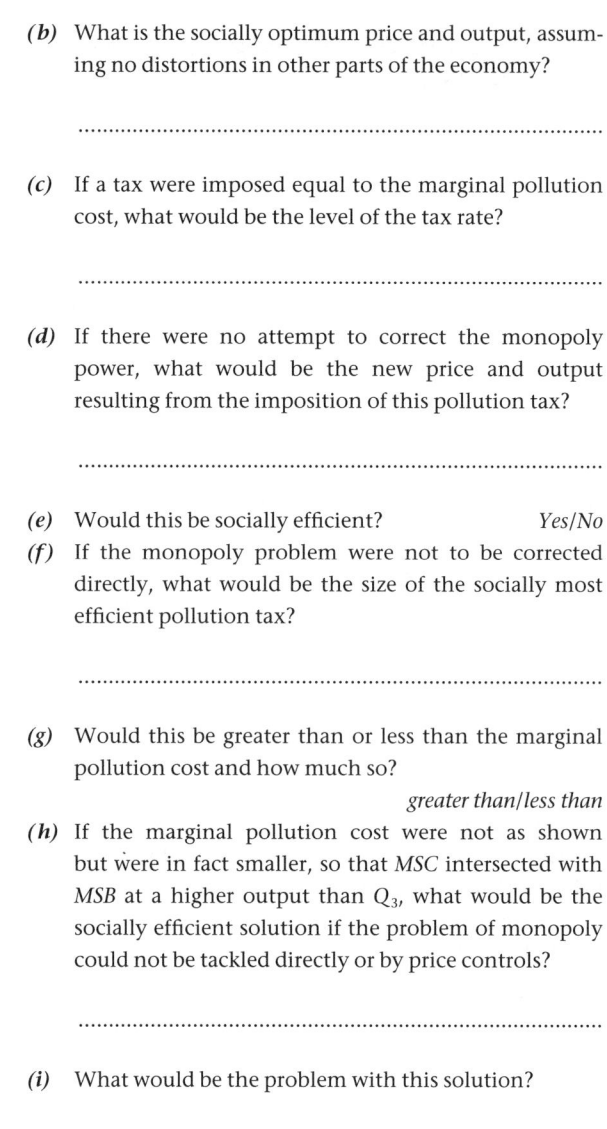

....

Figure 11.6 A monopoly causing pollution

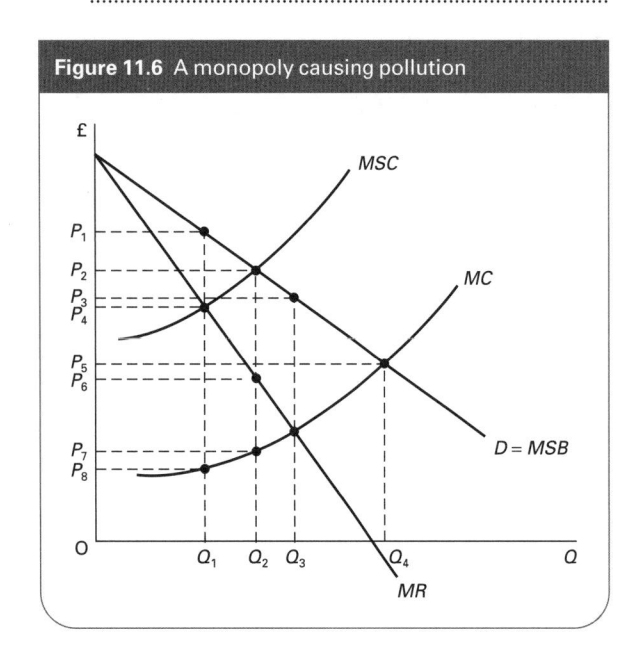

(b) What is the socially optimum price and output, assuming no distortions in other parts of the economy?

....

(c) If a tax were imposed equal to the marginal pollution cost, what would be the level of the tax rate?

....

(d) If there were no attempt to correct the monopoly power, what would be the new price and output resulting from the imposition of this pollution tax?

....

(e) Would this be socially efficient?   Yes/No

(f) If the monopoly problem were not to be corrected directly, what would be the size of the socially most efficient pollution tax?

....

(g) Would this be greater than or less than the marginal pollution cost and how much so?

                                                    greater than/less than

(h) If the marginal pollution cost were not as shown but were in fact smaller, so that *MSC* intersected with *MSB* at a higher output than Q_3, what would be the socially efficient solution if the problem of monopoly could not be tackled directly or by price controls?

....

(i) What would be the problem with this solution?

....

....

(j) How could this problem be dealt with without affecting the price and output (which with the subsidy would now be at the sociably optimal level)?

....

....

Q57. In groups of two or three, write a report on the consumption of fossil fuels in the UK (or another specific country) since 1980. You should conduct an Internet search to find information.

Your report should first include a description of the changing pattern of fossil fuel consumption over the period and then explain why this has occurred. Finally, you should describe and explain the likely consequences of an introduction of a carbon tax on fossil fuels (a tax on the use of fossil fuels).

C DISCUSSION TOPICS AND ESSAYS

Q58. Why is the Pareto test for social welfare said to be a 'weak' test?

Q59. Why will general equilibrium under perfect competition be socially efficient provided there are no externalities?

Q60. Would it be desirable for all pollution to be prevented?

Q61. Why will a free market fail to achieve an optimum allocation of resources in education? Is this an argument for the abolition of private education?

Q62. Examine the case for a 'carbon tax' (i.e. a tax on the use of fossil fuels). Why might different groups of people take opposing views on the desirability of such a tax?

Q63. Compare the relative advantages and disadvantages of taxation and regulation as means of dealing with the problem of external costs.

*Q64. How would you set about measuring the value of a human life?

Q65. Go through each of the types of failings of a free-market economy and assess whether a government is more or less likely to fail in these respects if it tries to take over from the market.

Q66. Consider the neo-Austrian argument that the possibility of large monopoly profits is of vital importance for encouraging risk taking and innovation. Does this imply that criticising a market economy for being imperfect and allocatively inefficient is to focus on the wrong issues?

Q67. Debate
Despite the weaknesses of a free market, replacing the market by the government generally makes the problem worse.

D ARTICLES

Economic success in a modern high-technology economy is as much determined by the skills of its workforce as by its stock of physical capital. The article below is taken from *The Economist* of 26 March 1994 and considers the case for government involvement in helping to provide a greater level of training and education.

Investing in people

In recent years the term 'human capital' has become almost drearily familiar. It entered into common usage among economists 30 years ago, thanks to Gary Becker, a Nobel laureate and professor of economics and sociology at the University of Chicago; he made it the title of a seminal book on the economics of education and training.

As Mr Becker points out in the third edition of *Human Capital* (published this month by the University of Chicago Press), the term was controversial in the beginning. Many said it treated people as slaves or machines. Now, the notion that people and firms invest in skills in much the same way that they invest in plant and machinery – i.e. weighing the costs against the expected returns – seems too obvious to need stating.

Yet one of Mr Becker's most telling insights remains widely ignored. Discussion of policy towards education and training usually takes it for granted that markets fail in a particular way. Mr Becker showed otherwise.

Typically, the argument goes as follows. When a firm pays for workers to be trained, the trainees become more productive not only in their present employment, but also in any number of different jobs, with different employers. If a trained worker should be poached by another firm, the employer that paid for the training has merely subsidised a competitor. The fact that the firm cannot capture the benefits of its spending is a kind of market failure – and firms will spend less on training than they otherwise would. Hence, there is a case for public subsidy.

The argument has an impressive pedigree: as far back as 1920, A.C. Pigou, one of this century's most brilliant economic theorists, said that training was a classic case of 'externality'. But the argument is wrong.

True, employers cannot directly capture the benefits of their spending on training – but the workers who receive the training can. Once equipped with new skills, they will be paid more than untrained workers, either by their present employer or by some other. So the benefits of training do accrue chiefly to one of the parties in the transaction; they are not sprayed over the economy at large.

As far as the decision to invest is concerned, it does not matter whether this capturing of benefits is done by employers or by workers. If the benefits are captured by workers, Mr Becker showed, the market succeeds.

The market's answer is simple: workers undergoing an expensive training will be paid less, for the time being, than the value of their work to the firm. This came as a surprise to economists, but will strike trainee lawyers, accountants, architects – and anybody else receiving an education in highly marketable skills – as terribly obvious.

All such people gain skills that are not firm-specific; skills, in other words, that will be as valuable to other employers as they are to the firm that pays for the training. That being so, the market-failure

Trade-off

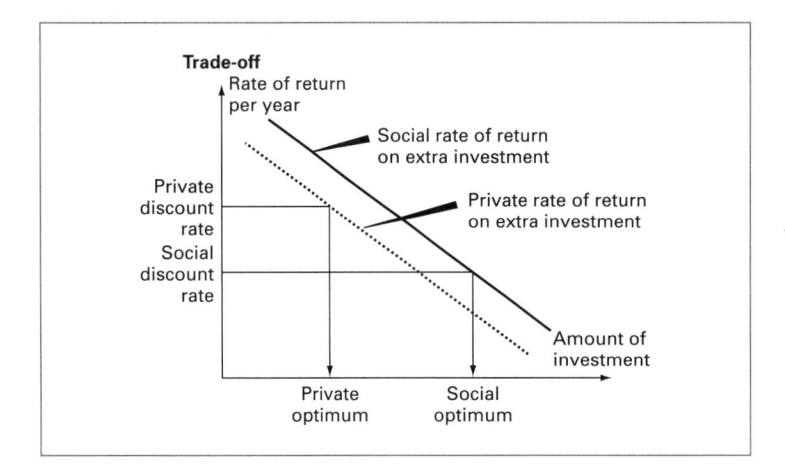

[Chart: Rate of return per year on vertical axis; Amount of investment on horizontal axis. Shows Social rate of return on extra investment (solid line) above Private rate of return on extra investment (dashed line), both sloping downward. Horizontal lines mark Private discount rate (higher) and Social discount rate (lower). Intersections define the Private optimum (left) and Social optimum (right).]

argument suggests that little on-the-job training should take place. But lawyers, at least, are hardly in short supply. The reason is that workers, not employers, meet the cost – by accepting low wages during the period of training.

Less than perfect

The standard market-failure argument for subsidising investment in human capital may be wrong, but this does not mean that market forces get everything right. Markets may fail in other, subtler ways. If they do, this will just as surely upset the calculations that society makes about how much to invest in training and education.

In principle, an economy should invest in human capital (as in any other kind of capital) up to the point where the rate of return yielded by the last bit of investment is just equal to the rate of return yielded by the best alternative use of the resources. It should invest, that is, up to the point where the marginal benefit equals the marginal cost. Please note: the idea that you can never have enough investment in human (or any other sort of) capital is nonsense. Investment is not free. You can have too much as well as too little.

To the private investor, weighing costs and benefits means investing so long as the rate of return exceeds the private discount rate (the cost of borrowing, plus an allowance for risk). For the economy as a whole, it means investing so long as the social return (which includes broader benefits to society, net of all costs) is greater than the social discount rate (which is the preference that society as a whole has for spending now rather than spending in the future). Plainly, these criteria are not the same.

The chart plots private and social rates of return against the amount of investment undertaken.* Both rates of return fall as investment increases (i.e. the two lines slope downwards). This reflects the law of diminishing returns – a truth that economists take to be self-evident. Also, at every level of investment, the chart says that the social return is higher than the private return. There are five reasons why this might be true. In each case, the cause is indeed a sort of market failure – though not always an obvious one.

- A big **stock of skilled** labour may deliver economy-wide benefits over and above the private ones that spring from the fact that skilled labour is therefore cheaper to buy – the benefit, for instance, of greater flexibility in responding to economic change. (Michael Porter's best-selling study, *The Competitive Advantage of Nations*, made much of this point.)
- Perhaps, for lack of information, would-be trainees simply **underestimate** the return to investing in skills.
- Income taxes, especially 'progressive' ones, reduce the private (post-tax) return to training, relative to the social return. This is a good example of one form of government intervention creating a 'market failure' that another form of intervention may then be called upon to remedy.
- If unskilled workers are more likely to be **unemployed** than skilled ones (as they are), then it

*The chart and the explanation that follows are drawn from a forthcoming study, *Britain's Training Deficit*, edited by R. Layard, K. Mayhew and G. Owen for the Centre for Economic Performance at the London School of Economics.

follows that the social return to training will exceed the private return. Here, the economics gets complicated. The idea is that society gives up less (in terms of output) to train an extra worker than the typical trainee gives up (in terms of income).
- Another argument is too tricky to go into: if firms have a degree of **monopoly power** as buyers in the market for labour (and many do), it turns out that it will be profitable for them to meet some of the cost of their workers' training – but not as much as makes sense from society's point of view. In this roundabout way, a variant of Pigou's 'poaching' argument can be valid, after all.

As well as assuming that the social return to investing in human capital exceeds the private return, the chart says that the private discount rate is higher than the social discount rate. This is plausible for two main reasons. Again, the underlying causes are varieties of market failure:

- In several ways, the **capital market** may be imperfect. For instance, borrowing to finance an investment in human capital may be difficult because would-be trainees lack collateral, or because the costs of administration and collection make such loans unattractive to private lenders. (These costs, it might be argued, would be lower if the lending were undertaken by the government, with subsequent debt-collection through the tax system.)
- Potential trainees may be unduly discouraged by the **risk** they would incur if they were to give up some of their income today in return for higher income (maybe) tomorrow. The idea is that private risks can be pooled, and thereby reduced: it follows that society as a whole should be less influenced by risk than individuals acting alone.

What is the net effect of all this? If, as in the chart, (a) the private return to investing in human capital is lower than the social return and (b) the private discount rate is higher than the social discount rate, then there will be too little investment. The investment that is actually undertaken (the 'private optimum') will be lower than makes sense for the whole economy (the 'social optimum').

© *The Economist*, London (26.3.94).

(a) The traditional argument states that the market will fail to provide the desirable level of education and training. What is this argument?
(b) How does Becker's argument concerning the level of education and training differ from the traditional view?
(c) Explain why the private rate of return from education and training is less than the social rate of return.
(d) If the social optimum level of education and training is greater than the private optimum, how might the government encourage greater investment in human capital? (Hint: consider what factors determine the private discount rate.)
(e) Given the arguments you have considered above, outline a case both for and against the operation of student loans in higher education.

In the article below, taken from the *Financial Times* of 2 September 1999, Richard Tomkins assesses why taxation as a means of changing social habits like smoking and car use is unlikely to succeed.

Taxation road to nowhere

Cars, you could say, are like cigarettes. They pollute the air we breathe; they kill large numbers of people; and they are associated with high levels of dependency among users.

But does it follow that governments should treat drivers like smokers, portraying their habit as anti-social and trying to discourage it with punitively high taxes?

In Britain, where traffic congestion has become a troublesome political issue, the response of governments has been to try to price motorists off the roads. The country already has some of the world's highest fuel taxes, and John Prescott, the deputy prime minister, is proposing further levies, such as charging for the use of the roads on a pay-as-you-go basis.

The idea of using price to regulate people's behaviour grew in popularity in the 1980s, when – at least in the US and UK – free-market economics replaced government regulation as the favoured means of achieving social objectives.

As traffic congestion worsened, economists in the UK started arguing for a 'market' solution. Congestion imposed heavy costs on society, they said, and in a socially efficient market, motorists should meet these costs directly.

An attractive precedent appeared to have been set by attempts to control smoking, another habit with high social costs. In the 1980s, big rises in cigarette taxes had been accompanied by a gradual decline in smoking, and the government was praised by anti-smoking advocates for discouraging socially undesirable behaviour.

But, with hindsight, it seems likely that smokers who quit were motivated more by concerns about their health than by the government's price signal. In Britain, smoking also declined in the 1970s, even though the real price of cigarettes fell during the decade. And over the years, smoking prevalence has followed similar trends in the US, Canada and the UK, even though these countries have taxed tobacco at differing rates.

Moreover, in the 1990s, the long decline in smoking has ended in Britain in spite of further big tax increases. It seems that smoking has now settled at a level where those who indulge in it cannot or will not give up. Each successive tax increase simply results in higher levels of criminal activity: namely, soaring imports of contraband tobacco, now said to account for at least 10 per cent of the UK market.

The same sort of resistance to price increases is evident in people's driving behaviour. According to Britain's office for national statistics, motoring costs for the average household rose 96 per cent in the 10 years to financial year 1997–98, or 27 per cent in real terms. But the rise was not accompanied by a fall in traffic: the number of miles travelled by people in cars rose 24 per cent over the same period.

It is also interesting to note that people's ability to absorb higher motoring costs is not just a side-effect of rising incomes. Instead, it has come at the expense of spending in other areas. The percentage of household expenditure taken by motoring rose from 12.6 per cent to 14.2 per cent over the decade to 1997–98: so it seems people would rather economise on food, heat or holidays than cut down on their driving.

At this point, economists usually start talking about elasticity of demand, pointing to neat charts tracking the relationship between price and consumption.

This is fine when applied to goods for which an acceptable alternative exists, or that do not involve a high level of dependency. It is less successful at predicting outcomes when governments use taxes to stop people using things they cannot or will not go without.

In theory, economists are right: there is a point at which price will cut demand for road transport. The trouble is that such a price is by definition unacceptable. If it were not, it would fail to cut consumption.

And so, to political realities. We have seen already what happens when tobacco taxes reach the limit of acceptability: people resort to crime to avoid them, leading to social disorder.

There are signs, too, that levies on road transport are reaching the point at which the public is questioning their legitimacy. Truck drivers have taken to blockading London's streets in protest at rising taxes. Private motorists are a less cohesive community, but they are making their views known in opinion polls. And long before they stop driving, their anger will find its outlet – if nowhere else, then at the ballot box.

So if the government cannot tax traffic growth out of existence, what is the alternative?

Some people think better public transport is a panacea. Unfortunately, it is not. Motorists like governments to spend money on public transport because they think it will encourage the idiot in the car in front to catch the train instead. But for most drivers, public transport is like the nicotine-free cigarette: it's nice to know it's there, but you would never want to use it.

Instead, the first priority should be to recognise that, contrary to popular perceptions, traffic growth is not inexorable. It will cease when everybody is driving 24 hours a day, and probably long before that. In the meantime, better traffic management will help absorb the extra traffic, and roads should be built or widened where environmental considerations permit.

But there is no magic bullet that will end traffic jams. Congestion is a part of modern life: we find it at the supermarket, the airport, the burger bar and the hospital, and the art of modern life is to learn how to deal with it.

Motorists are already doing this quite well. No new roads have been built in central London for decades, yet traffic speeds in the capital have not fallen greatly. Instead, the rush-hour has expanded to the point where it lasts all day, and is now stretching into the night.

Drivers themselves are the best judges of how to deal with congestion. They will adjust their journey times to maximise the use of the available road space, or they will change their lifestyles to minimise their travel needs.

Eventually, like smokers, they may even decide to quit. But if they do, it will be when they are ready, not when the government tells them to.

(a) Explain why taxation has been ineffective in cutting smoking beyond a certain level. Why does the article suggest that similar problems will be encountered if government attempts to price cars off the road?

(b) Why might policies to make demand for car use more price elastic fail to have much effect?

(c) What solutions to congestion does Richard Tomkins argue should be adopted (or will emerge)?

How can you price a river? Not easily is the answer. In the following article, taken from *The Guardian* of 4 March 1998, Oliver Tickell considers a recent cost–benefit analysis of the River Kennet and examines the difficulties in calculating the costs of its use by Thames Water.

Stream of abuse

How much is the river Kennet worth? The question may at first seem abstruse. But last week, following a long public inquiry in autumn 1996, the Department of the Environment put a value on the river's environmental quality. And it is now using it to uphold Thames Water's licence to pump more than 13 million litres of water from the Kennet a day, no matter how low its flow.

The move is supported by Environment Secretary John Prescott, who, speaking at last July's Water Summit, promised to 'shift the balance to help the environment', to 'give more power to the regulator' and to review abstraction licences so as to 'provide full protection for the environment'.

The Kennet, a chalk stream running west into the Thames from the Marlborough Downs, is one of England's finest trout streams. It is also of high ecological value, and has been designated a Site of Special Scientific Interest. However, low flows are contributing to the siltation of its gravel beds and the prolific growth of blanket weed.

The Environment Agency wanted to restrict Thames Water's licence to pump water from aquifers under the river to increase flows downstream of the Axford pumping station, near Marlborough, estimating that the river would be 'worth' an additional £13.6 million as a result. The sum was based on an extra 'use value' from recreation and angling of £400 000, and an extra 'non-use value' of £13.2 million.

But the head of the DETR's Water Supply and Regulation Division, Richard Vincent, determined otherwise. While accepting the EA's use-value estimate, he reduced the non-use value to £300 000, producing a total benefit worth just £700 000.

He then compared the figure with the £6.2 million cost to Thames Water of developing new infrastructure to compensate for the reduced pumping. Accordingly, he struck out the EA's attempt to reduce pumping to 3 million litres a day at times of low flow, ruling that Thames Water could continue to pump 13.1 million litres a day for the indefinite future.

But is it right to compare the value of a river with the cost of an infrastructure investment? The latter is easily calculated, but the value of the environment is not so readily tied down – as the £12.9 million gulf between the EA's and DETR's estimates in the case of the Kennet demonstrates.

The EA's non-use value was founded on the assertion that the 3 million households in Thames Water's area would be willing to pay 32p a year for the environmental benefits of reduced pumping. Taken over 30 years at the 6 per cent Treasury discount rate, that produces a capital value of £13.2 million. Vincent reduced the number of people to 100 000, each judged willing to pay 25p per year, producing a value of £300 000.

In fact, neither figure is satisfactory: both are based on arbitrary figures unsupported by credible research. And neither even begins to refloat the intrinsic value of the river, its wildlife and its landscape.

Yet the EA is stuck with the cost/benefit approach. Section 39 of the 1995 Environment Act, which brought the EA into being, requires it, in deciding whether or not to exercise a power, to 'take into account the likely costs and benefits of the exercise or non-exercise of the power or its exercise in the manner in question'.

In that it forces the EA into a cod science of dubious environmental valuation, Prescott would do well to be rid of Section 39. But the baby should not be thrown out with the bathwater. Cost–benefit analysis can usefully be deployed in comparing the relative costs and benefits of different means of achieving environmental quality targets.

At the Kennet inquiry, for example, Thames Water argued that the same benefits that would arise from reduced pumping would also result from redesigning the river channel and weirs to increase water velocity and create pools and riffles, and from reducing soil erosion and agrochemical use in the Kennet catchment – all at far lower cost.

In fact, measures such as these are promoted by the EA itself. But its powers to undertake in-channel improvements are limited, and it has no influence on farming practice. So the sensible option, that it should select the cheapest approaches to river restoration, is simply not open to it. If John Prescott wants the EA to bring about cost-efficient improvements in river quality, he needs to extend its powers.

Back to the Kennet, all is not lost. Thames Water is installing phosphate-stripping at its Marlborough sewage works. And its environment manager, Dr Peter Spillett, has told the *Guardian* of his company's willingness to fund improvements such as those he proposed at the inquiry. The way is now open for the warring parties and others (including local farmers and the Ministry of Agriculture) to come together and agree on a catchment-wide plan for the Kennet's restoration.

(a) What is the role of cost–benefit analysis?
(b) Why is it difficult to calculate the costs of using a natural resource, such as the River Kennet, by a large user, such as Thames Water?
(c) What is meant by 'non-use value'? How do you explain the difference between the Environmental Agency's and the DETR's estimation of the non-use value of restricting pumping from the river (£13.2 billion and £300 000, respectively)?
(d) If it is so difficult to calculate costs and benefits, should we continue to use cost–benefit analysis in order to make judgements concerning use and value? Would it be better merely to set environmental targets and then find the cheapest way of achieving them?

Socks from Granny again! Would you have preferred the money? In the following article, taken from *The Economist* of 20 December 2001, the author assesses whether Christmas is a waste of money.

Is Santa a deadweight loss?

Are all those Christmas gifts just a waste of resources?

Economics has long been known as the dismal science. But is any economist so dreary as to criticise Christmas? At first glance, the holiday season in western economies seems a treat for those concerned with such vagaries as GDP growth. After all, everyone is spending; in America, retailers make 25% of their yearly sales and 60% of their profits between Thanksgiving and Christmas. Even so, economists find something to worry about in the nature of the purchases being made.

Much of the holiday spending is on gifts for others. At the simplest level, giving gifts involves the giver thinking of something that the recipient would like – he tries to guess her preferences, as economists say – and then buying the gift and delivering it. Yet this guessing of preferences is no mean feat; indeed, it is often done badly. Every year, ties go unworn and books unread. And even if a gift is enjoyed, it may not be what the recipient would have bought had they spent the money themselves.

Intrigued by this mismatch between wants and gifts, in 1993 Joel Waldfogel, then an economist at Yale University, sought to estimate the disparity in dollar terms. In a paper* that has proved seminal in the literature on the issue, he asked students two questions at the end of a holiday season: first, estimate the total amount paid (by the givers) for all the holiday gifts you received; second, apart from the sentimental value of the items, if you did not have them, how much would you be willing to pay to get them? His results were gloomy: on average, a gift was valued by the recipient well below the price paid by the giver.

The most conservative estimate put the average receiver's valuation at 90%

* 'The Deadweight Loss of Christmas', *American Economic Review*, December 1993, vol. 83, no. 5.

of the buying price. The missing 10% is what economists call a deadweight loss: a waste of resources that could be averted without making anyone worse off. In other words, if the giver gave the cash value of the purchase instead of the gift itself, the recipient could then buy what she really wants, and be better off for no extra cost.

Perhaps not surprisingly, the most efficient gifts (those with the smallest deadweight loss) were those from close friends and relations, while non-cash gifts from extended family were the least efficient. As the age difference between giver and recipient grew, so did the inefficiency. All of which suggests what many grandparents know: when buying gifts for someone with largely unknown preferences, the best present is one that is totally flexible (cash) or very flexible (gift vouchers).

If the results are generalised, a waste of one dollar in ten represents a huge aggregate loss to society. It suggests that in America, where givers spend $40 billion on Christmas gifts, $4 billion is being lost annually in the process of gift-giving. Add in birthdays, weddings and non-Christian occasions, and the figure would balloon. So should economists advocate an end to gift-giving, or at least press for money to become the gift of choice?

Sentimental value

There are a number of reasons to think not. First, recipients may not know their own preferences very well. Some of the best gifts, after all, are the unexpected items that you would never have thought of buying, but which turn out to be especially well picked. And preferences can change. So by giving a jazz CD, for example, the giver may be encouraging the recipient to enjoy something that was shunned before. This, and a desire to build skills, is presumably the hope held by the many parents who ignore their children's pleas for video games and buy them books instead.

Second, the giver may have access to items – because of travel or an employee discount, for example – that the recipient does not know existed, cannot buy, or can only buy at a higher price. Finally, there are items that a recipient would like to receive but not purchase. If someone else buys them, however, they can be enjoyed guilt-free. This might explain the high volume of chocolate that changes hands over the holidays.

But there is a more powerful argument for gift-giving, deliberately ignored by most surveys. Gift-giving, some economists think, is a process that adds value to an item over and above what it would otherwise be worth to the recipient. Intuition backs this up, of course. A gift's worth is not only a function of its price, but also of the giver and the circumstances in which it is given.

Hence a wedding ring is more valuable to its owner than to a jeweller, and the imprint of a child's hand on dried clay is priceless to a loving grandparent. Moreover, not only can gift-giving add value for the recipient, but it can be fun for the giver too. It is good, in other words, to give as well as to receive.

The lesson, then, for gift-givers? Try hard to guess the preferences of each person on your list and then choose a gift that will have a high sentimental value. As economists have studied hard to tell you, it's the thought that counts.

© *The Economist*, London (20.12.01)

(a) What are the findings of the 1993 research by Waldfogel concerning the gifts his students received for Christmas?

(b) Does the article support the view that the concept of consumer surplus should be extended to include the giver and the receiver of gifts?

(c) What do you understand by the term 'deadweight loss'? How does deadweight loss relate to Waldfogel's findings?

(d) Is deadweight loss a relevant concept when presents or gifts have more than a financial dimension to their giving? For example, are Granny's socks great because they came from Granny?

E ANSWERS

Q1. E. This is the case when all Pareto improvements have been made. A Pareto improvement is where it is possible to make people better off *without* making anyone worse off. Note that B is not correct because if improvements can still be made the optimum cannot yet have been reached. A and C are not correct: Pareto optimality has to do with efficiency, not fairness. D is not correct because Pareto optimality is concerned with *allocative* efficiency not X efficiency.

Q2. True. The Pareto criterion is concerned with *efficiency* not with equity. A totally equal and a highly unequal distribution of income can both be Pareto optimal (i.e. efficient).

Q3. *(a)* A, C and E. Compared with point X, C represents a gain to both Bill and Ben. A and E represent a gain to one but no loss to the other.

(b) D, F and G. Compared with point F, X represents a gain to both. Compared with points D and G, X represents a gain to one and no loss to the other.

(c) No. Bill's gain is Ben's loss. The choice then is one of distribution rather than efficiency.

Q4. 1. Perfect competition in all markets.
2. No externalities.

Q5. *marginal cost.*

Q6. *less than.*

Q7. *marginal benefit.*

Q8. D. It is merely an extension of the general proposition that the optimum level of any activity will be where $MB = MC$, only in this case it is marginal *social* costs and marginal *social* benefits that are relevant. (Note that A would be true in the absence of externalities.)

Q9. *marginal utility.*

Q10. *marginal cost.*

Q11. *(a)* People would consume more. MU (and MSB) would fall (diminishing marginal utility) and price would rise until once more $MSB = P$.

(b) The rise in the price of the good would raise the MRP of factors and thus the demand for factors would rise. The resulting shortage would increase the price of factors and encourage more supply of factors until $MRP_f = P_f = MC_f$ (where MRP_f is the marginal benefit from using a factor and MC_f is the marginal cost of supplying

a factor (= *MDU* in the case of labour). With no externalities this means that *MSB* of factor use equals *MSC* of factor supply.

(c) To the extent that good X is a complement or substitute for other goods, so the changes in the price of good X will affect the *MU* of other goods. To the extent that factors used for producing good X are used for producing other goods, so the change in factor prices will affect the *MC* of other goods. The resulting disequilibria will lead to adjustments in these other goods markets until in each case *MSB* = *MSC* once more.

(d) To the extent that factors used for good X are complements or substitutes for other factors, so the demand for these other factors will change. The resulting disequilibria will lead to adjustments in these other factor markets until in each case $MSB_f = MSC_f$ once more.

(e) These ripple effects will continue until a general equilibrium is restored where *MSB* = *MSC* in all goods and factor markets.

Q12. Buy relatively more X and relatively less Y until $MU_X/MU_Y = P_X/P_Y$.

Q13. Produce relatively more Y and relatively less X until $MC_X/MC_Y = P_X/P_Y$.

Q14. *(a)* By B giving A some X in exchange for some Y. Both A and B would gain.
(b) Where MU_X/MU_Y for person A equals MU_X/MU_Y for person B.

Q15. *True.* For any pair of goods, where *MRS* = *MRT* there are no further Pareto improvements that can be made.

Q16. *(a)* (social) $MRS = MU_X/MU_Y = MSB_X/MSB_Y$.
(b) (social) $MRT = MC_X/MC_Y = MSC_X/MSC_Y$.
(c) The line is the tangent to point *A* since this is the point where *MRS* equals *MRT*.
(d) Because production cannot take place beyond the production possibility curve and point *A* is the point where the production possibility curve reaches the highest social indifference curve.
(e) (i) By moving out towards the production possibility curve. There could be a gain in production by some producers with no loss in production by others. (ii) There could be a move to a higher social indifference curve. A reallocation of consumption could lead to some consumers gaining with no one losing.

Q17. Examples include: greater equality, faster economic growth and stable prices.

Q18. (a) (v), (i); (b) (iv), (ii); (c) (i); (d) (iii), (iv); (e) (vi); (f) (viii), (iv); (g) (ii); (h) (i); (i) (vii), (ii) (but there are the benefits of economies of scale: for example, if another family member buys you the wrong flavour of yoghurt, the disappointment of this may be outweighed by the fact that you did not have to go out and buy it!); (j) (iv).

Q19. *(a)* I.
(b) Q_2 (where *P* = *MC*).
(c) £$_2$ – £$_3$.
(d) Q_1 (where *P* = *MSC*).

Q20. See pages 291–2 of Sloman, *Economics* (5th edition). Two additional examples of each are:
(a) An attractive new shopping centre built on previously ugly derelict land; the use of new cheaper, but less polluting, technology.
(b) A person decorating the outside of their house (thus making the street more attractive); travel by bus (thus relieving congestion).
(c) People visiting beauty spots and causing damage to wildlife; the consumption of alcohol and the effects of drunken behaviour on other people.

Q21. *True.* See Figure 11.7 on page 294 of Sloman, *Economics* (5th edition).

Q22. A. Large external costs relative to private costs make the goods socially desirable but privately unprofitable to produce. Once provided it is not possible to exclude people from consuming the goods or services without paying (i.e. from getting a 'free ride').

Q23. *Yes*: (b), (d), (f) and (g). In each of these cases the free market would simply not provide these services.
No: (a), (c), (e) and (h). In each of these cases the free market would provide the good or service, but probably imperfectly. There would be only a relatively small free-rider problem.

Q24. *True.* Since people cannot be excluded from consuming the good without paying, the market price would be zero (and hence it would be privately unprofitable to produce the good).

Q25. *overused.*

Q26. *rivalry*. One person's use of the resource will reduce its yield for others.

Q27. *negative externalities*. People's use of the resource adversely affects other people.

Q28. *(a)* Q_3 (where *MC* equals the marginal revenue to the *individual* user, which will be the *ARP* of the land, given that the individual user is too small to affect the yield. The individual owner is a 'yield taker'.)
(b) *Negative.*
(c) Q_1 (where *MC* = *MRP*).
(d) *Less.* This is a classic example of positive externalities. Why should the individual spend money on improving the land if most of the gain is going to *other* owners, who will therefore gain a 'free ride'?

Q29. E. It is the loss in *total* surplus. The gain in producers' surplus (profit) will be more than offset by a loss in consumers' surplus, giving an overall net loss.

Q30. *(a)* People with infectious diseases passing them on to other people.

- (b) Hospitals or doctors colluding to keep up the price of treatment.
- (c) Patient ignorance about their condition. They may be persuaded to have more expensive treatment than is necessary.
- (d) People taking out expensive private insurance for fear of their future health.
- (e) Uncaring parents not buying adequate treatment for their children. Children not buying adequate treatment for their elderly parents.
- (f) Poor people not being able to afford reasonable health. The belief that people have a moral right to health care according to need and not ability to pay.
- (g) People may neglect their health. The government may regard health care as a merit good.

Q31. The solution of correcting a specific market distortion so as to restore the condition that *MSB* = *MSC* in all parts of the economy.

Q32. D. Thus if prices in the rest of the economy are on average 10 per cent above marginal cost, the minimum *relative* distortion would be for prices in this industry to be set at 10 per cent above marginal cost.

Q33. False. The tax should be equal to marginal *external* cost. (Marginal *social* cost equals marginal external cost *plus* marginal private cost.) Likewise the subsidy should be equal to marginal *external* benefit not marginal *social* benefit.

Q34. (a) $£_3 - £_4$.
(b) None: it will remain at $£_3$.

Q35. Advantages: they 'internalise externalities'; rates can be adjusted according to the magnitude of the problem, thus allowing *MSB* to equal *MSC*; firms are encouraged to find ways of reducing external costs and of increasing external benefits.
Disadvantages: impractical to use when a different tax or subsidy rate is required for each case; rates would have to be frequently adjusted as external costs and benefits changed; knowledge is imperfect (for example, there is a danger of underestimating external costs such as pollution) – it might be safer to ban certain activities.

Q36. *many* (it will be difficult to co-ordinate their actions).

Q37. *slightly* (it may not be worth the effort of pursuing the culprits).

Q38. *many* (it makes pursuing the culprits more difficult and costly).

Q39. (a) (i) (it is illegal to have below a minimum tread).
(b) (ii) ('resale price maintenance' is against the law).

(c) (i) (cigarette advertising is banned on television and is being phased out on hoardings and in magazines).

Q40. (a) (vi), (b) (viii), (c) (iv), (d) (iii), (e) (vii), (f) (i), (g) (ii), (h) (v).

Q41. (a) (ii), (b) (iv), (c) (iii), (d) (v), (e) (vii), (f) (i), (g) (vi).

Q42. (b) and (c). These can give an indication of the non-monetary benefits to local residents from a quieter village – (b); and to road users from the time saved – (c).

Q43. *Ignorance*: people are unlikely to know beforehand just how much they will gain or lose. *Dishonesty*: people may exaggerate the costs or benefits to them in order to influence the outcome.

Q44. True.

Q45. (a) No. No matter whether the uncertain costs turned out to be £4 or £10, the project would still be *profitable*.
(b) Yes. The project would be profitable only if the uncertain costs turned out to be less than £6m.
(c) No. No matter whether the uncertain costs turned out to be £4 or £10, the project would still be *unprofitable*.

Q46. 1 (c), 2 (e), 3 (a), 4 (d), 5 (b).

Q47. Two or three alternative discount rates can be tried to see if the project's desirability is sensitive to the choice of discount rate. If it is, then the project will be seen as borderline.

Q48. D. The criterion is merely that there be a *potential* Pareto improvement. The question of *actual* compensation is seen to be a question of equity and should thus be considered separately from the social efficiency of the project.

Q49. In practice compensation may not be paid. An actual Pareto improvement, therefore, may not take place.

Q50. Reasons include: shortages and surpluses, poor information, bureaucracy and government inefficiency, lack of market incentives, inconsistent government policy, unrepresentative government, unaccountable government and voters' ignorance.

Q51. (a) efficiency, (b) free-market, (c) dynamic, (d) monopoly, (e)–(g) risk taking, innovation, growth, (h) longer-term, (i) oligopolies.

Q52. A. This will *strengthen* its power: it is a barrier to the entry of new firms. Any new entrants (at less than the output of the existing firm) would find that their costs were higher than this firm's and would thus find it hard to survive.

Chapter Twelve

12

Applied Microeconomics

A REVIEW

This chapter examines five topics that illustrate well the possible strengths and weaknesses of both the market and government intervention. These are: (1) the economics of the environment, (2) traffic congestion and urban transport policies, (3) monopolies and oligopolies and government policy to encourage greater competition, (4) privatisation and regulation and (5) privatisation in transition economies.

12.1 Economics of the environment

(Pages 320–2) People draw various benefits from the environment. The three main benefits are: (1) as an amenity; (2) as a source of primary products; (3) as a dump for waste. These three uses, however, tend to conflict with each other.

Q1. In what ways do the above uses come into conflict?

....

....

Q2. As population increases, so environmental degradation is likely to:
A. reduce.
B. stay constant.
C. increase at a decelerating rate.
D. increase at a constant rate.
E. increase at an accelerating rate.

Q3. Which of the following are likely to reduce pressures on the environment?
(a) An increased price of non-renewable resources. Yes/No
(b) Growth in national income. Yes/No
(c) Technological progress. Yes/No
(d) An increase in living standards in developing countries. Yes/No
(e) An increased recognition of global interdependence. Yes/No

(Pages 322–4) What is the optimum use of the environment? The answer depends on people's attitudes towards sustainability.

Q4. The following are four different approaches to sustainability:
(i) The free-market approach.
(ii) The social efficiency approach.
(iii) The conservationist approach.
(iv) The Gaia approach.

Match each one of the following four descriptions to one of the above approaches:
(a) Downplaying the importance of material consumption and economic growth and putting greater emphasis on the maintenance of the ecosystems.

....

(b) Emphasising the importance of private property and the pressures this puts on using the environment as a

---

Multiple choice | Written answer | Delete wrong word | Diagram/table manipulation | Calculation | Matching/ordering

166 CHAPTER 12 APPLIED MICROECONOMICS

productive resource – a resource which, like other resources, should not be wasted.

....

(c) Regarding the environment as having rights of its own, with humans having an obligation to live in harmony with it.

....

(d) Taking explicit account of environmental costs and benefits in decision making.

....

Q5. Figure 12.1 shows the net private benefit from producing a good (curve $MB - MC$) and the marginal pollution cost to society ($MC_{pollution}$). Which output would be seen as optimum under each of the following approaches?

Figure 12.1 Optimum level of an activity that involves pollution

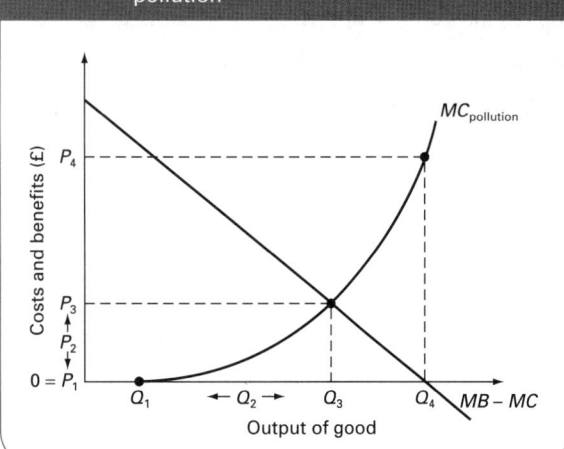

(a) The social efficiency approach $Q_1/Q_2/Q_3/Q_4$
(b) The Gaia approach $Q_1/Q_2/Q_3/Q_4$
(c) The conservationist approach $Q_1/Q_2/Q_3/Q_4$
(d) The free-market approach $Q_1/Q_2/Q_3/Q_4$

(Pages 324–8) There are various policy alternatives for dealing with environmental problems. One is to extend private property rights; another is to use green taxes. The next two questions again refer to Figure 12.1.

Q6. According to the Coase theorem, the extension of private property rights to sufferers from pollution would allow them to levy a charge on the polluter which would (a) fully compensate the sufferers and (b) result in a profit-maximising output:
A. of Q_1.
B. between Q_1 and Q_3.
C. of Q_3.
D. between Q_3 and Q_4.
E. of Q_4.

Q7. The socially efficient green tax would of an amount equal to:

A. zero.
B. OP_4.
C. $MB - MC$.
D. $MC_{pollution}$.
E. $OP_4 - OP_3$.

(Pages 328–9) An alternative means of protecting the environment is to use command-and-control systems. Minimum environmental standards could be set. These could be any of three types: technology-based standards, ambient-based standards, social-impact standards.

Q8. Define these terms:

Technology-based standards ....

....

Ambient-based standards ....

....

Social-impact standards ....

....

Q9. Command-and-control systems have the following advantages over green taxes:
(a) They are more appropriate when it is impossible to predict the precise environmental impact of pollution. *True/False*
(b) They have the effect of making the polluter pay for the amount of pollution generated. *True/False*
(c) They are easier to administer than green taxes. *True/False*
(d) They act as a continuous incentive for polluters to reduce the amount of pollution they generate. *True/False*

(Pages 329–30) An alternative that has been much debated in recent years is the use of tradable permits.

Q10. Assume that two firms, A and B, are currently emitting 100 units of a pollutant each. Now assume that a standard is set permitting them to emit only 50 units of pollutant each. If either firm emits less than 50 units, it will be given a credit for the difference. This credit can then be sold to the other firm allowing it to go over the 50-unit limit by the amount of the credit. Assume that the marginal cost of pollution reduction for firm A is £2000 per unit and for firm B it is £1000 per unit, irrespective of the current level of emission.
(a) How many units of pollution will each firm emit after trade in credits between the two firms has taken place?

Firm A............... Firm B ....

Table 12.1 Marginal cost of pollution reduction by firms A and B

Number of units of pollutant emitted	MC of reducing pollution by 1 unit (£000)	
	Firm A	Firm B
100	4	1
90	4	2
80	4	3
70	4	4
60	4	5
50	4	6
40	4	7
30	4	8
20	4	9
10	4	10

(b) What can we say about the price at which the credits will be traded?

....

Now assume that the marginal private cost to the firms of reducing pollution below 100 units is given in Table 12.1. (Assume for firm B that there is a straight-line *MC* curve: for example, the *MC* of reducing emissions by a 25th unit to 75 units is £4500.)

(c) How many units of pollution will each firm emit this time after trade has taken place in the permits?

Firm A .... Firm B ....

(d) What can we say about the price at which the credits will be traded?

....

(*Pages 330–2*) It is difficult to reach international agreements on pollution reduction.

Q11. Give three reasons why.

1. ....
2. ....
3. ....

Q12. Assume that a country is considering whether to honour a new international agreement to cut the emission of greenhouse gases. Assume also that it is considering purely its own domestic gains from the cutting of these gases and its own domestic costs of so doing.
(a) What would be the *maximax* strategy?
    Stick to agreement/Break the agreement
(b) What would be the *maximin* strategy?
    Stick to agreement/Break the agreement

(c) Why could this be described as a *prisoners' dilemma* game?

....

....

12.2 Traffic congestion and urban transport policies

(*Pages 333–5*) The demand for road space can be seen largely as a *derived* demand.

Q13. Which one of the following demands for road space is *not* a derived demand?
A. Using a car to go to work.
B. Using a bus to go to work.
C. Using a car to go for a Sunday afternoon drive.
D. Using a car to go shopping.
E. Lorries using roads to deliver goods.

There are various determinants of the demand for road space by car users. One of the most important is the 'price' to the motorist of the journey. This is not paid directly for using a particular stretch of road, except in the case of **Q14.** *tolls/taxes/congestion/the price paid for the car*, but instead can be seen as the various **Q15.** *total/average/marginal* **Q16.** *costs/benefits* to the motorist.

Q17. This 'price' will vary according to the level of congestion. *True/False*

Q18. Which of the following motoring costs are marginal (private) costs to the motorist?
(a) Fuel consumption. *Yes/No*
(b) Fuel tax. *Yes/No*
(c) Road fund tax. *Yes/No*
(d) Congestion. *Yes/No*
(e) Car maintenance costs. *Yes/No*
(f) Depreciation due to wear and tear. *Yes/No*
(g) Depreciation due to ageing of the vehicle. *Yes/No*
(h) Time spent making a journey. *Yes/No*

One of the reasons why it is difficult to tackle the problem of a growing level of traffic has to do with elasticity of demand.

Q19. Which one of the following is likely to be elastic?
A. Price elasticity of demand for road space (with respect to the direct marginal motoring costs).
B. Income elasticity of demand for road space.
C. Cross-price elasticity of demand for road space with respect to rail fares.
D. Cross-price elasticity of demand for road space for private cars with respect to bus fares.
E. Cross-price elasticity of demand for road space with respect to the price of new cars.

168 CHAPTER 12 APPLIED MICROECONOMICS

(Pages 335–7) A problem is that when people use their cars they impose external costs on other people.

(?) Q20. Give three examples of external costs of motoring.

1. ....
2. ....
3. ....

What, then, is the optimum level of road usage?

Q21. The optimum level of road usage would be that at which the external costs of motoring were zero.

True/False

⊖ Q22. Figure 12.2 shows the effects of increasing traffic along a particular stretch of road. At first additional cars have no effect on the speed of traffic: it flows freely. But after a point, additional cars slow down the traffic and thus impose a 'congestion cost' (an externality) on other car users. Beyond this point, therefore, the marginal social cost (*MSC*) of using the road is greater than the marginal private cost (*MC*).

(a) Assuming that there are no externalities on the demand side, so that marginal social benefit and marginal private benefit are the same, what will be the actual level of road use?

....

(b) What is the socially optimal level of road use?

....

(c) What is the marginal external cost at *OH*?

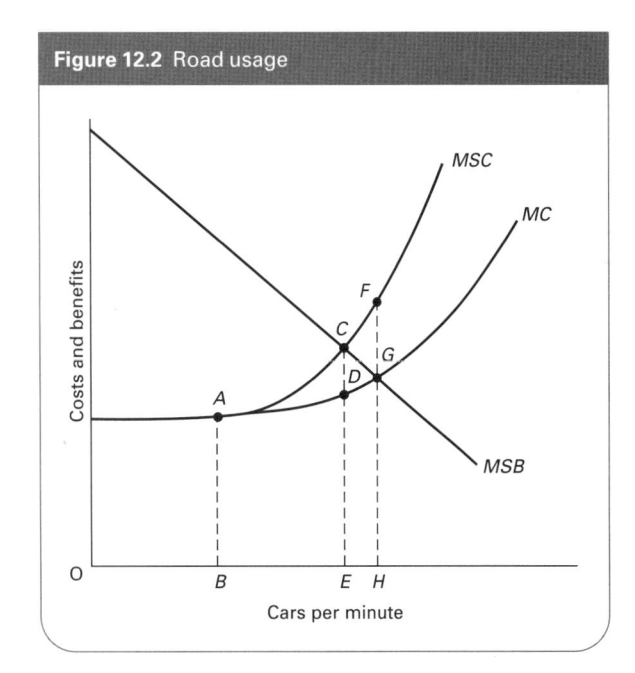

....

Figure 12.2 Road usage

(d) What level of 'congestion tax' (e.g. tolls) would be necessary to achieve the optimal level of road use?

....

(Pages 337–41) Various policies have been adopted for tackling the problem of traffic congestion.

(?) Q23. Give three problems of building more roads as the means of reducing traffic congestion.

1. ....
2. ....
3. ....

Q24. In order to reduce congestion, the marginal tax rate must increase as the level of congestion increases.

True/False

Q25. Four of the following are advantages of electronic road pricing. Which one is not?
A. The charge can be varied according to the time of day.
B. The charge can be varied according to the level of congestion.
C. The socially efficient rate to charge can easily be ascertained.
D. The revenues can be used to subsidise public transport.
E. It can be used to 'internalise' motoring externalities.

(?) Q26. Under what circumstances will electronic road pricing be most effective in reducing the level of traffic congestion?

....
....
....

12.3 Competition policy

(Pages 342–4) There are a number of possible targets of government policy concerning competition and market power.

Q27. The following are problems that have been the target of various government policies:
  (i) An increase in industrial concentration.
  (ii) The exercise of monopoly power.
  (iii) Restrictive practices.
  (iv) Resale price maintenance.
  (v) Excessive industrial concentration.
  (vi) Natural monopolies.
  (vii) Cross-subsidisation.

On which of the above problems would each of the following policies be primarily targeted?

(a) A government makes it illegal for manufacturers to set the price at which their products must be sold by shops. ....

(b) A government nationalises the national electricity grid. ....

(c) A government makes collusive agreements between oligopolists illegal. ....

(d) A government sets up a body which can investigate any firm with a share of the market above a certain level. ....

(e) Firms are prohibited from using 'unfair competitive practices' whereby they use profits in one market to charge prices below cost in another, and thereby to drive competitors out of business. ....

(f) A regulatory body has the power to limit a firm's price increases where this would result in 'excessive' supernormal profits. ....

(g) A government passes legislation that enables an investigation of any mergers that will lead to the merged firms having more than a certain percentage share of the market. ....

Competition policy is concerned with three main problem areas: (i) the abuse by a firm of a dominant position in the market; (ii) oligopolistic collusion between firms; (iii) the growth of market power through mergers and acquisitions.

Q28. Which one of the above three problems is addressed by the following types of policy?
(a) Restrictive practices policy   (i)/(ii)/(iii)
(b) Monopoly policy   (i)/(ii)/(iii)
(c) Merger policy   (i)/(ii)/(iii)

Q29. Monopoly policy, under both EU and UK legislation, is directed purely towards monopolies. *True/False*

(Pages 344–51) Because the relative costs and benefits of monopolies and oligopolies will differ from firm to firm and industry to industry, governments in the UK, like many other governments round the world, have tended to prefer to judge each case on its merits.

Q30. What is the main criterion used under both EU and UK legislation when deciding whether action should be taken against a firm with monopoly power?

A. The firm's market share.
B. Whether its behaviour is anti-competitive.
C. Whether it is achieving economies of scale.
D. Whether it engages in excessive advertising.
E. How high its profits are.

There are various types of anti-competitive practice in which firms can engage.

Q31. The following is a list of anti-competitive practices:
  (i) Tie-in sales.
 (ii) Collusive tendering.
(iii) Selective distribution.
(iv) Price rings.
 (v) Price discrimination.
(vi) Rental-only contracts.
(vii) Market-sharing agreements.
(viii) Vertical price squeezing.
(ix) Predatory pricing.

Match the above practices to the following definitions.

(a) Where a firm is only prepared to supply certain selected retail outlets. ....

(b) Where a vertically integrated firm, which controls the supply of an input, charges competitors a high price for that input so that they cannot compete with it in selling the finished good. ....

(c) Where firms divide up the market between them, agreeing not to compete in each other's part of the market. ....

(d) Where firms bidding for a contract (e.g. to supply building materials for a new office development) agree beforehand all to bid high prices. ....

(e) Where a firm sells the same good at a different price (relative to costs) in different sectors of the market. ....

(f) Where a firm is only prepared to hire out equipment and not sell it outright. ....

(g) Where a firm controlling the supply of a first product insists that its customers also buy a second product from it rather than from its rivals. ....

(h) Selling a product below cost in order to drive competitors from the industry. ....

(i) Where firms get together to agree on a common price. ....

Q32. Which of the nine anti-competitive practices in Q31 are:
(a) forms of oligopolistic collusion (restrictive practices)?

....

(b) directly concerned with controlling prices?

....

(c) directly concerned with controlling supply or sales?

....

Q33. The EU and UK approaches to restrictive practices are very similar. Article 81 of the Treaty of Amsterdam and Chapter I of the UK's 1998 Competition Act do not seek to ban all agreements between oligopolies but rather to ban various types of anti-competitive *behaviour* by oligopolists.
True/False

Q34. Which type of merger is likely to be most damaging to competition? *horizontal/vertical/conglomerate*

Q35. Give three ways in which a merger could be in the public interest.

1. ....
2. ....
3. ....

Q36. Article 82 of the Treaty of Amsterdam is concerned with European monopolies and mergers. Under this Article, what is the main criterion in judging the desirability of a merger?

....

Q37. In 1990 the EU adopted new merger control measures. These were criticised in a European Commission Green Paper of December 2001, which proposed reform of the regulations. Which of the following criticisms of the 1990 measures are valid, or at least have some validity?
(a) The investigations are expensive to conduct. *Yes/No*
(b) The Commission can too easily be persuaded by firms that the merger is not anti-competitive. *Yes/No*
(c) The conditions attached by the Commission to mergers that are allowed to proceed often rely too heavily on co-operation by the firms concerned. *Yes/No*
(d) The investigations are very time consuming. *Yes/No*
(e) Only a very limited number of cases meeting the minimum ECU5 billion turnover criterion are considered.
Yes/No

(f) Not enough emphasis is placed on questions of possible cost reductions from the mergers. Instead the stress is almost exclusively on questions of competition.
Yes/No

Q38. If, under the 1990 regulations, the European Commission decides on a full investigation of a proposed merger, it can prevent the merger if it is found to be anti-competitive. *True/False*

Q39. Under UK legislation governing mergers (covered by the 1973 Fair Trading Act):
(a) Companies must give details of any proposed merger to the Office of Fair Trading. *True/False*
(b) The Director General of Fair Trading then makes recommendations to the Secretary of State for Trade and Industry. *True/False*
(c) The Secretary of State must then refer the merger proposal to the Competition Commission (CC).
True/False
(d) When the CC investigates merger proposals, there is no initial assumption that the merger is against the public interest. Instead the arguments for and against are weighed up. *True/False*
(e) The CC reports its findings to the Secretary of State, who must then carry out the wishes of the CC and either prevent or permit the merger. *True/False*

12.4 Privatisation and regulation

(Pages 351–5) Privatisation can take various forms.

Q40. Give three forms that privatisation can take other than the complete sale of state-owned corporations by a public sale of shares.

1. ....
2. ....
3. ....

One of the major arguments used to justify privatisation was the low level of profits of nationalised industries.

Q41. Give three reasons why the level of profits may have been a poor indicator of the economic performance of nationalised industries.

1. ....
2. ....
3. ....

Q42. Imagine you are an economic consultant given the responsibility of preparing a report on the desirability of privatising the railways in a country where the railways are currently wholly stated owned. Classify the following arguments as being generally for privatisation, against privatisation or inconclusive.
(a) Many socially desirable lines are currently being run at a loss. *for/against/inconclusive*
(b) There are various ways in which competition could be injected into the industry. *for/against/inconclusive*
(c) The 'price' per mile to road users is well below the marginal social cost. *for/against/inconclusive*
(d) Studies show that the efficiency of the railways has been approximately the same as that in other countries. *for/against/inconclusive*
(e) The proceeds from the privatisation sale can be used to reduce taxes. *for/against/inconclusive*
(f) There would no longer be any government interference in setting fares. *for/against/inconclusive*
(g) The railways have had a very poor profit record. *for/against/inconclusive*
(h) A new genuinely independent body OFRAIL would be given substantial regulatory powers. *for/against/inconclusive*

Q43. Assume that a government wants to raise the maximum revenue from a privatisation sale and also wants to inject the maximum amount of competition into the industry. Why may these two objectives come into conflict?

....

....

Q44. Ownership is a less important determinant of the efficiency of an industry than the degree of competition it faces and the attitude of the government towards it. *True/False*

(Pages 355–6) If a nationalised industry is run 'in the public interest', or if the industry is privately owned but regulated so that it is required to operate in the public interest, how much should it produce and at what price? Take the case of industry X.

Q45. If all other industries were operating under perfect competition and there were no externalities, then the 'first-best' policy for industry X would be to produce where:
A. $P = AR$
B. $AR = AC$
C. $MR = MC$
D. $MC = P$
E. $MC = AC$

Q46. Consider now what price industry X should charge when the first-best situation does not apply. Assume that firms typically throughout the economy (including related industries to industry X) charge a price 15 per cent above marginal cost and that industry X's marginal cost is 5 per cent above its marginal social cost. Assume also that on average other firms' externalities are zero. The second-best price for industry X will be:
A. 10 per cent above its marginal cost.
B. 10 per cent above its average cost.
C. 20 per cent above its marginal cost.
D. 20 per cent above its average cost.
E. 15 per cent above its marginal cost.

Q47. If it is regarded as socially desirable for reasons of equity to provide loss-making rural bus services, what is the least distortionary solution to this problem?
A. Raise the fares on the urban bus services to cover the losses of the rural services so as to retain the same overall level of profit as before.
B. Keep urban fares the same and pay for the rural services from reduced bus company profits.
C. Subsidise the rural services from increased local taxes in rural areas.
D. Subsidise the rural services from increased income tax.
E. Subsidise the rural services from increased taxes on the motorist.

(Pages 356–62) In the UK, the major privatised industries have had substantial market power. It was felt at the time of their privatisation that the OFT and the MMC would not be sufficient to ensure that they operate in the public interest, and so the government set up independent bodies to regulate their behaviour.

Q48. Which of the following are features of UK regulation?
(a) Each regulatory body is responsible for just one industry. *Yes/No*
(b) *All* pricing decisions in the regulated industries are subject to regulation. *Yes/No*
(c) Price regulation is normally of the form: *RPI plus X*. *Yes/No*
(d) The *X* in the formula is designed to take account of expected increases in efficiency. *Yes/No*
(e) Price regulation takes account of cost increases beyond the control of the industries. *Yes/No*
(f) Price regulation can involve industries having to reduce their prices even when there is inflation. *Yes/No*
(g) If there is no agreement between the regulator and the industry when reviewing price-setting formulae, an appeal can be made to the Competition Commission for settlement of the dispute. *Yes/No*

(h) Once the price-setting formula has been set for a specified number of years, it cannot be changed until the end of that period. *Yes/No*

(i) Regulators are only concerned with pricing decisions. *Yes/No*

(j) The system of regulation is discretionary, with the regulator able to judge individual examples of the behaviour of the industry on their own merits. *Yes/No*

Q49. In the USA, the main form of regulation has been 'rate-of-return' regulation, which involves restricting the amount of profit a firm can make. This has the major advantage that it encourages firms to find ways of reducing costs. *True/False*

Q50. One of the dangers with regulation is that of 'regulatory capture'. This can be defined as a situation where:
A. the regulator is only concerned about carrying out government policy.
B. the regulator totally dominates the industry, leaving the managers no discretion to make pricing and investment decisions which might be in the *long-term* interests of the industry and the country.
C. the regulator captures an ever *increasing* amount of the decisions of the industry.
D. the managers become obsessed with doing what the regulator wants rather than what is genuinely in the interests of the industry.
E. the regulator starts seeing things from the managers' point of view rather than the consumers'.

Q51. Give three advantages and three disadvantages of the UK system of regulation.
Advantages

1. ....
2. ....
3. ....

Disadvantages

1. ....
2. ....
3. ....

Q52. Assume that a country has a single interconnected system of natural gas pipelines owned by a recently privatised company. Give three ways in which the government could attempt to inject competition into the supply of gas to customers.

1. ....
2. ....
3. ....

12.5 Privatisation in transition economies

(Pages 363–7) Virtually all of the previously centrally planned economies of central and eastern Europe and the former Soviet Union have been pursuing large-scale programmes of privatisation.

Q53. Which of the following problems occurred under central planning?
(a) Prices did not reflect opportunity costs. *Yes/No*
(b) Planners had insufficient information about individual workplaces. *Yes/No*
(c) Investment rates were very low. *Yes/No*
(d) It was often in managers' interests to provide planners with inaccurate information. *Yes/No*
(e) Inappropriate units were used for targets to be met by managers. *Yes/No*
(f) Bonuses were rarely awarded. *Yes/No*
(g) The prices set by the state were often above the equilibrium level. *Yes/No*

Q54. Privatisation has taken a number of forms. Which of the following forms are examples of 'insider' privatisation and which of 'outsider' privatisation?
(a) Selling an enterprise to its managers and/or workers. *Insider/Outsider*
(b) Issuing vouchers to the general public and then auctioning shares in enterprises for vouchers. *Insider/Outsider*
(c) Transferring ownership directly to the workers/managers of enterprises, with no sale of shares involved. *Insider/Outsider*
(d) Open public sale of an enterprise for cash. *Insider/Outsider*
(e) Selling an enterprise to an independent national investment trust. *Insider/Outsider*
(f) Selling an enterprise to a foreign company. *Insider/Outsider*

(Pages 367–8) There have been various problems associated with privatisation and the move to a market economy in the transition economies.

Q55. Which of the following have been problems arising from privatisation and market liberalisation?
(a) Inequality has increased. *Yes/No*
(b) Shortages have increased. *Yes/No*
(c) Inflation is higher than before. *Yes/No*
(d) Unemployment is higher than before. *Yes/No*

(e) Output fell (at least initially). Yes/No
(f) Relative prices are more distorted than before. Yes/No

(?) **Q56.** Name three ways in which the environment in which privatisation takes place could be made more conducive to the success of that privatisation in building a competitive market economy.

1. ....

2. ....

3. ....

B PROBLEMS, EXERCISES AND PROJECTS

Table 12.2 Time taken to travel between two points along a given road

Cars per minute (1)	Marginal private time cost: in minutes (2)	Total time cost: in minutes (3)	Marginal social time cost: in minutes (4)	Marginal external time cost: in minutes (5)
1	4	...	...	...
2	4	...	...	...
3	5	...	...	...
4	7	...	...	...
5	10	...	...	...
6	15	...	...	...
7	25	...	...	...

Q57. Table 12.2 shows the time taken to travel between two points along a given road.

Column (1) gives the traffic density: i.e. the number of cars per minute entering that stretch of road.

Column (2) gives the journey time per car: i.e. the number of minutes taken for a car to travel along that stretch of road.

Column (3) gives the sum of the journey times: i.e. the total number of minutes for *all* the cars per minute entering the road to travel along that stretch of road.

Column (4) gives the extra total journey time as traffic density increases by one more car.

Column (5) gives the additional time costs imposed on *other* road users by one more car entering that stretch of road: i.e. column (4) minus column (2).

(a) Fill in the figures for columns (3), (4) and (5).
(b) Assume that tolls are now imposed on this road in order to reduce congestion to the socially optimal level. If time were valued at 10p per minute, what level of toll should be imposed per car when traffic density reaches:

  (i) 6 cars per minute? ....

  (ii) 7 cars per minute? ....

(c) Assume that the non-time costs of using the road are constant at 40p per car, that the marginal social benefit for the first car per minute using the road is £2.00, and that this decreases by 10p for each additional car per minute. What is the socially optimal level of road use (in cars per minute)?

....

(d) What level of toll should be imposed per car to achieve the socially optimal level of traffic on this road?

....

Q58. Figure 12.3 shows an industry that was originally perfectly competitive, but which has been taken over by a monopoly. It is assumed that this has resulted in lower costs of production. (This is illustrated by the two sets of *MC* curves.) It is also assumed that the monopoly produces no external costs or benefits. The government decides to regulate the firm's pricing behaviour.

(a) What price will the unregulated monopoly charge if it wishes to maximise profits?

....

(b) What price will the government set if it wishes the monopoly to charge the socially efficient price?

....

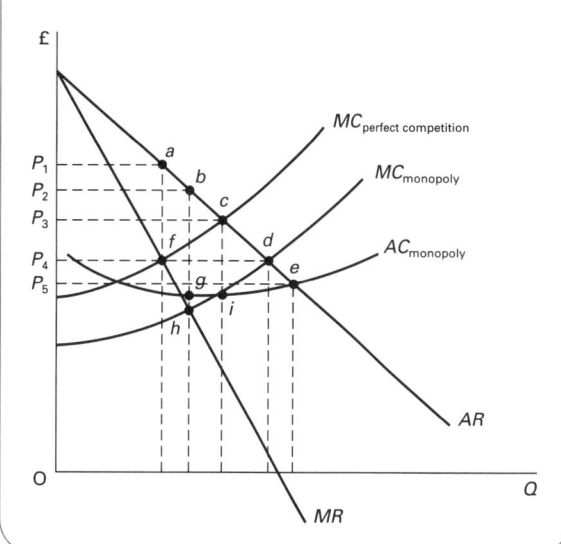

Figure 12.3 Industry under perfect competition and monopoly

(c) What price will the government set if it wishes the monopoly to make only normal profits?

....

(d) What price will the government set if it wishes the price to be that which would have occurred had the industry remained under perfect competition?

....

Q59. Select an industry that has been privatised and which has a government regulatory agency (such as OFWAT) concerned with its activities. Do a library and/or Web search to find articles on the industry's performance and pricing policies and on any competition it faces. See the hotlinks section of the Sloman Web site (www.booksites.net/sloman) for useful Web sites.

You should use these articles to write two brief reports on the industry's performance in the private sector, and on the effectiveness of regulation and attempts to inject competition into the industry. One report should be critical of the industry's performance and one should be in support. You should then write a conclusion stating (a) where the balance of the arguments lies; (b) in what ways regulation could be made more effective; (c) in what ways additional competition could be introduced into the industry.

Q60. Do a web search to find out up-to-date reports on the progress of privatisation and progress towards a competitive market in one or more central and eastern European countries or countries of the former Soviet Union. You could use the Web sites referred to in the hotlinks section of the Sloman Web site (www.booksites.net/sloman), especially from sections A, I and J. Sites G1 (European Economy), H14 and B32 are also useful.

In small groups, produce a report on the consequences of and further prospects for privatisation and market liberalisation in a transitional country. In this report, you should do the following: (a) describe the current progress of privatisation and market liberalisation; (b) using case studies, identify the costs and benefits of the policies that have been adopted; (c) assess the likely costs and benefits of any proposed privatisations and market liberalisation.

C DISCUSSION TOPICS AND ESSAYS

Q61. Compare the relative merits of green taxes and command-and-control systems as means of achieving an optimum use of the environment.

Q62. (a) For what reasons is it difficult to reach international agreements on global environmental protection? (b) Why is it difficult to stop overfishing in international waters?

Q63. To what extent are urban traffic problems the result of externalities?

Q64. Compare the relative merits of road pricing in cities with schemes to restrict the entry of traffic into city centres.

Q65. Imagine you were called upon by the government to offer advice on (i) whether to introduce tolls and, if so, at what rate on a particular motorway; (ii) whether to build an extra lane on a congested motorway. On what basis would you arrive at your recommendations?

Q66. To what extent can the provision of public transport solve the problem of urban traffic congestion?

Q67. Should certain monopolistic and restrictive practices be banned or should firms' practices be judged on a case-by-case basis? Use relevant examples to illustrate your answer.

Q68. Is it best to define the 'public interest' in terms of the level of deadweight welfare loss, when considering whether a firm should be referred to the Competition Commission?

Q69. Compare the differences of approach to (a) monopolies and restrictive practices and (b) mergers, in UK and EU legislation.

Q70. Give two examples of industries that are in part natural monopolies and which were once nationalised and then privatised. In each case consider whether any competition has been injected into the industry by or since privatisation. Consider ways of injecting further competition and any difficulties in so doing.

Q71. 'In the UK of today, there is no economic justification for nationalisation.' Discuss.

Q72. How successfully does the UK system of regulating privatised utilities protect the consumer's interest?

Q73. For what reasons have the transition economies of eastern Europe suffered from de-industrialisation, high unemployment and growing inequality after the introduction of privatisation and market liberalisation? Why have privatisation and market liberalisation helped to improve productivity in these countries?

Q74. Debate
Regulation is always inferior to competition as a means of protecting the consumers' interests.

ARTICLES

With electrical goods waste growing three times as fast as municipal waste, the environmental impact of this cannot be overlooked. The European Parliament is taking an increasingly strong line in trying to ensure that as much electrical goods waste as possible is recycled. It now seems that the issue is not whether such recycling should take place but who is going to pay for it. The following article, taken from *The Independent* of 9 April 2002, evaluates moves within the EU to ensure that the recycling of electrical goods takes place within the European marketplace.

Toasters, PCs, radios: everything must go in the EU recycling bin. But who foots the bill?

Stephen Castle

First it was cars, then it was fridges. This week everything from toasters to cellphones, from radios to steam irons, will fall under the scope of Europe's great push for recycling.

Tomorrow, MEPs in Strasbourg will vote on a complex piece of legislation destined to change for ever the way that businesses, governments and consumers deal with the mountains of rubbish we discard. Put simply, it will force firms to cover the expense of collecting, dismantling and then recycling all household electronic and electrical goods.

This being the EU, tomorrow's vote will hardly be the end of the story. With the extra costs estimated variously at between €500m (£305m) and €7.5bn (£4.5bn) a year, industry is haggling over the detail. There is a dispute over whether companies should pick up the tab for their own products' recycling or contribute to a collective pot. Months of further complicated negotiations are in store. But, after 20 years of pressure from Brussels, and in the face of obstruction from industry and governments, the principle that the polluter should pay will come a big step closer to reality.

That this is coming to pass is an acceptance of the looming environmental crisis posed by an inexorable rise in consumption of electrical goods. Since 1998 more than 6 million tons of electrical waste has been produced in the 15 EU member states each year, and the figure has been rising by 5 per cent a year. With the sale of information age electrical and electronic goods booming, it is estimated that by the end of the decade 8 per cent of all waste will be from this category of goods alone.

Meanwhile little effort is going into recycling. Today 90 per cent of electrical waste is put into landfills, incinerated or sent for scrap metal without prior treatment. These solutions constitute an ecological time bomb. Incinerated electrical goods release an estimated 36 tons of mercury and 16 tons of cadmium into the air within the EU each year, and are the biggest source of emissions of dioxins into the atmosphere. Landfill presents similar problems, as no site is completely watertight.

For this pattern to change requires a revolution in attitudes. As David Bowe, a Labour MEP and member of the European Parliament's environment committee, puts it: 'Volumes of waste are increasing drastically because we are buying more consumables and throwing away vast quantities of plastic and metals which are going into landfills.' There is, he says, a need for 'a culture of recycling which we don't have in the UK'. Whereas Germans or Belgians will routinely sort out their paper, glass and plastics from their other household trash, Britons do so rarely.

Predictably, the initiative has come not from the UK but from Brussels, which has been pressing this agenda for two decades against varying degrees of opposition. Roberto Ferrigno, EU policy director of the European Environmental Bureau, a federation of 135 environmental groups, argues: 'This was a package that the European Commission started tabling in the 1980s. The aim at the time was to reach a consensus with industry and avoid legislation. The early drafts of this directive came out about nine years ago. Traditionally, industry has been very successful at lobbying government to prevent them having to pay the full costs of recycling.'

For years motor manufacturers fought tooth and nail, backed by the German government, to oppose a directive on the recycling of old vehicles. Even now the legislation is agreed, argument continues about who should pay. EU governments will pay up to 2005 and manufacturers are due to take over the responsibility in 2006, but no one can agree what will happen for the year in between.

Another piece of EU law designed to control substances that deplete the ozone layer has thrown the British Government into disarray after a bureaucratic mix-up. Although the Government signed up to the measure it failed to prepare for one key provision, arguing (alone of the 15 member states) that the wording of the text was imprecise. Without the necessary equipment to tackle the recycling of foam, fridges have been piling up around the British countryside.

But the latest initiative is the most far-reaching yet. As the draft legislation puts it: 'All equipment which needs electricity to work properly is either electrical or electronic,' and could be covered by 2006.

The European Commission wants to balance the need to reduce pressure on the environment with its citizenry's insatiable desire to consume. The aim, says Pia Ahrenkilde Hansen, spokeswoman for the European commissioner for the environment, Margot Wallström, is that 'people can enjoy high standards of living by buying products which are designed in a way which can be easily dismantled and then recycled'. Because the polluter will have to pay for disposing of their products, they will have an incentive to design goods that are easy to recycle. As firms will pass on the costs of disposal to customers, those that are more environmentally friendly will be the cheapest.

But how will it actually work? With dozens of amendments being debated this week in the European Parliament, the detail of the plan will become clearer. In Britain an estimated 25,000 companies will be affected, and prices will rise anything from 1 to 5 per cent. Electrolux estimates that a fridge retailing at €500 (£300) will cost an extra €10–€20 (£6–£12) depending on which modifications are adopted.

Key issues remain to be resolved and, under EU procedures, this week's vote will lead to a new round of negotiations with EU states. One question is whether all consumers should be forced to sort their rubbish into different categories.

Governments are battling for the right to decide whether firms should pick up the tab for just their own recycling or contribute to a general fund.

Either way, industry will be responsible for contracting out the collection of their goods and their eventual recycling. Collection points will be made available in shops or via local authorities.

Industry is fighting to avoid liability for waste already on the market before the directive comes into force. And there is the issue of what to do with goods produced by firms that have gone out of business (the latest thinking is that each firm should put up a guarantee to cover the costs).

Some big firms are already backing the measure. Viktor Sundberg, director of European affairs for Electrolux, says: 'We realised that, sooner or later, we were going to get some form of producer-responsibility measure. We thought it would be better if it were constructive. This gives us a motivation to build better products.'

(a) Explain the arguments behind the principle that the polluter ought to pay. What are the implications of adopting this principle for (i) business and (ii) consumers?

(b) What are identified as some of the long-term advantages of insisting that businesses pay for the recycling of their products?

(c) What difficulties are there in achieving environmental policy objectives, such as those outlined above, when they involve a number of different countries?

(d) Other than direct laws, are there any other policy initiatives that governments might adopt to encourage firms to recycle?

The congested state of Britain's roads and how to relieve this problem have taxed economists and politicians alike for many years. Some economists have argued that the only way to deal with this problem is to return to the price mechanism and to ensure that road use is reflected in the cost that a motorist pays. The greater the congestion and environmental damage, the greater the cost. In the following article, taken from the *Journal of the Institute of Economic Affairs*, volume 18, number 4 (December 1998), Alan Day considers the issues involved in road pricing and some of the implications of its use.

The case for road pricing

The basic economic argument for using the price mechanism wherever possible, in order to co-ordinate the decisions and actions of millions of individuals, is that it provides a flexible and subtle information system, on the basis of which the myriad decisions are made. Moreover, the rational reactions of individuals to this information interact in order to produce a social optimum in which the efficient use of resources is maximised. Clearly, the problem of transport co-ordination is an excellent example of the more general problem of co-ordinating innumerable individual decisions, about both the present and the future. The fundamental rule of classical microeconomics is that it is rational to carry out an activity right up to (but not beyond) the point at which the marginal cost of taking the activity any further just equals the marginal benefit enjoyed from taking it further. A classical example is that a firm acting in this way will necessarily maximise profits. More generally, welfare economics has long taught that the rule for society as a whole is to push to the point where marginal social cost equals marginal social benefit. Since long before environmentalism was even heard of, economists have argued that social costs (as opposed to purely private costs which enter into the profit and loss accounts of an ordinary firm) include the adverse impact on others of pollution and other externalities. These external costs are not borne by the polluter in normal commercial practice, unlike the way it pays for costs it imposes on the rest of society for which there is a market price, such as ordinary inputs of labour and materials. Welfare economists have long concluded that external costs (and benefits) should be charged to (or credited to) the individual or firm responsible for their creation. For many decades, economists have argued that the polluter should pay.

Roads and external costs

Economists have long tended to accept that roads must be seen as public goods (except for limited-access toll roads where twentieth-century motorways in several countries have revived the eighteenth-century tradition, as a means of financing new road construction). In the late 1950s and early 1960s, a considerable number of economists came to realise that electronics was developing to the point where much more subtle charging methods than old-fashioned toll gates could be used, on any part of the road network, and that the toll charged could vary with factors such as the distance travelled, the degree of congestion, and other external costs imposed on the rest of society such as noise, pollution and accidents. Despite attempts at obfuscation by politicians, there is now no doubt about the feasibility of a variety of suitable electronic devices, of which perhaps the most attractive is the replacement of the licence disc by the purchase of a transponder whose units of electronic charge would be progressively used up as the vehicle is driven on congested roads. The economic argument is generally presented in terms of congestion costs – each additional vehicle on a road above some level of free flow will impose additional costs on every other vehicle on the road, by making their journeys slower and so less efficient than they would otherwise be. But the argument extends naturally to other external costs – for example, accident costs, where it would be logical and probably practical for insurance premiums for vehicles to be paid at least in part out of the road charge. In general, this road charge on the individual user should be related to the marginal costs imposed on the rest of society – highest in congested conditions, lower in uncongested conditions but still calculated to cover pollution, noise, accident and road repair costs.

The fundamental economic argument considers that congestion, pollution and other similar externalities should be treated in exactly the same way as other costs, such as the use of scarce resources of labour or capital. This implies several things. One is that the charges should be paid by all road users, including trucks and buses, at levels reflecting as accurately as possible the relative costs imposed by different kinds of vehicle. Thus trucks and buses, which use more road space per vehicle-mile, would pay more. Another implication is that it is right that the charges are passed on in selling prices, just like any other cost. A firm whose productive activities cause congestion to others is imposing greater costs on the rest of society than another firm using different techniques. Another implication is that these external costs should be balanced against other, equally real, costs. For example, public transport may cause less pollution than private but it uses more labour, because private transport is a perfect example of DIY. The two costs – and many others – need to enter into the balance and the outcome needs to be duly weighed. The process of weighing will commonly lead to answers which do not accord with commonly held prejudices. For example, 'everyone knows' that public transport is more economical than private. But is it, when labour costs enter the picture? Indeed, it is not even clear that the pollution costs are on average in favour of public transport. Pollution is roughly proportional to fuel consumption. An average bus carries a load of about 9 passengers and does 7–9 miles per gallon (mpg) in urban conditions – say 60–70 traveller-miles on a gallon of fuel. A small car will do up to 50 mpg in similar conditions – so with a driver alone as the only traveller in the car, it pollutes rather more than a bus to achieve a given distance of travel, but with a driver and one passenger it causes less pollution per traveller-mile. This simple example should indicate that untutored common sense and *a priori* reasoning are no substitute for careful calculation.

Another lesson from all this line of argument is that the case for road pricing is not limited to congested city centres. Undoubtedly, the appropriate price would be higher there. Public transport is far and away the most competitive with private on 'line hauls' where large numbers of people (or loads of goods for that matter) are being carried together from A to B, or in very congested areas where trains can be run underground. It seems, however, that our society is developing away from these kinds of transport demands to one of a complex pattern of criss-cross journeys – as a result of factors such as greater job mobility, the now normal situation where both husbands and wives go out to work and the choice of most people for suburban and exurban living. I have little doubt that if the traffic Origin and Destination surveys that were fashionable in the 1960s were done again today, the apparent daily tidal flow towards and from the centre of cities and conurbations would break down into much more complex cross flows with the average movement being from farther out to nearer in to the centre – simply because most people live rather further out from the centre than their work places, but with relatively few people travelling all the way from periphery to centre.

Guiding investment decisions

The last lesson of the application of basic microeconomics to road pricing is in many ways the most fundamental and the one most often ignored. In the short run, the function of the price mechanism is to allocate existing resources. But in the medium and long term, its function is also to guide decisions about adding to our productive resources (investment) or allowing existing resources to wear out (disinvestment). It is quite indefensible to argue, as many do, that road pricing should simply be used to ration existing road space. Road pricing should be used, both as an allocative device and as a measure of whether or not to add to (or, indeed, subtract from) the existing road space: it can and should be used as an investment criterion. All this means – but this 'all' is a great deal – is that if road users are prepared to pay a price for the use of roads that is greater than the costs of providing additional road space (including all the costs, externalities, land costs, a sensible measure of the costs of disturbing any areas with special wildlife and all the other genuine costs which can be identified) then the additional road space should be built, and as in any other economic activity, the charge for the use of the new facility should be sufficient to finance its cost.

This point – pricing as an investment criterion – is the one where we economists start to lose some of our conventionally-minded supporters. Will not new roads lead to an indefinite demand and renewed congestion? One answer is that this only happens when the pressure of frustrated demand has built up to enormous proportions. Certainly, road traffic can be expected to grow with real incomes – but why should this growth be so wrong (as long as, one must repeat, external costs are all paid by road users) when growth in demand for and consumption of other good things is accepted as a normal part of the growth of prosperity. Indeed, it is true that transport, both private and public, is a considerable user of depletable resources – but so are very many other economic activities. The basic lesson is that all economic activities – transport or non-transport, private or public – should follow so far as is possible the rule of marginal social cost equals marginal social benefit.

(a) Why is the current system of allocating road space socially inefficient?
(b) Identify the external costs of using a car to travel to work.
(c) How could road pricing ensure that external costs would be borne by the motorist? Can you see any difficulties in administrating such a system?
(d) If road pricing were to guide investment in transport infrastructure, would it matter if this resulted in the building of many more roads?
(e) The article does not talk about equity, and whether road pricing is a fair way to allocate road space. What arguments might be made against road pricing in this respect?

In the article below, taken from *The Economist* of 18 April 2002, the author assesses the global move towards a tougher approach to cartels and price fixing, and the difficulties that new technology will raise for competition authorities.

Fixing for a fight

Bosses beware: price-fixing and other dodgy dealings are under fire from governments everywhere, as regulators cast a wider net for culprits.

Until recently, the world of art seemed an unlikely place to find a cartel. For a long time, shady price-fixing deals were the province of the decidedly less chic: industries such as steel tubes, animal feed, graphite electrodes and construction are just a few recent examples. So it must be particularly galling for Alfred Taubman, a former chairman of Sotheby's, an auctioneer, to have been convicted last December in America of fixing prices with his ostensible arch-rival, Christie's. But Mr Taubman, who faces a probable prison term when he is sentenced on April 22nd, will not be the last colluding boss to come in for a nasty surprise. Many see his case as a sign of things to come.

To see why, consider Mr Taubman's alleged co-conspirator in the case, Christie's former chief, Sir Anthony Tennant, who remains safely at home in Britain. Price-fixing in Britain, as in most countries, is not yet treated as a crime. But that is changing across the world, as a wave of new rules and stronger enforcement seeks to stamp out anti-competitive practices.

Just a few years ago, America seemed uniquely obsessed with price-fixing. Today, new measures against cartel behaviour (which includes bid-rigging and deals to carve up market share, as well as price-fixing) are being taken from Sweden to South Korea, where the competition body levied its first fine against a foreign firm earlier this year. In Britain, a planned law will introduce jail sentences for cartel conspirators.

In the past few years, the European Commission has crusaded with new fervour against cartels, levying the biggest fines in its history, totalling €1.8 billion ($1.6 billion) in 2001 alone (see chart).

Moreover, these days it is not only manufacturers and commodity-mongers who can expect a visit from the competition cops. Recent inquiries have led them to brewers, banks and even bus operators. The current attack on cartels comes at a time when the temptation to strike cosy deals with competitors is stronger than ever, as pricing power remains weak and excess capacity abounds in the wake of the global economic slowdown.

The costs of collusion should make any boss think twice, though. The European Commission can levy fines of up to 10% of a company's turnover for cartel offences. Dawn raids are running at about one a month in the European Union. In America, fines are based on the size of the market affected, but private lawsuits can be far more costly: Sotheby's was hit by a $45m fine by the American government, but its customers' lawsuits have cost it hundreds of millions more. Such private lawsuits are on the rise in Europe, says Elizabeth Morony of Clifford Chance, a law firm.

International cartels – those in which member firms are headquartered all over

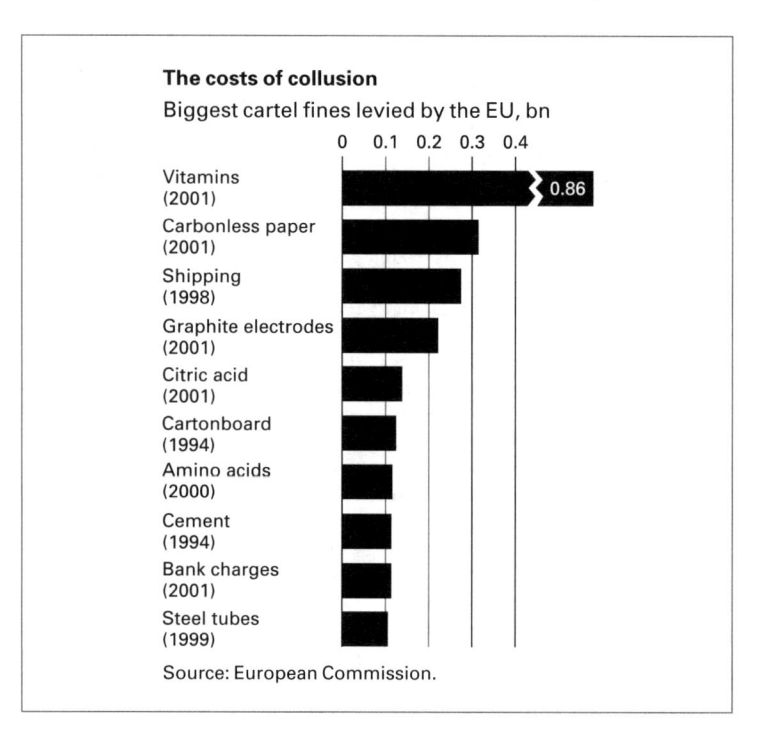

The costs of collusion
Biggest cartel fines levied by the EU, bn

Vitamins (2001)	0.86
Carbonless paper (2001)	
Shipping (1998)	
Graphite electrodes (2001)	
Citric acid (2001)	
Cartonboard (1994)	
Amino acids (2000)	
Cement (1994)	
Bank charges (2001)	
Steel tubes (1999)	

Source: European Commission.

the world – face new attack too. Last year, eight vitamin makers from France, Germany, Japan and Switzerland, including Aventis, BASF and Roche, were fined €855m by the European Commission for fixing prices and setting sales quotas. The cartel had earlier been fined in America, and several executives have served time in American prisons. America's Department of Justice estimates that 70% of its cartel targets last year were foreign-based, compared with none in 1990.

Global telecoms companies may soon receive similar treatment. Last summer, European enforcers raided the offices of mobile-phone companies, including Britain's Vodafone and a division of Deutsche Telekom, seeking evidence of price-fixing in international roaming charges. Mario Monti, Europe's competition commissioner, now plans to go after the industry over connection fees for fixed-line calls. Pharmaceutical companies, already humbled by the fines for the vitamin cartel, became the target of yet another investigation in Britain, earlier this month, into the alleged price-fixing of generic drugs.

Several things are driving the anti-cartel push. One is the desire to create a genuine single market in Europe, where geographic 'market sharing' is seen as particularly damaging, according to Alec Burnside of Linklaters, a law firm. Last month, for example, the commission accused Carlsberg, a Danish brewer, and Heineken, a Dutch rival, of plotting not to compete on each other's home turf.

Secondly, regulators have become more sympathetic to consumer lobbies, and have turned their attention to retail goods. Britain's Office of Fair Trading claims to be running 25 cartel probes, with a shift towards recognisable household names.

Another snag for would-be price-fixers is legislation to make whistleblowing more attractive. Many countries have now followed America in encouraging guilty parties to spill the beans: the first member of a cartel to come forward now wins leniency, a concession taken advantage of in both the vitamin and auctioneering cases.

New technologies, new concerns

The smoke-filled room is the fabled venue for hatching cartels, but new technologies such as the Internet, once seen as sources of price transparency, have ironically created new concerns about collusion. Covisint, the car industry's online parts exchange, was scrutinised by America's Federal Trade Commission last year, with these fears in mind. One way to avoid problems with such exchanges is to ensure anonymity and to stop competing firms from seeing each other's bids. E-mail should also worry company bosses, as it may create an appearance of collusion if salesmen from competing firms casually correspond about, say, pricing patterns – and e-mails are hard to delete.

Given regulators' aggressive new approach to cartels, companies are having to educate themselves. Roche, a member of the vitamin cartel, has put thousands of its managers in training to teach them to follow the law. In truth, avoiding cartels such as the one for vitamins should not be so difficult. The best advice, as one lawyer puts it, is: 'Don't talk to the competition.'

But there are shades of grey. Trade associations and annual conventions are one source of problems; sugar companies once came under scrutiny after such a meeting. Bosses are often keen to hear about the state of demand in their industry, but comments about price and volume targets can be taken as a tacit attempt at collusion. Joint ventures and merger negotiations are another possible minefield. When, as Adam Smith once put it, talk turns to 'some contrivance to raise prices', the best policy these days is just to say no.

© *The Economist*, London (18.4.02)

(a) What reasons are given in the article to explain the growth in global cartels?

(b) Why are competition authorities throughout the world adopting the more hard-line American approach to dealing with cartels and price fixing?

(c) What issues does use of the Internet raise for competition authorities and for companies seeking to avoid suspicion of collusion?

Privatisation has been, and continues to be, a contentious issue. The article below, taken from *The Economist* of 13 June 1998, shows why it is becoming increasingly difficult for those who argue against it to make a case.

The end of privatisation?

Labour's reluctance to use the p-word is oddly out of tune with its usual tendency to trumpet any successful British export. For privatisation is one British invention that continues to be emulated around the world. Flotations of privatised assets are expected to take place in more than 100 countries in 1995–2000 and to raise over £120 billion ($200 billion). The reasons for this are not hard to understand: privatisation works, as any fair reading of the British record amply illustrates.

First, the benefits to British public finances over the past two decades have been considerable. The cumulative proceeds from privatisation between 1979 and 1997 were more than £90 billion (at current prices). And the benefits go far wider than the capital account.

According to a 1997 study by National Economic Research Associates (NERA), in the first year of Mrs Thatcher's government (i.e. 1979–80) 33 state enterprises, all later to be privatised, absorbed £500m of public funds as well as more than £1 billion in loan finance. By 1987, these same companies were contributing £8 billion a year to the Treasury in share sales, tax receipts and dividends. This dramatic improvement conceals some striking individual achievements. British Steel, which ate up an annual subsidy of £600m–£1 billion on a turnover of less than £3 billion before privatisation, is now one of the lowest-cost steel producers in the world. British Airways is the world's most profitable airline, and is cited as a model by the would-be privatisers running Air France.

Customers have also benefited. A 1996 study from the National Audit Office found that service had improved significantly in telecoms and to a lesser extent in electricity, gas and water since privatisation. Since privatisation of telecoms and the introduction of digital exchanges, there has been a 50-fold reduction in faults in trunk calls and a 30-fold reduction in faults in local ones.

Most customers are also paying less for their utility bills. Since privatisation, the average telephone bill has declined in real terms by 49 per cent. But even in industries where it has taken time to introduce competition, regulation has meant that prices have fallen – the average domestic gas bill is down by 31 per cent since privatisation, and the average domestic electricity bill by 20 per cent. Real competition is just beginning in these markets, and should force prices down further. Water and sewerage are the exceptions: average domestic household bills rose by 36 per cent and 42 per cent respectively. But this is largely a result of having to meet European environmental standards, and to make up for decades of under-investment.

Water apart, the dramatic improvements in price and service give the lie to the claim that customers have been the prime victims of privatisation. Another frequently voiced fear was that privatisation would lead to a deterioration in safety. The evidence points the other way. In most privatised industries there have been 'widespread and sustained improvements in occupational safety,' according to NERA. Its 1997 study points out that the safety records at British Gas, British Steel, and in the supply of electricity and water, have also been significantly better than in the economy as a whole.

There is, of course, a valid argument that many of these post-privatisation improvements and price cuts owed as much to changes in technology and the decline in fossil-fuel prices as they did to changes in ownership. And it is also true that the performance of many of the privatised industries improved in the run-up to their sale. Yet would these improvements have taken place if the threat of privatisation had been removed? Dieter Helm, director of Oxford Economic Research Associates, is doubtful. He says the speed of change achieved could not have been matched in the public sector. Any government, whatever its ideological hue, would have been limited by public-sector borrowing constraints, as well as by the fear of industrial unrest.

Yet facts alone do not seem enough to win the argument. Poll evidence suggests that privatisation has never been wildly popular, and that it has been getting less so as time goes by. In 1983 MORI found that 43 per cent of people wanted more privatisation; by 1992 that was down to 24 per cent and last year a poll found just 19 per cent in favour of privatising the Underground.

Why is this? Many people believe that the most recent privatisations do not make sense, because it is hard to introduce competition in some industries, such as rail. But this ignores the role of regulation in mimicking competition – something that has improved the electricity and gas industries, even though the introduction of real competition is only now being completed.

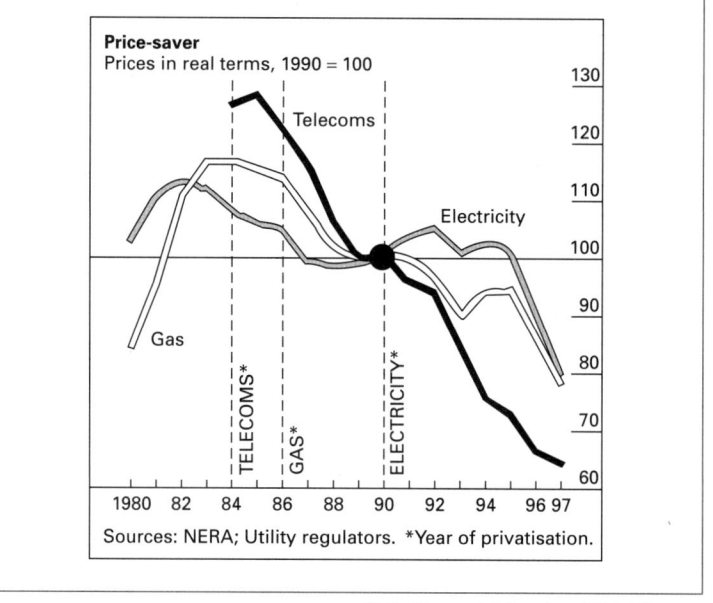

Price-saver
Prices in real terms, 1990 = 100

[Graph showing Telecoms, Electricity, and Gas price indices from 1980 to 1997, with vertical dashed lines marking years of privatisation: TELECOMS*, GAS*, ELECTRICITY*. Y-axis values: 60, 70, 80, 90, 100, 110, 120, 130.]

Sources: NERA; Utility regulators. *Year of privatisation.

© *The Economist*, London (13.6.98)

(a) Outline the main arguments in favour of privatisation.
(b) What evidence does the article present to support its case that privatisation has been successful?
(c) Why is regulation so important in ensuring that the benefits of privatisation continue?

The importance of privatisation for the economies of eastern Europe is clearly illustrated in the following article, taken from the *OECD Observer* of August/September 1998. It describes how the Polish economy will need further privatisation, if it is to maintain its impressive growth record of the past few years.

Poland: privatisation as the key to efficiency

A thriving private sector is the force behind Poland's buoyant economy, which is now in its seventh year of continuous expansion. The number of new private firms soared in the first half of the 1990s and has continued to increase rapidly since. Meanwhile, privatisation has reduced the size of the public sector, which nonetheless is still quite prominent across the economy, with a strong presence in mining, fuels, power generation, defence, heavy chemicals, telecommunications, air and rail transport, sugar, spirits and insurance.

Corporate performance in the public sector has been much weaker than in private enterprises and has acted as a brake on the economy as a whole. Profitability has improved in the private sector since 1995 and deteriorated in the public sector, and while investment in the private sector has soared, it has stagnated in public enterprises. Yet the firms in the public sector have received most of the subsidies. This difference in performance might be partly explained by the fact that privatisation began with the strongest companies, leaving the rest to struggle on under public ownership. However, some empirical studies suggest that there was no such selection bias.

Another possible reason lies in the inherited liabilities carried by some traditional heavy industries which the newly emerged private firms do not have, such as an antiquated capital stock and environmental drawbacks. Arguably a more important cause of the discrepancy in performance is poor corporate governance in the public sector. Even unprofitable public enterprises can award relatively high wages, and spending priorities are not always geared to restructuring, as documented by Poland's Supreme Board of Inspection, which recently published a list of cases of ill-judged expenditure.

In short, financial discipline is an ingredient in short supply in Poland's public enterprises. Wages are negotiated according to a national norm established between social partners. This practice is not that unusual in Europe, but in Poland the leverage of the unions in the negotiations is particularly strong, limiting the influence of market forces on public pay deals. As a result, the national norm, which is intended to act as a ceiling to wage deals, in fact works as a floor. Also, in some firms, the remuneration of managers is set as a multiple of the workers' average wage rather than as a function of corporate performance. Moreover, a number of public enterprises do not honour their tax and social security obligations, which is a *de facto* and quite perverse form of subsidy. Admittedly such arrears, and more importantly, outright evasion, are also observed in the private sector.

Although the state or the local government nominally owns those firms, in practice it fails to control them. Its inability to sanction mismanagement is in part due to political pressure from a broad range of sectoral lobbies. The fact that their demands are accommodated quite easily is helped by the lack of transparency in the handling of public money. This is a weakness which a new draft law is trying to correct. On top of that, the public administration is not equipped well enough, whether it be in logistics or skills, to be able to keep up with operations in the several thousand enterprises that are still in the public sector.

The renewed momentum

To overcome these problems the government, formed after the parliamentary elections in September 1997, has decided to accelerate privatisation. After all, private investors, be they foreign or domestic, would be in a better position than the cash-strapped state to provide the money, skills and know-how Polish firms need to boost their competitiveness. And these new stakeholders would obviously have strong incentives to impose hard budgetary constraints and would, if necessary, be freer to liquidate non-viable activities.

The menu of privatisation formulae on offer is an impressive one, but its diversity has not always helped to speed up the sales. Although the proliferation of schemes to transfer ownership reflects a multi-track approach with strong pragmatic merits, it has in some cases resulted in procrastination, slowing the process down. The new government is determined to push privatisation along quickly, since it faces strong budgetary pressures from ambitious reforms in pensions, health and education, as well as decentralisation. Moreover, the State still owes very large amounts to those whose property was illegally confiscated under communism and on account of past unpaid pension and wage hikes.

After the sale of a major bank and a large copper company last year, a whole series of important enterprises are to be privatised in the near future, particularly in banking, insurance, telecommunications, power supply and air transport. In addition, the government is considering sell-offs in sectors, such as mining, which were previously off-bounds. It is also contemplating removing some of the legal strictures which hold up privatisation, such as the approval of the Council of Ministers, which is obligatory even for some relatively small deals.

Although faster privatisation may be both feasible and desirable in Poland, it will not take place overnight. It is an inherently complex process, involving a redistribution of property and other rights on an enormous scale. It is intertwined with restructuring, deregulation and demonopolisation, each of which is a challenge on its own. Moreover, privatisation alone is not a sufficient condition of good governance; other factors include managerial skills, the existence of performance incentives, transparency and a sound legal and business environment. But can the government really afford delays? Probably not. Poland's own experience to date, as well as that of some other OECD countries, strongly suggests that the benefits of postponing the divestiture of state assets – even for prior restructuring or consolidation into larger entities – would be dwarfed by the costs. Privatising sooner, while the economy is growing strongly, rather than letting the costs build up further, would seem to be the best way forward.

182 CHAPTER 12 APPLIED MICROECONOMICS

(a) What forms can privatisation take in a transition economy?

(b) What weaknesses do Poland's public-sector enterprises have, and how do these weaknesses impinge upon the performance of the economy in general?

(c) What difficulties are there in achieving a faster rate of privatisation in Poland?

E ANSWERS

Q1. Use of the environment for mining, farming, etc. reduces its amenity value. Use of the environment as a dump reduces its productivity for producing primary products. Use of the environment as a dump reduces its amenity value.

Q2. E.

Q3. *Yes*: (a), (c) and (e); *No*: (b) and (d). In the case of (c), technological progress has tended to be environmentally friendly (but not always so). The reasons include: greater miniaturisation, and hence a lower demand for raw materials; higher raw material prices leading to pressures to develop more resource-efficient products and processes; the pressure of public opinion; government policies (laws, taxes and subsidies promoting more environmentally friendly technology).

Q4. (a) (iii), (b) (i), (c) (iv), (d) (ii).

Q5. (a) Q_3, (b) Q_1, (c) Q_2, (d) Q_4.

Q6. C. By levying a charge that would fully compensate sufferers (i.e. a charge equal to the marginal pollution cost), the *MB – MC* line would shift downwards by the amount of the charge (i.e. by the height of the $MC_{pollution}$ curve). Profits for the polluter would be maximised where the new *MB – MC* curve crosses the horizontal axis: at Q_3.

Q7. D. The socially efficient tax rate is equal to the marginal external cost of pollution: i.e. $MC_{pollution}$. At the socially efficient level of output (Q_3), this will be equal to an amount OP_3.

Q8. *Technology-based standards*. Here the focus is on restricting the amount of pollution generated, irrespective of its impact.
Ambient-based standards. Here the focus is on restricting the environmental impact of the pollution.
Social-impact standards. Here the focus is on restricting the undesirable effects on people.

Q9. (a) and (c) *True*.
(b) and (d) *False*.

Q10. (a) Firm A 100 units; Firm B zero. (It is more expensive for firm A to reduce the emission of the pollutant than for firm B, and so it would be profitable for both firms if firm B reduced its emission by the full 100 units and then sold its 50 units of credits to firm A, permitting firm A to continue emitting 100 units.)

(b) The price would be somewhere between £1000 per unit (the lower limit for firm B to gain) and £2000 per unit (the upper limit for firm A to gain). This is a bilateral monopoly situation (i.e. only one seller and one buyer) and thus there is no unique equilibrium price. The actual price would depend on the outcome of negotiations between A and B.

(c) Firm A 30 units (a reduction of 70 units); Firm B 70 units (a reduction of 30 units). Firm B can reduce emissions of the pollutant by up to 30 units at an *MC* less than £4000, and hence more cheaply than A. Beyond this level, however, it would be cheaper for A to make the necessary reductions and sell the credits to B (allowing B to continue emitting 70 units).

(d) Again, given that the firms are operating under bilateral monopoly, the price would be negotiated. If a separate price is negotiated for each credit traded, then the upper price limit for each one would be the *MC* to B and the lower limit would be £4000, the *MC* to A.

Q11. There may not be the political will, given that governments are concerned about *domestic* interests; it is difficult to measure the amount of pollution caused by each country; it is difficult to identify the global effects of individual countries reducing their pollution; it is difficult to agree on the amount that each country should reduce emissions.

Q12. (a) Break the agreement. (If it is assumed that other countries will stick to the agreement, this country would save costs by not sticking to the agreement, but would gain most of the benefits from the other countries sticking to it.)

(b) Break the agreement. (If it is assumed that other countries will *not* stick to the agreement, this country will save costs by not sticking to it, and would only sacrifice the small benefit it would get directly by sticking to it.)

(c) Because either strategy would lead to a breakdown of the agreement and hence all countries being worse off than without the agreement.

Q13. C. In all the other cases the demand for roads is to serve some *other* purpose than mere travelling: whether to go to work, to go shopping or to deliver goods. In the case of going for a Sunday afternoon drive, the pleasure is gained directly from the journey.

Q14. tolls (note that some taxes are nevertheless included in the 'price' of motoring, even though the motorist does not pay them for using a particular stretch of road).

Q15. marginal.

Q16. costs.

Q17. *True*. The higher the level of congestion, the longer will be the time taken to make a journey and the greater will be the level of frustration experienced. These are both costs to the motorists of that specific journey and are thus marginal costs.

Q18. (c) and (g) *No*. These are *fixed* costs of owning a car. There is no *additional* cost incurred under these two headings each time the motorist makes a journey. All the other costs, however, *are* variable costs with respect to car usage and therefore have a positive marginal cost. Note that (d) and (h) are not direct *monetary* costs, but nevertheless are a cost to the motorist of making the journey. In the case of (d) we are only referring to the cost the specific motorist experiences from the congestion; we are not referring to the congestion costs imposed on others by the motorist's journey.

Q19. B. As incomes grow so the demand for road use grows rapidly: more people feel they can afford private transport rather than public transport; people use cars increasingly for leisure purposes; more families can afford more than one car. The price and cross-price elasticities of demand, on the other hand, are relatively inelastic: many people feel that there is no close substitute for private motoring.

Q20. Examples include: congestion; pollution (from exhaust fumes); accidents; noise.

Q21. *False*. The optimum level would be that where the marginal social benefit is equal to the marginal social cost. This may well be at a level of road use where there are some external costs. (If environmentalists object that this involves putting too little weight on protecting the environment, an economist would reply that the answer would be simply to attach a higher value to these external costs. This value, however, would have to be very high indeed, if not infinite, if the optimum level of road use were to generate *no* environmental externalities.)

Q22. *(a)* OH: where marginal private cost (MC) equals marginal private benefit, which, in the absence of externalities on the demand side, equals marginal social benefit (MSB).
(b) OE: where MSC = MSB.
(c) FG.
(d) A level equal to the marginal external cost: i.e. CD at the optimum level of road use, OE.

Q23. Environmental costs.
Equity: losers are unlikely to be compensated.

Congestion may not be solved. It may encourage a faster rate of growth of traffic.

Q24. *False*. Any positive marginal congestion tax rate will *reduce* congestion. To reduce congestion to the *optimum* level, however, the congestion tax would have to equal the size of the congestion externality at the optimum level of road use.

Q25. C. It is very difficult to measure the exact size of the congestion externalities and therefore difficult to determine the socially optimal level of charge.

Q26. When there are ready alternatives for the motorist: in terms of altering the timing of journeys, or the route, or the means of transport. For example, road pricing will be more effective if there is an attractive form of public transport available.

Q27. (a) (iv), (b) (vi), (c) (iii), (d) (v), (e) (vii), (f) (ii), (g) (i).

Q28. (a) (ii), (b) (i), (c) (iii).

Q29. *False*. Any firm in a dominant market position (whether a monopolist or an oligopolist) can be investigated if it is suspected of abusing its market power.

Q30. B. The mere possession of power is not seen to be important. What is important is how the firm exercises its power: whether it abuses its power by acting to restrict competition.

Q31. (a) (iii), (b) (viii), (c) (vii), (d) (ii), (e) (v), (f) (vi), (g) (i), (h) (ix), (i) (iv).

Q32. *(a)* (ii), (iv) and (vii).
(b) (ii), (iv), (v), (viii) and (ix).
(c) (i), (iii), (vi) and (vii).

Q33. *True*.

Q34. horizontal. This type of merger will reduce the number of firms in the relevant segment of the market.

Q35. Ways include: economies of scale from rationalisation, greater countervailing power to drive down prices charged by suppliers to the firm, increased power to compete more effectively against an already established large firm, increased ability to afford costly research and development.

Q36. Whether the merger is likely to impede effective competition.

Q37. *Yes*: (b), (c), (f). *No*: (a), (d), (e). (See Sloman *Economics* (5th edition) pages 344–5.)

Q38. *True*. It can decide to block the merger, permit it, or permit it subject to various conditions to safeguard competition.

Q39. *True*. (a), (b) and (d). *False* (c) (the Secretary of State can choose whether or not to refer the proposed merger to the CC), (e) (the Secretary of State can choose whether or not to accept the recommendations of the CC).

Q40. Ways include: sale of a nationalised firm directly to a private-sector firm (e.g. Rover Group to British Aerospace); sale of government's shares in otherwise private company (e.g. BP); introduction of private contractors into parts of the public sector (e.g.

contract cleaners in National Health Service hospitals); introduction of private firms selling directly to the public in otherwise nationalised industries (e.g. private canteens); sale of public sector assets (e.g. council houses).

Q41. Reasons include: poor profitability may be a reflection of low demand rather than ownership; prices may be kept deliberately low by the government for social/political/macroeconomic reasons; costs may be similarly high if it were under private ownership.

Q42. Although (b), (e), (f), (g) and (h) would seem at first sight to be arguments in favour of privatisation and (a) and (c) against, most of the arguments are inconclusive (which is part of the reason why politicians will continue to argue). The extent to which any industry, private or public, operates in the public interest depends on the way in which it is run, the degree of government intervention and the amount of competition faced, and these will not necessarily depend on whether the industry is publicly or privately owned. (How would you reply to argument (e)?)

Q43. To maximise revenue from the sale, the government will want the industry to be as attractive (profitable) as possible to potential shareholders. This will be the case if the industry is sold as a monopoly with the prospect of large supernormal profits. But this will conflict with the second objective of making the industry as competitive as possible.

Q44. *True*. Monopolies can be inefficient in both the public sector and the private sector. Similarly the government can be 'tough' or take a *laissez-faire* approach with both public and private industries.

Q45. D. The socially efficient output for a firm is where $MSB = MSC$. In the absence of externalities and in the first-best situation this will be where $P = MC$.

Q46. A. The second-best pricing formula is $P = MSC + X$ (where X is the average of other industries' price above their MSC). Given that, on average, other firm's externalities are zero, this formula gives $P = (MC - 5\%) + 15\% = MC + 10\%$.

Q47. D. If for reasons of equity it is desired to help a particular section of the community, it is best (*ceteris paribus*) to do this from *general* taxation, otherwise it would be unfair on those who have to pay the subsidy. For example, in A, why should urban bus users have any greater obligation than others to help the rural users?

Q48. *(a)* Yes. There are separate regulatory bodies for each regulated industry, such as OFGEM for the fuel (gas and electricity) industry, OFTEL for the telecommunications industry and OFWAT for the water industry.
(b) No. Only those parts where it is felt by the government that there is inadequate competition.
(c) No. It is of the form *RPI* minus *X*.
(d) Yes.
(e) Yes. This enters the formula as an extra term *Y*, so that the formula becomes $RPI - X + Y$.
(f) Yes, if $X - Y$ is greater than the rate of inflation.
(g) Yes.
(h) No. The price-setting formula may be changed before the end of the period if circumstances change, such as a larger value for *X* than had been anticipated.
(i) No. They are also concerned to prevent practices which could be anti-competitive (e.g. attempts to compete unfairly against rivals in order to prevent them getting a larger share of the market).
(j) Yes.

Q49. *False*. It does just the opposite: it removes the incentive to reduce costs. What is the point of reducing costs if the regulators simply reduce prices to prevent profits rising?

Q50. E. The regulator is 'captured' by the industry.

Q51. Advantages: it gives the regulator discretion to take account of the specific circumstances of the industry; it is flexible, allowing the licence and price formula to be changed as circumstances change; the price formula gives the industry an incentive to be as efficient as possible, since that way it will be able to make more profit *and keep it* (provided that this does not then lead to a higher value being given to *X*).

Disadvantages: if the value of *X* is too low (which it might become if there are substantial technical advances in the industry), the firm might make excessive profits; if, on the other hand, *X* is changed to reflect reductions in costs, this then removes the incentive referred to above in the list of advantages; a large amount of power is vested in the regulator, who is not democratically accountable; regulation has become increasingly complex, which makes it more difficult for the industries to plan; regulation can involve a time-consuming 'game' between the regulator and the industry; regulatory capture.

Q52. Dividing up the industry into a separate company owning the pipelines and other companies using the pipelines and supplying the customers; forcing the pipeline company to charge the same rates to all companies using the pipelines (including itself, if it is still allowed to supply gas); forcing the pipeline company to allow any supplier meeting safety standards to use the pipelines; breaking up the part of the industry producing gas and supplying gas to customers into several companies; allowing customers to choose from a number of different suppliers (this is possible through metering, provided that central records are kept of the gas metered into the system by each company and the gas used by each consumer allocated to that company).

Q53. *Yes*: (a), (b), (d) and (e).

No: (c), (f) and (g). In the case of (f), bonuses were nearly always awarded. The problem was that they were often awarded even though targets had not been met, or had only been met by using bogus figures. In the case of (g), the problem was that prices were often set *below* equilibrium. This resulted in shortages and queues.

Q54. (a) and (c) are examples of insider privatisation: where ownership passes to management and/or workers. The rest are examples of outsider privatisation: where the new shareholders are not employees of the company.

Q55. *Yes*: (a), (c), (d) and (e).

No: (b) and (f). Although output has fallen in many industries, shortages have been reduced or eliminated as a result of prices rising towards or to equilibrium.

Q56. Ways include: careful management of the economy to avoid inflation; creating as much competition as possible, and not merely privatising firms as monopolies; introducing a regulatory regime that will prevent the abuse of monopoly/oligopoly power; encouraging systems of corporate governance that are responsive to consumers and other outside stakeholders; improving incentives for inward investment; improving the financial, communications and transport infrastructure.

Chapter Thirteen

13

The National Economy

A REVIEW

Chapters 13 to 15 offer a basic overview of the principal macroeconomic issues: *growth, unemployment, inflation* and *the balance of payments*. In this chapter we focus on the first: economic growth. We look at why growth fluctuates in the short term and what causes economies to grow over the longer term. We also look at how national output and income are measured.

13.1 The scope of macroeconomics
(Pages 374–6)

Q1. Which of the following are macroeconomics issues?
(a) An increase in the number of job vacancies. Yes/No
(b) The problems faced by a firm relocating in the south of England. Yes/No
(c) Industrial action by the teaching unions. Yes/No
(d) An increase in the level of taxation. Yes/No
(e) A slowdown in the growth of the economy. Yes/No
(f) The privatisation of the electricity industry. Yes/No
(g) Unemployment in the coal industry. Yes/No
(h) A rise in interest rates. Yes/No

Q2. (Actual) economic growth is defined as ....

....

Q3. In which two decades between 1930 and 2000 was unemployment the lowest in most industrialised economies?

....

Q4. Inflation is defined as:
A. The difference in the price level this year compared with the same time last year.
B. The rise in costs over the previous twelve months.
C. The absolute increase in *average* prices over the previous twelve months.
D. The percentage increase in the average level of prices over the previous twelve months.
E. The percentage expansion of the economy over the previous twelve months.

13.2 The circular flow of income
(Pages 376–8) An important diagram for understanding how the macroeconomy works is the *circular flow of income diagram*. It can be used to show the relationship between changes in aggregate demand and the four macroeconomic objectives.

Q5. Figure 13.1 shows a circular flow of income. Attach the correct label (C_d, G, I, M, S, T, X, Y) to each of the eight flows.

▤ Multiple choice   ? Written answer   ◐ Delete wrong word   ⊖ Diagram/table manipulation   ✕ Calculation   ⬢ Matching/ordering

Figure 13.1 The circular flow of income

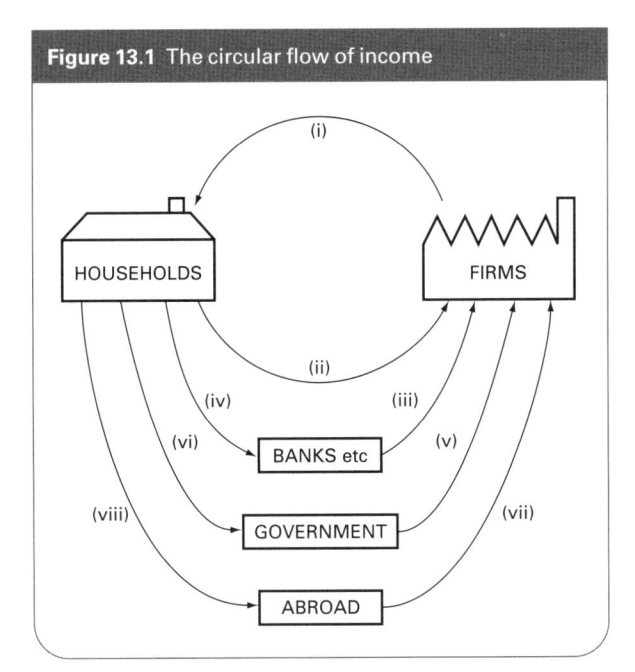

[Diagram showing households and firms with flows (i)-(viii) through Banks, Government, and Abroad]

Q6. Which of the following are changes in injections and which are changes in withdrawals in the UK circular flow of income? In each case specify whether the change is an increase or a decrease. In each case assume *ceteris paribus*.

(a) The government raises tax allowances.
Withdrawal/Injection   Increase/Decrease

(b) The government cuts spending on roads.
Withdrawal/Injection   Increase/Decrease

(c) Firms borrow more money in order to build up their stocks in preparation for an anticipated rise in consumer demand.
Withdrawal/Injection   Increase/Decrease

(d) A depreciation in the exchange rate affects the popularity of holidays abroad.
Withdrawal/Injection   Increase/Decrease

(e) Saving is affected by a redistribution of income from the rich to the poor.
Withdrawal/Injection   Increase/Decrease

(f) Consumers demand more goods that are domestically produced (but total consumption does not change).
Withdrawal/Injection   Increase/Decrease

(g) People invest more money in building societies.
Withdrawal/Injection   Increase/Decrease

Q7. The following represent flows in the economy of a small country:

	(£m)
Saving	200
Consumption of domestic goods	1550
Income tax revenue	750
Indirect tax revenue	475
Import expenditure	600
Export expenditure	850
Government expenditure	900
Investment	575

(where government expenditure and investment include only the amount spent in the domestic economy: i.e. exclude any imported component).

Calculate the level of withdrawals from the circular flow.

....

Q8. Referring to the data in Q7, what is the level of aggregate demand?

A. £4075m
B. £3875m
C. £3275m
D. £2325m
E. £1550m

(Pages 377–9) Assume initially that injections equal withdrawals. Now assume that injections rise (or withdrawals fall), so that injections exceed withdrawals. This will cause a **Q9.** *rise/fall* in national income. This in turn will cause a **Q10.** *rise/fall* in **Q11.** *injections/withdrawals/both injections and withdrawals* until a new equilibrium level of income is reached where withdrawals once more equal injections. This change in income will tend to be **Q12.** *larger/smaller* than the initial change in injections.

Q13. What will happen to the level of national income in an economy if the following changes occur? (In each case assume other things remain unchanged.)

(a) The Chancellor of the Exchequer raises income tax.
Rise/Fall/Impossible to tell without more information

(b) Firms are encouraged by lower interest rates to build new factories.
Rise/Fall/Impossible to tell without more information

(c) French buyers are deterred from buying British-made goods.
Rise/Fall/Impossible to tell without more information

(d) Both taxation and government expenditure are reduced.
Rise/Fall/Impossible to tell without more information

(e) People decide to save a larger proportion of their income.
Rise/Fall/Impossible to tell without more information

(f) Other countries begin to recover from recession.
Rise/Fall/Impossible to tell without more information

13.3 Measuring national income and output

(Pages 380–3)

Q14. Gross domestic product (GDP) may be defined as

....

....

When calculating real GDP we must use the *GDP deflator* for that year. This allows us to adjust figures measured in current prices for the rate of inflation, and show them in terms of a base year.

188 CHAPTER 13 THE NATIONAL ECONOMY

Q15. The GDP deflator is the same as the retail price index (RPI). *True/False*

Q16. Assume that GDP in current prices grows from £120bn in year 1 to £160bn in year 2 and that the GDP deflator rises from 100 in year 1 to 130 in year 2. By how much has real GDP grown (as a percentage)?

....

When comparing national income statistics of different countries, they have to be converted into a common currency (e.g. dollars or euros). But the current market exchange rate may be a poor indicator of the purchasing power of a country's currency. To correct for this, *purchasing-power parity* (PPP) exchange rates can be used. PPP rates are those at which a given amount of money would buy the same in any country after exchanging it into the local currency. GDP measured at PPP exchange rates is known as *purchasing-power standard* GDP (PPS GDP).

Q17. If country A has a national income of $10bn and country B has a national income of $12bn at current exchange rates, and if, in PPP terms, current exchange rates overvalue the currency of B relative to A by 1.5 times, what is the ratio of the PPS GDP of country A to country B?

....

13.4 Short-term economic growth and the business cycle

(Pages 384–6) When discussing economic growth we need to distinguish between *actual* and *potential* economic growth.

Q18. What would be the result of each of the following events: actual growth, potential growth, both or neither? (In each case assume that other things remain constant.)

(a) The discovery of new raw materials.
  Actual growth/potential growth/both/neither
(b) Firms take on more labour in response to an increase in consumer demand.
  Actual growth/potential growth/both/neither
(c) A reduction in the number of vacancies in the economy. *Actual growth/potential growth/both/neither*
(d) An increase in the level of investment.
  Actual growth/potential growth/both/neither
(e) A reduction in the working week.
  Actual growth/potential growth/both/neither
(f) The discovery of new more efficient techniques which could benefit industry generally.
  Actual growth/potential growth/both/neither
(g) Increased expenditure on training.
  Actual growth/potential growth/both/neither

Q19. Actual growth can never be greater than potential growth. *True/False*

Figure 13.2 A production possibility curve

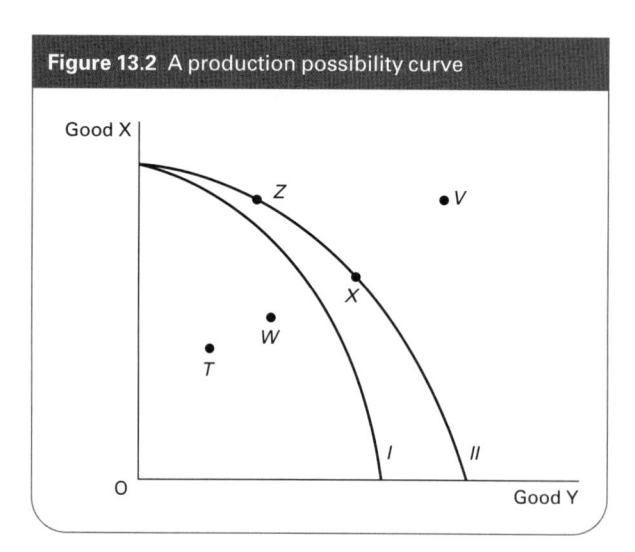

(Page 386) The production possibility curve can be used to illustrate the difference between actual and potential output.

Questions 20–22 refer to Figure 13.2.

Q20. A movement from *T* to *W* (but no movement in the production possibility curve) represents:
(a) An increase in potential output. *True/False*
(b) An increase in actual output. *True/False*
(c) A more efficient point of production. *True/False*

Q21. A movement from *W* to *X* and a shift of the curve from curve *I* to curve *II*, represents:
A. an increase in potential output.
B. an increase in actual output.
C. a more efficient point of production.
D. A, B and C.
E. B and C.
F. none of the above.

Q22. A movement from *X* to *Z* represents:
A. an increase in potential output.
B. an increase in actual output.
C. a more efficient point of production.
D. A, B and C.
E. B and C.
F. none of the above.

(Pages 386–90) Actual growth will tend to fluctuate over the course of the business cycle. The cycle can be broken down into four phases: the upturn, the boom, the peaking out and the slowdown or recession. In the **Q23.** *upturn/ expansion/peaking out/slowdown or recession* phase the rate of growth will be at its highest, whereas in the **Q24.** *upturn/expansion/peaking out/slowdown or recession* phase growth may actually cease or even become negative. Actual and potential outputs are closest during the **Q25.** *upturn/expansion/peaking out/slowdown or recession* phase of the business cycle.

Q26. Why is it unlikely that actual and potential outputs would ever be equal?

....

....

Q27. One of the major influences on the rate of actual growth within the economy is consumer spending.
True/False

13.5 Long-term economic growth

(Pages 390–2) When we look at economic growth over the *longer* term, it is growth in *potential* output that we need to examine.

Q28. The potential output of an economy depends upon which two factors?

1. ....

2. ....

Q29. The relationship between investment as a proportion of national income (*i*) and the potential rate of economic growth (g_p) is given by the formula:

A. $g_p = i/MEC$
B. $g_p = MEC/i$
C. $g_p = MEC - i$
D. $g_p = i - MEC$
E. $g_p = i \times MEC$

where *MEC* stands for the marginal efficiency of capital: the annual extra income (ΔY) as a proportion of the investment (*i*) that yielded it.

Q30. Given that investment of £100m yields an extra £50m annual national income, and given that 25 per cent of national income is put into new investment, what will be the growth in potential output?

....

Q31. If there is an increase in the size of the population, this will cause the level of output per head to increase.
True/False

Appendix: Calculating GDP

There are three methods of calculating GDP: the product method, the income method and the expenditure method.

(Pages 393–4) The product method
In order to avoid double counting we measure the value added to a product or service as it passes through each phase of its production.

Q32. If a raw material supplier, firm A, sells some raw materials to firm B for £120, which then processes them and sells them to firm C for £160; and if firm C fashions them and sells them to firm D for £240, which uses them to produce a finished good which it sells to a wholesaler for £300, which then sells it to a retailer for £350, which then adds a £25 mark-up – what has been the total value of production? Use a value-added approach to work out the answer.

....

Q33. Which of the following would be included in the measurement of the UK's GDP?
(a) The appreciation of stock due to price increases. *Yes/No*
(b) A service provided by government. *Yes/No*
(c) A raw material that is imported. *Yes/No*
(d) Stocks carried over from previous years. *Yes/No*
(e) The profits from the output produced in the UK by foreign-owned firms. *Yes/No*
(f) The benefits derived by owner occupiers from living in a property. *Yes/No*
(g) Additions to stocks made during the year. *Yes/No*
(h) The incomes earned by UK residents from the production of overseas companies. *Yes/No*

(Pages 394–5) The income approach
Q34. The factor incomes generated from the production of goods and services will be exactly equal to the sum of all values added. *True/False*

Q35. Table 13.1 represents a simplified national income account for an economy.
(a) What is the level of gross value added?

....

(b) What is the level of gross domestic product (at market prices)?

....

Table 13.1 Items from a national income account

	(£m)
Compensation of employees	3000
Gross profit	500
Gross rent and interest	100
Mixed incomes	90
Taxes on products	150
Subsidies on products	60

(Page 395) The expenditure approach
Q36. Which of the following items would be included in measuring the UK's GDP by the expenditure method?
(a) Spending on domestically produced consumer durables. *Yes/No*
(b) The purchase of British clothes in Europe. *Yes/No*
(c) Government spending on social security. *Yes/No*
(d) Government spending on educational services. *Yes/No*

(e) The purchase of new machinery by private industry. Yes/No
(f) Expenditure on new private housing. Yes/No
(g) Local government expenditure on new council housing. Yes/No
(h) Private expenditure on old (unimproved) housing. Yes/No

Q37. Table 13.2 shows GDP by category of expenditure. Calculate

(a) GDP (at market prices) ....

(b) GVA ....

Table 13.2 GDP by category of expenditure

	(£m)
Consumer expenditure	1050
Government final consumption	600
Gross domestic fixed capital formation	500
Exports of goods and services	850
Imports of goods and services	950
Taxes on products	500
Subsidies on products	50
Net income from abroad	60
Capital consumption (depreciation)	120

(Pages 395–8) Other measures

Three other measures that are frequently used are gross national income (GNY), net national income (NNY) and households' disposable income.

Q38. Using the figures in Table 13.2, calculate the following:

(a) GNY ....

(b) NNY ....

Q39. Households' disposable income is:
A. GDP (at market prices) + taxes paid by firms − subsidies received by firms + personal taxes − benefits.
B. GDP (at market prices) − taxes paid by firms + subsidies received by firms − depreciation − undistributed profits + personal taxes − benefits.
C. GDP (at market prices) − taxes paid by firms + subsidies received by firms − depreciation − undistributed profits − personal taxes + benefits.
D. GNY (at market prices) − taxes paid by firms + subsidies received by firms − undistributed profits + personal taxes − benefits.
E. GDY (at market prices) − taxes paid by firms + subsidies received by firms − depreciation − undistributed profits − personal taxes + benefits.

B PROBLEMS, EXERCISES AND PROJECTS

Q40. In small groups, find four items from this week's newspapers that are macroeconomic items. What makes them macroeconomic? To what extent is each of the items related to any of the four macroeconomic objectives that we have identified? Are any of the items related to macroeconomic policy and, if so, how is the policy supposed to improve the macroeconomic situation?

Q41. Given the following data:

	£million
Consumers' expenditure	290 000
Government final consumption	91 000
Gross domestic fixed capital formation	80 000
Exports of goods and services	110 000
Imports of goods and services	125 000

Calculate the level of aggregate demand (AD) ....

Q42. Using available statistical sources, find time-series data for the last ten years for the following macroeconomic variables:
- Consumer expenditure.
- Government expenditure.
- Gross domestic fixed capital formation.
- Imports and exports.

Calculate the level of aggregate demand for each of the years found (a bar chart may be effective here) and describe the implications of your findings. Does there appear to be a regular business cycle? What is the length of time between peaks? Data may be obtained from the *Annual Abstract of Statistics* (NS), *Economic Trends* (NS), *UK National Accounts* (NS) and the *National Institute Economic Review* (NIESR). National Statistics data are all available on the Web at www.statistics.gov.uk. See, in particular, the 'Bookshelf' and 'Statbase' sections.

Q43. In small groups, find data for economic growth, unemployment, inflation and current account deficits as a proportion of GDP for the UK and two other developed countries from 1980 to the current time. Data can be found from *OECD Economic Outlook* (http://www.oecd.org) and from *European Economy* (http://europa.eu.int/comm/economy_finance/publications/europeaneconomy_en.htm).

(a) When has economic growth been the highest in the UK and when has it been negative? Has the pattern been cyclical? Have the 'ups and downs' in economic growth since 1980 been similar in all three countries?

(b) Which of the countries has had the highest long-term growth?
(c) What explanations can you offer for (i) differences in the amount by which economic growth fluctuates in the three countries; (ii) differences in long-term economic growth in the three countries?
(d) How do the four indicators vary with each other over the course of the business cycle in the three countries?

Q44. Table 13.3 shows UK National Income Accounts for 2001 by category of expenditure. Calculate the following:
(a) GDP.
(b) GVA.
(c) GNY.
(d) NNY.

Table 13.3 UK national income by category of expenditure

	(£m)
Consumption of households and NPISH	655 265
General government final consumption	190 663
Gross domestic fixed capital formation	162 244
Value of physical increase in stocks and work in progress	1 804
Exports of goods and services	268 451
Imports of goods and services	290 912
Statistical discrepancy	499
Taxes on products	114 824
Subsidies on products	3 827
Net income from abroad	5 756
Capital consumption	112 431

C DISCUSSION TOPICS AND ESSAYS

Q45. Assume that country A has higher economic growth, lower unemployment and lower inflation than country B. Discuss whether this makes country A (a) more successful economically; (b) a better place to live in than country B.

Q46. Sketch a circular flow of income diagram and describe its components. Explain the effect of (a) a decrease in saving and (b) an increase in direct taxation.

Q47. Suppose that the proportion of the 18–30 age group participating in higher education rises from 40 to 50 per cent. Explain what is likely to happen to the level and rate of growth of GDP in (a) the short run and (b) the long run. Specify your assumptions.

Q48. (a) What is the relationship between actual and potential output? (b) What is the relationship between actual and potential growth?

Q49. At what stage of the business cycle is the economy at the present time? Are all the macroeconomic variables behaving in the way you would expect?

Q50. How might the government set about increasing the overall level of investment in the economy? What problems is it likely to encounter in attempting to do so?

Q51. Why can GDP be measured in three different ways? What adjustments have to be made to ensure that all these methods yield the same figure?

Q52. There are difficulties in making useful national income comparisons not only of different countries, but also of the same country over time. Why?

Q53. Debate
Comparing the welfare of different countries' citizens by the use of GNY statistics is so misleading that it is better not to use these statistics at all for comparative purposes.

Q54. Debate
The pursuit of economic growth is not in society's best long-term interests.

D ARTICLES

Business cycles are no longer purely domestic phenomena. With the progressive globalisation of trade and industry, the world economy invariably swings between boom and slump. The more a country embraces globalisation and opens its economy to trade and foreign investment, the more sensitive it will become to these global shifts in output. The article below by Marc Lopatin, taken from *The Independent* of 13 October 1998, describes the vulnerability of the UK economy to such cycles, following its willingness to embrace high levels of inward investment in the 1980s and 1990s.

The crisis – a crash course in globalisation

As factories shut, Britain's reliance on inward investment has been exposed.

'World trade and the opening of markets has been going on for centuries. Globalisation in that sense is not new. What is new is its pace and scope. It is as if someone has pressed the fast forward button on the video, and there is no sign of it stopping.' This was how Tony Blair explained the impact of globalisation to Japanese business leaders when in opposition.

Two years on, Mr Blair's words have come back to haunt him in his own Sedgefield constituency. Addressing 570 workers made redundant by the Japanese semiconductor firm Fujitsu two weeks ago, he trotted out the same rhetoric as its disconsolate casualties of globalisation listened.

UK plc has suddenly lost some of its most high-profile inward investments. In the past three months Siemens, Fujitsu, Viasystems, and National Semiconductors have all closed hi-tech plants or scaled back production, despite investing billions of pounds in state-of-the-art assembly plants.

The closures stem from a sharp cyclical downturn in the semiconductor industry caused by massive oversupply and rock-bottom prices. The bad news is one of the first manifestations of a truly globalised industry succumbing to the acute effects of a global downturn. While semiconductor makers are unlikely to be in the doldrums for long, the same cannot be said of countries left to support redundant workers each time production is switched elsewhere.

Despite Government assurances, the stream of plant closures raise serious questions about the future of inward – or foreign direct investment (FDI) – in the UK. The nation is no stranger to closing factories. But the closures of cutting edge technologies are a world away from those of shipyards and textile factories.

Government strategy has been to lure the foreign owners to use Britain as a European base of operations. But it has not yet addressed what Britain should do when these same investors cut back on their world-wide operations.

Robert Crawford, head of inward investment at accountant Ernst & Young, believes the closures are an inevitable part of globalisation. 'The semiconductor business is not a spent industry: it's a blueprint for the future of global manufacturing,' he says. 'The firms fabricate in the UK, assemble and test components in Asia, before selling chips worldwide. They must have global reach and be able to shift resources, or risk losing their foothold altogether.'

In a downturn, 'shifting risk' means deciding which plants in which countries to close. Stephen Regan, a Cranfield School of Management lecturer, says: 'When companies seek to be truly global they leave themselves nowhere to hide. So drastic action is required.'

Andrew Fraser, chief executive of the Invest in Britain Bureau (IBB), says the closures are unique to the semiconductor industry. 'Billions of pounds spent on rolling investment in new plant and products coupled with an unforeseen downturn caused the closures.'

But Mr Regan argues that other foreign investors in other cyclical industries, including commodities, oil and pharmaceuticals, may soon be copying the semiconductor business. Should this happen, Britain's impressive record in FDI might look very different. There are some 8100 foreign-owned firms in the UK generating 40 per cent of all exported manufactured goods, and 400 000 jobs in 13 years. United Nations figures show Britain has an impressive 10.66 per cent of the world's $400bn (£232bn) FDI stock, achieved with just 1 per cent of world's population and about 5 per cent of world trade.

Economists predict that, despite the crisis, global foreign direct investment will continue to grow as markets' ears are opened to the deafening mantra of free trade. Before the Asia crisis, FDI was growing at 9 per cent a year, over twice as fast as the world economy.

The IBB is bringing record levels of investment to the UK – £9.42bn for 1997/98. But with boom turning to bust the challenge is defensive: to prevent foreign companies from quitting the UK, and to persuade firms to cut production elsewhere. The IBB says the UK is still creating more FDI jobs than it is losing. But there are no loyalty cards in a global economy.

In this sense Britain could be heavily exposed. In the 1980s Britain stole a march on other Europeans by attracting massive amounts of foreign investment. A cheap workforce and generous grant packages lured many a multi-national to the UK. But Sean Ricard, head of management economics at Cranfield School of Management, says: 'The UK has been importing industrial expertise using FDI, instead of strengthening domestic manufacturing.'

The point is not lost on Peter Mandelson, Secretary of State for Trade and Industry: 'I want to see more home-grown hi-tech industries where British know-how can be harnessed to develop and launch our own manufactured products in the UK.'

Mr Crawford says: 'For the last 20 years big assembly plants have been the order of the day. But the UK will not hold on to companies that simply assemble or manufacture products. There will always be somewhere cheaper to go. We have to provide the infrastructure and a labour force for design and development – the life blood of any manufacturer.'

The UK is now the call centre capital of Europe, but Mr Crawford says: '[They] are not connected to core product development. They are mobile assets which can be set up anywhere and will probably be gone within five years.' The IBB refutes this, but is well aware of the need to embed inward investors in the UK.

Mr Fraser, of the IBB, says: 'Fifteen years ago Nissan set up a plant factory which critics labelled a screwdriver factory. It is now the most productive car factory in Europe, exporting 80 per cent of production and sourcing 200 British suppliers. That is embeddedness.'

More recently Microsoft spent £12m setting up its first research and development facility at Cambridge Science Park where no financial inducements are on offer. The park brings together academia, training and industry to deliver an integrated long-term approach to attracting FDI.

Mr Fraser believes clustering related firms is the way forward. 'It becomes a magnet for inward investment. In the same way the City of London is a must for international finance.' Vicky Pryce, chief economist at accountant KPMG, agress: 'The growing diversity of FDI will force countries to create domestic centres of excellence.'

(a) Explain how a business cycle might be transmitted between the world's economies. For example, consider the impact on the UK of the collapse in the economies of south-east Asia in 1997/8.
(b) What strategies does the article suggest that a country, such as the UK, can adopt in order to reduce its vulnerability to a downturn in global economic activity?
(c) Should the UK restrict both inward and outward investment, and encourage more domestic investment, in order to become less vulnerable to global economic upheavals?
(d) How does the UK's membership or non-membership of the euro affect its vulnerability to turbulence within the global economy?

The following article, taken from the *Investors Chronicle* of 5 April 1996, explores the problems of using the output gap of an economy as a guide to informing economic policy action.

Minding the output gap mythology

The so-called output gap – the difference between actual output and its potential level – is widely considered a key influence upon inflation. 'Roughly speaking, inflation is likely to decelerate if the output gap is negative and to accelerate if it is positive,' says Tim Congdon, one of the chancellor's panel of independent forecasters. He believes that output is currently around 3 per cent below its potential. 'On this basis, good inflation numbers are likely to be reported for the rest of 1996 and most of 1997,' he says.

However, it does not follow that interest rates should be cut further. One reason for this is that there are many problems with the idea that the output gap does determine inflation.

Not least of these is that the gap is very hard to measure. The simplest, and most popular, way of doing it is to take the peak of two economic cycles and estimate the growth rate between the two. This gives the potential growth rate. Extrapolating this rate forward gives us the current level of potential output, with which actual output can be compared.

Unfortunately, this method, and its more sophisticated counterparts, fails to give an unambiguous answer. A particular problem is that it cannot tell us whether there has been an increase in the potential growth rate since the last economic cycle. But frequently, this is precisely the point at issue between inflation optimists and pessimists, with the former claiming that structural change will enable growth to stay low, and the latter denying it.

Measures of the output gap also frequently conflict with the trade deficit. Both should show the same thing – whether supply is greater than demand. The mere existence of a trade deficit suggests that demand is greater than supply. But most measures of the output gap suggest the opposite. This could, of course, mean that there is no output gap in manufacturing, but that there is in services. And sure enough, the RPI figures, showing goods inflation rising and services inflation falling, lend credence to this claim. But this means that there is no single output gap, and no single implication for inflation.

A further problem lies in the mechanism through which the output gap influences prices. It should be simple. If output is above potential, demand exceeds supply and prices rise. If output is below potential, supply exceeds demand and prices fall. But nothing is that simple. In deciding whether to cut prices, firms consider much more than whether they have spare capacity. What will be the response of their rivals? How many more customers will they get? Will the increased demand be enough to compensate for the loss of immediate cash flow? The output gap is silent on such important questions.

But even if we reject all of these problems, and continue to hold faith in the output gap as a determinant of inflation, it does not follow that we should support lower interest rates. Indeed, Professor Congdon himself is opposed to rate cuts.

One reason for this is that it takes a long time for monetary policy to affect inflation; most estimates put the lag at around two years. In setting rates now, therefore, the government needs to know where inflation will be from April 1998 onwards. But the output gap can only tell us this if the lags between it and inflation are longer than those between monetary policy and inflation. This is improbable, not least because interest rates affect inflation through their impact on the output gap. So we need much more than the output gap to tell us where interest rates should be.

It may seem odd, therefore, that policy makers attach so much weight to the output gap. Not so. Consider the chancellor's dilemma. On the one hand, the only economic target he has is low inflation; there is no official target for growth or unemployment. On the other hand, there are political pressures to cut rates whenever the economy seems weak. How better to reconcile these conflicts than by claiming that a weak economy will eventually reduce inflation? Output gap theories may or may not be true. But they are extremely useful.

(a) What is the output gap and how can it be measured?
(b) Why is it difficult to measure the rate of *potential* economic growth?
(c) Why would we expect inflation to rise when an economy nears its potential output?
(d) What would you expect to be the relationship between the output gap and the size of the trade deficit (or surplus)?
(e) What argument does Professor Congdon advance to suggest that the existence of an output gap should not automatically lead to a cut in interest rates?
(f) Given your answers to the above questions, of what use is the output gap to the policy maker?

Environmental economists are highly critical of conventional methods of calculating GDP. They argue that GDP should reflect the full social costs of production, which include the impact on the natural environment and its resources. In the article below, taken from *Nature* of October 1998, the issues involved, and the problems of constructing a green GDP, are considered.

Progress and pitfalls along the path towards a 'greener' method of calculating national productivity

One goal that unites most ecological economists is the desire to develop a system of national accounting that embraces environmental factors excluded from current definitions of gross domestic product (GDP).

The conventional assessment of GDP, which is around 50 years old, works by adding up all the final demands for goods and services produced annually by a nation. Although widely used by economists, journalists and politicians as the measure of the economic health of a country, GDP has been much criticized by environmentalist groups – backed by some sympathetic economists – on the grounds that it paints a potentially misleading picture of a society's health when seen in environmental terms.

'A country could exhaust its mineral resources, cut down its forests, erode its soils, pollute its aquifers, and hunt its wildlife and fisheries to extinction, but its GDP would not be affected as these assets disappeared,' says Robert Repetto, an environmental and resource economist at the World Resources Institute, an independent research organization in Washington DC.

Repetto has pioneered work on a greener GDP. His study in Indonesia in 1989 concluded that annual GDP growth corrected for depreciation in timber, petroleum and soil resources was 3 per cent lower than the conventionally calculated figure of 7.1 per cent between 1971 and 1984.

More radical ecological economists such as Herman Daly take a different view. They criticize the idea that a country's wealth can be measured just in terms of how much its citizens produce.

Daly has helped to develop what he and colleagues refer to as the index of sustainable economic welfare (ISEW). Although this takes GDP as its starting point, it adds the value of unpaid household work, and then subtracts the cost of pollution, as well as urbanization, road accidents and advertising.

But, for all its intellectual attractions, the ISEW has had little success among policy-makers. It has also been criticized by more mainstream economists, mainly because of questions about the accuracy of measuring some of its components.

Despite such shortcomings, since the beginning of the decade, calls for a green GDP have been getting louder. In 1993, in response to such suggestions, the United Nations (UN) Statistical Division in New York, which is responsible for setting guidelines for national accounting systems, carried out a review of possible alternatives.

But the review concluded that there was a lack of sufficient data to be able to recommend that countries adopt a green index, or, indeed, a new welfare index.

Instead, countries were encouraged merely to publish separate indicators on the state of key environmental services, as well as their associated monetary values, in parallel with conventional measurements of GDP.

In response to such suggestions, the European Commission is already working on 60 environmental 'pressure indices' intended to act as a measure of the health of various natural resources.

In parallel, the commission is working with the UN and the Organization for Economic Cooperation and Development (OECD) on so-called 'satellite accounts' that attempt to put monetary values on different aspects of environmental degradation.

There are several other reasons why a green GDP has not been taken up. One is the lack of agreement on its components and on how the index would be calculated.

A second reason is that GDP was never intended to be used as an indicator of environmental health, or indeed of prosperity. And some policymakers see little point in trying to turn it into something that was not originally intended.

Third, there has been unexpected enthusiasm among governments for the human development index (HDI), a quality-of-life indicator that is based on average life expectancy at birth, literacy level, number of years at school and GDP per capita.

Another equally important reason for scepticism about a new green index is the lack of detailed knowledge of its

How green is your country?

Country	GNP	Green NNP ($ per capita 1993)	% fall on GNP
Japan	31 449	27 374	−13.0
Norway	25 947	21 045	−18.9
United States	24 716	21 365	−11.5
Germany	23 494	20 844	−11.3
South Korea	7 681	7 041	−8.3
South Africa	3 582	2 997	−16.3
Brazil	2 936	2 579	−12.2
Indonesia	732	616	−15.8
China	490	411	−10.4
India	293	242	−17.4

Green net national product (NNP) is gross national product (GNP) minus depreciation of produced assets, depletion of forests and subsoil assets, and damage from carbon dioxide emissions.

potential components, such as an accurate measure of water pollution, or the climate change potential of greenhouse gases. The UN review team felt that the work on parallel indicators – which many countries are now carrying out – would help to address most of these issues.

'There was a feeling at the time that if we want to include environmental resources in GDP, we must have comprehensive information,' says Kirk Hamilton, a senior economist at the environment department of the World Bank. 'That means having detailed knowledge of each type of damage by each pollutant.'

Many of these gaps are now being filled. But Hamilton points out that most rich countries remain unconvinced about the desirability of a new index, partly because they derive a smaller share of their earnings from natural resources than developing countries, but also because the parallel indicators are, in themselves, an adequate guide to environmental health.

Despite the setbacks, environmental and ecological economists continue to argue the case for a single index that integrates a measure of the wealth of a country's citizens and the health of its natural environment. Progress towards this goal has been slow. But few have given up hope that it can be achieved in a generally acceptable way.

(a) In what ways do current calculations of GDP ignore environmental considerations?

(b) If GDP calculations did include some environmental estimation, what implications would this have for the level of countries' GDP? Would the gap between the GDP of rich and poor countries narrow or widen?

(c) Why has a green measure of GDP not been adopted by governments and international agencies?

ANSWERS

Q1. (a), (d), (e) and (h) are macroeconomic issues as they concern the whole economy rather than a segment of it.

Q2. Economic growth can be defined as the percentage increase in national output over a twelve-month period.

Q3. 1950–69.

Q4. D.

Q5. (i) Y, (ii) C_d, (iii) I, (iv) S, (v) G, (vi) T, (vii) X, (viii) M.

Q6. (a) *withdrawal, decrease*; (b) *injection, decrease*; (c) *injection, increase* (building up stocks counts as investment); (d) *withdrawal, decrease*; (e) *withdrawal, decrease* (the poor save proportionally less and spend proportionally more than the rich); (f) *withdrawal (imports), decrease*; (g) *withdrawal (saving), increase* (note that whereas it is normal in everyday language to refer to depositors 'investing' in building societies, economists refer to this as 'saving'; they reserve the term 'investment' to refer to the spending by firms on capital (plant, equipment, stocks, etc.) which is an *injection*).

Q7. £2025m ($S + T$ (both) + M).

Q8. B. $C_d + I + G + X$. Notice that C_d excludes imports: if the consumption figure was for *total* consumption, we would have to subtract imports: i.e. $C - M + I + G + X$.

Q9. *rise*.

Q10. *rise*.

Q11. *withdrawals*. (In the simple model, injections are not affected by the level of income.)

Q12. *larger*. The reason is that additional injections will subsequently flow round and round the circular flow of income generating additional expenditure and additional income. There is a 'multiplied' rise in income (see Chapter 17). But the process will not go on for ever, because eventually all the additional injections will leak away as additional withdrawals.

Q13. (a) *fall* (increase in withdrawals); (b) *rise* (increase in injections); (c) *fall* (fall in injections); (d) *impossible to tell without further information* (both withdrawals and injections fall); (e) *fall* (increase in withdrawals); (f) *rise* (increase in injections: i.e. exports to these countries rise as a result of their increased incomes).

Q14. The value of output produced within the economy over a twelve-month period.

Q15. *False*. The GDP deflator, unlike the RPI, includes not just the prices of consumer goods, but also the prices of investment goods, the prices of goods and services consumed by the government and the prices of exports: in other words, it includes the weighted prices of all the components of GDP.

Q16. 2.56 per cent.
This is calculated as follows:
Real GDP = Nominal GDP/GDP deflator × 100
Thus in year 1, real GDP = £120bn/100 × 100 = £120bn and in year 2, real GDP = £160n/130 × 100 = £123.07bn
∴ real GDP has grown by (123.07 − 120)/120 × 100 = 2.56%.

Q17. The ratio of country A's GDP to country B's is 10/12 at current exchange rates. Given, however, that country B's currency is overvalued by 1.5 times in PPP terms, the ratio of country A's PPS GDP to country B's PPS GDP is 10/12 × 1.5 = 1.25.

Q18. (a) *potential growth*. (Only if they are *used* will there be actual growth.)
(b) *actual growth*.
(c) *neither*. (A reduction in vacancies usually signals a reduction in output. It *could*, however, be a sign of increased labour productivity, in which case there would be *potential growth* or more vacancies being filled, in which case there would be *actual growth*.)
(d) *both*. (Increased inestment, by increasing the stock of capital, increases potential output. The purchase of new machinery and equipment stimulates growth in the industries producing the equipment.)
(e) *neither*. (Other things being equal, it will lead to a *reduction* in output.)
(f) *potential*. (It would only lead to actual growth if these techniques were used.)
(g) *both*. (It will increase labour productivity and hence lead to potential growth. The employment of instructors and other money spent on the training will stimulate demand and hence encourage an increased output in the economy.)

Q19. *False*. Provided there is some slack in the economy (i.e. production is inside the production possibility curve), actual growth can take place by using some of the idle capacity. Only when the economy is operating at full capacity will potential growth be a necessary condition for actual growth.

Q20. (a) *False*; (b) *True*; (c) *True*.

Q21. D. The movement outwards of the production point from W to X represents an increase in potential output. Since W was inside curve I, whereas X is on curve II, X represents a more efficient point of production than W. Finally, the outward shift in the production possibility curve represents an increase in potential output.

Q22. F. In this case consumers select a new combination of X and Y. (Actual output of X has increased, but actual output of Y has *decreased*.) Potential output remains unaffected.

Q23. The *expansion* phase.

Q24. The *peaking out* and the *slowdown or recession* phases.

Q25. The *peaking out* phase. During this phase the economy will be running closest to full capacity.

Q26. In a perfect market situation it might be possible for all resources to be fully utilised. In real-world markets, however, either as a result of imperfect information, or as a consequence of other market failures, some resources will remain idle.

Q27. *True*. A major determinant of actual growth is aggregate demand, of which consumer spending is the biggest element.

Q28. Potential output depends upon the level of resources available and the state of technology.

Q29. E.

Q30. The $MEC = 50/100 = 0.5$. In order to find the potential growth rate we use the formula $g = i \times MEC$, where i is the level of investment as a percentage of national income ($i = 25\%$). Thus $g = 25\% \times 0.5 = 12.5\%$.

Q31. *False*. Whether output per head rises or not depends upon the proportion of the population as a whole that is working, and whether the marginal product of labour of new workers is above the average product of labour.

Q32. £120 + £40 + £80 + £60 + £50 + £25 = £375 (which is the retail price).

Q33. *Yes*: (b), (e), (f) and (g). (Note that if we had been referring to gross *national income*, then (e) would not have been included but (h) would have been.)

Q34. *True*. The value added in production is simply the difference between a firm's revenue from sales and the costs of its purchases from other firms. This difference is made up of the wages, rent, interest and profit generated in the production process.

Q35. (a) £3690m: i.e. income from employment + gross profits + gross rent and interest + mixed incomes.
(b) £3780m, i.e. *GVA* + taxes on products − subsidies on products.

Q36. All except (c) and (h) would be included in the expenditure method of calculating GDP (since all except (c) and (h) involve the production of goods and/or services).

Q37. (a) £2050m (i.e. $C + G + I + X - M$).
(b) £1600m (i.e. GDP − taxes on products + subsidies on products).

Q38. (a) £2110m (i.e. GDP at market prices + net income from abroad).
(b) £1990m (i.e. GNY − depreciation).

Q39. E. It is the income available for people to spend after all deductions and additions.

Chapter Fourteen

14

Unemployment and Inflation

A REVIEW

At the beginning of Chapter 13, we identified four main macroeconomic issues: economic growth, unemployment, inflation and the balance of payments. In this chapter we turn to the second two – unemployment and inflation. We examine the nature of unemployment and inflation and take a preliminary look at their causes.

14.1 The nature of unemployment
(Pages 401–5) We start by examining the meaning and measurement of unemployment.

Q1. If there are 3 million people unemployed and 24 million people employed, the rate of unemployment will be:
A. 3 per cent
B. 8 per cent
C. 9 per cent
D. 11.1 per cent
E. 12.5 per cent

Q2. There are two major measures of unemployment: the claimant count and the standardised measure used by the ILO and OECD. Why is claimant unemployment likely to be lower than standardised unemployment?

....

....

Q3. The stock of unemployment at the end of year *t* equals the stock of unemployment at the beginning of year *t* minus the outflows of people from unemployment to work or to outside the labour force, plus the inflows of people to unemployment from jobs and from outside the labour force. *True/False*

Q4. Which one of the following will increase the level of unemployment?
A. More people retire.
B. More unemployed people become disheartened and give up looking for work.
C. The school leaving age is raised.
D. The retirement age is lowered.
E. More people resign from low-paid jobs.

14.2 Causes of unemployment
(Pages 406–11) We now turn to the different types of unemployment.

Q5. Which of the following defines *real-wage* unemployment?
A. Real wages being set above the equilibrium level by trade unions, or minimum wage legislation.
B. Inflation causing an erosion of real wages and hence a rise in unemployment.
C. Increased aggregate demand in the economy driving up equilibrium real wages.
D. Increased aggregate demand in the economy causing money wages to rise faster than real wages.

≡ Multiple choice   ? Written answer   ◐ Delete wrong word   ⊖ Diagram/table manipulation   ⊗ Calculation   ▨ Matching/ordering

E. Real wages falling below the equilibrium level as a result of deficiency of demand.

Q6. Why is demand-deficient unemployment sometimes referred to as *cyclical unemployment*?

....

Q7. Frictional unemployment is the result of:
A. a shift in the pattern of consumer demand.
B. workers and employers being ill-informed about the labour market.
C. the introduction of new technology.
D. the economy entering the recessionary phase of the business cycle.
E. employers responding to the time of year and cutting back on their level of production.

Q8. Which of the following will affect the level of *structural* unemployment?
(a) The concentration of a particular industry within a particular region. Yes/No
(b) The speed at which structural change within the economy is taking place. Yes/No
(c) The immobility of labour. Yes/No

Q9. Given the following possible types of unemployment – *demand-deficient/real-wage/frictional/structural/technological/seasonal* – which one is likely to worsen in which of the following cases?
(a) The introduction of robots in manufacturing.

....

(b) The economy moves into recession.

....

(c) Legislation is passed guaranteeing everyone a minimum wage rate that is 60 per cent of the national average.

....

(d) The development of the single market in Europe leads to a movement of capital to the 'centre of gravity' in Europe.

....

(e) The government decides to close job centres in an attempt to save money.

....

(f) The government raises interest rates.

....

(g) More people are forced to take their annual holidays when the schools are on holiday.

....

14.3 Aggregate demand and supply and the price level

(Pages 411–14) Before we examine the causes of inflation (the rate of increase in prices), we need to look at how the *level* of prices in the economy is determined.

It is determined by the interaction of aggregate demand and aggregate supply.

Q10. As the price level in the economy rises, which of the following will occur?
(i) The quantity of 'real money' decreases.
(ii) Real aggregate demand decreases.
(iii) Total spending in *money* terms decreases.

A. (i) only.
B. (ii) only.
C. (i) and (ii).
D. (i) and (iii).
E. (i), (ii) and (iii).

The aggregate demand curve slopes downwards. This is largely because of a *substitution effect* of a rise in the price level.

Q11. Of the following, which account for the substitution effect of a rise in the price level?
(a) Higher domestic prices lead to people purchasing fewer domestic goods and more imports. Yes/No
(b) Exports become less competitive and thus fewer are sold. Yes/No
(c) People cannot afford to buy so much at higher prices. Yes/No
(d) As the price level rises, so the value of people's money balances will fall. They will therefore *spend* less in order to increase their money balances and go some way to protecting their real value. Yes/No
(e) The government is likely to raise taxes as prices rise. Higher taxes will mean that people will be able to purchase less. Yes/No
(f) Higher wages and prices cause a higher demand for money. With a given supply of money in the economy, this will drive up interest rates and encourage people to spend less and save more. This will have the effect of reducing real aggregate demand. Yes/No
(g) Higher prices will encourage the government to reduce the money supply in an attempt to reduce inflation. The reduction in money supply will reduce spending. Yes/No

Q12. There are various factors that can cause the aggregate demand curve to shift. What effect will the following have on the aggregate demand curve?

(a) The government increases the money supply.
Leftward shift/rightward shift/ no shift (movement along)

(b) The government increases taxes.
Leftward shift/rightward shift/ no shift (movement along)

(c) The government increases its spending.
Leftward shift/rightward shift/ no shift (movement along)

(d) People anticipate a rise in the rate of inflation.
Leftward shift/rightward shift/ no shift (movement along)

(e) Higher prices lead to higher interest rates.
Leftward shift/rightward shift/ no shift (movement along)

(f) The government reduces interest rates.
Leftward shift/rightward shift/ no shift (movement along)

(g) Higher UK prices lead to a fall in the exchange rate.
Leftward shift/rightward shift/ no shift (movement along)

(h) A reduction in prices abroad leads to a fall in the demand for UK exports.
Leftward shift/rightward shift/ no shift (movement along)

Q13. Why is the aggregate supply curve upward sloping?

....

....

14.4 Inflation

(Pages 414–16) The rate of inflation in the UK is normally calculated by taking the percentage increase in the retail price index (RPI).

Q14. If the RPI increased by 14 points over a 12-month period, the standard of living must have fallen.
True/False

Q15. In a period of rapid inflation which of the following would be the least desirable store of wealth?
A. Vintage wine.
B. Money.
C. Property.
D. Land.
E. Stocks and shares.

Q16. Debtors are likely to benefit from inflation.
True/False

Q17. Why is a high rate of domestic inflation likely to make the country's foreign trade balance (exports minus imports) worse?

....

....

Q18. Why might a higher rate of inflation cause economic growth to slow down?

....

....

(Pages 416–21) Inflation is caused by persistent **Q19.** *rightward/leftward* shifts in the aggregate demand curve and/or persistent **Q20.** *rightward/leftward* shifts in the aggregate supply curve.

Q21. Assume that the following factors lead to inflation. Which ones will result in demand-pull inflation and which will result in cost-push inflation? (In each case assume *ceteris paribus*.)
(a) A cut in the rate of income tax. *demand-pull/cost-push*
(b) The expansion of public-sector works. *demand-pull/cost-push*
(c) An attempt by unions to increase real wages. *demand-pull/cost-push*
(d) An increase in the price of oil. *demand-pull/cost-push*
(e) VAT is imposed on domestic fuel. *demand-pull/cost-push*
(f) A company decides to increase its profits by increasing its prices. *demand-pull/cost-push*

Q22. Explain the phenomenon of the wage–price spiral.

....

....

Anti-inflationary policy can focus on reducing the rate of growth in aggregate demand ('demand-side policy') or on reducing the rate of increase in costs ('supply-side policy').

Q23. Which of the following are examples of demand-side policies and which of supply-side policies?
(a) A cut in government expenditure. *demand-side/supply-side*
(b) A rise in taxation. *demand-side/supply-side*
(c) Tougher anti-monopoly policy. *demand-side/supply-side*
(d) Reducing the bargaining power of trade unions. *demand-side/supply-side*
(e) Increasing the rate of interest. *demand-side/supply-side*
(f) Offering tax incentives to encourage increased productivity. *demand-side/supply-side*

Q24. How will expectations influence the rate of inflation?

....

....

14.5 The relationship between inflation and unemployment

(Pages 421–4) In this section we take a prelimary look at the relationship between inflation and unemployment.

Q25. What use could a Phillips curve serve for economic policy makers (assuming that it painted an accurate picture)?
A. Predicting the phase of the business cycle.
B. Showing the relationship between the level of aggregate demand and aggregate supply.
C. Showing the relationship between rates of unemployment and rates of inflation.
D. Showing the relationship between overseas trade and economic growth.
E. Showing the effects of expectations on the level of investment.

During the late 1950s and 1960s, policy makers interpreted the Phillips curve as follows: demand management policy would lead to a **Q26.** *shift in/movement along* the Phillips curve. Thus it would only be possible to reduce both inflation and unemployment together by **Q27.** *expansionary demand management policies/contractionary demand management policies/keeping the level of aggregate demand the same/using policies to influence non-demand factors causing inflation and unemployment.*

After 1966 the Phillips curve appeared to break down, and economies began to experience both higher unemployment *and* higher inflation.

Q28. Today the evidence suggests that there is no longer any relationship between inflation and unemployment.
True/False

B PROBLEMS, EXERCISES AND PROJECTS

Q29. Referring Table 14.1, how did the duration of unemployment change between 1979 and 2001? How did this relate to the rate of unemployment?

Table 14.1 UK claimant unemployment by duration

	Up to 26 weeks	Over 26 weeks and up to 52 weeks	Over 52 weeks	Total
Oct 1979 (thousands)	771.6	194.2	337.0	1302.8
(per cent)	59.2	14.9	25.9	100.0
Oct 1981 (thousands)	1514.5	689.5	784.6	2988.6
(per cent)	50.7	23.1	26.2	100.0
Oct 1988 (thousands)	873.0	360.4	885.5	2118.9
(per cent)	41.2	17.0	41.8	100.0
Oct 1990 (thousands)	873.4	289.5	507.7	1670.6
(per cent)	52.3	17.3	30.4	100.0
Oct 1992 (thousands)	1293.1	565.7	955.6	2814.4
(per cent)	45.9	20.1	34.0	100.0
Oct 1994 (thousands)	1057.7	440.9	956.5	2455.0
(per cent)	43.1	17.9	39.0	100.0
Oct 1998 (thousands)	704.2	229.7	352.4	1286.3
(per cent)	54.7	17.9	27.4	100.0
Oct 2001 (thousands)	581.4	149.5	177.1	908.0
(per cent)	64.0	16.5	19.5	100.0

Source: *Labour Market Trends* (National Statistics).

Q30. Table 14.2 shows the aggregate demand and supply of labour at various average wage rates.

Table 14.2

Average real wage (£ per hour)	Labour demand (000s)	Labour supply (000s)	Labour force (000s)
3.00	200	100	118
3.50	170	120	136
4.00	140	140	154
4.50	110	160	172
5.00	80	180	190

(a) Plot the labour demand and labour supply curves.
(b) How might we explain the inelastic nature of the labour supply curve?

....

(c) If the wage rate were set at £4.00, what would be the level of employment and unemployment?

employment = ... unemployment = ...

(d) What type of *unemployment* is this? ....
(e) If the wage level were to increase to £4.50, how many workers would be classified as *disequilibrium* and how many as *equilibrium* unemployed?

disequilibrium = ... equilibrium = ...

Q31. From the information in Table 14.3 calculate the price index in year *X* for the basket of commodities.

....

Table 14.3

Commodity	Average price in base year	Average price in year X	Weight
A	£0.70	£0.75	4
B	£1.20	£1.35	1
C	£45.00	£55.00	1
D	£0.35	£0.37	2
E	£3.20	£3.55	2

Q32. In small groups, write a report on changes in unemployment since 1980. Your report should include the following: (a) a description of changes in the unemployment rate over the period; (b) a description of changes in (i) the duration of unemployment and (ii) the gender balance of unemployment since 1990; (c) an assessment of the extent to which unemployment is cyclical; (d) an explanation of changes in unemployment from 1980 to the present day.

The best sources of information are *Labour Market Trends*, *The Annual Abstract of Statistics* and *Economic Trends Annual Supplement*. All three are taken by most university libraries and all are available on the National Statistics site (www.statistics.gov.uk): the first two in the 'Bookshelf' section of the site and *Economic Trends* as separate time-series tables in the 'Statbase', 'Time series data' section. The *Economic Trends* data set goes back to 1979, while the other two have data only back to 1990.

C DISCUSSION TOPICS AND ESSAYS

Q33. How do the (a) the flows into and out of unemployment and (b) the average duration of unemployment vary with the course of the business cycle?

Q34. To what extent is it appropriate to classify either some or all of unemployment as 'voluntary'?

Q35. What are the arguments for and against raising the benefits paid to (a) the unemployed; (b) their families?

Q36. What factors have been most important in explaining the changing level of unemployment in the UK over the last 10 years?

Q37. If we were to devise a series of policies to tackle the plight of the unemployed, what factors other than the actual *number* unemployed ought we to take into account?

Q38. Solutions to the unemployment problem can be classified as interventionist or market orientated, although there is some common ground. List as many solutions to unemployment as you can, suggesting which would be supported by 'free marketeers' and which by 'interventionists'.

Q39. What are the economic consequences of inflation?

Q40. Would it be desirable to achieve a permanent zero rate of inflation? Explain.

Q41. If the government insisted that everyone had wage increases to match the rate of inflation, would it matter how high the rate of inflation was?

Q42. Distinguish between demand-pull and cost-push inflation. Why in practice might it be difficult to establish the extent to which a given rate of inflation were demand-pull or cost-push?

Q43. For what reasons were both inflation and unemployment generally higher in the 1980s than in the 1960s? For what reasons are both generally lower in the 2000s than in the 1980s?

Q44. Under what circumstances are policies to reduce unemployment likely to lead to higher inflation? Are there any policies that a government could pursue that would reduce both inflation and unemployment?

Q45. Debate
Keeping inflation low should be the overriding macroeconomic objective of the government.

D ARTICLES

In the following article, taken from *The Guardian* of 28 March 1999, Mauricio Rojas attempts to dispel widely held fallacies that work, as we know it, is coming to an end. In fact, he argues that a *shortage* of labour, rather than mass unemployment, is likely to be the norm in the future.

The death of work has been greatly exaggerated

It is a remarkable epoch we are living in. Never have so many jobs been created as in the past quarter of a century. Never have so many people improved their standard of living so radically in such a short time as in the past two decades.

But instead of acclaiming this breakthrough, more and more people in the developed countries of Europe seem to be transfixed by doom-mongering about globalisation and the demise of work – often combined as one big threat. But these depressing predictions are fallacies.

Fallacy 1: work to end
Millions of old jobs are disappearing and very few new ones are created. Eventually, most of the world population will be excluded from the labour market in a world without work.

In fact, quite a number of developed countries have shown an excellent capacity for creating many new jobs. Employment in the United States, Canada, Australia and Japan grew by a startling high total of 58 million jobs between 1975 and 1995.

The assertion that work is ending will not entirely stand up, even in the case of the European Union. Some EU countries – the Netherlands, Austria and Ireland, for example – display a considerable capacity for creating new jobs. (In the UK, more people are employed now than ever.)

The end-of-work thesis becomes more remarkable still if you consider global progress over the past 20 years. We find a startling expansion of employment which, despite a rise in unemployment in the less dynamic, developing countries, has successfully absorbed the most dramatic growth ever of the employable population.

Fallacy 2: technology is taking our jobs
It is because of the information technology revolution that economic growth is not creating more jobs than are being lost. We have entered an epoch of jobless growth.

If this proposition had the slightest connection with reality, the US and Japan, which have dominated IT development since the seventies, ought to be especially hard hit. They are not.

On the contrary, tens of millions of new jobs have begun in these countries since the arrival of the computer age.

Apologists for this fallacy might, perhaps, say there are still fewer than before the IT breakthrough. But that isn't true, either. Both in Japan and the US, more jobs were created in between 1975 and 1995 than in the previous 20 years.

This is especially remarkable, given that economic growth in Japan and the US was slower between 1975 and 1995 than from 1955 to 1975. So there was a considerable increase in the job creation effect of growth.

After extensive studies, the International Labour Organisation has also concluded that growth generally is creating more jobs today than in the golden age of Fordism (mass production), the sixties.

The main reason for this is the transition from industrial to service societies. It is the highly labour-intensive services that are the backbone of the caring and educational sector which, in terms of work, have expanded most during the IT revolution.

Fallacy 3: the US creates 'trash' work
Most of the new jobs which, despite everything, are created in the developed economies are low-skilled, low-paid service work. The US typifies an economy that creates jobs through an expansive service sector consisting more and more of the 'working poor'.

The American economy, which has created tens of millions of new jobs, is frequently dismissed like this. It gives the impression that they are almost exclusively 'trash jobs' that really ought not to exist.

But this picture is profoundly misleading. Nearly half of all the new posts created in the US between 1983 and 1995 belonged to the most highly skilled occupational groups.

Nearly 12m highly qualified jobs were created in only 12 years. Seven out of 10 new jobs – just over 16.7m out of a total job growth of 24 million – came in the occupational categories of the upper income half of the American economy.

I am not condoning American poverty, of course, nor denying the existence of low-skilled jobs – only seeking to give a fair overall picture of US labour developments.

Fallacy 4: they're taking our work
Jobs are disappearing or paying less and less, owing to the pressure from new producers in poor countries. Capital and enterprise are migrating to nations where labour is cheap, using them to put developed countries out of business.

The jobs crisis is defined here as a problem of the industrialised countries, caused by the increasing mobility of capital and the ability of the transnational corporations to exploit the impoverished masses of the Third World – and Eastern Europe, too – as alternative labour.

The scene is set for a life-and-death struggle between 'us' and 'them', a struggle which we are doomed to lose because 'they' are so much cheaper. Which is why we are becoming unemployed, poorer and more desperate.

If the fallacy had anything significant to say about real developments, the industrialised countries ought to have experienced a dramatic fall in their share of world trade over the past 15 years. However, reports of our global collapse are great exaggerations – we have slipped only very slightly. But as world exports almost doubled between 1980 and 1994, that means we made enormous gains.

What is true of trade also applies to world industrial output. In 1995 the affluent countries accounted for four-fifths of that output (80.3 per cent), roughly the same share as in 1980 (82.8 per cent), despite the enormous successes during these years by China and other Asian countries.

The relocation of certain traditional industries – textile manufacturing is a typical example – has in most cases been paralleled by the establishment of new industries. Asian successes have not been achieved at our expense.

This is not all. Even if we imported everything that was exported by South, South East and East Asia and this knocked out our own production without any compensation, it would still not impoverish us much. In 1994 the exports of this immense region equalled only 3.41 per cent of the developed world's gross domestic product.

In any case, the idea of cheap industrial products from the Third World taking away our industrial jobs conceals a fundamental fact: we export far more industrial goods to these countries than they export to us – $550 billion in 1992, while from them we imported the equivalent of $330bn.

(a) Why might technology create more jobs than it destroys?
(b) Is there *any* truth in any of the four fallacies?
(c) Given the four fallacies, what policies might governments pursue in order to ensure employment and job creation are maintained?

In the following article, taken from BBC News Online of 16 January 2002, Evan Davis charts the UK's rise to having the lowest unemployment rate of the Group of 7 (G7) leading industrial economies.

Unemployment: UK leads the pack

Evan Davis, BBC economics editor

Unemployment rose for the third consecutive month in December, although the rise was small.

The number out of work and claiming benefit rose by 3200 – the third consecutive month it has increased.

International unemployment

UK: 5.1%
USA: 5.4%
Japan: 5.4%
Canada: 7.3%
Germany: 8.0%
France: 9.1%
Italy: 9.3%

Source: OECD (October 2001).

On the internationally recognised measure of unemployment, the rate of joblessness in the UK is now 5.1%.

But it also emerged today that that rate of unemployment is now the lowest of any of the big industrial nations, for the first time in a generation.

Manufacturing under pressure

It's hard to know whether to greet the rise in unemployment with gloom because any job losses are bad news. Or to greet the figures with relief, because so far they have not been as bad as expected.

The truth is that the jobless total tends to have a delayed reaction to the wider economy, and unemployment will continue to grow.

It's also true, that manufacturing jobs are being lost at a rapid rate, even services are struggling. Most of the good news on jobs is in growth of employment in public services and in education and health.

Britain stands out

But in one important sense, today is a momentous one in Britain's unemployment history.

For the first time since 1966, on the best comparable figures drawn up by the official group, the Organisation of Economic Cooperation and Development in Paris, Britain's latest unemployment rate is the lowest of all the large industrial countries.

Japan and the US have become accustomed to enjoying far lower unemployment than the UK, but the economic slowdown has been so severe in those countries, they have now passed Britain.

And in the rest of Europe, France, Germany and Italy all have many more unemployed than in the UK.

While some smaller European countries have lower unemployment, overall unemployment in the twelve countries of the eurozone is 8.5%, compared to 5.1% in the UK.

Of course, that other countries' unemployment is rising faster than ours may not be much consolation to anyone here, whose job is going, or about to go.

Whatever Britain's performance relative to other countries, the number out of work is expected to continue rising as the slowdown late last year works its way through the labour market.

(a) What factors might explain the UK's success in reducing unemployment?
(b) Why is Evan Davis reluctant to claim that unemployment will remain at such a low level in the near future?
(c) Find out the UK's current unemployment rate. How does it currently compare with the other G7 economies? What factors might explain differences in unemployment rates between the G7 countries?

The article below, taken from Management Today of March 1995, explores the implications for management in operating within a low-inflation economy and the problems that businesses are likely to face in maintaining levels of profit.

The low-inflation challenge

For Sir James Blyth, chief executive of Boots, low inflation is not a glint in a politician's eye. It is the reality he has been living with for the past three or four years, and he expects it to continue. 'It has been with us for some time,' he says, 'and we've set out to try and plan strategies within a low-inflation environment'. The highly competitive high-street market in which Boots operates means that the company, in Blyth's words, 'under-recovers inflation'.

In other words, prices rise by less than general inflation. When general inflation is low, this can mean stable or falling prices for Boots.

Initial scepticism about whether Britain's inflationary leopard had truly changed its spots is now giving way to a general acceptance that things have changed. And even those who subscribe to the cock-up theory of economic policy – which is that when governments have an opportunity to mess things up they generally do so – accept that the scope for politicians to throw away the present low-inflation advantage is limited.

The Bank of England's enhanced role in the policy process has produced a permanent anti-inflationary bias in policy. Wage bargaining behaviour has changed for the better, partly because of the labour market reforms of the 1980s. Credit growth, which reached runaway proportions during the Lawson boom, has come up against the brick wall of corporate and personal sector debt aversion. And consumers are more price-sensitive than for a generation.

But the adjustment to a low-inflation era is far from painless, even for those companies who have lived with it for some time. For Blyth of Boots, it means tough control of costs: 'We're operating on the basis of matching our wage bill to inflation and, as long as our productivity is growing by between 2 per cent and 5 per cent, our margin is very well-protected.'

Milton Friedman, the father of modern monetarist economics, drew the analogy between inflation and drug or alcohol addiction. At first, he said, the effects can appear pleasant, even benign, but very soon it gets nasty. No one doubts that they would be better off without it.

But inflation, like addiction, becomes a hard habit to kick. Right now, Britain is in the painful, cold-turkey phase of kicking a long-standing habit. Many say it would be far easier to slip back into the habit. The scepticism over Britain's ability to become a stable-price economy is being overcome, but now comes the hard part: rewriting strategies that were developed during an inflationary era.

Pressure from international forces is one factor that is forcing new thinking on companies. Increasing industrial output from newly emerging economies such as China and India will drive up the demand, and hence the price, for raw materials. At the same time, because these countries are low-cost manufacturers, their impact on world markets will be to exert downward pressure on the prices of manufactured goods. This provides Lesson One of the low-inflation era, that cost-cutting becomes a way of life. 'Most companies will find that they will have to work as hard to reduce costs during "normal" times as they ever did during the recession,' says McWilliams. 'Not surprisingly, many managers regard this as very unfair.'

Nick Morris, director of the consultancy London Economics, takes this point further: 'Many businessmen, having got used to inflation, find it hard to believe in price elasticities (the fact that demand responds to price changes). If your product isn't selling and we are in a period of no inflation, holding prices is not enough – you have to cut them.' And, because price-cutting has in the past often been regarded as a desperate throw, or as undermining a reputation for quality, it does not come easily.

Roger Bootle, chief economist at HSBC Markets (the money-market arm of the Hong Kong & Shanghai Bank) recently published a paper, *The End of the Inflationary Era*. In it he described the new psychology of low inflation among consumers, which is forcing companies to change their pricing behaviour.

'Areas which have discovered the power of price include clothing and footwear outlets, supermarkets, newspapers and insurance,' he says. 'But there are whole swathes which have yet to catch on. If they are in a line of business where demand has seemed inelastic in the past (unresponsive to price changes), they find it difficult to realise that they have become price-uncompetitive in an economy where consumers have become more sensitive to price.' Bootle believes the realisation that this is a new era will come in stages. At first, he says, many firms are reluctant to openly cut prices: 'Instead, they resort to discounts, special offers, tokens, gifts and other forms of disguised price reduction, perhaps because they regard the current "value sensitivity" in the market as temporary and wish to preserve the image of their posted price as the real price.'

The result of this, he says, is that for some time there have been two price levels in existence – the official price level, which he dubs the fictional price level because very little business is done at it. The other price level, with discounts, special deals and sales packages, is significantly lower and is one at which most business is conducted. Over time, these two price levels will inevitably converge, Bootle predicts.

One example is in the motor trade. Traditionally, retail buyers of new cars were accustomed to regarding the manufacturers' list as a ceiling from which a discount, often a very hefty one, could be negotiated. The real price was well below the official price. In 1993, Vauxhall pioneered a shift towards more realistic list prices by cutting dealer markups. Other manufacturers followed.

Keen pricing, then, has to be the strategy in a low-inflation era. But that isn't the end of the management process. The fundamental question is how to keep prices stable, or reduce them, and still improve earnings.

Cost control, as the CEBR's McWilliams says, has to be as tough in recovery as in recession. Inevitably, one of the hardest areas in which to achieve this will be with wages. The labour market is subject to what economists call the 'money illusion', where people feel better off if they are getting a 10 per cent pay rise alongside 8 per cent inflation than if the two figures are 3 per cent and 1 per cent respectively.

Bootle points out that the cards are heavily stacked in favour of management. Widespread job insecurity has curbed labour militancy. 'The new technological revolution is labour-saving. The demand for button-pushers and lever-pullers is substantially reduced. Smaller and smaller numbers are employed in manufacturing. Even in the office, technology has made possible substantial economy in the use of clerks and typists. The structural changes stretch deep into the service sector. In transport, for instance, computerisation greatly reduces the number of people needed to run a railway system. And the potential developments are huge.'

One of the difficulties of low inflation is that it is harder to establish the differentials needed to retain key staff. In a period of moderately high inflation, the difference between a 10 per cent rise for those who could be poached by other firms and a pay freeze for others is significant. But when the total wage has to be frozen, it is hard to single out vital staff.

A low-inflation environment should also lend itself to long-term pay deals. In practice, however, both management and unions have been reluctant to commit themselves to deals stretching for more than two years. Long-term deals have not, so far, worked to the obvious benefit of companies, because in a period where both inflation and pay settlements have come in below expectations, second-year increases have tended to be higher than those that could have been freely negotiated at the time. The combination of long-term deals for basic pay coupled with a substantial profit-related element is now suggesting itself as the way forward.

Do low prices effectively take over as the main selling-point in the new era, or is there still value in brands? Boots's Blyth has no doubt that brands are a bigger advantage in a stable price era. 'They are a very large advantage,' he says. 'When you've established a reputation for very high quality, this works even more to your advantage when prices are not rising.' He cites the fact that Boots successfully saw off a pure cut-price challenge, in perfumes and other products, from Superdrug. Another example is provided by the low-price strategies of Sainsbury, Tesco and Asda, which have meant that the challenge from new discount entrants into the market, including the German retailer Aldi and the club warehouses, has been far less significant than many expected.

In the end, the challenge of low inflation has to be met by good management, which has at its heart the containment of costs and responding to the needs of increasingly price-sensitive but brand-loyal customers. This can be presented as a re-engineering task.

(a) Why is low and stable inflation economically advantageous?
(b) How are businesses able to maintain high profits during periods of inflation?
(c) What new strategies have businesses been forced to adopt in order to maintain profits in a low-inflation economy?

In the following article, taken from *The Guardian* of 24 December 2001, Tony Thirlwall considers whether the policy objective of achieving low inflation is misplaced. He suggests that the problems of Japan, and the eurozone countries too, could be cured by a good dose of inflationary medicine.

Inflation is no devil in monetary policy detail

Tony Thirlwall

Most of the world's major economies – apart from Britain – are in recession. The rapid growth of the United States has come to a halt, at least temporarily; and Japan, Germany, France and Italy have experienced disappointing growth over the last decade. Inflation is also quiescent, and in Japan prices are actually falling.

Despite the deflationary environment, economic policy-making throughout the world still seems to be dominated by the view that inflation is harmful to economic growth – not the least in euroland, where the sole objective of the European Central Bank is to achieve price stability, defined as a rate of inflation between zero and 2%. Yet the contemporary cross-country evidence and historical research suggests a positive relation between inflation and growth at least up to 6 to 8% inflation.

Keynes remarked in the second volume of his *Treatise on Money* that he was struck by the 'extraordinary' correspondence in history between periods of profit inflation and deflation and national rise and decline, respectively.

The distinguished economic historian, Walt Rostow, showed in his book, *The Stages of Economic Growth*, that historical take-offs into self-sustaining growth have invariably been associated with periods of relatively high inflation.

Today, Japanese businessmen might concur with Keynes's observation in his *General Theory* that there is nothing worse for investor confidence than a 'slowly sagging price level'.

There are sound theoretical reasons for expecting a positive relation between inflation and growth. The first point to make is that growth involves structural change, and inflation is a natural concomitant of resource shifts from contracting to expanding sectors of an economy if costs and prices are more flexible upwards than downwards. In this sense, inflation is part of the growth process.

Secondly, a mild demand inflation acts as a stimulus to investment by reducing real interest rates and raising prospective yields on investment. There is nothing that discourages investment more than the anticipation by business that the monetary authorities or government will clamp down on demand as soon as there is any upward movement of the price level.

This is the unfortunate signal that the ECB has been transmitting in euroland for the last two years, which is why growth there languishes below productive potential.

There is no lasting solution to the high unemployment being experienced in the major countries of euroland without an acceleration of the growth of output to at least 3% a year for the next few years.

Even if inflation accelerated beyond the target 2%, why should the alleged costs be regarded as higher or more serious than the costs of lost output and unemployment? The ECB has never given a satisfactory answer.

Another reason why inflation may be beneficial for growth is that it gives a greater degree of real wage flexibility if that is necessary for employment creation in activities subject to diminishing returns and rising marginal costs. Given these theoretical points, it is no wonder that all the most recent empirical studies, including those coming out of the inflation-averse International Monetary Fund – for instance, Sarel, IMF Staff Papers 1996 and Ghosh and Phillips, IMF Staff Papers 1998 – point to a non-linear relation between inflation and growth, with growth first positively related to inflation and then turning negative as the costs of inflation start to exceed the benefits.

But the 'optimum' rate of inflation from these studies is considerably higher than the ECB's arbitrary 2% target or, for that matter, the 3.5% maximum set by the Monetary Policy Committee in the UK.

Countries should not be seduced into believing that a necessary condition for achieving their growth of productive potential is price stability. Indeed, it could turn out to be a recipe for perpetual stagnation.

What Japan needs now is a strong dose of inflationary medicine – and it would act as a tonic for the countries of euroland, too. The task of economic management should be to choose an economic policy mix and targets based on evidence and pragmatism, not to pursue a dogma without scientific foundations.

(a) Why would you expect there to be a positive relationship between inflation and economic growth?
(b) Why could the goal of price stability result in stagnation?
(c) What policies could the Japanese government use to promote 'a strong dose of inflationary medicine'?

ANSWERS

Q1. D. The formula is $U/(U + E) \times 100\%$ (where U is the number unemployed and E is the number employed): i.e. $3/(3 + 24) \times 100\% = 11.1\%$.

Q2. The claimant figures exclude those who are unemployed but are ineligible for benefit. In the UK the following categories of unemployed people are ineligible for benefit: people returning to the workforce, people over 55, people temporarily unemployed, people seeking part-time work rather than full-time work.

Q3. *True*. The level of unemployment at the end of a period is equal to that at the beginning plus the inflows and minus the outflows.

Q4. E. (Note that A will have no effect, B will have the effect of reducing unemployment, and C and D will either reduce unemployment or leave it the same depending on whether those now staying on at school and retiring were previously recorded in the statistics.)

Q5. A. The result is that the supply of labour exceeds the demand, causing disequilibrium unemployment.

Q6. Because such unemployment is closely related to the business cycle and grows in periods of recession.

Q7. B. Frictional unemployment would be reduced if workers had better knowledge of jobs available and employers had better knowledge of what workers were available. This improved knowledge would reduce the search time of workers looking for a job and firms in recruiting labour.

Q8. (a), (b) and (c). The more industrially diverse a region, the slower the rate of change, and the more flexible the workforce, the less of a problem structural unemployment will be. Those made unemployed over a period of time can more easily move to alternative employment either within the existing area or elsewhere.

Q9. (a) *technological*; (b) *demand-deficient*; (c) *real-wage*; (d) *structural*; (e) *frictional*; (f) *demand-deficient*; (g) *seasonal* (holiday areas have higher unemployment during school terms).

Q10. C. The higher prices will mean that the current stock of money will purchase fewer goods and services: i.e. the 'real' money supply has decreased (i). The movement up along the aggregate demand curve shows that fewer goods and services will be demanded: i.e. that real aggregate demand has decreased (ii). With the rise in prices and a constant nominal money supply, however, it is highly unlikely that *money* expenditure will decrease (iii).

Q11. *(a)* *Yes*. This is part of the *foreign trade substitution effect*. People substitute imports for home-produced goods and services.
(b) *Yes*. This is the other part of the foreign trade substitution effect. People abroad substitute non-UK goods for UK exports.
(c) *No*. This is the income effect. (For this to occur, prices would have to rise faster than wages.)
(d) *Yes*. This is the *real balance effect*. People substitute increased money balances for expenditure on goods and services.
(e) *No*. This will shift the curve. It is not a direct consequence of the rise in the price level: it is something the government chooses to do.
(f) *Yes*. The higher interest rates are a direct consequence of the higher price level.
(g) *No*. The reason is the same as in the case of (e).

***Q*12.** *Leftward shift* (b), (h). (These are causes of a fall in aggregate demand other than a rise in the price level.)

Rightward shift (a), (c), (d), (f). (These are causes of a rise in aggregate demand other than a fall in the price level.) Note in the case of (d), if people believe that inflation is going to rise, they will buy more now in order to beat the price rises.

No shift (movement along) (e), (g). (These are changes in the price level that will affect aggregate demand and will thus be shown by the curve itself.)

***Q*13.** Firms' marginal cost curves are likely to slope upwards. They would thus need to receive higher prices to encourage them to produce more. (This assumes that they believe that their cost curves will not *shift*: only that costs will rise as they move upward *along* their marginal cost curves.)

***Q*14.** *False*. The RPI does not measure the standard of living as it takes no account of incomes.

***Q*15.** B. In a period of rapid inflation the real value of money falls.

***Q*16.** *True*. Debtors will see the value of their debt fall as prices rise. High inflation is often accompanied by low *real* rates of interest (i.e. interest rates relative to the rate of inflation). This benefits debtors.

***Q*17.** A high rate of domestic inflation relative to those with whom we trade will cause the competitiveness of exports to fall as they become more expensive. Equally the demand for imported goods will increase since they will appear relatively cheaper than domestically produced products.

***Q*18.** Inflation creates uncertainty for businesspeople: costs and hence profits are difficult to predict. As a consequence businesses may be reluctant to invest, thereby reducing the actual and potential levels of growth.

***Q*19.** *Rightward.*

***Q*20.** *Leftward.*

***Q*21.** (a) and (b) are demand-pull while the rest are cost-push.

***Q*22.** Higher wages increase firms' costs of production and thus cause them to put up their prices. These higher prices then cause unions to demand higher wages to compensate for the higher cost of living. Thus wages and prices chase each other in a spiral.

***Q*23.** (a), (b) and (e) are demand-side policies. They have the effect of reducing the growth in aggregate demand. The others are supply-side policies. If successful, they will reduce the rate of increase in costs.

***Q*24.** The higher the rate of inflation that employers and employees expect, the bigger will be the rate of increase in wages and prices that are set. The higher the current rate of inflation, the higher people will expect it to be in the future. (This question is examined in Chapter 21.)

***Q*25.** C. The Phillips curve showed the apparent trade-off between rates of unemployment and rates of inflation.

***Q*26.** *movement along*. In other words, the government could trade off inflation against unemployment.

***Q*27.** *using policies to influence non-demand factors causing inflation and unemployment*. It was believed that demand management policies could only be used to trade off inflation against unemployment: i.e. to cause a movement along the curve. Thus if the government wanted to reduce *both* inflation *and* unemployment, it would have to attempt to shift the curve inwards. This would involve policies other than demand management policies: policies to tackle cost-push inflation and equilibrium unemployment.

***Q*28.** *False*. There is still an apparent inverse relationship between them, albeit a worse trade-off than in the 1950s and 1960s but better than in the 1980s.

Chapter Fifteen
15
The Open Economy

A REVIEW

A country's economy does not operate in isolation. It is affected by the state of the international economy. What is more, the macroeconomic policies it pursues will have effects on other countries, which in turn will have effects on it.

In this chapter we look at macroeconomic issues in the context of an 'open economy'. We start by examining the balance of payments and then see how it affects and is affected by the rate of exchange. These related topics of the balance of payments and exchange rates can be seen as the fourth major macroeconomic issue (economic growth, unemployment and inflation being the other three).

We then group these four issues together and see how they are related, and in particular examine the relationship between inflation and unemployment. We then look at the circular flow of income, a useful model for helping to understand the role of aggregate demand in the economy and its effects on the four issues. Finally we turn to the methods used to measure national income and its various components: again, this is done in the open-economy context.

15.1 The balance of payments account
(Page 427)

Q1. The balance of payments for country A is defined as the balance of all money transactions between the residents of country A and the residents of all other countries over a specified period of time. *True/False*

Q2. Receipts of money from abroad are counted as *credits* on the balance of payments, whereas outflows of money are regarded as *debits*. *True/False*

Q3. Which of the following are debit items and which are credit items on the UK balance of payments account?

(a) The purchase of imports. *debit/credit*
(b) Loans made to non-UK residents by UK banks. *debit/credit*
(c) Investment by UK companies abroad. *debit/credit*
(d) Dividends earned by UK shareholders on overseas investment by UK companies. *debit/credit*
(e) Investment in the UK by non-UK companies. *debit/credit*
(f) Money placed on short-term deposit in the UK by non-residents. *debit/credit*
(g) Drawing on reserves. *debit/credit*

(Pages 427–30) The balance of payments account is composed of a number of parts.

Q4. A country has the following items in its balance of payments:

Exports of goods	£120m
Imports of services	£60m
Income flows and current transfers from abroad	£80m
Imports of goods	£150m
Exports of services	£50m
Income flows and current transfers going abroad	£30m

Its balance on trade in goods and services is a:
A. deficit of £40m.
B. deficit of £30m.
C. deficit of £20m.
D. deficit of £10m.
E. surplus of £10m.

Q5. Referring to the data of Q4, the country's balance of payments on current account is a:
A. deficit of £40m.
B. deficit of £30m.
C. deficit of £20m.
D. deficit of £10m.
E. surplus of £10m.

Q6. If there is a current account deficit of £1bn, then:
A. there must be a surplus of £1bn on trade in services.
B. there must be an equivalent deficit on the capital plus financial accounts.
C. there must be a net errors and omissions item of +£1bn.
D. the overall capital plus financial accounts (including net errors and omissions) must be in surplus by £1bn.
E. the financial account must be +£1bn.

Q7. The following are the various elements in the UK balance of payments account:
(i) Imports of goods (−)
(ii) Exports of goods (+)
(iii) Imports of services (−)
(iv) Exports of services (+)
(v) Incomes and current transfers to the UK from abroad (+)
(vi) Incomes and current transfers abroad from the UK (−)
(vii) Transfers of capital to the UK from abroad (+)
(viii) Transfers of capital abroad from the UK (−)
(ix) Long-term UK investment abroad (−)
(x) Long-term investment in UK from abroad (+)
(xi) Short-term financial outflows (−)
(xii) Short-term financial inflows (+)
(xiii) Adding to reserves (−)
(xiv) Drawing on reserves (+)

Into which of the above categories would you put the following items (there can be more than one item in each category)?

(a) Car imported from Germany.

....

(b) Insurance cover purchased by overseas company at Lloyds in London.

....

(c) UK pays contribution to EU Budget.

....

(d) Japanese car company builds factory in UK.

....

(e) UK resident takes a holiday in Florida.

....

(f) Interest earned by non-UK residents on assets held in UK.

....

(g) UK insurance company sets up branch in Canada.

....

(h) Running down the stock of foreign exchange in the Bank of England.

....

(i) Deposits in UK banks by foreigners.

....

(j) Scotch whisky sold in France.

....

(k) Aid given by the UK to developing countries for the construction of infrastructure.

....

Q8. Table 15.1 shows the internationally accepted way of setting out a balance of payments account.
The following are the items in country X's 2000 balance of payments:

210 CHAPTER 15 THE OPEN ECONOMY

Table 15.1

Credits	Debits
(1) Exports of goods	(2) Imports of goods
1 − 2 = Balance on trade in goods	
(3) Exports of services	(4) Imports of services
(1 + 3) − (2 + 4) = Balance on trade in goods and services	
(5) Incomes and current transfers from abroad	(6) Incomes and current transfers going abroad
(1 + 3 + 5) − (2 + 4 + 6) = Current account balance	
(7) Transfers of capital to UK from abroad	(8) Transfers of capital abroad from UK
7 − 8 = Capital account balance	
(9) Net direct and portfolio investment in UK from abroad	(10) Net direct and portfolio investment by UK abroad
(11) Other financial inflows (mainly short term)	(12) Other financial outflows (mainly short term)
either	*or*
(13) Drawing on reserves	(14) Building up reserves
(9 + 11 + 13) − (10 + 12 + 14) = Financial account balance	
(15) Net errors and omissions	
Current + capital + financial account balances + net errors and omissions = 0	

Exports of services	£80m
Exports of goods	£74m
Income flows and current transfers from abroad to country X	£43m
Net investment abroad by country X	£70m
Imports of services	£78m
Imports of goods	£82m
Net investment in country X from abroad	£56m
Short-term financial inflows to country X	£96m
Short-term financial outflows from country X	£84m
Drawing on reserves	£1m
Income flows and current transfers abroad from country X	£40m
Transfers of capital to country X from abroad	£7m
Transfers of capital abroad from country X	£5m

By referring to Table 15.1, work out the following balances in country X's balance of payments.

(a) the balance on trade in goods

....

(b) the balance on trade in goods and services

....

(c) the balance of payments on current account

....

(d) the capital account balance

....

(e) the financial account balance

....

(f) the current plus capital plus financial account balances

....

(g) net errors and omissions

....

(?) **Q9.** Explain why the overall balance of payments always balances.

....

....

Q10. The current account of the balance of payments tends to fluctuate with the business cycle. The current account tends to improve during a recession and deteriorate during a boom. *True/False*

15.2 Exchange rates

(Pages 430–4) The balance of payments is closely related to the rate of exchange. The rate of exchange is the rate at which one currency exchanges for another. If the rate of exchange of a pound sterling alters from 200 to 210 Japanese yen, this means that the pound has **Q11.** *appreciated/depreciated* relative to the yen, and that the yen has **Q12.** *appreciated/depreciated* relative to the pound. This means that Japanese imports will now be **Q13.** *cheaper/more expensive* in the UK and that, therefore, they will **Q14.** *rise/fall* in volume.

⊖ **Q15.** Sketch a demand curve for sterling and a supply curve of sterling against the euro on Figure 15.1 and mark the equilibrium exchange rate. Make sure you label the axes correctly.

Figure 15.1 Demand for and supply of sterling

(a) Who is demanding sterling in the diagram and for what purpose?

....

(b) Who is supplying sterling in the diagram and for what purpose?

....

(c) Now illustrate what happens to the exchange rate when there is an increased demand for sterling and a decreased supply.

Q16. The demand for sterling results from the credit items in the UK balance of payments and the supply of sterling results from the debit items. *True/False*

Q17. Only one of the following flows represents a *demand* for sterling. Which one?
A. Imports of goods and services into the UK.
B. UK investment abroad.
C. Short-term financial outflows from the UK.
D. Profit earned from UK investment abroad.
E. Overseas aid by the UK government.

Q18. Assume that there is a free-floating exchange rate. Will the following cause the exchange rate to appreciate or depreciate? In each case you should consider whether there is a shift in the demand or supply curves of sterling (or both) and which way the curve(s) shift(s).

(a) More video recorders are imported from Japan.
　　Demand curve shift *left/right/no shift*
　　Supply curve shift *left/right/no shift*
　　Exchange rate *appreciates/depreciates*

(b) Non-UK residents increase their purchases of UK government securities.
　　Demand curve shift *left/right/no shift*
　　Supply curve shift *left/right/no shift*
　　Exchange rate *appreciates/depreciates*

(c) UK interest rates fall relative to those abroad.
　　Demand curve shift *left/right/no shift*
　　Supply curve shift *left/right/no shift*
　　Exchange rate *appreciates/depreciates*

(d) The UK experiences a higher rate of inflation than other countries.
　　Demand curve shift *left/right/no shift*
　　Supply curve shift *left/right/no shift*
　　Exchange rate *appreciates/depreciates*

(e) The result of the development of the single market in the EU is for investment in the UK by the rest of the EU to increase by a greater amount than UK investment in other EU countries.
　　Demand curve shift *left/right/no shift*
　　Supply curve shift *left/right/no shift*
　　Exchange rate *appreciates/depreciates*

(f) Speculators believe that the rate of exchange will fall.
　　Demand curve shift *left/right/no shift*
　　Supply curve shift *left/right/no shift*
　　Exchange rate *appreciates/depreciates*

(Pages 434–5) The government may be unwilling to let the pound float freely. Instead it may attempt to fix the exchange rate, or at least attempt to reduce exchange rate fluctuations.

Q19. Which one of the following is likely to lead to persistent balance of payments deficits for country X under fixed exchange rates?
A. A lower income elasticity of demand for the country's exports than for its imports.
B. A lower rate of growth at home than abroad.
C. A higher rate of inflation abroad than in the domestic economy.
D. The long-term development of import substitutes at home.
E. A growth in the country's monopoly power in the export market.

Q20. Which one of the following would help to prevent an appreciation of sterling resulting from an excess demand for sterling?
A. An increase in interest rates.
B. Building up reserves.
C. The Bank of England purchasing sterling on the foreign exchange market.
D. A reduction in government expenditure and an increase in taxation, but with no change in interest rates.
E. A decrease in the supply of money.

Q21. Assume that, as a result of inflation, there was downward pressure on the exchange rate. List three short-term measures the government could adopt in order to prevent the exchange rate depreciating.

1. ....

2. ....

3. ....

15.3 The relationship between the four macroeconomic objectives

(Pages 435–7) In the short term, the four macroeconomic objectives – faster economic growth, lower unemployment, lower inflation and the avoidance of excessive current account balance of payments deficits – are all related.

212 CHAPTER 15 THE OPEN ECONOMY

Q22. Fill in the blanks in Table 15.2, which relates the state of the economy to each phase of the business cycle. You should insert one of the following words in each of the blanks: *high/low/rising/falling/surplus/deficit*.

Table 15.2

	The upturn	The expansion	The peaking out	The slow-down
Inflation	.....	.....	.....	.....
Unemployment	.....	.....	.....	.....
Balance of trade	.....	.....	.....	.....
Growth	.....	.....	.....	.....
Investment	.....	.....	.....	.....
Business confidence	.....	.....	.....	.....

There are, however, various time lags involved in the response of the four objectives to changes in aggregate demand. This means that at some points in the business cycle, the objectives are collectively looking more favourable than at other points.

Q23. At which of the following points in the business cycle would a government be more likely to call an election (assuming that it can choose)?
A. The bottom of a recession.
B. The peak of the boom.
C. Mid-recovery, where growth is fastest.
D. Shortly after the peak, where the economy is slowing down.
E. Where the economy is just beginning to recover from a recession.

B PROBLEMS, EXERCISES AND PROJECTS

Table 15.3 Current account balances (seasonally adjusted)

£ million

	Trade in goods and services			Income			Current transfers			Current balance
	Trade in goods	Trade in services	Total trade	Compensation of employees	Investment income	Total income	Central government	Other sectors	Total current transfers	
	BOKI	IKBD	IKBJ	IJAJ	HBOM	HBOJ	FNSV	FNTC	IKBP	HBOP
1992	−13 050	5 482	−7 568	−49	177	128	−1 632	−3 902	−5 534	−12 974
1993	−13 066	6 581	−6 485	35	−226	−191	−1 517	−3 726	−5 243	−11 919
1994	−11 126	6 379	−4 747	−170	3 518	3 348	−2 839	−2 530	−5 369	−6 768
1995	−12 023	8 481	−3 542	−296	2 397	2 101	−3 292	−4 282	−7 574	−9 015
1996	−13 722	9 597	−4 125	93	1 111	1 204	−2 469	−3 319	−5 788	−8 709
1997	−12 342	12 528	186	83	3 823	3 906	−3 087	−2 725	−5 812	−1 720
1998	−21 813	12 666	−9 147	−10	12 568	12 558	−4 844	−3 381	−8 225	−4 814
1999	−27 524	11 660	−15 864	201	3 818	4 019	−3 749	−3 497	−7 246	−19 091
2000	−30 023	13 779	−16 244	143	8 433	8 576	−5 552	−3 785	−9 337	−17 005
2001	−33 632	13 046	−20 586	..	..	..	..	..	..	..
1997 Q1	−2 303	3 195	892	1	537	538	−688	−1 148	−1 836	−406
Q2	−3 140	3 062	−78	18	1 724	1 742	−1 080	−131	−1 211	453
Q3	−2 777	3 225	448	22	1 847	1 869	−857	−808	−1 665	652
Q4	−4 122	3 046	−1 076	42	−285	−243	−462	−638	−1 100	−2 419
1998 Q1	−4 767	3 054	−1 713	75	1 605	1 680	−1 170	−1 253	−2 423	−2 456
Q2	−5 178	3 540	−1 638	−27	1 854	1 827	−748	−549	−1 297	−1 108
Q3	−5 686	3 531	−2 155	−29	4 857	4 828	−1 260	−430	−1 690	983
Q4	−6 182	2 541	−3 641	−29	4 252	4 223	−1 666	−1 149	−2 815	−2 233
1999 Q1	−7 746	2 654	−5 092	33	−45	−12	−503	−1 211	−1 714	−6 818
Q2	−6 322	3 104	−3 218	90	2 098	2 188	−906	−558	−1 464	−2 494
Q3	−6 268	2 971	−3 297	48	794	842	−1 122	−972	−2 094	−4 549
Q4	−7 188	2 931	−4 257	30	971	1 001	−1 218	−756	−1 974	−5 230
2000 Q1	−6 899	3 280	−3 619	11	2 945	2 956	−1 127	−935	−2 062	−2 725
Q2	−7 193	3 438	−3 755	82	361	443	−1 293	−757	−2 050	−5 362
Q3	−7 942	3 874	−4 068	28	3 074	3 102	−1 312	−1 179	−2 491	−3 457
Q4	−7 989	3 187	−4 802	22	2 033	2 055	−1 820	−914	−2 734	−5 481
2001 Q1	−7 749	3 315	−4 434	−60	4 122	4 062	−765	−1 129	−1 894	−2 266
Q2	−8 887	3 167	−5 720	100	3 150	3 250	−1 326	−1 420	−2 746	−5 216
Q3	−8 060	2 151	−5 909	79	3 739	3 818	709	−1 004	−295	−2 386
Q4	−8 352	3 070	−5 282	83	−62	21	−1 086	−1 225	−2 311	−7 572

Source: *Monthly Digest of Statistics* (National Statistics, 2000).

Q24. Table 15.3 is taken from *the Monthly Digest of Statistics* and shows the UK balance of payments on current account.
(a) Explain the terms 'Services', 'Income' and 'Current transfers'.
(b) Which parts of the current account are subject to the greatest short-term fluctuations? What explanations can you offer for this?
(c) Which parts of the current account fluctuate with the course of the business cycle and in which direction? What explanations can you offer for this? Why do other parts appear not to fluctuate with the course of the business cycle?

Q25. Table 15.4 shows a simplified balance of payments account for the UK in 2000.
(a) What was the UK's balance on trade in goods and services?

....

(b) Calculate the deficit/surplus on the current account.

....

(c) Calculate the deficit/surplus on the capital plus financial accounts (excluding reserves and net errors and omissions).

....

(d) Establish whether there was a loss or addition to the country's reserves and of how much. (You will first have to take net errors and omissions into account.)

....

Table 15.4 UK balance of payments (2000)

Item	£m
UK investment overseas	231 940
Balance of services	+13 779
Net capital transfers	+1 676
Net current transfers	−9 337
Net errors and omissions	−2 661
Overseas investment in the UK	245 996
Short-term capital inflows to UK	274 532
Short-term capital outflows from UK	266 663
Exports of goods	188 085
Imports of goods	218 108
Net income flows from abroad	+8 556
Changes in reserves	.....

Q26. Let us assume that there is a free-floating exchange rate: i.e. that the exchange rate is determined by free-market forces. The demand and supply schedules in Table 15.5 relate the price of sterling to the euro for a given day.
(a) What is the equilibrium rate of exchange? ....
(b) A sharp fall in UK interest rates causes the demand for sterling to fall by £8m per day at all exchange rates.

Table 15.5 Demand for and supply of sterling

Price of sterling in euros	1.10	1.20	1.30	1.40	1.50	1.60	1.70	1.80
£m demanded per day	40	36	32	28	24	20	16	12
£m supplied per day	16	20	24	28	32	36	40	44

Assuming other things remain equal, what will happen to the exchange rate for sterling in euros?

....

(c) If we relax the assumption that other things remain equal in (b) above, what might happen to the supply of sterling?

....

(d) Assume that, in addition to the fall in demand for sterling of £8m per day, the supply of sterling to purchase euros rises by £8m. What will the equilibrium exchange rate be now?

....

(e) Suppose now that the authorities decide to fix the exchange rate value between the pound and the euro. They decide on a rate of £1 = €1.60. How can the reserves be used to maintain this rate of exchange?

....

(f) What will be the effect on trade between the UK and the eurozone countries of this policy of fixing the exchange rate at £1 = €1.60?

....

(g) In order to address the problem of the over-valued pound, the authorities may be forced in the long run to reassess the fixed exchange-rate value. They might be forced to *devalue/revalue* the currency.

Q27. In pairs, find data for (i) economic growth and (ii) current account deficits as a percentage of GDP for four separate countries. Data can be found from the *OECD Economic Outlook* or from the *Statistical Annex* of the *European Economy*, which are also available to download from http://www.oecd.org and http://europa.eu.int/comm/economy_finance/publications_en.htm respectively.
(a) To what extent do the two indicators more together over time in each of the countries?
(b) Can you observe any time lags? If so, explain them.
(c) If an economy grows rapidly, what is likely to happen to (i) interest rates; (ii) the exchange rate? How will these impact on the current account?

C DISCUSSION TOPICS AND ESSAYS

Q28. In what sense is it true to say that a current account deficit will always be matched by an equal surplus elsewhere in the balance of payments?

Q29. What effect will a rise in interest rates be likely to have on the various parts of the balance of payments account?

Q30. For what reasons may the rate of exchange depreciate? What measures could the government adopt to prevent this depreciation?

Q31. Why should a government ever be concerned about the balance of payments, if a deficit on the current account is always offset exactly by a surplus on the capital plus financial account?

Q32. What are the advantages and disadvantages of a depreciation in the exchange rate? To what extent do these advantages and disadvantages depend on the causes, magnitude and timing of the depreciation?

Q33. If it is assumed that a Japanese firm opened a car plant in the UK, what would be the likely impacts on the various parts of the balance of payments in (a) the short term; (b) the long term?

Q34. Assume that the exchange rate has been depreciating over time. What are the likely causes of this? What are the likely economic consequences? What policies can the government introduce to stop the depreciation in the currency?

Q35. If a government or central bank decides to reduce unemployment through changing the interest rate, what should it do to the interest rate? Explain the likely consequences for the other macroeconomic objectives.

Q36. What is the relationship between the balance of payments and the rate of exchange?

Q37. What problems face a government in attempting to achieve all its principal macroeconomic objectives simultaneously?

Q38. At what point of the business cycle is the country at present? Do you think that the government has managed to get the economy to the right point of the cycle in order to improve its chances of success at the next general election?

Q39. Debate
A persistent and substantial current account deficit is a symptom of a fundamental weakness in the structure of the economy.

D ARTICLES

The USA has been running a massive trade deficit for many years, and there is every indication that it is getting worse. The article below, taken from *BusinessWeek* online of 11 March 2002, examines the dynamics behind the widening trade deficit and the failure of a depreciation of the dollar to help solve the problem.

US: There's a cloud inside that silver lining

A strengthening US economy will come with a cost – a wider trade gap

Recessions have always been both painful and salutary. While they bring distress to households and corporations, they also have a cleansing effect on the economy's imbalances, such as excess inventories and burdensome debt, that build up during the good times.

However, this business cycle is different in one key respect: the US trade deficit and the enormous external debt it created still hang ominously over the economy. Both the trade gap and its financing needs will swell further as the recovery picks up speed. That will hamper the upturn in manufacturing, and it could set up potential problems for the dollar later this year.

During a recession, currencies usually lose value and trade gaps typically narrow. True, the December deficit shrank by $3.3 billion, to $25.3 billion. But much of the shrinkage came from lower oil prices, and when adjusted for inflation, December's trade gap was not much lower than its year-ago level.

The amazingly strong performance of the US dollar has helped to keep the trade deficit wide. Since the economy began to slow in early 2000, the broad trade-weighted dollar has appreciated 12%, to levels not seen since the superdollar of the mid-1980s. Moreover, since the official start of the recession in March, 2001, the greenback has gained nearly 3%, a decidedly atypical recession pattern, especially for a country that has external debts totalling more than 4% of its gross domestic product.

The dollar's rise indicates foreigners are still willing to buy and hold American assets, in part because no other economy offers the potential payoffs the US does. And the strong greenback helps to finance the US's propensity to consume more than it produces, with no threat from inflation.

That windfall, though, comes at a price. In the short run, US manufacturers, who now export about 20% of their output, will continue to get hammered by the strong dollar, which makes their goods less competitive in foreign markets. Plus, since the recovery in the rest of the world will lag behind the US upturn, foreign demand will be slow to strengthen. At the same time, a pickup in US demand will draw in cheaper imports at a faster rate.

The result will be a wider trade gap by the end of this year, which may trigger a longer-run cost for the US. Financing the trade gap will require one of two things: ever-increasing amounts of foreign capital attracted by high expected rates of return, or a weaker dollar that would force a realignment of the US trade balance. The worry: a suddenly weaker dollar that could lift inflation and interest rates in 2003, and choke off the recovery.

For now, investors are not thinking that far ahead. Instead, they are focused on the economy's increasingly bright recovery prospects, a key factor keeping the dollar strong. The latest data on the leading index, consumer confidence, and durable goods orders are generally upbeat. And Federal Reserve Chairman Alan Greenspan sounded cautiously optimistic when he delivered his semi-annual report on monetary policy and the economy to Congress on February 27, which included the Fed's latest economic forecast.

The Fed chief suggested that any tightening of monetary policy this year won't come anytime soon, because the Fed expects only a moderate recovery and because the inflation outlook is excellent. In fact, the dollar's brawn in the past year is a key reason for inflation's subdued performance. Over the past year, prices of imported goods excluding petroleum have plunged 5.2%, the largest yearly drop since records began in 1988. Plus, inflation tends to decline in the first year of a recovery, because the economic slack created by the recession limits pricing power.

Greenspan's comments were consistent with the latest data, which suggest that the upturn is coming on a bit stronger than anyone thought possible late last year. In particular, the Conference Board's composite index of leading indicators, those that foreshadow the economy's path, rose 0.6% in January, following jumps of 1.3% in December and 0.8% in November. That adds up to the strongest three-month advance since 1982, just before the powerful 1983 recovery.

Consumers say they were more cautious in February, according to the latest reading of consumer confidence. But that hasn't stopped them from shopping. Store sales remain healthy, and car sales are holding up far better than anyone thought possible after the late-2001 boost from dealer incentives. As a result, more and more economists are boosting their forecasts for first-quarter and first-half economic growth.

However, what's good for the recovery will not be so good for the trade gap. The US still imports 34% more goods and services than it exports. That means, just to keep the deficit from widening further in the coming year, exports will have to grow a third faster than imports. But that's not going to happen, as the US leads the global recovery.

The capital-goods sector will probably account for much of the trade gap's deterioration this year. Both imports and exports of tech equipment stabilized at the end of 2001, after declining for a year. And the recent increases in factory orders, including a 2.6% gain in January bookings for durable goods and another rise in capital-goods orders, suggest that US companies are starting to lift their capital spending. That means imports of business equipment, especially high-tech goods, should bounce back before exports do.

Despite the worsening outlook for trade, the dollar is likely to retain its lofty status among the world's currencies at least through most of this year. That's because the US is still the world's preeminent site for investment opportunities.

Clearly, the Japanese yen will offer no competition this year. Japan's economy remains a basket case, with little progress on restoring health to its banking sector or on broader reform efforts. In fact, much of the dollar's appreciation in the past year has come at the expense of the yen. The greenback's main potential challenge will come from the euro. But even here, Europe's recovery will be restrained by tight monetary policy, growing fiscal excess, and only a modicum of reforms to its labor markets and pension systems.

As the trade deficit widens, though, the US will continue to pile up debts owed to the rest of the world. By the end of next year, the current account deficit, the broadest definition of US foreign obligations, is likely to hit a record 5% of GDP.

At some point, investors will bring about a balancing of the lopsided US position, most likely by bidding down the dollar. But with US growth prospects for 2002 looking better than those of anyplace else, the dollar's day of reckoning is most likely to come later rather than sooner.

(a) Why, according to the article, was the USA's trade deficit likely to get worse before it got better?

(b) Explain why the USA, with a huge trade deficit (5 per cent of GDP), experienced a 12 per cent *appreciation* of the dollar from early 2000 to the end of 2001. Should the dollar not have fallen rather than risen in value over the period?

(c) Why does the article suggest that the dollar was unlikely to fall in the near future, even if the trade deficit continues to widen?

(d) Find out and explain what has happened to the value of the dollar since this article was written.

> In the following article, which appeared in *The Independent* of 30 June 1998, Lea Patterson assesses the nervousness of international currency markets and how the devaluation of one currency in one part of the world is likely to lead to a ripple effect of devaluation around the global economy.

Currency bomb is still ticking

On 2 July 1997, the Thai government devalued the baht in the face of intense pressure from currency speculators. By the end of the year, the Indonesian rupiah, the Korean won, the Malaysian ringgit and the Philippine peso had all depreciated by at least 40 per cent. The world at large was forced to face facts – the once-vaunted 'tiger' economies of the East were on decidedly shaky ground.

Almost exactly a year on, currency speculators are in the news again – the Russian rouble is faltering, the Pakistan government devalued the rupee by 4.2 per cent at the weekend, and the South African rand yesterday hit an all-time low, at 6.155 to the dollar. Are we about to see a second, perhaps more widespread, round of devaluations? And what, if anything, can the authorities do to stave off the speculators?

The amount of money traded on the world's foreign exchange markets is nothing short of phenomenal. Harry Shutt, in his newly-published book *The Trouble with Capitalism*, estimates that the daily volume of business on the world's currency markets stood at around $1500bn in 1995, a figure which exceeds the annual gross domestic product of all but three of the world's economies.

As a result, currency speculators have immense power. When the markets become convinced that a country's currency is fundamentally overvalued, as recently has been the case in South Africa, there is little the authorities can do to avert a currency collapse.

Notwithstanding the Malaysian Prime Minister's view that the markets' attack on the ringgit was a Jewish conspiracy aimed at the Far East, most experts are now convinced that last year's Asian devaluations were inevitable, given the fundamentals. In its recently published 1997 annual report, the Asian Development Bank argues that globalisation, and the consequent rapid inflow of capital into the tiger economies, merely 'heightened the risks associated with failing to address inappropriate policies, weaknesses in financial sector institutions and problems in corporate and public governance'.

Globalisation, and the free movement of capital, may have been a spur to the heady economic growth enjoyed by the region in the early 1990s, but it also opened up the economies to an unprecedented degree of public scrutiny and evaluation. When the bubble burst in Asia, and when investor confidence began to falter, capital flowed out of the region as fast as it had flowed in just a few months before, and devaluations became inevitable.

A combination of increased globalisation – with the accompanying increase in global scrutiny – and weak economic fundamentals also lies behind the latest round of currency speculation in the emerging markets.

In Russia, the rouble yesterday steadied at around 6.22 to the dollar after the government raised interest rates on Friday to 80 per cent from 60 per cent, but analysts were gloomy about the country's long-term prospects. Paul McNamara, emerging markets economist at Julius Baer Investments, commented: 'Policy is king and neither in Asia nor Russia are we seeing any positive steps.'

In South Africa, meanwhile, the rand pulled itself off its earlier lows after the central bank raised its repo rate by almost 2 per cent but, as with Russia, experts say the outlook for the economy is negative. The central bank's use of interest rates is predicted to slow economic growth in an already fragile economy, while the fall in the exchange rate is likely to fuel inflation.

There has also been pressure on the Australian dollar, where economists are predicting that the Asian crisis will continue to hit growth. In Pakistan, meanwhile, the reasons for the currency slide are also economic in nature, albeit of a slightly different variety. Most experts have been attributing the weakness in the rupee to the economic sanctions imposed on Pakistan in the wake of its nuclear tests.

But although economic fundamentals would seem to provide the reasons for the latest bout of speculative attacks, they do not fully explain the timing. The markets have known about the weaknesses in certain of the emerging markets for some time. So why has the speculation started now? The answer here lies in the Japanese economy, and in particular in the recent bout of weakness in the Japanese yen.

David Brickman, international economist at PaineWebber, explained: 'The weakness in the yen has changed the attitude to risk in the global currency markets. There has been a flight to quality, and the markets have begun to reassess the weaker economies.' Ask the experts which of the emerging markets economies are the weakest, and the names South Africa and Russia are on almost everybody's lips.

As it is Japan that lies behind the renewed attacks by the currency speculators, so it is Japan that will determine how far the latest slump in emerging market currencies will go.

If the yen depreciates rapidly, the signs are that China will devalue the yuan. And if China devalues, this is likely to spark not only another round of devaluations in the East, but also sharp falls in global stock markets. Further emerging market gloom will also hit export demand in the developed countries, re-awakening fears of a worldwide slowdown.

It is this spectre of Chinese devaluation that prompted the US Federal Reserve to intervene in the world currency markets 10 days ago in an attempt to stem the rapid fall in the yen. The apparent success of the US intervention – the yen has not rallied but neither has it gone into free-fall – seems surprising, given the funds the currency speculators have at their disposal.

Most analysts attribute this to a mixture of nervousness in the markets, which believe that there may be no ceiling on the Fed's willingness to intervene and buy up the yen, and, perhaps more significantly, to the signals the intervention sent to the speculators. Some believe the West is now committed to rescuing the Japanese economy – and that Japan is committed to making the necessary reforms.

In sum, depreciation in the South African rand and the Russian rouble may be inevitable, given the power of the currency speculators, the renewed risk-averseness in the markets and the weak economic fundamentals.

What is less clear is whether a devaluation in the yuan is inevitable, at least in the near term. Policymakers the world over hope that co-ordinated central bank intervention combined with rapid and wide-ranging structural reforms in Japan will be sufficient to stave off the speculators. If it is not, the economic consequences may be nothing short of disastrous.

(a) What reasons does the article give to explain why currencies collapsed in south-east Asia?
(b) Why, according to the article, was Japan to blame for the uncertainty in international currency markets?
(c) 'If the yen depreciates rapidly, the signs are that China will devalue the yuan. And if China devalues, this is likely to spark not only another round of devaluations in the East, but also sharp falls in global stock markets.' Why would a round of competitive currency devaluations have very limited benefit to any country in the longer term?

Large and small companies alike, if they trade abroad, have the problem of foreign exchange risk. The article below, taken from *CBI News* of July/August 1999, considers the foreign exchange problems faced by businesses and how they might deal with them.

The critical difference

The strong pound has been wreaking havoc with British businesses for months. Furthermore, the British exporter faces two major risks: firstly from exchange rate volatility and secondly, the way in which the markets are structured. Foreign exchange is the world's largest traded market with a daily turnover of approximately £1600bn. The market is dominated by the big US and European banks led by the likes of Citibank, ABN Amro and United Bank of Switzerland. Surprisingly, 95 per cent of this enormous turnover is speculative, where trading is not based upon the sale or purchase of real goods. Therefore, even the largest exporting firms are minorities in this huge, complex flow of money around the world.

Smaller firms are even more vulnerable, and it makes no sense for hard-pressed sales staff to bring in new business if already tight margins are then frittered away by ill-timed foreign exchange deals. Many firms, like clothing manufacturers Fruit of the Loom, operate the most careful hedging strategy they can, as Stephen Grisman, the company's assistant treasurer responsible for European Treasury explains. 'We are a multinational company with an American base. World-wide our sales total £1.4bn. Our European division employs about 3500 people and we have annual sales of £168m.

'I manage our integrated, centralised European cash management system and we operate a foreign exchange hedging policy. I need to be aware of where the foreign exchange markets are and I need to look ahead about 12 months. I use a mixture of spot trades, forwards and options. Historically I have worked on information from three sources, *Financial Times*, an online information system and material received from my banks.'

Stephen Grisman's problem, like that of many smaller company treasurers, is that he does not have sufficient transactions to warrant operating his own dealing room. All the time he is faced with interpreting the information he receives from his various sources, he has other tasks to perform in his working day. This means that he cannot spend long periods poring over statistics and analysing the market.

'I suppose my banks are impartial! But I am dealing with the people who want to do a trade with my money,' he adds. That, he admits, is not ideal. He is always likely to be at a disadvantage when dealing with experienced and specialist foreign exchange dealers.

'There is always a conflict of interest when banks provide foreign exchange to their clients,' says Laurence Butcher, managing director of Windsor-based Halewood International Market Strategies Ltd (HIMS). 'It is a fact that the best time for any company to sell a currency is, by the very nature of the transaction, the worst time for the bank to be buying it.'

HIMS works closely with Grisman to level up the odds. HIMS provides Fruit of the Loom's European treasury with professional expertise and analysis to assist Grisman to get the best results from the currency markets and the banks.

Nick Warburton, financial accountant at ARM Holdings Plc, the Cambridge microchip designer, faces a similar challenge. Last year the company had sales of £42m. Dual listed in London and New York's NASDAQ, ARM is mainly a sterling-based operation; however, virtually all its revenues are in dollars.

With an ongoing requirement to sell dollars for sterling, staying in tune with the market is crucial. Like Fruit of the Loom, ARM is risk averse when it comes to foreign exchange and has established clear guidelines; avoiding foreign exchange risk as far as possible. When doing a deal, Nick Warburton, for whom foreign exchange cannot be a full-time job, needs to make vital decisions.

'The main decision is when to sell US dollars. We may be in a better position to negotiate if we understand what the market is likely to do.' In other words, he needs to know more than simply the spot price. He needs to be able to understand trends in the market in order to time his sale, and protect against negative price movements. Having assessed the expected range of trade over a period of time, whether hours, days or weeks, it can make a considerable difference in protecting profits and getting the best out of the trading conditions.

Mr Warburton knows that by outsourcing advice and up-to-the-minute information, he can assess whether the banks are giving him a fair price and making reasonable forward adjustments. 'It gives me assurance and takes the worry off my shoulders because I know that the market is being monitored all the time.'

'Simply knowing where exchange rates are is only part of the story,' explains Laurence Butcher. 'To make a decision or take action without knowing why the movement has taken place and where it is expected to move from there is pure speculation. Our clients benefit from us keeping them fully updated with real-time information where it affects their exchange rates.

They know where the market is and why it is moving.

'Historically, companies have been reactive, basing their decisions on past events seen in the FT or heard on the news. Their policies tended to be based on prices quoted by their bands. Trading so blindly very often results in trades being completed at the worst price of the day, week or month in question. This bad timing is a direct result of the client being unaware of the factors and sentiment in the market at the time of the trade.

'At HIMS, we make our clients aware of the range of movement and the reasons behind the range. Then we monitor the developing trend and inform our clients when the exchange rate is at the top or bottom of expectations. This objective overview ensures that our clients never trade blind. They can make well-informed decisions on their exposure and protect against risk whenever necessary.'

Renishaw Plc is a high-technology engineering company making precision meteorology equipment with a world headquarters in Wootton-under-Edge, Gloucestershire. Sales in 1998 were £92m in dollars, deutschemarks, yen and Irish punts. The company exports about 90 per cent of its turnover.

Looking after foreign exchange is one of group financial accountant Rob Hume's jobs. 'Because we've got currencies coming in on a regular basis, and our costs are all sterling based, we have to convert the currencies to sterling. We use Halewood as an "insurance policy", they inform us of where rates are and where they are likely to move.'

Deals vary from £250 000 to £1m. Hume uses a screen-based pricing system but Halewood's information is delivered real-time with an added dimension of interaction with the analysts – something that his bankers do not supply.

'It is critical that we sell currency at the right time. HIMS inform us as to which way the currencies are moving,' says Mr Hume, 'so then we are able to optimise our dealings'.

Predicting where exchange rates may be at any given time is a pointless and exceptionally risky practice, says Laurence Butcher. 'Traditionally, the information and analysis given to UK corporates by their banks has fallen into that category. This will invariably be wrong as these guess-timates are based on variables subject to change.

'If the risk for a currency is to appreciate or depreciate, then we need to know by how much it could realistically move. From there a company can establish logical parameters of movement over any given time frame. Too many times, companies just book forward and live to regret it.'

At a time when UK companies are struggling to preserve their sales and their margins against the burden of spiralling exchange rates, good advice and specialist analysis is critical. Moreover, in the battle against the big financial institutions, who run the world's foreign exchange markets, exporters, even very large exporters, need all the help they can get.

(a) Explain how a firm's foreign trading profits might be influenced by: (i) an appreciation; (ii) a depreciation of the currency.

(b) How might a firm set about reducing its exposure to foreign exchange risk?

(c) What impact is the euro likely to have on the stability of profits for firms within the eurozone?

ANSWERS

Q1. True.

Q2. True.

Q3. *debits* (a), (b), (c). These all represent a monetary flow from the UK to the rest of the world.

credits (d), (e), (f), (g). These all represent a monetary flow to the UK. Note that drawing on reserves is a credit item because it credits the balance of payments (even though it represents a debit to the reserves).

Q4. A. The balance on trade in goods and services equals exports of goods and services minus imports of goods and services: i.e. (£120m + £50m) − (£150m + £60m) = −£40m.

Q5. E. It equals the balance on trade in goods and services plus net income flows and current transfers: i.e. −£40 + £80m − £30m = +£10m.

Q6. D. The three accounts, the current account, capital account and financial account (plus any net errors and omissions), must add up to zero: they must balance. Thus a deficit on the current account must be balanced by a surplus of the same amount on the sum of the other two accounts plus net errors and omissions.

Q7. (a) (i), (b) (iv), (c) (vi), (d) (x), (e) (iii), (f) (vi), (g) (ix), (h) (xiv), (i) (xii), (j) (ii), (k) (viii).

Q8. *(a)* £74m − £82m = −£8m.
(b) £74m − £82m + £80m − £78m = −£6m.
(c) £74m − £82m + £80m − £78m + £43m − £40m = −£3m.
(d) £7m − £5m = £2m.
(e) £56m − £70m + £96m − £84m + £1m = −£1m.
(f) −£3m + £2m − £1m = −£2m.
(g) +£2m.

Q9. After taking account of any errors and omissions, any deficit on the current account must be matched by an equal and opposite surplus on the total of the other two accounts, and vice versa.

Q10. True. In a boom, higher incomes lead to more imports, and higher inflation leads to both less exports and more imports. Therefore the balance of payments on current account tends to deteriorate. The reverse is true in a recession.

Q11. *appreciated*.

Q12. *depreciated*.

Q13. *cheaper*.

Q14. *rise*.

Q15. *(a)* Non-UK residents are buying sterling with euros in order to obtain UK exports of goods and services and to invest in the UK.

(b) UK residents are supplying sterling in order to purchase euros in order to obtain imports of goods and services from the eurozone countries and to invest in the eurozone.

(c) The demand and supply curves in Figure A15.1 shift to D_2 and S_2 respectively. The exchange rate will appreciate to r/e_2.

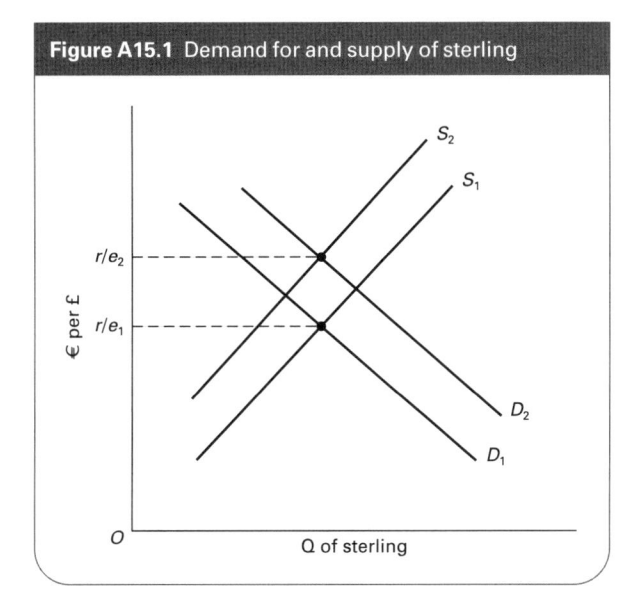

Figure A15.1 Demand for and supply of sterling

Q16. *True*.

Q17. D. It is a credit item on the balance of payments. The others are debit items. The profit earned abroad on UK investment will be in foreign currency. When this is exchanged for sterling in order to pay the dividends to UK shareholders, this will create a demand for sterling.

Q18. *(a)* Demand curve *no shift*; supply curve shifts to the *right*; exchange rate *depreciates*.

(b) Demand curve shifts to the *right*; supply curve *no shift*; exchange rate *appreciates*.

(c) Demand curve shifts to the *left*; supply curve shifts to the *right*; exchange rate *depreciates*.

(d) Demand curve shifts to the *left*; supply curve shifts to the *right*; exchange rate *depreciates*.

(e) Demand curve shifts to the *right*; supply curve shifts to the *right* (but less so than the demand curve); exchange rate *appreciates*.

(f) Demand curve shifts to the *left*; supply curve shifts the *right*; exchange rate *depreciates*.

Q19. A. This will mean that as world incomes grow, exports will grow less rapidly than imports. Note in the case of B that a lower rate of growth in country X will lead to a lower rate of growth in demand for imports than in other countries, and hence a lower rate of growth in demand for country X's imports than its exports.

Q20. B. Building up reserves results from the Bank of England selling sterling on the foreign exchange market. This increased supply of sterling helps to prevent an appreciation. All the other options will tend to *cause* an appreciation. In the case of option A, higher interest rates increase the demand for sterling and decrease the supply, as short-term finance flows into the country. With option C, the Bank of England is adding to the demand for sterling. With option D, there will be reduction in aggregate demand and hence a reduction in the demand for imports (and hence the supply of sterling) and, via lower prices, an increase in exports (and hence the demand for sterling).

Q21. 1. The use of reserves to buy sterling.
2. Borrowing from abroad to buy sterling.
3. Increased interest rates to attract short-term money inflows.

Q22.

	The upturn	The expansion	The peaking out	The slow-down
Inflation	low	rising	high	falling
Unemployment	high	falling	low	rising
Balance of trade	surplus	deficit	deficit	surplus
Growth	rising	high	falling	low
Investment	rising	high	falling	low
Business confidence	rising	high	low	low

Q23. C. In mid-recovery, growth is fastest and unemployment is falling (both popular with the electorate), but inflation has probably not started rising yet, given the fact that most firms are still able to respond to the higher demand by raising their output. Also, there is unlikely to be a severe current account deficit and downward pressure on the exchange rate. Thus there is good news and no bad news – yet!

Chapter Sixteen

16

The Roots of Modern Macroeconomics

A REVIEW

'The ideas of economists and political philosophers, both when they are right and when they are wrong, are more powerful than is commonly understood. Indeed the world is ruled by little else. Practical men, who believe themselves to be quite exempt from any intellectual influences, are usually the slaves of some defunct economist.'

J.M. Keynes, The General Theory of Employment, Interest and Money (1936)

In this chapter we examine the development of macroeconomic ideas and their influence on economic policy.

16.1 Setting the scene: three key issues

(Pages 442–4) The different schools of economic thought make different assumptions about how the economy operates. The classical and new classical schools argue that prices and wages are **Q1.** *flexible/inflexible*; that aggregate supply is **Q2.** *responsive/unresponsive* to a change in aggregate demand; and that individual producers and consumers have **Q3.** *quickly adjusting/slowly adjusting* expectations concerning economic events. As a result of these assumptions, supporters of the classical position argue that the main role of government economic policy is **Q4.** *to manage the level of aggregate demand so as to maintain full employment/remove impediments to the free play of market forces/ensure that no slack is allowed to develop in the economy*. This they argue is the only way to guarantee long-term growth.

Q5. Go through questions 1–4 and summarise the key assumptions of the *Keynesian* school.

....

....

Much of the disagreement between the different schools of thought centres on the responsiveness of aggregate supply to changes in aggregate demand.

Q6. Aggregate supply may be defined as ....

....

Q7. Consider the aggregate supply curves shown in Figure 16.1.

Which of the three curves would be most likely to represent the views of:

(a) Extreme free-market economists?

....

(b) Those who argue that an expansion of demand will have no effect upon inflation?

....

Multiple choice | Written answer | Delete wrong word | Diagram/table manipulation | Calculation | Matching/ordering

Figure 16.1 Aggregate supply curves

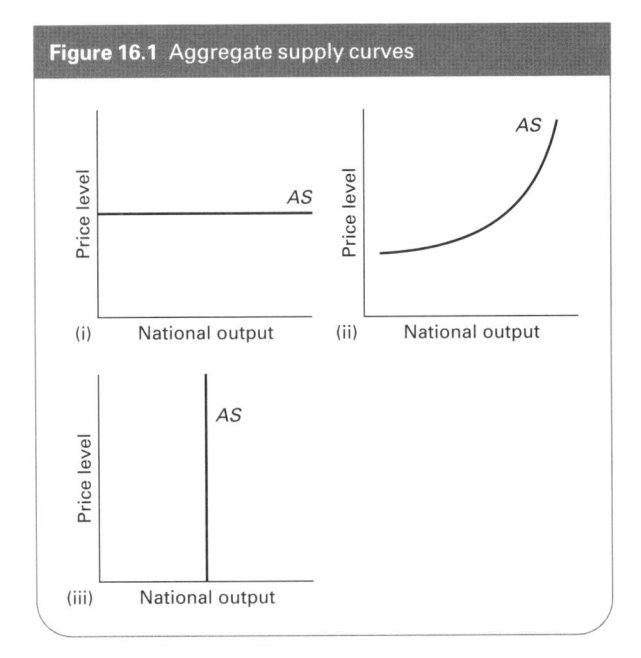

(i) horizontal AS curve; (ii) upward-sloping AS curve; (iii) vertical AS curve.

(c) Those who argue that the degree of slack in the economy will determine the impact of a change in aggregate demand on aggregate supply?

....

Q8. One of the arguments used by those advocating government intervention in the economy is that people's expectations are slow to adjust to changes in the economic environment. *True/False*

16.2 Classical macroeconomics

(Pages 444–5) The classical school of the nineteenth and early twentieth centuries advocated minimal state intervention in the running of economic affairs, and the development of a system of free trade. Providing the government balanced its budget, in other words that it made *T* equal to **Q9.** *I/G/X/S/M/C*, achievement of full-employment macroeconomic equilibrium could be left to the free market. The free market would ensure that *S* was equal to **Q10.** *I/T/G/X/M/C*, and that *M* was equal to **Q11.** *I/T/G/X/S/C*.

Q12. What, according to the classical economists, would be the effect of a rise in saving on the level of investment?

....

....

The operation of the gold standard was supposed to ensure that the balance of payments was kept in equilibrium (*X = M*). The gold standard was a system of **Q13.** *fixed/freely flexible/partly flexible* exchange rates.

Q14. Assume that there is a balance of payments deficit (*M > X*). Trace through the steps by which the gold standard could correct this deficit.
(a) The deficit leads to an *inflow/outflow* of gold.
(b) This leads to an *increase/decrease* in interest rates.
(c) This leads to an *increase/decrease* in the price level.
(d) This leads to an *increase/decrease* in imports and an *increase/decrease* in exports.

(Pages 445–6) The classical economists argued that because the markets for loanable funds and for imports and exports would clear, then Say's law would apply.

Q15. Say's law states that, at a macroeconomic level:
A. supply will always adjust to equal demand.
B. markets are always in a state of disequilibrium.
C. demand creates its own supply.
D. supply creates its own demand.
E. price and quantity are directly related.

Q16. Say's law implied that there could be no deficiency of demand in the economy. *True/False*

Q17. In terms of the circular flow of income diagram, Say's law would imply that *flexible prices* (as opposed to changes in national income) would ensure that withdrawals equalled injections. *True/False*

(Pages 447–50) The classical economists also supported the *quantity theory of money*.

Q18. This states that $MV = PY$. *True/False*

Q19. If real national income (i.e. measured in base-year prices) were £30bn, if prices had doubled since the base year, and if the velocity of circulation were 5, then the level of money supply would be:
A. £300bn
B. £75bn
C. £60bn
D. £12bn
E. £3bn

The classical economists had predicted that, provided markets were allowed to clear, there would never be a problem of **Q20.** *high inflation/mass unemployment*.

Q21. Which of the following policy decisions would have been characteristic of the classical economists' approach to the Great Depression?
(a) Encourage workers to take wage cuts. *Yes/No*
(b) Increase the rate of interest. *Yes/No*
(c) Expand the public sector's provision of goods and services. *Yes/No*
(d) Reduce unemployment benefits. *Yes/No*

(e) Increase the supply of money in circulation. Yes/No
(f) The government should aim to balance its budget. Yes/No
(g) Encourage people to save. Yes/No

16.3 The Keynesian revolution

(Pages 451–2) J.M. Keynes rejected many of the assumptions made by the classical school, key among which was the notion that markets would clear. According to Keynes, disequilibrium was the natural state of the market and such disequilibrium would persist unless the government intervened. For example, in the labour market, if there were a fall in aggregate demand, as occurred during the Great Depression, workers would resist wage cuts and the result would be demand-deficient unemployment.

Q22. Show, using Figure 16.2, the effect of a fall in the aggregate demand for labour and the subsequent level of disequilibrium unemployment that would result. (Assume that the labour market is initially in equilibrium.)

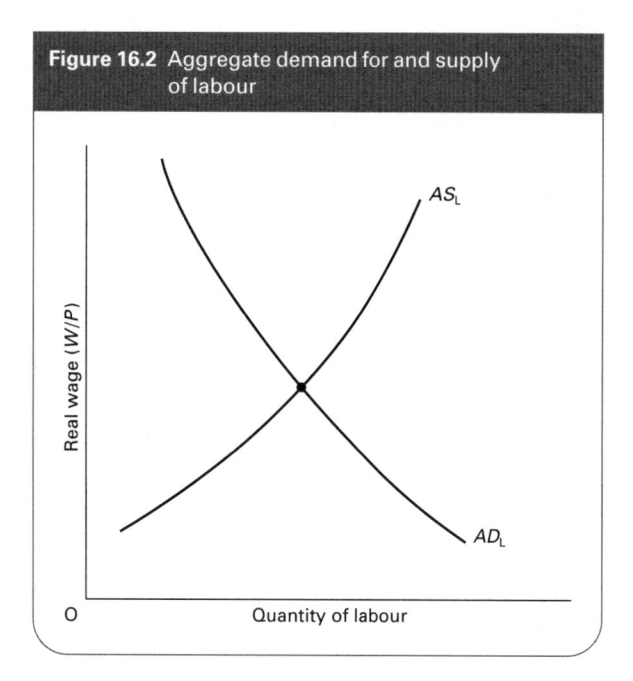

Figure 16.2 Aggregate demand for and supply of labour

[Graph: Real wage (W/P) on vertical axis, Quantity of labour on horizontal axis, showing AS_L upward sloping and AD_L downward sloping curves intersecting]

But even if workers *were* willing to accept cuts in real wages, there would still be a problem of unemployment.

Q23. Why, according to Keynes, might a successful cut in workers' wages, as advocated by the classical school, deepen the recession and not improve it?

....

....

Q24. Disequilibrium could also persist in the market for loanable funds. Assume, for example, that there was an increase in saving. Why might the resulting fall in interest rates fail to stimulate a rise in investment and restore equilibrium?

....

....

(Page 452) Keynes also rejected the simple quantity theory of money. Under certain circumstances, a rise in money supply may have little or no effect on prices.

Q25. If there was an expansion of the money supply, what, according to Keynes, would happen to each of the following?
(a) V rise/fall/stay the same
(b) Y – if there was substantial unemployment
 rise/fall/stay the same
(c) Y – if there was full employment
 rise/fall/stay the same

(Pages 452–4) Keynesian theory stresses that equilibrium in the economy is brought about, not so much by changes in prices, but by changes in the level of national income.

Q26. Describe the process whereby a new equilibrium national income will be achieved, following a rise in aggregate demand.

....

....

....

....

(Pages 454–6) Keynesian theory emphasised an active role for government in maintaining the full-employment level of national income. There are two major methods a government can use to control the level of aggregate demand. These are *fiscal policy* and *monetary policy*.

Q27. Fiscal policy involves

....

Q28. Monetary policy involves

....

Following the Second World War, Keynesian views became the accepted orthodoxy. If the economy was experiencing rising inflation then **Q29.** *expansionary/deflationary* fiscal and monetary policy was to be used. Alternatively, an economy suffering low rates of growth and unemployment would require **Q30.** *expansionary/deflationary* policy measures.

Because of the cyclical nature of the economy, the policies alternated between deflationary and reflationary (i.e. expansionary) measures.

Q31. As a result the policies became known as

....

Q32. List four criticisms of Keynesian demand management policy that were to grow over the 1960s.

1. ....

2. ....

3. ....

4. ....

16.4 The Monetarist–Keynesian debate

(Pages 456–8) The problems encountered with the Keynesian model of the economy led certain economists to return to the old classical theory of income determination. The monetarists, led by Milton Friedman, returned to the quantity theory of money. They reasserted that both V (the velocity of circulation) and Y (the level of real national income) were **Q33.** *endogenous/exogenous* variables, meaning that V and Y are determined **Q34.** *by the supply of money/independently of the supply of money*. The implication was that any change in the money supply would have a direct effect upon the level of **Q35.** *prices/national income*.

An important element of the monetarist analysis was that there was no trade-off in the long run between unemployment and inflation: that the long-run Phillips curve is **Q36.** *horizontal/vertical/upward sloping/a downward-sloping line at 45° to the axes*.

Q37. What arguments do monetarists use to justify a long-run Phillips curve of this shape?

....

....

....

Q38. What effect would the following have on the natural rate of unemployment?
(a) A reduction in the level of information concerning available work. *Rise/Fall*
(b) The decline in traditional heavy industry. *Rise/Fall*
(c) An increase in the power trade unions have within the wage-negotiating process. *Rise/Fall*
(d) An expansion of job retraining schemes. *Rise/Fall*
(e) A more rapid and widespread introduction of new technology into the workplace. *Rise/Fall*
(f) An increase in unemployment benefits. *Rise/Fall*

(Pages 458–60) Not surprisingly, modern-day Keynesians reject much of the monetarist analysis.

Q39. The modern *Keynesian* analysis of a rightward shift in the Phillips curve since 1970 focuses on a *variety* of factors, some that are argued to have influenced the rate of inflation and some the level of unemployment. List three causes of inflation and three of unemployment given by Keynesians to explain higher levels of both occurring simultaneously.
(a) Inflation

1. ....

2. ....

3. ....

(b) Unemployment

1. ....

2. ....

3. ....

One reason given by Keynesians for unemployment being higher in the 1980s and early 1990s than in the 1970s was the problem of *hysteresis*.

Q40. In the context of unemployment, hysteresis can be defined as the persistence of unemployment that occurred in a recession even when the economy has recovered from the recession. *True/False*

Q41. Keynesians offer various explanations for hysteresis. These include:
(a) A decline in capital stock during the recession. *True/False*
(b) A balance of payments problem in the recession that persists in the recovery. *True/False*
(c) Having experienced a recession, firms are cautious about taking on more labour. *True/False*
(d) Insiders in firms bidding up the wage rate and making it less profitable to take on extra labour. *True/False*
(e) The unemployed have become deskilled and hence less employable. *True/False*

16.5 The current position: an emerging consensus?

(Pages 461–3) Today there is a whole range of viewpoints concerning the functioning of the macroeconomy and the most appropriate macroeconomic policies to pursue.

Q42. The following are four schools of thought:
(i) New classical
(ii) Moderate monetarist
(iii) Moderate Keynesian/new Keynesian
(iv) Extreme Keynesians

Members of which school of thought hold each of the following views?
(a) A rise in aggregate demand (caused by an increase in money supply) can lead only to a temporary reduction in unemployment. As price expectations adjust upwards, so within a few months the extra demand will be translated into higher prices and unemployment will return to the natural level. *(i)/(ii)/(iii)/(iv)*
(b) Equilibrium in the economy can persist at a very high level of unemployment and there is no automatic mechanism for bringing the economy out of recession. Indeed, recessions are likely to persist as expectations remain pessimistic. It is important, therefore, for the government to take an active role in maintaining sufficient aggregate demand. This will help to stimulate investment and lead to faster long-term growth. *(i)/(ii)/(iii)/(iv)*
(c) Markets clear virtually instantaneously. Any increase in aggregate demand by the government will be entirely reflected in higher prices. *(i)/(ii)/(iii)/(iv)*
(d) Wage rates are sticky downwards. Unemployment can take a long time, therefore, to be eliminated by a fall in real wages. The government should take responsibility for maintaining an adequate (but not excessive) level of aggregate demand. *(i)/(ii)/(iii)/(iv)*

Q43. New classical 'real business cycle theory' explains cyclical fluctuations in the economy in terms of *shifts in aggregate demand/shifts in aggregate supply/changes in the output of goods rather than services*.

Despite disagreements between economists, some general points of agreement have emerged in recent years.

Q44. Which of the following propositions are part of this 'mainstream consensus'?
(a) Excessive growth in the money supply will lead to inflation. Yes/No
(b) Governments' ability to control their country's economy is being increasingly eroded by the process of globalisation. Yes/No
(c) In the short run, changes in aggregate demand will have only a minor effect on output and employment. Yes/No
(d) There is a clear long-run trade-off between inflation and unemployment. Yes/No
(e) Long-term growth depends primarily on changes in aggregate supply. Yes/No
(f) Expectations have an important effect on the economy. Yes/No

B PROBLEMS, EXERCISES AND PROJECTS

Q45. In the version of the quantity theory of money $MV = PY$:
(a) What are meant by the following terms?
   (i) M

   (ii) V

   (iii) P

   (iv) Y

(b) If the money supply were £20bn and money on average were spent 5 times per year on buying goods and services that make up national income, what would be the level of national income (in nominal terms)?

(c) Continuing with the same assumptions as in (b), what would be the price index if real national income, measured in base-year prices, were £50bn?

(d) If money supply increases by 50 per cent and neither the price level nor the velocity of circulation changes, how much will real national income increase?
more than 50 per cent/50 per cent/ less than 50 per cent
(e) If money supply increases by 50 per cent and neither real income nor the velocity of circulation changes, how much will the price level rise?
more than 50 per cent/50 per cent/ less than 50 per cent
(f) What did the classical economists assume about:
   (i) V?

   (ii) Y?

(g) What do Keynesian economists assume about:
   (i) V?

   ....

   (ii) Y?

   ....

Q46. The kingdom of Never Had It So Good is having it bad! Inflation has risen steadily following a series of expansionary budgets and the current account of the balance of payments has slipped into deficit. High interest rates, used to tackle the high inflation by curbing domestic demand, have led to a steady fall in household consumption. Firms have responded by cutting back on production and reducing their demand for labour, as well as postponing future investment.

Write two reports advising the chancellor of Never Had It So Good on a course of action to solve the country's economic problems. One report should emphasise the policies and beliefs of the classical school of economics, whereas the second should focus on Keynesian strategies.

C DISCUSSION TOPICS AND ESSAYS

Q47. Explain the contrasting views of Keynesians and new classical economists concerning the nature of the aggregate supply curve. What implications do their respective analyses have for the effect of a rise in aggregate demand on prices and output?

Q48. What are the implications of the quantity theory of money for (a) the control of inflation, and (b) the use of monetary policy to stimulate an economy in recession?

Q49. What assumptions must be made about the terms in the equation of exchange if the strict quantity theory of money is to hold? How would changes in the money supply affect the economy if you changed these assumptions?

Q50. Describe the working of the economy using classical economic theory. Clearly state your assumptions. Why did classical economists maintain that the economy would tend towards a situation of full employment?

Q51. Explain the reasoning behind Keynes' rejection of Say's law.

Q52. Keynesian demand management policies, although initially appearing to be successful, began to run into problems in the mid-1960s. What were these problems?

Q53. 'The monetarist counter-revolution is simply the restating of classical theory.' Discuss.

Q54. Describe how monetarist and Keynesian views differ regarding the Phillips curve.

Q55. What are the distinguishing features of the following schools of thought: new classical economists, moderate monetarists, moderate Keynesians, extreme Keynesians?

Q56. What is meant by 'hysteresis' (in the context of unemployment)? How do Keynesians explain this phenomenon?

Q57. To what extent is there common ground between economists over the following: (a) the effect of changes in aggregate demand on real national income; (b) the relationship between inflation and unemployment; (c) appropriate policies for increasing the rate of economic growth over the longer term?

Q58. Debate

Leaving the economy to private enterprise and the market system is more likely to lead to recessions and instability than to sustained economic growth.

D ARTICLES

The following extracts are taken from the work of John Maynard Keynes.

We have, as a rule, only the vaguest idea of any but the most direct consequences of our acts ... our knowledge of the future is fluctuating, vague and uncertain ... the sense in which I am using the term (uncertain) is that in which the prospect of a European war is uncertain, or the price of copper and the rate of interest twenty years hence, or the obsolescence of a new invention, or the position of private wealth-owners in the social system in 1970. About these matters there is no scientific basis on which to form any calculable probability whatever. We simply do not know.[1]

Many of the greatest economic evils of our time are the fruits of uncertainty, and ignorance. It is because particular individuals, fortunate in situation or in abilities, are able to take advantage of uncertainty and ignorance, and also because for the same reason big business is often a lottery, that great inequalities of wealth come about; and these same factors are also the cause of the unemployment of labour, or the disappointment of reasonable expectations, and of the impairment of efficiency and production. Yet the cure lies outside the operation of individuals; it may even be to the interest of individuals to aggravate the disease. I believe that the cure for these things is partly to be sought in the deliberate control of the currency and of credit by a central institution, and partly in the collection and dissemination on a great scale of data relating to the business situation, including the full publicity, by law if necessary, of all business facts which it is useful to know. These measures would involve society in exercising directive intelligence through some appropriate organ of action over many of the inner intricacies of private business, yet it would leave private initiative and enterprise unhindered. Even if these measures prove insufficient, nevertheless, they will furnish us with better knowledge than we have now for taking the next step.[2]

1. Keynes (1937) in W. Hutton, *The Revolution That Never Was* (1986), p. 95.

2. Keynes in A.P. Thirlwall, Keynes and *Laissez-Faire* (1978), pp. 39–40.

Using the extracts, answer the following questions:
(a) According to Keynes, what problems did ignorance and uncertainty create?
(b) What were Keynes' remedies for ignorance and uncertainty?
(c) How would Keynes' views have differed from the classical economic orthodoxy of the day?

The conflict between monetarists and Keynesians has lasted many years. At different points in history, one view or the other has tended to dominate economic opinion. Keynesianism occupied this position throughout the 1950s and 1960s, and more recently monetarism has been the dominant theory. Between these eras of dominance we can identify a transition period in which ideas and theories are redefined. The article below, taken from *The Guardian* of 7 April 1994, assesses the relevance of Keynesian economics after 14 years of economic policy being based largely upon monetarist assumptions.

Free lunch as Keynes makes a comeback

Tony Thirlwall

Not so long ago, many economists of Keynesian persuasion, myself included, felt as if they belonged to an endangered species, with the prospect of extinction in the face of the onslaught from the doctrine of monetarism.

This argued that economies are inherently self-regulating, that governments have no role to play in the stabilisation of output and employment at the macro level, and all that matters for the control of inflation is the control of the money supply.

From the mid-1970s, this doctrine spread from the shores of America, infecting academia and policy-making in several parts of the globe. It looks now, however, that the tide is beginning to turn.

Monetarism, in its various guises, seems to be dying a slow death. Books and articles are being written on the rise and fall and rise again of Keynesian economics, and the empirical evidence of deep recession in the UK and slump in Europe is focusing again on what Keynes had to say about unemployment and how to tackle it.

The Keynesian tide should never have ebbed away in the first place, and wouldn't have done so had the 1970s not been so inflation prone and Keynesian economics been properly understood, particularly on the other side of the Atlantic.

If American monetarists had absorbed their Keynesian economics from Keynes himself and not from text book versions, how could it ever have been seriously argued (as Milton Friedman used to) that 'money doesn't matter' in Keynes, or that Keynes's central message that capitalist economies may get stuck in depression for long periods of time depends on the assumption that wages and prices are rigid, and that Keynesian economics cannot explain stagflation? None of these claims bears textual scrutiny.

The basic proposition that mainstream monetarism has always denied is that there can be such a thing as involuntary unemployment, defined as unemployed people willing to work at the going money wage (and a lower real wage if necessary) given the opportunity.

Attempts by governments to reduce unemployment by higher levels of public spending will simply raise prices and lead to money wages chasing prices in an ever-accelerating spiral of inflation with no effect on employment.

Monetarist models assume to start with what must be proved – that the labour market always clears on the basis of voluntary exchange.

But if we look back to Mrs Thatcher's 'miracle economy' in the 1980s, when unemployment peaked at nearly 3.5 million in 1986 and then fell to 1.5 million in 1990 with expansionary monetary and fiscal policy, were the two million unemployed absorbed into the system voluntarily unemployed? Clearly not.

Unemployment responded in exactly the way one would have predicted from a Keynesian model. The notion of continuous market clearing and no involuntary unemployment has been totally discredited by the bitter experience of the 1980s, and continues to be discredited today as unemployment in the UK hovers around the three million mark and unemployment in the European Community approaches 20 million.

If we want to understand what is going on in the British economy today, and the great difficulties of reconciling low unemployment with low inflation, we cannot continue to embrace the pre-Keynesian assumptions of monetarism: that all unemployment is voluntary due to a refusal of workers to accept cuts in their wages; that there are automatic mechanisms that guarantee enough private expenditure in the economy to generate sufficient demand for goods and services to ensure full employment; that all cycles in economic activity are the result of supply shocks; and that inflation is always and everywhere a monetary phenomenon in a casual sense as if trade unions and monopolies don't exist, and money is totally exogenous to an economic system.

For the past 14 years, economic policy-making in Britain has been dominated largely by this monetarist thinking. If the primitive application of monetarism had worked in the early 1980s, it should have reduced the growth of the money supply and the rate of inflation without, in the long run, affecting the level of unemployment and the real economy.

Instead, there was an almighty slump that destroyed large sections of manufacturing industry and made thousands of workers virtually unemployable, just as a Keynesian model would have predicted. Good old-fashioned demand mismanagement then produced an unsustainable boom in the late 1980s, and we are now in the longest, if not the deepest, recession since the 1930s. All in the name of the rejection of Keynesianism.

The fundamental Keynesian message remains that, in conditions of heavy, involuntary unemployment, there is such a thing as a free lunch; stone can be turned into bread; expenditure will generate multiplier effects; and there will be the crowding in of resources, not crowding out.

If only the Government could grasp this message, it would be a blow for monetarism but a victory for common sense.

Tony Thirlwall is Professor of Applied Economics at the University of Kent.

(a) What economic assumptions does the article suggest underpin monetarist and Keynesian views?

(b) What is the difference between voluntary and involuntary unemployment? Why is this distinction seen by the author as crucial in refuting the monetarist case?

(c) What evidence does the author cite to support his Keynesian position?

E ANSWERS

Q1. flexible.

Q2. unresponsive.

Q3. quickly adjusting.

Q4. to remove impediments to the free play of market forces.

Q5. The Keynesian school argues that prices and wages are relatively inflexible; that aggregate supply is relatively responsive to changes in aggregate demand; and that expectations are relatively slow to adjust. Keynesians advocate government intervention to manage aggregate demand so as to avoid recessions.

Q6. Aggregate supply may be defined as the quantity of goods and services that the nation's producers would be willing to supply at any given price.

Q7. *(a)* (iii). They argue that changes in aggregate demand will have no effect on output and therefore the aggregate supply 'curve' is vertical.

(b) (i). They argue that aggregate supply is totally elastic and that therefore output depends entirely on aggregate demand.

(c) (ii). The lower the level of output and the higher the level of unemployment, and hence the greater the degree of 'slack' in the economy, the more will output be able to increase in response to an increase in aggregate demand, and hence the shallower the curve will be. As full employment is approached, however, the curve will get steeper, as firms find it increasingly difficult to increase output and instead respond to an increase in aggregate demand by putting up their prices.

Q8. Ture. Because expectations take time to adjust, interventionist policies can have a significant impact on the economy. For example, a rise in aggregate demand can lead to firms producing more if they do not expect that the rise in aggregate demand is also likely to raise inflation and hence raise their costs of production.

Q9. G.

Q10. I.

Q11. X.

Q12. The rise in saving would cause a surplus of loanable funds. This would drive the rate of interest down. This in turn would cause an increase in the level of investment and a reduction in the level of saving

Q13. *Fixed.* The value of each country's currency was fixed in terms of a certain amount of gold. Each country's exchange rate was therefore fixed.

Q14. (a) *outflow*; (b) *increase*; (c) *decrease*; (d) *decrease* in imports, *increase* in exports.

Q15. D. The production of goods and services will generate incomes, which in turn will generate spending, thereby creating a demand for the goods and services which have been produced. Any proportion of income that is saved will generate extra investment, and any proportion going on imports, via the gold standard, will generate extra exports. Thus, when production generates extra income, *all* of it will come back as extra spending.

Q16. *True.* Any change in aggregate supply would automatically bring about a corresponding change in aggregate demand, via the effects on aggregate demand of a change in prices and interest rates.

Q17. *True.*

Q18. *False.* The quantity theory of money states that the level of prices (P) depends on the quantity of money: if money supply increases faster than output, then prices will rise. The equation $MV = PY$ is called the 'quantity equation', not the 'quantity theory of money'.

Q19. D. The level of national income (at current prices) is equal to the real level of national income at base-year prices ($Y = £30$bn) multiplied by the price level as a proportion of the base year price ($P = 2$): $PY = £60$bn. Thus MV is also equal to £60bn. Given that the velocity of circulation (V) = 5, money supply must be £60bn/5 = £12bn.

Q20. *mass unemployment.*

Q21. Yes (a), (b), (d), (f) and (g). These were all advocated by classical economists during the 1920s and early 1930s.

Q22. The AD_L curve shifts to the left, but, with no resulting fall in the real wage rate, the level of aggregate labour supply now exceeds the level of aggregate labour demand, the gap between them giving the level of disequilibrium unemployment.

Q23. As workers took a wage cut, their ability to consume goods and services would fall. This would deepen the recession as firms would consequently have less demand for their output.

Q24. As saving increased, consumers would consequently have less money to spend on consumption of domestic goods and services. Businesses would respond to this fall in demand by cutting back on their level of investment.

Q25. *(a)* *fall.* The average speed at which money circulates may slow down. (The reasons for this are examined in Chapter 19.)

(b) *rise.* The increased spending will stimulate extra production and extra employment.

(c) *stay the same.* Output and employment cannot be stimulated by a rise in spending as there is no slack in the economy.

Q26. The rise in injections will mean that injections exceed withdrawals. This will cause a rise in national income. This will cause withdrawals (and consumption) to rise until withdrawals equal injections. At that point income will stop rising: income will be in equilibrium.

Q27. Changing government expenditure (an injection) and/or taxes (a withdrawal).

Q28. Changing money supply or interest rates, and thereby affecting the level of spending.

Q29. *deflationary.*

Q30. *expansionary.*

Q31. *Stop/go policies,* or less provocatively, *demand management policies.*

Q32. Criticisms included: policies failed to stabilise the economy; policies were short term rather than long term; the Phillips curve relationship appeared to be breaking down; balance of payments problems meant that deflationary policies had to be pursued even when unemployment was high; it was difficult to predict the magnitude of the effects of the policy (difficult to predict size of the multiplier); there were time lags involved with the policy (see Chapter 20, section 20.2).

Q33. *exogenous.*

Q34. *independently of the supply of money.*

Q35. *prices.*

Q36. *vertical.*

Q37. If the government expands aggregate demand in order to reduce unemployment, eventually people's expectations of inflation will increase until all the extra demand is absorbed in higher prices with no increase in output or employment. Thus in the long run the Phillips curve is vertical.

Q38. All will cause the natural rate of unemployment to rise except (d), which will cause it to fall.

Q39. *(a)* Examples include: rising costs, changes in the pattern of demand in the economy and expectations.

(b) Examples include: deficient demand, poor business expectations, structural changes in the economy, hysteresis.

Q40. *True.*

Q41. *True.* All except (b). In the case of (a), a decline in investment, and hence the capital stock, during the recession means that when the recovery comes firms reach full employment of existing capital before there is full employment of labour.

Q42. (a) (ii), (b) (iv), (c) (i), (d) (iii).

Q43. *shifts in aggregate supply.*

Q44. *Yes* (a), (b), (f) and (g).
No (c) and (d).

Chapter Seventeen

17

Short-run Macroeconomic Equilibrium

A REVIEW

17.1 Background to the theory

(Pages 466–7) In order to understand the Keynesian model, it is necessary that you are fully familiar with the circular flow of income diagram that we looked at in Chapter 13.

Q1. By way of revision, sketch the circular flow diagram and label the inner flow and all the injections and withdrawals.

The relationship between national income and the various components of the circular flow are shown in the *Keynesian 45° line diagram*.

Q2. In the model, it is assumed that consumption and withdrawals are determined by the level of national income, whereas injections are not. Which would we classify as endogenous and which as exogenous variables?
(a) Withdrawals are *endogenous/exogenous*
(b) Injections are *endogenous/exogenous*
(c) Consumption is *endogenous/exogenous*

Q3. In the 45° line diagram, which of the following is given by the 45° line?
A. National expenditure.
B. Consumption of domestic goods and services.
C. Consumption of domestic goods and services plus withdrawals.
D. Consumption of domestic goods and services plus injections.
E. Withdrawals plus injections.

(Pages 467–9) The consumption function
The consumption function shows the relationship between consumption and national income.

Q4. This question is based on Table 17.1.
(a) Plot the consumption function shown in Table 17.1 on Figure 17.1 and add the 45° line.
(b) Explain why the consumption function lies above the 45° line at low levels of national income and below it at high levels.

....

....

(c) What is meant by the term *marginal propensity to consume*? Give its formula.

....

....

(d) Calculate the marginal propensity to consume between the following levels of national income:

(i) £50bn and £75bn ....

(ii) £125bn and £150bn ....

(e) The marginal propensity to consume is given by *the slope of the consumption function/the height of the consumption function above the horizontal axis*.
(f) If the marginal propensity to consume diminished as national income rose, what shape would the consumption function be?

....

....

Multiple choice | Written answer | Delete wrong word | Diagram/table manipulation | Calculation | Matching/ordering

Table 17.1

National income (£bn)	Consumption (£bn)	
50	70	...
75	90	...
100	110	...
125	130	...
150	150	...
175	170	...
200	190	...
225	210	...
250	230	...

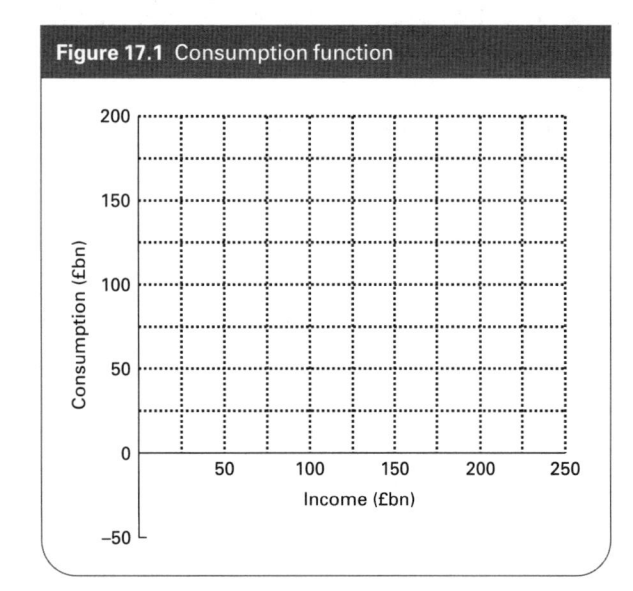

Figure 17.1 Consumption function

In the long run the marginal propensity to consume will be **Q5.** *higher/lower* than in the short run. This is the result of individuals responding relatively **Q6.** *quickly/slowly* to changes in their level of income.

(?) **Q7.** What is the difference between the marginal propensity to consume (*mpc*) and the marginal propensity to consume domestically produced goods and services (mpc_d)?

....

(Pages 469–74) Withdrawals and injections
(?) **Q8.** The major determinant of saving in the Keynesian model is

....

⊖ **Q9.** Label the last column in Table 17.1 'Saving (£bn)'.
(a) Assuming that saving is the only withdrawal, fill in the figures for saving in Table 17.1.

(b) Plot the saving function on Figure 17.1.
(c) Over which range of national income is there dissaving?

....

(d) What is the marginal propensity to save between a national income of £175bn and £200bn?

....

◐ **Q10.** What effect will the following have on saving? In each case state whether there will be a rise or fall in saving and whether there will be a shift in or a movement along the saving function.
(a) An increase in personal taxation.
    rise/fall; shift/movement along
(b) Christmas. *rise/fall; shift/movement along*
(c) An increase in the rate of interest.
    rise/fall; shift/movement along
(d) Expectations of a fall in prices.
    rise/fall; shift/movement along
(e) Moving into the recessionary phase of the business cycle. *rise/fall; shift/movement along*

◐ **Q11.** The marginal propensity to pay taxes (*mpt*) is the same as the marginal tax rate. *True/False*

(?) **Q12.** The marginal propensity to import is the proportion of a rise in national income that goes on imports. If a country were predominantly an importer of luxury goods, what effect would this have on (a) the shape of the import function and (b) the marginal propensity to import?

(a) ....

(b) ....

◐ **Q13.** Injections are assumed in the Keynesian model to be exogenously determined. This means:
(a) That injections are constant with respect to changes in national income. *True/False*
(b) That injections are constant with respect to time. *True/False*
(c) That injections in the 45° line diagram are given by a horizontal straight line. *True/False*

17.2 The determination of national income

(Pages 475–8) The injections and withdrawals approach
⊖ **Q14.** Figure 17.2 shows a withdrawals and an injections function.
(a) Equilibrium national income is

....

Figure 17.2 National income determination: withdrawals and injections approach

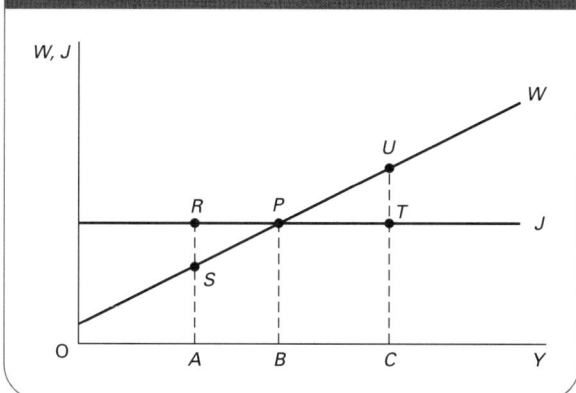

(b) Assume that the current level of national income is OA. Describe the process whereby equilibrium will be achieved.

....

(c) Illustrate on Figure 17.2 the effect of an increase in government spending by an amount UT on the level of national income.

(?) **Q15.** The multiplier can be defined as

....

Q16. In symbols the (injections) multiplier can be defined as:
A. $\Delta Y/\Delta J$
B. $\Delta J/\Delta Y$
C. $\Delta J/\Delta W$
D. $\Delta W/\Delta J$
E. $\Delta W \times \Delta J$

Q17. Referring back to Figure 17.2, the multiplier is given by:
A. UT/PT
B. PT/UT
C. PU/PT
D. PU/UT
E. PT/PU

Q18. The multiplier is the inverse of the *mpw*.
True/False

Q19. What are the answers to the following?
(a) $mpw + mpc_d =$

....

(b) $(1 - mpc_d) - (mps + mpm + mpt) =$

....

(where *mps*, *mpm* and *mpt* are from gross income).

Q20. What is the value of the multiplier in the following cases?
(a) $mpw = 1/3$

....

(b) $mpc_d = 0.75$

....

The full multiplier effect does not occur instantaneously. It takes time for the additional incomes to build up as they go round and round the circular flow of income. The following question demonstrates this process.

Q21. Assume that the $mpw = 1/2$ and that there is an initial injection of £200m into the economy. Fill in the missing values in Table 17.2 and calculate by how much income has increased after five periods.

Table 17.2 The multiplier

Period	ΔJ(£m)	ΔY(£m)	ΔC_d(£m)	ΔW(£m)
1	200	200	...	...
2	–	...	...	...
3	–	...	...	...
4	–	...	...	...
5	–	...	...	...
Totals				

Q22. Which of the following would cause the value of the multiplier to fall?
A. A cut in the level of government spending.
B. An increase in the marginal propensity to consume.
C. A fall in the level of investment.
D. The population becomes more thrifty, and saves a larger proportion of any rise in income.
E. A balance of payments surplus.

(Page 478) The income and expenditure approach
The multiplier can also be demonstrated using the income/expenditure approach.

(?) **Q23.** Consumption of domestically produced goods and services plus injections ($C_d + J$) is otherwise known as:

....

Q24. Figure 17.3 shows a Keynesian national income and expenditure diagram.
(a) Assuming that the expenditure function is given by E_1 by how much do injections exceed withdrawals at an income of OC?

....

232 CHAPTER 17 SHORT-RUN MACROECONOMIC EQUILIBRIUM

Figure 17.3 National income determination: income and expenditure approach

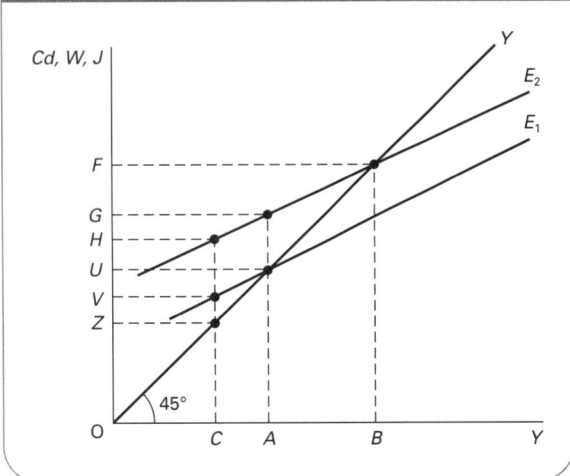

Identify the correct letters for each of the following:
(a) Equilibrium national income. OA/OB/OD/OF
(b) Injections at income OA. AQ/AH/QH/(AQ−QH)
(c) Withdrawals at income OF. FT/TN/TM/NM/VT
(d) mpc_d. RU ÷ SU/SU ÷ RU/TM ÷ LT/RT ÷ VT
(e) The amount that withdrawals rise when national income rises from OD to OF. TN/NM/TM/LN/LM
(f) mpw. TN ÷ DF/NM ÷ DF/DF ÷ TN/DF ÷ NM
(g) The multiplier. TN ÷ DF/NM ÷ DF/DF ÷ TN/DF ÷ NM

(Pages 478–9) *The formula for the multiplier is $1/(1 - mpc_d)$. Remember that mpc_d refers to consumption of *domestic* goods, from *gross* income and after the deduction of indirect taxes. When people decide how much of a rise in income to spend (their *mpc*), however, their decision is based on *disposable* income: they do not distinguish between domestic and imported goods and their spending includes the indirect taxes on the goods they purchase. How, then, do we derive the mpc_d from the *mpc* (from disposable income)? We use the formula:

$$mpc_d = mpc\,(1 - t_E)(1 - t_Y) - mpm$$

where t_Y is the marginal rate of income tax, and t_E is the marginal rate of expenditure tax.

(b) If the expenditure line now shifts upwards from E_1 to E_2 as the result of an increase in planned consumer spending, what will be the new equilibrium level of national income?

....

(c) What is the size of the multiplier given a rise in expenditure from E_1 to E_2?

....

Q25. A rise in the marginal propensity to save is shown by a swing downwards of the expenditure function (i.e. the curve becomes less steep). *True/False*

Q26. Examine Figure 17.4.

Figure 17.4 Income and expenditure

*Q27.** If the *mpc* is 0.75, the *mpm* is 0.1, the rate of expenditure tax is 10 per cent and the rate of income tax is 25 per cent:
(a) What is the mpc_d?

....

(b) What is the size of the multiplier?

....

17.3 The simple Keynesian analysis of unemployment and inflation

(Pages 481–4)

Q28. When the economy is at the 'full-employment' level of national income, this means that:
A. everybody is employed.
B. there is no deficiency of demand.
C. the amount of money in the economy is at its maximum level.
D. the economy is in the expansionary phase of the business cycle.
E. the multiplier effect will generate a large number of jobs.

If the equilibrium level of national income (Y_e) is below the full-employment level (Y_f), there will be a **Q29.** *deflationary gap/inflationary gap*. Alternatively, if the level of national expenditure exceeds the full-employment level of national income, there will be a **Q30.** *deflationary gap/inflationary gap*.

Q31. Which of the following define a *deflationary* gap?
 (i) The amount by which equilibrium national income exceeds the full-employment level.
 (ii) The amount by which the full-employment level of national income exceeds the equilibrium level.
 (iii) The amount by which injections exceed withdrawals at the full-employment level of national income.
 (iv) The amount by which withdrawals exceed injections at the full-employment level of national income.
 (v) The amount by which national income exceeds national expenditure at the full-employment level of national income.
 (vi) The amount by which national expenditure exceeds national income at the full-employment level of national income.

A. (ii)
B. (ii) + (v)
C. (iv)
D. (iv) + (v)
E. (iii) + (vi)

Q32. Referring to the same list as in Q31, which define an *inflationary* gap?
A. (i)
B. (i) + (vi)
C. (iii)
D. (iv) + (v)
E. (iii) + (vi)

Q33. Using Figure 17.5:
(a) Mark a full-employment level of national income above Y_e. Identify the deflationary gap. Use two methods to do this.
(b) Now assume that injections rise such as to increase equilibrium national income beyond Y_f. Illustrate this and identify the resulting inflationary gap. Again use two methods to do this.

Figure 17.5 Deflationary and inflationary gaps

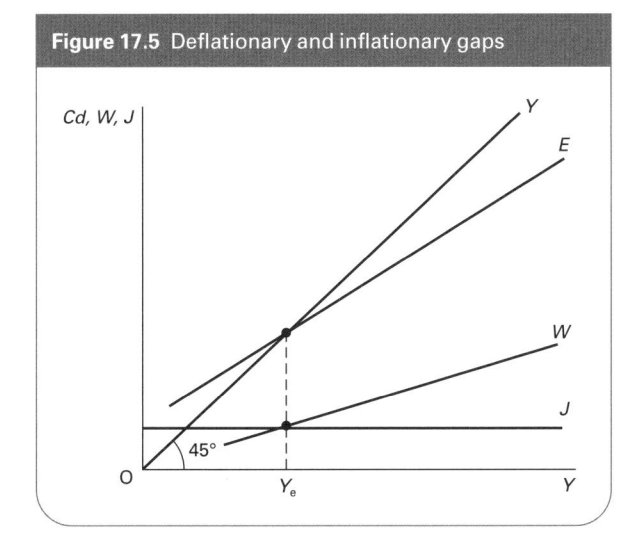

Table 17.3

National Income (£bn)	50	100	150	200	250	300	350	400
Withdrawals (£bn)		0	10	20	30	40	50	60	70

Q34. Table 17.3 gives country A's withdrawals schedule.
Assume that the full-employment level of national income is £250bn, and that there is an inflationary gap of £10bn.
(a) What is the size of the multiplier?

....

(b) What is the current equilibrium level of national income?

....

(c) If technological progress and increased labour productivity led to a rise of £150bn in the full-employment level of national income, and if there were no change in the equilibrium level of national income, what sort of gap would there be now and what would be its size?

....

Q35. An economy currently has a deflationary gap of £20bn and an equilibrium level of national income £60bn below the full-employment level of national income. This means that it must have an mpc_d of:
A. 3
B. 3/2
C. 2/3
D. 1/3
E. 1/6

In practice, inflation is likely to occur before the full-employment level of national income is reached. This means that the aggregate supply curve, rather than being horizontal up to the full-employment level of national income and then vertical at that point, is in fact upward sloping. How do we analyse this using a 45° line diagram?

Q36. Figure 17.6 shows an aggregate demand and supply diagram and a 45° line diagram. Assume that national income is initially in equilibrium at Y_{e_1} where $Y = E_1$ and $AS = AD_1$. Now assume that there is an increase in injections such that expenditure increases to E_2.
(a) Illustrate the effect on national income in diagram (b), assuming *no* rise in prices.
(b) Draw in the new *AD* curve on diagram (a) and again assuming no rise in the price level (i.e. a horizontal *AS* curve) mark the equilibrium level of national income.
(c) Now allowing for the fact that the *AS* curve is upward sloping, show the actual effect on income of the shift in the *AD* curve that you drew in question (b).

234 CHAPTER 17 SHORT-RUN MACROECONOMIC EQUILIBRIUM

Figure 17.6 National income determination: upward-sloping AS curve

(a)

(b)

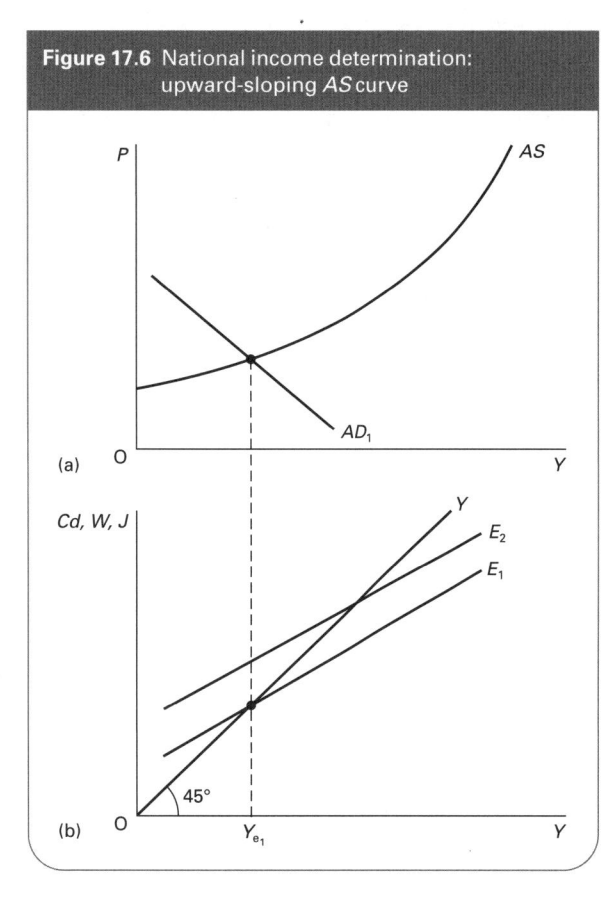

(d) Given that diagram (b) shows *real* national income and expenditure, mark the eventual (reduced) rise in the expenditure curve after allowing for the price rise.

17.4 The Keynesian analysis of the business cycle

(Pages 484–6) Keynesians seek to manage the level of aggregate demand and thereby stabilise the fluctuations in the business cycle. They argue that one of the major causes of cyclical fluctuations is the instability of investment.

Q37. The *accelerator* theory of investment states that the level of investment depends upon:
A. the rate of interest.
B. the level of saving.
C. the level of national income.
D. the size of changes in national income.
E. the degree of slack in the economy.

Q38. The marginal capital/output ratio refers to:
A. the change in investment.
B. the change in investment over a year.
C. the amount output must change in order to lead to more investment.
D. the amount of additional capital required to produce an additional unit of output.
E. the level of investment needed to achieve full employment.

The relationship between induced investment (I_i) and changes in national income (ΔY) can be expressed in the formula:

$$I_i = \alpha \Delta Y$$

where α is known as the 'accelerator coefficient'.

Q39. The accelerator coefficient is the marginal capital/output ratio. *True/False*

Q40. The accelerator gets its title because of the amount by which investment changes following a change in national income. *True/False*

Q41. Table 17.4 illustrates the accelerator effect by looking at the case of an individual firm. Assume that each of its machines produces 100 units of output and that one machine each year will need replacing.

Table 17.4 The accelerator effect

	0	1	2	3	4	5	6
Quantity demanded by consumers	500	500	1000	2000	2500	2500	2300
Number of machines required	...	...	...	...	...	...	...
Induced investment (I_i)	...	...	...	...	...	...	...
Replacement investment (I_r)	...	...	...	...	...	...	...
Total investment ($I_i + I_r$)							

Assume that the firm decides to increase the number of machines as necessary in order to supply consumer demand.
(a) Fill in the missing values.
(b) Between years 3 and 4 demand has continued to grow but total investment has fallen. Why is this?

....

....

Q42. List four difficulties we might encounter when trying to calculate the size of the real-world accelerator effect.

1. ....
2. ....
3. ....
4. ....

(Pages 486–9) The multiplier/accelerator interaction is important when analysing changes in national income. A single injection will cause a cycle of economic activity.

Q43. Describe the interaction between the multiplier and accelerator following an increase in government spending.

....

....

....

Q44. The magnitude of cyclical fluctuations resulting from any initial shock to the economy will be greater:
A. the greater the value of both the multiplier and the accelerator.
B. the smaller the value of both the multiplier and the accelerator.
C. the greater the value of the multiplier and the smaller the value of the accelerator.
D. the smaller the value of the multiplier and the greater the value of the accelerator.
E. the greater the difference in the values of the multiplier and accelerator.

Q45. If firms hold stocks, this will increase the speed with which the economy will recover from recession.
True/False

Q46. Decide in which phase of the business cycle (*upturn/expansion/peaking out/recession*) each of the following effects is most likely to appear.
(a) The accelerator leads to an increase in investment.

....

(b) Low interest rates result from only limited borrowing.

....

(c) Firms reach their full productive capacity.

....

(d) Rising stocks force firms to cut back on production.

....

(e) Firms attempt to rebuild their level of stocks.

....

(f) Replacement investment re-emerges.

....

B PROBLEMS, EXERCISES AND PROJECTS

Table 17.5

Income (Y)(£m)	20	40	60	80	100	120
Consumption (C_d)(£m)	25	40	55	70	85	100
Withdrawals (W) (£m)	...	...	...	...	...	...
Injections (J) (£m)	...	...	...	...	...	...
Expenditure (E) (£m)	...	...	...	...	...	...

Figure 17.7 National income and expenditure

Q47. Table 17.5 shows how national income and the consumption of domestically produced goods and services (C_d) are related. Government expenditure is £5 million, investment is £2 million and exports are £3 million.
(a) Fill in the missing figures in Table 17.5.
(b) Equilibrium national income is at a level of £40 million. *True/False*
(c) Using Figure 17.7 plot the line showing $C_d + W$ against income (the 45° line).
(d) Plot the J, W and E functions.
(e) Identify the equilibrium level of national income from the diagram, verifying that the same result is obtained using both the injections and withdrawals approach and the income and expenditure approach.

....

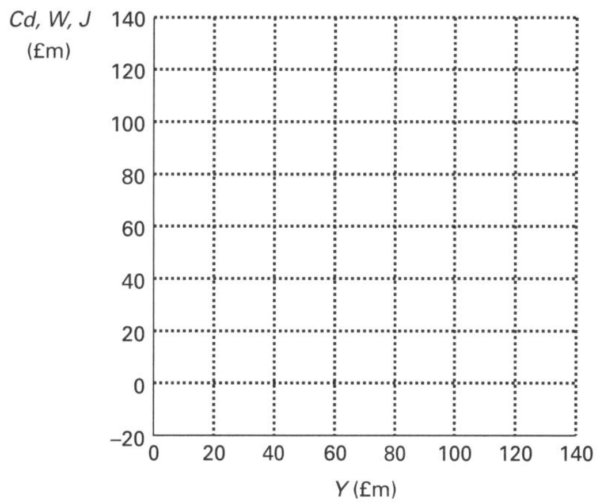

(f) Assume that withdrawals now fall by £5 million at all levels of national income. Plot the new W and E functions on Figure 17.7.
(g) What is the new equilibrium level of national income?

....

(h) What is the value of the mpc_d? ....

(i) What is the value of the *mpw*? ....

(j) What is the value of the multiplier? ....

(k) Verify that the rise in equilibrium in question (g) accords with the value of the multiplier you have just given.

....

....

Q48. At present a country has the following: exports £15bn, investment £1.5bn, government expenditure £6.5bn, *total* consumer expenditure £42bn, imports £10bn, indirect taxes £6bn. The economy is currently in equilibrium. It is estimated that the full-employment level of national income is £60bn. The *mpw* is 0.5.

(a) What is the equilibrium level of national income?

....

(b) Is there an inflationary or deflationary gap?

inflationary/deflationary

(c) What is the size of the gap?

....

(d) If the government wished to close this gap by fiscal policy but did not want to alter taxes, by how much would it have to adjust its level of spending?

....

Q49. Assume that there is an initial increase in injections to the economy of £100m. Assume that the mpc_d is 0.5 and the accelerator coefficient (α) is 1.5. Each period, therefore, C_d rises by 0.5 times the rise in income last period (i.e. $\Delta C_{dt} = 0.5 \Delta Y_{t-1}$). The level of I is 1.5 times the rise in income last period (i.e. $I_t = 1.5 \Delta Y_{t-1}$); this means that the *rise in I* is 1.5 times the rise in ΔY.

The effects of the initial rise in J are shown in Table 17.6 for three periods.

(a) Fill in the figures up to period 7.

(b) Does a cyclical effect occur?

Table 17.6 Effects of a rise in injections (£m)

Period	Initial rise in J	ΔC_d ($C_{dt} - C_{dt-1}$)	ΔI ($I_t - I_{t-1}$)	ΔY ($Y_t - Y_{t-1}$)	Cumulative rise in income ($Y_t - Y_0$)
1	100	–	–	100	100
2	–	50	150	200	300
3	–	100	150	250	550
4	–	...	...	...	...
5	–	...	...	...	...
6	–	...	...	...	...
7	–	...	...	...	...

Q50. Table 17.7 gives data comparing the investment performance of six industrialised countries.

(a) Plot the UK's investment performance, plus that of two other countries. How does the UK compare?

(b) Using Table 17.8, assess how investment changes with output. Can you identify any time lags between changes in output and the level of investment?

(c) What are the implications for an economy of a lower level of investment than that of its main rivals?

Table 17.7 Growth of total gross fixed capital formation (real percentage change over 12 months)

	1980	1981	1982	1983	1984	1985	1986	1987	1988	1989	1990	1991	1992	1993	1994	1995	1996	1997	1998	1999	2000	2001	2002
USA	−5.6	0.5	−7.4	7.6	15.8	5.4	1.4	−0.1	3.6	3.1	−0.4	−5.4	5.8	6.8	8.0	5.9	8.6	9.5	10.5	7.9	6.8	−1.0	0.0
Japan	−0.4	2.3	−0.1	−1.1	4.4	5.1	5.1	9.4	12.0	8.6	8.8	2.2	−2.5	−3.1	−1.4	0.3	6.8	1.0	−4.0	−0.8	3.2	−1.7	−5.3
Germany	2.2	−5.0	−5.4	3.1	0.1	−0.5	3.3	1.8	4.4	6.3	8.5	6.0	4.5	−4.4	4.0	−0.6	−0.8	0.6	3.0	4.2	2.3	−4.8	−2.4
France	4.2	−0.6	0.0	−2.2	−0.8	3.1	6.0	6.0	9.5	7.3	3.3	−1.5	−1.6	−6.4	1.5	2.0	0.0	−0.1	7.0	6.2	6.1	2.8	−0.1
Italy	3.0	−1.2	−3.5	−1.1	3.4	0.4	2.3	4.2	6.7	4.2	4.0	1.0	−1.4	−10.9	0.1	6.0	3.6	2.1	4.0	5.7	6.5	2.4	2.8
UK	−4.7	−8.9	5.9	5.1	9.2	4.1	1.9	9.3	14.9	6.0	−2.6	−8.2	−0.9	0.3	4.7	3.1	4.7	7.1	13.2	0.9	3.9	0.1	2.1

Source: *European Economy* (European Commission).

Table 17.8 Growth of real GDP (percentage change over 12 months)

	1980	1981	1982	1983	1984	1985	1986	1987	1988	1989	1990	1991	1992	1993	1994	1995	1996	1997	1998	1999	2000	2001	2002
USA	−0.2	2.5	−2.1	4.3	7.3	3.8	3.4	3.4	4.2	3.5	1.7	−0.5	3.1	2.7	4.1	2.7	3.6	4.5	4.3	4.1	4.2	1.2	2.7
Japan	2.8	2.8	3.1	2.3	3.8	4.4	3.0	4.5	6.5	5.3	5.3	3.1	0.9	0.4	1.0	1.6	3.5	1.8	−1.1	0.7	2.4	−0.5	−0.8
Germany	1.0	0.1	−0.9	1.8	2.8	2.0	2.3	1.5	3.7	3.6	5.7	5.0	2.2	−1.1	2.3	1.7	0.8	1.4	2.0	1.8	3.0	0.6	0.8
France	1.6	1.2	2.6	1.5	1.6	1.5	2.4	2.5	4.6	4.2	2.6	1.0	1.5	−0.9	2.1	1.7	1.1	1.9	3.4	2.9	3.1	2.0	1.6
Italy	3.5	0.8	0.6	1.2	2.8	3.0	2.5	3.0	3.9	2.9	2.0	1.4	0.8	−0.9	2.2	2.9	1.1	2.0	1.8	1.6	2.9	1.8	1.4
UK	−2.1	−1.5	2.0	3.6	2.5	3.6	3.9	4.5	5.2	2.2	0.8	−1.4	0.2	2.5	4.7	2.9	2.6	3.4	3.0	2.1	3.0	2.2	2.0

Source: *European Economy* (European Commission).

C DISCUSSION TOPICS AND ESSAYS

Q51. Describe the main determinants of consumption and consider whether changes in these determinants are likely to cause simply a parallel shift in the consumption function or whether they will also affect the *mpc*.

Q52. In what ways and for what reasons is a country's long-run consumption function likely to differ from its short-run consumption function?

Q53. The simple Keynesian model assumes that injections are exogenously determined. What does this mean? Are there any elements of injections that might in fact be *endogenously* determined?

Q54. Using (a) a withdrawals and injections diagram and (b) an income and expenditure diagram, illustrate and explain what you understand by the 'multiplier' effect and what determines its magnitude.

Q55. Why is it difficult to predict the size of the multiplier?

Q56. Why does the size of the multiplier vary from country to country? Which country is likely to have the bigger multiplier: the USA or Singapore? Explain.

Q57. Distinguish between an inflationary gap and a deflationary gap and explain the importance of this information for policy makers. What are the weaknesses of the analysis?

Q58. Explain the accelerator theory of investment and suggest some of the reasons why it is difficult to forecast the accelerator effect with any degree of accuracy.

Q59. Fluctuations in the level of stocks are an important feature of the business cycle. Explain how stocks are likely to change over the course of a business cycle and what effect these changes have on the cycle.

Q60. Why do booms and recessions come to an end?

Q61. Identify three key 'leading' indicators which are likely to signal the end of a recession and the recovery of the economy. Explain why they act as indicators and consider how reliable they are.

Q62. Debate
The Keynesian model presents such a simplified view of reality that it is misleading.

D ARTICLES

The central aim of UK economic policy throughout the 1950s, 1960s and 1970s was the achievement of 'full employment'. Only for short periods, however, was this goal attained. In the article below, taken from *Management Today* of August 1999, David Smith argues we are approaching full employment again, only this time it might be more long lasting.

Nirvana is not so unattainable

About 15 years ago I took part in one of those residential conferences where movers and shakers, and a few others, gather to discuss the big issues. At one point, the question came up: would we see full employment again in Britain in our lifetimes?

The movers and shakers, who included top business people, trade union general secretaries, politicians and senior civil servants, all shook their heads gravely. I, as one of the 'others', suggested tentatively that this was too gloomy a view and that when the unfavourable demographic factors unwound (baby-boomers entering the workforce), the picture might be transformed.

I say this not to boast of any forecasting triumph but merely to underline the depth of gloom into which it was all too easy to fall regarding unemployment.

For a while, it looked as if my optimism would be vindicated. Between 1986 and early 1990, unemployment virtually halved to 1.6 million and talk even turned to labour shortages in the 1990s. It was not to be. The recession of 1990–92 intervened to push the jobless total up to within a whisker of three million, and the gloomy view seemed justified once more. In the first half of the 1990s, job insecurity was again in vogue.

Now, however, it is possible to be optimistic again. Although the economy skirted recession last winter, unemployment has continued to fall. There are 1.2 million claimant unemployed and the unemployment rate is 4.5 per cent. Since full employment is reckoned by economists to occur at an unemployment rate of 2–3 per cent (there is always some frictional – people moving between jobs – and seasonal unemployment), Britain is within sight of it. So too is the US, where the rate is a shade over 4 per cent.

Europe, by some distance, is not – average EU unemployment is still in double figures. And Japan, which until recently had full employment, is moving away from it.

There are caveats to be applied to Britain's current condition of near full employment. On the other measure of unemployment produced by the Government, based on the Labour Force Survey, the jobless rate is more than 6 per cent, and some argue that true unemployment, based on all those who say they would like a job, is between four million and five million. I take the latter with a sack of salt, and I have my doubts about the LFS measure. Just as many arguments can be used to say that even the lower claimant count overstates true unemployment – not least the fact that many unemployed people apparently melt away when faced with, for example, a New Deal interview.

A more telling argument is that the unemployment figures have been massaged down by early retirement and rising numbers on sickness and disability benefits. But the fastest-growing employment age group in the 1990s has been the over-fifties, and only partly because of rising numbers of people in this age group. Meanwhile, the labour market has had to cope in the 1990s with something as dramatic as the coming of the baby-boomers in the 1980s – a sharp rise in female participation.

Compared with the golden age of the 1950s and 1960s, when the workforce was largely made up of men and pre-childbirth women, employment has reached out hugely to parts of the population for whom the norm was to stay at home.

Can this last, and what will be the consequences if it does? There is, as in the late 1980s, a sticky patch to go through before we can be said to have reached full employment nirvana. The surprise so far is that the economy's slowdown has produced no significant rise in unemployment. That doesn't mean it will not – unemployment is a lagging indicator. There is also the small matter of what happens to Britain and the rest of the global economy if, or when, the US economic bubble bursts.

If these hurdles can be overcome, and the pattern of strongly rising service-sector employment more than offsetting falling manufacturing jobs persists, would a move towards full employment bring with it an end to the present benign inflation environment? After all, 3 per cent unemployment would be significantly below what the Bank of England, Treasury and most economists believe to be Britain's natural rate. When unemployment falls below that rate, inflation tends to rise as the wage–price spiral kicks in.

It would certainly be a test, so why am I optimistic about both unemployment and inflation? For two reasons. The first is that there are a few examples, even in Britain's chequered economic history, of a tight labour market triggering higher inflation on its own. Only in combination with other inflation-boosting factors has this happened. Second, I believe we have seen a fundamental change in inflationary psychology and, because of that, in wage behaviour.

Full employment, however, throws up new challenges, not least in raising skills levels to minimise labour shortages, and avoiding mismatches between jobs and the people capable of filling them. Like old age, however, full employment is far better than the alternative.

(a) What is meant by the term 'full employment', and why is it such an important concept in Keynesian economics?

(b) What reservations does the article suggest we should have when considering unemployment statistics and using them to identify full employment?

(c) Why does Smith argue that we are unlikely to see a wage spiral as we near full employment?

(d) If full employment is to be maintained without rising inflationary pressure, what kinds of policy will governments need to pursue?

In the following article, taken from *BusinessWeek Online* of 8 July 2002, the author laments the return of the twin deficits to the US economy, and how they are likely to shape US economic policy for the foreseeable future.

US: the twin deficits are back – and as dangerous as ever

Widening budget and trade gaps could jeopardize growth

The twin deficits have returned. A ballooning federal budget shortfall and a widening trade gap are towering, Godzilla-like, over the nascent recovery. These two deficits, if unchecked, could cause trouble for the financial markets, the US dollar, monetary policy, and US growth.

The US shouldered these twin burdens before. In the mid-1980s, the federal and trade deficits mushroomed, with serious consequences. Interest rates were higher than they should have been, and massive foreign inflows boosted the dollar to a level that clobbered US exporters. Consequently, US businesses had little incentive to invest. Spending on new equipment was flat from the end of 1984 until the start of 1987.

A similar outcome could spell danger for the economy, which is looking vulnerable right now. New allegations of accounting fraud at WorldCom have further heightened investor uncertainty and pushed stock indexes to new lows for the year. Consumers are feeling less confident about the recovery and job prospects. Real gross domestic product may have grown at less than a 2% annual rate in the second quarter. And while the Federal Reserve Board kept interest rates unchanged at the June 25–26 meeting, they warned the lift from 'inventory investment and the growth in final demand appear to have moderated.'

Economists are betting on a turn-around in capital spending to give the recovery the extra oomph needed to power it into 2003 and beyond. But less foreign money coming into the US and a bigger government presence in the bond market means funds for new capital projects will not be as plentiful. Access to cheap money fueled the New Economy boom. But thanks to the twin deficits, financing the economy may not be as easy in the future as it was in the 1990s.

The 180-degree turn in Washington's finances has been particularly stunning. The budget for fiscal 2002, which will end on September 30, is on track to post its first deficit since 1997. Total spending from October to May is up 10% from the same period the year before, while revenues have sunk by 11.7%. The Congressional Budget Office projects a shortfall well above $100 billion, and private forecasters put the total at more than $150 billion in both 2002 and 2003, a sharp reversal from the $127 billion surplus for 2001. Indeed, the $277 billion swing would be the largest on record.

But while some of the rise in outlays and fall in revenues is due to the economy's cyclical slowdown, some is structural, created by permanent tax cuts and new defense and security priorities. According to the CBO, a rise in unemployment insurance is leading the spending jump. Once the economy is strong enough to generate a healthy pace of new jobs, these expenditures will shrink. But Washington will spend more on the war against terrorism, homeland security, and perhaps a military initiative against Iraq. As a result, Washington's outlays will continue to rise, but growth probably will slow back down to the 4% to 5% pace of the last few years.

At the same time, the White House wants to make a permanent and significant cut to revenues. To be sure, in this fiscal year, much of the loss in tax revenues was the result of layoffs, pay cuts, fewer exercised stock options, and a fall in capital gains. But the CBO estimates that between '$35 billion and $40 billion of the $161 billion decline in total receipts through May, 2002, resulted from changes in tax laws.' The stimulus plan now before Congress will reduce tax rates for upper-income households even further. So even when the economy gathers momentum, Washington won't see a commensurate pickup in tax revenues.

The dangers to the economy from these fiscal woes are twofold. First, to fund outlays, Washington will have to draw more deeply on the credit markets. That means the US Treasury will take funds away from corporate borrowers. This crowding-out could result in higher interest rates paid on all types of borrowing, from US bonds to business loans to mortgages.

Second, Washington has lost its ability to respond rapidly to economic swings. A major reason for the mildness of last year's slump was the tax rebate quickly enacted by the White House and Congress. Those checks were possible because the government had piled up cash during four years of surpluses. Without that cushion, the government will not be able to react nimbly if the economy stumbles.

The other deficit clouding the expansion's future is the trade gap – along with its much broader cousin, the current-account deficit, which also includes the balances for portfolio income and foreign transfers. The gaping current-account deficit reflects both the 1990s boom in investment and consumption and the foreign funds that helped to finance it.

Now, though, fewer foreign funds are available just when the US needs them the most. US external financing requirements ballooned in the first quarter, as the current-account deficit hit a record $112.5 billion. The gap may swell further as the year progresses. The April trade gap increased to $35.9 billion after averaging $31.6 billion per month during the first quarter. A wider trade deficit will subtract a percentage point or more from second-quarter GDP growth.

The longer-term problem is that less abundant foreign financing could limit the US expansion. Foreign financing in the late 1990s allowed the US to consume more than it produced, and it helped provide investment funds for tech startups and productivity-enhancing systems at nontech companies. From 1995 to early 2001, foreign net purchases of stocks and corporate bonds increased almost tenfold, and foreign direct investment rose sixfold.

But in the past year, foreign purchases of stocks and bonds are down 24%, and foreign direct investment is off 63%. Geopolitical risks and mistrust of Corporate America take some blame for this reduced inflow. And a key victim is the dollar, down 12% vs the euro and 10% vs the yen since late February.

The dollar will decline further, but it should do so in a gradual and orderly fashion. Why? US prospects for growth, productivity, and profits remain better than those in either Japan or Europe. Unit labor costs in Europe are rising, while in the US they are falling. A lower dollar will make the country's producers more competitive, lift the earnings of its multinationals, and reduce its dependence on foreign funds by narrowing the trade gap.

The price of that narrowing, however, could be slower growth in US investment and consumption, especially if Uncle Sam skims off more private savings, which could lift interest rates. The US weathered the effects of the twin deficits in the mid-1980s. But given the new uncertainty of the stock market, battling them this time around could be tougher.

(a) How far are the budget and trade deficits the result of cyclical changes in the economy?

(b) Why does the author suggest that the deficits may be more difficult to deal with this time round, compared to when the deficits last afflicted the economy in the 1980s?

(c) What are the implications of the USA's twin deficits for the global economy and its performance over the next few years?

CHAPTER 17 SHORT-RUN MACROECONOMIC EQUILIBRIUM

ANSWERS

Q1. See Chapter 13, Q5.

Q2. Withdrawals and consumption are endogenous in the model of national income determination: that is, they are determined (in part) by the level of national income. Injections, however, are exogenous: that is, they are determined by factors other than the level of national income.

Q3. C. Assuming that the scale of the two axes is the same, then a 45° line shows that whatever is measured on one axis *must* under all circumstances equal what is measured on the other axis. With national income measured on the horizontal axis, a 45° line shows whatever must equal national income. This is consumption of domestic goods and services plus withdrawals ($C_d + W$): income must be either spent on domestically produced goods and services or withdrawn – there is nothing else that can happen to income.

Q4. *(a)* See Figure A17.1.

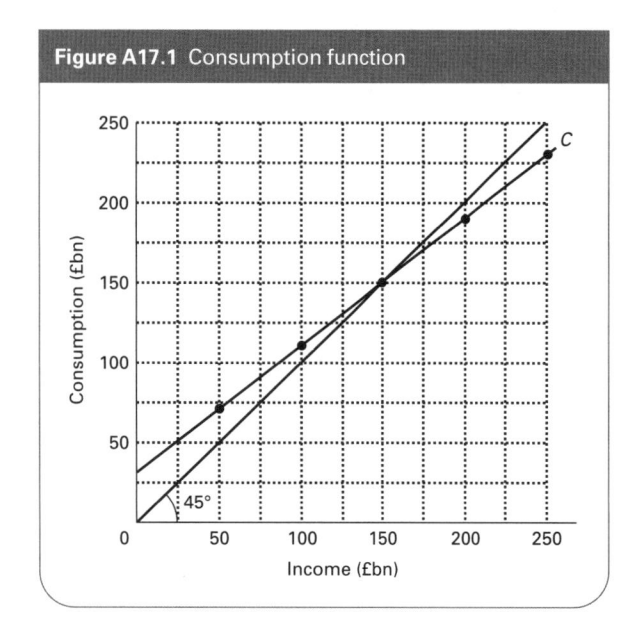

Figure A17.1 Consumption function

(b) At low levels of income, people may be forced to spend more than they earn, by either borrowing or drawing on savings. By contrast, at high levels of income individuals will be able to save part of their income.

(c) The marginal propensity to consume represents the proportion of a rise in national income that goes on consumption. The formula is $\Delta C/\Delta Y$.

(d) (i) $(90 - 70) \div (75 - 50) = 0.8$
(ii) $(150 - 130) \div (150 - 125) = 0.8$

(e) the slope of the consumption function.

(f) It would be curved, with the slope diminishing as national income rose.

Q5. *higher.* In the long run, individuals will have time to adjust their consumption patterns.

Q6. Slowly.

Q7. The mpc_d includes only that part of a rise in national income that accrues to domestic firms. It thus excludes that part of a rise in consumption that goes in expenditure taxes (VAT, excise duties, etc.) and also excludes the consumption of imports. It includes, however, sales subsidies to firms.

Q8. Income.

Q9. *(a)* See the following table.

National income (£bn)	Saving (£bn)
50	−20
75	−15
100	−10
125	−5
150	0
175	5
200	10
225	15
250	20

(b) See Figure A17.2.
(c) At levels of national income below £150bn.
(d) $mps = \Delta S/\Delta Y = (10 - 5) \div (200 - 175) = 0.2$.

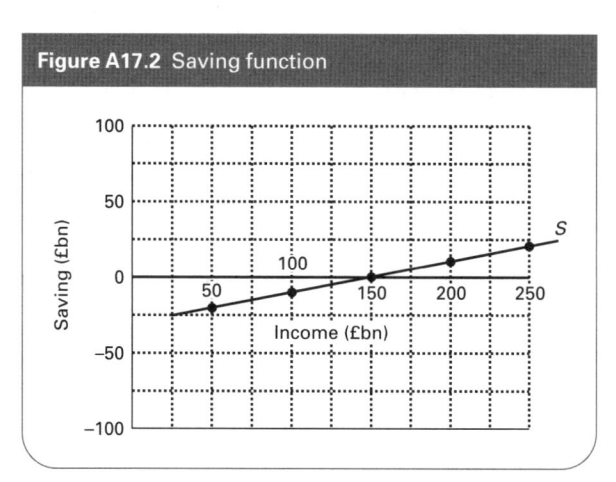

Figure A17.2 Saving function

Q10. *(a)* fall; shift.
(b) fall; shift.
(c) rise; shift.
(d) rise; shift.
(e) fall; movement along. (The fall in saving is due to the fall in income.)

Q11. *True.* It is the weighted average of all the marginal tax rates for each person in the country.

Q12. The import function would become progressively steeper as imports would account for a larger proportion of any rise in national income. The *mpm* would thus rise as income rose.

Q13. (a) *True* (b) *False* (c) *True*.

Q14. *(a)* OB (where W = J).

(b) At income OA injections exceed withdrawals. There will be a movement towards point P as the additional net expenditures (J – W) encourage producers to increase output, which in turn lead to higher levels of national income. As income rises, so will the level of withdrawals (a movement along the W curve). The movement along the withdrawals curve will continue until W = J.

(c) The injections curve will shift upwards by an amount UT. Equilibrium will now be achieved at point U (where the new injections curve intersects the withdrawals curve). National income will thus have risen by an amount BC.

Q15. The ratio of a rise in national income to the rise in injections that caused it.

Q16. A.

Q17. B.

Q18. *True.* The multiplier = 1/*mpw*. The larger the *mpw*, the less of any rise in income will be spent on domestic goods and services, and thus the less will recirculate round the circular flow of income each time.

Q19. *(a)* 1.
(b) 0.

Q20. *(a)* 3.
(b) 4 (i.e. 1/(1 – 0.75)).

Q21. See Table A17.1.

Table A17.1 The multiplier

Period	ΔJ(£m)	ΔY(£m)	ΔC_d(£m)	ΔW(£m)
1	200	200	100	100
2	–	100	50	50
3	–	50	25	25
4	–	25	12.5	12.5
5	–	12.5	6.25	6.25
Totals		387.5	193.75	193.75

Q22. D. An increase in the marginal propensity to save will cause the *mpw* to increase: hence the value of the multiplier will fall.

Q23. *National expenditure* (which is the same as aggregate demand).

Q24. (a) VZ (b) OB (c) AB/UG.

Q25. *True.* The *mpc*_d will fall, and thus the slope of the C_d function and hence the E function will fall.

Q26. *(a)* OD (where Y = E).
(b) QH (i.e. E – C_d).
(c) TM (i.e. Y – C_d).
(d) SU ÷ RU (i.e. ΔC_d ÷ ΔY).
(e) NM (i.e. TM – SL).
(f) NM ÷ DF (i.e. ΔW ÷ ΔY).
(g) DF ÷ NM (i.e. 1 ÷ *mpw*).

Q27. *(a)* (0.75 × 0.9 × 0.75) – 0.1 = 0.40625.
(b) 1/(1 – 0.40625) = 1.68.

Q28. B. National output is at a maximum and the level of national income is such as to ensure that all such output produced is bought, i.e. there is no deficiency in demand.

Q29. *deflationary gap.*

Q30. *inflationary gap.*

Q31. D. Note that (ii) is *not* a definition. The deflationary gap will be less than the shortfall of national income below the full-employment level. If the government adopts policies to close the deflationary gap, the multiplier will then ensure that the full shortfall is made up.

Q32. E.

Q33. *(a)* See Figure A17.3.

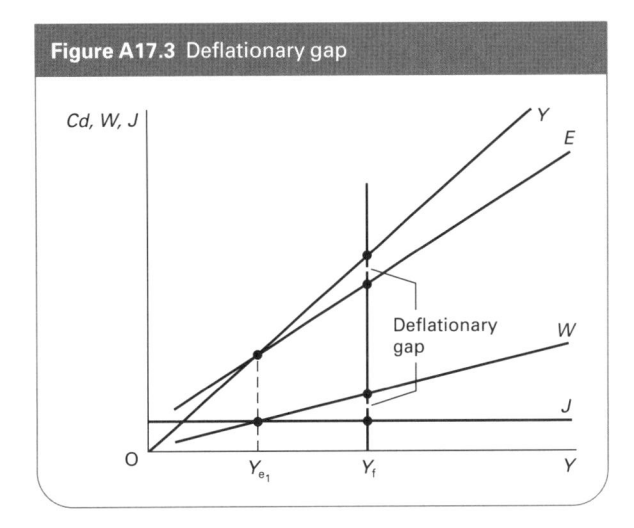

Figure A17.3 Deflationary gap

(b) The J and E lines will shift upward so that they now intersect with the W and Y lines respectively to the right of Y_f. The inflationary gap is now the amount by which E exceeds Y and J exceeds W at Y_f.

Q34. *(a)* 5. (i.e. 1/*mpw*. The *mpw* is 1/5, since for every rise in national income of £50bn, withdrawals rise by £10bn.)

(b) £300bn. (With an inflationary gap of £10bn and a multiplier of 5, the equilibrium national income must be £50bn above the full-employment level.)

(c) *Deflationary gap of £20bn.* (The full-employment level of national income has risen by £150bn to £400bn. This means that the full-employment level of national income is now £100bn above the equilibrium level of national income (of £300bn). With a multiplier of 5, the deflationary gap must be £100bn/5 = £20bn.)

Q35. C. If an increase in injections to fill a gap of £20bn leads to a rise in national income of £60bn, the multiplier must have a value of 3. Given that the multiplier = $1/(1 - mpc_d)$, the mpc_d must equal $2/3$.

Q36. *(a)* In Figure A17.4(b), national income rises to Y_{e_2}.

(b) The *AD* curve shifts to AD_2, and if the price level remained at P_1 (i.e. if the *AS* curve were horizontal), income would rise to Y_{e_2}.

(c) With the upward-sloping aggregate supply curve illustrated, equilibrium will be at point *X*. National income will be Y_{e_3}.

(d) The expenditure curve will be E_3.

Figure A17.4 National income determination: upward-sloping *AS* curve

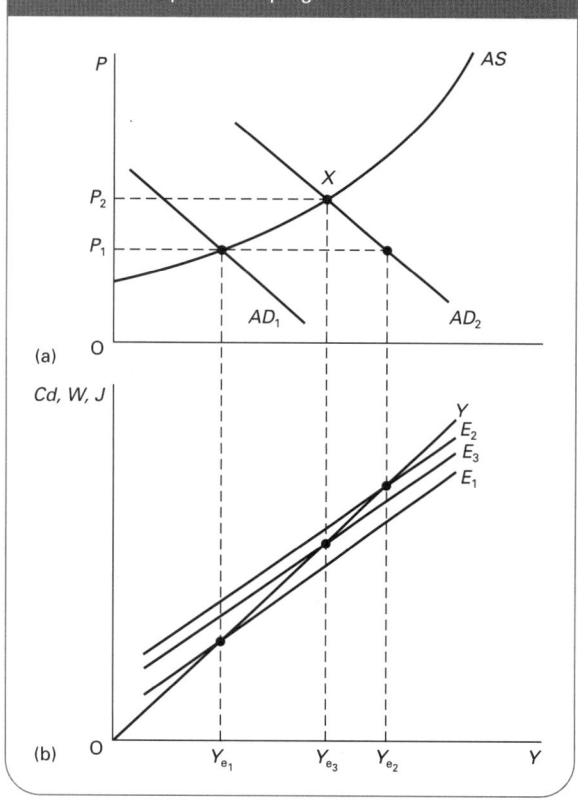

Table A17.2 The accelerator effect

	0	1	2	3	4	5	6
Quantity demanded by consumers	500	500	1000	2000	2500	2500	2300
Number of machines required	5	5	10	20	25	25	23
Induced investment (I_i)	–	0	5	10	5	0	0
Replacement investment (I_r)	–	1	1	1	1	1	0
Total investment ($I_i + I_r$)		1	6	11	6	1	0

(b) Even though demand has continued to grow, it has done so at a slower rate. Induced investment is determined by the rate of growth of demand.

Q42. Firms often have spare capacity or carry stocks and thus do not need to invest more when demand rises; expectations of future demand will vary; producer goods industries may not be able to supply additional machines; replacement investment is unpredictable; firms make investment plans into the future and it may take time to change them.

Q43. Following an increase in government spending, national income will rise (multiplier effect). This rise in national income will stimulate investment (the accelerator effect). This represents a further injection into the circular flow (causing a multiplier effect). Whether the subsequent effect on national income is greater than the previous change in national income will determine whether investment continues to increase. If the change in national income is bigger, investment will rise and there will be a resulting multiplied rise in income. If it is smaller, investment will fall and there will be a resulting multiplied fall in income. The interactions continue indefinitely.

Q37. D.
Q38. D.
Q39. *True.*
Q40. *True.* Relatively small changes in national income can lead to relatively large changes in the level of investment, which in turn lead to further rises in national income.
Q41. *(a)* See Table A17.2.

Q44. A.
Q45. *False.* It will slow down the recovery. The firm, rather than employing more labour to increase output, may simply draw on its stocks to meet the additional rise in demand.
Q46. *(a) expansion*; *(b) recession or early part of upturn*; *(c) peaking out*; *(d) recession*; *(e) expansion*; *(f) upturn*.

Chapter Eighteen
18
Money and Interest Rates

A REVIEW

The financial sector has changed a great deal in recent years, primarily as a result of the introduction of new technology and of the policy of deregulation.

This chapter and the next will review the monetary sector of the economy, examining how it operates and how it is controlled. We will also consider the relationship between money and interest rates, and examine the importance of money and interest rates in determining the level of activity in the economy.

18.1 The meaning and functions of money
(Pages 492–4)

◐ **Q1.** The supply of money in the economy is a flow concept since money circulates by being passed from hand to hand. *True/False*

? **Q2.** Money has four main functions. These are:

1. ....

2. ....

3. ....

4. ....

♚ **Q3.** Which of the following items would be included in:
 (i) both narrow and broad definitions of money?
 (ii) broad definitions alone?
 (iii) neither narrow nor broad definitions?

(a) Current accounts in banks. ....

(b) Share certificates. ....

(c) Cash in banks' tills. ....

(d) Cash in a person's pocket. ....

(e) Deposits in savings accounts in banks and building societies. ....

(f) A debit card. ....

(g) Wholesale deposits in financial institutions. ....

The amount of money in the economy influences the level of economic activity. It does this by affecting aggregate demand.

Before we can examine just how money supply affects the economy, we must see what determines money supply

≡ *Multiple choice*   ? *Written answer*   ◐ *Delete wrong word*   ⊖ *Diagram/table manipulation*   ✗ *Calculation*   ♚ *Matching/ordering*

18.2 The financial system

(Pages 494–6) Financial intermediaries provide a number of important services, two of which are in providing expert advice to their customers, and channelling funds to those areas that will yield the greatest return. They also lend long and borrow short. This is known as **Q4.** *risk transformation/ maturity transformation/credit creation*. Also by lending to a large number of individuals they reduce the impact of loan defaults by any one borrower. This is known as **Q5.** *risk transformation/maturity transformation/credit creation*.

There are several different types of institution in the financial sector.

Q6. Match the following financial institutions with the role in which they tend to specialise.
 (i) Finance houses
 (ii) Wholesale banks
 (iii) Retail banks
 (iv) Building societies

(a) They provide branch banking facilities, current accounts and overdraft facilities.
....

(b) They receive large deposits from and make large loans to industry. They also provide assistance to firms when raising new capital through an issue of shares.
....

(c) They specialise in granting loans for house purchase
....

(d) They specialise in providing hire-purchase finance for consumer durables.
....

(Pages 496–500) The deposits made in banks and building societies are **Q7.** *liabilities/losses/costs/assets/profits* of these institutions. The loans they make to their customers are **Q8.** *liabilities/losses/costs/assets/profits* of these institutions.

An important distinction is between wholesale and retail loans and deposits.

Q9. Which of the following are wholesale and which are retail?
(a) Large-scale deposits made by firms at negotiated rates of interest. *retail/wholesale*
(b) Loans made by high street banks at published rates of interest. *retail/wholesale*
(c) Deposits in savings accounts in high street banks. *retail/wholesale*
(d) Deposits in savings accounts in building societies. *retail/wholesale*
(e) Large-scale loans to industry syndicated through several banks. *retail/wholesale*

Financial institutions keep a range of liabilities and assets. The balance of items is dictated by considerations of *profitability* and *liquidity*.

Q10. Rank the following assets of a commercial bank in order of decreasing liquidity.
(a) Money at call with money market institutions.
(b) Government bonds.
(c) Bills of exchange.
(d) Operational balances with the Bank of England.
(e) Cash.
(f) Personal loans.

High liquidity

 (i) ....

 (ii) ....

 (iii) ....

 (iv) ....

 (v) ....

 (vi) ....

Low liquidity

Q11. Profitability is the major aim of most financial institutions. Why does the motive of profitability tend to conflict with the need for liquidity?

....

....

....

Q12. The liquidity ratio of a bank refers to:
A. the ratio of Treasury bills to government bonds that it holds.
B. the ratio of liquid to illiquid assets.
C. the ratio of cash to advances.
D. the ratio of liquid assets to total liabilities.
E. the ratio of total assets to total liabilities.

Q13. What adverse consequence for a bank might follow if it maintained a liquidity ratio that was:

(a) too low? ....

....

(b) higher than necessary? ....

....

(Pages 500–3) The *money market* plays a central role in the financial system. The money market is **Q14.** *the market for short-term loans and deposits/the Issue Department of the Bank of England/the institutions dealing specifically in cash transactions.*

Q15. There are two parts of the London money market:

(a) the.., and

(b) the..

Q16. Bills of exchange are one major type of monetary instrument. Bills pay no interest. Why, then, is it profitable for banks to buy bills (thereby providing liquidity to the issuers of the bills – the government in the case of Treasury bills and firms in the case of commercial bills)?

....

Q17. The process of purchasing bills from the banks and discount houses by the Bank of England is known as 'rediscounting'. *True/False*

Q18. Another major type of monetary instrument is a sale and repurchase agreement (repo). Which of the following describes a repo?
A. Where a bank agrees to buy certain assets from an institution for cash in return for being able to borrow from that institution in the future.
B. Where a bank sells some assets (e.g. bonds) and agrees to buy them back at a particular price after a set period of time.
C. Where bank A lends to bank B provided that bank B is prepared to lend to bank A in the future.
D. Where a bank sells assets to person or institution A in return for buying assets from person or institution B.
E. All of the above.

Q19. Give three reasons why the parallel money market has grown in importance in recent years.

1. ....
2. ....
3. ....

Behind the scenes, acting as overseer to the monetary and financial system, is the Bank of England.

Q20. Which of the following statements about the Bank of England are true?

(a) The Bank of England is the sole issuer of banknotes in the UK. *True/False*
(b) The Bank of England acts as banker to the banks. *True/False*
(c) No matter whether the government runs a budget surplus or a budget deficit, the Bank of England still has to manage the national debt. *True/False*
(d) The Bank of England is lender of last resort to the banking system. *True/False*
(e) The Bank of England not only operates domestic monetary policy but also manages the country's exchange rate policy. *True/False*

18.3 The supply of money

(Pages 504–7) If the money supply is to be monitored and controlled then it must be measured.

Q21. Match the following UK money supply measures:
(i) M0
(ii) M2
(iii) M4

with the descriptions below.
(a) Notes and coin in circulation + private-sector retail and wholesale sterling bank and building society deposits and certificates of deposit

....

(b) Notes and coin in circulation + banks' till money + banks' operational balances in the Bank of England

....

(c) Notes and coin in circulation + private-sector retail sterling bank and building society deposits

....

(Pages 505–9) The process by which banks increase the money supply is known as **Q22.** *maturity transformation/credit creation/profit generation/liquidity preference.* The amount by which the money supply can increase depends on their liquidity ratio.

Q23. If banks operate with a liquidity ratio of 20 per cent, by how much would they eventually increase their advances if they received an additional £175m from a government investment project?

....

Q24. If the banks decide to hold a lower liquidity ratio, what effect will this have on the bank multiplier?
Increase it/Reduce it

Explain ....

....

Q25. Which of the following will cause the UK money supply to rise; which will cause it to fall; and which will cause no direct change?
(a) A fixed exchange rate where the demand for sterling is greater than the supply. *Rise/Fall/No change*
(b) The government finances its PSBR by selling securities to the Bank of England. *Rise/Fall/No change*
(c) The government decides to increase the proportion of the national debt financed by bonds rather than by bills. *Rise/Fall/No change*
(d) The government finances its PSBR by selling bonds and bills to the general public and non-bank private sector. *Rise/Fall/No change*
(e) The government imposes a statutory liquidity ratio on banks higher than their current ratio.
Rise/Fall/No change

(Pages 509–10) The various effects on money supply can be shown in a *flow-of-funds equation*.

Q26. Decide whether each of the following elements should be added (+) or subtracted (–) to arrive at the total change in money supply.
(a) The PSNCR. +/–
(b) Sales of public-sector debt to the non-bank private sector. +/–
(c) Bank lending to the private sector. +/–
(d) A total currency flow deficit (on the balance of payments). +/–

(Pages 510–11) The relationship between the money supply and the rate of interest is one of debate.

Q27. What does it mean in simple monetary theory when it is assumed that the money supply is *exogenously* determined?

....

....

Q28. Give two reasons why Keynesian models assume that the money supply is *endogenous*.

1. ....
2. ....

18.4 The demand for money

(Pages 512–15)
Q29. What do we mean by the term the 'demand for money'? Is it:

A. the demand by individuals for greater wealth?
B. the demand to hold financial assets in money form?
C. a means of controlling the money supply?
D. a sign of individuals wishing to change from sight to time deposits?
E. a term used by the Bank of England to refer to the demands placed upon it by the banking sector?

It is common to distinguish three motives for holding money: the transactions motive, the precautionary motive and the speculative motive. The principal determinant of the size of transactions balances is **Q30.** *national income/interest rates/the exchange rate/tastes*, and the principal determinant of the size of speculative balances is **Q31.** *national income/interest rates/the exchange rate/tastes*.

Q32. Peter and Jane receive the same annual income, but Peter, who gets paid monthly, will have a much higher demand for active balances than Jane, who gets paid weekly. *True/False*

Q33. Indicate whether the following reasons for holding money are based on the transactions, precautionary or speculative motive.
(a) To purchase household items.
Transactions/Precautionary/Speculative
(b) To purchase shares at some future date.
Transactions/Precautionary/Speculative
(c) To pay rent. *Transactions/Precautionary/Speculative*
(d) To be able to purchase goods and services if your wages are not paid on time.
Transactions/Precautionary/Speculative

Q34. What will be the effect on the demand for money curve (L) of the following?
(a) An increase in nominal GDP.
Shift right/Shift left/Movement up along/ Movement down along
(b) A rise in interest rates.
Shift right/Shift left/Movement up along/ Movement down along
(c) Growing expectations that share prices will fall.
Shift right/Shift left/Movement up along/ Movement down along
(d) A rise in bond prices.
Shift right/Shift left/Movement up along/ Movement down along
(e) People believe that foreign interest rates will fall, while domestic interest rates will be unchanged.
Shift right/Shift left/Movement up along/ Movement down along

18.5 Equilibrium

Equilibrium in the money market is achieved where the demand for money is equal to the supply of money. This is illustrated in Figure 18.1

Figure 18.1 The money market

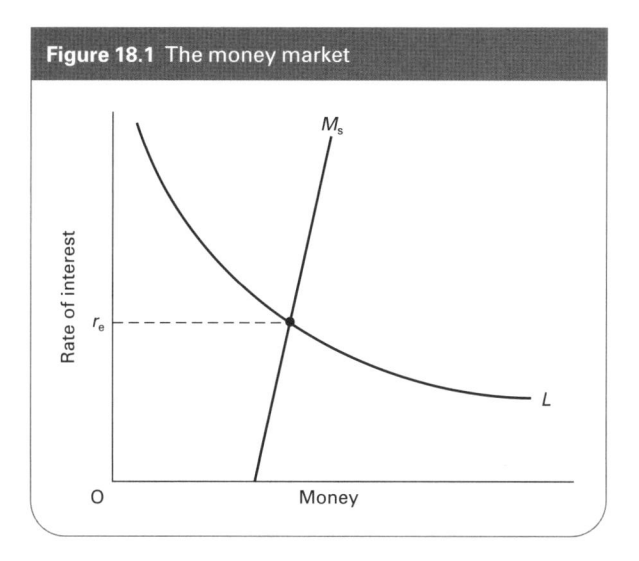

Q35. In each of the following cases, state which curve shifts and what the effect will be on the equilibrium rate of interest.

(a) The government funds the PSNCR by borrowing from the Bank of England.

....

(b) A rise in national income.

....

(c) Speculation that the domestic currency will appreciate on the foreign exchange market.

....

(d) The Bank of England sells more securities through open market operations.

....

Q36. An excess supply of money will cause people to buy securities, hence increasing their price and causing interest rates to fall. The lower interest rates eliminate the excess supply of money so that equilibrium in the money market is restored. *True/False*

Q37. Short-term rates of interest will rise relative to long-term rates of interest if the demand for long-term bonds increases relative to bills. *True/False*

Q38. Trace through the effects of a reduction in money supply on the rate of exchange.

....

....

B PROBLEMS, EXERCISES AND PROJECTS

Q39. Consider the items in Table 18.1 selected from Bank A's balance sheet.
(a) Using these items, compile a balance sheet for the bank. When doing so make sure you order the sterling assets in descending order of liquidity.
(b) What are the bank's total sterling assets (and liabilities)?
(c) What is the liquidity ratio?

Table 18.1 A range of sterling assets and liabilities of Bank A

	£bn
Notes and coin	3.5
Sight deposits by UK private sector	100.0
Time deposits by UK private sector	120.0
Investments in the public sector	16.0
Certificates of deposit in Bank A	50.0
Advances to UK private sector	200.0
Bills of exchange	14.0
Debit items in suspense and transmission	9.0
Time deposits by overseas customers	57.0
Operational balances with Bank of England	0.5
Market loans	102.0

Q40. Assuming that banks choose to maintain a liquidity ratio of 25 per cent, that new cash deposits of £100m are made in the banking system and that all loans made are redeposited in the banking system:
(a) Complete Table 18.2.

Table 18.2 The creation of money

	£m		£m
Banks receive	100	Hold	25
		Lend	75
Second round deposits rise by	...	Hold	...
		Lend	...
Third round deposits rise by	...	Hold	...
		Lend	...
Fourth round deposits rise by	...	Hold	...
		Lend	...
Fifth round deposits rise by	...	Hold	...
		Lend	...
Total deposits after five rounds	...		

(b) To what level will total deposits eventually increase (after an infinite number of rounds!)?

....

(c) How much credit will have been created?

....

(d) What is the size of the bank multiplier?

....

Q41. Look up the liabilities and assets of the banking sector for the most recent month available and for 10 and 20 years ago. You will find the information in *Financial Statistics* (NS) and the *Bank of England Monetary and Financial Statistics*. You can download this from Table B1.2 in the Bankstats section of the Bank of England Website at http://www.bankofengland.co.uk/mfsd/ How has the balance of items changed over the years? How have the cash and liquidity ratios changed? What explanations can you offer for these changes?

C DISCUSSION TOPICS AND ESSAYS

Q42. Describe the main functions of money. What attributes should money have if it is to fulfil these functions?

Q43. 'The aims of profitability and liquidity tend to conflict.' Explain this statement in respect of the banking sector.

Q44. Define the term 'liquidity ratio'. How will changes in the liquidity ratio affect the process of credit creation? Why might a bank's liquidity ratio vary over time?

Q45. What have been the government's objectives in encouraging greater competition in the banking sector? How are these objectives likely to conflict with the government's/central bank's objectives of maintaining stability and security in the banking sector and of carrying out effective control of the money supply?

Q46. What factors might cause the money supply to rise and why? To what extent are these factors within the government's (or central bank's) control?

Q47. Describe the main motives for holding money and the main determinants of each of these money balances.

Q48. Trace through the effects of an increase in money supply on interest rates and exchange rates. How does the elasticity of demand for money affect the outcome? What determines this elasticity?

Q49. Debate
Total deregulation of banks is in the interests of their customers as it is the best way of ensuring maximum competition between banks.

D ARTICLES

The internet is set to revolutionise all aspects of economic life. One sector that is currently witnessing a flurry of internet activity is banking and financial services, as providers attempt to establish a presence in this new marketplace. The article below, by Stephen Timewell and Kung Young, taken from *The Banker* of June 1999, considers some of the implications for those banks that are shifting services on to the internet.

How the internet redefines banking

The internet is not particularly new but, for the financial sector, the last few months have witnessed not only a massive surge of interest from banks around the globe but also an explosive growth in online activities.

As the technology focus of banks shifts away from preoccupation with projects on the euro and year 2000, institutions are beginning to realise the full potential of the internet. Some online enthusiasts predict that the internet will reshape the global economy over the next five years but while this may be over-optimistic, it would be dangerous for financial institutions to underestimate the impact of Internet technology and e-commerce.

Internet commerce is already changing companies' approach to business: take, for example, the shift in buying books from the bookstore to online supplier amazon.com. And this is only the beginning.

Tim Jones, the retail head of NatWest Bank, says: 'We expect that the two fundamental impacts of these technologies will be a massive reduction in transaction costs and the dramatically lessening importance of geography. At present, many people's horizons are governed by their capital cities since this is where they are governed from and often where their money is managed.

'In future, people's horizons may diverge, getting larger and smaller simultaneously. They may use some extremely large pan-national financial services companies but also perhaps some very local, personalised financial services.'

So, what is happening now at banks and in banking as competition increases, the 'end of geography' is at hand and non-traditional players enter the fray? Banks have been somewhat slow to realise the full potential of the internet and have been distracted by preparations for the euro but recent months have seen a quantum shift in both attitudes towards activities on the internet.

While the actual number of online customers is still relatively small (the bank with the largest number of online customers at the end of March was BankAmerica with 1.2 million), the rate of growth in online customer accounts in the first quarter of 1999 amongst the largest banks in the US shows that, across the board, online accounts will more than double this year.

The median growth is put at 118 per cent for the year with banks such as First Union and US Bancorp showing large annualised growth rates of 253 per cent and 400 per cent respectively.

For retail banking leaders, such as Wells Fargo, the accelerating customer growth implies a year end total of 1.5 million accounts compared with 700 000 at the end of 1998.

The growth surge is not just in the US. According to Sandra Alzetta, senior vice president for electronic commerce at Visa International, internet sales on Visa worldwide doubled in 1998 to $15 billion and are forecast to reach $100 billion by 2002.

Visa believes that although e-commerce accounts for only 1 per cent of total sales volume now, it will reach 10–15 per cent in the next five years.

And many countries are well advanced in their online usage, especially countries in northern Europe. Recent reports on Nua Internet Surveys showed that the percentage of the population connected online was (at the end of March, 1999): Iceland (45 per cent), Sweden (38 per cent), Finland (28 per cent), Denmark (22 per cent) – compared with the UK (18 per cent).

Nua noted in May that of the 3.6 million people online in Sweden, 3.1 million use the internet once a month and 950 000 have made an online purchase. Another May 1999 report showed that 64.2 million US adults, representing 42.2 per cent of the adult population in the US, were regular internet users, a 20 per cent increase on the previous year.

The acceptance of the internet reflects a need in the market that is redefining the relationship between the institution and the customer and in turn redefining the banking industry.

According to Robert Baldock, a partner in Andersen Consulting's financial services practice, banks up until now had driven the process, deciding what products customers would have and what prices they would be at. Now, with the internet and e-commerce, the customer will be able to drive the process: 'In the 21st century the customer is going to be the dictator, not the banks.'

With customers becoming more intelligent and sophisticated, their behaviour suggests that they will demand many more product offerings than the simple savings account. The internet allows for much more transparency in assessing products, where customers can now peruse their screens for the best products, services and prices for their banking needs.

This new-found ability for customers to choose rather than have products chosen for them represents a critical shift in the customer relationship and will be vital to an institution's future survival. The crucial issue is that if a product or service is not offered or priced competitively online, then customers will go elsewhere at the click of a mouse button.

The ability to win or lose customers at the click of a mouse poses critical challenges for banks. Customers will demand even more control over their personal finances. They will value 'anytime, anyplace, anywhere' customised access to financial services and those institutions that can satisfy this demand will be rewarded, they hope, by the benefits of profitable customer loyalty. But what mix of products, channels of distribution and technology will be rewarding for banks?

BankAmerica, for example, provides the following products and services online: bill payment, credit cards, discount brokerage, and mutual funds. This is contrasted by Wells Fargo's larger online offerings, which include: bill payment, bill presentment, credit cards, home equity, mortgages, other loans, discount brokerage and mutual funds.

According to management at Wells Fargo, online banking customers are on average more profitable – they generate 50 per cent more revenue than the bank average, hold 20 per cent higher balances and use 50 per cent more products; at the same time, their attrition is 50 per cent of the bank rate and their servicing costs are, on average, 14 per cent lower once online.

But banks will have to offer more products and services on the internet because customers are likely to be loyal to more than one bank. There may be a direct correlation between the number of products/services offered online and customer loyalty but this may not necessarily apply.

A new institution may focus on a narrow product range and with good marketing and brand recognition carve out market share at the expense of traditional suppliers. In the UK, the Prudential's new direct banking arm, called Egg, has accumulated a massive £5 billion ($8 billion) in deposits and 500 000 customers since its launch last October; the fact that it appears to have also accumulated enormous losses in the process may not necessarily be important in the long run if it can maintain customer satisfaction.

The convenience factor of the internet, coupled with customer demand, is changing how banks do business. Instead of being product-centric, they are becoming more customer-centric.

Customer satisfaction is key and banks are looking at different mediums, including the internet, to consolidate information to customise products and services suited to the customer's specific needs. This is consistent with the idea of 'convergence', where ideally, different electronic mediums such as web TV, call centres, mobile phone and other internet-related networks begin to converge to form a common 'customer destination point' or 'portal'.

The idea is to provide customers with a single contact point to alert them about new product offerings. The scope of internet technologies has no boundaries.

(a) The authors argue that the internet will have two major impacts on banking; (i) reduced transaction costs, and (ii) the decline in the importance of geography. Explain what they mean by these changes and how they will change the face of banking.

(b) Why is it suggested that banking with the internet will become a more consumer-driven, rather than bank-driven process?

(c) How is the expansion of internet banking services likely to affect the amount of credit created?

The City of London, one of the world's major financial centres, has undergone huge changes since the 'Big Bang' of 1986. The following article, taken from *The Independent* of 27 October 2001, looks at these changes and assesses whether they have all been for the better.

The City: a British success or a study in failure?

Reforming the city

Just in case you hadn't noticed, today [27 October 2001] is the 15th anniversary of Big Bang, an event that changed the face of the City for ever.

On one level, it was an innocuous enough event. By today's standards, the existence of a system that required all stock brokers to charge a minimum rate of commission, forbade brokers from making a market in shares, and stopped outsiders from owning a stock market firm, was absurd, and even at the time it seemed hard to defend.

Even so, few would have predicted the seismic shift in ownership, power and culture that dismantling this system would bring about. Over the intervening years the City has changed beyond recognition from a closed shop of exclusively British-owned securities firms and merchant banks into an international financial centre which is almost entirely controlled by the bulge bracket firms of Wall Street and their European counterparts.

Whether Margaret Thatcher and her then Trade and Industry Secretary, Cecil Parkinson, would so wholeheartedly have backed the reforms had they realised they would give rise to such a root and branch structural shift is anyone's guess. But what is not in doubt is that by the mid-1980s, the City was slipping into the sea and without modernisation, the place would almost certainly have been doomed.

To her eternal credit, Mrs Thatcher was always as hostile to the closed shops of big business and wealth as to those of organised labour. The City had become an inward looking, uncompetitive, class-ridden oligopoly and yes, in its culture of long lunches, and its toleration of sloppy and untoward practice, both unprofessional and out of date.

The process of capital market reform that began with the dismantling of exchange controls ended with deregulation of the Square Mile. Without these reforms, the City would not today be describing itself as the world's most preeminent international financial centre.

That position would instead have belonged to Frankfurt, Paris or somewhere else.

Not everything about the old City was bad. As Philip Augur has remarked in his excellent book on this period of the City's history, *The Death of Gentlemanly Capitalism*, there was much to admire in its culture of honour, decency and service.

But the Stock Exchange's refusal up until Big Bang to contemplate change of any sort left the partnerships that then ruled the roost totally unprepared for the onslaught that was about to hit them.

Of the major stock broking and jobbing partnerships that then existed, only one is still around in its original form, Cazenove. The same goes for the merchant banks. All but NM Rothschild and Lazards have sold out.

A myriad of once glorious, old City names is now largely lost in the mists of time. This didn't happen all at once. There were two distinct phases to the transformation of the City that subsequently took place.

In the first, there was a mad scramble among the big commercial banks, both British and foreign, to buy up the best of the Stock Exchange partnerships and City merchant banks and mould them into something akin to an integrated, American-style investment bank covering all aspects of securities trading, corporate advice and capital raising.

Very few of them understood what they were doing and most of them lost their shirts. Some £500m was spent in the first wave of acquisitions.

Another £500m was lost in the subsequent downturn, and then hundreds of millions more written off in the programme of closures and withdrawal that followed.

In the second phase, there was a more structured assault by the big investment banks of Wall Street and some of their European counterparts, much of it a green field attempt to build a presence from scratch. The Americans brought in their own people, their own systems, their own methods and their own salaries.

Rather than buy existing franchises, they poached the most able and up and coming talent around, often on salary and bonus packages with which the old City couldn't even begin to compete, and then applied it more effectively. What subsequently happened was a massacre, and like all massacres, it was unfair and arbitrary.

The bulge bracket firms of Wall Street have their own cartel and hugely lucrative it is too. Throughout the 1990s they poured the fruits of their American monopoly into the great globalisation project. The City was a centre of their attentions. The old City was razed to the ground and a new foreign-owned one constructed in its place.

Today the City and its Canary Wharf satellite are among the most cosmopolitan places on earth – a wealth of different nations, languages and interests – and there's hardly a banking transaction anywhere of size or complexity that doesn't pass through its byways and systems in some shape or form.

The City always does best when it is looking out rather than in, when it is open to rest of the world rather than closed to it. Big Bang came in the nick of time. Of that there is no doubt. But it is also a potent symbol of British failure, incompetence and loss of nerve.

The British seem to make great traders, corporate financiers and wheeler dealers, but post the collapse of empire, they don't seem to be much good at running anything. There have been all kinds of recent examples of it – Marconi and Equitable Life to name but two – but the City is perhaps the biggest of the lot.

Fifteen years ago, the City was dominated by British controlled players. Today the Brits are only fringe operators in their own market place. There isn't a single example of a big league, British-owned investment bank. In pharmaceuticals we have GlaxoSmithKline, in oil we have BP.

But there's nothing comparable in an industry the British are meant to excel in, the capital markets. Those that describe the City as these days just a wholly owned subsidiary of Wall Street aren't too far from the truth.

The Americans have brought great wealth and expertise back to the City, but they could just as easily withdraw it again. The present downturn is likely to provide the first significant test. What we have seen so far in terms of job losses and closures is no worse than during previous setbacks in the capital markets. Investment banking is a highly cyclical industry.

It expands like topsy in the good times and cuts back like a deranged gardener in the bad. The worry is that this one is going to prove a good deal more serious. So far, investment banks have deliberately held off from more draconian cuts because of past experience.

There's no point in cutting back sharply just to rehire again six months later. The trouble is that the anticipated upturn should by now be happening but it is not.

Wall Street cannot afford to hold back the axe forever and there is a palpable sense of anticipation in the City of swathes of cuts to come. The City has been a big beneficiary of globalisation, a process that has at its heart the free movement of capital around the world.

The events of 11 September dealt that process a huge blow. It remains to be seen how the City as a financial centre fares in the more cautious, anxious world in which we now find ourselves.

(a) What was the Big Bang? What were the two phases in the subsequent transformation of the City?

(b) What benefits has the transformation of the City brought?

(c) What dangers exist from what has transpired?

Broad money is a key element in determining the level of economic activity. But just what is meant by 'broad money', and what determines changes in the amount of it that is held? The following extract considers these issues. It is taken from an article by Ryland Thomas appearing in the May 1996 edition of the *Bank of England Quarterly Bulletin*.

Understanding broad money

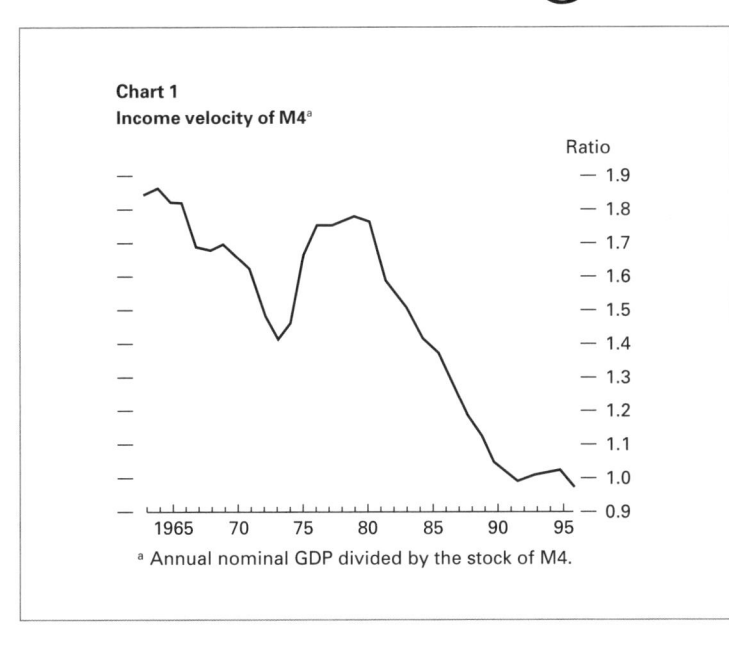

Chart 1
Income velocity of M4[a]

Ratio: 1.9, 1.8, 1.7, 1.6, 1.5, 1.4, 1.3, 1.2, 1.1, 1.0, 0.9

Years: 1965, 70, 75, 80, 85, 90, 95

[a] Annual nominal GDP divided by the stock of M4.

Broad money and its sectoral components and counterparts

The measure of broad money used by the UK authorities, M4, consists of holdings by the 'M4 private sector'[1] of sterling notes and coin, and of sterling deposits (including certificates of deposit and similar bank and building society deposits) held at banks and building societies in the United Kingdom. At the end of December 1995, the stock of M4 totalled £623 billion, roughly equal to one year's nominal GDP and almost 30 times the size of the stock of sterling notes and coin in circulation.

The relationship between the growth of M4 and the growth of nominal activity has been quite variable over the past 30 years. The income velocity of M4,

1. All UK residents except the public sector, banks and building societies.

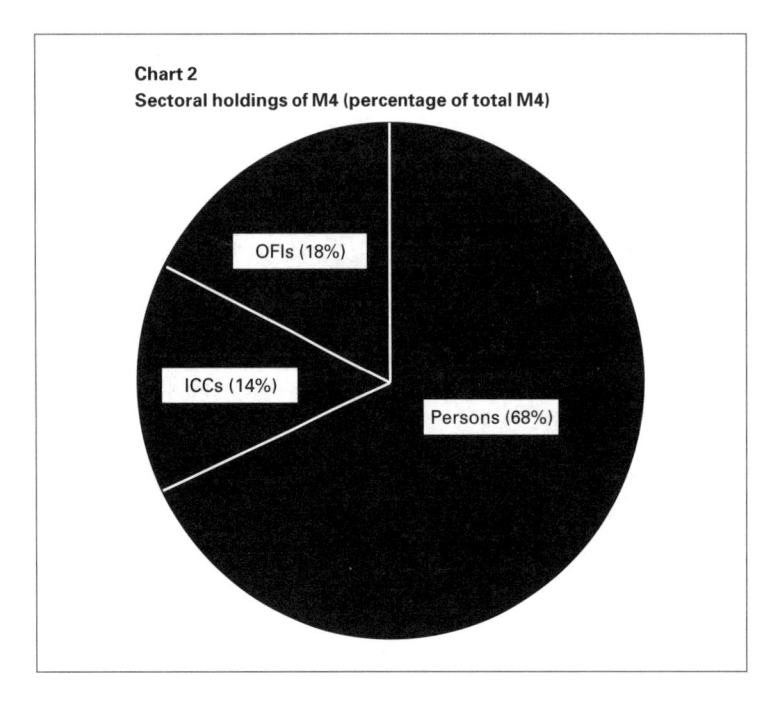

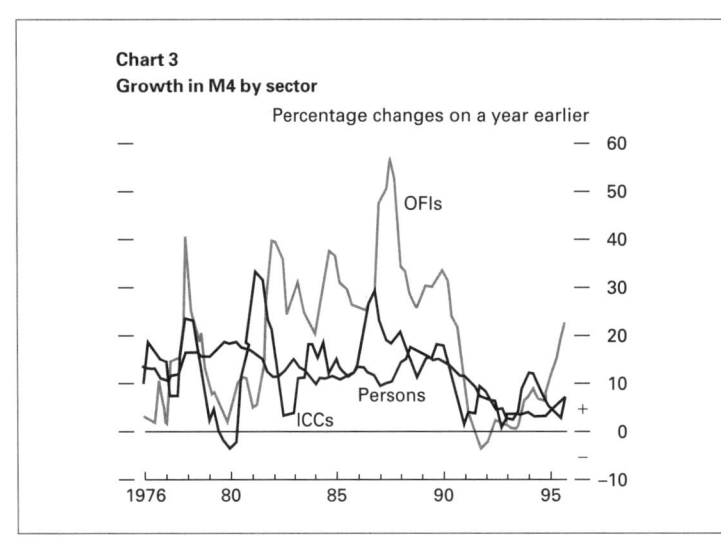

Chart 2
Sectoral holdings of M4 (percentage of total M4)

- OFIs (18%)
- ICCs (14%)
- Persons (68%)

Chart 3
Growth in M4 by sector
Percentage changes on a year earlier

which measures the ratio of nominal GDP to the stock of M4, has shown several distinct phases (see Chart 1). In the period before 1980, velocity did not exhibit any consistent trend. But it declined steadily during the 1980s when – in response to financial deregulation and liberalisation – banks' and building societies' balance sheets expanded more rapidly than nominal income. Between 1991 and 1994, M4 velocity was fairly stable. But during 1995, velocity started to decline once more, raising the issue of whether this indicates incipient inflationary pressures or is simply a reflection of further changes in the structure of the financial sector.

Within M4, there have also been some interesting patterns in *sectoral* money holdings. Chart 2 shows a breakdown of M4 holdings by sector. At the end of 1995, the personal sector was the dominant holder of M4 assets, accounting for roughly two-thirds of the stock of M4. Of the remainder, 14 per cent was held by industrial and commercial companies (ICCs), and 18 per cent by other financial institutions (OFIs).

The pattern of growth for each of these three sectors has been quite different over the past 20 years (see Chart 3). Personal sector M4 growth has been much less volatile than the growth of corporate sector holdings (both ICCs and OFIs). In particular, OFIs' M4 holdings have grown at a considerably faster and more erratic rate than those of either ICCs or persons. Thus, although personal sector holdings are important in determining trend movements in M4, shorter-term fluctuations in M4 are typically dominated by changes in corporate sector money holdings. That was again true in 1995.

Another way of decomposing M4 holdings is to look at its 'counterparts' on the bank and building society sector balance sheet. As Chart 4 shows, the most important counterpart to M4 growth has been sterling lending to the M4 private sector – 'M4 lending'. This too has exhibited interesting sectoral patterns over the recent past. Chart 5 shows that corporate sector (ICCs and OFIs) borrowing, like corporate sector M4 deposits, has historically been more volatile than personal sector borrowing; it has also been the most important factor driving recent fluctuations in M4 lending. In particular, there has been a rapid turnaround in the position of ICCs from being net repayers of debt for much of 1992–94 to substantial net borrowers during 1995. The growth of personal sector borrowing, by contrast, has remained subdued for much of the 1990s.

Money, credit and the transmission mechanism

In general, movements in M4 will depend on both the *demand* for broad money and on its *supply*. The second of these can be linked to developments in the credit market, given the way in which banks and building societies typically manage their balance sheets.

Looking first at the *demand* side, broad money balances are held for two main reasons. First, they serve as a medium of exchange, since banks' and building societies' deposit liabilities are generally accepted as a final means of settlement, in much the same way as cash. Second, bank and building society deposits can serve as a store of value. A large proportion of M4 is interest bearing, so agents will hold broad money as part of a diversified wealth portfolio alongside other financial (such as equities) and real (such as houses) assets. Taken together, these two roles suggest

Chart 4
M4 and M4 lending
- M4
- M4 lending

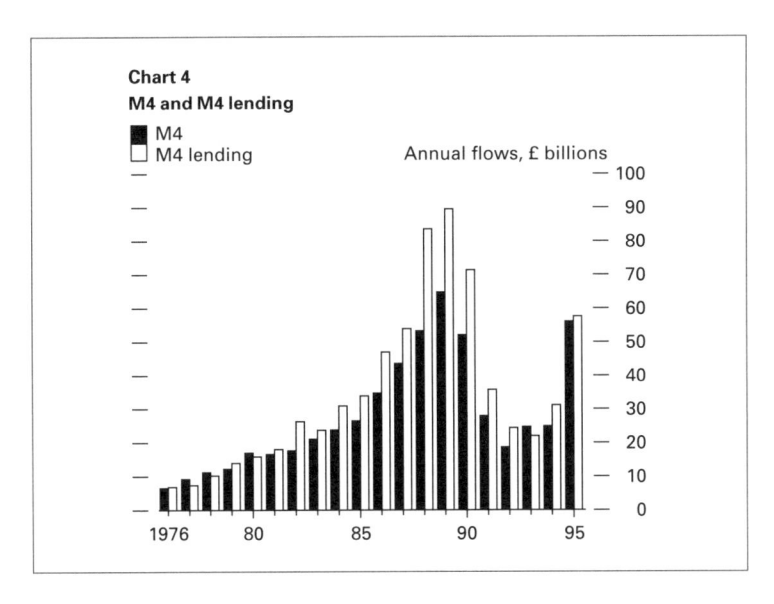

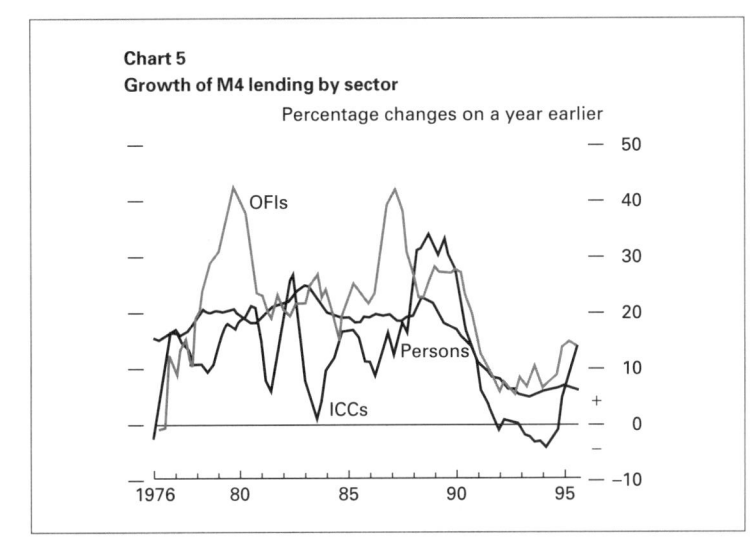

Annual flows, £ billions

(bar chart, 1976–95, values 0 to 100)

Chart 5
Growth of M4 lending by sector
Percentage changes on a year earlier

(line chart showing OFIs, Persons, ICCs, 1976–95, values −10 to 50)

that the aggregate demand for broad money is likely to be determined by real spending, prices, wealth and the opportunity cost of holding money (the difference between the return on money and the return on non-monetary assets, real and financial).

The *supply* of broad money depends on the behaviour of banks and building societies. A useful approach in this context is to think of the banking system as managing its liabilities. The banking system undertakes profitable lending opportunities at the prevailing level of interest rates and this, in turn, determines the extent to which it needs to bid for deposits from the rest of the private sector. This implies that conditions in the credit market determine the supply of broad money. The demand for credit – borrowing from banks and building societies – is likely to depend on the current and expected future level of activity in the economy, (real) borrowing rates, and the difference between the cost of credit from banks and building societies and other forms of finance, such as retained earnings or capital market issues. For certain types of borrowers, most notably small businesses and consumers, substitution possibilities between borrowing from banks and building societies and other forms of finance are likely to be limited. The amount of lending will then also depend on the willingness of banks and building societies to provide credit. Ultimately, it is the interaction of these demand and supply – or money and credit – factors which determine holdings of broad money at any one time.

(a) What is the definition of M4?
(b) How has the proportion of total M4 held by different sectors of the economy changed over time?
(c) What is meant by 'counterparts' to M4?
(d) What are the main determinants of the demand and supply of broad money?

E ANSWERS

Q1. *False.* The amount of money in supply is a stock concept. At any one point in time there is a given amount of money in circulation.

Q2. The four main functions of money are: as a medium of exchange, a store of wealth, a means of valuing different types of goods and services, and a means of establishing future claims and payments, e.g. the setting of wages or an estimate from a builder tendering for a future contract.

Q3. *(a)* (i).
(b) (iii).
(c) (iii). Cash in banks is not included as a separate item because it has *already* been included under the heading of accounts. To count it again would be a case of 'double counting'.
(d) (i).
(e) (i). Under old definitions deposits in savings accounts were only included in broad

definitions of money. Now, however, since savings accounts can normally be accessed rapidly (albeit with some loss of interest) they are also included in the narrow definition of money, M2. (M2 includes all *retail* deposits: i.e. deposits in branches of banks and building societies at published interest rates.)

(f) (iii).

(g) (ii).

Q4. *maturity transformation*. This process is possible because not all depositors wish to withdraw their deposits at the same time. If they did, the financial intermediary would be unable to return their money!

Q5. *risk transformation*. This is where the risks of lending are spread over a large number of borrowers.

Q6. (a) (iii), (b) (ii), (c) (iv), (d) (i).

Q7. *liabilities*. Institutions that take depositors' money are liable to the claims that the individuals may make on their money.

Q8. *assets*. These are claims that the financial institution has on others, e.g. personal loans to customers.

Q9. (a) *wholesale*, (b) *retail*, (c) *retail*, (d) *retail*, (e) *wholesale*.

Q10. (i) (e) Cash, (ii) (d) Operational balances with the Bank of England, (iii) (a) Money at call, (iv) (c) Bills of exchange, (v) (b) Bonds, (vi) (f) Personal loans.

Q11. The more liquid an asset, the less profitable it is (the less interest it will earn). However, banks and other financial institutions must keep part of their assets liquid, e.g. to act as till money and cover day-to-day transactions.

Q12. D. The liquidity ratio refers to the bank's total assets held in liquid form as a percentage of the bank's total assets or liabilities (total assets equal total liabilities).

Q13. *(a)* The consequence of a liquidity ratio that is too low might be that customers' demands for cash cannot all be met. The bank may be forced to borrow, or in an extreme case it may be driven out of business.

(b) If the liquidity ratio is excessively high, the bank will not be making as much profit as it might.

Q14. *the market for short-term loans and deposits*.

Q15. (a) the *discount and repo markets*, (b) the *parallel money markets*.

Q16. The banks buy them at a discount (i.e. below their face value) but sell them back to the issuer on maturity at face value. The difference is the equivalent to interest. The rate of discount (i.e. the annualised return relative to the face value) will be determined by demand and supply and will reflect market rates of interest.

Q17. True. Rediscounting refers to the buying of bills by the Bank of England before they reach maturity. Banks and discount houses will only sell to the Bank of England in this way if they are short of liquidity as the rediscount rate will be a penal one (i.e. the Bank of England will pay a low price for these bills).

Q18. B. As with bills, the difference between the sale and repurchase price is the equivalent of interest. Repo rates may be determined by demand and supply. Alternatively, the central bank can set the repo rates at which it deals with the banks, and thereby seek to influence interest rates generally. Here we are talking about government bond (or 'gilt') repos between banks and the central bank (the Bank of England in the case of the UK). This is a means whereby the central bank, by temporarily buying back government bonds from the banks, provides them with a short-term source of liquidity.

Q19. The parallel money market has grown due to: the abolition of exchange controls and the expansion of international dealing, the deregulation of the money market, and the volatility of interest rates and exchange rates making it more desirable to have a stock of funds that can be quickly converted from one asset to another and from one currency to another.

Q20. *(a) False*. The Bank of England is the sole issuer of banknotes in England and Wales. In Scotland and Northern Ireland the clearing banks can also issue notes.

(b) True. The banks keep operational balances with the Bank of England for clearing purposes.

(c) True. When the government runs a budget deficit, the Bank of England arranges the necessary borrowing. But even when the government runs a budget surplus, the Bank of England will still need to manage the national debt and the issuing of new bonds if the budget surplus is insufficient to repay all maturing bonds.

(d) True. The Bank of England thereby ensures there is always sufficient liquidity within the banking system.

(e) True. The Bank of England manages the nation's stock of foreign currency and its gold reserves.

Q21. (a) M4, (b) M0, (c) M2.

Q22. *Credit creation* is the process whereby bank deposits expand by more than the cash base.

Q23. £700m. The *total* increase in bank deposits will equal $1/L \times \Delta R$ (where R = the change in the reserve base). $1/0.2 \times £175m = £875m$. The additional advances are found by deducting the initial increase in the reserve base (£175m).

Q24. If the bank decides to hold a lower liquidity ratio, the bank multiplier will increase. More will be lent to customers, thereby creating more money when it is redeposited back in the banking system.

Q25. *(a) Rise*. If the exchange rate is to be maintained at this value, additional pounds will need to be supplied to the market. These additional pounds will then find their way back to banks as deposits by those that trade overseas.

(b) *Rise*. If the government finances its PSBR in this way, this will lead to the creation of new money. When the government spends the money, banks' accounts in the Bank of England will be credited, thereby increasing their liquid assets and allowing credit to be created.

(c) *Fall*. Changing the way the national debt is funded by substituting bonds for bills will cause the asset base of banks to become more illiquid. As a result, advances to customers will be reduced.

(d) *No change*. Funding the PSBR in this manner will simply lead to a reshuffling of money between individuals and government. No new money is created.

(e) *Fall*. Statutory reserve requirements effectively mean that banks cannot lend as much as they would like to. Thus the initial imposition of such a ratio will cause the money supply to fall.

Q26. (a) *added*, (b) *subtracted* (given that this is the part of the PSBR that does *not* lead to an increase in the money supply), (c) *added* (this is credit creation), (d) *subtracted* (a balance of payments deficit will mean that the Bank of England has to *purchase* the excess pounds on the foreign exchange market, thereby 'retiring' them from circulation).

Q27. That the level of the money supply is determined by government rather than by the demand for money.

Q28. Reasons include: higher demand for credit will force up interest rates, encouraging banks to supply more credit and causing the money supply to expand as a consequence; higher interest rates may encourage depositors to switch deposits from sight to time accounts, but since such money is less likely to be withdrawn quickly from time accounts, banks may be encouraged to lower their liquidity ratio and create more credit as a result; higher interest rates will attract deposits from overseas.

Q29. B. The term 'demand for money' reflects the desire by individuals to hold their assets in money form as opposed to any other (such as stocks and shares or property).

Q30. *national income*.

Q31. *interest rates*.

Q32. *True*. Peter will receive just over four times as much on each pay day as Jane, but this will have to last him a whole month. On average, therefore, he will hold a larger transactions balance of money than Jane.

Q33. (a) *Transactions*; (b) *Speculative*; (c) *Transactions*; (d) *Precautionary*

Q34. (a) *Shift right*; (b) *Movement up along*; (c) *Shift right* (instead of buying shares now, people will prefer to hold money while they wait for share prices to fall); (d) *Movement down along* (bond prices and interest rates move inversely to each other; thus interest rates will fall, causing a movement down along the *L* curve); (e) *Shift right* (the demand for the domestic currency will rise as people anticipate that the fall in interest rates abroad will cause the domestic currency to appreciate).

Q35. *(a)* Supply curve shifts to the right; rate of interest falls.

(b) Demand curve shifts to the right; rate of interest rises.

(c) Demand curve shifts to the right; rate of interest rises.

(d) Supply curve shifts to the left; rate of interest rises.

Q36. *True*. As security prices rise, so the return on them (i.e. the interest relative to the price paid for the) falls. The lower interest rate will increase the demand for money, and possibly decrease the supply, until the demand for money equals the supply.

Q37. *True*. The increased demand for long-term bonds will drive up their price, and hence reduce their return (i.e. the long-term interest rate) relative to bills. In other words, short-term interest rates will rise relative to long-term ones.

Q38. A reduction in money supply will lead to fewer assets, including foreign ones, being purchased: the supply of the domestic currency on the foreign exchange market will fall. The reduction in money supply will also drive up the rate of interest: this will increase the demand for the domestic currency on the foreign exchange market. The net effect will be a rise in the rate of exchange. This will be compounded by the actions of speculators.

Chapter Nineteen

19

The Relationship between the Money and Goods Markets

A REVIEW

In Chapter 17 we saw how equilibrium national output was determined. In other words, we looked at macroeconomic equilibrium in goods markets. In Chapter 18 we saw how equilibrium was determined in the money market. In this chapter we combine the analysis of the two chapters. We see how monetary changes affect goods markets and how changes in the goods market affect interest rates.

19.1 The effects of monetary changes on real national income

(Pages 519) The quantity theory of money
The possible effects of monetary changes on aggregate demand can be shown by considering the *quantity theory of money*. This states that **Q1.** money supply/the average level of prices is a function of **Q2.** money supply/the average level of prices/the velocity of circulation.

Q3. The relationship between money supply and prices can be expressed in the *quantity equation*. One version is as follows:
A. $M/V = PY$
B. $M/V = Y/P$
C. $MY = VP$
D. $MV = PY$
E. $MP = VY$

Q4. If the money supply as measured by M4 = £150bn and GDP at current prices (nominal GDP) = £300bn:
(a) What will be the (GDP) velocity of circulation (of M4)?

....

(b) If the money supply were cut by 50 per cent, what must happen to the velocity of circulation if there were no change in the current value of final goods and services sold?

....

Q5. Monetarists and Keynesians disagree over the nature of V and Y. Who argues the following cases?
(a) Changes in V are small and predictable, hence any increase in the money supply M will have a significant effect upon total spending.
Keynesian view/monetarist view
(b) M and V vary inversely.
Keynesian view/monetarist view
(c) V is determined by people's desire to hold speculative balances, which in turn is determined by expectations.
Keynesian view/monetarist view
(d) V is exogenously determined.
Keynesian view/monetarist view
(e) If MV falls as a result of a tight monetary policy, then Y will fall as well as P.
Keynesian view/monetarist view

(f) In the long run, Y is determined independently of the level of aggregate demand, such that any rise in MV will ultimately simply lead to a rise in prices.

Keynesian view/monetarist view

(Pages 519–22) The interest-rate transmission mechanism (the traditional Keynesian mechanism)

According to the interest-rate transmission mechanism, a rise in money supply will lead to a **Q6.** *rise/fall* in interest rates, which, in turn, will lead to a **Q7.** *rise/fall* in investment and hence a **Q8.** a *rise/fall* in aggregate demand. These effects of monetary policy on aggregate demand depend upon the elasticity of the money demand curve and the responsiveness of investment to a change in interest rates.

⊖ **Q9.** Figure 19.1 shows the relationship between changes in the money supply and the level of national income.
(a) On diagram (ii) draw a curve relating investment to the rate of interest. On diagram (iii) draw an injections 'curve' and a withdrawals curve.
(b) On diagram (i) illustrate the effect of a decrease in the money supply. Trace through the effects on to diagrams (ii) and (iii).
(c) The effect on national income will be greater:
   (i) The *steeper/flatter* the liquidity preference (demand for money) curve.
   (ii) The *steeper/flatter* the investment demand curve.

Keynesians and monetarists disagree over the shape and stability of the liquidity preference curve (the demand-for-money curve).

Figure 19.1 The effect of a change in money supply: the interest rate mechanism

⊖ **Q10.** Distinguish which of the four propositions below reflect Keynesian views and which monetarist views.
(a) 'Money and financial assets are relatively close substitutes for each other. Thus, as interest rates rise, so will the demand for financial assets. Consequently the demand for money will fall significantly. The liquidity preference curve is therefore relatively elastic.'

Keynesian/monetarist

(b) 'Expectations concerning changes in the exchange rate, in interest rates and in inflation have important effects upon the holding of speculative balances.'

Keynesian/monetarist

(c) 'Money is not a close substitute for financial assets. Hence changes in the rate of interest will have little effect upon money demand. The liquidity preference curve is thus relatively inelastic.' *Keynesian/monetarist*

(d) 'The liquidity preference curve is stable and relatively inelastic, as speculative balances are relatively insignificant.' *Keynesian/monetarist*

⊖ **Q11.** Figure 19.2 illustrates the interest-rate transmission mechanism.
(a) Of the four curves, L_A, L_B, I_A and I_B in Figure 19.2, which two are based on monetarist assumptions?

....
(The other two are based on Keynesian assumptions.)
(b) Using Figure 19.2, show the effect of an increase in the money supply on the level of national income using both monetarist and Keynesian curves.
(c) Under which assumption does a change in money supply have the greater impact?

monetarist/Keynesian

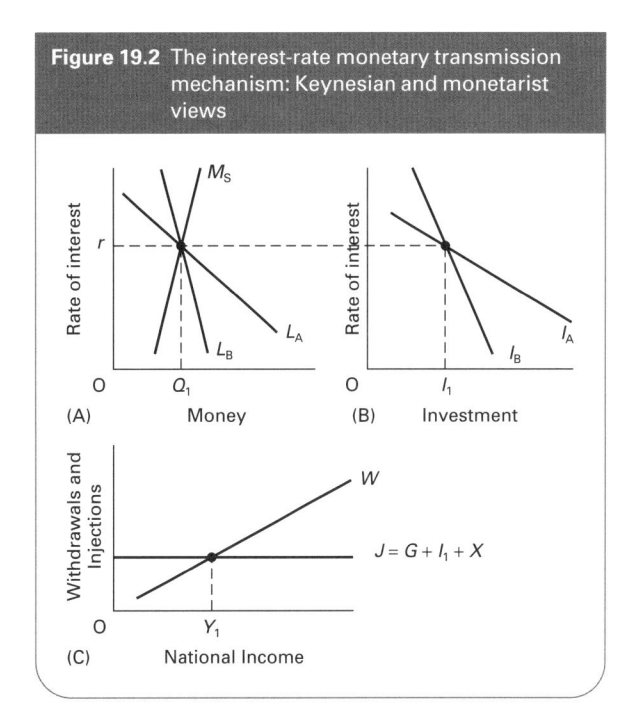

Figure 19.2 The interest-rate monetary transmission mechanism: Keynesian and monetarist views

(d) The money supply curve in diagram (a) has been drawn as upward sloping (albeit steeply) rather than vertical. The assumption here is that money supply in the model is: *endogenous/exogenous*

(e) If the money supply curve had been drawn under strict monetarist assumptions, would there have been a bigger or smaller effect on national income from an increase in money supply? *bigger/smaller*

Q12. Keynesians argue not only that changes in money supply will have a relatively small effect on investment, but also that the relationship between money supply and investment is an *unstable* one. Why?

....

....

(Pages 522–3) The Keynesian analysis of the open economy transmission mechanism

Q13. Order the following points in a logical sequence, assuming that there is a free-floating exchange rate.
(a) A rise in demand for exports and a fall in demand for imports.
(b) A fall in interest rates leading to an outflow of finance overseas.
(c) A rise in the money supply.
(d) A multiplied rise in national income.
(e) A depreciation of the exchange rate.

Order: (c) ....

Q14. What effect would a fixed exchange rate have on the exchange-rate transmission mechanism?

....

....

(Pages 523–4) Portfolio balance: a more direct transmission mechanism

Q15. The monetarist analysis is based on the theory of portfolio balance. This states that:
A. in times of recession individuals will use up their savings rather than cutting down on excess spending.
B. people hold their wealth in a number of different forms, the balance depending on their relative profitability and liquidity.
C. individuals will keep an equal balance between financial assets and money in their portfolios, irrespective of the rate of interest.
D. individuals with stocks and shares spread their risks by having a broadly balanced portfolio of equities.
E. high inflation will cause people to sell their low-earning financial assets and substitute them for cash, which, by definition, is totally liquid.

Q16. How does the theory of portfolio balances help to explain the direct transmission mechanism between money supply and aggregate demand?

....

....

....

Q17. Many economists claim that the velocity of circulation (*V*) is relatively stable over the longer run. Of the following, which can be used to support this claim?
(i) Sufficient time has elapsed for the direct mechanism to have worked fully through.
(ii) The demand for money is relatively elastic in the long run.
(iii) Increased money supply would lead to inflation and hence a higher nominal rate of interest, thus offsetting any fall in the real rate of interest (and any initial fall in *V*).
(iv) Increased money supply would lead to inflation and hence people holding smaller money balances, thus offsetting any initial tendency for *V* to rise.

A. (i) and (ii).
B. (i) and (iii).
C. (ii) and (iii).
D. (ii) and (iv).
E. (iii) and (iv).

19.2 The monetary effects of changes in the goods market

(Pages 526–9)

Q18. Assume that the government runs a budget deficit. Describe what will happen to:

(a) The supply of money ....

....

(b) The demand for money ....

....

(c) Interest rates *rise/fall/either/neither*

Explain ....

....

Assume that, despite an increase in government expenditure and a resulting budget deficit, the government does not allow the money supply to increase. Interest rates will **Q19.** *rise/fall*. This in turn will cause the level of investment to **Q20.** *rise/fall*. As a consequence **Q21.** *crowding in/crowding* *out/additional investment/pump priming* will occur. The level of injections into the circular flow will **Q22.** *increase further/fall back again*, causing the level of national income to **Q23.** *increase further/fall back again*.

If the government operates an expansionary fiscal policy but does not allow money supply to increase at all, this is known as *pure* fiscal policy.

◐ **Q24.** Which of the following analyses of the crowding-out effects of pure fiscal policy are Keynesian and which are monetarist?
(a) The increased demand for money will cause a relatively large rise in interest rates. *Keynesian/monetarist*
(b) The increased demand for money will cause a relatively small rise in interest rates. *Keynesian/monetarist*
(c) The increased interest rates will cause a relatively large fall in investment. *Keynesian/monetarist*
(d) The increased interest rates will cause a relatively small fall in investment. *Keynesian/monetarist*
(e) Crowding out is thus substantial and possibly total. *Keynesian/monetarist*
(f) Crowding out is thus relatively minor and may even be non-existent. *Keynesian/monetarist*

*19.3 ISLM *analysis: the integration of the goods and money market models*

The *ISLM* model is an attempt to combine in one diagram the analysis of the goods market (i.e. the injections/withdrawals model) with the analysis of the money market (i.e. the demand and supply of money model). The *ISLM* model involves two curves: an *IS* curve and an *LM* curve. Let us look at each in turn.

(Pages 530–1) The IS *curve*
The *IS* curve represents equilibrium in the **Q25.** *goods market/money market*.

(?) **Q26.** The *IS* curve slopes downwards from left to right because, as interest rates fall,

....

....

The elasticity of the *IS* curve is determined by the responsiveness of investment (and saving) to changes in the rate of interest and by the size of the multiplier. The more responsive are investment and saving to changes in interest rates, the more **Q27.** *elastic/inelastic* will the *IS* curve be. The smaller the value of the multiplier, the more **Q28.** *elastic/inelastic* will the *IS* curve be.

Keynesians argue that the *IS* curve is relatively **Q29.** *elastic/inelastic*. Monetarists by contrast argue that the *IS* curve is relatively **Q30.** *elastic/inelastic*.

(?) **Q31.** Why do Keynesians and monetarists disagree over the slope of the *IS* curve?

....

....

....

◐ **Q32.** What effect will the following have on the *IS* curve?
(a) Business expectations of the future improve. *Shift left/Shift right*
(b) Minimum deposits are required before mortgages are given. *Shift left/Shift right*
(c) Consumer durables fall in price as VAT is cut. *Shift left/Shift right*
(d) The economy experiences a consumer boom. *Shift left/Shift right*
(e) Firms anticipate an oncoming recession. *Shift left/Shift right*

(Pages 531–2) The LM *curve*
◐ **Q33.** The *LM* curve represents those points where the demand for money is equal to the equilibrium rate of interest. *True/False*

(?) **Q34.** The *LM* curve slopes upwards from left to right because, as national income rises,

....

....

The elasticity of the *LM* curve is determined by (i) the responsiveness of the demand for money to changes in national income and (ii) the responsiveness of the demand for money to changes in the rate of interest.

In the case of (i), the greater the marginal propensity to consume, the more the money demand curve (*L*) will shift to the **Q35.** *left/right* with a given increase in national income. Hence the more will the equilibrium rate of interest rise and the **Q36.** *steeper/shallower* will the *LM* curve become.

In the case of (ii), the more elastic the money demand curve, the **Q37.** *more/less* will the equilibrium interest rate change from a given shift in the money demand curve caused by an increase in national income. Hence the **Q38.** *steeper/shallower* will the *LM* curve be.

The Keynesians argue that the *LM* curve is relatively **Q39.** *steep/shallow*, whereas the monetarists argue that it is relatively **Q40.** *steep/shallow*.

(?) **Q41.** Why do Keynesians and monetarists disagree over the slope of the *LM* curve?

....

....

....

260 CHAPTER 19 THE RELATIONSHIP BETWEEN THE MONEY AND GOODS MARKETS

◐ **Q42.** What effect will the following have on the *LM* curve?

(a) Banks decide to hold a higher liquidity ratio.
Shift upwards/Shift downwards

(b) Speculation that the price of securities is about to fall.
Shift upwards/Shift downwards

(c) The government funds the PSNCR by selling bonds to overseas purchasers. *Shift upwards/Shift downwards*

(d) People are paid on a less frequent basis.
Shift upwards/Shift downwards

(e) It is expected that the foreign exchange value of the domestic currency will fall.
Shift upwards/Shift downwards

(Pages 532–3) Equilibrium in the ISLM *model*

⊖ **Q43.** Figure 19.3 shows an *IS* and an *LM* curve, with equilibrium in the goods and money markets respectively.

(a) Equilibrium in both markets simultaneously is identified by which point?

....

(b) Describe the position of the economy at point *A*, referring to both the goods and the money markets.

....

....

(c) By what process would the economy return to an equilibrium position?

....

(d) Describe the position of the economy at point *C*, again referring to both the goods and the money markets.

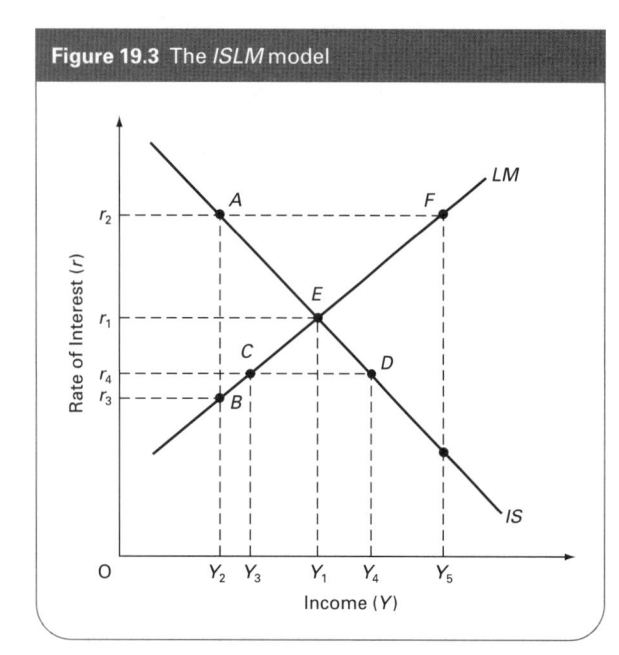

....

....

(e) By what process would the economy return to an equilibrium position this time?

....

....

(f) Using Figure 19.3, demonstrate the effects of the following:
  (i) An inflow of funds coming from abroad as the result of a balance of payments surplus.
  (ii) An increase in business confidence.

19.4 Taking inflation into account

(Pages 537–40) Many countries today have inflation targets and change interest rates as necessary to keep inflation at its target rate. What will be the implications of a change in aggregate demand under these circumstances?

◐ **Q44.** When inflation is above target, action by the central bank will lead to a fall in aggregate demand and hence a fall in real national income. *True/False*

Figure 19.4 shows the impact of changes in aggregate demand when inflation is targeted at the rate of $\dot{P}_{target}$.

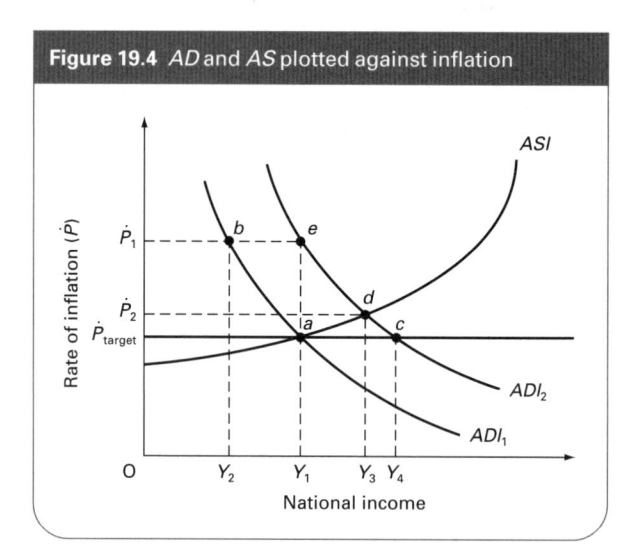

Figure 19.3 The *ISLM* model

Figure 19.4 *AD* and *AS* plotted against inflation

Q45. The *ADI* curve is downward sloping because:

A. A higher national income will cause inflation to fall.
B. The central bank will raise interest rates if national income falls.
C. The government will set a lower inflation target if national income rises above its sustainable level.
D. The central bank will lower interest rates if inflation falls below its target level.
E. A lower level of aggregate demand will cause national income to fall and inflation to rise.

Q46. The *ADI* curve will be steeper:
(a) the more quickly the central bank wants to get inflation back on target if it should diverge from the target. *True/False*
(b) the more the central bank is concerned to avoid a recession if inflation is above target. *True/False*
(c) the more responsive the components of aggregate demand are to a change in interest rates. *True/False*

Q47. Assume in Figure 19.4 that equilibrium is initially at point *a*, but that inflation is currently at $\dot{P}_1$ with national income at Y_2. Explain what will cause a movement from point *b* to point *a*.

....

....

Q48. All of the following except one would cause the *ADI* curve to shift to the right (e.g. from ADI_1 to ADI_2 in Figure 19.4). Which one would not?
A. A reduction in interest rates because inflation is currently below target.
B. The government sets a higher target rate of inflation.
C. An increase in government expenditure because real income is below the level the government desires.
D. An increase in business confidence.
E. An increase in consumer confidence.

Q49. Assume that equilibrium in Figure 19.4 is initially at point *a*. Now assume that aggregate demand rises to ADI_2.
(a) Assuming *no* initial change in inflation, what will be the new initial level of real national income?
$Y_1/Y_2/Y_3/Y_4$
(b) What will be the new equilibrium level of national income after prices have responded to this new higher level of aggregate demand? $Y_1/Y_2/Y_3/Y_4$
(c) Assuming that the central bank adjusts its target rate of interest in order to keep inflation at the target level, what will be the equilibrium level after the economy has adjusted to the central bank's actions?
$Y_1/Y_2/Y_3/Y_4$

Q50. On Figure 19.4, draw the effect of a permanent increase in aggregate supply in (a) the short run; (b) the long run.

Q51. A temporary supply shock will cause a movement along the *ADI* curve, whereas a permanent supply-side change will lead to a shift in the *ADI* curve. *True/False*

B PROBLEMS, EXERCISES AND PROJECTS

Q52. Using diagrams (such as those in Figure 19.6 of Sloman, *Economics*, 5th edn), illustrate the effect on aggregate demand, via the exchange-rate transmission mechanism, of a contraction in the money supply, making (a) Keynesian assumptions; (b) monetarist/new classical assumptions.

Q53. Using data for the money supply (M4) and GDP (where $GDP = PY$), calculate values for the velocity of circulation for each of the last 15 years. How has the value of V changed over the period? What explanations can you offer for these changes?

How does the velocity of circulation alter when different measures of the money supply are used in its calculation? Use M0 as an alternative to M4. What are the consequences of your findings for the quantity theory of money?

Figures for GDP and the various money supply measures can be found in *Economic Trends* (NS), the *Annual Abstract of Statistics* (NS) and *Financial Statistics* (NS). All three are taken by most university libraries and all are available on the National Statistics site (www.statistics.gov.uk): the *Annual Abstract* in the 'Bookshelf' section of the site and *Economic Trends* and *Financial Statistics* as separate time-series tables in the 'Statbase', 'Time series data' section. See also the Bank of England Web site, http://www.bankofengland.co.uk/mfsd/

*Q54. In Figure 19.5, simultaneous goods and money market equilibria are achieved at point E (r_1, Y_1). Two alternative *LM* curves are shown, one representing the monetarist position, the other the Keynesian position.

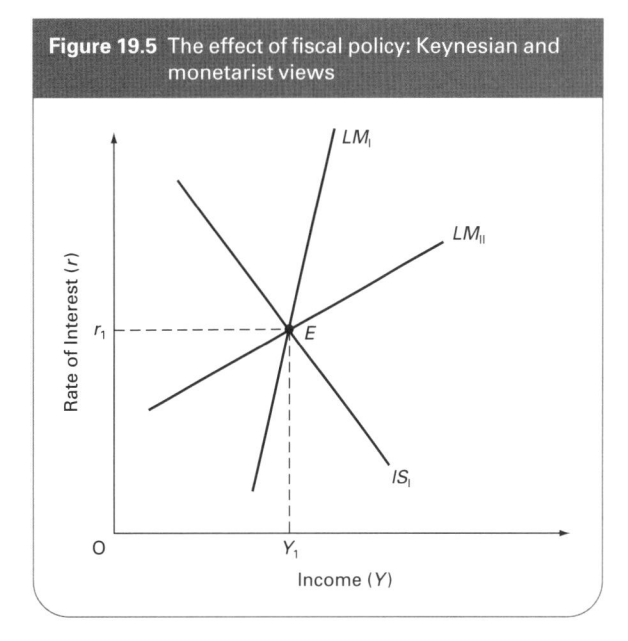

Figure 19.5 The effect of fiscal policy: Keynesian and monetarist views

(a) Which *LM* curve represents the monetarist position?

LM_I/LM_{II}

(b) Which *LM* curve represents the Keynesian position?

LM_I/LM_{II}

(c) Draw on Figure 19.5 the new *IS* curve following an expansionary fiscal policy. Clearly identify the new rates of interest and levels of national income for each *LM* curve.

(d) Extend the line from r_1 to the new *IS* curve. What would be the full multiplied rise in national income from the shift in *IS*, assuming that money supply expanded sufficiently to keep the rate of interest at r_1?

....

(e) Dropping the assumption of a constant rate of interest, identify the crowding out that occurs from the shift in the *IS* curve if the *LM* curve is:

  (i) LM_I ....

  (ii) LM_{II} ....

(f) What would the *LM* curve look like if there were no crowding out?

....

(g) What would the *LM* curve look like if crowding out were total?

....

C. DISCUSSION TOPICS AND ESSAYS

Q55. 'The dismantling of controls on international financial flows and the integration of international financial markets have made the transmission mechanism from exchange rates to the money supply to prices far more important.' Discuss and consider the implications for the conduct of monetary policy.

Q56. 'The quantity equation $MV = PY$ is true by definition.' Explain why this is so. Does it imply that a rise in money supply will necessarily lead to a rise in the price level? Discuss how monetarists and Keynesians have disagreed over the nature of V and Y. What are the implications of this disagreement for the effectiveness of monetary policy in controlling inflation?

Q57. 'The effectiveness of discretionary fiscal policy is reduced by the phenomenon of crowding out.' Explain what is meant by 'crowding out'. What determines its magnitude?

Q58. How does a change in money supply affect the output of goods and services? How does the size of this effect depend on (a) the responsiveness of the demand for money to changes in interest rates; (b) the responsiveness of aggregate demand to changes in interest rates; (c) the size of the multiplier; (d) the responsiveness of international financial flows into and out of the country to changes interest rates; (e) the responsiveness of the demand for imports and exports to changes in the exchange rate?

Q59. To what extent has Japan been suffering from a 'liquidity trap'? In this context, why may monetary policy be totally ineffective in bringing an economy out of recession?

Q60. Explain the 'portfolio balance' transmission mechanism. What determines the strength of this mechanism?

Q61. Under what circumstances would an increase in private investment lead to a reduction in private investment elsewhere in the economy? How does the size of this effect depend on the government's/central bank's attitude towards the size of the money supply and the rate of interest?

Q62. Why and how much does crowding out depend on the central bank's attitudes towards the money supply and interest rates? If the money supply were totally endogenous, would there be any crowding out?

Q63. How does inflation targeting affect the impact of (a) a temporary supply-side shock; (b) a permanent increase in aggregate supply?

Q64. If inflation is targeted and if the aggregate supply curve (with respect to inflation) does not shift, explain why a reduction in aggregate demand will lead to only a temporary decrease in real national income. What determines the speed with which the economy rises back to the sustainable level of real national income?

Q65. Debate

An increase in aggregate demand can never lead to more than a temporary increase in real national income.

ARTICLES

Monetary authorities around the world have less control over their economies than in the past. Increasingly, as governments and central banks struggle to tame the business cycle, they are having to rely not simply on changing current interest rates, but on talking about possible *future* interest rate changes that might be necessary if people fail to respond sufficiently to current changes. In the following article, taken from *The Guardian* of 4 September 1999, Edmond Warner (chief executive of Albert E. Sharp Securities) argues that attempting to control people's expectations in this way is virtually impossible to do with any precision.

The danger of growing up quickly

Like a gangly teenager, the global economy is experiencing its share of growing pains. All the signs are that the world is in the middle of a growth spurt. Although this brings immediate benefits it also carries the threat of dislocation. Much hinges on the skills of the policy masseurs.

Although impossible to measure it seems as if each major statistical release in the US is awaited with yet greater trepidation. This is a sure sign that investors appreciate how much they have riding on a continuation of the 'new paradigm' – strong growth and low inflation. It is as if markets have begun to expect an acceleration in the rate of inflation while continuing to pray for the opposite.

Inflation is a notoriously difficult variable to model. Sure, it is too much money chasing too few goods, but what makes the money *want* to do the chasing? What, in the modern economy, determines the total quantum of money available to join the chase? The explosion in sources of credit and electronic commerce have transformed money creation. The monetary authorities have less direct control over economies than ever before.

Economic management increasingly involves the manipulation of inflation expectations. Interest rate rises of 25 basis points ($^1/_4$ per cent) are unlikely, in themselves, to effect a significant change in the behaviour of an economy's participants. It is the accompanying rhetoric that magnifies the import of rate changes. Employers, employees and consumers are encouraged to display restraint by threats of future action from policymakers.

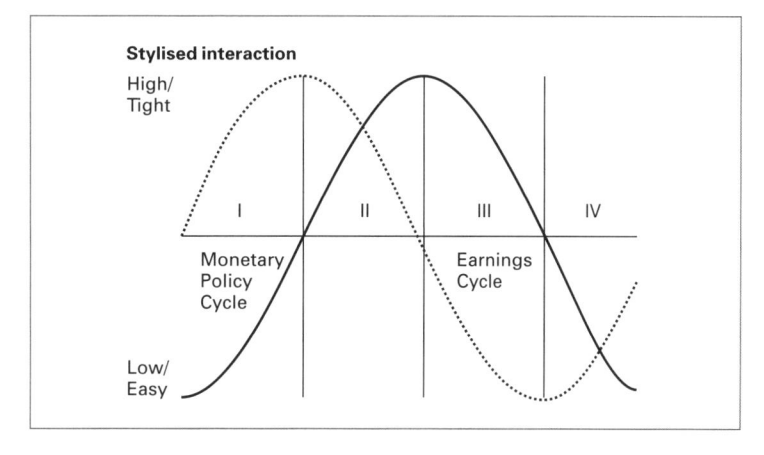

This fine-tuning approach is fraught with difficulties, not least because any individual within an economy might assume the masses will exercise restraint – leaving him or her to borrow, spend and issue extravagant wage demands at will.

It is not just in America that monetary authorities are responding to stronger economic growth with dark hints of higher rates. Wim Duisenberg, president of the European central bank, has responded to the recovery by signalling the need for policy tightening at some point in the future. One of the Bank of England's deputy governors, Mervyn King, is fulfilling the same role of inflation hard man in Britain.

This policy shadow-boxing is typical of the present stage of the global economic cycle. The chart shows the stylised interaction of the cycles of monetary policy and corporate earnings. The world is now in stage I, a period of rising profits and easy but tightening monetary policy. This stage normally witnesses equities outperforming cash, and both cash and equities outperforming bonds. This has indeed been the experience this year.

The challenge for investors is to assess whether inflation can be averted without tighter policy crushing corporate profitability in the process. If this is possible then the cycles can be stretched and their amplitude compressed.

History suggests this is a difficult stunt to pull off – although that is just what America's Federal Reserve has managed in recent years.

If the authorities fail to avert inflation and hence are forced to raise rates dramatically to reassert control, corporate profits are likely to pop.

In this stage of the global cycle – stage II in the chart – falling corporate earnings and tightening monetary policy typically push equities to the bottom of the performance pile and cash to the top.

(a) Why is the relationship between money supply and inflation very difficult to model?

(b) Why is the fine-tuning approach to managing the business cycle 'fraught with difficulties'?

(c) Explain the relationship between the two cycles in the chart.

The following extract is from an article entitled 'Monetary policy instruments: the UK experience', appearing in the *Bank of England Quarterly* of August 1994. The author, Mervyn King, argues that whereas the transmission mechanism between money and aggregate demand and prices is itself relatively uncontroversial, the size and timing of the effects are far from certain, depending as they do on expectations.

Money, aggregate demand and prices

If money were neutral – in the sense that a change in the money supply produced an immediate equiproportionate change in the price level – then the uncertainties of the transmission mechanism would be reduced to the link between the discretionary actions of the authorities and the behaviour of money. In practice, of course, the link between money and activity and inflation is far from clear.

The traditional view of the transmission mechanism of monetary policy is, at least *qualitatively*, relatively uncontroversial. A decrease in the monetary base or, equivalently, higher short-term official interest rates, will feed through to interest rates at all maturities and alter asset prices. Given some inertia in the setting of nominal wages and prices, the higher level of nominal interest rates will, in the short run, imply a higher level of real interest rates. Higher nominal interest rates will reduce the demand for money, and higher real rates will reduce the demand for credit. Real asset prices will fall, and there will be a process of substitution among various real and financial assets, and between assets and spending. With fewer profitable lending opportunities, the banks will wish to attract fewer deposits, and the broad money supply will fall.

The fall in money has as its counterpart a fall in nominal incomes, as households and companies adjust their portfolios and spending plans to the new levels of real money balances and interest rates. How does this come about? The rise in real interest rates and fall in asset prices will reduce real aggregate demand in three ways.

First, the higher real rate of interest will lead to a switch of spending from the present to the future, as saving becomes more attractive. Second, higher real interest rates will lower asset prices and hence wealth. Both effects will reduce consumer spending and private investment. Third, the rise in real short-term interest rates is also likely to lead to an appreciation of the exchange rate to a level from which it will be expected to revert slowly to its original real level. In turn, this will lead to lower prices for imports in terms of domestic currency and also a depressing effect on the economy through a reduction in the net trade balance. Eventually, the contraction of the real economy will affect prices and wages, and real demand and output can, in the long run, return to their original levels.

As I mentioned, there is nothing particularly controversial here. Turning this qualitative story into a *quantitative* account of how monetary policy affects the economy is, however, a different story. And both recent research and experience have made us aware of the importance of expectations about future inflation in determining how long and how variable are the lags between changes in interest rates and their effect on inflation.

One of the most contentious issues in assessing the role of money is the direction of causation between money and demand. Textbooks assume that money is exogenous. It is sometimes dropped by helicopters, as in Friedman's analysis of a 'pure' monetary expansion, or its supply is altered by open-market operations. In the United Kingdom, money is endogenous – the Bank supplies base money on demand at its prevailing interest rate, and broad money is created by the banking system. The endogeneity of money has caused great confusion and led some critics to argue that money is unimportant. This is a serious mistake. In his latest (April 1994) forecast, Tim Congdon[1] – who could never be accused of understanding the role of money – argues that 'the upturn in monetary growth has done its usual work in bolstering balance sheets and encouraging more spending on big-ticket capital items'. Some of his critics might reverse the causation and say 'the upturn in spending on big-ticket capital items and the bolstering of balance sheets had done its usual work in raising monetary growth'. In other words, spending and activity determine money, not the other way round.[2] I would prefer to say that interest rates have been kept at a level such that monetary growth has turned up, balance sheets have improved and there has been an increase in spending on big-ticket capital items.

Monetary policy does affect nominal growth in the economy, but the point is that money and interest rates are twins – two sides of the same coin. Many of those who find it difficult to accept that money plays a key role find it quite natural to assign great importance to the role of interest rates in determining expenditure and output. And equally, some of those for whom money is the key driving variable in the economy sometimes overlook the crucial role of interest rates in the transmission mechanism.

Of course, there may be times when the relevant interest rates are unobservable, either because of lack of data on rates charged to certain types of borrower or because of credit rationing – in which case the observed monetary flows will contain unique information. This was especially true in the circumstances of the credit crunch in the early 1990s, which affected particularly the banking systems of Japan, the United States and the Nordic countries. But this issue concerns the question of which variables we should be monitoring, rather than the underlying transmission mechanism.

1. Professor Congdon is the Managing Director of Lombard Street Research.

2. Kaldor, N. (1982) *The Scourge of Monetarism*, Oxford University Press.

(a) What is the connection between changes in money supply and changes in aggregate demand?

(b) Does the direction of causation between money supply and aggregate demand matter as far as the operation of monetary policy is concerned?

(c) Does the endogeneity of money mean that monetary policy is not important?

The following article, taken from *The Guardian* of 21 January 2002, looks at the faltering US economy and what would be necessary to bring a rise in aggregate demand. Will the boosts that were given to the economy be enough or will a more long-term strategy of boosting aggregate demand be required?

Kick-start strategy fails to fire spluttering US economic motor

Wynne Godley

Recovery in the recession-hit US economy will be under way by the second half of the year, if share prices on Wall Street are to be believed. But what, exactly, does 'recovery' mean?

'Recession' in the US is defined as two consecutive quarters of negative growth, with the corollary that positive growth, however small, qualifies as a recovery. But there is no significant difference between a decline of 0.1% per annum and growth of 0.1%; both are so far below the growth of productive potential that they would be experienced as increasingly severe recession if continued for any length of time. No growth rate much below 3% should be called 'recovery' at all, since unemployment would be rising; profits and capacity utilisation falling.

Public discussion is further distorted by Wall Street's obsession with the very short term. People who want to make money on the stock exchange try to predict what will happen during the next few months. But strategic policy formation, particularly with regard to fiscal policy, requires a time horizon several years ahead. 'Fine tuning' has decisively and permanently been discredited.

Taking such a strategic view, my belief is that, in the absence of a further large and rising stimulus from fiscal policy, the US recession will continue for several more years, at least in the form of seriously sub-normal growth, while it is easy to imagine circumstances (a world slump or a stock market crash) which would cause the absolute decline to continue.

The 90s expansion was powered uniquely and exceptionally by a huge fall in the net saving of the private sector, the scale of which is illustrated in the chart. Vertical lines mark the first quarter of 1992, when the expansion really got going, and the third quarter of 2000, when the slowdown started.

During this period the balance between the private sector's income and expenditure fell by 11.5% of GDP; in the third quarter of 2000, private expenditure exceeded income by an amount equal to 6.2% of GDP, never having exceeded it significantly at all during the previous 30 years or more. This could not have happened without a huge rise in borrowing, which made the private sector as a whole far more indebted than ever before.

The subsequent recession has clearly been associated with a reversal of this tendency. There has been a sharp fall in private expenditure relative to income since the third quarter of 2000. Yet, in the third quarter of 2001, the private sector deficit was still nearly 2.5% of GDP; much higher than in any earlier period and still enough to require so much borrowing that private debt relative to GDP rose to another peak.

The private deficit will probably recover all the way back to its normal condition of surplus, implying a continued fall in private expenditure relative to income, withdrawing 4.5%–5%, up to $500bn (£342bn), from aggregate demand. But even if the private deficit were not to recover at all, my main conclusion would still stand because the US economy would remain deprived of the motor which drove it through the 90s.

Total demand and output in the rest of the world is unusually stagnant, so net export demand may not rise at all, while the Congressional Office's fiscal projections imply no stimulus beyond the injections under consideration.

A number of factors may combine to lift aggregate demand in the very short term. A tax rebate has put $40bn into the hands of US consumers in the third quarter of 2001. This has been written off as too small to count, with GDP at about $10 trillion per annum. But while

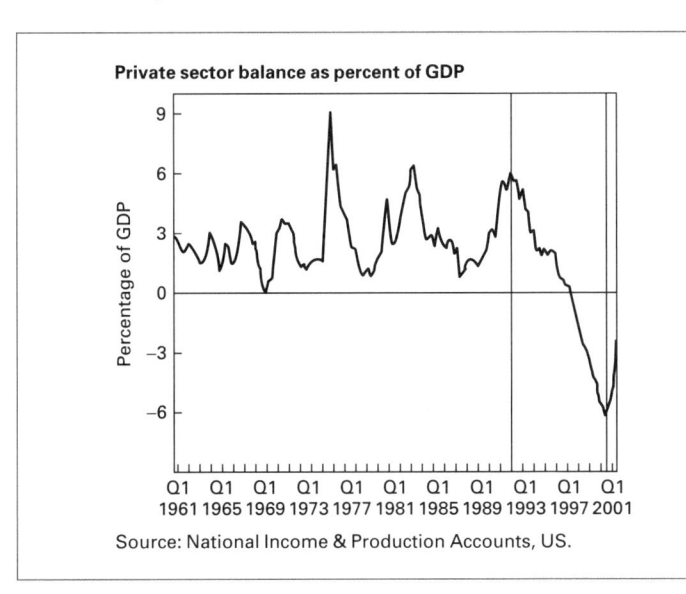

Private sector balance as percent of GDP

Source: National Income & Production Accounts, US.

the rebate is indeed less than half of 1% of a year's flow of GDP, it was 1.6% of GDP arising in the third quarter – quite enough to have a perceptible effect on spending.

Second, the huge fall in short-term interest rates has reduced mortgage rates to their lowest level for decades, lowering the interest burden on households and resulting in substantial withdrawals of equity from the housing market.

Third, there is bound soon to be a recovery in inventory investment which was heavily negative in the third quarter. And car-buying has surged as a result of zero-interest credit inducements.

All of these influences will be having a positive effect in the immediate future. However, some of them (the rebate, the equity withdrawal) will be 'blips' in the sense that their effects are once-for-all and self-reversing. Others (lower interest payments and the rise in inventory investment) while not self-reversing are nevertheless once-for-all steps, while the car splurge is likely to be self-cancelling since sales have been 'stolen' from 2002.

So, none of the factors tending to stem the recession in the short term will generate any enduring motor for expansion over the next few years. There is a strategic need, if 'growth recession' is to be avoided, for a new motor to drive the economy, particularly if there is a further decline in private expenditure relative to income which could generate a further hole in aggregate demand worth $400–$500bn. So don't get overexcited if the US gets a few good looking numbers in the next two or three months.

Professor Wynne Godley works at Cambridge Endowment for Research in Finance.

(a) What powered the 1990s expansion in the USA?
(b) Why might US aggregate demand increase in the very short term after the article was written?
(c) Why might these effects rapidly peter out?
(d) What 'enduring motor' could drive the economy so as to bring sustained expansion over the long term?

E ANSWERS

Q1. the average level of prices.
Q2. the money supply.
Q3. D. The quantity theory of money is $MV = PY$. PY, the money value of national output, is equal to MV, the total spending on national output.
Q4. (a) If we rearrange the quantity theory of money equation, then $V = PY/M$. Thus if PY = GDP at current prices = £300bn and M = M4 = £150, V = 300/150 = 2. Hence money (M4) is spent, on average, twice a year on final goods and services.
(b) If the money supply were to be cut by 50 per cent, then the velocity of circulation would have to *double* in order for total spending to remain the same and hence there to be no change in the value of final goods and services sold.
Q5. (a), (d) and (f) are all monetarist arguments, (b), (c) and (e) are Keynesian. (For a full explanation of these views, see Sloman, *Economics*, 5th edn, pp. 519–24.)
Q6. fall.
Q7. rise.
Q8. rise.
Q9. (a) and (b). See Figure A19.1.
(c) (i) *steeper*. The steeper the demand for money curve, the bigger the change in interest rates for any given change in money supply.
(ii) *flatter*. The flatter the demand for investment curve, the bigger the effect on investment for any given change in interest rates.

Figure A19.1 The effect of a change in money supply: the interest rate mechanism

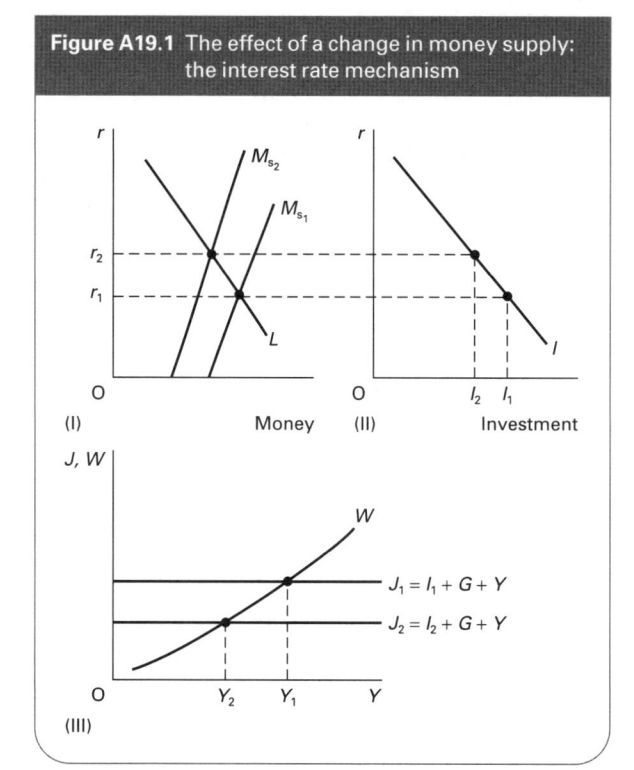

Q10. (a) and (b) are the Keynesian views. The demand-for-money curve is elastic and unstable. By contrast the monetarists see the demand-for-money curve as inelastic and stable. (The reasons for this can be found in Sloman, *Economics* (5th edn), pp. 528–9.)

Figure A19.2 The interest-rate monetary transmission mechanism

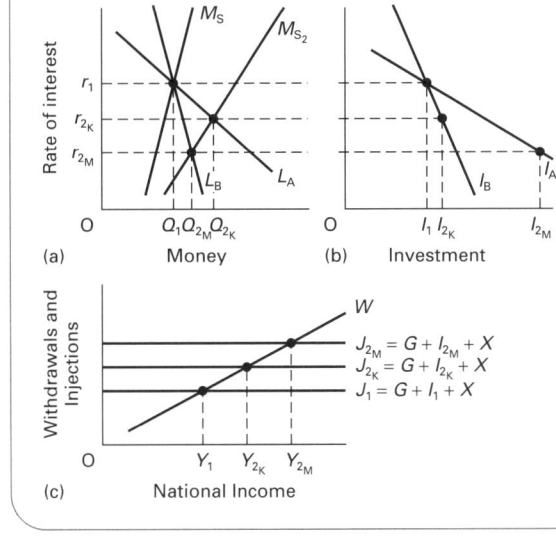

(a) Rate of interest vs Money: curves M_S, M_{S_2}, L_B, L_A; points r_1, r_{2_K}, r_{2_M} and Q_1, Q_{2_M}, Q_{2_K}.

(b) Investment: curves I_B, I_A; points I_1, I_{2_K}, I_{2_M}.

(c) Withdrawals and Injections vs National Income: line W; lines $J_{2_M} = G + I_{2_M} + X$, $J_{2_K} = G + I_{2_K} + X$, $J_1 = G + I_1 + X$; points Y_1, Y_{2_K}, Y_{2_M}.

Q11. (a) The monetarist curves are L_B and I_A. The Keynesian curves are L_A and I_B.

(b) See Figure A19.2. A rise in money supply to M_{S_2} leads to a fall in the rate of interest to r_{2_K} (Keynesian assumptions about L) or r_{2_M} (monetarist assumptions about L). This fall in the rate of interest leads to a rise in investment to I_{2_K} (Keynesian assumptions about I) or I_{2_M} (monetarist assumptions about I). This rise in investment leads to a rise in injections to J_{2_K} (Keynesian assumptions about I) or J_{2_K} (monetarist assumptions about I) and a resulting rise in national income to Y_{2_K} (Keynesian assumptions) or Y_{2_M} (monetarist assumptions).

(c) *monetarist*. (National income rises to Y_{2_M} in Figure A19.2(c).)

(d) *endogenous*. With an upward-sloping M_S curve, the level of money supply depends on the rate of interest, which in turn depends on the demand for money.

(e) *bigger*. If the money supply were exogenous (the strict monetarist assumption), the M_S curve would be vertical. A given rightward shift would lead to a bigger reduction in the rate of interest and hence a bigger increase in aggregate demand.

Q12. Because the other determinants of investment, and especially business confidence, are themselves subject to considerable fluctuations.

Q13. The points should be ordered in the following sequence; (c), (b), (e), (a) and (d). They show the effect of an increase in money supply on national income via the exchange-rate transmission mechanism.

Q14. The more rigidly fixed the exchange rate, the less its value will appreciate or depreciate. Hence the less effect changes in money supply will have via this mechanism. In fact, any attempt to alter the money supply will be largely frustrated. For example, a rise in the money supply would cause the balance of payments to go into deficit. This would then cause the money supply to fall again as reserves were used to buy in excess sterling and as interest rates had to rise again to protect the overvalued exchange rate (see Sloman, *Economics*, 5th edn, Chapter 24, Section 24.2).

Q15. B. The theory of portfolio balances argues that individuals hold their assets in various forms – money, financial assets and physical assets such as housing.

Q16. Assume that the money supply expands. As it does so, people find that their portfolios change as well: they become more liquid. The additional money may be used to purchase more securities (driving up their price and forcing down the rate of interest), or more goods and services. This readjusting of individuals' portfolios will continue until balance has been restored. In the process, spending will have increased.

Q17. B. In the case of (ii), monetarists argue that the demand for money is relatively *inelastic*. In the case of (iv), the initial tendency would be for V to *fall* as increased money supply drove down the rate of interest and encouraged people to hold *larger* money balances.

Q18. (a) The increased PSNCR will lead to an increase in the money supply if it is financed by borrowing from the Bank of England or by selling bills to the banking sector.

(b) The increased aggregate demand will lead to an increased transactions demand for money.

(c) *either*. The effect of (b) will be to increase interest rates. The effect of (a) will be to offset this. Whether interest rates do rise, and whether as a result some crowding out will occur, will depend on just how much the money supply increases.

Q19. *rise*.

Q20. *fall*.

Q21. *crowding out*.

Q22. *fall back again*.

Q23. *fall back again*.

Q24. (a), (c) and (e) are monetarist. (b), (d) and (f) are Keynesian.

Q25. *goods market*.

Q26. As interest rates fall, investment will expand and the level of saving will decrease. Both will cause a multiplied rise in national income.

Q27. *elastic*.

Q28. *inelastic*.

Q29. *inelastic*.

Q30. *elastic*.

Q31. They disagree over the responsiveness of investment and saving to changes in the rate of interest. Keynesians argue that investment and saving are relatively unresponsive, whereas the monetarists argue that they are relatively responsive.

Q32. (a), (c) and (d) will all lead to shifts to the right. They will all lead to a higher level of national income for any given rate of interest.

Q33. False. The *LM* curve shows all the various combinations of interest rates and national income at which the demand for money equals the supply ($L = M$).

Q34. As national income rises, transactions and precautionary demands for money increase, shifting the liquidity preference curve to the right. Assuming the money supply is fixed, this will lead to a rise in the rate of interest.

Q35. right.

Q36. steeper.

Q37. less.

Q38. shallower.

Q39. shallow.

Q40. steep.

Q41. The disagreement between the two groups centres on the speculative demand for money and its responsiveness to changes in the rate of interest. Keynesians argue that the speculative demand is significant and responsive to interest rate changes, and that the *LM* curve is therefore correspondingly shallow. Monetarists argue that the demand for money is relatively inelastic, and that therefore the *LM* curve is relatively steep.

Q42. *(a)* *Shift upwards*. A higher liquidity ratio will cause the supply of money to fall. This, in turn, will cause the rate of interest to rise. Thus for any given level of national income the rate of interest will be higher.

(b) *Shift upwards*. As speculation mounts, there will be an increase in the demand for money. This will cause the money demand curve to shift to the right. The rate of interest will rise at the current level of national income.

(c) *Shift downwards*. If the PSNCR is funded in this manner, the money supply will increase. The rate of interest will fall at the current level of national income.

(d) *Shift upwards*. The transactions demand for money will rise. Thus the same reasoning as in (b) applies.

(e) *Shift downwards*. If domestic currency is expected to fall in value, the demand for it will fall. The liquidity preference curve will shift left, causing the rate of interest to fall at the current level of national income.

Q43. *(a)* E.

(b) At point *A*, given national income of Y_2 and a rate of interest of r_2, the economy is in goods market equilibrium and money market disequilibrium. The rate of interest r_2 would lead to a national income of Y_2. But at this level of income the demand for money is less than the supply (point *A* is above the *LM* curve). At this level of income, the money market would be in equilibrium at point *B*, at a rate of interest of r_3.

(c) The excess supply of money will cause the rate of interest to fall. This will lead to a movement along the *IS* curve as saving declines and investment picks up. National income will rise. The higher national income will lead to an increased transactions demand for money and hence a movement up along the *LM* curve. The process will continue until point *E* is reached.

(d) At point *C*, given national income of Y_3 and a rate of interest of r_4, the economy is in money market equilibrium and goods market disequilibrium. At this low rate of interest, the desired level of investment and saving are equal at point *D*.

(e) The excess of investment over saving at point *C* will cause the level of national income to rise. This will lead to a movement up along the *LM* curve and a rise in the rate of interest. As the rate of interest rises, the desired level of investment will fall and saving increase. This will cause a movement back along the *IS* curve until equilibrium is reached at point *E*.

(f) (i) This will cause the *LM* curve to shift downwards (towards a point such as *D*) as the money supply expands. The equilibrium rate of interest will fall and the level of national income will rise. The new equilibrium in both markets will be where the new *LM* curve intersects with the *IS* curve. (Thus in the case of point *D*, the equilibrium rate of interest would be r_4 and the equilibrium level of national income would be Y_4.)

(ii) This will cause the *IS* curve to shift right, towards a point such as *F*. This pushes interest rates and national income upwards. The new equilibrium is where the new *IS* curve intersects with the *LM* curve. In the case of point *F*, this would give a national income of Y_5 and a rate of interest of r_2.

Q44. True. This is shown by a movement up along the *ADI* curve (e.g. from point *a* to point *b* in Figure 19.4).

Q45. D. The lower interest rates will cause a higher level of aggregate demand (a movement down along the curve) and hence a higher level of real national income. Similarly, the central bank will raise interest rates if inflation rises above its target level, thereby reducing real national income.

Q46. (a) *False.* The more rapidly the central bank wants to get inflation back to target, the more it will change interest rates and hence the more real income will change and hence the *shallower* will be the curve.

(b) *True.* It will only change the rate of interest by a small amount, so as not to have a big effect on aggregate demand and hence on real national income.

(c) *False.* The more responsive the components of aggregate demand are to a change in interest rates, the bigger will be the effect on real national income and hence the *shallower* the curve.

Q47. Real national income is at Y_2 because the central bank has raised interest rates in response to the higher inflation. As inflation falls in response to the higher interest rate, so the rate of interest can be reduced somewhat. There will be a move back down the curve towards point *a*.

Q48. A. This is a movement along the curve. A rate of inflation below target will cause the central bank to reduce interest rates. This will raise real national income. Note that in B, a higher target rate of inflation will lead to a lower interest rate being set for each rate of inflation, thereby shifting the *ADI* curve to the right.

Q49. (a) Y_4 (where ADI_2 crosses the target rate of inflation line).

(b) Y_3. The upward-sloping *ASI* curve illustrates the effects of both quantity *and* inflation adjustment to changes in the level of aggregate demand. Equilibrium is at point *b*.

(c) Y_2. Since point *b* is above the target rate of inflation, the central bank will have to raise its target rate of interest, so as to shift the *ADI* curve back to ADI_1, giving equilibrium back at point *a*.

Q50. (a) The rightward shift in the *ASI* curve will cause it to cross the *ADI* curve (ADI_1) at a rate of inflation below target.

(b) Assume that the permanent increase in aggregate supply is represented by a new *ASI* curve passing through point *c*. Once the central bank realises that this is a permanent increase in aggregate supply, it will lower the target rate of interest. This will shift the *ADI* curve to the right. Long-run equilibrium will be at point *c*.

Q51. *True.* In the case of a temporary supply shock, the central bank will adjust the actual rate of interest to bring the economy back to target at the sustainable level of real national income. There will be a movement along the *ADI* curve. In the case of a permanent supply-side change, the target rate of interest will have to be changed in order to cause a shift in the *ADI* curve to match the shift in the *ASI* curve.

Chapter Twenty

20

Fiscal and Monetary Policy

A REVIEW

In this chapter we look at the two types of policy for controlling aggregate demand: fiscal and monetary policy. Fiscal policy seeks to control aggregate demand by altering the balance between government expenditure (an injection into the circular flow of income) and taxation (a withdrawal). Monetary policy seeks to control aggregate demand by directly controlling the money supply, or by altering the rate of interest and then backing this up by any necessary change in money supply.

20.1 The nature of fiscal policy

(Pages 543–6) Fiscal policy involves altering the size of the *budget deficit* or *budget surplus*.

Q1. If the government runs a budget deficit, this will necessarily cause an increase in national income.

True/False

The size of the budget deficit or surplus is linked to the size of the *public-sector net cash requirement* (PSNCR).

Q2. The public-sector net cash requirement is defined as:
A. the amount central government has to borrow in a given year.
B. the national debt.
C. the increase in government securities in a given year.
D. the excess of public-sector spending over public-sector receipts in a given year.
E. the budget deficit in a given year.

Q3. Explain why the size of the public-sector deficit or surplus will be influenced by the level of national income.

....

....

Q4. Fiscal stance refers to:
A. the total level of government spending.
B. whether the government supports the use of fiscal policies to manage the economy.
C. the effect of the budget deficit or surplus on the level of aggregate demand.
D. the existence of inflationary or deflationary gaps in the economy.
E. the size of the government's budget surplus or deficit.

Q5. Those taxes and government expenditures that increase and decrease respectively as national income rises are called:

....

The more that taxes increase and government expenditure decreases as national income rises, the **Q6.** *larger/smaller* will be the multiplier. What is more, if taxes are progressive, then *ceteris paribus*, a rise in national income will cause the multiplier to **Q7.** *rise/fall*.

(Pages 547–8) Discretionary fiscal policy refers to the specific adjustment of government expenditure and/or taxation with the aim of influencing the level of aggregate demand.

≡ *Multiple choice*   ? *Written answer*   ◐ *Delete wrong word*   ⊖ *Diagram/table manipulation*   ✕ *Calculation*   ▨ *Matching/ordering*

Q8. Which of the following fiscal policy measures would have an expansionary and which a contractionary impact upon the level of economic activity?
(a) A cut in direct taxation.
expansionary/contractionary
(b) A rise in personal allowances.
expansionary/contractionary
(c) An increase in the PSBR.
expansionary/contractionary
(d) A reduction in social security benefits.
expansionary/contractionary
(e) A move from a budget deficit to a budget surplus.
expansionary/contractionary

The multiplier effect of increasing government expenditure by £xm is different from that of reducing taxes by £xm. The tax multiplier is given by $\Delta Y/\Delta T$.

Q9. The tax multiplier is smaller than the government expenditure multiplier. *True/False*

Q10. If the mpc_d is 0.75, the tax multiplier is:
A. 4
B. −4
C. 3
D. −3
E. −1⅓

Q11. If investment exceeds saving by £10m and there is a balance of payments surplus of £30m, then for the economy to be in equilibrium there must be a:
A. budget deficit of £40m.
B. budget surplus of £40m.
C. budget deficit of £20m.
D. budget surplus of £20m.
E. budget balance.

20.2 The effectiveness of fiscal policy
(Pages 549–56) One problem with fiscal policy is that it can lead to 'crowding out'.

Q12. Crowding out is defined as:
A. increased public expenditure replacing private-sector expenditure.
B. increased taxes pushing up interest rates.
C. when there are insufficient tax revenues to finance increased government expenditure.
D. the difficulty some people find in paying their taxes.
E. that part of public expenditure financed from borrowing.

Q13. Give three reasons why it is difficult to forecast the magnitude of the impact of fiscal policy on the economy.

1. ....
2. ....
3. ....

Q14. Fiscal policy suffers from a number of timing problems. Match the following problems to the various time lags between a problem occurring and the full final effect of fiscal policy measures taken to correct the problem.
 (i) The time taken for the multiplier process to work.
 (ii) The long-run consumption function is different from the short-run one.
(iii) The business cycle is irregular.
(iv) Administrative delays.
 (v) The Budget occurs only once a year.

(a) Time lag to recognition. ....
(b) Time lag between recognition and changes being announced.
....
(c) Time lag between changes being announced and changes coming into force.
....
(d) Time lag between changes in taxes and government expenditure and the resulting changes in national income.
....
(e) Time lag before people's spending patterns adjust fully to changes in incomes.
....

20.3 Varieties of monetary policy
(Page 556)
Q15. Which of the following would be classified as monetary policy? The attempt to:
(a) reduce the level of taxation. *Yes/No*
(b) control the supply of money by various means. *Yes/No*
(c) regulate wages by the use of formal agreements with unions. *Yes/No*
(d) ration credit. *Yes/No*
(e) manipulate aggregate demand via the use of interest rates. *Yes/No*
(f) regulate aggregate demand through changes in government spending. *Yes/No*

(Pages 556–7) Controlling the growth of the money supply over the medium and long term
Q16. Which one of the following would not be a cause of growth in the money supply?
A. The banks decide to hold a lower liquidity ratio.
B. There is a total currency flow surplus on the balance of payments.
C. The PSBR is financed by selling Treasury bills to the banking sector.
D. The government imposes a statutory reserve ratio on banks that is higher than their current reserve ratio.
E. National income rises and money supply is endogenous.

272 CHAPTER 20 FISCAL AND MONETARY POLICY

If over the longer term the government wishes to control the growth of the money supply, it will have to tackle the underlying causes.

? Q17. Give the two major sources of a long-term growth in the money supply.

1. ....

2. ....

One way of restricting the growth in private-sector borrowing would be to impose statutory reserve requirements on banks.

? Q18. Why do monetarists oppose statutory reserve requirements?

....

....

Q19. Goodhart's law states that 'to control an indicator is to distort its accuracy as an indicator'. An example of this law when applied to monetary policy is that:
A. all forms of intervention in financial markets will have little impact on the money supply.
B. regulation in one part of the financial system will divert business to other areas of the financial system.
C. government borrowing will lead to financial crowding out.
D. control of the money supply will not be possible without control of the PSNCR.
E. private-sector borrowing is a more important determinant of monetary growth than is public-sector borrowing.

If there is a substantial PSNCR, it is nevertheless possible to avoid an increase in the money supply by financing the PSNCR by government borrowing from **Q20.** *the banking sector/the non-bank private sector*. If the government does this, however, there is likely to be a problem of financial crowding out. This will involve **Q21.** *higher/lower* interest rates and **Q22.** *more/less* private-sector borrowing.

This financial crowding out will be reduced, however (but there will be less reduction in the growth of aggregate demand), if the velocity of circulation of circulation **Q23.** *increases/decreases*. This change in the velocity of circulation will be greater the **Q24.** *more/less* elastic the liquidity preference curve that we looked at in Chapter 18.

(Pages 558–64) Short-term methods of monetary control
There are three approaches to short-term monetary control: controlling the *supply* of money; controlling the *demand* for money by controlling interest rates; rationing credit.

Controlling the supply of money will involve manipulating the liquid assets of the banking sector.

Q25. The following are methods of controlling banks' liquidity base:
(i) open-market operations
(ii) the central bank changing the amount it lends to banks
(iii) funding
(iv) changing minimum reserve ratios

Match each of the following actions of a central bank to the above methods of control, and in each case state whether money supply will *increase* or *decrease*. (In each case, assume that the actions are not in response to changes in the PSNCR.)
(a) It sells more government bonds but reduces the value of Treasury Bills sold by the same amount thereby keeping total government borrowing the same.
(i)/(ii)/(iii)/(iv); increase/decrease
(b) It sells more government bonds (but the same amount of Treasury bills). *(i)/(ii)/(iii)/(iv); increase/decrease*
(c) It buys back bonds from banks under a repo agreement.
(i)/(ii)/(iii)/(iv); increase/decrease
(d) It requires banks to hold a larger proportion of liquid assets. *(i)/(ii)/(iii)/(iv); increase/decrease*
(e) It sells fewer bonds and bills.
(i)/(ii)/(iii)/(iv); increase/decrease
(f) It replaces £1m of gilts that are maturing with £1m extra Treasury bills. *(i)/(ii)/(iii)/(iv); increase/decrease*
(g) It keeps its interest rate to the banks below market rates, but then reduces the amount it allows banks to borrow at that rate. *(i)/(ii)/(iii)/(iv); increase/decrease*

Q26. If banks operate a rigid 10 per cent liquidity ratio and the Bank of England repurchases £10m of government bonds on the open market, what will be the eventual size of the change in the level of bank advances?

....

(Pages 564–5) The prime form of monetary policy in the UK has been to control *interest rates*.

Q27. Interest rates are controlled by the Bank of England through its operations in the discount and repo markets. *True/False*

Q28. Assume that the Bank of England decides that it wants a rise in the rate of interest and conducts open-market operations in the discount market to achieve this. What should it do if:
(a) banks have excess liquidity?
Buy/Sell more/fewer bills.
(b) banks are currently having to borrow from the Bank of England? *Buy/Sell more/fewer* bills.

Q29. On most days, there is a shortage of liquidity in the banking system. Which one of the following operations in the gilt repo market does the Bank of England conduct to maintain interest rates at the level chosen by the Monetary Policy Committee?

A. It buys bonds from the banks at its chosen interest rate on condition that the banks must sell the bonds to other banks later.
B. It sells bonds to the banks at its chosen interest rate on condition that the banks must sell the bonds to other banks later.
C. It buys bonds from the banks at its chosen interest rate on condition that the banks must buy them back again later from the Bank of England.
D. It sells bonds to the banks at its chosen interest rate on condition that the banks sell them back to the Bank of England later.
E. It buys bonds from the non-bank sector at its chosen interest rate on condition that the banks must buy them later from the Bank of England.

20.4 Problems of monetary policy

(Pages 565–6) It is difficult to control the growth of the money supply over the medium and longer term without controlling the size of the PSNCR. This can also be difficult, however.

Q30. Which of the following make the control of PSNCR difficult?
(a) The political desirability of cutting taxes. *Yes/No*
(b) The political desirability of increasing government expenditure. *Yes/No*
(c) Automatic fiscal stabilisers in times of a boom. *Yes/No*
(d) Automatic fiscal stabilisers in times of stagflation (recession plus inflation). *Yes/No*
(e) Pressure on the government to increase expenditure on education, R&D and transport infrastructure as a means of improving productivity and long-term growth. *Yes/No*
(f) An ageing population. *Yes/No*

(Pages 566–8) Controlling the money supply is difficult whether the authorities use monetary base control or attempt to control broad liquidity.

Q31. What is meant by 'monetary base control'?

....

....

Q32. Four of the following are problems associated with monetary base control. One is not. Which one?
A. Banks could currently have a cash ratio above their prudent (or statutory) level.
B. Goodhart's law.
C. Disintermediation.
D. There may be a high demand for liquidity in the financial system.
E. The Bank of England will always lend money to banks if demanded.

Q33. Give two problems for the authorities in attempting to control broad liquidity.

1. ....

2. ....

Q34. If the government is successful in keeping the money supply stable, it will have succeeded in keeping interest rates stable too. *True/False*

(Pages 568–9) Credit rationing may seem to be the solution to the problems of monetary control. Governments around the world, however, are increasingly opposed to it.

Q35. Which of the following statements about credit rationing are correct?
(a) It reduces competition and thus creates inefficiency. *True/False*
(b) It leads to interest rates being higher than they would be otherwise. *True/False*
(c) It will have an uneven impact upon different sectors of the economy. *True/False*
(d) Goodhart's law is likely to apply. *True/False*
(e) It only affects lending indirectly. *True/False*

Q36. In the short run the supply of money is to a large extent demand determined. Why?

....

....

(Pages 569–70) Because the supply of money is demand determined in the short run, monetary policy has tended to concentrate on controlling the demand for loans via the control of interest rates. This, however, may require the authorities setting very high interest rates. This is because the demand for loans is relatively interest **Q37.** *elastic/inelastic*.

Q38. A tight monetary policy involving high interest rates can lead to a number of related problems. Identify which of the following might be a consequence of such a policy.
(a) Reduced investment. *Yes/No*
(b) A deteriorating competitive position overseas. *Yes/No*
(c) Increased costs of production. *Yes/No*
(d) Slow growth in potential output. *Yes/No*
(e) Expensive for the government to maintain. *Yes/No*
(f) Increased cost-push pressures. *Yes/No*

*20.5 ISLM *analysis of fiscal and monetary policy*

(Pages 571–3) Fiscal and monetary poliy

Q39. Using the two diagrams in Figure 20.1, illustrate the following situations.

(a) Government expenditure grows and is financed by an expansion in the money supply. Avoid any crowding out in your model.

(b) Business expectations deteriorate and in response the government expands the money supply in order to maintain the level of aggregate demand.

Figure 20.1 (a) Increased government expenditure and increased money supply
(b) Deteriorating business expectations and increased money supply

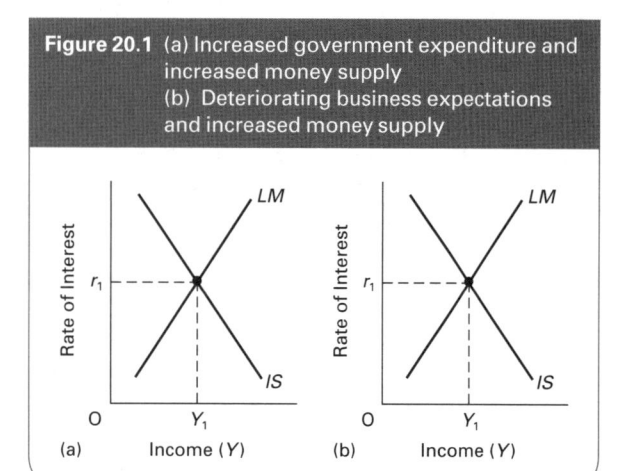

Q40. Using Figure 20.2 sketch the following effects of government policy. On diagrams (a) and (b) sketch *ISLM* curves to represent a contractionary fiscal and contractionary monetary policy from a Keynesian perspective. On (c) and (d) sketch *ISLM* curves to represent contractionary fiscal and contractionary monetary policy from a monetarist perspective.

Figure 20.2 Keynesian and monetarist views on fiscal and monetary policy

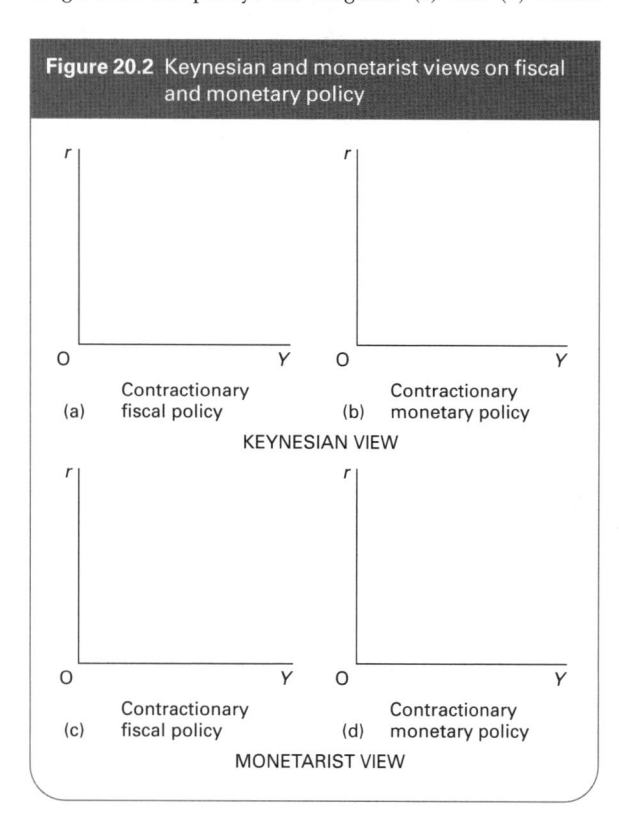

20.6 Fiscal and monetary policy in the UK

(Pages 573–81)

Q41. Which of the following arguments would a Keynesian use concerning government macroeconomic intervention in the economy?

(a) The management of aggregate demand by the government can reduce the degree of instability in the economy. *Yes/No*

(b) Control over the money supply is the best way to regulate aggregate demand in the short run. *Yes/No*

(c) Control over the money supply is the best way to regulate aggregate demand in long run. *Yes/No*

(d) The 'natural' state of the market system is one of disequilibrium. *Yes/No*

(e) 'Intervention' should focus on removing government barriers to the free operation of the market. *Yes/No*

(f) The business cycle is damaging to economic performance. *Yes/No*

(g) Fine tuning can reduce cyclical fluctuations. *Yes/No*

Q42. What was the dominant constraint on demand-led growth policies in the 1950s and 1960s?

A. The level of unemployment.
B. Time lags.
C. Money supply targets.
D. The balance of payments.
E. The size of the budget deficit.

Q43. List five possible causes of the stagflation experienced by the UK economy in the 1970s.

1. ....
2. ....
3. ....
4. ....
5. ....

Q44. Which of the following policies were pursued by the Thatcher government in the early 1980s?

(a) The setting of targets for the growth in the money supply. *Yes/No*

(b) Attempts to cut the PSNCR. *Yes/No*

(c) The implementation of statutory requirements. *Yes/No*

(d) Reductions in the rate of income tax. *Yes/No*

(e) The use of incomes policy to regulate the growth of wages. *Yes/No*

(f) The tendering of public-sector services to the private sector. *Yes/No*

Q45. List three problems that were encountered.

1. ....

2. ....

3. ....

Q46. Were any economic indicators targeted in the late 1980s, and if so, what?

....

Q47. UK entry into the ERM (the exchange rate mechanism of the European Monetary System) meant that government had less discretion in monetary policy than before. *True/False*

Q48. Which one of the following was a direct consequence of UK membership of the ERM?
A. The rate of inflation was driven up to the European average.
B. Fiscal policy was dominated by European budgetary issues.
C. The money supply grew more rapidly.
D. Aggregate demand was caused to expand faster than the government had wished.
E. Interest rates had to be set at whatever level was necessary to maintain the exchange rate.

Q49. Since 1992, the main focus of UK demand-side policy has been the control of inflation. *True/False*

Q50. If the UK rate of inflation is forecast to be below $2^{1}/_{2}$ per cent, the Monetary Policy Committee of the Bank of England is obliged to reduce the rate of interest. *True/False*

Q51. If the rate of inflation for the eurozone countries is forecast to be below 2 per cent, the ECB is obliged to reduce the rate of interest. *True/False*

20.7 Rules versus discretion
(Pages 582–6)

Q52. Outline the monetarist case in favour of rules.

....

....

....

Q53. Outline the Keynesian case in favour of discretion.

....

....

....

....

Q54. To take account of the fact that achieving the target rate of inflation may nevertheless still be consistent with fluctuations in national income, some economists have advocated following a 'Taylor rule'. This means that:
A. National output is targeted rather than inflation.
B. The central bank will *reduce* interest rates if inflation is above target, for fear of an impending recession.
C. Real national income and inflation will, as a result, vary inversely.
D. The amount that interest rates rise when inflation rises depends on the relative weights attached to divergences of inflation and real national income from their respective targets.
E. Inflation is less likely to diverge from its target.

B PROBLEMS, EXERCISES AND PROJECTS

Q55. Table 20.1 shows the consumption schedule for a closed economy (i.e. one that does not trade with other countries). Investment is currently £40bn.
(a) Assuming that the government is currently spending £20bn, what is the equilibrium level of national income?

....

Table 20.1 National income and consumption for country A (£bn)

National income	30	60	90	120	150	180	210	240	270	300
Consumption	20	40	60	80	100	120	140	160	180	200

(b) Assuming that at this equilibrium level of national income the government is running a budget deficit of £5bn, what must be the level of saving in the economy?

....

(c) What is the government expenditure multiplier?

....

(d) What is the tax multiplier?

....

Q56. Referring to Q55, assume that full employment is achieved at a national income of £240bn.

(a) What is the size of the deflationary gap?

....

(b) How much would government expenditure have to be raised (assuming no change in tax rates) in order to close this gap?

....

(c) Alternatively, how much would taxes have to be changed (assuming no change in government expenditure) in order to close the gap?

....

(d) Alternatively, assume now that the government decides that it wants to close the gap and *also* to balance its budget (i.e. to raise taxes £5bn more than it raises government expenditure). How much must it raise government expenditure and how much must it raise taxes?

....

....

Q57. The Budget is when the Chancellor of the Exchequer announces changes in taxation and government expenditure for the coming financial year commencing 5 April. Using references that you have available, find out the main fiscal measures in the most recent Budget. Assess how these measures related to the state of the economy at the time of the Budget, and how the economy was forecast to change in the future. This may require your referring to government statistics. These can be found in *Economic Trends* (NS), *Financial Statistics* (NS) and the *Annual Abstract of Statistics* (NS). Forecasts of economic performance can be found in the Treasury's *Financial Statement and Budget Report* (published at the time of the Budget). Independent forecasts and assessments can be found in the quality press. There is usually a wealth of information in the press concerning the Budget and the state of the economy at the end of March (when the Budget is usually held). Information on the Budget can also be found at the following two Web addresses:

http://www.hm-treasury.gov.uk/
http://www.ft.com/

Q58. Using relevant statistical sources, such as *Financial Statistics* (NS), the *Annual Abstract of Statistics* (NS) and the *Bank of England Quarterly Bulletin*, investigate recent movements in the various monetary aggregates. See also the National Statistics Web site at http://www.statistics.gov.uk and the Monetary and Financial Statistics part of the Bank of England's Web site at http://www.bankofengland.co.uk/mfsd/index.htm. How do such movements compare with those in earlier years? Does this tell you anything about the current tightness of monetary policy and the economic position of the UK economy?

Q59. Assume that the banking sector's assets and liabilities consist of the following items: cash £10m; advances £60m; time deposits £50m; bonds £15m; market loans £10m; bills £5m; sight deposits £40m; certificates of deposit in the banking system £10m. Assume that there are no other items.

(a) Compile a balance sheet for the banking sector.
(b) What is its current cash ratio?
(c) What is its current liquidity ratio?

Assume in each of the following that banks want to maintain the *cash* ratio in (b) above. What will be the effect of each of the following?

(d) An open-market purchase by the central bank of £1m of bonds.
(e) An open-market sale by the central bank of £5m of bonds.
(f) An open-market sale by the central bank of £2m of bills, where these bills are purchased by the banking sector.
(g) An open-market sale by the central bank of £2m of bills, where these bills are purchased by the non-banking sector.

Assume in each of the following that banks want to maintain the *liquidity* ratio in (c) above. What will be the effect of each of the following?

(h) An open-market purchase by the central bank of £1m of bonds.
(i) An open-market sale by the central bank of £5m of bonds.
(j) An open-market sale by the central bank of £2m of bills, where these bills are purchased by the banking sector.
(k) An open-market sale by the central bank of £2m of bills, where these bills are purchased by the non-banking sector.

Q60. Using the Bank of England and Treasury Web sites, http://www.bankofengland.co.uk/ and http://www.hm-treasury.gov.uk/, and the Bank of England's *Inflation Report*, trace the decisions of the Bank of England's Monetary Policy Committee on interest rates over the past two years. Why were the changes made? In retrospect, were they the correct decisions?

Alternatively you could answer this question in terms of the interest rate decisions of another central bank, such as the European Central Bank (see http://www.ecb.int/) or the US Federal Reserve Bank (see http://www.federalreserve.gov/).

Q61. In small groups, write a commentary on the use of demand management policy in the UK over the past three years.

The report should include (a) evidence on the performance of economic growth, unemployment and inflation and (b) a description of the fiscal and monetary policy measures that were taken.

By examining the evidence and reading commentaries, you should attempt to assess how successful the fiscal and monetary policies have been. Remember that fiscal and monetary policies take a time to work and therefore you will need to look at the lagged effects of policies taken some time before.

Consider whether there have been any 'economic shocks' (such as wars, trade disputes, stock market turbulence, etc.) and whether fiscal and monetary policies have been able to offset the effects of these shocks.

Good sources of evidence are the Treasury, Bank of England and Financial Times Web sites (see hotlinks section on the Sloman *Economics* Web site at http://www.booksites.net/sloman).

C   DISCUSSION TOPICS AND ESSAYS

Q62. 'The existence of a budget deficit or a budget surplus tells us very little about the stance of fiscal policy.' Explain and discuss.

Q63. What factors might prevent the government from effectively fine tuning the economy?

Q64. Adam Smith remarked in *The Wealth of Nations* concerning the balancing of budgets, 'What is prudence in the conduct of every private family can scarce be folly in that of a great kingdom.' Should the government follow a balanced budget approach to its spending?

Q65. Aaron Wildavsky refers to the Treasury's forecasting as 'a compound of knowledge, hunch and intuition'. What difficulties are there in forecasting the effects of changes in fiscal policy? What are the future policy implications if past and present policies are based on inaccurate forecasts? Give some hypothetical examples.

Q66. What are the advantages and disadvantages of the government sticking to a fiscal rule? (An example of such a rule is the UK Labour government's 'golden rule', whereby the government pledges that, over the economic cycle, it will borrow only to invest and not to fund current spending.)

Q67. 'The problems of magnitude and the problems of timing conspire to make fiscal policy unpredictable. As such, intervention of this sort should be avoided and the government should aim to balance its budget.' Discuss.

Q68. What is the relationship between the money supply and the public-sector net cash requirement?

Q69. When the Bank of England's Monetary Policy Committee announces that it is putting up interest rates, how will it achieve this, given that interest rates are determined by supply and demand?

Q70. How might the targeting of a foreign exchange rate value be a means of controlling inflation?

Q71. 'It is impossible to target both the money supply and the rate of interest. If you control one, you have to let the other be as it will.' Discuss.

Q72. Are targeting the rate of inflation and targeting the rate of growth in the money supply compatible policies?

Q73. Use *ISLM* analysis to explain the difference in monetarist and Keynesian views on the efficacy of fiscal and monetary policies.

Q74. What was stagflation? What reasons have been advanced to explain the stagflation experienced by the British economy during the 1970s? What problems did stagflation create for the management of economic affairs during this period?

Q75. Outline and assess the success or otherwise of the monetarist experiment in the 1980s.

Q76. 'Discretionary demand management policy in the UK between 1990 and 1992, like that in the early 1980s, was made virtually impossible by the adherence to a policy rule. The rule was a different one, but the effects were similar.' Do you agree?

Q77. To extent has the policy of targeting a $2^{1}/_{2}$ per cent rate of inflation in the UK, with the Bank of England independently setting interest rates to achieve this, been a successful macroeconomic strategy?

Q78. Debate
The only way of achieving a stable macroeconomic environment is to set clear macroeconomic targets and then stick to them.

Articles

In the following article, taken from the *Financial Times* of 18 April 2002, four economists evaluate the measures undertaken by the Chancellor in his April 2002 Budget.

Four economists have a say on Brown's measures

Juli Collins-Thompson
BNP Paribas

The 2002 Budget confirmed that 'Old Labour' style fiscal policy is slowly resurfacing. The massive rise in public expenditure was on the larger side of expectations but, unsurprisingly, directed at the NHS, after years of underspending and underinvestment. Gordon Brown also stuck by his characteristic run of micro-style measures – to the benefit of enterprise, pensioners, working families and the environment.

With regard to the implications for monetary policy, the key point is what this Budget implies for the overall fiscal stance. Mr Brown has largely offset the stimulus of spending cuts with tax increases, leaving the net fiscal position in the coming three years little changed from the projections in the pre-Budget report. The change in the cyclically-adjusted Budget balance out to 2004/05 indicates a fiscal ease of about 1 per cent of GDP. The Bank of England's monetary policy committee has already incorporated such a scenario in its economic outlook, and thus does not change my view that the Bank will hold off hiking rates until the third quarter.

However, there is the question of what the rise in national insurance taxation for employers will mean for the inflation profile further out, given the associated rise in employers' cost base. The improved outlook for growth, which looks realistic in our opinion, was behind the moderate downward revisions to the Treasury's borrowing projections out to 2003/04. Yet, public borrowing is expected to deteriorate further out to its highest levels since 1996/97.

Simon Rubinsohn
Chief economist, Gerrard

This was always going to be a Budget designed to provide more resources for the NHS and, in this respect, the chancellor did not disappoint. While the magnitudes involved are large, they are in truth not far away from expectations.

However, there were a number of surprises that could yet have ramifications for Gordon Brown's overall strategy. For a start, the increase in the trend rate of growth means that the fiscal arithmetic even on the most cautious case is based on more upbeat economic assumptions than was felt to be appropriate last year. Whether this change is warranted is a point for debate but it does crucially increase projected receipts and thus provides the scope to raise spending levels significantly while also lifting the projected surplus on the current Budget.

The other big unexpected development was the increase in national insurance contributions on employers. The risk here is the knock-on effect on profits could have some adverse impact on planned investment which, interestingly, the Treasury forecasts see as playing a key role in driving growth next year.

Although the actual level of borrowing for this financial year is slightly lower than projected in the pre-Budget report it is hard to make the case that the chancellor is tightening policy in the near term. The minutes of the April meeting of the monetary policy committee suggest that the authorities are willing to give consumers a little more time to moderate spending but it is improbable that the tax-raising measures designed to take effect from next year will have much immediate impact on high-street activity.

Ian McCafferty
Confederation of British Industry chief economic adviser

In opening his Budget, the chancellor highlighted the 'challenge of enterprise' – the need to stimulate entrepreneurship. He then announced a number of measures to achieve this aim. But, having given with one hand, he quickly took it all back with the other.

The measures on R&D tax credits and training initiatives were steps in the right direction, the additional help for smaller businesses to focus on employee training, through assistance with the costs of Investors in People, was very welcome. The CBI had also sought the R&D tax credit, though to be fully effective it needs to be big enough to change business behaviour. The amount allocated could have been closer to £1bn than the £400m announced. Other cuts in taxes for small and medium-size enterprises were also of value.

But the rise in employers' national insurance contributions from 2003 overshadows these benefits. As a result, rather than starting to roll back the business tax burden, this Budget has increased it by a further £2bn. Although delayed a year, the rising cost of employment will hit businesses hard. It could tip some companies from profit into loss, at which point tax credits on profits cease to have relevance.

Some of the increased spending on the NHS comes not from 'real' tax increases but from shifting the assumptions underlying the fiscal projections, with the underlying annual GDP growth assumption nudged up from 2.25 per cent to 2.5 per cent. This adds £1bn–£2bn to the annual pot in future years.

Nevertheless, consumers have also been hit, with a net tax rise of £500m over the next two years. The one silver lining is that the damping of consumer sentiment that will result should give the monetary policy committee more room to hold interest rates at current levels for some time.

Michael Hume,
Lehman Brothers Global Economics

This is the first tax-and-spend Budget since Denis Healey's inaugural Budget of 1974. It is highly redistributive, with middle- and high-income earners being asked to pay for higher spending on public services and welfare payments. So, is this a New Labour or an Old Labour Budget? Most definitely New Labour. Although bigger than expected, the tax-and-spend measures announced yesterday are still small, amounting to less than 1 per cent of GDP over four years. That is a mere fifth of what Old Labour put into effect in 1974–6. However, the chancellor has become less cautious in his projections. He has raised the trend rate of GDP growth and factored in about £1bn of extra revenues from anti-avoidance measures, both of which might prove hard to achieve. Consequently, while the government's finances remain on a sound footing in the near term, they are looking increasingly vulnerable to a downturn in economic fortunes further ahead.

The fiscal impact on the economy is negligible and will not alter the trend towards growing economic convergence between the UK and the euro area. Consequently, the chancellor has left the door wide open for a positive assessment of his 'five tests' early next year. However, he has done little to deal with the problem of sterling's overvaluation.

The tax hikes on the personal sector will encourage the Bank of England's monetary policy committee to expect a slowdown in consumer spending. But crucially, the interest rate outlook will be determined by what happens to the global economy over the next six months. On that front the signs remain positive, so base rates are still likely to end the year at more than 5 per cent.

(a) From the four views, how dependent is the success of the Chancellor's measures on the accuracy of the forecasts of growth made in the Budget? What problems are there in forecasting future growth?

(b) From the views expressed, would you say the Budget was expansionary, contractionary or neutral? Explain your answer.

(c) Some commentators claimed that the Budget was a tax on jobs and would reduce investment. What evidence would you need to test this claim?

As part of the process of convergence within the EU, the European heads of government agreed to balance their budgets by 2004. They recognised that the benefits to the euro and the European economy as a whole from such a move would be immense. However, words are cheap. The following article, taken from *BusinessWeek* of 3 June 2002, evaluates the difficulties facing a number of EU economies in meeting such a target.

So much for discipline

John Rossant and David Fairlamb

The EU is facing a crisis as budgets balloon and nations square off

Fiscal probity above all. That was the do-or-die pledge made by European heads of government at a meeting in Barcelona just last March. One by one, the key nations of Europe solemnly agreed to balance their budgets by 2004, even if it meant telling voters that generous benefits had to be cut. Welfare state largesse is nice, but balanced budgets translate into lower interest rates, investor confidence, a strong euro, and good growth. All that is needed is a little discipline. It's the next step in building a stronger Europe, a more united Europe.

Fat chance. Already, Germany, France, Portugal, and Italy are having problems reining in large budget deficits, mainly because of a stronger-than-expected economic downturn in the euro zone last year and an anemic recovery this year. The ever-vigilant European Commission triggered a kind of early warning mechanism in February by threatening to issue a formal reprimand to Germany and Portugal about their bulging deficits – which are fast approaching the 3% of GDP that is the ceiling for all euro zone countries.

Political pressure from Berlin, along with pledges to rein in spending, have forestalled punitive measures in Germany's case. Portugal, too, escaped rebuke, since its center-right government has promised to enact austerity measures. Yet the struggle for a new, more responsible Europe is far from over. In fact, it's just heating up. Since the high-water mark of European unity in 1992, when the Maastricht Treaty put the finishing touches on monetary union, European leaders have been postponing crucial decisions. From fiscal discipline and rules for bringing in new EU members, to new power arrangements in Brussels, 'the problems are now coming home to roost, and it's all looking a bit unpleasant,' says Charles Wyplosz, director of the International Center for Monetary & Banking Studies at the University of Geneva and an adviser to the French government.

That's an understatement. Things are getting downright nasty. Start with the core relationship in Europe – the nexus of power and authority that connects Germany and France. The two countries once set the pace for reform in Europe. Now, instead of planning with Paris how to restore the momentum on reform, the Germans are accusing the French of being the biggest budget-busters around. On May 14, only hours before French President Jacques Chirac's new Foreign Minister, Dominique de Villepin, was set to land in Berlin, German Finance Minister Hans Eichel launched an unprecedented public attack on Chirac. The French President plans to stimulate the economy through more government spending and tax cuts – even if that breaks commitments to the rest of Europe to balance the books. 'I don't see how Chirac can vote [to balance France's budget], and then say a month or two later it no longer applies,' said Eichel. 'If the French don't toe the line, all the euro zone states could lose credibility in the markets.' In private, German government officials have been even more scathing. 'France has lost the political leadership of Europe,' says one aide to Chancellor Gerhard Schröder.

Chirac is trying to repair the damage by renewing his pledge to rein in France's budget deficit. But the reality is that he must fulfill his campaign promise to cut 5% off French income taxes. Given this political bind, it's hard to see how Paris can balance the books before 2007. Such a delay would clearly violate the Growth & Stability Pact, the treaty everyone signed to ensure fiscal discipline. The Germans are left wondering why they should hold up their end of the bargain. 'It's bizarre that we and the Portuguese are trying to cut spending, whereas the French want to ride roughshod over the pact,' says an aide to Eichel.

Consumers and companies across the euro zone could end up paying the price. Already, yields on short-term euro zone government bonds have jumped by up to 10 basis points over the past month on fears that squabbles over budget deficits, coupled with higher-than-expected inflation, could force the European Central Bank to raise interest rates. 'It must be clear to all that an expansive fiscal policy always means a more restrictive monetary policy,' says Michael Schubert, a monetary economist at Frankfurt's Commerzbank. 'This will make it easier for the ECB to justify a rate hike.'

Another issue: French laxness could inspire other nations to loosen the purse strings. Italy, especially, seems set to fall short of its budget pledge, as its economy cools and the government of Prime Minister Silvio Berlusconi makes little headway in cutting spending or injecting flexibility into labor markets. He's even talking about assisting the floundering Fiat auto company – though he stresses that he doesn't want to run afoul of EU guidelines.

The fight with the French also draws attention away from the Germans' own wavering faith in the European idea. Center-left Chancellor Schröder, running hard for reelection in September, has been wasting no time bashing the European Commission and its president, Romano Prodi. When the EC proposed to pry open the cozy links between car dealerships and car manufacturers – a move that could force Germany's Volkswagen to cut prices in its home market – Schröder accused Brussels 'Eurocrats' of taking aim at German industry and jobs. 'With his Commission-bashing, Schröder is basically saying Germany needs to work out its own industrial policies,' says Ulrike Guérot, Europe specialist at Berlin's German Council on Foreign Relations. 'But that goes against 20 years of co-ordinating with the rest of the EU.'

Budget deficit as share of gross domestic product

	2001	2002*	2003*
France	–1.5%	–2.0%	–1.8%
Germany	–2.7	–2.8	–2.1
Italy	–1.4	–1.3	–1.3
Eurozone 12	–1.3	–1.5	–1.2

*Forecast.
Data: European Commission.

The squabbling is set to get even worse. In Brussels, the rolling constitutional convention meant to come up with new and improved institutional reforms is increasingly divided. Germans, for example, are putting their considerable weight behind federalist solutions that mirror their own country's constitutional makeup. France and Britain are backing solutions that emphasize national sovereignty. Some, like Germany and many smaller countries, want to see a stronger Commission and Parliament. Others, like France, favor an intergovernmental approach to decision-making. The convention, chaired by former French President Valéry Giscard d'Estaing, has until the end of 2003 to do its job. The current betting is that the convention will come up with muddled proposals in an effort to paper over divisions.

This stuff sounds abstruse, but it can determine whether Europe ever grows up politically and gets its member states to conform to common economic goals. The disagreements in Brussels are especially disruptive as the EU prepares to bring countries as far afield as Poland and Bulgaria into the union. The infighting also plays into the hands of Europe's far-right politicians, who think Brussels is a menace and who condemn the euro, the Maastricht treaty, and the Stability Pact out of hand.

Some see this as nothing less than make-or-break time for the EU. 'The next two years will be remembered as one of those defining moments in the history of Europe. Either it really gels, or you have real problems,' says Guérot. 'You could have a win-win situation, with a good constitutional convention, a recovering European economy, enlargement to the east, and a receding of right-wing populism,' she says. 'But the other scenario has Europe being sucked into rising populism, as no one dares to speak about more European integration. That leads to rising interest rates and even more problems on the far right. We end up in 2004 with nothing binding us together but a weak euro.' That decidedly unpretty picture is something Europe's fractious leaders ought to reflect on sooner rather than later.

(a) What difficulties do budget deficits create for economies?

(b) What reasons does the article advance to explain why various European economies will find it difficult to reduce their budget deficits?

(c) Why is a convergence of budget deficits vital for the long-term success of the euro?

In the following article, taken from *The Economist* of 28 January 2001, the increasing ineffectiveness of monetary policy within the USA, especially in the short term, is evaluated.

A blunt tool

Is monetary policy less effective these days?

The quarter-point cut in interest rates by America's Federal Reserve on June 27th takes the total reduction in rates over the past six months to 2.75 percentage points – one of the most aggressive easings in Fed history. Yet it seems to have done little, so far, to revive America's economy. Monetary policy always needs time to take effect. This time the wait seems especially nerve-wracking.

The latest batch of economic statistics paints a mixed picture. The economy may yet avoid recession, but hopes of a quick, strong bounce-back have faded.

One reason why interest-rate cuts may have been less effective than expected this year is that they have actually done little to ease financial conditions. The Fed's main policy tool is the federal-funds rate, the rate at which banks lend overnight to one another. However, this rate has little direct impact on the economy, since neither firms nor households pay it. The transmission mechanism through which changes in the federal-funds rate affect the economy is a good deal more complex. The size of a cut in the rate can be a poor measure of the likely impact of monetary policy.

Broadly, monetary policy affects the real economy through three channels:

- Through the cost of borrowing in the market which, if reduced, could be expected to spur consumer spending and investment. Interest rates on short-term loans do indeed tend to move in line with the federal-funds rate. But much other borrowing, by both firms and households, is linked to bond yields, which hang more on market expectations about future interest rates and inflation than on changes in short-term rates.
- Through the exchange rate. In theory, looser monetary policy should push down the the dollar, so boosting exports.
- Through the prices of financial assets, especially equities. If lower interest rates lift share prices, this may boost consumer spending as private shareholders feel wealthier, or spur corporate investment by reducing the cost of capital.

If changes in the federal-funds rate do not feed through into market rates, the dollar or share prices, they will have little effect upon the economy. Bruce Kasman at J.P. Morgan Chase has analysed the Fed's macroeconomic model of the American economy, derived from past behaviour. According to the model, a one percentage-point reduction in the federal-funds rate should raise the level of GDP by 1.7% after two years, but by only 0.6% after one year. This may suggest that America simply needs patience.

However, the model also suggests that, if lower interest rates are to revive the economy, a cut of 2.5 percentage points (the size of the cut until this week) would normally be expected to have lifted share prices by 22% within a year, reduced long-term bond yields by three-quarters of a point, and left the dollar 5% weaker. Yet since the Fed first started to slash interest rates on January 3rd, the S&P 500 has actually fallen by 10%, the dollar's trade-weighted value has gained 7%, and both bond yields and mortgage rates have remained broadly unchanged.

Stiff levers

In previous economic cycles, as much as two-fifths of the total impact of interest-rate cuts on GDP, on average, has come through the stockmarket and the dollar – two channels that now appear to be blocked. This suggests that the Fed will have to push even harder on the monetary lever to revive growth.

The Fed has another concern. Not only have long-term borrowing costs failed to follow short-term rates down, but households and firms may also be less responsive to lower rates. They may not want to borrow any more because they are already up to their ears in debt. With capacity utilisation in manufacturing at its lowest for 18 years, firms will also be reluctant to invest more.

Yet there is no need for too much gloom about the dwindling powers of the Fed. The economy does look fragile, but what if the Fed had done nothing? Share prices would have fallen more sharply, as would business and consumer confidence. As it is, consumer confidence has not, so far, been greatly dented. And the Fed's easing has helped to prop up the housing market. In other words, the Fed still carries clout.

Central bankers certainly think so. In April, the Federal Reserve Bank of New York held a conference on the monetary transmission mechanism. One paper[*] observed that, since the early 1980s, changes in the federal-funds rate seem to have had a smaller impact on output. However, the authors concluded that there was no evidence that firms and households had become less sensitive to changes in interest rates. Instead, the impact of changes in monetary policy seems to have declined because the conduct of policy has improved over the past two decades. The Fed now responds more quickly to changing economic expectations, which has helped to smooth out the effect of interest-rate shocks, reducing the variability of output and inflation. A reassuring conclusion for central bankers – but it will need revisiting in a year's time.

[*] 'The Monetary Transmission Mechanism: Has it Changed?', by Jean Boivin and Marc Giannoni.

© *The Economist*, London (28.1.01)

(a) What reasons are given in the article to explain why monetary policy in the USA appears to have become less effective in shaping economic performance in recent years?

(b) Why might the impact of monetary policy on economic performance be increasingly long term in its effect?

(c) Following 11 September 2001, the US recovery (which the article alludes to) stalled. The Fed aggressively

reduced interest rates in response. As the article might have predicted, the impact of these cuts on the economy's performance appeared negligible. There was a fear that US interest rates might have to approach zero to get the economy moving! And even then there was no guarantee that this policy course would work. At this point the US government decided that a fiscal stimulus was required. Investigate what happened to the US economy in the months following 11 September. Did the US economy recover from recession? Did US interest rates continue to fall? Explain and comment.

From its founding in June 1997 to May 2001, the Monetary Policy Committee (MPC) had taken 49 interest rate decisions and, of these, 19 changed the rate. On 9 occasions the rate was raised and on 10 the rate was reduced. Given its performance since 1997, has the MPC been successful in achieving price stability and meeting its inflation target? The article below is an extract from a House of Commons Research Paper 01/59 of June 2001, by Grahame Allen. The author evaluates the evidence.

Price stability

On the key point of whether the MPC has actually hit its stated inflation target the news is ambiguous. The inflation target that the MPC is required to meet is a 2.5% increase, over the previous twelve months, in the retail prices index excluding mortgage interest payments. Over the period covered by this paper the following monthly inflation rates, on the stated basis, have been recorded:

RPI(X) annual changes

		per cent	Meets target?	over/under target			per cent	Meets target?	over/under target
1997	June	2.7%	no	0.2%	1999	June	2.2%	no	−0.3%
	July	3.0%	no	0.5%		July	2.2%	no	−0.3%
	Aug	2.8%	no	0.3%		Aug	2.1%	no	−0.4%
	Sept	2.7%	no	0.2%		Sept	2.1%	no	−0.4%
	Oct	2.8%	no	0.3%		Oct	2.2%	no	−0.3%
	Nov	2.8%	no	0.3%		Nov	2.2%	no	−0.3%
	Dec	2.7%	no	0.2%		Dec	2.2%	no	−0.3%
1998	Jan	2.5%	yes	0.0%	2000	Jan	2.1%	no	−0.4%
	Feb	2.6%	no	0.1%		Feb	2.2%	no	−0.3%
	Mar	2.6%	no	0.1%		Mar	2.0%	no	−0.5%
	Apr	3.0%	no	0.5%		Apr	1.9%	no	−0.6%
	May	3.2%	no	0.7%		May	2.0%	no	−0.5%
	June	2.8%	no	0.3%		June	2.2%	no	−0.3%
	July	2.6%	no	0.1%		July	2.2%	no	−0.3%
	Aug	2.5%	no	0.0%		Aug	1.9%	no	−0.6%
	Sept	2.5%	yes	0.0%		Sept	2.2%	no	−0.3%
	Oct	2.5%	yes	0.0%		Oct	2.0%	no	−0.5%
	Nov	2.5%	yes	0.0%		Nov	2.2%	no	−0.3%
	Dec	2.6%	yes	0.1%		Dec	2.0%	no	−0.5%
1999	Jan	2.6%	no	0.1%	2001	Jan	1.8%	no	−0.7%
	Feb	2.4%	no	−0.1%		Feb	1.9%	no	−0.6%
	Mar	2.7%	no	0.2%		Mar	1.9%	no	−0.6%
	Apr	2.4%	no	−0.1%		Apr	2.0%	no	−0.5%
	May	2.1%	no	−0.4%		May	2.4%	no	−0.1%

Source: National Statistics First Releases, various dates.

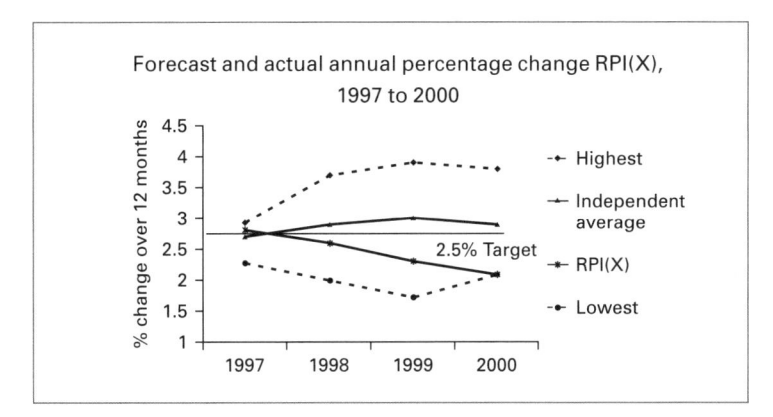

Forecast and actual annual percentage change RPI(X), 1997 to 2000

Is this good or a bad performance? Only four out of the forty-eight rates have met the target and thirty-five have been less than 0.5% away from the target. But, the last twenty-seven rates have all undershot the target and ten of the last fourteen rates have been 0.5% or more away from the target rate, suggesting that MPC policy may have been too 'tight'. All the inflation rates are good by historical standards. However, in the light of the downturn in both the UK and international economies and the general collapse in world commodity prices this has been a period in which background economic conditions have been conducive to low inflation.

Another way to compare the performance of the MPC is to compare inflation over the period with what had been the forecast immediately prior to its establishment. In the chart below, the actual average annual inflation rate RPI (X) is compared to the average and range of forecasts made by independent groups, themselves influenced by their state of knowledge about the then government's inflation target which, at the time, was a 1–2.5% target range.

The chart confirms the view that inflation has been substantially lower than most forecasts predicted in 1997. However, it is still just within the range that economists, four years ago, thought it would be. Of course this type of comparison is as much a test of the predictive abilities of a particular group of economists as it is of the MPC, indeed, perhaps, a greater test.

(a) Consider whether the MPC's performance in meeting the government's inflation target since 1997 could be judged a success.

(b) Bring the table in the article above up to date. The relevant information can be found at the Bank of England Web site (http://www.bankofengland.co.uk).

(c) Identify the most recent change in interest rates. What reasons did the MPC give to justify the interest rate change?

In 1997, the incoming Labour government made the Bank of England independent, giving its Monetary Policy Committee responsibility for setting interest rates. But, as Tony Thirlwall argues in the following article, taken from *The Guardian* of 5 October 1998, this leaves the government with both too little and too much power in determining macroeconomic policy.

Why the Government needs to get real on economic policy

It was a mistake to make the Bank of England independent, giving the Monetary Policy Committee (MPC) the sole task of achieving a target rate of inflation as low as 2.5 per cent per annum. I say this for two reasons.

First, the prime task of economic policy-making should be to maximise the growth of real living standards (i.e. the growth of real output per head) not to minimise the rate of inflation. There is no economic theory, or convincing empirical evidence, that a rate of inflation of 2.5 per cent is in any sense 'optimal' from the point of view of generating the maximum use of the country's resources.

Secondly, monetary and fiscal policy need to be co-ordinated if the macroeconomic goals of stable growth, low unemployment and low inflation are to be achieved simultaneously; now much more difficult with the Bank of England responsible for monetary policy and the Government in charge of fiscal policy, with apparently no effective dialogue between the two.

It would make more sense to depoliticise both monetary and fiscal policy and put economic policy-making into the hands of a group of technocrats which could be called the Real Economy Policy Committee. Such a group would be charged with the task of achieving a stable growth of GDP per head in line with the country's rate of growth of productive capacity, subject to a much more flexible target for inflation. The Real Economy Policy Committee would replace the MPC and take decisions on monetary policy consistent with decisions of fiscal policy and the overall state of the real economy.

The MPC was given a fruitless and too easy a task: fruitless because control of inflation is only one of many goals of economic policy; too easy because to control inflation through the use of interest rates, without regard to the real economy, requires no particular skills. (This is no criticism of the members of the MPC.)

The really difficult task is to control inflation while preserving growth, full employment and a healthy, tradeable goods sector. But these other objectives are outside the remit of the MPC. In the early days of independence, the MPC had an easy ride because growth was buoyant, unemployment was falling, and decisions to raise interest rates appeared benign. The situation is now very different, but the committee is powerless to change its stance.

How much more sensible it would be to have a Real Economy Policy Committee with a much wider brief.

Recent studies of the relation between inflation and economic growth within countries and across the world show that 2.5 per cent inflation is far below the rate at which inflation may damage the real economy. Studies by the IMF and World Bank* show a positive or neutral effect of inflation on growth up to about 8 per cent inflation. There are good economic reasons why this should be so. First, a mild demand inflation encourages investment by keeping entrepreneurs' expectations buoyant and real interest rates low. Second, inflation is to be expected in the process of growth and structural change.

Controlling inflation by monetary policy alone implicitly assumes that all inflation is monetary in origin, which clearly it is not.

It is also a grave mistake for economic policy-making to be indifferent to the exchange rate. If tight monetary policy raises the exchange rate to levels which damage the tradeable goods sector, this calls for other instruments to be used to achieve the inflation target: proper co-ordination of monetary and fiscal policy is needed.

It is ostrich-like to ignore the fortunes of the manufacturing sector on the grounds that it constitutes only 20 per cent or so of total output and employment. More than 50 per cent of foreign

* M Bruno and W Easterly, Inflation Crises and Long-run Growth, *Journal of Monetary Economics*, 1998; M Sarel, Non-Linear Effects of Inflation on Economic Growth, *IMF Staff Papers*, 1996.

exchange earnings still come from manufactured exports.

The current approach to economic policy-making which sets only a monetary target and no real targets, and which divorces monetary and fiscal policy, is doing great damage to the UK economy, as many economists predicted. There would appear to be three alternatives. The first would be to abolish the MPC and for the Government to once again co-ordinate monetary and fiscal policy itself. The second would be for both monetary and fiscal policy to be 'depoliticised' and for decision-making to be put in the hands of a Real Economy Policy Committee with the objective of achieving a high and stable rate of economic growth. The Government is unlikely, however, to relinquish control of fiscal, as well as monetary, policy, so a third (compromise) option would be a UK equivalent of the US Council of Economic Advisers with strong advisory powers, with the Government obliged to give reasons if the advice preferred is not taken. Macroeconomic policy as currently practised, effectively based on one target and one instrument, has no merit or logic.

(a) What are the disadvantages of having a low rate of inflation as the central goal of monetary policy?

(b) Why, according to Tony Thirlwall, is the current approach to economic policy-making doing 'great damage to the UK economy'?

(c) Critically evaluate the case made out in the article for a 'Real Economic Policy Committee'.

In the following article, taken from the *Financial Times* of 1 March 2001, Samuel Brittan evaluates the limitations of setting inflation targets and how the conduct of monetary policy might change in the future.

Alternatives to inflation targets

Samuel Brittan

Despite their recent success inflation targets are highly unlikely to be the last word in monetary policy

There is one prediction about the next Wednesday's British Budget which can be safely made. That is that no sooner has the Chancellor Gordon Brown sat down than financial discussion will shift to the likely decision of the Monetary Policy Committee, the very next day, on UK short-term interest rates.

In principle the decision must be guided by the Chancellor's directive that the inflation target is 'at all times' 2½ per cent and by the threat of having to write a letter of explanation to him if the recorded rate deviates by more than 1 percentage point on either side.

Indeed inflation targets have enjoyed such success in the last decade that it seems vain to query them. Yet it is just in such periods that it is most necessary to look at the weaknesses of the prevailing regime and ask what is to follow. It is not enough to go on blindly reiterating what the Chancellor said in 1997.

It was originally expected that explanations of target breaches would be quite frequent; and the deputy governor,

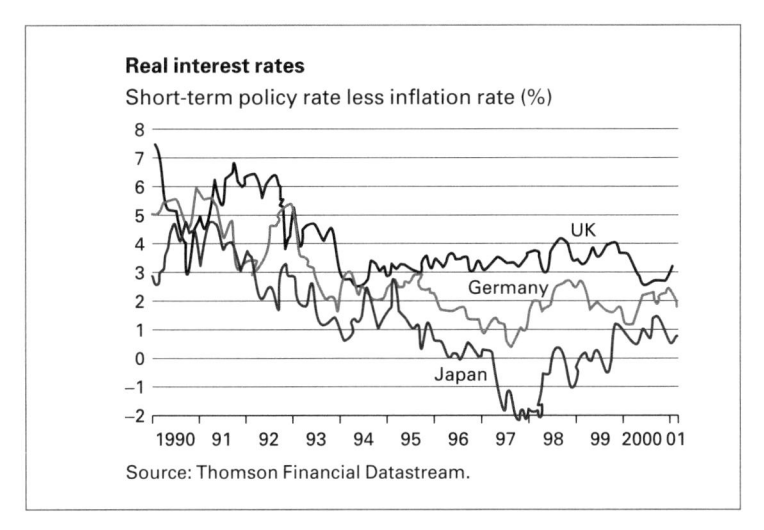

Real interest rates
Short-term policy rate less inflation rate (%)

[Chart showing real interest rates for UK, Germany, and Japan from 1990 to 2001, with values ranging from -2 to 8 percent]

Source: Thomson Financial Datastream.

Mervyn King even spoke about 'reviving the lost art of letter writing'. At his last press conference Mr King said that the probability of having to write a letter was now higher, a prospect he seemed almost to relish. The thought behind such remarks is that almost any monetary regime can be made to work if run intelligently. But already financial commentators are discussing the prospect of a letter from the Bank in terms of failure and humiliation; and so far the Chancellor has done nothing to discourage such discussion. Moreover we cannot always rely on enlightened people being in charge; and who knows what the political pressures of the next few years will bring. The number of countries with their own central banks is now running into hundreds; and there is a need for some guidelines which do not require the shrewdness of a Keynes or a Milton Friedman to operate.

The Chancellor introduced a 2$^{1}/_{2}$ per cent inflation target as a rough and ready way of preventing the Bank of England from being too contractionary in the face of recession, as it was in the 1920s. But circumstances in which this target would be inappropriate are easy to envisage.

Suppose that inflation is low or negative, not because of a recession but because the much heralded productivity takeoff has at last occurred. Competition between firms will still put a limit on profit margins and the benefits of the breakthrough will be felt in zero inflation or even falling prices. Would it be sensible then for the Bank to have to write a letter of abject humiliation and promise and to take steps to lever up inflation to 2$^{1}/_{2}$ per cent?. It is not stable or falling prices which are disliked by the public but the recessions which have often – but far from always – accompanied them.

Now take an opposite situation, an oil price explosion. Would it be sensible for central banks to force the inflation rate down quickly to where it was before? Yet one reason why the European Central Bank has been reluctant to cut interest rates is that the recorded euro area inflation rate has been running above the approved corridor of 0 to 2 per cent, entirely as a result of increased oil prices.

Or suppose that there is some event such as a Wall St crash or a collapse of an institution like Long Term Capital which induces a rush for liquidity. Should not the Fed supply this need even if there is no immediate danger of price deflation?

There was once an alternative theory of monetary policy different to both the inflation target version of monetarism and the Keynesian emphasis on stimulating output directly. This was the so-called 'Austrian' school, which in its turn drew on a Swedish economist of a century ago, Knut Wicksell. The latter distinguished between two rates of interest. There was the actual market rate; and there was also the unobservable 'natural rate' which would bring intended savings and investment into line if there were no distortions introduced by the monetary system.

The aim of monetary policy should be 'neutral'; in other words to try to minimise divergences between the natural and the market rates. The 'Austrians', in particular Von Mises and Heyek, emphasised that it was not sufficient to try to keep the general price level stable. Quite apart from index number problems – which they overemphasised – the main harmful effect of inflation and deflation came, they argued, from distortions in relative prices which could occur even if the overall price index remained fairly stable. They emphasised particularly the malinvestment which would result if production became either too capital intensive or not intensive enough.

One still controversial example is that of the behaviour of the Fed in the 1920s, leading up to the 1929 crash. While the monetarists believe that the Fed of those days was too tight, the 'Austrians' considered, even at the time, that it was from 1927 onwards, too expansionary in promoting an investment boom which could not last. A similar controversy surrounds the period since the mid-1990s, during which US inflation has remained low and stable, but when there were many signs of a rush into fashionable investments in IT and elsewhere.

During the interwar period the Austrian school discredited itself by insisting that the depression should run its course, to allow mistaken investment to be liquidated. Lionel Robbins of the London School of Economics, who had earlier supported such views, made a well-known recantation. Even 'assuming that the original diagnosis of successive financial ease and mistaken real investment was correct' to take no action against the ensuing depression, he remarked, was 'as unsuitable as denying blankets and stimulants to a drunk who had fallen into an icy pond, on the ground that his original trouble was overheating'.

Since the early 1970s there has however been a revival of Austrian economics, not anywhere near Vienna, but mostly in the United States where it is now a sufficiently important minority movement for respectable economic publishers to maintain sections of their lists devoted to it.

Like all such minority movements the new 'Austrians' have their quota of fanatics and cranks. Indeed when one of the more sophisticated of them attempted a semi-mathematical exposition of the school's teachings, he received hate mail from some who thought that he was being disloyal to the anti-mathematical gospel of von Mises.

But at the other end of the spectrum there are 'Austrians' well aware of modern techniques, as well as of mainstream economics and of what is going on in the economy. One of the best examples can be found in a book with the unnecessarily forbidding title of *Microfoundations and Macroeconomics*, by Steven Horwitz, (Routledge, 2000). The emphasis is on the need to shift from monetary or inflation targets to some attempt at neutral money. He is less convincing on how to do so.

Like many other modern Austrians he has endorsed Hayek's last idea of competitive private enterprise currencies to allow market forces to adjust the supply of money and other financial instruments to the desire of the public to hold them. Unlike Hayek, Horwitz wants these private enterprise suppliers to be firmly committed to convert on application any currency or deposits issued into actual stocks of commodities in specified bundles.

None of the apostles of free banking seem able to confront the following problem. Commercial banks are not usually allowed to issue notes and coins; but these are now the small change of the monetary circulation. The English legal tender laws place no obstacle to contracts in any chosen medium – whether gold, cowrie shells, euros or in the liabilities of any financial institution. A spirited debate on whether the emergence of competitive private enterprise money, free from central bank control, is one day likely to emerge from the development of electronic transmission processes can be found in the July issue of *International Finance*. The result is a draw. Meanwhile the evidence suggests that in present conditions it needs a runaway inflation to induce people to abandon their official currencies.

Yet we do not have to give up all attempt at a neutral monetary policy. A starting point would be the research, stimulated by people such as de Anne Julius of the MPC, on what a normal real short-term rate of interest might be. This would have to be based on the historical trend, abstracting from crisis years or periods of high inflation. Such an estimate will almost certainly come to somewhere in the range of 3 to 5 per cent.

This is only a beginning. Faced with developments such as a hectic scramble to invest in high tech industries or a scramble for liquidity, it would be clear that the natural rate has moved. There is no avoiding judgment about how much, but it would surely be possible to do something better than just plough on regardless with rigid inflation targets.

For the time being, estimates of normal and natural interest rates are unlikely to be good enough to replace inflation targets altogether; and they will have to come in as a supplement. But anything that can replace the parrot-like incantations about price stability at every European central bankers' gathering would be a move in the right direction.

(a) What does Brittan identify as the principal weaknesses of adhering to rigid inflation targets as a basis of monetary policy?

(b) Outline the Austrian school approach to monetary policy. How does it differ from the current system of inflation targeting?

(c) A movement towards the Austrian school of monetary policy may result in monetary policy once again becoming more discretionary in its operation. What are the drawbacks of such an approach to economic management?

ANSWERS

Q1. *False.* A budget deficit will only cause national income to rise if it results in *total* injections exceeding *total* withdrawals. Note, however, that an increase in the size of the budget deficit will, *ceteris paribus*, be expansionary.

Q2. D. The answer is not A, C or E, because the PSNCR refers to the borrowing of the *whole* public sector: central government, local government and public corporations. The answer is not B, because the national debt refers to the accumulated debt over the years, not just to this year's borrowing.

Q3. As national income rises, so tax revenue will rise. Conversely, if national income rises fast enough for unemployment to fall, government expenditure on transfer payments such as unemployment benefit will fall. The net effect is that the budget deficit will fall (or the surplus rise). The opposite will happen if national income falls.

Q4. C. Fiscal stance refers to the effect of the government's fiscal policy on total aggregate demand: will the effect be reflationary or deflationary, and how much so. The answer is not E because the mere size of the deficit or surplus alone is not enough to determine whether aggregate demand will increase or decrease and by how much. It is also necessary to know what is happening to the other two injections and the other two withdrawals.

Q5. *automatic fiscal stabilisers.*

Q6. *smaller.* The more that taxes increase, the higher the *mpt* and hence the higher the *mpw* and the smaller the multiplier. The smaller the multiplier, the more stable will the economy be.

Q7. *fall.* The *mpt* will rise.

Q8. (a), (b) and (c) are expansionary. (d) and (e) are contractionary.

Q9. *True.*

Q10. D. The full multiplier is 4, but only ³⁄₄ of the cut in taxes is spent on domestic goods and services. Thus the rise in income is only ³⁄₄ as much as with the full multiplier. In fact, you can easily demonstrate that the tax multiplier is always 1 less than the full multiplier. (Note that the tax multiplier is negative: this is because a *fall* in taxes leads to a *rise* in income and vice versa.)

Q11. B. In equilibrium $I + X + G = S + M + T$. Thus if I exceeds S by £10m, and X exceeds M by £30m, $I + X$ must exceed $S + M$ by £10m + £30m = £40m. Thus for the economy to be in equilibrium T must exceed G by £40m: i.e. there must be a budget surplus of £40m.

Q12. A. Increased public expenditure can lead to a shortage of resources available for the private sector (resource crowding out) or a shortage of finance for private sector borrowing (financial crowding out).

Q13. Reasons include: the amount of crowding out is difficult to predict; the impact of tax cuts (or benefit increases) will depend on how consumers decide to allocate additional incomes (which in turn depends on expectations of future price and income changes); the size of the accelerator is difficult to predict and subsequent multiplier/accelerator interactions are virtually impossible to predict; random shocks.

Q14. (a) (iii), (b) (v), (c) (iv), (d) (i), (e) (ii).

Q15. (b), (d) and (e) are all examples of monetary policy. (a) and (f) are examples of fiscal policy, and (c) incomes policy.

Q16. D. This will reduce the credit multiplier. For the current reserve base, banks will now have to reduce the amount of non-reserve assets (i.e. loans, etc.).

Q17. The two major sources are: increased government borrowing (a PSNCR) and increased private-sector borrowing (from banks being prepared to operate with a lower liquidity ratio).

Q18. Their main argument against statutory reserve requirements and other forms of direct monetary control is that they interfere with the working of the market and prevent competition. Such controls could become sources of inefficiency. Regulated institutions would be unable to expand, whereas non-regulated ones (and probably less efficient ones) would take business from them. Another reason is Goodhart's law (see next question).

Q19. B. Goodhart's law states that regulation of one part of the financial system would cause unregulated parts to expand. Thus the amount of lending by the regulated institutions would be a poor indicator of total lending: 'to control is to distort'.

Q20. *the non-bank private sector*. If the borrowing is not from the banks, there will be no expansion of the money base and no resulting credit creation.

Q21. *higher*. The excess government spending will increase the demand for money, and so, with no increase in the supply of money, there will be a rise in interest rates.

Q22. *less*. Higher interest rates will reduce private-sector borrowing, including private-sector investment. This 'crowding-out' of investment is seen by monetarists to be a serious problem of attempting to restrain the growth of the money supply *without* also reducing the PSBR.

Q23. *increases*. If existing money circulates faster, there will be less upward pressure on interest rates.

Q24. *more*. The more elastic the liquidity preference curve, the more will idle balances fall as the rate of interest rises, and hence the faster will money circulate.

Q25. (a) (iii): *decrease*, (b) (i): *decrease*, (c) (i): *increase*, (d) (iv): *decrease*, (e) (i): *increase*, (f) (iii): *increase*, (g) (ii): *decrease*.

Open-market operations will involve altering the total amount of government borrowing on the open market (as opposed to from the central bank). If the central bank deliberately keeps banks short of liquidity and then manipulates the amount that it lends to them, this will directly affect banks' liquid base. Funding involves altering the *type* of government borrowing (e.g. switching from bills to bonds). In some countries (but not the UK), the central bank requires banks to maintain a minimum ratio of reserve assets to total assets – a ratio which is above the ratio banks would choose. By raising this ratio it can force banks to contract credit.

Those actions that increase the liquidity base of the banking sector will increase the credit creation. Those that decrease the liquidity base will decrease credit creation.

Q26. £90m. The liquidity base will expand by £10m, on which banks can create £90m credit, making a total increase in the money supply of £100m (a bank multiplier of 10).

Q27. *True*. When banks run short of liquidity they will borrow from the Bank of England through gilt repos or offer bills of exchange for rediscounting. The Bank of England can dictate the repo and discount rates. This then has a knock-on effect on interest rates generally throughout the financial system.

Q28. *(a) Sell more*. If banks have surplus liquidity, they will be buying bills. If the Bank of England sells them more, this will force down the price of bills and hence force up the rate of discount and hence the rate of interest.

(b) Buy fewer. If banks are short of liquidity, they will be 'in the Bank' (selling bills to the Bank of England). If the Bank of England is prepared to buy fewer at any given price, this will force down the bill price and hence force up the rate of rediscount and hence the rate of interest.

Q29. C. Given that the Bank of England generally keeps banks short of liquidity, the banks have to borrow from the Bank of England. They do this through gilt repos. The Bank of England is prepared to buy bonds from the banks (thereby providing them with liquidity) on condition that the banks buy them back later (generally two weeks later). The price difference is set to be equivalent to the interest rate chosen by the Monetary Policy Committee.

Q30. *(a) Yes.* If the government cuts taxes, then other things being equal this will increase the PSBR.

(b) Yes. Similarly, if the government wants to increase government expenditure, this will increase the PSBR.

(c) No. A booming economy will automatically lead to higher tax revenues and reduced government expenditure (e.g. on unemployment benefits).

(d) Yes. In a recession, however, the PSBR will increase as tax revenues fall and government expenditure automatically rises.

(e) Yes (short term). The extra government expenditure will raise the PSBR.
No (long term). A faster growth in output will lead to a faster growth in tax revenues.

(f) Yes. This will reduce the tax base and increase government expenditure on health care, pensions and other benefits.

Q31. This is where the authorities seek to control cash and banks' balances with the central bank.

Q32. D. In this case, any reduction in the cash base is likely to 'bite' more effectively. In the case of A, banks could suffer a loss of liquidity without reducing loans; in the case of B and C, there is a diversion of business between institutions, which will limit the size of the total reduction in loans; in the case of E, the Bank of England is supplying liquidity on demand (albeit at a price).

Q33. Banks may reduce their liquidity ratios; they may initially have surplus liquidity; disintermediation may occur (possibly abroad).

Q34. *False.* If the supply of money is stable, but the *demand* for money is unstable, then the rate of interest will fluctuate as the level of demand fluctuates.

Q35. *(a) True.* Competition is stifled if only one part of the financial system is under regulation, whereas the rest is not. Uncontrolled (and possibly inefficient) institutions will be given an unfair advantage, which may allow them to charge monopolistic interest rates.

(b) False. Credit rationing will allow interest rates to be *below* the free-market equilibrium.

(c) True. Credit rationing will hit hardest those industries that depend upon consumer hire purchase to buy their goods. The car and other consumer durable industries are likely to be particularly hard hit by credit controls.

(d) True. Banks as well as other financial institutions will attempt to find ways around credit restrictions.

(e) False. Unlike interest rates, it directly affects the amount of bank lending.

Q36. If people wish to borrow (demand), then the financial institutions will attempt to lend (supply), even if controls are in place restricting institutions from doing so.

Q37. inelastic.

Q38. All are possible consequences of a policy of high interest rates. Note that in case of (b), higher interest rates will lead to an appreciation of the exchange rate, which will make exports and home-produced import substitutes less competitive. In the case of (d), higher interest rates will discourage investment, which will reduce the rate of growth of capital and of technical progress.

Q39. *(a)* In Figure A20.1(a), the increase in government expenditure causes an increase in aggregate demand and a rightward shift in the *IS* curve to IS_2. If it is financed by an increase in the money supply, the *LM* curve will shift to LM_2. The rate of interest remains at r_1. Hence there is no crowding out and there is a full multiplier rise in income to Y_2.

(b) In Figure A20.1(b), the deterioration in business expectations causes a leftward shift in the *IS* curve to IS_2. If the government increases the money supply, this will shift the *LM* curve downwards. If income is to be maintained at Y_1, the *LM* curve must shift downwards to LM_2 and the rate of interest fall to r_3.

Figure A20.1 (a) Increased government expenditure and increased money supply
(b) Deteriorating business expectations and increased money supply

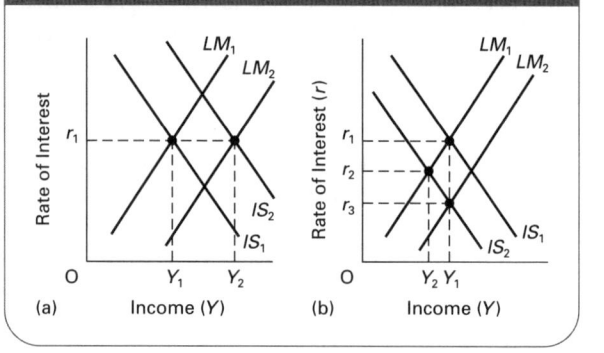

Q40. See Figure A20.2. Given their assumptions about the shapes of the curves. Keynesians conclude that fiscal policy has a relatively large effect on aggregate demand, whereas monetary policy has a relatively small effect. Monetarists conclude the opposite.

Q41. (a), (d), (f) and (g) are all justifications used by the Keynesians for government intervention in the economy.

Q42. D. As the balance of payments moved into deficit, a deflationary policy was adopted in order to stop

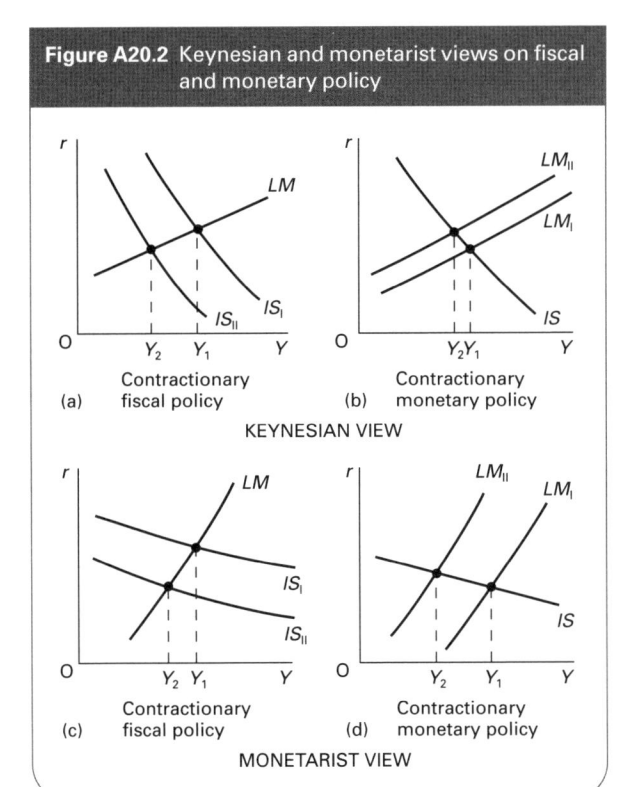

Figure A20.2 Keynesian and monetarist views on fiscal and monetary policy

(a) Contractionary fiscal policy
(b) Contractionary monetary policy
KEYNESIAN VIEW

(c) Contractionary fiscal policy
(d) Contractionary monetary policy
MONETARIST VIEW

people buying imports and to improve the competitive position of UK exports by reducing the rate of inflation. As the economy slowed down and inflation fell, the balance payments would move into surplus. This was the cue for government to reflate the economy, and the start of a new cycle.

Q43. There are many arguments put forward to explain the stagflation of the 1970s. These include: a relaxation of monetary controls; a massive increase in the money supply in 1972/3; the move to floating exchange rates; the rise in oil prices; rising costs in the domestic economy; the decline in the UK's competitive position overseas; the effects of technology on jobs; poor expectations of future economic performance. (For a more comprehensive consideration of these points, see Sloman, *Economics*, 5th edn, pp. 575–7.)

Q44. (a), (b), (d) and (f) are all policies that characterised the approach to economic management in the early 1980s.

Q45. A range of problems were encountered: the PSNCR was very difficult to reduce; money supply measures moved in different directions and proved difficult to control; the decision to allow the pound to float freely, and the subsequent large-scale appreciation, created a great deal of uncertainty for those businesses trading overseas; the removing of credit controls contributed to the credit boom of the mid-1980s that proved to be too large to be sustainable; the reliance on high interest rates to curb spending created great difficulties for businesses and consumers. (For a more comprehensive assessment of these policy problems, see Sloman, *Economics*, 5th edn, pp. 577–8.)

Q46. The D-Mark exchange rate was effectively targeted in the late 1980s (before entry to the ERM).

Q47. *True.* The ERM imposed an exchange rate band. If the exchange rate moved to the limits of its band, then the government had to adopt appropriate policies to maintain the exchange rate value. For example, it could have been forced to raise interest rates if the value of the pound moved towards the bottom of its band.

Q48. E. With a fixed exchange rate, monetary policy has to be geared to maintaining that exchange rate. This substantially reduces flexibility in the use of monetary policy. In the case of A, the UK inflation rate was *higher* than the European average. In the case of B, fiscal policy was largely dominated by the domestic issue of reducing the growing PSBR. In the case of C and D, maintaining the exchange rate meant maintaining high rates of interest, and this tended to reduce the growth of the money supply and the growth of aggregate demand.

Q49. *True.*

Q50. *True.* The Monetary Policy Committee (MPC) is charged with targeting a rate of inflation of $2^{1}/_{2}$ per cent. It has to reduce interest rates if it believes that otherwise inflation would be below $2^{1}/_{2}$ per cent, and raise interest rates if it believes that otherwise inflation would be above $2^{1}/_{2}$ per cent.

Q51. *False.* The ECB has set itself a target of maintaining inflation at no more than 2 per cent, but the rate can go *below* 2 per cent. Also, it has more discretion than the MPC in carrying out this policy.

Q52. Monetarists favour rules because, they argue, they will reduce inflationary expectations and create a stable environment for investment and growth. Discretionary policy, by contrast, owing to time lags and uncertainty, will at best be ineffective, and at worst actually destabilise rather than stabilise the economy.

Q53. Keynesians favour discretion because the economic environment is always changing; hence government must change its policy in response. Better forecasting and speedier action will help to increase the effectiveness of discretionary policy.

Q54. D. The Taylor rule seeks to obtain the optimum degree of stability of both inflation and real national income by assigning weights to each. The higher the weight attached to achieving the inflation target, the more the central bank will be prepared to allow real national income to fluctuate. The higher the weight attached to achieving stability in real national income, the more the central bank will be prepared to allow inflation to diverge from its target.

Chapter Twenty-one

21

Aggregate Supply, Unemployment and Inflation

A REVIEW

To what extent will aggregate supply respond to changes in aggregate demand? Will the effects be solely on prices? Or will they be solely on output and employment? Or will the effects be partly on prices and partly on output and employment, and if so, in what combination? As you will discover, the different schools of economics give different answers to these questions.

The nature of aggregate supply and its responsiveness to changes in aggregate demand will also determine the shape of the *Phillips curve*. It is the shape of the Phillips curve that has been at the centre of the *expectations revolution* in economics. Later in the chapter we will look at the theories of expectations and their implications for policies to tackle inflation and unemployment.

21.1 Aggregate supply
(Page 589) The effect that a change in aggregate demand has on the economy is determined by the nature and shape of the aggregate supply curve.

⬛ Figure 21.1 illustrates two extreme aggregate supply curves. Aggregate supply curve I represents the extreme **Q1.** *Keynesian/new classical* position, whereas aggregate supply curve II represents the extreme **Q2.** *Keynesian/new classical* position.

◐ **Q3.** Consider Figure 21.1. To which of the aggregate supply curves will the following statements apply?
(a) Up to the full-employment level of national income, an expansion in aggregate demand will progressively close a deflationary gap. AS_I/AS_{II}
(b) A rise in aggregate demand will have no effect on output and employment. AS_I/AS_{II}
(c) The only way to achieve higher levels of national income in the long run is through the use of supply-side policies. AS_I/AS_{II}

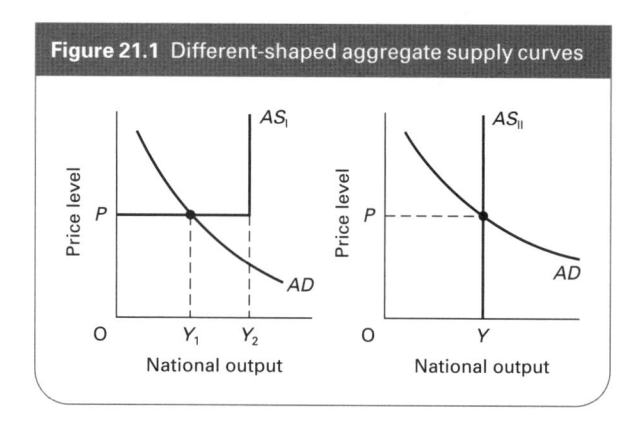

Figure 21.1 Different-shaped aggregate supply curves

(d) Fiscal and monetary policy used to regulate aggregate demand will have a significant effect upon economic activity. AS_I/AS_{II}

When looking at aggregate supply we must distinguish between short-run and long-run *AS* curves.

≡ Multiple choice ？ Written answer ◐ Delete wrong word ⊖ Diagram/table manipulation ✗ Calculation ⬛ Matching/ordering

(Pages 589–90) Short-run aggregate supply

To understand the short-run aggregate supply curve we need to look at its *microeconomic* foundations.

In the short run we assume that individual firms respond to a rise in demand for their product **Q4.** *by considering/without considering* the effects of a general rise in demand on their suppliers and on the economy as a whole.

⊖ **Q5.** Figure 21.2 shows the profit-maximising price and output of a firm facing a downward-sloping demand curve. Look back to Chapters 5 and 6 (sections 5.6 and 6.3) if you are uncertain of this material.

(a) Using Figure 21.2, show the effect of a rise in demand on price and output.
(b) Add a further *MC* curve that is flatter than the one already shown in the diagram (but still passes through point *x*). How does this influence the effect upon price and output of a rise in demand?

....

....

(c) Near full capacity, is the *MC* curve likely to become steeper or flatter? *steeper/flatter*
(d) Explain your answer to (c).

....

....

....

If there is now a *general* rise in demand in the economy, but firms assume that their cost curves are given (i.e. that the rise in demand for their products is not accompanied by a shift in their cost curves), then the aggregate supply curve will be **Q6.** *horizontal/similar in shape to the MC curve illustrated in Figure 21.2/horizontal then vertical/vertical*.

(Pages 590–1) Long-run aggregate supply

In the long run (which might not be very long at all), we cannot assume that firms' cost curves are unaffected by a change in aggregate demand. Three factors will have an important influence on the aggregate supply curve in the long run: the *interdependence* of firms, *investment* and *expectations*.

⊖ **Q7.** Figure 21.3 illustrates two situations (diagrams (a) and (b)) in which the slope of the long-run aggregate supply curve is different from that of the short-run *AS* curve. In each diagram there is an initial increase in aggregate demand. In each situation we assume that in the long run firms' cost curves are affected by the change in aggregate demand. One situation is the result of firms being interdependent; the other, the result of investment by firms in response to the change in aggregate demand.

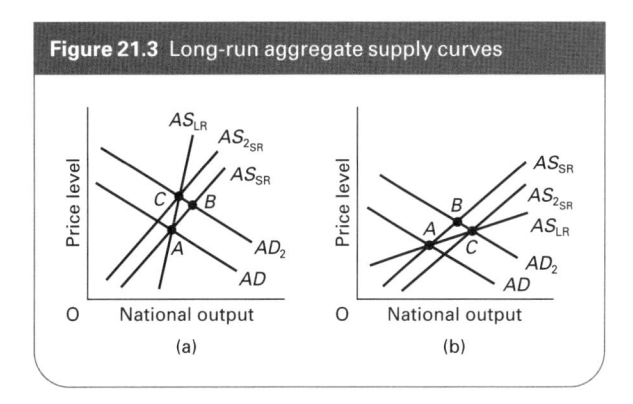

Figure 21.3 Long-run aggregate supply curves

Figure 21.2 Profit-maximising price and output for a firm in an imperfect market

(a) In which diagram is the interdependence of firms the dominant effect on the long-run *AS* curve?
Diagram(a)/Diagram(b)
(b) Explain the reason for your answer.

....

....

(c) Explain why the diagram you did not select in (a) represents the impact of new investment on aggregate supply.

....

....

....

◗ **Q8.** Expectations can make the long-run *AS* curve either steeper or shallower than the short-run *AS* curve. Which of the following effects of a rise in aggregate

292 CHAPTER 21 AGGREGATE SUPPLY, UNEMPLOYMENT AND INFLATION

demand will make the long-run *AS* curve steeper, and which will make it shallower?
(a) People expect that the rise in aggregate demand will lead to a general rise in prices. *steeper/shallower*
(b) People expect that the rise in aggregate demand will lead to firms increasing the level of investment. *steeper/shallower*
(c) People expect that the rise in aggregate demand will cause unemployment to fall. *steeper/shallower*
(d) People expect that the rise in aggregate demand will cause a general rise in wages throughout the economy. *steeper/shallower*
(e) People expect that the rise in aggregate demand will lead to increased economic growth. *steeper/shallower*
(f) People expect that the rise in aggregate demand will strengthen the bargaining position of trade unions. *steeper/shallower*

(Pages 591–3) Aggregate supply, the labour market and unemployment
What is the relationship between aggregate supply and unemployment?

Q9. Figure 21.4 shows short-run aggregate demand and supply of labour curves. The total labour force is shown by curve *N*; the effective supply of labour (those working plus others willing and able to work) is shown by curve AS_L. Aggregate demand for labour is initially given by AD_{L_1} and the wage rate by W_1.
(a) How much is equilibrium unemployment?

....

(b) How much is disequilibrium unemployment?

....

Figure 21.4 Short-run response to a fall in aggregate demand in the labour market

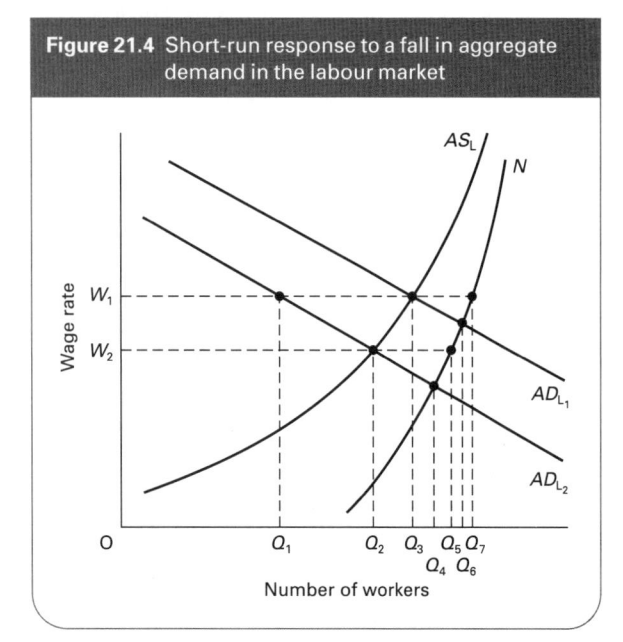

Now assume that aggregate demand falls to AD_{L_2} and that wages are *flexible* downwards.
(c) How much is total unemployment now? ....
(d) How much is disequilibrium unemployment?

....

(e) How much is equilibrium unemployment?

....

Now assume that aggregate demand has again fallen from AD_{L_1} to AD_{L_2}, but that this time wages are fixed at W_1.
(f) How much is total unemployment this time?

....

(g) How much is disequilibrium unemployment?

....

(h) How much is equilibrium unemployment?

....

Q10. Keynesian models of long-run aggregate supply make one or more of four assumptions. Which of the following is *not* one of these four?
A. The existence of money illusion.
B. Firms will take on more labour only if there is a fall in the real wage rate.
C. Downward stickiness of wages.
D. Expectations by firms that changes in aggregate demand will affect sales.
E. Hysteresis.

(Pages 593–5) Aggregate demand and supply, and inflation
So far we have used aggregate supply and demand analysis to illustrate the effect of a single increase in aggregate demand and a single increase in the price level. Aggregate demand and aggregate supply analysis can also be used to illustrate the causes of *inflation* (the rate of *increase* in prices). It can be used to distinguish between demand-pull and cost-push pressures on inflation.

Q11. This question is based on Figure 21.5 and illustrates an inflationary sequence that starts with *demand-pull* pressures. The economy is initially at point *X* on curves AD_1 and AS_1. Each of the following events will shift either the *AD* or the *AS* curve. Assuming they occur in a sequence, to which point on the diagram will the economy move after each event?
(a) The government undertakes an extensive new programme of public works.

point ....

(b) Subsequently the government decides to fund the programme by selling bonds to the banking sector in an attempt to prevent crowding out.

point ....

Figure 21.5 Shifts in aggregate demand and supply

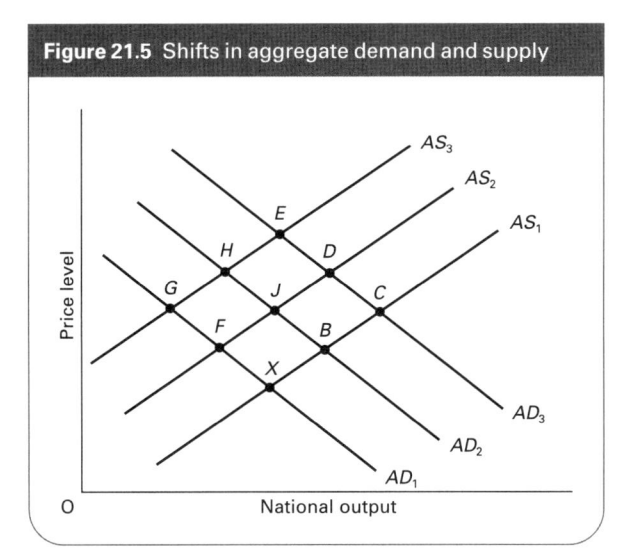

(c) Higher production costs have a knock-on effect throughout industry.

point ....

(d) Workers demand higher wages to cover rising costs of living.

point ....

Q12. This question is also based on Figure 21.5 but this time illustrates an inflationary sequence that starts with *cost-push* pressures. To which point on the diagram will the economy move after each of the following events, which, as before, shift either the *AD* or the *AS* curve? Again assume that point X is the starting point and that each event follows the previous one.

(a) Firms expect their suppliers' prices to rise following the collapse of an agreement between government and unions over pay restraint.

point ....

(b) Trade unions demand and get higher wages.

point ....

(c) Falling national output and rising unemployment persuade the government to increase public expenditure.

point ....

(d) The government, believing that its fiscal policy is inadequate, decides to cut interest rates.

point ....

21.2 The expectations-augmented Phillips curve

(Pages 596–601) The Phillips curve had an important influence upon economic thinking and analysis during the 1960s and 1970s.

Q13. The original Phillips curve showed:
A. the influence of fiscal policy on the level of inflation and unemployment.
B. the direct relationship between price inflation and unemployment.
C. the relationship between aggregate labour demand and aggregate labour supply in the long run.
D. the inverse relationship between wage inflation and unemployment.
E. the effect of expectations about changes in economic activity on the level of unemployment.

The main contribution of the monetarists to the study of the Phillips curve was to introduce the effects of expectations. They based their theory upon adaptive expectations.

Q14. Adaptive expectations state that:
A. people never make the same mistake twice.
B. people adapt their expectations according to the policies the government is currently pursuing.
C. expectations are formed on the basis of information from the past.
D. expectations are based upon forecasts made about the future performance of the economy.
E. government economic policy will always be predicted and hence people will adapt to it before it takes effect.

Q15. Which of the following equations are consistent with the adaptive expectations theory?
(i) $\dot{P}^e_t = a\dot{P}_t$
(ii) $\dot{P}^e_t = a\dot{P}_{t-1}$
(iii) $\dot{P}_t = b + c(1/U) + d\dot{P}^e_t$
(iv) $\dot{P}_t = b + c(1/U) + d\dot{P}^e_{t-1}$

where $\dot{P}$ is the percentage annual rate of inflation, $\dot{P}^e$ is the expected rate of inflation, t is the time period and U is the percentage rate of unemployment.
A. (i) and (iii).
B. (ii) and (iii).
C. (i) and (iv).
D. (ii) and (iv).
E. (iv) only.

Q16. Why is the adaptive expectations theory of the Phillips curve sometimes referred to as the *accelerationist theory*?

....

....

According to the adaptive expectations model, in the long run the Phillips curve is **Q17.** *horizontal/vertical*. At this rate of unemployment, real *AD* is equal to real *AS*. Monetarists call this rate of unemployment the **Q18.** *natural rate/accelerating rate* of unemployment. The implications this has for government policy are that expansionary monetary (and fiscal) policy will only have the effect of reducing unemployment in **Q19.** *the long run/the short run*. In the

294 CHAPTER 21 AGGREGATE SUPPLY, UNEMPLOYMENT AND INFLATION

Q20. *long run/short run*, the effect of expansionary policy will be purely inflationary.

⊖ **Q21.** Figure 21.6 shows an economy moving clockwise over time from points A to J and back to A again.

Figure 21.6 A Phillips curve loop

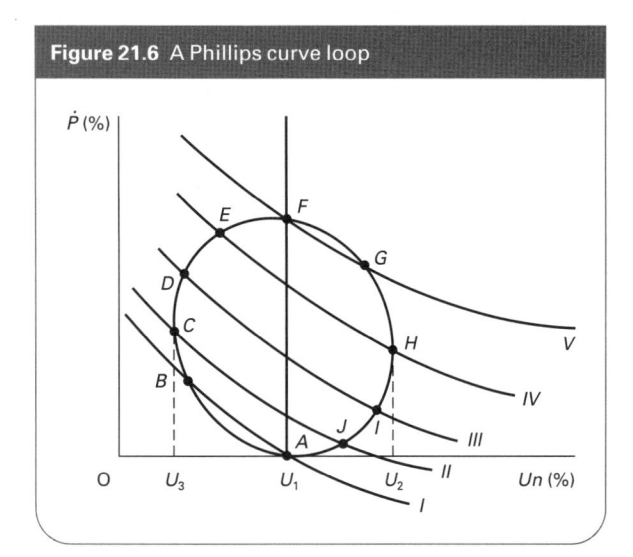

(a) What is the natural rate of unemployment? $U_1/U_2/U_3$
(b) What is the non-accelerating inflation rate of unemployment (NAIRU)? $U_1/U_2/U_3$
(c) Between what points will the economy experience positive demand-pull pressures on inflation?

....

(d) Between what points will the economy experience stagflation?

....

(e) How could the economy move from point F back to point A more rapidly?

....

◐ **Q22.** A fall in the rate of frictional unemployment will cause the Phillips curve to shift to the right. *True/False*

21.3 Inflation and unemployment: the new classical position

(Pages 601–5) The *new* classical economists take an extreme view of the Phillips curve and the aggregate supply curve. They argue that both curves are vertical in **Q23.** *the short run alone/the long run alone/both the short run and the long run/neither the short run nor the long run*. Therefore the effect of any expansionary monetary policy will be simply to **Q24.** *raise prices/increase output and employment*.

The new classical school assumes that markets clear **Q25.** *very slowly/virtually instantaneously*. Therefore all unemployment is **Q26.** *voluntary/involuntary*.

The new classical economists reject adaptive expectations theory. Instead they base their analysis on *rational expectations*.

◐ **Q27.** Rational expectations theory states that:
(a) Expectations are formed using currently available information. *True/False*
(b) Errors in prediction are made at random and therefore do not result in systematic divergences between the actual and expected rate of inflation. *True/False*
(c) The current economic situation will have only limited impact on expectations. *True/False*
(d) Expectations are based on imperfect information. *True/False*

⊖ **Q28.** Figure 21.7 shows the effects upon price and output of a rise in the level of aggregate demand under rational expectations. Aggregate demand rises from AD_1 to AD_2.

Figure 21.7 Rational expectations and the effect on prices and output of a change in aggregate demand

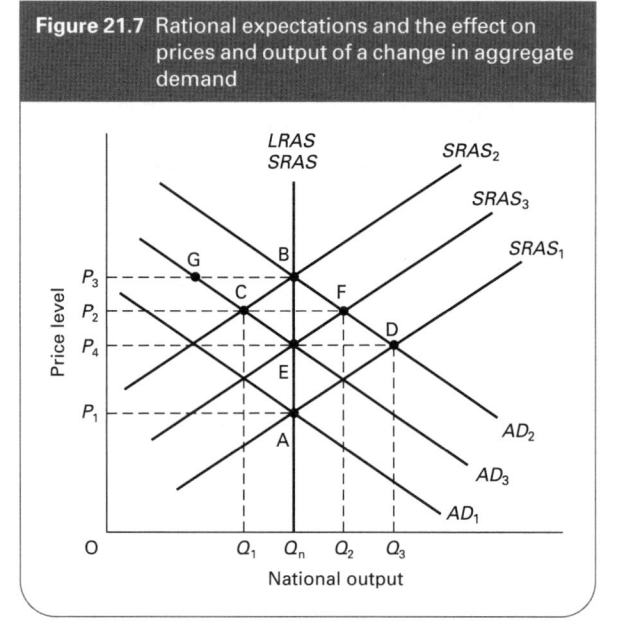

(a) Assuming the long-run AS curve is vertical, then given rational expectations theory, to which point on Figure 21.7 will the economy move in the *short run*, assuming that people correctly predict that the AD curve will shift to AD_2?

....

(b) If expectations prove to be incorrect, and people anticipate that aggregate demand will rise only to AD_3 and that the price level will rise only to P_4, to what point will the economy move in the short run?

....

(c) Returning to point A, assume now that aggregate demand in reality only increases to AD_3, but that people *over*predict the rate of inflation and believe in effect that aggregate demand will rise to AD_2 and that prices will rise to P_3. To what point will the economy move in the short run?

....

Q29. What happens to the Phillips curve if inflation is (a) underpredicted and (b) overpredicted?

(a) ....

....

(b) ....

....

One of the major criticisms made of the new classical approach concerns the assumption of perfect wage and price flexibility.

Q30. Why is total price and wage flexibility unrealistic?

....

....

....

(Page 605) Even with this criticism, the new classical school has had an important influence on attitudes towards government management of the economy.

Q31. According to the new classical school, governments should, in order to manage the economy:
A. use discretionary fiscal and monetary policy.
B. use only monetary policy when attempting to increase output and employment.
C. leave everything to market forces and not intervene at all.
D. announce monetary rules to control inflation and attempt to reduce voluntary unemployment by liberalising the market.
E. announce monetary rules to control inflation and otherwise do not interfere with the market.

(Pages 605–6) If new classical economists argue that unemployment deviates from its natural rate only very temporarily and by chance, how do they explain cyclical fluctuations in unemployment and output? They have developed 'real business cycle theory' to explain this.

Q32. Real business cycle theory explains cyclical fluctuations in terms of:
A. fluctuations in real aggregate demand (i.e. after correcting for inflation).
B. fluctuations in the money supply, caused by banks expanding credit in anticipation of real increases in output and hence demand.
C. the effects of changes in rational expectations on real output.
D. fluctuations in aggregate supply, caused by technological or structural changes in the economy that take place over a number of months.
E. fluctuations in real output causing changes in expectations.

21.4 Inflation and unemployment: the modern Keynesian position
(Pages 607–10)

Q33. Which of the following are given as reasons by Keynesians for the problem of both higher inflation and higher unemployment in the 1980s and 1990s (or at least a worse trade-off) than in the 1950s and 1960s?
(a) An increase in equilibrium unemployment (at least up to the early 1990s). Yes/No
(b) Expectations of higher inflation and/or higher unemployment. Yes/No
(c) High unemployment persisting after the end of a recession (hysteresis). Yes/No
(d) The absence of a trade-off, even in the short run, between inflation and unemployment. Yes/No

Q34. Why are 'insider workers' in firms able to secure higher wage rates, if there are 'outsiders' willing to work at lower wage rates?

....

....

Q35. According to Keynesians, which of the following are suitable policies to tackle the problem of hysteresis?
(a) An increase in aggregate demand. Yes/No
(b) Retraining programmes. Yes/No
(c) Grants to firms to take on the long-term unemployed. Yes/No
(d) A tight monetary policy. Yes/No

Q36. Modern Keynesians argue that structural changes experienced by the economy over recent years have resulted in higher levels of technological, structural and frictional unemployment. They argue that freer markets would solve this problem. *True/False*

Q37. Give two reasons why modern Keynesians reject the notion of a natural rate of unemployment.

1. ....

2. ....

Q38. Modern Keynesians are critical of free-market thinking, arguing that government policy should involve the maintenance of a steady expansion of demand. *True/False*

B PROBLEMS, EXERCISES AND PROJECTS

Table 21.1 An expectations-augmented inflation function: $\dot{P}_t = (40/U - 4) + \dot{P}_t^e$

Year	U	40/U − 4	+	$\dot{P}^e$	=	$\dot{P}$
0	...	...	+	...	=	...
1	...	...	+	...	=	...
2	...	...	+	...	=	...
3	...	...	+	...	=	...
4	...	...	+	...	=	...
5	...	...	+	...	=	...
6	...	...	+	...	=	...
7	...	...	+	...	=	...

Q39. Assume that inflation depends on two things: the level of aggregate demand, indicated by the inverse of the rate of unemployment (1/U), and the expected rate of inflation ($\dot{P}_t^e$). Assume that the rate of inflation ($\dot{P}_t$) is given by the equation:

$$\dot{P}_t = 40/U - 4 + \dot{P}_t^e$$

Assume initially (year 0) that the actual and expected rate of inflation is zero.

(a) What is the current (natural) rate of unemployment?

....

(b) Now assume in year 1 that the government wishes to reduce unemployment to 5 per cent and continues to expand aggregate demand by as much as is necessary to achieve this. Fill in the rows for years 0 to 4 of Table 21.1. It is assumed for simplicity that the expected rate of inflation in a given year ($\dot{P}_t^e$) is equal to the actual rate of inflation in the previous year ($\dot{P}_{t-1}$).

(c) Now assume in year 5 that the government, worried about rising inflation, reduces aggregate demand sufficiently to reduce inflation by 2 per cent in that year. What must the rate of unemployment be raised to in that year?

....

(d) Assuming that unemployment stays at this high level, continue Table 21.1 for years 5 to 7.

Q40. In Tables 21.2 and 21.3, you are provided with unemployment and consumer price inflation data for three countries.

Table 21.2 Unemployment rates (percentage)

	1971	1972	1973	1974	1975	1976	1977	1978	1979	1980	1981	1982	1983	1984	1985	1986
USA	6.0	5.6	4.9	5.6	8.3	7.7	7.0	6.1	5.8	7.2	7.6	9.7	9.6	7.1	7.1	7.0
Japan	1.2	1.4	1.3	1.4	1.9	2.0	2.0	2.2	2.1	2.0	2.2	2.3	2.7	2.6	2.6	2.8
France	2.7	2.8	2.7	3.0	4.3	4.5	5.0	5.4	6.0	6.4	7.6	8.2	7.9	9.4	9.8	9.9

	1987	1988	1989	1990	1991	1992	1993	1994	1995	1996	1997	1998	1999	2000	2001	2002
	6.2	5.5	5.3	5.6	6.8	7.5	6.9	6.0	5.6	5.4	4.9	4.5	4.2	4.0	4.8	5.6
	2.8	2.5	2.3	2.1	2.1	2.2	2.5	2.9	3.1	3.4	3.4	4.1	4.7	4.7	5.0	5.8
	10.1	9.6	9.1	8.6	9.1	10.0	11.3	11.8	11.4	11.9	11.8	11.4	10.7	9.3	8.6	9.1

Source: OECD. © OECD Publications.

Table 21.3 Consumer prices (annual percentage increase)

	1971	1972	1973	1974	1975	1976	1977	1978	1979	1980	1981	1982	1983	1984	1985	1986
USA	4.3	3.3	6.2	11.1	9.1	5.7	6.5	7.6	11.2	13.5	10.3	6.1	3.2	4.3	3.5	1.9
Japan	6.1	4.5	11.7	24.5	11.8	9.3	8.1	3.8	3.6	8.0	4.9	2.7	1.9	2.2	2.1	0.4
France	5.5	6.2	7.3	13.7	11.8	9.6	9.4	9.1	10.8	13.6	13.4	11.8	9.6	7.4	5.8	2.5

	1987	1988	1989	1990	1991	1992	1993	1994	1995	1996	1997	1998	1999	2000	2001	2002
	3.6	4.1	4.8	5.4	4.2	3.0	3.0	2.6	2.8	2.9	2.3	1.5	2.2	3.4	2.8	1.8
	−0.2	0.5	2.3	3.1	3.3	1.6	1.3	0.7	−0.1	0.0	1.7	0.7	−0.3	−0.7	−0.7	−1.2
	3.3	2.7	3.5	3.6	3.4	2.4	2.2	1.7	1.8	2.1	1.3	0.7	0.6	1.8	1.8	1.6

Source: OECD. © OECD Publications.

(a) Using the data, plot inflation against unemployment for each country, clearly marking the year of each point.
(b) Can you identify any Phillips curve loops?
(c) Does the evidence suggest that the Phillips curves have shifted to the right over time?
(d) Do you think that the Phillips curve relationship is of any value to economic policy makers?

Q41. Figure 21.8 gives a monetarist/adaptive expectations perspective of the relationship between real GDP, unemployment and inflation over the course of the business cycle.
(a) Explain the relationship between actual and real GDP, unemployment and inflation at each of the points 1–7 in the top part of the diagram. Why does the top of the curve in the top diagram (point 6) not correspond to the bottom and top respectively of the curves in the other two parts of the diagram (point 5)?
(b) If the magnitude of the cycle in the top part of the diagram became greater, would there be a similar change in magnitude in the fluctuations in unemployment and inflation?
(c) To what extent would (i) a Keynesian and (ii) a new classicist agree with the relationships portrayed in the diagram?

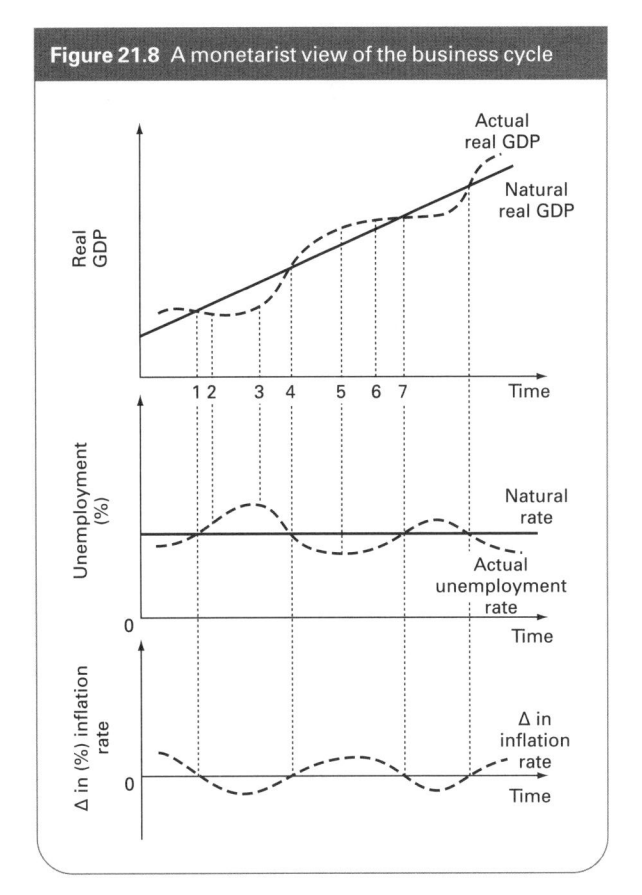

Figure 21.8 A monetarist view of the business cycle

C DISCUSSION TOPICS AND ESSAYS

Q42. How does the shape of the aggregate supply curve affect the relationship between inflation and unemployment?

Q43. Why will the long-run aggregate supply curve have a different slope from the short-run aggregate supply curve? What determines the relationship between the two?

Q44. What is meant by the 'natural' rate of unemployment? Is it possible to reduce unemployment below the natural rate in (a) the short run and (b) the long run?

Q45. Distinguish between adaptive and rational expectations and describe how they are formed. What effect will each type of expectation have on the relationship between inflation and unemployment?

Q46. Outline the main assumptions made by the new classical school and describe the implications these assumptions have for macroeconomic policy.

Q47. If real wages are 'sticky' downwards, what implications does this have for the shape of the Phillips curve and for government macroeconomic policy?

Q48. How do new Keynesians explain the persistence of unemployment in the recoveries of the mid-1980s and mid-1990s?

Q49. Discuss the proposition that the only effective way of reducing *both* inflation *and* unemployment is to use supply-side policies.

Q50. Debate
Governments invariably resort to demand-side policies for short-term political gain. But such policies are useless in the long run as a means of increasing aggregate supply.

D ARTICLES

In the following article, taken from *The Times* of 3 April 2001, Anatole Kaletsky reflects on the economic success of the UK economy over recent years and who is ultimately responsible for it.

Should the Tories claim credit for Labour's economic success?

Does the Government believe that interest rates and taxes should be managed to try to achieve the best possible tradeoff between inflation and unemployment? Or does Labour believe, as the Tories asserted in the 1980s under the influence of Milton Friedman and Nigel Lawson, that the level of unemployment is an inevitable product of market forces and that controlling inflation is the only legitimate macroeconomic goal? These abstract-sounding questions can be posed in a more concrete and politically relevant way. Has Labour merely benefited from the good work that began at the Treasury in 1993, when Norman Lamont was forced to reconstruct Britain's economic policies after sterling's providential expulsion from the European exchange-rate mechanism? Or did Brown make an indispensable contribution to the permanent improvement of Britain's economic performance with his bold decision to transfer responsibility for monetary policy from the Treasury to the Bank of England?

In the monetarist counter-revolution of the mid-1970s, the opponents of full-employment policies had one essential claim. They asserted that all efforts by governments or central banks to reduce unemployment through macroeconomic policy were doomed to failure. If interest rates were cut or public spending was increased in an effort to combat unemployment, higher inflation would be the only result. This view was illustrated with a diagram known as the Phillips Curve among economists. The curve simply plotted the combinations of inflation and unemployment by the economy during various years and then drew a line between these points to show how the economy moved from one combination of inflation and unemployment to another.

Until the mid-1970s, it was generally believed that a country could choose to achieve rather lower unemployment by permitting slightly higher inflation – in other words that the curve sloped down to the right. But the monetarists asserted that the curve was in fact vertical – that expansionary macroeconomic policy would simply result in an inflation moving upwards, without unemployment moving to the left at all. This was, in fact, true during the 1970s (from 1971 to 1978 in the chart).

But what the chart also shows is that the Phillips Curve has become completely horizontal since 1994. In the past seven years, expansion in macroeconomic policy has moved unemployment to the left without causing any increase in inflation. We now seem to live in a world, therefore, where inflation is effectively fixed by structural factors, while unemployment is mainly determined by the strength of economic demand.

This seems to be the precise opposite of the world imagined by the monetarists and Milton Friedman, and still described in the textbooks of economics. This is a world where the primary function of monetary policy is to determine the rate of economic growth and the level of unemployment, while inflation is set by structural factors such as the strength of competition and trade unions' power.

Does this mean that Mr Brown was wrong to make the Bank of England independent on the basis of a monetarist theory that is clearly no longer valid? Not necessarily. The Bank has been doing a pretty good job of managing unemployment and aggregate demand. At some point, however, events will expose the illusion that monetary policy has nothing to do with politics or government. The Bank cannot simply follow an inflation target that is rapidly losing its meaning, on the basis of a monetarist economic theory that no longer seems to apply to the real world.

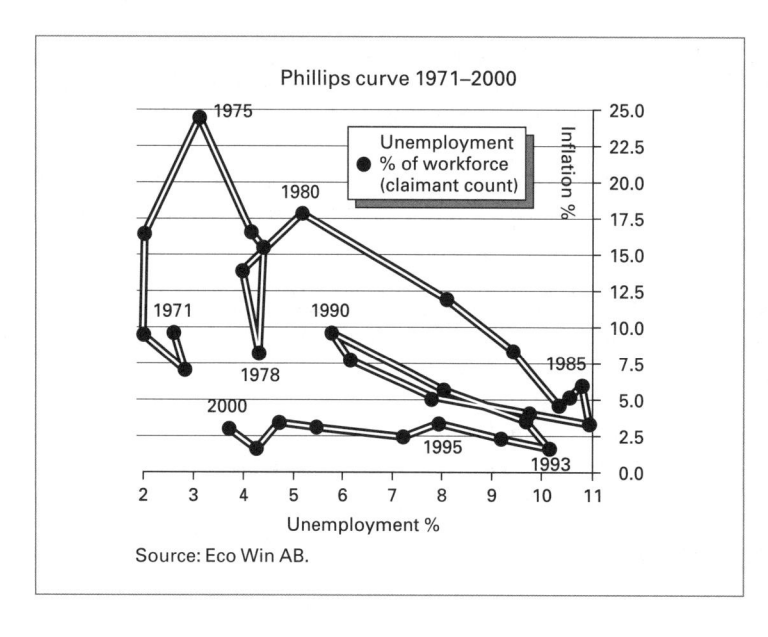

Phillips curve 1971–2000

Source: Eco Win AB.

(a) What were the apparent policy implications of the original Phillips curve?
(b) What did the accelerationist theory, developed by the monetarists, imply about the shape of the long-run Phillips curve?
(c) What arguments does Kaletsky advance to explain the performance of inflation and unemployment since the early 1990s?
(d) If Kaletsky is right and current monetarist theory no longer applies to the real world, what are the implications for the conduct of monetary policy?

One of the true strengths of a theory or idea is how it changes people's views and understanding of the world around them. Rational expectations is one such influential theory. The article below, taken from *The Economist* of 14 October 1995, assesses the work of Robert Lucas in developing rational expectations theory.

Great expectations, and rational too

Robert Lucas, a professor at the University of Chicago, is the most influential macroeconomist of his generation. Mr Lucas developed the idea known as 'rational expectations'. His work transformed both macroeconomic theory and the way that economists think about the effects of economic policies.

Expectations are fundamental to economic behaviour. A trade union negotiating with employers, say, will base its wage demands in part on its forecast of inflation. And the final deal will affect the actual inflation rate once it feeds through to prices. By definition, you might think, expectations are forward-looking. But until the 1970s, economists modelled expectations as if they were based on the past: next year's expected inflation rate might be a weighted average of current and past rates. That was not daft: it is impossible to observe expectations directly; and it is reasonable to suppose that they will be based largely on experience.

Yet it was wrong, because it supposed that people might go on believing what they knew to be false. Mr Lucas was not the first to see this. In the early 1960s, John Muth, another economist, argued that it would be better to assume that people have 'rational expectations'. These are forward-looking, in that they are based on all data to hand; expectations that are persistently wrong will be discarded.

Mr Lucas showed just how important this simple idea is. Governments' models of the economy are, of necessity, based on the past behaviour of consumers and firms. But unless they incorporate rational expectations, said Mr Lucas, they are useless for assessing changes in economic policy. This is because economic behaviour in the past will have depended on the economic policies of the time. When governments change their policies, expectations will change too; so the economy's response to a new policy may be different from what governments expect.

Although this principle is quite general, the best-known examples concern monetary policy. Until the 1970s, governments thought they could buy lower unemployment with a bit more inflation. That conceit had already been shredded by Milton Friedman, another Nobel prizewinner from Chicago, and Edmund Phelps, another American economist. But they had used backward-looking expectations. By applying rational expectations, Mr Lucas nailed the illusion for good.

In the short run, an inflationary monetary policy will boost jobs – but only because firms are fooled into thinking that a rise in the price they can charge signals stronger demand for their goods; in fact, it merely reflects a rise in prices in general. In the long run, under rational expectations, there can be no trade-off between inflation and unemployment, because people cannot be fooled for ever. Once they see that inflation has risen, unemployment will return to its old level.

Many forecasting models now include at least some element of rational expectations. For instance, predictions about the inflation rate that people will come to expect are typically made consistent with the model's own predictions of inflation. The one used by America's Federal Reserve is being revised to make its characterisation of the bond market more forward-looking; in the labour market, where adjustment to news is slower, expectations based on history will also still be used.

Warning governments against bad policy based on unreliable models is all very well. But how do rational expectations help them to choose a policy? To some economists and politicians in the early 1980s, one answer looked obvious. To reduce inflation, governments had to do little more than announce a strict monetary target. In the face of such a tough policy, workers, consumers and firms would expect lower inflation. They would moderate their wage demands and prices, and – hey presto – inflation would tumble at little cost in output and jobs.

How to be believed

That idea turned out to be wrong, but not because of any flaw in the notion of rational expectations. One reason was that markets do not always 'clear' quickly – i.e., supply and demand may be out of balance for a while – so unemployment may rise when monetary policy is tightened. 'New Keynesian' economists, such as Mr Mankiw, say that wages and prices take time to adjust, so that markets often clear only slowly. However, such theories often assume that expectations are rational.

The principle also explains why neither an announcement of tight money nor even a brief period of monetary stringency will lead quickly to low inflation: governments may not be believed. If people do not think that the government is in earnest, they will go on expecting high inflation. So financial markets will continue to demand high bond yields; workers will not curb their pay demands, nor will firms hold down prices.

Thus, again thanks to Mr Lucas, economists are now obsessed with the issues of credibility and sustainability. Can governments keep their promises, and for how long? Post-Lucasian economics recognises that governments are perpetually in temptation: although tough policies eventually bring the benefits of low inflation, politicians can earn popularity through an unexpected burst of inflation, which temporarily boosts incomes and employment; but if they succumb, their credibility is lost.

© *The Economist*, London (14.10.95)

(a) What makes rational expectations 'rational'?
(b) How did the theory of rational expectations, developed by Lucas, differ from the accepted way in which expectations were seen to be formed?
(c) How has the theory of rational expectations influenced the process of policy making?

In the article below, taken from *New Economy* of August 1999, Geoffrey Dicks and John O'Sullivan consider the value of NAIRU as a guide for policy, and how theory, reality and policy action do not always seem to correspond.

Is NAIRU worth a can of beans?

In the first half of 1998, unemployment was falling slowly and from August it was virtually stable at a rate of 4.6 per cent according to the claimant count, or 6.2 per cent on the ILO survey definition. Private-sector earnings growth peaked at 6.3 per cent in May 1998 and, on the headline measure, fell throughout the rest of the year. To anyone schooled in the NAIRU analytical framework, the implications are self-evident: since earnings were decelerating, unemployment must have been above the NAIRU.

The analysis could be refined by examining what was happening to real wages – falling, against the yardstick of underlying inflation which was stable at 2.5 to 2.6 per cent in the second half of the year – or to settlements which were edging lower. But without a more complex theory that brings in inflation expectations or lagged adjustment, the basic premise is inescapable. Unemployment at the start of 1999 had not fallen far enough to generate higher wage inflation – it must have been above the NAIRU.

In the first half of 1998 it all seemed very different. Interest rates reached a peak of 7.5 per cent in June 1998. The immediate cause of the final rate hike was the strength of earnings, particularly in the private sector, which confirmed the growing conviction of the Monetary Policy Committee (MPC) that output had risen significantly above trend and that unemployment had fallen below the level consistent with the inflation target.

Evidence has emerged over the last month that the cumulative tightening of the labour market has resulted in a rate of private sector earnings growth that jeopardises achievement of the inflation target over the medium term. (MPC statement accompanying the hike in interest rates to 7.5 per cent, 4 June 1998)

The next three months saw newspaper columnists and leader writers compete with City economists to produce the most hair-shirt estimate of how far unemployment would have to rise simply to stabilise inflation at the 2.5 per cent target.

How can the data from the second half of 1998 be interpreted? What seemed clear cut in June 1998 – that unemployment had fallen below the NAIRU and earnings were accelerating – was turned on its head as unemployment continued to fall and employment to rise. Yet all the froth went out of earnings. In the MPC's analysis, the labour market was at a 'turning point', begging the question as to whether a turning point was all that was necessary. In fact, is the whole analytical concept of the NAIRU worth a can of beans?

Nice concept . . .
Successive generations of MBA students at the London Business School in the 1980s were schooled in the NAIRU/output gap framework (by Alan Budd before us): that there is no trade-off between output and inflation in the long term; that there comes a point at which excess demand in the labour market results in accelerating wages, and that attempts to hold unemployment below the rate consistent with stable wage growth are ultimately self-defeating (since they produce rising inflation), all make intuitive sense. There seems to be no difficulty with the concept as such.

It came as no surprise therefore to read in the minutes of the MPC's December 1997 meeting (the first that Alan Budd attended as a member) that the focus of the discussion was shifting away from rates of growth of demand and output towards levels of output and unemployment. The following passage from the minutes sets out definitively how the MPC was looking at the economy in the first half of 1998.

The Committee began by discussing the importance to its assessment of the inflation outlook of levels of economic variables as well as their growth rates . . . Above-trend growth rates of output and employment need not entail short-run inflationary pressures when there was plenty of spare capacity, as was typically the case when the economy was coming out of a prolonged recession. But as spare capacity was used up, underlying inflationary pressures would increase.

Once the level of economic activity was above trend and/or the level of unemployment below the natural rate, increasing inflation would generally result. If the levels of output and employment then remained above trend, inflationary pressures would be exacerbated, requiring a more severe or prolonged slowdown to bring them back to trend levels.

From concept to application
The message is clear. A recovery that began in 1992 had, by early 1998, exhausted the spare capacity built up in the recession of the early 1990s. The MPC probably endorsed Treasury estimates which suggested that output was about on trend in the first half of 1997 and that by the turn of the year there was a (positive) output gap of around one per cent of GDP. Similarly, for the labour market. Unemployment had been falling steadily since early 1993 and, while the initial effect on wages was negligible, average earnings had, since early 1995, been on a rising trend. Put the two together and it was clear to the MPC that above-trend output and unsustainable low unemployment posed a major threat to the 2.5 per cent inflation target.

The MPC has been consistently cautious in its assessment. Even when it was spooked by a sudden jump in earnings growth last spring and raised rates to 7.5 per cent, its language was still that of central bankers: 'the earnings data *suggested* that it was *more likely* that unemployment was below the rate compatible with stable inflation. In that case, it was *probable* that unemployment would have to rise to hit the inflation target on a sustainable basis.' (MPC Minutes, June, 1998).

Where the MPC was cautious, others were more dogmatic, believing that the trend in average earnings growth, upwards since early 1995, said it all. The leader writers on the *Financial Times* typified the attitude: 'pay inflation has been rising since unemployment fell much below eight per cent [claimant count]. The labour market reforms of the past two decades seem to have left the structural rate of unemployment at between seven per cent and eight per cent, two to three percentage points greater than today.' (*Financial Times* 17 July)

Not content with that, they went on the offensive again two months later: '. . . unemployment must now be allowed to rise – perhaps by 500 000 – to bring the economy back to a non-inflationary path.' (*Financial Times* 11 September 1998) prompting our reply: 'by arguing for a 500 000 rise in unemployment you are implicitly saying that unemployment has been below the natural rate for two and a half years. If the strict theory of the NAIRU has any validity, by now inflation should surely be on an increasing (accelerating?) trend. Is it? Quite the reverse. Does this not imply that there is something wrong with the theory?' (*Financial Times* 15 September, 1998).

. . . shame about the application

Even if the concept of the NAIRU is acceptable or the output gap is a useful analytical tool, it is possible to take exception to the attempts by FT leader writers, who were typical of a whole strand of thinking, to translate this into an explicit policy prescription (or perhaps it was the prescription itself that we objected to). How can these two positions be reconciled?

Estimates of the natural rate of unemployment in Britain in the mid-1990s (as a percentage of the labour force (claimant count))

	%
Patrick Minford	3.5
Andrew Sentance	4–6
Tim Congdon	6–7
David Currie	6.5–7.5
Andrew Brittan	7–8
Gavyn Davies	7–8

The NAIRU is lower than has previously been estimated

It is very easy to obtain a spurious estimate for the NAIRU from an inappropriate regression specification. For example, by regressing inflation against lagged inflation and unemployment and solving out for the NAIRU. This may have been the approach of some of the Chancellor's 'Wise Men' in 1995 (see table). These estimates were made more than three years ago and it is possible that they (or some of them) were accurate at the time, but that the NAIRU has subsequently fallen. The MPC itself believes that there has been a reduction in the NAIRU: '. . . in each year of this recovery, the percentage increase in real unit labour costs has been lower than would have been expected based on the average relationship since 1980. The most likely reason for the shift in this trade-off is that the equilibrium, or natural rate, of unemployment is lower now than it was in the 1980s.' (*Inflation Report* February 1998).

There are many reasons why the NAIRU might have shifted down between the 1980s and the 1990s (changes in the benefits regime, lower rates of unionisation, the reduction in job protection legislation and so on). It is hard to argue, however, that the NAIRU has shifted in the last year to the extent that unemployment has fallen, yet at the same time moved from below to above the NAIRU. It is possible that unemployment is above the NAIRU, and has been throughout the recent experience, but the puzzle then becomes why earnings growth was on an upward trend from 1995 to 1998.

The answer is that earnings growth has not been rising *in real terms*. The wage bargain starts with the headline rate of inflation (rather than the underlying rate that the MPC is targeting) and, mainly as a result of interest rate increases, this was on a generally rising trend from about mid-1996 onwards. If real earnings are defined as the difference between the current rate of growth of nominal earnings and retail prices, real earnings growth has been approximately stable for the last two years at one to two per cent – less than trend productivity.

It makes sense to look at real wage costs, since unemployment is a real variable and should in theory be related to real, rather than nominal, wages. And if real wages are rising at less than trend productivity, they do not in themselves pose a threat to inflation. That is not to say that the six per cent-plus peak in private sector earnings growth seen in 1998 was consistent with the 2.5 per cent inflation target, but neither can it automatically be concluded that unemployment fell below the NAIRU. The distinction between nominal earnings growing too rapidly for the inflation target (which they were) and real earnings being pushed higher by levels of unemployment falling too low (which they were not), was lost on some commentators.

(a) What is NAIRU and how should it inform the economic policy of government?

(b) Why might the NAIRU have fallen in recent years?

(c) Why do the authors maintain that the true value of the NAIRU is lower than is generally accepted?

(d) Why might *real* wage increases be a better guide than simple price inflation as to whether unemployment is below the NAIRU?

> In the article below, taken from the *Financial Times* of 2 September 1999, Samuel Brittan takes a look at the current state of the Keynesian–monetarist debate. He suggests that the two sides tend to caricature each other's position in order to make their own position seem more reasonable and their opponent's position more extreme. Most *practising economic advisers*, however, take elements from both sides of the debate: indeed there has emerged a large measure of consensus about the need for government intervention on the one hand, and the adherence to inflation targets on the other.

Voices in the air

During the 1970s and 1980s there developed a counter-revolution against, not necessarily the core doctrines of Keynes, but against the 'Keynesianism' which governed official policy in so many countries, especially in the US and UK. It could better be described as a reaction against overambitious economic management.

The counter-revolutionary ideas were partially put into effect by the Reagan and Thatcher governments – which for some people was enough to condemn them. In fact the UK and US counter-revolutions started in the closing years of the Callaghan and Carter administrations – Callaghan's famous 1976 denial that governments could spend their way into full employment was a landmark.

The counter-revolution has indeed been carried forward by the present Labour government and has no keener exponent than the chancellor, Gordon Brown. Evidence is provided by his grant of operational independence to the Bank of England, his remit to the Bank to follow a strict inflation target, his devotion to a medium term financial framework limiting government borrowing, and his insistence on 'supply-side' cures for unemployment.

None of this prevents many leftwing economic intellectuals from disliking this counter-revolution intensely – a dislike which is shared by some on the right who are still attached to the postwar consensus. Hence the series of claims that Keynes is back and that free market and monetarist economists are discredited. How are these claims reconciled with the fact that in so many of the world economies there are independent central banks pursuing targets for inflation rather than for real growth?

Much of the battle reflects a 'Kulturkampf' among the economic chattering classes, which is a good deal fiercer than the ordinary party political battle. The most important rule of this game is to draw the dividing line between the Keynesian and the counter-revolutionary school in a way favourable to your own side.

If you want to exclaim that Keynes is alive and kicking you attribute to the counter-revolutionaries the most extreme doctrines possible: for instance that the economy automatically balances at full employment and is self-stabilising. They are also supposed to believe that the only instrument of economic policy is money supply rules, which have to be followed rigidly. As soon as it is clear that the money supply can neither be defined nor controlled so easily, and that in any case it cannot be the sole guide to policy, the other side exclaims with glee: 'Keynes is alive: classical economists fall down dead.' If, on the other hand, you want to pull down the Keynesian flag you pretend that any concern with inflation, other than by pay and price controls, is antipathetic to the Great Man's memory.

Those who want to claim victory for the anti-Keynesian side can point to the widespread agreement on what is called a 'nominal framework'. This means that even authorities such as the US Federal Reserve, which openly admit to a concern with the level of demand, think of it as demand in money terms. Those of us who would like the European Central Bank or the Bank of England to adopt similar objectives are really saying that at very low rates of inflation central banks should not be afraid of promoting output and employment; but this must be subject to an overriding concern with preventing an inflationary take-off.

A closer inspection shows that much of the argument is shadow boxing. The counter-revolutionaries have demonstrated that there is no long-run trade-off between unemployment and inflation and that there may even be a trade-off the other way at high and fluctuating inflation rates. That is their Big Idea. There is an underlying or structural rate of unemployment which cannot easily be treated by monetary, fiscal or exchange rate policy. This is sometimes called the natural rate, or more politely the NAIRU – non-accelerating inflation rate of unemployment.

Yet on reflection there is no incompatibility between the 'natural rate' and at least one reasonable interpretation of Keynes's doctrines in his 1936 *General Theory of Employment, Interest and Money*. The inclusion of 'employment' in the title was no accident. Before then economists believed that increases in savings could be nothing but beneficial. Interest rates would fall, investment rise and the growth rate increase. The heresy of Keynes was to demonstrate that these moralising tales might not always be true.

The traditional analysis, by focusing only on interest rates, overlooked other variables that could respond: namely output and employment. An attempted increase in savings might reduce national income and raise unemployment. This could happen because interest rates fail to fall enough or because investment is not sufficiently sensitive to them. It is this oversavings doctrine that was Keynes's Big Idea, for which he would have deserved a Nobel prize – had it existed in his lifetime for economics – several times over. In contemporary terms this means that you might not get unemployment even as low as the 'natural rate' if attempted savings are too high and demand is therefore inadequate.

There can be honest disagreement about how fast to try to restore price stability or squeeze inflation out of the system once it has taken hold. Similarly, when there is some depressive force, there can be disagreement on how aggressively governments should try to restore demand. But the interesting thing is that these arguments do not centre around any of the slogans used by the flagwavers of the two sides.

Those economists who still call themselves monetarists, including Milton Friedman himself, are often in the forefront of saying what Japan or the emerging countries should have done to restore activity.

There are almost no practising economic advisers who believe that the economy can be left on its own to approach an underlying equilibrium. It can be knocked off course by events ranging from oil price explosions to German reunification, not to speak of capital flights away from emerging countries or into western economies whose exchange rates then overshoot.

On the other side many practising Keynesians are now 'reconstructed'. This means that they do not believe that governments can promote full employment regardless of what is happening to inflation: and in practice they support the inflation targets now in force.

There is also a good deal of acceptance of the primary role of monetary policy in fighting both inflation and depression, although in some cases this is based on perceived political possibilities rather than genuine conviction. There are plenty of disagreements left on what remains for fiscal policy to do.

The most famous quotation from Keynes runs: 'The ideas of economists and political philosophers, both when they are right and when they are wrong are more powerful than is commonly understood. Indeed the world is ruled by little else. Practical men, who believe themselves to be quite exempt from any intellectual influences are usually the slaves of some defunct economist. Madmen in authority, who hear voices in the air, are distilling their frenzy from some academic scribbler from a few years back.' This remains true.

(a) Outline the arguments used by (i) Keynesians to criticise the monetarist counter-revolution; (ii) monetarists to criticise Keynesianism.

(b) Where do the counter-revolutionaries and Keynesians share common ground concerning how the economy operates and the role of government policy?

(c) Is the concept of the NAIRU consistent with the theory that aggregate demand might be inadequate if there is a high level of saving?

ANSWERS

Q1. Keynesian.

Q2. monetarist.

Q3. (a) and (d) relate to the Keynesian aggregate supply curve, AS_1. Changes in aggregate demand will have no effect on prices until the full-employment level of income (Y_2) is reached. (b) and (c) relate to the monetarist aggregate supply curve. Changes in aggregate demand will have no effect on output, but instead will be reflected solely in changes in the price level.

Q4. *without considering*. We assume that firms assume that a rise in demand is confined to their product.

Q5. *(a)* See Figure A21.1. The average and marginal curves shift to AR_2 and MR_2 respectively, giving a new profit-maximising price and output of P_2 and Q_2.

(b) See Figure A21.2. The flatter the MC curve, the more will a rise in demand affect output rather than price.

(c) steeper.

(d) The nearer a firm gets to full capacity, the more costs per unit will rise for each extra unit produced. This is in accordance with the principle of diminishing marginal returns.

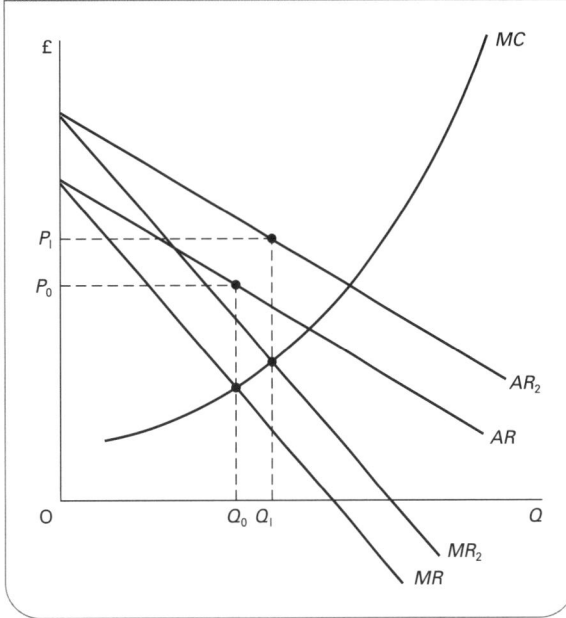

Figure A21.1 Profit-maximising price and output for a firm in an imperfect market following a rise in demand

Figure A21.2 Profit-maximising price and output for a firm with alternative cost curves

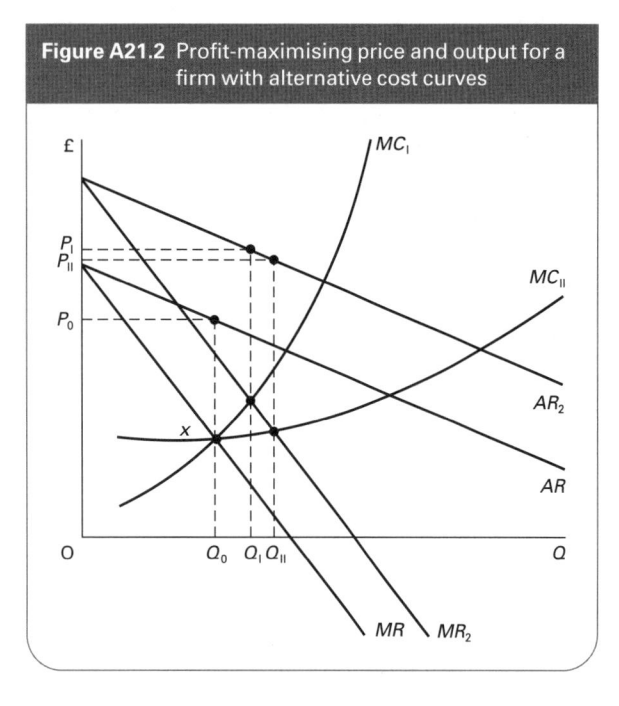

Q6. similar in shape to the MC curve illustrated in Figure 21.2.

Q7. *(a)* Diagram (a).
  (b) As AD rises, prices throughout the economy also rise. Because firms are interdependent, the price rise by one firm will be passed on as additional costs of production to another firm. This will cause the short-run AS curve to shift upwards.
  (c) As demand rises, firms will be encouraged to invest. As a result they will be able to increase output without significantly increasing prices.

Q8. (a), (d) and (f) will tend to make the AS curve *steeper*. All of these will tend to stimulate inflation and lead firms to believe that they can raise their prices without losing market share. The effect will therefore be to shift the short-run AS curve upwards and hence make the long-run AS curve steeper.
  (b), (c) and (e) will tend to make the AS curve shallower. They will all encourage firms to invest, in the belief that their market is expanding. The effect will therefore be to shift the short-run AS curve to the right and hence make the long-run AS curve shallower.

Q9. *(a)* $Q_7 - Q_3$ (the gap between AS_L and N at W_1).
  (b) There is no disequilibrium unemployment. The wage rate is at the equilibrium.
  (c) $Q_5 - Q_2$.
  (d) It is still zero, because the wage rate has fallen to the new equilibrium.
  (e) $Q_3 - Q_1$. Note that this is higher than before when the wage rate was W_1. Given that wages are lower, unemployed workers are inclined to search for longer before being prepared to accept job offers.
  (f) $Q_7 - Q_1$ ($N - AD_{L_2}$ at W_1).
  (g) $Q_3 - Q_1$.
  (h) $Q_7 - Q_3$.

Q10. B. Keynesians assume that firms will take on more labour in response to an increase in the demand for the goods that they produce. A fall in the real wage rate is not a precondition.

Q11. The economy will move from point X through points B, C, D and E. Both (a) and (b) will cause aggregate demand to shift to the right, whereas (c) and (d) will cause aggregate supply to shift upwards.

Q12. The economy will move from point X through points F, G, H and E. Both (a) and (b) will cause aggregate supply to shift upwards. If, in response to falling output and rising unemployment, the government then stimulates economic activity, as in (c) and (d), aggregate demand will shift to the right.

Q13. D. The Phillips curve showed the inverse relationship between wage inflation and unemployment. Wage inflation was replaced in later modifications by price inflation.

Q14. C. Adaptive expectations are based upon past events. It is assumed that people learn from experience. Hence, if the rate of inflation is under-predicted one year, the following year expectations will be adapted and revised upwards.

Q15. B. (ii) states that the expected rate of inflation ($\dot{P}^e$) depends on the actual rate of inflation in the last time period ($\dot{P}_{t-1}$): i.e. expectations adapt to what was actually the case previously.
  (iii) states that actual inflation ($\dot{P}_t$) depends on some constant amount (b), on the inverse of unemployment ($1/U$) and on the expected rate of inflation in the current time period ($\dot{P}^e_t$).

Q16. It is sometimes called the accelerationist theory because, in order to keep unemployment below the equilibrium rate, price increases must accelerate: i.e. inflation must rise. As long as unemployment is kept below the equilibrium rate, each year expectations will underpredict the rate of inflation and hence adapt and rise the following year. Thus the trade-off is not between unemployment and inflation but between unemployment and the rate of *increase* in inflation.

Q17. vertical.

Q18. natural rate.

Q19. short run.

Q20. long run.

Q21. *(a)* U_1. This is where real aggregate demand equals real aggregate supply.
  (b) U_1. In this model, the NAIRU is the same as the natural rate. It is the rate of unemployment consistent with a stable rate of inflation.

- (c) Between points *A* and *F*. Unemployment is reduced (temporarily) below the natural rate, but inflation rises.
- (d) Between points *C* and *F*. Between these points both inflation and unemployment rise.
- (e) By a more drastic contraction of aggregate demand. Unemployment would rise above U_2, but inflation would fall more rapidly.

Q22. *False*. A fall in the rate of frictional unemployment will shift the Phillips curve to the left.

Q23. *both the short run and the long run.*

Q24. *raise prices.*

Q25. *virtually instantaneously.*

Q26. *voluntary.*

Q27. (a) *True*. Expectations are formed using currently available information. People look not merely at what has happened to inflation in the past, but also at *current* economic indicators and government policies and project forward.
- (b) *True*. If errors in prediction are made at random, it can be assumed that on *average* forecasts will be correct. (The mean forecasted value will be correct over time, but there will be random divergences around the mean.)
- (c) *False*. Rational expectations theory argues that the current state of the economy, or the current policies being pursued by the government, will have a crucial impact upon expectations.
- (d) *True*. Expectations are based on the information available. Such information might well be incomplete or even wrong.

Q28. (a) The economy will move to point *B*. Here the effect of rising demand is correctly anticipated and simply causes aggregate supply to shift upwards to $SRAS_2$ as aggregate demand expands to AD_2. The price level rises to P_3.
- (b) *F*. Believing that aggregate demand will only rise to AD_3 and the price level to P_4 the aggregate supply curve will only shift up to $SRAS_3$. The excess demand at P_4 of $D - E$ will push up the level of prices. Believing that this represents a *real* rise in prices, firms increase output (they move up along $SRAS_3$.) Short-run equilibrium is achieved at point *F* with a higher price and output of P_2 and Q_2. Eventually, when people realise their mistake, long-run equilibrium will be achieved at point *B*.
- (c) *C*. The converse of (b) occurs. The *AS* curve shifts up to $SRAS_2$. Firms believe that there is a fall in real demand (they perceive a demand deficiency of $B - G$). They thus reduce prices and output. Short-run equilibrium is achieved at point *C* with a price and output of P_2 and Q_1. Eventually, when people realise their mistake, long-run equilibrium will be achieved at point *E*.

Q29. The Phillips curve will always be vertical in the long run as errors in prediction are made at random. However, underprediction will shift the short-run Phillips curve to the left: unemployment temporarily falls below the natural rate. Overprediction will shift the short-run Phillips curve to the right: unemployment will be temporarily above its natural rate.

Q30. There are a number of reasons why the assumption of price and wage flexibility is unrealistic. For example, wage contracts are negotiated on a yearly basis (hardly flexible); trade unions and monopoly producers of goods fix wages and prices; administrative costs in changing prices on a frequent basis would be very high, and may outweigh the advantage of adjusting prices.

Q31. D. The new classical school advocates the setting of clear monetary rules and the adoption of libertarian supply-side measures to reduce the natural rate of unemployment (e.g. reducing the power of trade unions).

Q32. D. The new classical school explains the business cycle in terms of fluctuations in aggregate supply, rather than fluctuations in aggregate demand. These changes in aggregate supply may be the result of changes in technology or other supply-side factors. The effects do not take place instantaneously, but over a period of time. These 'build-up' effects cause periods of expansion (or contraction) in the economy.

Q33. *Yes*. All except (e).

Q34. Because there would be additional costs to employers from employing outsiders, including training costs and the costs of demotivating the insiders. Also insiders may be members of unions who might be able to push their wage rates above market rates. Alternatively, insiders may simply have power and influence within the firm, as a result of having become established members of staff. For these reasons, firms may be willing to pay insiders more, rather than attempting to bring in outsiders.

Q35. (a) *No*; (b) *Yes*; (c) *Yes*; (d) *No*. Supply-side policies are needed to tackle the supply-side problems that have been caused by previous recessions.

Q36. *False*. Keynesians tend to argue that free markets will not offer sufficient incentives to cure this problem. They will fail to encourage sufficient people to retrain or move to where employment might be found.

Q37. Two reasons are: rising demand makes firms more confident about their future sales and encourages them to invest and consider expanding their labour force; if existing rates of unemployment include a high level of long-term unemployed or those unemployed due to structural change, the inflationary impact of their employment and retraining may be offset in the long run by higher levels of productivity.

Q38. *True*. Leaving things to the market is seen by modern Keynesians as a slow and highly ineffective way to deal with economic problems such as unemployment.

Chapter Twenty-two

22 Long-term Economic Growth and Supply-side Policies

A REVIEW

If an economy is to achieve sustained economic growth over the longer term, there must be a sustained increase in potential output. This means that there has to be a continuous rightward shift in the aggregate supply curve. But what causes such shifts and what policies can be adopted to encourage such shifts. This chapter examines these issues.

22.1 Economic growth in the long run
(Pages 614–20)

Although industrialised countries experienced recessions in the mid-1970s, the early 1980s, the early 1990s and early 2000s, OECD countries have averaged rates of economic growth of **Q1.** *between 0 and 2 per cent/2 and 4 per cent/over 4 per cent* per annum over the last 30 years.

Q2. Which of the following are major explanations of this sustained economic growth?
(a) A closing of the gap between actual and potential output. Yes/No
(b) Increases in labour productivity. Yes/No
(c) Technological progress. Yes/No
(d) Sustained increases in the capital stock. Yes/No
(e) Reductions in unemployment. Yes/No
(f) Increases in human capital. Yes/No

Q3. Figure 22.1 shows a simple model of economic growth. Assume that the economy currently has a capital stock of K_0.

(a) What is the level of total investment? ....

(b) What is the level of net investment? ....

(c) What is the current level of national income? ....

(d) Explain the process whereby national income increases.

....

....

(e) Will national income go on rising for ever? Explain.

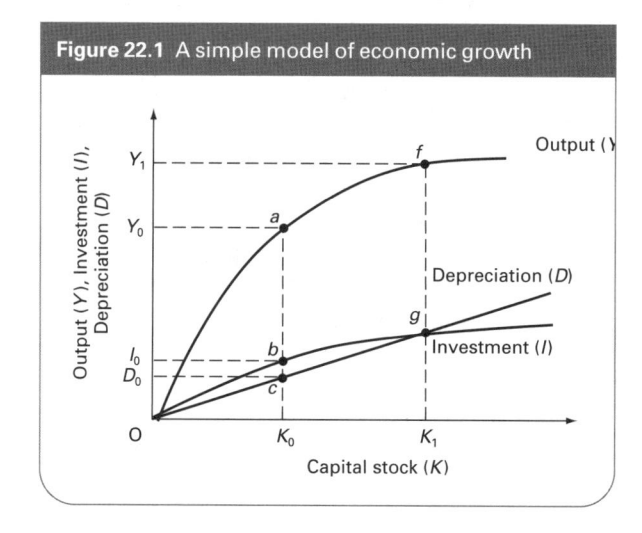

....

Figure 22.1 A simple model of economic growth

Multiple choice　?　Written answer　　Delete wrong word　　Diagram/table manipulation　✕　Calculation　　Matching/ordering

(f) Now assume that there is an increase in the rate of saving and hence investment. Illustrate the effect on Figure 22.1.

(g) Why will national income not go on rising for ever as a result of this higher rate of investment?

....

(h) Illustrate the effect of technological progress on Figure 22.1.

Q4. Given that an increase in saving means a reduction in current consumption, and has a declining effect in terms of extra long-term output, economists have developed the concept of a 'golden-rule saving rate'. This can be defined as the rate of saving that leads to:

A. the maximum level of output.
B. the maximum rate of growth.
C. the maximum level of consumption.
D. the minimum rate of depreciation.
E. the maximum level of investment.

Q5. An increase in technological progress is the main condition for achieving a faster rate of economic growth.
True/False

Q6. According to endogenous growth theory:
A. increases in aggregate supply depend on increases in aggregate demand.
B. the rate of technological progress depends purely on developments in science and engineering which, in turn, depend on random inventions and discoveries.
C. economic growth can only be a temporary phenomenon caused by 'one-off' discoveries.
D. the rate of technological progress and diffusion can be increased by appropriate incentives and government policies.
E. a faster rate of economic growth is likely to lead to a lower rate of technological progress.

22.2 Supply-side policies

(Pages 621–3) It is important to distinguish clearly between demand-side and supply-side solutions to economic problems.

Q7. Which of the following measures to cure unemployment would we call supply-side and which demand-side solutions, and which have elements of both?
(a) The encouragement of pay restraint to keep costs down by preventing excessive wage increases.
Supply-side/Demand-side/Both
(b) The launch of a new government training programme for school leavers.
Supply-side/Demand-side/Both
(c) A new computer network is set up to provide more detailed national information at job centres on vacancies.
Supply-side/Demand-side/Both
(d) A government investment programme targeted on key growth industries.
Supply-side/Demand-side/Both
(e) Income tax is cut by 2p in the pound.
Supply-side/Demand-side/Both
(f) Lower interest rates to prevent the exchange rate appreciating.
Supply-side/Demand-side/Both

Q8. What effect will successful supply-side measures have on the following curves?
(a) The production possibility curve.
Outward shift/Inward shift/Movement along
(b) The aggregate supply curve.
Rightward shift/Leftward shift/Movement up along/Movement down along
(c) The aggregate demand curve.
Rightward shift/Leftward shift/Movement up along/Movement down along
(d) The Phillips curve.
Rightward shift/Leftward shift/Movement up along/Movement down along
(e) The withdrawals curve in the Keynesian 45° line diagram.
Upward shift/Downward shift/No shift in
(f) The injections 'curve' in the Keynesian 45° line diagram.
Upward shift/Downward shift/No shift in
(g) The full-employment level of income in the Keynesian 45° line diagram.
Rightward shift/Leftward shift/No shift in

Q9. List three supply-side policies which might be used to achieve the effect on the production possibility curve in Q8 (a) above.

1. ....
2. ....
3. ....

Q10. Monetarists and new classical economists argue that there is a clear distinction between demand-side and supply-side policy. Which of the following would be maintained by such economists?
(a) In the long run, demand-side policy is suitable only for tackling inflation. *True/False*
(b) In the long run, only supply-side policy will reduce unemployment and increase output. *True/False*
(c) Supply-side policies will help to shift the Phillips curve to the right by reducing the natural rate of unemployment. *True/False*
(d) Supply-side policies should aim to make markets freer. *True/False*

Keynesian arguments concerning the nature and role of demand-side and supply-side policies differ considerably

308 CHAPTER 22 LONG-TERM ECONOMIC GROWTH AND SUPPLY-SIDE POLICIES

from those of the new classical economists. Keynesians argue that demand-side policies **Q11.** *can/cannot* cause increase in output and employment. They also argue that, on their own, supply-side policies **Q12.** *can/cannot* lead to increases in output and employment *and* a reduction in inflation.

◐ **Q13.** Keynesians maintain that supply-side policies can reduce the need for deflationary demand-side policies.
True/False

◐ **Q14.** 'Third way' supply-side policies aim to help people to help themselves. Such policies involve a mixture of government support and market incentives. *True/False*

22.3 Market-orientated supply-side policies

(Page 623) The main emphasis of the supply-side policies of the UK, the USA and many other countries in the 1980s was on the liberation of market forces.

▤ **Q15.** Which one of the following supply-side policies was not used in the UK in the 1980s?
A. Controls on both public- and private-sector prices and incomes to prevent inflation.
B. Deregulation and privatisation of British industry.
C. Attempts to reduce the PSNCR.
D. Regional grants to encourage industrial relocation.
E. Limiting the automatic entitlement to certain welfare benefits.

(Pages 623–5) Reducing government expenditure
(?) **Q16.** List four supply-side measures adopted by the UK government during the 1980s designed to reduce public expenditure.

1. ....
2. ....
3. ....
4. ....

▤ **Q17.** Reducing the level of government expenditure, while at the same time adopting a tight monetary policy to reduce inflation, proved to be difficult. Which one of the following help to explain why this was so?
A. The government also wanted to cut taxes.
B. Reducing the PSNCR was itself inflationary.
C. Reducing the PSNCR increased the money supply.
D. Statutory reserve ratios for banks had been abolished.
E. The deflationary monetary policy triggered automatic fiscal stabilisers.

(Pages 625–6) Tax cuts
◐ **Q18.** Cuts in the marginal rate of income tax are claimed to have various beneficial supply-side effects. These are:

(a) People work longer hours because the substitution effect from cutting the marginal rate of income tax is less than the income effect. *True/False*
(b) More people wish to work. *True/False*
(c) People work more enthusiastically. *True/False*
(d) Both equilibrium and disequilibrium unemployment fall even when wage rates are inflexible downwards. *True/False*
(e) Employment rises. *True/False*

(Page 626) Reducing the power of labour
◐ **Q19.** If the government succeeds in reducing the power of labour, equilibrium unemployment may well rise.
True/False

⊖ **Q20.** Figure 22.2 shows an aggregate labour market. N is the total labour force; AS_L is the effective demand for labour; AD_L is the aggregate demand for labour. Assume that wages are fixed above the equilibrium at a rate of W_1.

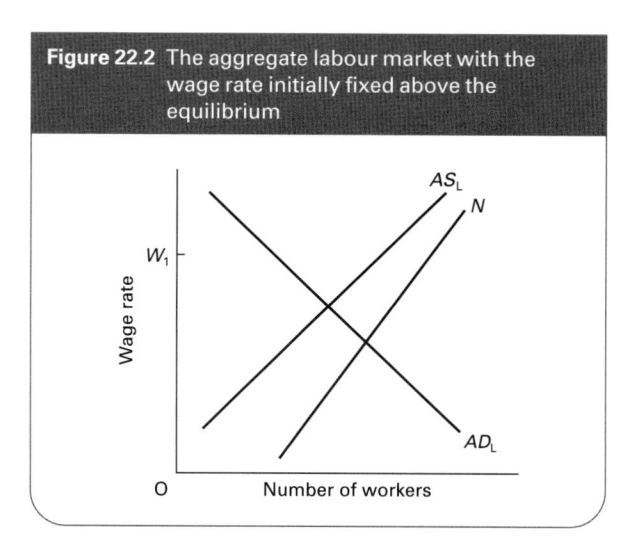

Figure 22.2 The aggregate labour market with the wage rate initially fixed above the equilibrium

(a) Mark on the diagram the levels of equilibrium and disequilibrium unemployment.
(b) Now assume that the government reduces union power, so that wages are freely set by forces of demand and supply. Mark the new wage rate and the resulting levels of equilibrium and disequilibrium unemployment.
(c) Now assume that the effect of reducing wages is to reduce the level of consumer expenditure. Illustrate the effect of this on aggregate demand.
(d) Illustrate the effect of this on employment (both equilibrium and disequilibrium), assuming that the wage rate is no longer flexible downwards below that in (b) above.
(e) Returning to (c) above, illustrate the effect of this on unemployment (both equilibrium and disequilibrium), assuming that the wage rate continues to be flexible downwards.

Q21. The disequilibrium unemployment in Q20(d) above is of which type?

....

(Pages 626–7) Reducing welfare
Monetarists argue that a **Q22.** *small/large* difference between wages and welfare benefits will cause a high level of **Q23.** *frictional/structural* unemployment. The extra income that an individual would receive from taking employment would be small. We would say these individuals are caught in a **Q24.** *poverty/unemployment* trap. If the level of benefits were cut, the effective labour supply curve (AS_L) would shift to the **Q25.** *left/right*.

(Pages 627–9) Encouraging competition
Q26. List three policies favoured by the Thatcher and Major governments as means of encouraging competition.

1. ....
2. ....
3. ....

22.4 Interventionist supply-side policy

(Pages 630–6) The UK has for decades had a **Q27.** *lower/higher* level of investment relative to national income than other industrialised countries.

Q28. The following series of points reflect the consequences of low investment. Order these points into a logical sequence of events. Number them from 1 to 6. (Number 1 is already shown.)

(a) Low investment.   1

(b) A widening balance of trade deficit. ....

(c) Low productivity growth. ....

(d) Low investment. ....

(e) Falling international competitiveness. ....

(f) The adoption of deflationary fiscal and monetary policy measures. ....

Q29. Deindustrialisation refers to:
A. the modernisation of manufacturing industry.
B. the growth in science parks where only high-technology industries are located.
C. the growth in the service sector.
D. the decline in the country's manufacturing base.
E. the movement back to an agriculturally based economy.

Q30. Give four arguments why the free market might lead to a sub-optimal level of investment.

1. ....
2. ....
3. ....
4. ....

Q31. Which of the following could be classified as *interventionist* supply-side policy?
(a) Government provision of infrastructure.   Yes/No
(b) Privatisation.   Yes/No
(c) Investment grants for private firms.   Yes/No
(d) A reduction in corporation tax.   Yes/No
(e) Government-funded workplace training schemes.   Yes/No

The most extreme form of interventionist supply-side policy is national economic planning.

Q32. Which of the following describes *indicative* planning?
A. A type of planning undertaken by a group of countries acting together.
B. Commands issued to different sectors of the economy to produce targeted amounts of output.
C. Consultation between government, business and unions in order to co-ordinate their policies and plans.
D. Government intervention in the operation of markets for short periods of time.
E. The nationalisation of large sections of the economy.

Q33. Although governments in most industrialised countries do not engage in national economic planning, virtually all intervene selectively in order to bring supply-side improvements.   *True/False*

Q34. Give three arguments against interventionist industrial policy.

1. ....
2. ....
3. ....

22.5 Regional and urban policy

(Pages 636–43) There are significant regional and local disparities in the UK economy, many of which grew over the 1980s and early 1990s.

Q35. If market prices were perfectly flexible, and there were perfect factor mobility:

(a) There would be no specifically regional or local unemployment problem. *True/False*

(b) There would be no problem of regional or local inequality of wage rates for given occupations. *True/False*

Q36. If market prices were perfectly flexible, but there was significant factor immobility:

(a) There would be no specifically regional or local unemployment problem. *True/False*

(b) There would be no problem of regional or local inequality. *True/False*

Q37. Which of the following regional or urban policies would be advocated by the radical right and which by interventionists?

(a) The offering of local facilities and improvement of local infrastructure for potential new business. *Radical right/Interventionist*

(b) The migration of labour should be encouraged by the reduction of benefit levels. *Radical right/Interventionist*

(c) High-spending local authorities, which impose excessive local taxation, should be capped. High taxation is a disincentive to firms locating in particular areas. *Radical right/Interventionist*

(d) Government should prevent the location of firms in already prosperous parts of the country. *Radical right/Interventionist*

(e) Nationally negotiated wage agreements should be replaced by locally negotiated ones. *Radical right/Interventionist*

(f) The provision of a range of local subsidies and grants to firms. *Radical right/Interventionist*

(g) The setting of a uniform business rate (local business tax) across the whole country. *Radical right/Interventionist*

Q38. Which of the following have been part of successive UK governments' approach to regional policy?

(a) Increasing government expenditure on regional assistance in *real* terms and targeting it more carefully. *Yes/No*

(b) Increasing government expenditure on regional assistance in *money* terms and targeting it more carefully. *Yes/No*

(c) Making regional assistance more cost-effective. *Yes/No*

(d) Abolishing Regional Development Grants (which were *automatically* available to firms in development areas.) *Yes/No*

(e) Abolishing Regional Selective Assistance (which was granted at the *discretion* of the government). *Yes/No*

(f) Increasing the reliance placed on grants from the European Regional Development Fund. *Yes/No*

(g) The introduction of a system of grants to small businesses in assisted areas. *Yes/No*

Q39. Give three factors that have limited the effectiveness of UK urban policy in regenerating deprived inner-city areas.

1. ....
2. ....
3. ....

B PROBLEMS, EXERCISES AND PROJECTS

Q40. Figure 22.3 illustrates the effect of a tax cut on the level of employment. N is the total labour force; AS_L is the effective aggregate supply of labour; AD_L is the aggregate demand for labour.

(a) Assume that Q_1 represents an equilibrium in the labour market, and that labour supply depends on the after-tax wage rate (W), whereas the demand for labour depends on unit labour costs: the pre-tax wage rate (Lc). What is the average level of income tax per worker?

....

(b) With employment at Q_1, what is the level of *equilibrium unemployment*?

....

(c) Assume now that income tax falls to $b - c$. What is the new unit labour cost to firms (pre-tax wage), assuming that wage rates are flexible?

....

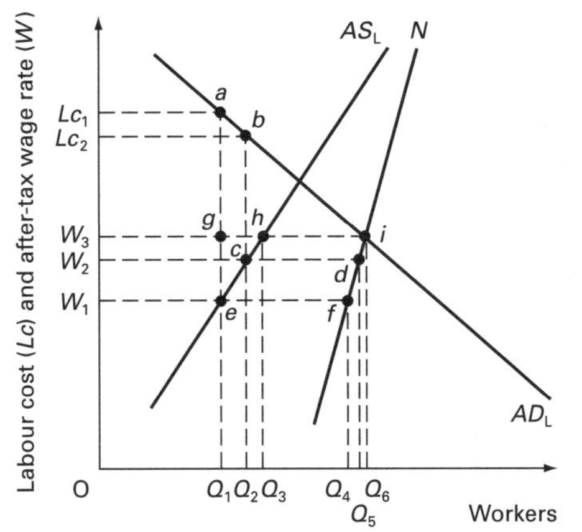

Figure 22.3 The effects of income tax cuts on employment

(d) How many workers will now be employed?

....

(e) Has equilibrium unemployment risen or fallen?
Risen/Fallen

Q41. Referring still to Figure 22.3, assume now that (pre-tax) wage rates are inflexible downwards.

(a) Still assuming a cut in income tax to $b - c$: if the pre-tax wage rate did not fall, but instead the after-tax wage rate rose to W_1 (i.e. $a - g = b - c$), how many workers would be willing to work at this wage now?

....

(b) What would be the level of disequilibrium unemployment?

....

(c) What would be the level of equilibrium unemployment?

....

(d) Has total unemployment risen or fallen as a result of the tax cut, given that the pre-tax wage rate is not flexible downwards?
Risen/Fallen

Q42. Either individually or in small groups, write a report on the changing geographical and social pattern of inequality in the UK (or some other country of your choice) since 1980.

Identify a range of economic and social inequalities and comment upon their growing (or declining) significance. Your report should include some assessment of whether these inequalities are likely to widen or narrow in the future. It should also review the main policies that might be adopted in order to remove or narrow such imbalances.

Sources of UK data for this question include *Social Trends* (NS), *Regional Trends* (NS) and *Economic Trends* (NS). The first two and selected articles from the third can be downloaded as PDF files from the 'Bookshelf' section of the National Statistics Web site at http://www.statistics.gov.uk.

DISCUSSION TOPICS AND ESSAYS

Q43. Under what circumstances will an increase in the rate of saving in an economy lead to a faster rate of *long-term* economic growth?

Q44. What do you understand by 'endogenous growth theory'? What implications does the theory have for government supply-side policy?

Q45. Describe how Keynesian and new classical approaches to supply-side policy differ. Illustrate this difference with reference to policies concerned with reducing unemployment and inflation.

Q46. Has there been a supply-side 'miracle' in the UK?

Q47. Outline the main supply-side policies introduced by the Thatcher and Major governments. Does the evidence suggest that they achieved what they set out to do?

Q48. In what ways do the supply-side policies of the Blair government differ from those of the previous Conservative governments? Provide a comparative critique of the two sets of policies.

Q49. What normative objections and justifications can be put forward to criticise and support market-orientated supply-side policies?

Q50. What do you understand by the term 'deindustrialisation'? What arguments have been advanced to explain the UK's experience of this phenomenon? What are the economic arguments for and against attempting to reverse the process? Consider the relative merits of alternative policies for reversing the process.

Q51. Given large regional and local variations in economic prosperity and economic performance, what problems might occur in using a free-market policy to rectify such imbalances?

Q52. To what extent is it possible for a government to make a significant impact on urban deprivation without spending considerable sums of money?

Q53. Debate
If supply-side policy is to be successful in achieving more rapid economic growth, it must inevitably lead to greater inequality.

ARTICLES

In the article below, taken from the *Investors Chronicle* of 31 May 2002, the author, Dan Oakley, reviews the observations made by Will Hutton on the recent performance of the US economy, and the implications for the UK if it were to try to emulate the US experience.

Wall Street's Faustian pact

Did faster computers really transform the US economy in the 1990s? In his new book, Will Hutton argues that the truth is far less flattering. He tells Dan Oakey why UK investors should think twice before they fall into the same trap.

We'll soon know if he's right. If he is, we may all have to change our view of companies, stock markets and investing strategies. He is Will Hutton, scourge of monetarist economics and a convinced sceptic that chasing shareholder value in the short term gets a business anywhere in the long run. Seven years ago, in *The State We're In* he argued that British firms needed to invest more to compete internationally. Now he's reserving his direst warnings for the US.

Mr Hutton thinks the US economy is in a bind and that investors there should rethink their exposure. At risk are not just individual stocks and the strong dollar, but also the very idea that America's new model economy is something we should try to emulate lock, stock and barrel.

In his book, *The World We're In*, Mr Hutton doesn't deny the success of the US economy in the 1990s – when stock markets grew an average 17 per cent a year, and when the economy grew 4 per cent annually between 1995–2000. Where he finds fault is the idea that this growth was sustainable and the result of a superior brand of American capitalism.

Mr Hutton argues that, in terms of productivity, innovation, incentivising workers and job creation, US companies are not the runaway commercial successes we believed them to be during the 1990s. In other words, the booming economy was not the simple result of dynamic entrepreneurs establishing a new form of capitalism inspired by massive financial incentives to new heights of technological innovation.

Widespread ignorance

There is, he contends, 'a widespread ignorance within the US about what has propelled its growth, a vast exaggeration of what has been achieved, an uncomprehending dismay at the consequences of the pricking of the epic 1990s financial bubble – and equal incomprehension of how something so irrational could ever have taken place'.

In the aftermath of that bubble, the salient features of the US economy are its record-breaking trade deficit and the indebtedness of its consumers. The Clinton boom, he argues, 'was more of an old-fashioned consumer boom built on record credit and a monumental inflow of foreign capital to finance the consequent trade deficit'. That trade deficit was both fuelled and justified by soaring share prices that made consumers feel wealthy and foreign investors long for a piece of the action.

Now the whole edifice is under threat. For a start, the US trade deficit cannot continue to grow. Borrowing ever more money to keep buying imports is not a sustainable option – even if US consumer confidence held up. As it is, unemployment is rising and the Bush administration is warning that further terrorist attacks and suicide bombers are inevitable.

Drip-drip effect

So far, falling share prices haven't changed US consumption habits, but a substantial slab of US savings still lies in the hands of Wall Street via equities. This is the same Wall Street that's currently horrifying the American public with tales of corruption at Enron, collusion at Andersen and apparent abuse of investor credulity at Merrill Lynch. So far this year, the US Securities and Exchange Commission has opened 49 major investigations of accounting fraud – treble the total at the same stage in 2001.

The drip-drip effect of financial scandals is taking its toll on perceptions of US equities. Recent surveys of fund managers have found that, for the first time, institutional investors believe European stocks have higher quality earnings than US ones, which are now rated on a par with companies from emerging markets.

In essence, Mr Hutton argues that US managers made a 'Faustian pact' with Wall Street which is now unravelling. Companies could only deliver the constant progress in earnings per share by stretching accounting standards to breaking point. 'Corporate America now no longer principally seeks to innovate, build and marshal resources over time to create value,' argues Mr Hutton, 'it tries to extract value by financial engineering'.

Financial engineering

To support his case he cites the contrast between Boeing and the Airbus consortium. Boeing's heyday came in the decade after 1978, when the long-term gamble to build the 747 jumbo jet finally paid off. But a cyclical business that needs huge upfront investment 'did not lend itself to quick dollars'. Boeing slashed R&D spending, froze plans for new planes and tried to rebrand itself as a provider of aerospace services. Meanwhile, the Airbus consortium is pushing ahead with plans to build the superjumbo A380 and now has the market for itself. The US company, believes Mr Hutton, 'is surrendering technological leadership to the European consortium, whose stabler ownership structure and long-term financing environment leaves open possibilities for Airbus that no longer exist for Boeing'.

In tune with a growing number of economists, he argues the likelihood of the US quickly resuming 5 per cent annual growth 'is severely limited by the sheer scale of the debt overhang and the size of the trade deficit, with the US's accompanying dependence on foreign capital'. Foreign capital inflows and Wall Street's buoyancy will reverse: 'The US will be forced towards an adjustment of its ambitions and living standards; it will resist; and things will get ugly,' he warns, citing President Bush's decisions to impose punitive taxes on steel imports and bail out American farmers with billions of dollars in subsidies.

Go along with this view of events and US assets begin to look perilously overvalued. 'The American economy rests on an enormous confidence trick,' he contends, 'and if either of its twin supporters – foreign investors or domestic consumers – were to withdraw their support, it would be set back for years while the imbalances worked themselves out'.

As for talk of surging productivity and job creation, he's sceptical that the US has as much to teach other countries as you might suppose. Most of the jobs created were in the poorly-paid service sector and went to women and immigrants from central or Latin America. Overall, US GDP rose because people were working far longer hours than in Europe (41 and 28 per cent more than French and German workers, respectively).

On the productivity front, the evidence is far harder to interpret than American triumphalists will allow. According to a report by McKinsey earlier this year, most of the productivity growth post-1995 was focused on six sectors (three of which were semiconductors, computer manufacturing and telecoms). For the remaining 70 per cent of the economy, there was little or no improvement.

Alternative theories

This counter argument runs that it was hard not to improve productivity if you were supplying internet equipment or services in the late 1990s. A small minority of companies made massive margins as the tech bubble fuelled an unprecedented splurge on servers, routers and fibreoptics. All too often they were selling their products to the very firms whose value – and spending power – were being inflated by the internet bubble.

Those business models are now derided and broken so we shouldn't expect productivity rises in those sectors to hold. As Mr Hutton points out: 'Yahoo!'s revenues came from other dot.coms advertising on its web pages; as they imploded with the collapse in stock market values, so they cut their spending.'

In this environment, American bosses did what wily managers have always done: claim credit for any success and demand an overblown share of the available rewards before someone finds them out.

So it is that some academic economists now stress the role of the strong dollar and weak oil may have had in accelerating US growth, while taming inflation and interest rates. At the same time, the US's main trading rivals in Europe were reining in their economies to prepare for the euro, while Japan was gripped by a decade-long deflationary slump.

If this is a more truthful picture, then the UK and other European countries could never reproduce the 1990s boom. The conditions that made it possible – a strong currency, vigorous credit expansion, the irrational optimism that fed the tech bubble – were unique to the US in the late 1990s.

There are problems with this assessment though. For a start, although you can argue over the statistical measures of productivity, you can't deny that the US economy grew strongly. And its businesses were quicker to exploit information technology than were European firms. The latest figures for US productivity show that it is still rising at robust rates.

Furthermore, the US still accounts for the lion's share of new patents – suggesting that it remains a hotbed of innovation. Mr Hutton doesn't contest that, but he's quick to highlight that 63 per cent of US patents rely on basic research conducted by the state through universities.

Lessons for the UK

What, then, can the UK learn from the US experience? For a start, incentive structures linking executive pay to short-term share prices don't always work. Although inconclusive, Mr Hutton points to a study by Scott Klinger which found that between 1993 and 2000 the majority of companies headed by the 10 highest-paid bosses underperformed the stock market over both one and three-year periods. Recruiting a boss to drive the business forward has more to do with finding people who are driven to succeed and have a passionate interest in the firm's mission – be it to make airliners, tyres, software or medicines. The next 18 months should reveal whether or not Mr Hutton is right on the immediate prospects for the US economy. But in line with his emphasis on the long term, it'll be years before we know the true cost of corporate America's love affair with financial engineering.

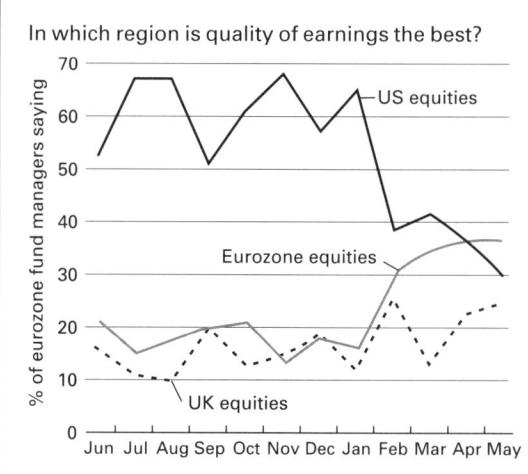

Source: Merrill Lynch survey of eurozone fund managers May 2002; 'quality' of earnings in terms of transparency, predictability and volatility.

(a) Why does Will Hutton think that the US growth and productivity performance throughout the 1990s was far less impressive than the statistics suggest?

(b) What is 'financial engineering' and what are its implications for the USA?

(c) What advice would you offer the government and business outside the USA in the light of Will Hutton's observations?

The following article, taken from the *Computer Bulletin* of March 2001, considers whether the UK economy is suffering an IT skills shortage or whether the problem in fact lies in the productivity of existing IT workers.

Skills shortage or productivity gap?

The UK has long been in the grip of a supposed IT skills shortage. But is there really a shortage of people, or is there instead a lack of good management, professional discipline and productivity? John McDermid takes a fresh look at the issue.

Much is made of the IT skills shortage, with one recent study saying the UK will be short of 300,000 IT practitioners by 2003 – but what does this mean? The UK IT industry is said to employ about 1m people – so do we need 300,000 more people, or a 30% gain in productivity from those we have, or something else?

The earliest data on individual productivity in software development showed that there is a huge difference between the most and least productive programmer. I know of nothing which suggests that this gulf is any narrower today. Indeed, as there are more people in the profession we might expect the gap to be wider.

I know of situations where individuals have contributed 'negative productivity' to a project: in one case a person did N hours of work, and others had to be employed to do a further $1.5N$ hours to rectify the problems he created; this may not seem too bad, but N was in four figures. Do we need another 300,000 people like that?

If we consider the productivity of projects, as opposed to individuals, where does the time go? Much of it goes into testing, much goes into fixing errors. There are gains to be had from improving testing techniques, but reducing the number of errors is perhaps the biggest lever.

It is not uncommon for more than 70% of the problems found after unit testing to have arisen in the requirements phase – so for most errors the whole development cycle needs to be repeated. Empirical evidence shows that reviews are the single most effective way of identifying errors. So if spending 5% of a project budget on additional reviews found only half these errors, that would achieve the 30% increase in productivity needed to solve the skills shortage. In fact 5% of the total budget on a large project allows a lot of time to spend on reviews, so the gain may be much bigger.

There are other factors in productivity. Tools are not a panacea, and some empirical data suggests that inappropriately chosen computer-aided systems engineering tools can actually slow projects down. However, I continue to be surprised at the number of projects that are hampered by inadequate tools.

A modern PC costs about a week's salary for a typical software developer. If it merely increases productivity by 2% it pays for itself in a year – and makes a net contribution in the subsequent two to three years of its life. If it increases productivity by 20%, it may be much more cost-effective than recruiting staff. Similar arguments can be made about software development tools.

The purchase of tools should not be indiscriminate, but international comparisons show the UK to be consistently behind its international competitors in capital investment – and in productivity. Might there be a causal link here?

Returning to basics, why is there said to be a skills shortage? It is presumably because the industry cannot develop everything that users want.

But what do they really need?

The 80:20 rule says we get 80% of the benefit for 20% of the cost. There are some development methods which exploit this. In general they give priorities to requirements and use various techniques to control developments so as to deliver something useful even if it does not meet all the requirements.

If we believe the 80:20 ratio, we should be delighted with only needing to save 30% of the effort. If we assume that an extra 20% of effort produces 80% of the previously unimplemented 20% of the functionality (that is, 16% of the total), then we get a 96:40 rule (80% plus 16%, for 20% plus 20% of the cost). Continuing this calculation, by the time we have spent 70% of the effort (saving 30%) we have implemented over 99% of what was wanted.

Perhaps some of the assumptions here are dubious, but think instead about the underlying principle. It seems unarguable that the 30% cost reduction can be had with a much less significant reduction in system features.

All this suggests that we need to consider not only the skills of individual developers but also the effect of managerial competence on productivity. Indeed, management education and training must be the best place to invest, as the effects of good or bad management affect the whole development team, and hence the project.

I am not saying that we do not need more people in the profession. I am merely saying that the message, 'we will be short by N people' is over-simplistic – and perhaps dangerously so, as it masks all sorts of factors which contribute to productivity.

Some of my own arguments here have been simplistic, but let me draw some conclusions, especially for the government.

First, we need education, not training. Providing short training courses for people with no background in computing will almost undoubtedly compound the problem, not solve it: remember those who contribute 'negative productivity'.

On this topic of education or training, there is considerable evidence that the MSc conversion courses run by a number of universities, teaching IT skills to graduates from other disciplines, are highly effective. The students are well motivated and often have the real world experience to hit the ground running on graduation. A year is enough to provide a reasonable education – not just training – even if it must fall short of the content of an undergraduate degree. Unfortunately, the Engineering and Physical Sciences Research Council no longer supports these successful and popular courses, because they are deemed to be inappropriate, so many of them are under threat of closure.

Next, educate the managers. If they are taught nothing else, get them to understand how to obtain metrics on error introduction and removal, as well as simply work hours per line of code. Doing this will enable them to see where there are problems in their processes, and focus effort on resolving the problems that waste scarce effort: that 30% improvement might be possible quickly.

After that, provide education on setting priorities for requirements, on evolutionary development, on project risk management. Provide such education to procurement managers as well as to developers, because they seem to be the source of many project problems.

Encourage companies to retain or recruit mature staff. They have desirable personal qualities and may actually know something about the business. The biggest source of problems in most projects is requirements errors. Employing people who understand the business is a good way of removing errors. If companies do not see that this is to their advantage, consider instituting schemes to encourage them to take on mature workers.

In this way we can perhaps address the skills shortage and productivity gap, not just the headcount shortage.

(a) What is 'negative productivity', and what are its implications?

(b) John McDermid suggests that the apparent shortage of skilled workers is in many respects the result of poor productivity. What arguments does he advance to support his claim?

(c) Why does McDermid argue that education rather than training is key to the long-run performance of the IT sector?

(d) What do you think are some of the implications of this article for current government thinking on training and its provision?

UK urban policy has received fresh impetus in recent years as the problem of social inequality has moved up the political agenda. In the following article, taken from *New Economy* of August 1999, Peter Lee examines the way in which urban deprivation is measured and how these measures are used as the basis for identifying target areas for urban policy. As he argues, 'a consistent measure is needed, which can regularly be updated to gauge changes in levels of deprivation and the success of regeneration initiatives'.

Social exclusion and urban policy

Since June 1998, three important policy changes have occurred within the context of debates on targeting deprivation and social exclusion:

- there has been a marked shift in language away from 'worst estates' to a discourse on 'poorest neighbourhoods', reflected in the Social Exclusion Unit's (SEU) Autumn 1998 report
- the launch of the New Deal for Communities has refocused and re-emphasised the competitive element of regeneration policy and resulted inadvertently in a competition *between* 'poorest neighbourhoods'
- changes in the measurement of deprivation have led to a shift in the location of the 'poorest neighbourhoods' away from London towards the North and Midlands.

A national strategy for neighbourhood renewal

In its report, the SEU set out an agenda on how to '. . . develop integrated and sustainable approaches to the problems of the worst housing estates, including crime, drugs, unemployment, community breakdown, and bad schools . . .'. Reference to the 'worst estates' is made only once, the language shifting away from tenure specific references towards the preferred 'poorest neighbourhoods' – a phrase which appears 13 times in the report. Identifying how many 'poorest neighbourhoods' there are in Britain depends on the thresholds and indicators used to identify them. The SEU report refers to three separate studies that estimate the size of the problem:

- 1370 'worst estates' in England (Department of the Environment, 1997)
- 3000 run-down neighbourhoods (English House Condition Survey)
- 1600 to 4000 neighbourhoods classified by socio-economic group (SEU, 1998).

The Index of Local Deprivation

The Index of Local Deprivation (ILD), released in the summer of 1998 as the official measure of deprivation (DETR, 1998), superseded the Index of Local Conditions (ILC). Like its predecessor, the ILD remains a multi-level index capturing deprivation at three spatial scales: local authority district, ward and enumeration district (ED). The main changes were made to the local authority district level of the index with data being added and updated. Changes at the local level (ward and ED) involved the dropping of one variable (children in unsuitable accommodation, which

Table 1 The 70 most deprived authorities on the ILD: movers up and down

Movers up the Index				Movers down the Index			
Local authority	ILC	ILD	Change in rank	Local authority	ILC	ILD	Change in rank
Liverpool	6	1	5	Newham	1	2	−1
Manchester	13	3	10	Hackney	3	4	−1
Tower Hamlets	7	6	1	Southwark	2	8	−6
Sandwell	9	7	2	Islington	4	10	−6
Knowsley	12	9	3	Lambeth	8	12	−4
Greenwich	14	11	3	Haringey	10	13	−3
Barking and Dagenham	18	15	3	Lewisham	11	14	−3
Nottingham	25	16	9	Camden	15	17	−2
Brent	29	20	9	Hammersmith and Fulham	16	18	−2
Sunderland	34	21	13	Newcastle upon Tyne	17	19	−2
Salford	28	23	5	Waltham Forest	20	22	−2
Sheffield	36	25	11	Bradford	23	28	−5
Kingston Upon Hull	31	26	5	Wandsworth	21	30	−9
Rochdale	50	29	21	Gateshead	33	35	−2
Walsall	44	31	13	Hartlepool	35	37	−2
Leicester	37	32	5	South Tyneside	22	38	−16
Oldham	39	33	6	Blackburn	32	41	−9
Halton	51	34	17	Blackpool	30	51	−21
Ealing	38	36	2	City of Westminster	26	57	−31
Doncaster	41	39	2	Brighton and Hove	40	60	−20
Coventry	46	40	6	North Tyneside	52	62	−10
Barnsley	54	42	12	Kensington and Chelsea	19	63	−44
Wirral	61	44	17	Burnley	57	65	−8
St Helens	55	45	10	Norwich	59	66	−7
Lincoln	48	46	2	Preston	47	68	−21
Bolton	49	47	2	Bristol	43	69	−26
Stoke-on-Trent	64	48	16				
Stockton-on-Tees	69	49	20				
Rotherham	60	50	10				
Easington	58	52	6				
Tameside	65	53	12				
Sefton	73	54	19				
Barrow-in-Furness	93	55	38				
Leeds	56	56	0				
Wansbeck	63	58	5				
Hounslow	99	59	40				
Wear Valley	75	61	14				
Thanet	81	64	17				
Mansfield	84	67	17				
Enfield	96	70	26				

Birmingham (ranked 5), Middlesborough (24) and Wolverhampton (27) had no change in ranking; Redcar and Cleveland, ranked 43rd on the ILD, had no ranking on the ILC.

referred mainly to children living in flats) following considerable criticism of the indicator.

Table 1 shows the 70 local authorities that make up the most deprived local authority districts according to the ILD. The overall trend, comparing the ILD with the ILC, shows some London boroughs moving down the index and appearing less deprived, while authorities in the North and Midlands have generally moved up. Among these:

- 13 London boroughs have moved down the index compared with seven moving up
- 13 north-western local authorities have moved up compared with three moving down
- 4 West Midlands authorities have moved up the ILD, with none moving down
- 8 authorities in Yorkshire and Humberside have moved up and one down.

Changes in the rankings at local authority level appear to show real changes in levels of deprivation. New

Table 2 Regional comparisons of the percentage share of EDs comparing the ILC and ILD

	ILC		ILD	
Region (% share of all EDs)	Most deprived 10%	Most deprived 5%	Most deprived 10%	Most deprived 5%
London (15)	47	59	31	34
North West (11)	8	6	13	12
Merseyside (3)	6	5	8	9
Yorkshire & Humberside (10)	8	6	12	13
North East (5)	4	3	8	7
West Midlands (11)	10	8	12	12
South West (11)	4	3	3	3
Eastern (11)	3	2	2	2
South East (15)	7	6	5	4
East Midlands (8)	3	2	5	4

ILC figures reproduced from Harvey, J. et al. (1997) *Mapping Local Authority Estates Using the Index of Local Conditions*, DoE: London.

data were added at the local authority level updating the index in some cases to 1997.

Analysis of the ILC at small area level showed that while London contained 15 per cent of England's EDs, it contained almost half (47 per cent) of EDs ranked in the top 10 per cent on the ILC (see Table 2). London's share of deprived EDs at the 10 per cent threshold on the ILD had dropped to just below a third. At the 5 per cent threshold, the differences in the spatial distribution of EDs, when comparing the ILC and ILD, changed more markedly. Almost 60 per cent of EDs, at the ILC 5 per cent threshold, were located in London, whereas less than 35 per cent were identified as such using the ILD. The North West, Yorkshire and Humberside, the North East and East Midlands regions all doubled their share of deprived EDs at the 5 per cent threshold. The evidence on deprivation, therefore, shows a shift from London and the South to the Midlands and the North using both the updated local authority level index and the adjusted small area index.

New Deal for Communities

These changes in the rankings at both local authority and small area level are important as the ILD is used as the basis for identifying targets for regeneration policies. The 70 most deprived local authorities in Table 1 were used as the basis for selecting 'Pathfinder' authorities to take part in the New Deal for Communities (NDC) by the DETR.

The NDC was launched in the same month as the SEU report and will give £800 million to the most deprived neighbourhoods over the 1999 to 2001 period. To ensure a 'geographical spread of Pathfinder districts across England,' the DETR identified at least one local authority area in each region of England from the list in Table 1. Regions with disproportionate shares of deprivation were awarded additional Pathfinder authorities.

A more divisive strategy?

The NDC represents just one arm of regeneration policy. The most significant arm, the Single Regeneration Budget, introduced a competitive bidding process to determine the allocation of resources. Previous policies, such as City Challenge, were based largely on levels of urban deprivation, with funding limited to the most deprived local authorities.

Writing about the competition for resources in inner-city policy, with particular reference to the SRB, Edwards (1997) argues that there are '... moral grounds on which the use of competition in social policy gives rise to disquiet. They concern rights and justice and derive from the precepts that if people have rights to things, then they should not have to compete for them or be subject to random selection or arbitrary power to get them ...'.

Competition continues to be at the heart of government policy and in this respect it is difficult to side step the argument that the NDC has created a more divisive regeneration strategy than the SRB, by intensifying competition for resources between deprived communities. In the case of the NDC the stakes have been raised and the level of disappointment sharpened as a few communities scrap for the top prize.

The most deprived communities may lose out in this process because NDC Pathfinders have been chosen on the basis of previous regeneration spending, with a clear preference for 'spreading resources around'. Judgement on the ability of 'competitors' to succeed – their capacity to form partnerships in addition to having the most exploitable mix of economic and demographic factors – could also rule out the 'worst' areas.

'Form over substance'

Urban policy has increasingly emphasised the use of partnerships involving local authorities, the private sector and voluntary agencies whilst a consensus has emerged which has championed the role that community involvement and sustainability plays in regeneration. Edwards claims this is a victory of form over substance, where urban policy has lost sight of the principle objectives of regeneration: the reduction of poverty and deprivation.

Some local authorities used the ILD to determine which areas should be considered, whilst others used a combination of the ILD and previous spending on regeneration. However, where local authorities have attempted to be objective in their choice of NDC areas, how confident can we be that the areas chosen are the *most* deprived? The ILD identifies growing problems of deprivation in the northern regions and the Midlands, while the small area index identifies proportionally more deprived areas in these areas than does its predecessor, the ILC. The latter had been used as the basis for identifying the 'worst estates' and much press attention focused on the fact that 60 per cent of the worst areas were in London.

Clearly, a consistent measure is needed, which can regularly be updated to gauge changes in levels of deprivation and the success of regeneration initiatives. Additionally, a contract between government and *all* deprived areas should be established, to avoid leaving desperate communities to fight over scraps.

(a) What is the aim of urban policy?

(b) If you were constructing an index by which to measure social exclusion and urban deprivation, what variables would you include in your index?

(c) What reservations does the author have about the system whereby areas have to bid for money from the SRB?

E ANSWERS

Q1. *between 2 and 4 per cent* per annum. The average growth rate of the OECD countries between 1970 and 1999 was 2.94 per cent.

Q2. *Yes*: (b), (c), (d) and (f). These all help to explain the rightward shifts in the aggregate supply curve. In the case of (a), closing the gap between actual and potential output has not taken place, and even if it had, would be insignificant over the long run compared with increases in potential output. In the case of (e), reductions in unemployment have not occurred, except in the last few years, and do not help to explain long-term growth.

Q3. *(a)* I_0 (point *b*).

(b) $I_0 - D_0$ (points *b – c*). D_0 has to be subtracted for capital depreciation.

(c) Y_0.

(d) The net investment of $I_0 - D_0$ leads to an expansion of the capital stock and hence a rise in national income. As national income rises, however, diminishing returns to capital take place (the *Y* and *I* curves get less and less steep). Eventually all the new investment is taken up with replacing worn-out capital (it all goes on depreciation) and national income stops rising. A steady state has been reached at Y_1 and K_1.

(e) No (see answer to (d)).

(f) The *I* line will shift upwards and a new equilibrium will be reached where it crosses the *D* line.

(g) Because all the extra investment will be eventually absorbed by depreciation (see answer to (d)).

(h) The *Y* line will shift upwards and there will be a corresponding upward shift in the *I* line. If it is a 'one-off' technological advance, rather than progress that goes on building over several years, there will be a single upward shift in the *Y* and *I* curves and a 'one-off' increase in national income. The new equilibrium national income will correspond to the level of capital stock where the new *I* line crosses the *D* line.

Q4. C (see Figure 22.4 on page 617 in Sloman, *Economics*, 5th edn).

Q5. *True.*

Q6. D. It is important for the government to create the right climate (through appropriate supply-side policies) to encourage more research and development and a correspondingly faster rate of technological progress and hence economic growth.

Q7. (a), (b) and (c) are supply-side solutions. (f) is a demand-side solution. (d) and (e) can have an effect upon both the demand side and the supply side. In the case of (d), investment will stimulate aggregate demand, but it will also increase potential output and/or reduce costs by increasing the capital stock, especially if investment is targeted on key growth industries or to bottleneck sectors. In the case of (e), tax cuts, as well as stimulating aggregate demand, will also offer an incentive for workers to work (assuming the substitution effect outweighs the income effect). In the case of (f), lower interest rates will increase demand generally, and a lower exchange rate will increase the demand for exports at existing *sterling* prices. A lower exchange rate, however, will *not* reduce costs.

Q8. *(a) Outward shift.*

(b) Rightward shift.

(c) Movement down along (caused by the rightward shift in the aggregate supply curve).

(d) Leftward shift and/or *Movement down along*. The leftward shift would result from a lower equilibrium level of unemployment. The movement down along would result from increased output from a given quantity of labour, and thus less employment for any given level of real aggregate demand.

(e) No shift in (except as a side-effect: e.g. tax cuts to provide greater incentives would, *ceteris paribus*, shift the withdrawals curve downwards).

(f) No shift in (except as a side-effect: e.g. incentives for firms to conduct research and development or training may lead to an increase in net investment and hence a vertical shift upwards in the injections line).

(g) Rightward shift.

Q9. Three supply-side policies that could be used to push the production possibility curve outward are: incentives to encourage investment; the expansion of labour training programmes; the use of taxation policy to encourage more people to work or the same people to work harder.

Q10. *(a) True.* Demand-side policy for the monetarist is monetary policy which should be directed to the control of inflation. Given a long-run

vertical Phillips curve, demand-side policy cannot be used to control long-run output and unemployment.
- (b) *True*. In the long run only by shifting the natural rate of unemployment to the left will unemployment fall, or by shifting the production possibility curve outward will output rise.
- (c) *False*. If supply-side policy causes the natural rate of unemployment to fall, the Phillips curve will shift to the *left*.
- (d) *True*. Free-market philosophy dominates the monetarist view of supply-side policy.

Q11. can.

Q12. can. With an upward-sloping aggregate supply curve, a rightward shift in the curve will both reduce prices and increase output. With a downward-sloping Phillips curve, a leftward shift in the curve can lead to lower unemployment and lower inflation too.

Q13. *True*. If supply-side policies can reduce inflation, there is less need for deflationary policies and the attendant problems of higher unemployment.

Q14. *True*. An example is the use of mixture of tax incentives and the provision of training to encourage unemployed people to take up unemployment.

Q15. A. Prices and incomes policy was not used during the 1980s. Note in the case of D, that regional grants were substantially reduced: see section 22.5 of Sloman (5th edition).

Q16. Examples included: cash limits on government departments; reductions in grants and subsidies to private industry; reductions in central government grants to local authorities as a proportion of local authority revenue; reductions in public-sector capital projects; cuts in the size of the civil service; tough stance on public-sector pay; reductions in the amount of government support given to nationalised industries; rate capping of local authorities; privatisation.

Q17. E. As the deflationary monetary policy led to increased unemployment, so the expenditure on unemployment and other social security benefits increased. (In the case of A, the desire to cut taxes would further stimulate the need to cut government expenditure; in the case of B and C, reducing the PSBR tends to lead to *reductions* in the money supply; in the case of D, this had no direct effect on government expenditure.)

Q18.
- (a) *False*. The supposed beneficial effect is that the tax cut will act as an incentive for workers to work more. This will occur only if the substitution effect (substituting work for leisure) is *larger* than the income effect (being able to afford to work less).
- (b) *True*. Lower tax rates are seen as a work incentive to those who are not the main income earners: for example, parents looking after children.
- (c) *Unsure*. This is very difficult to prove or disprove. The argument is that people will be prepared to put more effort into their work if they can keep more of their pay.
- (d) *False*. If tax rates are cut, take-home pay will increase, and thus it becomes more worthwhile for unemployed people to accept job offers. The level of *equilibrium* unemployment will fall. However, if (pre-tax) wage rates are sticky downwards, firms will not be willing to take on the extra supply of labour. Thus *disequilibrium* unemployment will *rise*.
- (e) *True*. Provided the increased supply of labour has some downward effect on *pre-tax* wages, firms will take on extra labour.

Q19. *True*. As union power is reduced, wages will fall, leading to a fall in the incentive to find employment. (Note, however, that disequilibrium unemployment will fall.)

Q20. The following answers refer to Figure A22.1:
- (a) Equilibrium unemployment equals $c - b$. Disequilibrium unemployment equals $b - a$.
- (b) Wage equals W_2. Equilibrium unemployment equals $e - d$. There is no disequilibrium unemployment.
- (c) The aggregate demand for labour shifts to the left (e.g. to AD_{L_2}).
- (d) Equilibrium unemployment equals $e - d$. Disequilibrium unemployment equals $d - f$.
- (e) Assuming no further fall in AD_L, the wage rate will fall to W_3.

    There will be no disequilibrium unemployment, but equilibrium unemployment will now be $h - g$. (In practice, there may be a further fall in consumer demand – given a further redistribution away from wages to profits – and thus there will be a further leftward movement in AD_L. If there is any sluggishness downwards in wages, further disequilibrium unemployment will occur.)

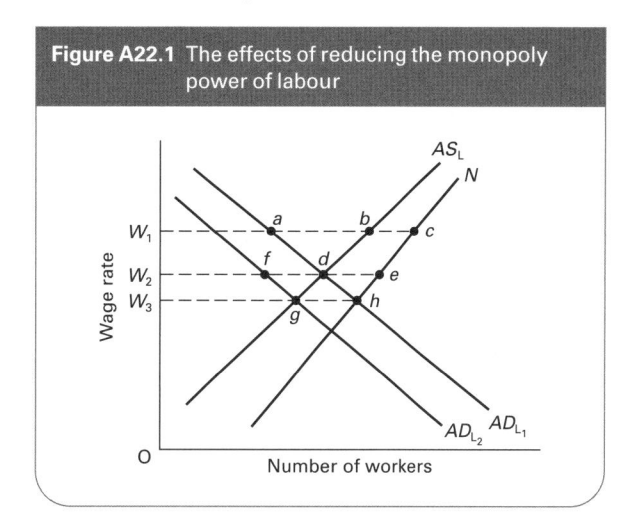

Figure A22.1 The effects of reducing the monopoly power of labour

Q21. Demand deficient.
Q22. *small.*
Q23. *frictional.*
Q24. *poverty.*
Q25. *right.* (More people would feel forced to look for a job.)
Q26. Examples include: privatisation; deregulation (e.g. financial markets and the bus industry); introducing market relationships into parts of the public sector, such as health and eduction; removing barriers to trade and international capital movements.
Q27. *lower.*
Q28. 1 (a); 2 (c); 3 (e); 4 (b); 5 (f); 6 (d).
Q29. D.
Q30. Reasons include: many markets are monopolistic (this removes some of the incentive for investment); firms may only be interested in short-term profits; investment might appear too risky, especially if the free market is subject to cyclical fluctuations; investment decisions by private firms may not take into account the social rate of return (for example, the full benefits from the training of labour); financial institutions may be unwilling to finance long-term investment.
Q31. (a), (c) and (e).
Q32. C. The key feature of indicative planning is one of consultation. Targets and goals are agreed upon between government, firms and possibly unions, and become the basis of a national plan.
Q33. *True.* Examples include: government-financed training schemes, financing research and development, providing assistance to small firms, increasing expenditure on infrastructure projects as a means of increasing national productivity.
Q34. Arguments include: firms have no incentive to be efficient if they know they can rely on government subsidies; the provision of grants and subsidies distorts economic signals; the government may finance extravagant projects that would otherwise not be economically viable.
Q35. *(a) True(?).* Prices and wages would simply adjust to equate demand and supply. There would be no disequilibrium unemployment. There would merely be a residual frictional unemployment, which nevertheless could vary from one locality to another.
(b) True(?). Workers would migrate to where wages were highest and businesses would locate where labour was cheapest. Any disparity in wages would be largely eliminated in this manner (unless there were significant non-monetary benefits from staying in the areas of reduced demand).
Q36. *(a) True(?).* Prices and wages would simply adjust to equate demand and supply. There would be no disequilibrium unemployment. To the extent, however, that wages differed from one region to another, the lower-wage regions might have a slightly higher frictional unemployment (but expectations of a normal wage would also be lower in these regions, which might make people more willing to accept lower-paid jobs).
(b) False. Considerable regional disparities in wages might continue to exist if some regions were more productive/more rapidly growing than others.
Q37. (a), (d) and (f) are all interventionist strategies. They have in common the fact that they all interfere with the free working of the market. The remainder are radical-right proposals as they all attempt to limit state or local authority intervention and/or to free up the market. Note that (g) was designed in part to prevent 'high-spending' local authorities in areas of high unemployment charging higher than average business rates and thereby discouraging the inflow of capital to those regions.
Q38. *(a)* and *(b) No.* There was a decline in government expenditure, not only in real terms, but in money terms also. Part of the reason for this has been an increase in expenditure on urban policy.
(c) and *(d) Yes.* The intention has been not only to save money, but also to target the money more carefully to investments that will be effective in promoting jobs.
(e) No.
(f) Yes.
(g) Yes.
Q39. Factors include the following: government restrictions on local authority expenditure have reduced the support that the local authorities can give to deprived areas; the total amount of government spending on urban policy has been relatively low compared with other areas of government expenditure; many of the jobs 'created' may have been merely diverted from marginally less deprived areas nearby which did not receive support; some of the new jobs may have been filled not by local residents, but by people commuting into the area.

Chapter Twenty-three

23

International Trade

A REVIEW

In this chapter we will look at the advantages and disadvantages of international trade. We start by examining the arguments in favour of trade and then ask, if trade is potentially beneficial to all participating countries, why do countries frequently seek to restrict trade? We then turn to examine the case for establishing trading blocs between countries where the members give each other preferential treatment. The final topic is the European Union, probably the most famous of all preferential trading arrangements.

23.1 The advantages of trade

(Pages 648–53) The theory of comparative advantage
Countries can gain from trade if they specialise in producing those goods in which they have a comparative advantage.

Q1. A country has a comparative advantage in good X compared with good Y if:
A. it can produce more X than Y in total.
B. it can produce more X than Y for a given amount of resources.
C. it can produce more X than other countries.
D. it can produce more X relative to Y than other countries.
E. it can produce X with less resources than other countries.

Q2. Consider the following five situations for a world with just two countries. Each one shows alternative amounts of goods X and Y that the two countries F and G can produce for a given amount of resources. Assume constant costs. In each case give the (pre-trade) opportunity cost of X in terms of Y.

(i) Country F: 10 units of X or 20 units of Y.
$1X = \ldots\ldots Y$
Country G: 10 units of X or 10 units of Y.
$1X = \ldots\ldots Y$

(ii) Country F: 12 units of X or 12 units of Y.
$1X = \ldots\ldots Y$
Country G: 6 units of X or 8 units of Y.
$1X = \ldots\ldots Y$

(iii) Country F: 8 units of X or 8 units of Y.
$1X = \ldots\ldots Y$
Country G: 10 units of X or 10 units of Y.
$1X = \ldots\ldots Y$

(iv) Country F: 20 units of X or 5 units of Y.
$1X = \ldots\ldots Y$
Country G: 18 units of X or 2 units of Y.
$1X = \ldots\ldots Y$

(v) Country F: 10 units of X or 8 units of Y.
$1X = \ldots\ldots Y$
Country G: 6 units of X or 6 units of Y.
$1X = \ldots\ldots Y$

Q3. Referring to the six different situations given in Q2, and assuming no transport costs:

Multiple choice | *Written answer* | *Delete wrong word* | *Diagram/table manipulation* | *Calculation* | *Matching/ordering*

(a) In which situations will country F export good X and import good Y?

....

(b) In which situations will country F export good Y and import good X?

....

(c) In which situations will country F either import or export both goods?

....

(d) In which situations will no trade take place?

....

Q4. In situation (i) in Q2, assume that before trade the price ratios of the two goods were equal to their opportunity cost ratios.

(a) What would the pre-trade price ratio (P_X/P_Y) be in country F?

....

(b) What would the pre-trade price ratio (P_X/P_Y) be in country G?

....

(c) Now assume that trade is opened up and that 1 unit of X exchanges for 1.5 of Y. Demonstrate how both countries have gained.

....

....

In what type of goods will countries have a comparative advantage? Which goods will they be able to produce at a low opportunity cost?

Q5. The following are four items that are traded internationally:
 (i) Wheat
 (ii) Computers
 (iii) Textiles
 (iv) Insurance

In which one of the four is each of the following most likely to have a comparative advantage?

(a) India ....

(b) UK ....

(c) Canada ....

(d) Japan ....

These four countries have a comparative advantage in these four products because they are intensive in the respective country's **Q6.** *scarce/abundant/intermediate* factor.

Specialising in these goods and exporting them will have the effect of **Q7.** *reducing/increasing/maintaining* existing factor price inequalities.

In practice there will be a limit to specialisation and trade. This will result in part from **Q8.** *increasing/decreasing/constant* opportunity costs. In other words the country will face a **Q9.** *bowed in/bowed out/straight line* production possibility curve. As a country specialises and has to use resources that are less and less suited to producing its exports, so its comparative advantage will **Q10.** *increase/remain constant/disappear*.

Q11. There are other factors also which will have the effect of limiting specialisation and trade. Name two.

1. ....

2. ....

(Pages 653–5) The terms of trade
What will be the relative price of exports and imports? This is given by the *terms of trade*.

Q12. In a simple world of just one export (X) and one import (M) the terms of trade are defined as P_M/P_X.
True/False

Q13. If 2 units of exports exchange for 3 units of imports, what are the terms of trade?

....

In the real world where countries have many imports and exports, the terms of trade are given by a weighted average price of exports divided by a weighted average price of imports, expressed as indices.

Q14. If in year 1 (the base year) the terms of trade index is 100, what will it be in year 5 if, over the period, the weighted average price of exports doubled while the weighted average price of imports went up by 50 per cent?

....

How will the trade price of each individual import and export be determined? Let us again assume for simplicity that there are just two countries.

Q15. Figure 23.1 shows the demand and supply of good Z in the two countries F and G.
(a) Which country will export the good?

....

Figure 23.1 The demand and supply of good Z in countries F and G

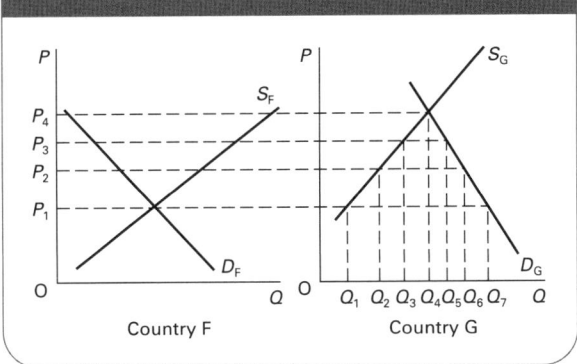

(b) What will be the equilibrium trade price?

....

(c) How much of good Z will be consumed in country G?

....

(d) How much will be traded? ....

The relative price of imports and exports, and hence the terms of trade, will also depend on the rate of exchange. For example, if the rate of exchange changes from £1 = €1.50 to £1 = €1.30, then, other things being equal, the UK terms of trade will have **Q16.** *improved/deteriorated*.

(Page 656) Other reasons for trade
Current comparative cost differences are not the only basis for trade.

🏁 **Q17.** The following is a list of other factors that can make trade beneficial:
  (i) Decreasing costs.
  (ii) Differences in demand.
  (iii) Increased competition.
  (iv) Trade is an engine of growth.
  (v) Non-economic factors.

Into which one of these five categories do the following examples fit?
(a) When the rest-of-the-world economy expands, this will increase the demand for a country's exports and also improve its terms of trade.

....

(b) By specialising in certain exports, the country may become increasingly skilled in their production.

....

(c) Free trade between countries may encourage closer political co-operation.

....

(d) Allowing imports freely into a country may stimulate domestic producers to be more efficient.

....

(e) The marginal utility ratios for products differ between different countries.

....

23.2 Arguments for restricting trade

(Pages 657–61) Many arguments are used by governments to justify restricting imports or giving specific help to domestic industries. These arguments can be put into four categories: (i) those arguments with some general validity in a world context, (ii) those arguments with validity for specific countries, but where there is nevertheless a net world loss, (iii) non-economic arguments, (iv) fallacious arguments.

🏁 **Q18.** Into which of the above four categories do the following arguments belong?
(a) Putting tariffs on certain imports is desirable if it can thereby drive down the price-less-tariff.

....

(b) Industries that are subject to external economies of scale should be protected or promoted if that will result in their gaining a comparative advantage.

....

(c) Trade sanctions are desirable against countries that abuse human rights.

....

(d) The international community should permit countries to retaliate with equivalent-sized tariffs against countries that subsidise their exports.

....

(e) If imported goods undercut the price of home-produced goods, it is desirable to put tariffs on them to bring them up to the price of home-produced goods.

....

(f) A domestic computer firm should be protected from a giant competitor abroad if there is the danger that the domestic one will not survive the competition.

....

Q19. Figure 23.2 shows a large country that as a whole has monopsony power in the purchase of a given import. Assume, however, that *individual* consumers in the country are price takers. What would be the size of the optimum tariff (assuming no externalities) to allow the country best to exploit its power?
A. HJ
B. OJ – FH
C. GH
D. FH
E. GJ – FH

324 CHAPTER 23 INTERNATIONAL TRADE

Figure 23.2 Country with monopsony power in the purchase of an import

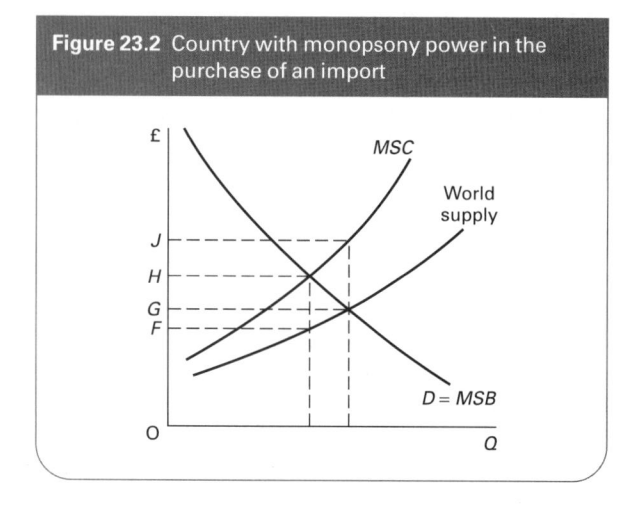

(Pages 661–3) Even if there are valid arguments for government intervention, protection through trade restrictions will rarely be the optimum solution. The point is that trade restrictions impose costs. Take the case of a tariff.

⊖ **Q20.** Figure 23.3 shows a country's domestic demand and supply curves (D_{dom} and S_{dom}) for a product. Part of demand is satisfied by imports. The country is a price taker and the world price for the product is given by P_w with the world supply curve given by S_w. A tariff is then imposed on the product whose amount is shown by the vertical difference between S_w and $S_w + t$.

Figure 23.3 A country's demand for and supply of an importable good

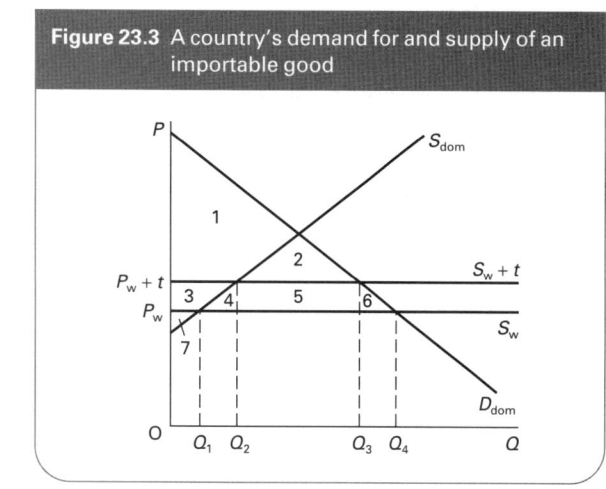

(a) How much is imported before the tariff is imposed?

....

(b) How much is imported after the tariff is imposed?

....

(c) What area(s) represent(s) total consumer surplus before the tariff is imposed?

....

(d) What area(s) represent(s) total consumer surplus after the tariff is imposed?

....

(e) What area(s) represent(s) the loss in consumer surplus from the imposition of the tariff?

....

(f) What area(s) represent(s) the producer surplus before the tariff is imposed?

....

(g) What area(s) represent(s) the producer surplus after the tariff is imposed?

....

(h) What area(s) represent(s) the gain in producer surplus from the imposition of the tariff?

....

(i) How much revenue does the government gain from the imposition of the tariff?

....

(j) What area(s) represent(s) the total net loss from the tariff?

....

Part of these 'costs' may be warranted. For example, if there were negative externalities in consumption (e.g. from cars), then it might be desirable to reduce consumption to Q_3 in Figure 23.3. But it is not *also* desirable to increase domestic production from Q_1 to Q_2. This, after all, involves diverting production from **Q21.** *high-cost producers to low-cost producers/low-cost producers to high-cost producers.* Thus protection in this case would be **Q22.** *first best/definitely second best/at most second best.*

📄 **Q23.** Referring to Figure 23.3, if there were external benefits of domestic production equal to $P_w + t - P_w$, but no externalities in domestic consumption such that $D_{dom} = MSB$, what would be the optimum form of government intervention?
A. A consumption tax so as to reduce consumption to Q_3 but leave production unchanged.
B. A tariff on imports, equal to $P_w + t - P_w$.
C. A production subsidy, equal to $P_w + t - P_w$.
D. A tax on the product, equal to $P_w + t - P_w$.
E. A complete ban on all imports of this product.

(?) **Q24.** What would be the 'first-best' solution to negative externalities in consumption (as in Q21 and Q22)?

....

(?) **Q25.** Name three other possible drawbacks from protectionism.

1. ....

2. ....

3. ....

23.3 Preferential trading

(Pages 667–8) Countries may make a partial move towards free trade by removing trade restriction with selected other countries. These *preferential trading arrangements* may take different forms, but there are four broad types.

Q26. The four types of arrangement are as follows.
(i) Free trade areas.
(ii) Customs unions.
(iii) Common markets without full economic and monetary union.
(iv) Common markets with full economic and monetary union.

Match each of the above to the following definitions:
(a) Where countries have no tariffs or quotas between themselves and have common external tariffs and quotas with non-members.

....

(b) Where countries have no trade barriers whatsoever between themselves, whether in terms of tariffs, quotas, differences in regulations governing the activities of firms, restrictions on factor movements or differences in indirect taxation.

....

(c) Where countries have no tariffs or quotas between themselves and are free to impose whatever restrictions they each individually choose on non-members.

....

(d) Where countries have no trade or other economic restrictions between themselves, have a fixed exchange rate or even a common currency, and pursue common economic policies: fiscal, monetary, labour and industrial.

....

(Pages 668–70) When a country joins a preferential trading system its trading patterns will change. The result can be either *trade creation* or *trade diversion*.

Q27. Trade creation is defined as a situation where production shifts from a higher-cost to a lower-cost source.
True/False

Q28. Which of the following defines a situation of trade diversion resulting from the formation of a customs union?
A. Production is diverted from a higher-cost producer outside the union to a lower-cost producer within the union.
B. Production is diverted from a lower-cost producer outside the union to a higher-cost producer within the union.
C. Production is diverted away from trade within the union to trade with non-union members.
D. Production is diverted away from tradable goods to those which are not traded.
E. Trade between non-union members is diverted to trade with union members.

Q29. Figure 23.4 illustrates the process of trade diversion. It shows a product that country A partly produces itself and partly imports. Before joining the union, country A imposed a common tariff on imports of the product from all countries. This had the effect of shifting the supply curve of imports from S_w to S_w + tariff. After joining the union, the country faced a (tariff-free) supply curve of the product from within the union of S_{union} (this curve includes the country's own domestic supply).

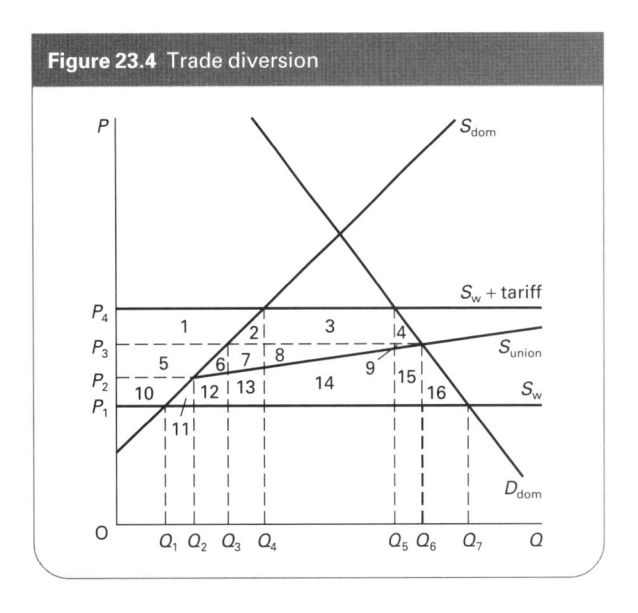

Figure 23.4 Trade diversion

(a) Before it joined the customs union, how much did country A import?

....

(b) Did it import the product from union countries or the rest of the world?
union countries/rest of the world

(c) Which are the higher-cost producers: union countries or the rest of the world?
union countries/rest of the world

(d) After joining the union, at what price could it now import the product?

....

(e) After it joined the customs union, how much did it import?

....

(f) Did production move to a higher- or a lower-cost producer?
higher-cost producer/lower-cost producer

(g) What area(s) represent the gain/loss in consumers' surplus from joining the union?
gain/loss of area(s) ....

(h) What area(s) represent the gain/loss in domestic producers' surplus from joining the union?
gain/loss of area(s) ....

(i) What area(s) represent the loss in tariff revenue for the government?

area(s) ....

(j) What area(s) represent the net gain or loss from the trade diversion?

area(s) ....

Q30. A customs union is more likely to lead to trade diversion rather than trade creation when

(a) the union's external tariff is very high.   *True/False*

(b) there is a substantial cost difference between goods produced within and outside the union.   *True/False*

23.4 The European Union
(Pages 672–8)

Q31. Which of the following best describes the European Community as it was in the 1980s?
A. A customs union.
B. A common market.
C. A free trade area.
D. An economic and monetary union.
E. A monetary system.

In 1993 the European Community (EC) was renamed the European Union (EU).

Q32. Referring to the list in Q31, which one best describes the European Union today as envisaged in the Single European Act of 1987?

A/B/C/D/E

Despite the elimination of tariffs between member states, there were significant *non-tariff* barriers before the completion of the single European market after 1992.

Q33. The following are various types of non-tariff barrier:
(i) Market-distorting barriers.
(ii) Quotas imposed by individual members on imports from outside the EU.
(iii) Tax barriers.
(iv) Labour market barriers.
(v) Regulations and norms.
(vi) State procurement bias.
(vii) Licensing.
(viii) Financial barriers.
(ix) Customs formalities.

Match each of the following examples from the pre-single market EU to the above types of barrier. There is one example of each type.

(a) A requirement by an EU country that all new buildings must be constructed using a certain type of girder made only in that country.

....

(b) The delays experienced by checking paperwork when goods cross from one EU country to another.

....

(c) Higher rates of excise duty on alcoholic drinks not produced in the country in question but produced elsewhere in the EU.

....

(d) A restriction on the quantity of shoes that one EU country allows to be imported from Poland, thereby encouraging Polish shoes to be diverted to other EU countries, making it harder for their domestic shoe industries to compete.

....

(e) Subsidies granted to domestic sheep farmers to enable them to compete unfairly in the EU lamb and wool markets.

....

(f) Professions that only recognise their own national qualifications.

....

(g) Governments or local authorities permitting only national firms to operate domestic coach and bus services.

....

(h) Governments preferring to buy military equipment from domestic armaments manufacturers.

....

(i) Credit controls that favour domestic firms.

....

Q34. Give three advantages of the completion of the single market in the EU.

1. ....

2. ....

3. ....

A complete common market also entails problems.

Q35. In which of the following cases are there most likely to be adverse regional multiplier effects from the development of the single market?

(a) Capital and labour move towards the geographical centre of the Union.   *Yes/No*

(b) Firms gain substantial plant economies by centralising production.   *Yes/No*

(c) Rents and land prices are flexible.   *Yes/No*

(d) A larger proportion of the EU budget is spent on regional policy.   *Yes/No*

(e) The impossibility of eurozone countries altering exchange rates between themselves.   *Yes/No*

(f) The development of information technology reduces communication costs. *Yes/No*
(g) Infrastructure expenditure is financed locally. *Yes/No*

Although the development of the single market encourages trade creation, it can also encourage trade diversion.

Q36. Which of the following cases would make trade diversion more likely?

(a) Substantial initial internal barriers to trade are now completely abolished. *Yes/No*
(b) External barriers remain high. *Yes/No*
(c) European industries have a wide range of available technologies and skills. *Yes/No*
(d) Many European industries experience decreasing costs at the level of individual national markets. *Yes/No*

B PROBLEMS, EXERCISES AND PROJECTS

Table 23.1 Pre-trade production possibilities for goods X and Y in countries F and G (per period of time)

Country F		Country G	
Good X (units)	Good Y (units)	Good X (units)	Good Y (units)
180	0	200	0
135	90	150	50
90	180	100	100
45	270	50	150
0	360	0	200

Q37. Table 23.1 shows the pre-trade production possibilities of countries F and G per period of time.

(a) Which country has a comparative advantage in good Y? *Country F/Country G*
(b) Assuming that $P = MC$, what would be the pre-trade price ratio (P_X/P_Y) in country F?
....
(c) Draw the production possibility curves for the two countries on Figure 23.5.
(d) Assuming that the exchange ratio after trade which balances the supply and demand for both imports and exports is $2X = 3Y$, draw a new line on each diagram showing the post-trade consumption possibilities if each country specialises completely in the good in which it has a comparative advantage.

Figure 23.5 Production possibilities for goods X and Y in countries F and G

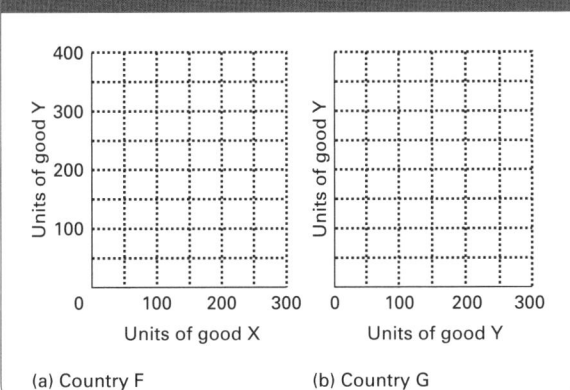

(a) Country F
(b) Country G

(e) What will be the level of production and consumption in each country after trade has commenced, assuming that country F consumes 240 units of good Y?

Country F produces .... units of X and .... units of Y.
Country F consumes .... units of X and 240 units of Y.
Country G produces .... units of X and .... units of Y.
Country G consumes .... units of X and .... units of Y.

.... units of X are exported by country ....

.... units of Y are exported by country ....

(f) Mark the level of imports and exports of each country on diagrams (a) and (b) of Figure 23.5.

Q38. A country's domestic supply and demand schedules for good X are as follows:

$$Qs_{dom} = -10 + 10P$$
$$Qd_{dom} = 130 - 10P$$

(a) Using these two equations, fill in the figures in Table 23.2.

Table 23.2 Demand and supply of good X

Price (£)	0	1	2	3	4	5	6	7	8
Qs_{dom}	...	...	...	...	30	...	...	...	...
Qd_{dom}	...	...	110	...	...	...	...	...	...

(b) What is the equilibrium price and quantity?

$P = $ .... $Q = $ ....

(c) Plot the curves on Figure 23.6.

Now assume that the country starts to trade and faces an infinitely elastic world supply curve at a price of £3 per unit.

(d) How much will the country now consume?

.... units

Figure 23.6 Demand and supply of good X

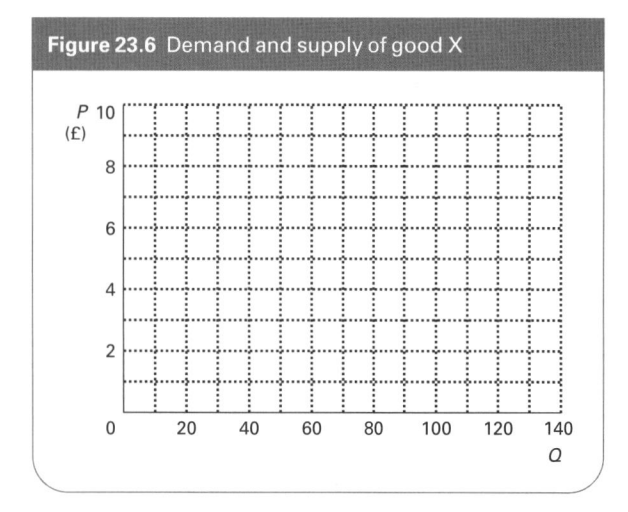

(e) How much will the country now produce?

.... units

(f) How much will the country now import?

.... units

(g) How much extra consumer surplus will consumers now gain?

....

(Clue: look at Figure 23.6 and work out the extra area gained.)

(h) How much producer surplus do domestic producers lose?

....

(i) What is the net welfare gain?

....

Q39. Given the information in Q38, now assume that a tariff of £2 per unit is imposed on the good.
(a) What will be the new market price?

....

(b) What will be the new level of imports?

.... units

(c) What is the reduction in consumer surplus?

....

(d) What is the increase in producer surplus?

....

(e) What is the tariff revenue for the government?

....

(f) What is the net welfare loss from the imposition of the tariff?

....

Now assume that the country joins a customs union, which has an infinitely elastic supply of good X at a price of £4.
(g) What is the new market price?

....

(h) What will be the new level of imports?

.... units

(i) Has there been trade creation or trade diversion?

trade creation/trade diversion

(j) What is the increase in consumer surplus?

....

(k) What is the reduction in producer surplus?

....

(l) What is the reduction in tariff revenue?

....

(m) What is the net gain or loss in terms of good X from joining the customs union?

....

Q40. Either individually or in small groups, find out how the composition of UK imports and exports has changed over the last 25 years. The best sources are *United Kingdom Balance of Payments (the 'Pink Book')* (NS) and *Annual Abstract of Statistics* (NS). Both of these can be downloaded as PDF files from the 'Bookshelf' part of the National Statistics site (www.statistics.gov.uk).
(a) How has the *area* composition changed? (What proportions of imports and exports come from which areas of the world?) Attempt an explanation for these changes.
(b) How has the *commodity* composition changed in primary products, semi-manufactures, manufactures and services? Have such changes reflected changes in comparative costs?

Q41. Find out what has happened to the UK's terms of trade over the last 15 years. Details are given in *Economic Trends Annual Supplement* (ONS).
(a) Have these changes reflected changes in the exchange rate index (also given in *Economic Trends Annual Supplement*)?
(b) What else determines the terms of trade? Are the figures consistent with your answer here?

DISCUSSION TOPICS AND ESSAYS

Q42. Can different endowments of factors of production fully explain countries' differences in comparative costs?

Q43. Make out a case for restricting trade between the USA and the UK. Are there any arguments here that could not equally apply to a case for restricting trade between Scotland and England or between Liverpool and Manchester?

Q44. 'Far from leading to specialisation by country, free trade simply leads to a proliferation of products within any one country. The result is the relatively minor gain of an increased number of brands to choose from.' Discuss.

Q45. Are any of the arguments for restricting trade based on the criticism that free trade *prevents* countries from fully exploiting their comparative advantage?

Q46. Are import restriction ever a first-best policy for aiding declining industries?

Q47. Discuss the economic consequences of the imposition of a tariff on a particular product. You should consider the effects on various types of consumers, firms and workers. Are tariffs ever superior to subsidies as a means of correcting market distortions?

Q48. 'Administrative barriers are a much more damaging form of protection than tariffs.' Discuss.

Q49. Discuss the economic implications for all relevant economic agents of a country joining a free trade area.

Q50. Are there any disadvantages from the development of the single market in the EU?

Q51. To what extent do non-EU countries gain or lose from the existence of the EU?

Q52. Is enlargement of the EU to include countries of eastern Europe likely to result in trade creation or trade diversion?

Q53. **Debate**
All arguments for restricting trade boil down to special pleading for particular interest groups. Ultimately there will be a net social cost from any trade restrictions.

Q54. **Debate**
Free trade reinforces the pattern of the rich countries becoming richer and the poor countries becoming relatively poorer.

D ARTICLES

The division of the world trading system into clearly defined regional trading blocs is not a new phenomenon, but it is a process that has intensified in recent years. The following article, taken from *Management Today* of December 1995, examines this trend and the implications for world trade and the WTO.

The balance of trade

The World Trade Organisation (WTO) is 'alive and functioning' says Dr Vincent Cable, director of International Economics at Chatham House. Yet, in the past two years, there have been a series of dramatic new initiatives to try and create regional free trade areas (FTAs) in North America and the Asia-Pacific region. Do these initiatives herald the demise of an open world trading system and the transition to a more conflictual, tripolar system of trading blocs? Or can British companies have some faith in the durability of the multilateral principles embodied in the new World Trade Organisation (WTO)?

While the WTO digests the Uruguay Round, what scope is there for an increase in trading ties between countries in the same geographical region? Contrary to the WTO's multilateral approach, the perceived advantage of FTAs is that they permit countries to choose their closest trading companions. Ideally, members of an FTA should be economically homogeneous either in trade patterns or in levels of economic development. Countries can then reap the benefits of an expanded market base, while minimising the problems that tend to flow from the desire of one nation's manufacturers to relocate to the markets of other FTA members with lower labour costs.

The FTAs have the advantage of being flexible. Member states need not lose the right to use ADDs or safeguards against other FTA members in case of a sudden surge of imports. FTAs are also accompanied by detailed negotiations on the 'rules of origin' for products that will be eligible for preferential treatment within the FTA. This means that national border controls can still prevent third countries from using neighbouring FTA members as launching pads for preferentially priced imports. Instead, those countries which are part of an FTA find their membership acts as a magnet to attract direct investment from foreign companies seeking to gain a foothold within the FTA.

Despite these advantages, there will still be winners and losers in an FTA. Successful FTAs, therefore, must rely upon a certain level of shared political cohesion in order to smooth over the disputes which are bound to surface periodically as economic interpenetration accelerates.

European Union
The European Union offers the clearest example of a regional agreement that blends economic and political self-interest. EU member states operate from the principle that their national economies cannot compete effectively either in domestic or in global markets unless they give their companies a wider regional base from which to operate.

The European Union is a customs union rather than an FTA. This means that member states have dismantled most national trade barriers and replaced them with a Common External Tariff (CET). EC member states also pooled control over their national trade policies into a Common Commercial Policy in which the European Commission acts as the single representative of the collective wishes of EC governments in international trade negotiations. As part of the drive for 'ever closer union', EC governments also extended freedom of movement to three other areas: services, capital and labour.

NAFTA

Regional integration in other parts of the Western hemisphere does not yet face the complex dilemmas which currently trouble the EU. The North American Free Trade Area (NAFTA) between Canada, Mexico and the United States was signed as recently as January 1994. It is a free trade area and not a customs union, and hence aims at a lower level of economic interpenetration at this stage. Nevertheless, reflecting the importance of foreign direct investment for all signatories, NAFTA's parameters go well beyond the mere liberalisation of tariffs. The agreement provides a detailed framework to remove barriers to direct investment, the free flow of services (including financial services) and the free movement of transportation. It also tackles the issues of environmental and labour standards, and has established an effective dispute settlement mechanism.

NAFTA has much in its favour. The US cannot afford to see Mexico's political and economic reform programmes descend into chaos, and has clear political and economic reasons to want NAFTA to succeed.

First, Mexico offers US multinationals a low-labour cost, contiguous market from which to import components for final assembly in the US. Second, the potential for trade-led growth in the Americas is enormous. NAFTA makes good economic sense for any other Latin American countries. Participation in NAFTA will help them to sidestep the worst excesses of future US unilateral trade actions. More fundamentally, most Latin American governments want to use a deepening of regional trade to encourage imports and to attract foreign direct investment.

However, NAFTA faces a number of challenges. The disparity in incomes between Mexico and its northern American partners, although part of the reason for integration, may also become a source of friction (in 1994, US GDP per capita stood at $25 000 and Canada's at $21 000, while Mexico's was $5000). In the short term, it seems unlikely that NAFTA can meet the wealth-creating expectations placed on it by Mexican politicians. Unlike the EU, NAFTA lacks any formal financial redistributive mechanisms to assist Mexico adapt to the rigours of a market economy.

East Asia

Regional trade arrangements in East Asia are far less developed than either in Europe or the Americas. The Association of South East Asian Nations (ASEAN) pledged in January 1992 to trim intra-regional tariffs to a mere 5 per cent by 2003 and to create a free trade area for manufactured goods by 2007. Subsequently, the Prime Minister of Malaysia, Dr Mohamad Mahathir, proposed the creation of an East Asian Economic Caucus (EAEC) to include ASEAN members and also Japan. However, strong US opposition to this 'Caucus without Caucasians' has kept the initiative on the backburner. Instead, the US has given its backing to a broader regional initiative entitled Asia-Pacific Economic Co-operation (APEC) which is designed to link the economies of ASEAN, NAFTA, Japan, China, some other East Asian states, Australia and New Zealand.

At their summit in November 1994, leaders of APEC committed themselves to create a free trade area across the Pacific by the year 2010 for industrialised members, and by 2020 for the rest. From the American perspective, APEC would prevent the emergence of an exclusionary regional agreement that might be detrimental not only to US business interests, but also to its regional political influence.

The primary logic for Asian regionalism, however, is market-driven. It is based, in particular, on increasing levels of foreign direct investment by the most advanced East Asian states, such as Japan and Singapore. Some 61 per cent of FDI flows into East Asian economies in 1986–90 were from within the region and such trade within East Asia has increased at a faster rate than in the other two blocs, averaging 20 per cent a year to reach 50 per cent of total Asian trade in 1993. A large part of this growth in FDI and in trade generally simply reflects the rapid growth of the economies in the region. It is nevertheless striking that when North America is included, trade within the entire Asia-Pacific region accounts for 65 per cent of world trade, making it comfortably the largest trading 'zone' in the world.

It would be wrong, however, to deduce from these figures that either the Asia-Pacific region or East Asia itself is developing into some form of institutionalised trade bloc. First, the region is riven by unresolved disputes and political fault-lines. Second, Asian nations are extremely cautious about US intentions. Singapore, Malaysia and China, in particular, suspect the US of plotting to force through Western standards of democratic accountability on the back of APEC trade initiatives.

Low levels of economic institutionalisation in East Asia also reflect the differing levels of development that exist there. In ASEAN alone, annual GNP per capita ranges from $22 250 in Singapore, $2315 in Thailand, to $220 in Vietnam.

Regionalism and the WTO

Looking in detail at the dynamics behind the EU, NAFTA, APEC and ASEAN, it is easy to agree with the view of Dr Vincent Cable that the concept of three neat 'trade blocs' is flawed. 'Vast differences exist between the EU, NAFTA and East Asia,' he argues, 'both in terms of the depth of economic integration and the political underpinnings of economic regionalism'.

Statistically speaking, however, a 'tripolarisation' of the world economy is taking place around the EU, NAFTA and the Asia-Pacific region. At the corporate level, multinationals have lobbied for regional integration, seeing regionalism as an integral part of the changing structure of international trade. This new structure is based partly upon the growing dependence of companies on international trade. It is also based upon the growing importance to companies of being able to invest in as many countries as possible. Between 1985–1993, foreign direct investment (FDI) by firms grew twice as fast as their direct exports.

Assisted by rapid technological modernisation, FDI serves many purposes, among them to allow firms to produce goods for local, regional or global markets in the most competitive manner; to produce or co-produce intermediate products in the most efficient locations, then move them across borders for final assembly; and to provide services on an international basis. The importance of the interaction between international trade and FDI is illustrated by the fact that one-third of world exports in 1993 consisted of trade within multinationals.

From the corporate viewpoint, anything which facilitates international trade and investment is to be welcomed – whether on a regional or global basis.

(a) Outline the economic benefits that countries might gain from joining together in a free trade area (FTA).
(b) How might the objectives of FTAs conflict with those of the WTO?
(c) Compare and contrast the three major trading blocs, the EU, NAFTA and East Asia. What factors are likely to determine their success?

Trade relations between Europe and the USA have been strained for many years, whether over bananas, GMOs or hormone-injected beef. To this list you can now add steel. In the article below, taken from *The Washington Times* of 27 March 2002, the responses to the US decision to protect its steel industry are analysed and the global implications of the action considered.

US steel protectionism angers

Shihoko Goto, UPI Senior Business Correspondent

Washington, March 27 (UPI) – Tension over the US decision to introduce hefty duties against imported steel products is mounting, and opposition to the Bush administration's policy is coming from across the globe, and not just from the European Union.

'There is no economic justification to the (Republican administration's) decision,' said the European Commission delegation's chief trade counselor to the United States, Petros Sourmelis, Wednesday at a steel dispute forum hosted by the Global Business Dialogue.

Sourmelis added that the US decision to protect steel makers was solely a political one, rather than one based on economics, noting that Congress is now eyeing the mid-term November elections and means to muster political support from key constituencies.

In retaliation against the US move to slap tariffs of up to 30 percent on a range of foreign steel imports to protect its domestic market, the EU will be imposing levies of up to 26 percent on steel products next week.

While the EU does not necessarily want to take such drastic measures to counter US actions, 'we do need to convince the US to remove the tariffs,' Sourmelis said. He added that putting up trade barriers would not only hurt the European economy, but also discourage US steel makers from restructuring their operations and growing in the longer term.

Moreover, the Europeans are not alone in their disgruntlement with the US protectionist measures.

New Zealand's Prime Minister Helen Clark – who met with President Bush Tuesday and who will be meeting with US Trade Representative Robert Zoellick later Wednesday – also voiced her concern about the levies.

'New Zealand's steel mills are unsubsidized, but the (administration's) decision is affecting all steel makers, who are being lumped together,' Clark told reporters following a speech at the US Chamber of Commerce Wednesday.

As a result, while New Zealand would 'not like taking action . . . it has been known to do so in the past,' Clark said, suggesting that the country too could take similarly retaliatory measures.

Other steel-producing countries have also been vocal in their opposition against the US decision to put up trade barriers, including Japan, South Korea and Switzerland.

'We intend to work closely with Europe . . . and we would welcome the participation of other concerned countries to actively argue this problem,' stated Japan's Economy Minister Takeo Hiranuma, shortly after the US decision to levy tariffs on steel products not only when the country's steel imports are actually dropping, but also as it has excluded Canada and Mexico from the tariff hikes as part of the North Atlantic Free Trade Agreement.

Meanwhile, South Korea's government made clear that it would continue to press Washington to lift the levies both through official and unofficial channels.

As for China, it is seeking compensation for the $350 million in steel sales it is expected to lose as a result of the higher US steel import tariffs, which would become still steeper if the EU also discriminates against its products as a result of the European dispute with the United States. The Chinese government has also threatened to file a complaint with the WTO, which would be the first action it would pursue with the global entity since China became a member last December.

Another country that could suffer a double blow as a result of the latest international trade dispute is Brazil, one of the world's biggest steel producers.

Earlier Wednesday, Brazilian Trade Minister Sergio Amaral said that the government could adopt its own measures to protect the country's steelmakers, pointing out that there was already an noticeable increase in steel exports to Brazil since March 20, when the United States first introduced its tariffs. That could increase still further when the EU also introduces levies on steel imports.

Nearly 12 percent of Brazil's steel exports are destined for the United States, and the government foresees a loss of at least $90 million in export revenue as a result of the US actions. Amaral estimated a further loss of $48 million in revenue this year from exports to the EU if the bloc's tariffs kick in.

But while global opposition against the US protectionist action increases, the Bush administration has challenged the European tit-for-tat reaction.

'The EU is levying tariffs without analyzing how much the (US import tariffs) could cost to European steel makers,' said Kevin Demsey, an attorney at Dewey Ballantine LLP who represents US flat-roll steel producers. He added that the EU should first take their complaint to the WTO, then decide whether to impose levies or not.

Demsey also defended the US decision to impose tariffs in the first place by pointing out that global steel-producing capacity is excessive, and countries have been eager to export their products to the United States particularly since the East Asian economies began to sour in the mid-1990s.

Given that many other steel-producing countries heavily subsidize their manufacturers, Demsey said that it was only fair for US steel makers to be similarly protected through the tariffs.

The WTO is expected to give its final ruling on the steel dispute between the United States and the EU by June 2003. In the meantime, countries heavily dependent on exporting steel – which ironically applies to neither the United States nor the EU – are likely to suffer the consequences the most.

(a) On what grounds does the USA justify its actions to protect its steel industry? What are the global implications of its actions?

(b) If the US steel industry is designated a 'senile industry', is protectionism in any way justified? Explain your answer.

(c) Visit the WTO Web site (http://www.wto.int) and evaluate its stance on this issue.

Many people criticise the policy of free trade as one that benefits the strong (large countries and powerful multinationals) and penalises the weak (small poor countries and firms with little or no economic power, such as small farmers). In the following article, taken from *The Independent* of 13 September 1999, Diane Coyle challenges these arguments and maintains that it is often the poorest who have most to gain from the law of comparative advantage and from the activities of the World Trade Organisation.

Free-trade supporters must speak frankly

The idea of free trade is under attack as never before in the post-war era

One of the many fresh starts in the next century will be the launch of a millennium trade round, a three-year negotiation intended to reduce barriers to trade in more areas, particularly services and agriculture. The annual meeting of the World Trade Organisation in early December is meant to agree the scope and terms of the negotiations, and it is no exaggeration to say its success will determine whether the 21st century will see extended to developing countries the improvements in welfare and prosperity enjoyed by the populations of developed countries these past hundred years.

Trade growth that gives them access to the world's big markets is one of the main ways that poorer countries can capture some of the benefits of globalisation. For very many countries, exports have been the engine of long-term growth. As the chart shows, for developing countries as a whole trade has been the motor for the past two decades, growing faster than national income, and its share rising most rapidly during the years of fastest growth.

Yet the idea of free trade is under attack as never before in the post-war era. The WTO's meeting in Seattle is likely to turn into a zoo of protest, as a coalition of campaigners, including aid charities and environmental groups, converge to proclaim their view that the world trading system is organised to benefit the rich and powerful through exploiting the poor. This could not be more wrong.

Yet the campaigners' false and malicious view of the WTO, and the continuing process of liberalisation, is in danger of becoming conventional wisdom. Few commentators bother to engage with it, or to correct it. Some even exploit it irresponsibly. For example, a recent discussion paper by economists Francisco Rodriguez and Dani Rodrik, published by the Centre for Economic Policy Research, challenged the methodology used in earlier research claiming countries with lower trade barriers grow faster. This rather technical paper was gleefully and wrongly acclaimed in some quarters as proving the stronger counter-claim that trade does not help boost growth.

The time has come for the supporters of free trade and globalisation to speak out. The global trading system has in fact been weighted very much more in favour of the developing countries by the establishment of the WTO. The reason is that it is a rule-based system, which does create a formally level playing field for all those who sign up to it. Systems based on rules, rather than negotiating weight, work to the advantage of the weak. In practice, of course, it is not quite so fair. For example, as the forthcoming World Development Report from the World Bank will point out, developing countries have very many fewer officials at the WTO than the industrial countries. Most are not in such a good position to exploit the opportunities.

Even so, the poorest country has, formally, the same market access as the richest. Poorer countries will be aided further by the fact that trade liberalisation is being extended to sectors in which they should have a comparative advantage, notably agriculture. If trade barriers and government subsidies can be reduced in farming, the whole world will benefit. Consumers everywhere will get cheaper food. Farmers in the rich countries, the lame-duck industry of the turn of the century, will no longer be diverted into unprofitable lines of business by daft subsidies. Taxpayers will save billions. And farmers in the developing countries will enjoy a much bigger market for their produce.

Unfortunately, the politics of trade are notoriously complicated even if the economic analysis is straightforward. There are always potential losers as well as winners, with the losers often an identifiable and powerful group able to lobby government effectively. And not only is there protest against trade liberalisation from campaigning organisations, the radical fringe of modern politics, there are currently serious tensions between the EU and US that could derail the new round of talks.

The banana case was an example. The American producer Chiquita was backed by the US government in a complaint that the EU had not fulfilled pledges to allow imports of its Latin American bananas. After a 10-year transition period the EU rules were still weighted in favour of former colonial producers in the West Indies and Africa. Portrayed as a big, bad US multinational throwing its weight around, the WTO nevertheless ruled in favour of the US. On this one the EU was in the wrong.

Potential future rows could make the bananas look like peanuts. Disputes over hormone-treated meat, genetically modified foods and aircraft are all in the pipeline. On the one hand is the EU's usual suspicion of free trade, reinforced

TRADE GROWTH VS NATIONAL INCOME

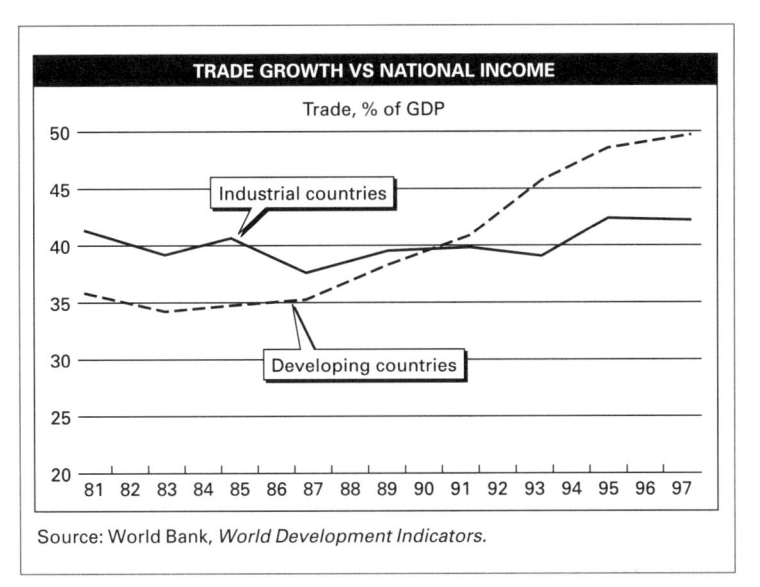

Trade, % of GDP

Source: World Bank, *World Development Indicators*.

now by the fact that the strongest liberal voice in Europe, the UK, is in the second division of decision making thanks to its decision not to join the euro in the first wave. On the other is a US administration with basically liberal instincts and a good record but a yawning trade deficit and an impending presidential election campaign. Between candidate Pat Buchanan's rhetoric and the need for union contributions to the campaign, there will be little scope for the American negotiators to make a strong push for further trade liberalisation in the early stages of the millennium round.

Even worse, one area on which the EU and US have reached agreement is the need to incorporate minimum labour standards in the trading rules. This means outlawing the use of child or slave labour, for example. Awful as these practices are, linking their abolition to access to world markets is potentially catastrophic, according to experienced and senior trade experts.

They warn that it is a disaster, that the decision will open up a chasm between the developed countries and the developing. The latter see the labour standards link as backdoor protectionism, especially as its most fervent advocates have been unions in industries in the rich countries most at risk from cheap imports.

After all, low wages are the core comparative advantage of developing nations. While it might be possible enough to identify, say, the use of prisoners paid no wages in export industries as unacceptable, other aspects are not so clear-cut. What if children's incomes are essential to families in a country where all children over a certain age do work? It would be considered abhorrent in the industrialised countries, but these countries are rich enough for households to have several dependents. Poor countries have to be allowed the opportunity to enjoy enough economic growth to reach that state of wealth themselves. That growth will come through exports of cheap goods.

The auguries for trade in the new millennium are not all that good. In the end, however, trade liberalisation is so important that policy makers will almost certainly hesitate to throw away its benefits. But they must not be diverted by the ill-informed and damaging circus of anti-trade campaigners descending on the negotiations.

(a) How can free trade help to reduce income inequality?
(b) In what ways has protectionism been weighted in favour of the richer and more powerful countries or groups?
(c) What are the arguments for and against outlawing child labour in developing countries?

E ANSWERS

Q1. D. A country will have a comparative advantage over another in the production of a good if it can produce it at a lower opportunity cost. This will apply to case D: the opportunity cost of X in terms of Y is lower. Note that B does not apply because other countries could possibly produce even more X relative to Y. Also E does not apply because the country could produce Y with even less resources than other countries.

Q2. (i) Country F: $1X = 2Y$.
Country G: $1X = 1Y$.
(ii) Country F: $1X = 1Y$.
Country G: $1X = 1.33Y$.
(iii) Country F: $1X = 1Y$.
Country G: $1X = 1Y$.
(iv) Country F: $1X = 0.25Y$.
Country G: $1X = 0.11Y$.
(v) Country F: $1X = 0.8Y$.
Country G: $1X = 1Y$.

Q3. *(a)* (ii) and (v). In these cases the opportunity cost of X in terms of Y is lower in country F than country G. Thus F specialises in good X and G in good Y.
(b) (i) and (iv). In these cases the opportunity cost of X in terms of Y is lower in country G than country F. Thus G specialises in good X and F in good Y.

(c) None. If there are only two goods and two countries, trade must involve one good being exported in return for the other being imported.

(d) (iii). In this case the opportunity cost of X in terms of Y is the same in both countries. Thus although country G has an *absolute* advantage in both cases, no trade will take place.

Q4. *(a)* $P_X/P_Y = 2$. Since 1 unit of X exchanges for 2 of Y, X must be twice the price of Y.

(b) $P_X/P_Y = 1$.

(c) Country F has gained because, before trade, to obtain 1 unit of X it had to sacrifice 2 units of Y (the opportunity cost of X was $2Y$); whereas with trade, it can import 1 unit of X by exporting only 1.5 units of Y (the opportunity cost of X is now only $1.5Y$).

Country G has gained because, before trade, to obtain 1 unit of Y, it had to sacrifice 1 unit of X (the opportunity cost of Y was $1X$); whereas with trade, it can import 1 unit of Y by exporting only 2/3 of a unit of X (the opportunity cost of Y is now only $0.67X$).

Q5. (a) (iii), (b) (iv), (c) (i), (d) (ii).

Q6. *abundant*. Abundant factors will tend to have a relatively low price as will goods that are intensive in them.

Q7. *reducing*. The effect of countries specialising in goods that are abundant in their relatively cheap factor will be to increase the demand for this factor and push up its price, thereby reducing factor price differentials.

Q8. *increasing*.

Q9. *bowed out*.

Q10. *disappear*.

Q11. Factors include: transport costs; factors of production moving rather than goods (e.g. labour migration); government restrictions.

Q12. *False*. The terms of trade are defined as P_X/P_M.

Q13. If $2X$ exchange for $3M$, then P_X/P_M must be 3/2.

Q14. Terms of trade equal $P_{\text{index of exports}} \div P_{\text{index of imports}} = 200/150 \times 100 = 133.3$.

Q15. *(a)* Country F.

(b) P_2 (where the exports from country F $(S_F - D_F)$ equal the imports to country G $(D_G - S_G)$.

(c) Q_6.

(d) $Q_6 - Q_2$.

Q16. *deteriorated*. If the exchange rate depreciates, then less imports can be purchased for a given quantity of exports: P_X/P_M has fallen. This is known as deterioration in the terms of trade.

Q17. (a) (iv), (b) (i), (c) (v), (d) (iii), (e) (ii).

Q18. *(a)* (ii) This is where the country is able to exercise its monopsony power.

(b) (i) This is the infant industry argument. It is justifying short-term protection (or better promotion) in order to be able to experience long-term comparative advantage.

(c) (iii) This is a political/moral argument.

(d) (i) This will prevent the move *away* from comparative advantage that dumping tends to create. Note, however, that the losers from dumping are *not* the consumers in the importing countries: they get the goods at a lower price! The losers are the firms in the importing country and the taxpayers in the dumping country.

(e) (iv) If followed, this policy would lead to a huge decline in trade, with no imports (however much more efficiently produced) being able to gain a price advantage.

(f) (i) This will help to prevent the establishment of a monopoly situation.

Q19. D. This is the amount of the tariff necessary to bring consumption to the point where $MSC = MSB$.

Q20. *(a)* $Q_4 - Q_1$.

(b) $Q_3 - Q_2$.

(c) $1 + 2 + 3 + 4 + 5 + 6$.

(d) $1 + 2$.

(e) $3 + 4 + 5 + 6$.

(f) 7.

(g) $3 + 7$.

(h) 3.

(i) 5.

(j) $4 + 6$ (i.e. the gain in producer surplus (3), plus revenue to the government from the tariff (5), minus the loss in consumer surplus $(3 + 4 + 5 + 6)$).

Q21. *low-cost* (foreign) *producers to high-cost* (domestic) *producers*.

Q22. *at most second best*. Some other policy (if such existed) which only increased production part of the way to Q_2 would be second best.

Q23. C. The production externalities but no consumption externalities imply that consumption should remain at Q_4 (where $P = MSB$), but that domestic production should be increased to Q_2. Both a production subsidy and a tariff (alternative B) will achieve the required increase in production, but a tariff, by raising the price to $P_w + t$, will also reduce consumption – side-effect distortion. A production subsidy, however, will not raise the price of imports. The product will continue to be sold at the world price of P_w.

Q24. A tax on consumption. This will have the desired effect on consumption, but by leaving the *producer* price unchanged, domestic production will remain unchanged and the reduced consumption will simply mean reduced imports. In terms of Figure 23.3, D_{dom} will shift downward by the amount of the tax, but domestic production will remain at Q_1.

Q25. Examples include: deflationary effects on the world economy may reduce demand for the country's exports; other countries may retaliate; protection may reduce competition and encourage firms to remain inefficient; protection may involve high administrative costs; it may encourage corruption as firms bribe officials to waive restrictions.

Q26. (a) (ii), (b) (iii), (c) (i), (d) (iv).

Q27. *True*. Trade creation is where the removal of trade barriers allows greater specialisation according to comparative advantage.

Q28. B. The reduction in tariffs within the union may mean that members now buy imports from each other rather than from outside the union, even if the non-union members were more efficient producers of the product.

Q29. *(a)* $Q_5 - Q_4$ at a price of P_4.
(b) *rest of the world*. (S_{union} is at a higher price for each output than S_w. If there were equal tariffs, therefore, on both union and non-union imports, the country would import from non-union countries.)
(c) *union countries*.
(d) P_3.
(e) $Q_6 - Q_3$.
(f) *higher-cost producer*. Trade is diverted from non-union suppliers who without tariffs would have supplied at the lower price of P_1.
(g) *gain* of areas $1 + 2 + 3 + 4$.
(h) *loss* of area 1.
(i) $3 + 8 + 14$. (Since nothing is now imported from outside the union, the government loses the whole of the tariff revenue it had previously earned.)
(j) $(1 + 2 + 3 + 4) - 1 - (3 + 8 + 14) = 2 + 4 - 8 - 14$.

Q30. *(a)* *True*. The abolition of such a tariff between union members will lead to a large reduction in the price of goods imported from other union members.
(b) *False*. If there is a substantial cost difference, the abolition of tariffs between union members is less likely to divert trade away from the (very) low-cost non-union producers.

Q31. A. There was an absence of tariffs and quotas within the EC and common tariffs with the outside world.

Q32. B. The Act envisaged the complete abandonment of all barriers to inter-EC trade and factor movements.

Q33. (a) (v), (b) (ix), (c) (iii), (d) (ii), (e) (i), (f) (iv), (g) (vii), (h) (vi), (i) (viii).

Q34. Advantages include: trade creation; reduction in the direct costs associated with barriers (such as administrative costs and delays); economies of scale, with firms better able to operate on an EU-wide scale; greater competition.

Q35. *(a)* *Yes*. If firms now see their market as the EU as a whole rather than mainly just their own country, they are likely to want to locate nearer the geographical centre of the EU.
(b) *Yes*. This encourages firms to merge and again to locate towards the geographical centre of the EU.
(c) *No*. A fall in rents and land prices tends to attract capital to the regions.
(d) *No*. This helps to offset regional problems.
(e) *Yes*. Individual eurozone countries with severe regional problems are unable to devalue in order to gain competitiveness.
(f) *No*. This reduces the need for centralising office functions.
(g) *Yes*. Depressed regions may be unable to afford the improvements to their infrastructure necessary to attract enough capital to halt their decline.

Q36. *(a)* *Yes*. This is likely to lead to a bigger switch in consumption from non-EU goods to EU goods, irrespective of whether many of them may be produced at higher cost. (On the other hand, the substantial increase in inter-EU competition may, over time, significantly reduce EU costs.)
(b) *Yes*. This would prevent low-cost non-EU products competing with higher-cost EU products.
(c) *No*. This tends to lead to trade creation as consumers are now able to purchase from lower-cost producers.
(d) *No*. The economies of scale from serving an EU-wide market tend to reduce costs of production and hence encourage trade creation.

Chapter Twenty-four

24

The Balance of Payments and Exchange Rates

A REVIEW

In this chapter we will look at ways of dealing with problems of the balance of payments and exchange rates. We begin with an overview of the range of alternative types of exchange rate 'regime' and how the balance of payments is corrected under each. We then look in detail first at fixed exchange rates and then at free-floating exchange rates.

Next we look at the various intermediate exchange rate regimes that have been tried since 1945. We start with the adjustable peg – a semi-fixed exchange rate system that was used round the world from 1945 to 1971. Then we consider the system of 'dirty' floating that has been used since 1971.

Finally, there are some optional questions on the extension of the *ISLM* model (see Chapter 20) to take account of balance of payments issues.

24.1 Alternative exchange rate regimes

(Pages 682–4) Correction under fixed exchange rates
In order to maintain the exchange rate at a fixed level, the central bank will have to intervene in the foreign exchange market whenever there is a **Q1.** *current account/capital account/currency flow* deficit or surplus. If the UK has a currency flow deficit, the Bank of England will have to **Q2.** *buy/sell* sterling.

Central bank intervention to maintain a fixed exchange rate will tend to affect the money supply.

Q3. Other things being equal, central bank intervention in the foreign exchange market to prevent a deficit leading to a depreciation in the exchange rate will increase the money supply. *True/False*

The effects on money supply can be offset by a process of *sterilisation*.

Q4. Assume that there is a currency flow surplus and that the Bank of England intervenes in the foreign exchange market to prevent the pound appreciating. Which of the following additional actions by the Bank of England would sterilise (i.e. offset) the consequent effects on money supply?
A. A reduction in interest rates.
B. Buying government securities on the open market.
C. Selling government securities on the open market.
D. Buying pounds on the foreign exchange market.
E. Selling pounds on the foreign exchange market.

If a currency flow deficit persists and if the government is to maintain the fixed exchange rate, it will have to tackle the underlying deficit. One approach is to try to improve the current account balance. It can use **Q5.** *deflationary/reflationary* fiscal or monetary policy for this purpose. This will lead to both 'expenditure changing' and 'expenditure switching' (an income effect and a substitution effect respectively).

Multiple choice | *Written answer* | *Delete wrong word* | *Diagram/table manipulation* | *Calculation* | *Matching/ordering*

◐ **Q6.** Which of the following are examples of expenditure changing and which are examples of expenditure switching?
(a) Relatively lower export prices lead to an increase in exports. *expenditure changing/expenditure switching*
(b) Lower aggregate demand leads to less imports.
expenditure changing/expenditure switching
(c) The resulting slowdown in economic activity leads to less demand for imports of raw materials and capital equipment from abroad.
expenditure changing/expenditure switching
(d) A fall in the rate of inflation makes home-produced goods more competitive relative to imports.
expenditure changing/expenditure switching

◐ **Q7.** Unlike expenditure changing, expenditure switching from deflationary policy will not have an adverse effect on unemployment. *True/False*

(Pages 684–6) Correction under free-floating exchange rates
Free-floating exchange rates automatically correct any balance of payments deficit or surplus by depreciation or appreciation respectively. As with a regime of fixed exchange rates, expenditure changing and expenditure switching will occur.

◐ **Q8.** Unlike with a fixed exchange rate, only expenditure changing will help to correct the disequilibrium: expenditure switching will make the problem worse.
True/False

◐ **Q9.** The greater the price elasticities of demand for imports and exports, the greater will be the level of expenditure switching from a depreciation and the smaller will be the amount of depreciation necessary to restore equilibrium. *True/False*

(Pages 686–7) Intermediate exchange rate regimes
There are a number of alternative exchange rate regimes between the extremes of a completely fixed and a completely free-floating exchange rate.

♟ **Q10.** The following is a list of exchange rate regimes:
(i) Crawling peg.
(ii) Free floating.
(iii) Adjustable peg.
(iv) Totally fixed.
(v) Dirty floating.
(vi) Exchange rate band.
(vii) Joint float.

Match the above to each of the following descriptions.
(a) Where a currency is allowed to float between an upper and lower exchange rate but is not allowed to move outside these limits.
....
(b) Where countries peg their exchange rate permanently to gold or to another currency.
....
(c) Where exchange rates are fixed for a period of time, but may be devalued (or revalued) if a deficit (or surplus) becomes substantial.
....
(d) Where a group of currencies are pegged to each other but collectively are free to fluctuate against other currencies.
....
(e) Where governments do not intervene at all in foreign exchange markets.
....
(f) Where the government allows a gradual adjustment of the exchange rate by small amounts.
....
(g) Where the government intervenes in the foreign exchange market to prevent excessive exchange rate fluctuations.
....

24.2 Fixed exchange rates

*(Pages 688–9) The effects of internal and external shocks under fixed exchange rates are analysed differently by new classical and Keynesian economists.

▤ ***Q11.** Assume that there is an *internal* shock under fixed exchange rates. According to new classical economists, if the government does not intervene, which of the following will occur?
(i) Internal balance will be restored.
(ii) Current account balance will be restored.
(iii) Overall external balance will be restored.

A. None.
B. (i) only.
C. (i) and (iii).
D. (ii) and (iii).
E. (i), (ii) and (iii).

▤ ***Q12.** What answer would Keynesian economists give to Q11? *A/B/C/D/E*

* Now consider the effect of an *external* shock under fixed exchange rates. Assume that there is a rise in demand for UK exports. According to new classical economists, the current account will to into **Q13.** *surplus/deficit*. The **Q14.** *higher/lower* aggregate demand will **Q15.** *reduce/increase* wages and prices. This will therefore tend to **Q16.** *increase/reduce/eliminate* the current account imbalance.

The rise in demand for exports will have a **Q17.** *small/large* effect on the financial account depending on whether there is any net pressure on interest rates. The current account surplus will tend to **Q18.** *increase/reduce* the money supply, putting **Q19.** *upward/downward* pressure on interest rates. A rise in prices, however, will increase the transactions demand for money, putting **Q20.** *upward/downward* pressure on interest rates. Thus the restoration of overall external balance is **Q21.** *assured/possible* and the restoration of current account balance is **Q22.** *assured/possible*.

*Q23. Keynesian economists argue that an external shock will, via the multiplier, destroy internal balance and may lead to a persistent current account imbalance given the inflexibility of prices. *True/False*

(Pages 689–90) Balance of payments problems do not simply arise from 'one-off' shocks. There are other factors that can lead to *persistent* balance of payments problems under fixed exchange rates.

Q24. Which one of the following is likely to lead to persistent current account deficits under fixed exchange rates?
A. A lower income elasticity of demand for the country's exports than for its imports.
B. A lower rate of growth at home than abroad.
C. A higher rate of inflation abroad than in the domestic economy.
D. The long-term development of import substitutes at home.
E. A growth in the country's monopoly power in the export market.

(Pages 690–2) Under fixed exchange rates the government will probably have to use fiscal and/or monetary policy to control the level of demand for imports and the level of inflation.

Q25. Assume that there is a balance of payments deficit caused by a high rate of domestic inflation.
(a) What effect will a deflationary *monetary* policy (a reduction in money supply) have on interest rates?
Raise/Lower them.
(b) What effect will this have on the financial account?
Cause an *inflow/outflow* of finance.
(c) What effect will this have on the money supply?
Increase it again/Reduce it further.
(d) What effect will this have on inflation?
Help to reduce it/Increase it.
(e) What effect will a deflationary *fiscal* policy have on interest rates? *Raise/Lower* them.
(f) What effect will this have on the financial account?
Cause an *inflow/outflow* of finance.
(g) What effect will this have on money supply?
Increase/Reduce it.
(h) What effect will this have on inflation?
Help to reduce it/increase it.
(i) Which will be more effective under fixed exchange rates: fiscal or monetary policy? *fiscal/monetary*

Q26. Give three advantages of fixed exchange rates.

1. ....
2. ....
3. ....

Q27. Give three disadvantages of fixed exchange rates from a new classical perspective.

1. ....
2. ....
3. ....

Q28. Give three disadvantages of fixed exchange rates from a Keynesian perspective.

1. ....
2. ....
3. ....

24.3 Free-floating exchange rates

(Pages 693–8) Under a free-floating exchange rate, the balance of payments will automatically be kept in balance by movements in the exchange rate.

If there are any internal shocks, then, provided that monetary policy maintains interest rates at international levels, the purchasing-power parity theory will hold.

Q29. The purchasing-power parity theory states that
A. inflation will adjust to the level of that abroad.
B. exchange rates will adjust so that the same quantity of internationally traded goods can be bought in all countries with a given amount of one currency.
C. interest rates will adjust so that the inflation rate is equalised in all countries so as to maintain the relative value of real incomes.
D. the exchange rate between currency A and B and between B and C and between C and A will be such that all three rates are consistent.
E. the exchange rate between any two currencies at any one time will be the same in all foreign exchange dealing centres in any part of the world.

Q30. Assume initially that the exchange rate is £1 = $1.50. Assume also that UK inflation is 50 per cent, but that US inflation (and also that in other countries) is zero. According to the purchasing-power parity theory, what will be the exchange rate after one year?

....

If we drop the assumption that interest rates are maintained at the same level at home as abroad, the purchasing-power parity theory will break down.

Q31. Assume that UK inflation is 10 per cent more than the (trade-weighted) average of that in other countries and that there is an expansion of domestic money supply that forces interest rates below the level of those abroad.
(a) What will happen to the current account balance (assuming it was initially in balance)?
Move into *deficit/surplus*.
(b) What will happen to the capital account balance (assuming it was initially in balance)?
Move into *deficit/surplus*.
(c) By how much will sterling depreciate?
more than 10 per cent/10 per cent/less than 10 per cent

(Pages 698–700) Let us consider how effective monetary and fiscal policies will be under free-floating exchange rates.

Q32. Exchange rate movements will reinforce monetary policy but will dampen fiscal policy. *True/False*

Q33. Assume that the government wishes to pursue a deflationary policy.
(a) What will happen to the exchange rate if it uses deflationary *monetary* policy? *Appreciate/Depreciate*
(b) What effect will this exchange rate movement have on aggregate demand? *Increase it/Decrease it*
(c) What will happen to the exchange rate if it uses deflationary *fiscal* policy? *Appreciate/Depreciate*
(d) What effect will this exchange rate movement have on aggregate demand? *Increase it/Decrease it*

Q34. Give three advantages of free-floating exchange rates.

1. ....
2. ....
3. ....

Q35. Under which of the following conditions are fluctuations in exchange rates likely to be severe?
(a) The demand for imports and exports is highly price inelastic. *Yes/No*
(b) Speculators believe that fluctuations in exchange rates are likely to be considerable. *Yes/No*
(c) Governments pursue a policy of setting interest rates in accordance with international interest rates. *Yes/No*
(d) Large amounts of the country's currency are held abroad. *Yes/No*
(e) There are many substitutes abroad for the country's exports. *Yes/No*

The uncertainty for importers and exporters associated with fluctuating exchange rates can be lessened in the **Q36.** *short term/long term* by firms dealing in the **Q37.** *spot/forward* exchange market. This allows traders to plan future purchases of imports and sales of exports at a known **Q38.** *price/exchange rate/interest rate/inflation rate*.

24.4 Exchange rate systems in practice

(Pages 700–2) After the Second World War, the world adopted an adjustable peg system where currencies were pegged to the US dollar. This was the Bretton Woods System (named after the town in the USA where the system was devised).

Q39. The following are various measures that can be taken under an adjustable peg system:
(i) Drawing on reserves.
(ii) Building up reserves.
(iii) Deflation.
(iv) Reflation.
(v) Devaluation.
(vi) Revaluation.

Which of the above measures is suitable for each of the following balance of payments problems?
(a) A severe and fundamental deficit.
....
(b) A temporary balance of payments surplus.
....
(c) A moderate surplus arising from the economy operating with a low level of aggregate demand.
....
(d) A mild deficit that is expected to disappear as the world economy recovers from recession.
....
(e) A large and persistent surplus because of the country's much lower underlying rate of inflation.
....
(f) A moderate deficit associated with a too rapid recovery from recession.
....

There were serious problems with the system.

Q40. Governments were sometimes reluctant to devalue, even when a deficit was fundamental. Why?

....
....

Q41. One problem of devaluation was the so-called 'J-curve effect'. This effect arose because:
A. governments tended to back up devaluation with deflationary fiscal and monetary policies.

340 CHAPTER 24 THE BALANCE OF PAYMENTS AND EXCHANGE RATES

B. after several months speculators came to believe that the balance of payments would begin to move into deficit again.
C. devaluation tended to make inflation worse in the long run.
D. the IMF only provided support for the exchange rate on a temporary basis.
E. the Marshall–Lerner condition was only satisfied in the long run.

? Q42. Why was there a problem of excess liquidity in the late 1960s and early 1970s?

....

(Pages 702–7) Since 1972 the world has been largely on a dirty floating exchange rate system (although groups of countries, such as those in the former European Monetary System, may peg their rates to each other).

? Q43. What are the two major ways in which countries seek to prevent short-term fluctuations in their exchange rate?

1. ....

2. ....

Q44. Floating exchange rates after 1972, by reducing the need for international liquid assets, reduced the inflationary pressures that were building up in the international economy. *True/False*

Q45. One of the problems experienced in the 1970s and 1980s was the growth in 'hot money'. Hot money may be defined as:
A. illegal exchange rate transactions designed to circumvent exchange controls.
B. currency deposits earning very high interest rates.
C. dollars that are used for international trade rather than transactions in the USA.
D. currency used for buying property and other assets abroad.
E. money put on short-term deposit in the country paying the most favourable interest rates relative to expected movements in the exchange rate.

The use of interest rates as the main weapon for stabilising the exchange rate has often led to conflicts with internal policy objectives.

Q46. In which of the following cases is there a clear conflict between internal and external policy objectives if interest rate changes are the only weapon available to the government?

(a) The government wants to prevent an appreciation of the exchange rate and to reduce demand-deficient unemployment. *Yes/No*
(b) The government wants to help UK exporters and to reduce the rate of inflation. *Yes/No*
(c) The government wants to reduce the price of imports and to curb the rate of growth in the money supply. *Yes/No*
(d) The government wants to prevent a depreciation of the exchange rate and to stimulate investment. *Yes/No*
(e) The government wants to halt a rise in the exchange rate and to reduce the rate of growth of the money supply. *Yes/No*
(f) The government wants to reverse a recent fall in the exchange rate and to reduce its unpopularity with home owners. *Yes/No*

Q47. Which of the following are likely to contribute to the volatility of exchange rates between the major currencies?
(a) A growth in the size of short-term financial flows relative to current account flows. *Yes/No*
(b) The abolition of exchange controls. *Yes/No*
(c) A harmonisation of international macroeconomic policies. *Yes/No*
(d) The adoption of money supply targets by individual countries. *Yes/No*
(e) The adoption of exchange rate targets by individual countries. *Yes/No*
(f) The adoption of inflation targets by individual countries. *Yes/No*
(g) A growing belief that speculation against exchange rate movements is likely to be stabilising. *Yes/No*
(h) A growing belief that speculation against exchange rates movements is likely to be destabilising. *Yes/No*
(i) A growing ease of international transfers of funds. *Yes/No*
(j) Countries' business cycles become more synchronised with each other. *Yes/No*

Appendix: The open economy and ISLM analysis

(Pages 708–11) *ISLM* analysis (see Chapter 20) can be extended to incorporate the balance of payments. This is done by introducing an additional curve to the *IS* and *LM* curves: this third curve is the *BP* curve.

Q48. Figure 24.1 illustrates a *BP* curve (we will look at the other two curves in the next question).
(a) What does the *BP* curve show?

....

(b) What will happen to the balance of payments if the rate of interest increases?
Current account/Financial account moves into *deficit/surplus*.

Figure 24.1 The open economy *IS/LM* model

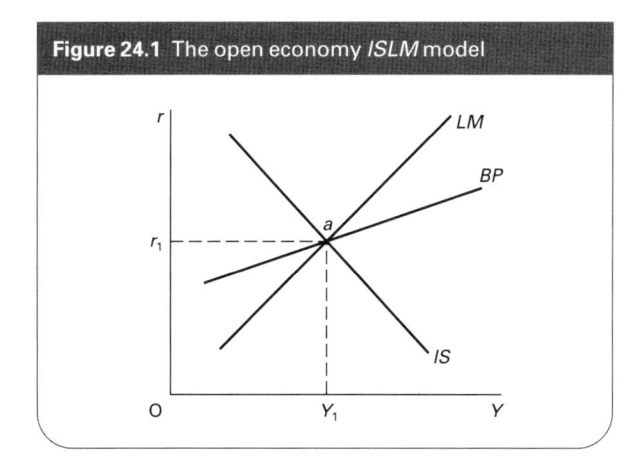

(c) What will happen to the balance of payments if the level of national income increases?

Current account/Financial account moves into *deficit/surplus*.

(d) Why does the *BP* curve slope upwards?

....

....

(e) What combinations of interest rate and national income would cause a surplus on the balance of payments?

Combinations in area of diagram *above/below BP* curve

(f) What will happen to the slope of the *BP* curve if the marginal propensity to import increases?

It will get *steeper/shallower*.

(g) What will happen to the slope of the curve if the elasticity of supply of international finance decreases?

It will get *steeper/shallower*.

(h) What will happen to the curve if there is an autonomous increase in exports?

It will shift *upwards/downwards*.

(i) What will happen to the cruve if there is an appreciation of the exchange rate?

It will shift *upwards/downwards*.

⊖ **Q49.** Figure 24.1 shows an economy which initially has an interest rate of r_1 and a level of income of Y_1 (point *a*). This is an equilibrium position because it is where *IS = LM*. Let us assume that the balance of payments is also in equilibrium (the *BP* curve passes through point *a* too). Assume a system of fixed exchange rates.

(a) What curve would initially shift and in which direction if the government pursued a deflationary fiscal policy? (It may help you answer the following questions if you draw the effects on Figure 24.1.)

The *IS/LM* curve would shift to the *left/right*.

(b) What effect would this have on the rate of interest?

rise/fall

(c) What effect would this have on national income?

rise/fall

(d) What effect would this have on the current account of the balance of payments? *improve/deteriorate*

(e) What effect would this have on the financial account of the balance of payments? *improve/deteriorate*

(f) The way the diagram is drawn, what would be the overall effect on the balance of payments?

Move into *deficit/surplus*.

(g) If there were to be the opposite effect on the balance of payments, how would the diagram have to have been drawn?

....

(h) What effect will the balance of payments position in (f) above have on the money supply?

increase/decrease

(i) What effect will this have on the *LM* curve?

Shift it to the *left/right*.

(j) Where will equilibrium finally be achieved?

....

(k) Will the secondary monetary effects of a fixed exchange rate (i.e. the shift in the *LM* curve) have strengthened or weakened the deflationary effects of the fiscal policy? *strengthened/weakened*

▤ **Q50.** Monetary policy under fixed exchange rates will be ineffective because:
A. any initial shift in the *LM* curve will simply be reversed because of the monetary effects of the change in the balance of payments.
B. the *BP* curve will shift so as to eliminate the effect of any shift in the *LM* curve.
C. the *IS* curve will shift so as to eliminate the effect of any shift in the *LM* curve.
D. the *BP* curve is steeper than the *LM* curve.
E. the *BP* curve is shallower than the *LM* curve.

⊖ **Q51.** Illustrate on a diagram like Figure 24.1 the effects of a deflationary fiscal policy under a system of free-floating exchange rates. Assume initially that the economy is in equilibrium at a national income of Y_1 with a rate of interest of r_1.

B PROBLEMS, EXERCISES AND PROJECTS

Figure 24.2 Expenditure switching and expenditure changing

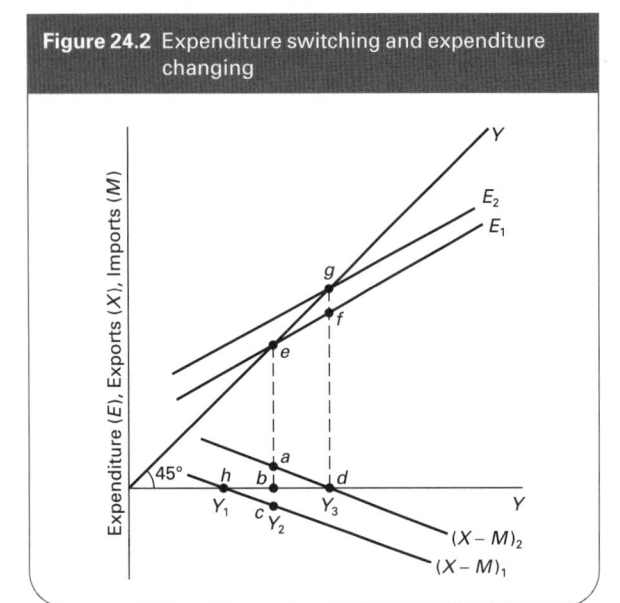

Q52. Expenditure switching and expenditure changing are shown diagrammatically in Figure 24.2.

Assume initially that the total expenditure function is given by E_1. The balance of payments is given by the line $(X - M)_1$. This shows that the higher the level of national income, the higher the level of imports relative to exports.

(a) What is the initial equilibrium level of national income?

....

(b) What is the balance of payments surplus or deficit at this initial equilibrium level of income?
surplus/deficit of ....

(c) Beyond what level of national income will there be a balance of payments deficit?

....

Now assume that there is depreciation of the exchange rate. This will alter the relative price of imports and exports and cause expenditure switching.

(d) How is this expenditure switching illustrated in the diagram?

....

(e) Why will the E line shift upwards as a result of the expenditure switching?

....

(f) Why does the E line shift upwards to E_2, but no further?

....

(g) What is the size of the multiplier? ....
(h) What is the size of the substitution effect (expenditure switching) on the balance of payments from the depreciation?
positive/negative effect of ....
(i) What is the size of the income effect (expenditure changing) on the balance of payments from the depreciation?
positive/negative effect of ....
(j) What is the total effect on the balance of payments of the depreciation?
positive/negative effect of ....

Q53. Free-floating exchange rates are likely to give rise to speculation. The two diagrams of Figure 24.3 both show an original demand and supply curve for sterling and an exchange rate of r_1. Assume that the UK experiences a lower rate of inflation than other countries.

(a) Show on each diagram the effect on the demand and supply curves and the exchange rate.
(b) Now assume that, as a result of the change in the exchange rate, people expect the government to cut interest rates and reflate the economy. On Figure 24.3(a) illustrate the effect on the demand and supply curves of these expectations.
(c) Alternatively assume that people expect inflation to continue falling and that as a result the exchange rate will continue to move in the same direction as in question (a). Use Figure 24.3(b) to illustrate the effect of these expectations.
(d) Which of the two diagrams represents destabilising speculation? *Figure 24.3(a)/Figure 24.3(b)*
(e) In which of the two diagrams is speculation self-fulfilling? *Figure 24.3(a)/Figure 24.3(b)/both/neither*

Figure 24.3 Alternative effects of exchange rate speculation

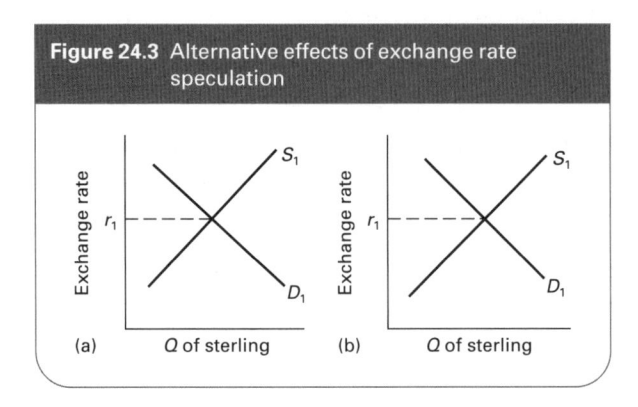

Q54. Construct a table showing the following figures for the UK economy since 1975: the exchange rate index, interest rates, the current account on the balance of payments, the rate of economic growth, the rate of growth in

money supply (M4), the rate of inflation. Plot the figures on a graph (or two or three graphs if it is easier). The graph(s) should show time on the horizontal axis and the other variables on the vertical axis (you can use different scales up the *same* axis for the different variables).

(a) Comment on the movement of these variables over time and whether there are any apparent relationships between them.

(b) Are these relationships as you would expect? Explain.

(c) What other factors would influence the movement of these variables and explain any apparent unexpected movements of one variable relative to others?

Sources: *Economic Trends Annual Supplement* (ONS); *Financial Statistics (Monthly)* (ONS); *National Institute Economic Review (Quarterly)* (NIESR). These statistics can also be obtained from the National Statistics Web site (www.statistics.gov.uk)

Q55. Compare movements in the volume of exports, the volume of imports, consumer prices, average earnings and the effective exchange rate over the last ten years for Germany, Japan, the UK and the USA. Plot these relationships on a separate graph for each country. (See Q54.) Explain the relative performance of the three countries.

Sources: *OECD Economic Outlook* (OECD); *European Economy* (Commission of the European Union); *National Institute Economic Review (Quarterly)* (NIESR). The first two of these can be downloaded from the respective Web sites: www.oecd.org and http://europa.eu.int/comm/economy_finance/publications/europeaneconomy_en.htm

DISCUSSION TOPICS AND ESSAYS

Q56. Discuss the effect on the balance of payments in both the short and long run of an increase in the domestic interest rate.

Q57. Why may an expansion of aggregate demand lead to a balance of payments surplus under a fixed exchange rate system?

Q58. What are the arguments for and against of pursuing a policy of maintaining a high fixed exchange rate?

Q59. Explain whether it is a problem for a country to have a persistent current account balance of payments deficit over the long term (i.e. a structural deficit rather than a mere cyclical deficit). What policies could a government pursue to remove a structural current account deficit?

Q60. To what extent can dealing in forward exchange markets remove the problems of a free-floating exchange rate?

Q61. 'If a country moves from a system of floating exchange rates to fixed or pegged exchange rates, it should switch its emphasis from monetary policy to fiscal policy when attempting to manage the level of aggregate demand.' Discuss.

Q62. How do elasticities of demand and supply for imports and exports influence the effectiveness of (a) depreciation and (b) deflation as means of correcting a balance of payments disequilibrium?

Q63. Was a system of managed flexibility (dirty floating) the best compromise between fixed and free-floating exchange rates in the 1970s? Is it the best compromise today?

Q64. What are the causes of exchange rate volatility? What are the adverse effects of exchange rate volatility? Has the problem of exchange rate volatility become worse in the last ten years?

*****Q65.** Using *ISLMBP* analysis, compare the relative effectiveness of fiscal and monetary policy as means of controlling aggregate demand (a) under a system of fixed exchange rates and (b) under a system of free-floating exchange rates.

Q66. Debate

A movement towards fixed exchange rates is to be wholly regretted. It is a denial of political and economic sovereignty and can force countries to adopt quite inappropriate domestic macroeconomic policies.

In praise of the international monetary non-system

The floating exchange rate non-system comes of age this month. It was 21 years ago, in March 1973, that the attempt to sustain the postwar system of fixed but adjustable exchange rates was abandoned. But that is not the only anniversary. It was also 50 years ago, in July 1944, that the conference at Bretton Woods, New Hampshire, designed the system that expired in 1973.

It is timely, therefore, to ask whether the global system of dirty floating either will, or should, endure for the next 21 years, or more. The answer is that it both will and should.

Floating exchange rates have had relatively few friends and many enemies. Yet nothing successful has been put in their place. Small countries are able to make credible commitments to fixed exchange rates, be it through currency boards (in the case of Hong Kong, for example), the ERM (in the case of the Netherlands) or just a unilateral target (in the case of Austria). Large countries find it far more difficult. Even France, most devoted to the cause of fixed exchange rates of the members of the group of seven leading industrial countries, had to concede 15 per cent fluctuation bands within the ERM last summer.

It looks as though the world must learn to stop worrying and love floating exchange rates. Would that be so bad?

The chart shows what has happened to exchange rates of the three major currencies – the dollar, the yen and the D-Mark – since 1971, the year when President Nixon's administration devalued the dollar, a decision that led ultimately to generalised floating. Five points emerge:

- there is a considerable amount of short-term 'noise' in the movement of nominal exchange rates;
- there was one huge swing in nominal exchange rates, which began in 1980 and ended in 1987;
- that swing went into reverse in early 1985, well before the celebrated meeting of the G7 finance ministers at the Plaza Hotel in New York;
- there has been a fairly close correlation between swings in nominal and real exchange rates, although this has been less true for the D-Mark than for the other two, because Germany is shielded by the ERM;
- there have now been some seven years of reasonable exchange rate stability.

This last fact explains why schemes to reform the international monetary system – common in the mid-1980s – have ceased to attract much attention today. But it also helps put the earlier dollar 'bubble' in proper perspective.

Neither credible exchange rate commitments nor intervention explain the long period of relative stability, at least after 1987. This underlines the point made by Professor Max Corden of the Johns Hopkins University School of Advanced International Studies in Washington DC, in a book to be published later this year, that 'managed floating is not incompatible with considerable exchange rate stability'.*

The conditions for this are low and stable inflation in all participants and the absence of major shocks. Destabilising shocks do have to be major ones. Even the fall of the Berlin Wall resulted in only a modest appreciation of the D-Mark against the dollar, though it did lead to a melt-down in the more rigid ERM.

In the mid-1980s, the non-system looked far more erratic. Now it is possible to recognise that the ultimate cause of the rise of the dollar was an exceptionally large shock in the world's biggest economy: the tightening of monetary policy under Paul Volcker, chairman of the Federal Reserve, combined with the loosening of fiscal policy under President Ronald Reagan.

It is also unlikely that any other exchange rate system could have coped

* W. Max Corden, *Economic Policy, Exchange Rates and the International System* (Oxford: Oxford University Press, forthcoming).

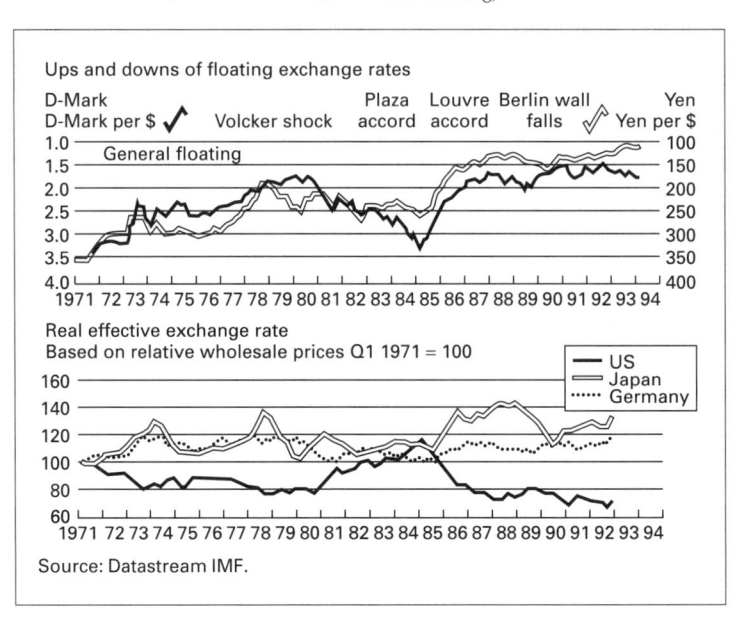

better with such a shock. Professor Corden's book, which shows just how economic analysis ought to be used to clarify important questions for an educated general public, indicates why.

Suppose that it is accepted that the dollar had begun to overshoot seriously by 1983 and 1984, what would have been the consequences of using monetary policy to stop the trend? The likely answer, as we know from British experience with a similar bubble in 1987 and 1988, is that US inflation would have risen instead. It is possible that the total real exchange rate appreciation would then have been smaller. What is much more important is that the loss of competitiveness would have been more difficult to reverse under greater exchange rate stability. It would have required falling prices or at the least rapidly falling inflation, rather than the depreciation of the nominal exchange rate that occurred.

Not only has the present non-system been functioning quite well for some years, it is also difficult to conceive of any workable alternatives. The fate of the ERM has demonstrated the vulnerability of any fixed exchange rate system with imperfect credibility and free capital movement. One alternative would be a credibly fixed exchange rate system, such as a currency board or, for large countries, a currency union. The only other would be a float, but the more explicitly the exchange rate is managed within the float, the greater its vulnerability to speculation.

As Professor Corden puts it, 'the current laissez-faire international monetary system is simply a market system, which co-ordinates the decentralised decisions reached by private and public actors, and is likely to be as efficient at this as the market system within the domestic economy'. In other words, floating exchange rates among major currencies offer the worst possible system, except for all the others.

(a) Using the two graphs presented in the article, explain what happened to the exchange rate value of the D-Mark (the old German mark), dollar and yen from 1971 to 1994.

(b) Does the evidence support the view that 'managed floating is not incompatible with considerable exchange rate stability'? What other conditions might be necessary for such a claim to be made?

(c) Did the events within the ERM in the 1990s confirm that semi-fixed or fixed exchange rate systems are doomed to failure?

The following article, taken from the *Investors Chronicle* of 15 March 2002, analyses the collapse of the Argentinian economy in recent years, and how the difficulties it faces are unlikely to improve in the near future.

No silver lining

Argentina has plummeted from its position as the seventh richest nation in the world to a debt-ridden also-ran among emerging markets. Even now, it would take a brave investor to call the bottom, argues Dan Oakey.

You have scrimped and saved for a lifetime. Not trusting your government's ability to control inflation, you keep your savings in US dollars. Finally you have a sizeable nest egg.

Then the government decrees that your bank account will be frozen and your dollar savings converted to pesos. You know that within a few days the government will also scrap the fixed-dollar exchange rate. The peso is bound to tumble, and with it the value of your savings. It could be by 40, 50 or 60 per cent. Welcome to the 'corralito' – the cattle-fold or investment dead-end into which Argentina's middle classes have been herded.

No one invests in emerging markets because of their perfect economies. We expect a few wrinkles like corruption, debt and a dodgy inflation record. The reason for putting your cash there is that things are moving in the right direction. And the ultimate destination could be a bright, shiny, modern market economy like Ireland or South Korea.

Applying that logic to Argentina, we would discount the $141bn owed to foreign creditors, ignore the country's four-year-old recession, 22 per cent unemployment rate and tumbling currency. Instead, we'd watch for turning points. So long as the Argentine senate passes this week's austerity budget, thus helping to win an emergency IMF loan, we might argue the path was clear to a tremulous recovery.

Free fall

Unfortunately not. Emerging market fund managers in the City are far from convinced that the country is on the rebound.

'Investors should not be touching Argentina right now, it's still significantly overvalued,' says Emily McLaughlin, F&C's director of Latin America. Since the government froze dollar savings accounts and banned capital from leaving the country, many people have been buying shares in companies with a dual-listing in Buenos Aires and New York. They can then convert the shares into American Depository Receipts and resell them for dollars in New York.

It's a desperate ploy that has created a false market in many Argentine stocks, lifting the index beyond any reasonable measure of fair value.

Besides, the Argentine economy as a whole is still in freefall. Industrial production, business investment and consumer spending are still crashing down. Richard Keery, Edinburgh Fund

Managers' emerging markets expert, is wary of calling the bottom.

'Buying at the point of maximum pessimism is a very brave strategy for any investor,' says Richard Keery. 'I'm 99 per cent sure we've not hit the bottom for Argentina.'

The peso devaluation and free-floating exchange rate should, in time, adjust prices to make Argentina's exports competitive again. But that will take years, especially if president Eduardo Duhalde goes ahead with plans for a windfall tax on exporters.

In the meantime, 90 per cent of gross domestic product (GDP) is internally consumed. Middle-class spending has, in effect, propped up the economy. Now that consumer confidence is plummeting, there is scant chance that the country can spend its way out of recession.

That leaves no obvious catalyst for a recovery except the kinds of painful structural reforms that will raise tax returns, cut government spending and lead to thousands of job losses (civil servant salaries make up 70 per cent of government spending). Whether Mr Duhalde has the will, or the power, to push through such reforms remains to be seen. But the omens are not good.

Having asset-stripped private investors, the government is now 'fleecing everyone they can get their hands on', says Ms McLaughlin, citing recent moves to use national lottery funds to pay public sector employees. Mr Duhalde has also just raised his own salary at the same time as calling for pay restraint for everyone else. Pulled between the conflicting demands of the IMF and his own back-stabbing colleagues, Ms McLaughlin doubts he'll see out the year.

Missed opportunities

It could all have been so different had Argentina's rulers tackled their budgetary problems 10 years ago when the dollar–peso peg was first introduced. Argentina's debt back then was technically fairly low. Where it tripped up was in its ability to pay it back. The dollar peg helped cure the country of hyperinflation, but regional and state governments failed to free up the labour market or improve tax collection.

As the country fell behind with repayments, it had to borrow more to pay back arrears. The risk premium grew for Argentinian debt, making it more and more expensive to service.

Argentina's public sector workers continued on their chronically unproductive ways. Stories of state employees swanning into work on the 29th of each month just to pick up their pay cheque are no myth. They still earn 50 per cent more than in the private sector.

But the private sector is also to blame for its failure to carve out any export niche.

'Argentina missed the boat,' argues Mr Keery. 'It's not producing anything the world can't get cheaper elsewhere.' Without a technological niche, core competence or significant natural resource, the country was living beyond its means.

Last year's financial crisis came as no surprise. Most UK fund managers had moved out of Argentina or written off their investments a year, or more, ago. 'It was an accident waiting to happen,' says Chris Jenkins, who manages Rothschild's Five arrows global emerging market fund.

There was no mad scramble to get out. Partly for that reason, there was little risk of contagion of Argentina's woes to other emerging markets. Floating exchange rates in Brazil and the rest of Latin America also allowed the market to adjust to developments in Argentina as they happened, rather than storing up trouble. But the sad fact is that what was once the world's seventh richest country has ceased to matter to financial markets. Viewed as a 'province of Brazil' by global asset managers, its GDP has shrunk to virtual irrelevance.

'Small, dangerous and not terribly significant,' said one City fund manager; a 'potential hand-grenade,' said another.

Signs of encouragement

But there are some voices of relative optimism about this peripheral economy. 'We're at the start of a process that has been delayed for a decade,' admits Five Arrows' Mr Jenkins. And if the right kind of reform comes then it will be painful for Argentines, the government and investors. However, Mr Jenkins maintains that from 'past experience of other countries, which have found themselves in similar messes, we know that there is a well-established way out'.

Comparisons with neighbouring Brazil are certainly encouraging. Devaluation of the Brazilian real gave a tangible boost to the export sector without stoking serious inflation. Brazil's lower labour costs also helped, as did its sound monetary and fiscal policy. In essence, it 'played the game' by the rules set down by the World Bank and IMF, reckons Mr Keery. As a result, emerging market watchers are generally bullish about Brazil in the coming months.

A drought last year hit the country's hydroelectricity capacity and led to power rationing, hurting industrial production. But rationing should end this year and inflation has fallen, leaving room for interest rates to come down too. The government of president Cardoso is now riding high in opinion polls, which should give it the confidence to embark on reforms with long-term benefits.

Global interest rate falls have also created a large flow of cheap money with no obvious targets in developed Western economies. Significant amounts have already gone to Asia, although Latin America has done well, too. If the US economy does pick up towards the end of this year, emerging markets offer a highly-leveraged play. Mexico and Asia stand to gain the most, but Brazil's cheap labour and vast commodities mean it should pick up too.

While the key emerging markets gear up for a party, Argentina will have to slash government spending if it wants another bail out from the IMF.

If the government sticks to its guns that can only swell the ranks of the jobless, depress the economy and fuel popular resentment. If it resorts to the printing presses, hyperinflation lies waiting in the wings.

Strong leadership will be essential, but the balance of power between the regions and the centre creates a stalemate, and leaves any government without the means to enact reform. Street protests have already scuppered four presidential careers in the space of a few weeks. The mob may have to rule before it learns the painful truths of political economy for itself.

'How is it going to recover? Where's the catalyst?' asks Mr Keery. 'The outlook is more bearish than I care to fully absorb.'

(a) What does the article identify as the source of Argentina's woes?
(b) Argentina operated a currency board for a number of years prior to the current crisis. Within such a system the peso was effectively fixed against the US dollar. What are the strengths and weaknesses of such a fixed exchange rate system? How are the problems with such a system affecting the Argentinian economy at present?
(c) What reforms are necessary in order to set the Argentinian economy back on the road to recovery?

In the article below, taken from *BBC News Online* of 14 February 2002, the topic is the rapid depreciation of a currency, its causes and consequences. The country is Venezuela and the currency, the bolivar.

Venezuela's currency in freefall

News that the bolivar would float spread quickly

Venezuela's currency has plummeted 25% against the US dollar after the government scrapped five-year-old exchange rate controls.

President Hugo Chavez made the surprise decision to scrap the bolivar's trading band on Tuesday.

The bolivar weakened to as low as 1001 to the dollar on Wednesday before closing at 981 compared with 795 on Friday, the Central Bank of Venezuela reported.

The mood on the street was angry and frustrated, with Venezuelans warning of dire consequences to come, after weeks of strikes.

'This is actually a devaluation and Venezuelans now should get used to higher prices,' said Janet Kelly, professor of public policy at the Caracas Graduate Institute of Advanced Management.

Financial markets pleased

The currency has been under increasing pressure as the international financial markets showed their disapproval of recent government policies.

'My first impression is that the economic measures are very positive, including allowing the [currency] to float,' Graciana del Castillo, Standard & Poor's lead Venezuela analyst, said.

'But there is still the political concern.'

The International Monetary Fund welcomed Venezuela's decision to float its currency.

'We have taken note of the flotation of the bolivar . . . We believe the measures go in the right direction but we do need to evaluate them as more details become available,' said the IMF's external relations director Tom Dawson.

The foreign reserves of Latin America's fourth largest economy have dropped by $6bn (£4.2bn) since November to $13bn, largely as a result of propping up the currency.

The director of the Venezuelan Central Bank has said the bank would not spend any more of its foreign reserves to shore up the bolivar.

'The central bank is not going to risk any more of its foreign reserves to feed capital flight,' Central Bank director Domingo Maza told local television.

Venezuela's stock market closed 10% higher as investors sought a haven for their investments aside from US currency.

Outlook worsens

The capital flight has been partly driven by Venezuela's volatile political situation, and also demands from business groups for a devaluation to boost domestic and foreign demand for Venezuelan goods.

The floatation is expected to stoke inflation to levels that Venezuelans, 80% of whom live in poverty, can ill afford.

One of Mr Chavez's chief policy aims was to tame inflation, which ran at 10% in 2001, as part of a populist platform of improving the lot of the poor and cracking down on endemic corruption.

The economy has been deteriorating, as falling international oil prices slowed down an economic boom, and there have been large-scale anti-Chavez strikes.

Oil is Venezuela's main export. It is the biggest supplier of oil to the US.

Chavez moves

President Hugo Chavez said the move was necessary to 'improve the competitiveness' of Venezuela's exports which had been 'buffeted by low oil prices'.

On Tuesday, Mr Chavez also announced budget cuts of 7% to tackle the deficit, which is expected to hit $8bn this year.

Venezuela is the second Latin American country to permit its currency to float against the US dollar within a week.

On Monday, Argentina finally floated the peso after it scrapped its 10-year-old peg to the US dollar and defaulted on $141bn of debts at the start of the year.

(a) Using evidence from the article, explain why the bolivar depreciated after it was floated.
(b) What are the likely economic consequences for Venezuela of the depreciation of the bolivar?
(c) Explain how the economic performance of the USA has a significant impact on Venezuela's exchange rate.
(d) How would the depreciation affect Venezuela's oil export earnings in (a) US dollars; (b) bolivars?

ANSWERS

Q1. *currency flow.* Note that if a deficit on current account is offset by a surplus on the capital plus financial accounts (excluding reserves) or vice versa, there will be no need for intervention.

Q2. *buy* sterling (with currencies in the reserves).

Q3. *False.* Purchases of domestic currency by the central bank to support the exchange rate will reduce the money supply.

Q4. C. To prevent the pound rising on the foreign exchange market the Bank of England will sell pounds. This will increase the money supply; so to offset this – sterilise it – the Bank of England must reduce the money supply by selling government securities.

Q5. *deflationary.*

Q6. (a) and (d) are examples of *expenditure switching*.
(b) and (c) are examples of *expenditure changing*.

Q7. *True.* Lower domestic prices will lead to an *increase* in demand for domestically produced goods.

Q8. *False.* It is the other way round. Expenditure changing from increased export demand and reduced import demand will, via the multiplier, cause an increase in national income and an *increase* in the demand for imports.

Q9. *True.*

Q10. (a) (vi), (b) (iv), (c) (iii), (d) (vii), (e) (ii), (f) (i), (g) (v).

Q11. C. Flexible wages and prices will restore internal balance. Any current account deficit (surplus) will put upward (downward) pressure on interest rates which will lead to a financial (plus capital) account surplus (deficit) which will offset the current account imbalance and restore overall external balance.

Q12. A. Wage and price rigidity will prevent internal balance being restored: a recession could persist. An endogenous money supply will remove the pressure on interest rates which would otherwise cause changes in the financial account to offset a current account imbalance.

Q13. *surplus.*

Q14. *higher.*

Q15. *increase.*

Q16. *reduce.*

Q17. *small.*

Q18. *increase.*

Q19. *downward.*

Q20. *upward.*

Q21. *assured.*

Q22. *possible.*

Q23. *True.*

Q24. A. As the world economy grows, so the growth in the country's exports will be less than the growth in its imports if the income elasticity of demand for exports is lower than that for imports.

Q25. (a) *Raise* them.
(b) Cause an *inflow* of finance.
(c) *Increase it again.*
(d) *Increase it.*
(e) *Lower* them.
(f) Cause an *outflow* of finance.
(g) *Reduce* it.
(h) *Help to reduce it.*
(i) *fiscal.*

Q26. Advantages include: certainty for the business community; little or no speculation (provided people believe that the rate will remain fixed); automatic correction of monetary errors; prevention of the government pursuing 'irresponsible' macroeconomic policies.

Q27. Disadvantages from the new classical perspective include: they make monetary policy totally ineffective; an imbalance between current and financial accounts may persist; they contradict the objective of having free markets.

Q28. Disadvantages from the Keynesian perspective include: deficits can lead to a recession, or if severe, to a depression; there may be problems of international liquidity to finance deficits; inability to adjust to shocks given sticky wages and prices; speculation if people believe that the fixed rate cannot be maintained.

Q29. B. The theory implies that the exchange rate will adjust so as to offset the effects of different inflation rates in different countries.

Q30. $1.00. To keep the purchasing power of the pound the same abroad as at home, the 50 per cent reduction in the purchasing power of the pound at home as a result of the 50 per cent inflation must be matched by a 50 per cent depreciation in the exchange rate (i.e. whereas originally £1 exchanged for $1.50, now £1.50 must exchange for $1.00).

Q31. (a) Move into *deficit.*
(b) Move into *deficit.*
(c) *more than 10 per cent.* The deficit on the capital account will cause the exchange rate to depreciate by more than that necessary to restore purchasing power parity.

Q32. *True.*

Q33. (a) *Appreciate.* A deflationary monetary policy will lead to higher interest rates, which will cause an inflow of finance and thus extra demand for (and reduced supply of) the domestic currency on the foreign exchange market.
(b) *Decrease it.* The higher exchange rate will discourage exports (an injection) and encourage imports (a withdrawal).

(c) Depreciate. A deflationary fiscal policy will lead to a lower transactions demand for money and hence a lower interest rate. This will encourage an outflow of finance and thus an increased supply of (and reduced demand for) the domestic currency on the foreign exchange market.

(d) Increase it. The lower exchange rate will lead to increased exports and reduced imports.

Q34. Advantages include: automatic correction of external disequilibria; elimination of the need for reserves; governments have a greater independence to pursue their chosen domestic policy.

Q35. *(a) Yes*: the inelasticities of currency demand and supply will cause severe fluctuations unless changes in interest rates or other factors affecting the financial account caused the curves to shift in such a way as to offset exchange rate movements.

(b) Yes: speculation tends to be self-fulfilling.

(c) No: this will tend to prevent large-scale financial movements and thus avoid large-scale exchange rate fluctuations.

(d) Yes: this can cause large-scale financial movements.

(e) No: this will make the demand for the currency more elastic and thus the exchange rate more stable.

Q36. *short term*: long-term movements in exchange rates over a number of years *cannot* be offset by forward currency dealing. Forward exchange deals are only for a few weeks or months hence.

Q37. *forward*.

Q38. *exchange rate*.

Q39. (a) (v), (b) (ii), (c) (iv), (d) (i), (e) (vi), (f) (iii).

Q40. It could be very disruptive to firms and might be seen as a sign of weakness of the economy and of the government's political failure. If so, it could possibly lead to speculation about a further devaluation. Also it would be inflationary.

Q41. E. In the short run, the demand for both imports and exports may be relatively inelastic, given that consumers and producers take time to adjust to price changes (arising from the devaluation). Thus the current account may deteriorate directly after the devaluation and only improve after a number of months (the J-curve).

Q42. Because the USA ran persistent balance of payments deficits.

Q43. Using reserves to intervene on the foreign exchange market; changes in interest rates.

Q44. *False*. By reducing the need to deflate if a country was experiencing a deficit, the system encouraged the expansion of countries' money supply.

Q45. E. It is 'hot' because it can easily be switched from one country to another as interest rates or expected exchange rates change.

Q46. *(a)* No: external and internal $r \downarrow$.
(b) Yes: external $r \downarrow$; internal $r \uparrow$.
(c) No: external and internal $r \uparrow$.
(d) Yes: external $r \uparrow$; internal $r \downarrow$.
(e) Yes: external $r \downarrow$; internal $r \uparrow$
(f) Yes: external $r \uparrow$; internal $r \downarrow$.

Q47. Yes: (a), (b), (d), (h) and (i).
No: (c), (e), (f), (g) and (j).
Note in the case of (d) that the adoption of money supply targets is likely to involve the government having to adjust interest rates to keep money supply within the target range and that this could lead to large inflows or outflows of short-term finance with a resulting effect on the exchange rate. In the case of (f) the adoption of inflation targets by countries (assuming that the targets are similar) will lead to greater harmonisation. In the short run, it could lead to greater exchange rate volatily if countries had different underlying inflation rates, but in the long run, it should lead to greater exchange rate stability as harmonisation increases. In the case of (j), if business cycles become more synchronised, countries' consumption, interest rates and inflation rates are likely to be more synchronised.

Q48. *(a)* All those combinations of national income (Y) and the rate of interest (r) where the balance of payments is in equilibrium.

(b) Financial account moves into *surplus* (as finance is attracted into the country).

(c) Current account moves into *deficit* (as higher incomes cause an increase in imports).

(d) Because an increase in national income causes the current account to move into deficit and therefore if the balance of payments is to stay in balance there must be a rise in the rate of interest to cause a counterbalancing surplus on the financial account.

(e) Combinations in area of diagram *above* the BP curve. This area shows higher interest rates or lower levels of national income than are necessary to achieve a balance. Higher interest rates will improve the financial account. Lower national income will improve the current account.

(f) It will get *steeper*. A rise in national income will cause a bigger rise in imports and thus there will have to be a bigger rise in interest rates to cause the necessary counterbalancing inflow of finance.

(g) It will get *steeper*. A bigger rise in interest rates will be needed to attract the necessary inflow of finance to offset any deterioration on the current account from an increase in income.

(h) It will shift *downwards*. The current account will improve at any level of national income and thus a lower interest rate will be necessary to

achieve the counterbalancing level on the financial account.

(i) It will shift *upwards*. If there is currently a balance of payments surplus (the economy is in the part of the diagram above the BP curve) the exchange rate will appreciate. The resulting increased imports and reduced exports will cause the balance of payments surplus to disappear. The BP curve will shift upwards.

Q49. (a) The IS curve would shift to the *left*.
(b) It would *fall*.
(c) It would *fall*.
(d) It would *improve*. A lower income would mean that less imports were purchased.
(e) It would *deteriorate*. A lower rate of interest will encourage an outflow of finance.
(f) It would move into *deficit*. The intersection of the new IS curve with LM is below the BP curve. The financial account effect is stronger than the current account effect (this is likely in the short run, given the massive financial flows that take place on the foreign exchanges).
(g) The BP curve would have to be steeper than the LM curve.
(h) *Decrease* as finance flows out of the country.
(i) Shift it to the *left*.
(j) Where the LM curve has shifted far enough to the left so that it intersects with the new IS curve *along* the BP curve. Only then will the balance of payments deficit be eliminated and thus money supply stop falling.
(k) *Strengthened*. The leftward shift of the LM curve will cause a further fall in equilibrium national income.

Q50. A. A rise in money supply (a rightward shift in the LM curve) will reduce interest rates. This will encourage an outflow of finance, which will reduce money supply again (a leftward shift in the LM curve).

Q51. See Figure A24.1. The deflationary fiscal policy shifts the IS curve to the left (say to IS_2). The resulting lower interest rate causes a balance of payments deficit (point *b* is below the BP curve). This causes the exchange rate to depreciate and thus the BP curve to shift downwards. But the depreciation will encourage more exports (an injection) and discourage imports (a withdrawal) and thus cause a rise in aggregate demand. The IS curve will shift back towards the right, reducing the original deflationary effect. Eventual equilibrium is reached at a point such as *c*, where all three curves intersect.

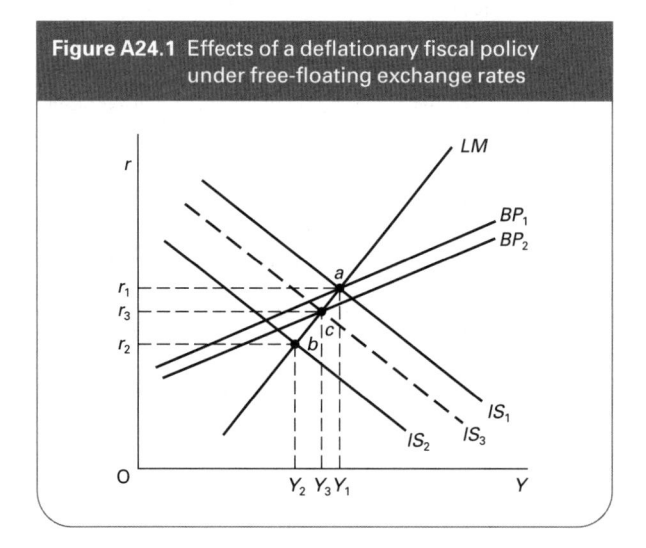

Figure A24.1 Effects of a deflationary fiscal policy under free-floating exchange rates

Chapter Twenty-five
25
Global and Regional Interdependence

A REVIEW

A rapid growth in international trade and financial flows has made countries much more interdependent. The result has been that countries' domestic economies are increasingly being governed by the world economy and by world international financial movements. We start by seeing just how countries are inter-related. We then look at what can be done to create a greater co-ordination of international economic policies. The extreme solution to currency instability is for countries to adopt a common currency. We then turn to look at the euro and how economic and monetary union (EMU) operates. Finally we look at some alternative suggestions for reducing currency fluctuations.

25.1 Globalisation and the problem of instability

(Pages 714–15) There are two main ways in which countries are economically interdependent: through trade and through international financial markets.

When the US economy expands, assuming no change in US interest rates, this will lead to **Q1.** *an expansion of output in other countries/a contraction in other countries approximately equal to the expansion in the USA.* This is the international trade multiplier effect.

Q2. Which one of the following defines the international trade multiplier?
A. The amount by which international trade expands for each $1 expansion in exports of country A.
B. The amount that country A's income expands for each $1 increase in its exports.
C. The amount that country A's income declines for each $1 increase in its imports.
D. The amount that country B's imports grow for each $1 increase in country A's national income.
E. The amount that country B's national income rises (via an increase in exports to A) for each $1 rise in country A's national income.

The effects of the international trade multiplier may be amplified by, or more than offset by, international financial flows.

Q3. Assume that the US economy expands. Assume also that the US Federal Reserve Bank (the central bank of the USA), worried by rising inflation, raises interest rates. What will be the consequences?
(a) There will be an outflow of finance from the USA.
 True/False/Uncertain
(b) The US dollar will appreciate. *True/False/Uncertain*
(c) This will lead to a fall in US exports.
 True/False/Uncertain
(d) As a result of the action of the Federal Reserve Bank, US national income will fall below what it would otherwise have been. *True/False/Uncertain*
(e) There will also be a fall in US imports.
 True/False/Uncertain

(f) The current account of the USA's trading partners will improve. *True/False/Uncertain*

(g) Interest rates in other countries will fall. *True/False/Uncertain*

(h) Investment in other countries will rise. *True/False/Uncertain*

(i) Other countries' national incomes rise. *True/False/Uncertain*

From the example given in Q3, it can be seen that a change in US monetary policy will probably have a **Q4.** *similar/opposite* effect on *other* countries' national incomes to that on US national income. This is the result of **Q5.** *the international trade multiplier effect/international financial flows*. The larger the level of international financial flows, the **Q6.** *more/less* will interest rate changes in one country affect the economies of other countries.

Q7. Consider the following policy changes in the USA:
(i) an expansionary fiscal policy, combined with lower interest rates.
(ii) an expansionary fiscal policy, combined with higher interest rates.
(iii) a contractionary fiscal policy, combined with lower interest rates.
(iv) a contractionary fiscal policy, combined with higher interest rates.

In which case(s) will international financial flows amplify the foreign trade multiplier effect on other countries?
A. (i) and (ii)
B. (iii) and (iv)
C. (i) and (iv)
D. (ii) and (iii)
E. (i) and (iii)

(Pages 715–18) Given the growing economic interdependence of nations of the world, it is important for countries to adopt complementary economic policies and not to engage in 'beggar-my-neighbour' tactics.

Q8. Assume that the world is suffering from a recession. Which of the following policies adopted by country A would benefit other countries and which would hinder them in attempting to pull out of recession?
(a) An expansionary fiscal and monetary policy. *benefit/hinder* other countries
(b) A devaluation of the currency. *benefit/hinder* other countries
(c) Raising interest rates in an attempt to reduce inflation and make exports more competitive. *benefit/hinder* other countries
(d) Using protectionism to help domestic industry. *benefit/hinder* other countries
(e) Giving investment grants to industry. *benefit/hinder* other countries

25.2 Concerted international action to stabilise exchange rates

(Pages 718–19) Currency fluctuations could be lessened if countries' economies were harmonised: in other words, if they were at a similar stage in the business cycle and if they did not experience excessive exchange rate fluctuations. In order to achieve these objectives, the Group of 7 major industrialised countries (Canada, France, Germany, Italy, Japan, the UK and the USA) meet periodically to discuss joint economic policies.

Q9. For which of the following reasons is it likely to be difficult for the G7 countries to achieve harmonisation of their economies?
(a) The G7 countries are usually more concerned about their own national interests than international ones. *Yes/No*
(b) Countries today have little power, given the huge scale of international financial flows. *Yes/No*
(c) Monetary policy is generally determined by central banks. *Yes/No*
(d) Achieving similar rates of economic growth may involve considerable differences between the countries with respect to other macroeconomic indicators. *Yes/No*
(e) General harmonisation of policies is possible only if there is convergence of the G7 countries, and that has not been achieved. *Yes/No*

Q10. For each of the following pairs of objectives, explain why it may be difficult to achieve harmonisation of *both* simultaneously.
(a) Interest rates and inflation rates

....

(b) Budget deficits and economic growth

....

(c) Inflation rates and exchange rate stability

....

Q11. If countries attempt to achieve similar rates of economic growth through demand management policy, for which of the following reasons may the equilibrium rate of exchange change over the longer term?
(i) The marginal propensity to import differs from one country to another.
(ii) The relative income elasticities of demand for imports and exports differ from one country to another.
(iii) The rate of growth of productivity differs from one country to another.

A. (i) and (ii).
B. (i) and (iii).
C. (ii) and (iii).
D. (ii) alone.
E. (i), (ii) and (iii).

(Pages 719–22) One example of an attempt to achieve greater exchange rate stability was the exchange rate mechanism (the ERM) of the European Monetary System (EMS).

Q12. Which one of the following describes the ERM?
A. A fixed exchange rate system between member countries and a joint float with the rest of the world.
B. A dirty floating system between member countries and a clean float with the rest of the world.
C. A pegged exchange rate system at a single point between member countries and a joint float with the rest of the world.
D. A pegged exchange rate system within bands between member countries and a joint float with the rest of the world.
E. A fixed exchange rate system within bands between member countries and a crawling peg with a basket of rest-of-the-world currencies.

Q13. Under an exchange rate mechanism, which of the following could be used to reduce inflation if there is upward pressure on the exchange rate and if it is already near the top of its band?
(i) Raising interest rates.
(ii) Reducing aggregate demand through fiscal policy.
(iii) A prices and incomes policy.

A. (i) only.
B. (i) and (ii).
C. (i) and (iii).
D. (ii) and (iii).
E. (i), (ii) and (iii).

Q14. Which of the following were reasons for the crisis in the ERM in September 1992 which led to the withdrawal of Italy and the UK from the system?
(i) Speculators perceived that Italy and the UK were not committed to maintaining their exchange rates within their bands.
(ii) The Bundesbank (the German central bank) felt obliged to maintain high rates of interest in order to dampen the inflationary effects of German reunification.
(iii) US interest rates were cut in order to halt the slide into recession.
(iv) There were worries that the Maastricht Treaty would not be ratified.

A. (i) and (ii).
B. (i), (ii) and (iv).
C. (ii) and (iii).
D. (ii), (iii) and (iv).
E. (i) and (iv).

Q15. The main reason behind the crises in the ERM in September 1992 and July/August 1993 was the lack of convergence of the economies of the ERM members.
True/False

Q16. As 1999 approached, so convergence between the economies of the ERM countries grew and exchange rate fluctuations diminished. *True/False*

25.3 European economic and monetary union (EMU)

(Pages 723–6)
Q17. The Maastricht Treaty set out three stages in the process of achieving full economic and monetary union. According to the treaty, which of the following would apply to those countries adopting full EMU in Stage 3?
(a) A fixed exchange rate between their currencies.
Yes/No
(b) A pegged exchange rate between their currencies.
Yes/No
(c) A single central bank for all the countries. *Yes/No*
(d) A single currency for all the countries. *Yes/No*
(e) Identical tax rates. *Yes/No*
(f) Free trade between the countries. *Yes/No*
(g) Free financial movements between the countries.
Yes/No
(h) Common external tariffs. *Yes/No*
(i) The abolition of all special EU help for different regions of the various countries. *Yes/No*
(j) A common monetary policy. *Yes/No*

Q18. Give two advantages of monetary union.

1. ....
2. ....

Q19. Give two disadvantages of monetary union.

1. ....
2. ....

The success or otherwise of having a single currency in Europe will depend on how close the eurozone is to an 'optimal currency area'.

Q20. An optimal currency area can be defined as one which:
A. maximises the growth rates of the member countries.
B. minimises the degree of economic fluctuations between member countries.
C. maximises the amount of trade between the member countries.
D. minimises the average inflation rate between member countries.
E. would involve a decrease in net benefits from having a single currency if the size of the area were either to grow or diminish.

25.4 Achieving greater currency stability

(Page 727) If there is a consensus in markets that a currency will depreciate, there is very little in the short term that governments can do to stop it.

Q21. If there were a 50 per cent chance that by this time next week a currency will have depreciated by 20 per cent, then selling the currency now will give an expected return of approximately 10 per cent for the week. *True/False*

Q22. The weekly interest in Q21 is equivalent to approximately 520 per cent per annum. *True/False*

Q23. If neither changes in interest rates nor central bank intervention from the reserves can halt a depreciation/appreciation of a currency that is perceived to be not at its equilibrium exchange rate, then which of the following exchange rate regimes are viable over the longer term?
(a) Free-floating exchange rate. *Yes/No*
(b) Adjustable peg system (with just occasional adjustments). *Yes/No*
(c) Fixed with an independent monetary policy. *Yes/No*
(d) Adopting the dollar or the euro or some other international currency as the domestic currency. *Yes/No*

(Pages 727–30) What then can be done to reduce the scale of speculative flows and create greater currency stability? One approach is reduce the *mobility* of international finance by introducing controls over financial flows. Such controls pose problems of their own.

Q24. Identify two problems of using controls over financial flows (sometimes known as 'capital controls').

1. ....
2. ....

Q25. One type of control is known as a 'Tobin tax' (named after James Tobin). This is a small tax on foreign exchange transactions. *True/False*

Q26. Controls are likely to dampen speculation, not eliminate it. Why might this be seen to be a desirable outcome?

....

....

Q27. An alternative to controlling financial flows would be to use a system of exchange rate target zones. This system would have the following features:
(a) Currencies would be allowed to fluctuate within bands. *True/False*
(b) These bands would be very narrow, say ±1 per cent. *True/False*
(c) Central parity would be set so as to maintain it at the 'fundamental equilibrium exchange rate'. *True/False*
(d) The central parity would be adjusted very infrequently. *True/False*
(e) There would be 'soft buffers', with exchange rates occasionally allowed to move outside their bands. *True/False*

Q28. Give two problems of the system of exchange rate target zones.

1. ....
2. ....

B PROBLEMS, EXERCISES AND PROJECTS

Q29. Construct a table and four graphs showing the movements of the following rates of exchange over the last three years: $/€, ¥/$, €/£, $/£. Plot the exchange rates at monthly intervals. Now plot interest rates for the four countries/areas over the same period. How closely have the exchange rate movements reflected interest rate movements? Identify any rapid changes in exchange rates and do a search through newspapers to find articles explaining such changes.

Sources: *International Financial Statistics* (IMF); *Datastream*; *The Economist*; newspapers; various Web sites, including the *Financial Times* (http://www.ft.com), Bank of England (http://www.bankofengland.co.uk), European Central Bank (http://www.ecb.int), Bank of Japan (http://www.boj.or.jp/en/index.htm), US Federal Reserve Bank (http://www.federalreserve.gov), International Monetary Fund (http://www.imf.org), Treasury Pocket Databank (http://www.hm-treasury.gov.uk). Hotlinks to all these sites can be found in the hotlinks section of this book's Web site at http://www.booksites.net/sloman.

Q30. Do a Web search to find articles considering whether or not the UK should adopt the euro. Prepare two reports, one putting the case for the UK adopting the euro and one putting the case against.

Sources: various newspapers (see Web addresses in Appendix 2 of Sloman, *Economics* (5th edition)); see also http://www.euro-emu.net.

C DISCUSSION TOPICS AND ESSAYS

Q31. Under what circumstances will the effect of international financial flows reinforce the international trade multiplier effect? Under what circumstances will the effect of such flows offset the international trade multiplier effect?

Q32. Why is it important for countries' economic policies to be harmonised?

Q33. What are the economic (as opposed to political) difficulties in achieving an international harmonisation of economic policies?

Q34. Using appropriate examples, explain how an economic crisis in one part of the world might lead to a global economic crisis. What would be the appropriate response by the G7 economies to a 'regional' economic crisis?

Q35. To what extent were the benefits and costs of membership of the exchange rate mechanism of the European Monetary System similar to those experienced under the old Bretton Woods system?

Q36. Why did the ERM with narrow bands collapse in 1993? Could this have been avoided?

Q37. Would economic and monetary union between a group of countries reduce any individual country's economic problems to those of a region *within* a country?

Q38. What are the arguments for and against a common currency for (a) the whole of the existing EU; (b) a considerably enlarged EU; (c) the whole world?

Q39. What difficulties are there for the eurozone countries in achieving continued convergence of their economies?

Q40. Consider the arguments for and against the worldwide adoption of a Tobin tax.

Q41. Debate
A world of just three currencies (the dollar, euro and yen) would be one which was much more stable economically, where international economic policies could be much more easily harmonised and where international economic growth could be higher.

D ARTICLES

The article below by Martin Woolf, taken from the *Financial Times* of 1 October 1997, examines how and why the world economy has become more integrated and open. In particular he focuses on the role of the multinational corporation in this process.

The heart of the new world economy

Globalisation is a word that now leaps readily to every tongue. Like the idea or loathe it, few deny its existence or understate its significance. But how far has it progressed? And what role do companies play?

Behind the growing integration of the world economy lies the decline in the costs of transport and communication. Between 1930 and 1990 average revenue per mile in air transport fell from 68 US cents to 11 cents, in 1990 dollars. The cost of a three-minute telephone call between New York and London fell from $244.65 to $3.32. Between 1960 and 1990, the cost of a unit of computing power fell 99 per cent.

Technological change makes globalisation feasible. Liberalisation allows it to happen. Under the agreement reached at the end of the Uruguay round of multilateral trade negotiations, average advanced country tariffs on imports of manufactures will be reduced to under 4 per cent. Tariffs of developing countries are set to fall from 34 per cent between 1984 and 1987 to 14 per cent. Between 1970 and 1997, the number of countries that eliminated exchange controls affecting imports of goods and services jumped from 35 to 137.

Restrictions on investment have been reduced virtually everywhere. Around the world, there have been some 570 liberalising changes in regulations governing foreign direct investment since 1991. Some 1330 bilateral investment treaties involving 162 countries are now in effect, a threefold increase in half a decade.

Technology and deregulation work together. The unit cost of sea freight, for example, fell 70 per cent in real terms between the beginning of the 1980s and 1996. Behind this sharp decline lay not just technical innovations, but increased competition generated by bigger, more liberal markets.

The extent of globalisation must not be exaggerated. At its pre-1914 peak, the

Crossing borders: trade inside the global company

Share of multinational affiliates in world output
- GDP
- Manufacturing
- Share in developing country GDP

Years: 1970, 77, 82, 88, 90, 92, 95

Source: World Bank, Global Economic Prospects *1983 **1989

International intrafirm trade's share in total country trade
- Exports
- Imports

JAPAN*: 1983, 1992
US: 1982, 1992

*Excludes firms engaged in commerce.

In 1996, the global stock of foreign direct investment (FDI) was valued at $3200bn. Its rate of growth over the previous decade was more than twice that of gross fixed capital formation. FDI flows grew at 12 per cent a year between 1991 and 1996, while global exports grew at 7 per cent. FDI is also widely spread: last year, 37 per cent of total FDI went to developing countries.

Investment leads to production. By 1995, 280 000 foreign affiliates generated $7000bn in global sales, which exceeded global exports of goods and services by 20 per cent. According to the World Bank, the share in world output of multi-national affiliates jumped from 4.5 per cent in 1970 to 7.5 per cent in 1995. Their share in manufacturing output was 18 per cent in 1992, up from 12 per cent in 1977.

Multinational production generates further international transactions. In the US, intra-firm imports were more than 40 per cent of total imports by the early 1990s. Similarly, an estimated 70 per cent of global payments of royalties and fees are transactions between parent firms and their foreign affiliates.

Large companies have long dominated industries characterised by economies of scale and scope, by firm-specific skills in innovation, production or sales or by valuable trademarks or brands. Companies usually find it more profitable to exploit such assets in-house than sell or license them to other companies or engage in joint ventures.

As sophisticated and more differentiated goods and services become more important in demand, output and trade, so do companies with the capacity to supply these competitively. Inevitably, it is the most successful companies of the most advanced economies that do best beyond the borders of their country of origin.

The largest 100 multi-nationals, ranked on the basis of their foreign assets, own $1700bn in their foreign affiliates, one-fifth of global foreign assets. All but two of the companies are from advanced countries, 30 from the US alone. The top 25 US multinationals are responsible for half of the country's stock of foreign capital – a share that has remained almost unchanged over four decades.

The big change in recent years, however, is a shift in the reasons why companies move production overseas. Historically, companies have located production abroad in order to overcome

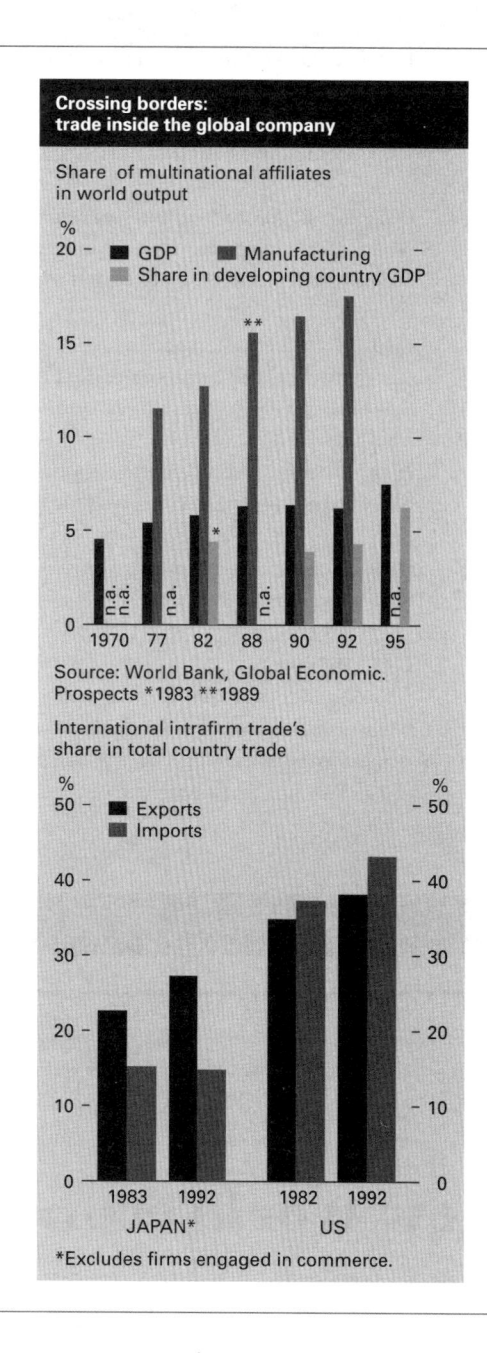

UK's net capital outflow was 9 per cent of gross domestic product, twice as big a share of GDP as outflows from Germany and Japan in the 1980s. In the same period the number of workers moving across frontiers was greater than now.

Nevertheless, international economic integration has, on balance, probably gone further than ever before. According to Angus Maddison, an economic historian, ratios of exports to global output were 9 per cent in 1913, 7 per cent in 1950, 11 per cent in 1973 and 14 per cent in the early 1990s. Financial markets are ever more closely linked; and governments are increasingly bound by a web of multilateral agreements and institutions.

Such constraints are one difference between today and a century ago. More fundamental still is the role of companies. Where once integration tended to take the form of trade and capital movements at arm's length, it now occurs increasingly within companies.

natural or artificial barriers to trade. If production efficiency were the only criterion, it would have made sense for many companies to locate all their production at a single base, to maximise economies of scale. In practice, however, governments in consuming countries have pushed them to spread production more widely.

For example, much of the Japanese investment in the US and the European Union was a response to protection against its exports. The same is true of investment in many developing countries – in car and truck production, for example.

Other barriers to centralised production were inherent in the nature of the business. The provision of many services used to require face-to-face contact. Expansion of service firms therefore required the creation of elaborate overseas networks. Similarly, fear of fluctuations in real exchange rates encouraged the spread of production capacity across frontiers.

Many of these trends are now changing. Trade liberalisation makes traditional protection-jumping production unnecessary. Improvements in communications are eliminating natural barriers to long-distance commerce; services can now be produced in one country and exported to another, just like manufactured goods. And in Europe, at least, economic and monetary union will eliminate exchange rate fluctuations.

So, creating overseas production sites merely in order to meet local consumption looks an increasingly fragile base for foreign investment. A much better one is the ability to make the best use of a company's competitive advantage by locating production wherever it is most efficient. Today's multi-nationals create widely spread networks of research, component production, assembly and distribution.

Evidence of this trend can be seen in the growing role of exports in multi-national production. Between 1966 and 1993, exports from US-majority owned foreign affiliates rose from about 20 per cent of sales to 40 per cent. For affiliates in developing countries, exports rose from 10 per cent to close to 40 per cent.

This sort of internationalisation reflects – and augments – the economic liberalisation and technical change binding the world's economies closer together. To the extent that reflects such forces, globalisation of companies is here to stay.

(a) What do you understand by the term 'globalisation'?
(b) How far is technology responsible for this globalising tendency?
(c) Why does Woolf see multinational corporations as central to the process of globalisation?
(d) Woolf argues that the reasons why businesses go multinational are changing. What are these changes and what are their implications?

In 1978 James Tobin proposed, in the face of growing foreign exchange turbulence, that all foreign exchange deals should be subject to a small tax in order to minimise speculative currency movements. Today his idea is still being debated. In the article below, which is an extract from an Oxfam Discussion Paper of May 1999, the value of the Tobin tax in helping to create greater financial stability, and also to reduce global poverty, is assessed.

Time for a Tobin tax? Some practical and political arguments

James Tobin, a Nobel Prize winner for economics, first submitted his proposal for a levy on international currency transactions in 1978. The tax was designed to deter the speculation that causes sharp exchange rate fluctuations and serious damage to economies. The idea was not greeted with enthusiasm, as it was a period of optimism and confidence in floating exchange rates. Yet, whenever currency crises erupted in the following years, the proposal for a levy to reduce volatility would again arise.

In the 1990s, two additional facts have sharpened interest in Tobin's proposal and its variants. First is the huge growth in foreign exchange trading to about $1.8 trillion per day (BIS, 1998) and the corresponding increase in currency instability, such as the 1992 crisis in the European Monetary System and the 1994 Mexican 'peso' crisis.

Second, since the tax could generate substantial sums, the idea has attracted the attention of those concerned with the public financing of development – a concern accentuated by the fiscal challenges faced by the state as well as by the growing need for international co-operation on problems such as the environment, poverty, peace and security. Depending on the formula, Tobin tax revenues could generate between $150–300 billion annually. The UN and World Bank estimated in 1997 that the cost of wiping out the worst forms of poverty and providing basic environmental protection would be about $225 billion p.a. (cf. Halifax 1998).

What are the economic benefits of a currency tax?

According to its advocates, a currency transaction tax would be a strategic element of global financial management since it can:
- reduce short-term, speculative currency and capital flows
- enhance national policy autonomy
- restore the taxation capacity of nation-states affected by the internationalisation of markets.

The tax is an attractively simple formula for reducing destabilising flows. The revenue base consists of very short-term, two-way speculative and financial arbitrage transactions in the inter-bank market. The greater the frequency of transactions, the higher the tax charge. Its appeal consists in being a disincentive to short-term transactions while not inhibiting international trade, long-term capital flows, or currency price adjustments based on changes in the real economy. The burden on 'normal business' would not be significant because of the low tax rate of 0.1–0.5% (depending on the specific proposal). According to the German Green calculation, if one assumes a tax rate of 0.2%, a speculator who works on a daily basis would be charged tax of 48% p.a.; an investor with a weekly time horizon would pay 10% p.a. and with a monthly horizon only 2.4%. Since 40% of currency transactions have a time horizon of less than two days and 80% have less than seven days, the tax would have a calming effect.

A currency tax is a levy on international capital flows and, as such, is a regulatory and fiscal counterpart to capital liberalisation and globalisation. In an environment of diminished nation-state economic sovereignty, the idea offers the opportunity to restore some of governments' lost taxation power and potentially raises the challenge of supranational taxation and redistribution of revenues within the international community.

The Spahn variation: two-tier currency taxes

Critics of the Tobin proposal point out that in the 'emerging market' world of extremely high currency risks, investors who expect a short-term devaluation of as little as 3% or 4% would not be deterred from a speculative transaction by a Tobin tax set at 0.1 to 0.5%. Indeed, given the scale of recent 'emerging market' devaluations (50% in Thailand and Indonesia, 40% in Brazil), the tax would be totally irrelevant. Though the Tobin tax would reduce pre-crisis speculative short-term flows and thus help avoid the problem of overvalued exchange rates in the first place, the point is valid. A higher tax rate is not the answer since it would deter 'normal' transactions.

In response to the problem, Paul Bernd Spahn, a German economist, proposes a 'two-tier structure: a minimal-rate transaction tax and an exchange surcharge that, as an anti-speculation device, would be triggered only during periods of exchange rate turbulence and on the basis of well-established quantitative criteria. The minimal-rate transaction tax would function on a continuing basis and raise substantial, stable revenues without necessarily impairing the normal liquidity function of world financial markets. It would also serve as a monitoring and controlling device for the exchange surcharge, which would be administered jointly with the transaction tax. The exchange surcharge, which would be dormant so long as foreign exchange markets were operating normally, would not be used to raise revenue, it would function as an automatic circuit-breaker whenever speculative attacks against currencies occurred (if they occurred at all under this regime). The two taxes would thus be fully integrated, with the former constituting the operational and computational vehicle for the latter' (Spahn, 1996).

Whatever the relative merits of the Tobin/Spahn proposals, it is clear that a Tobin tax on its own will not stop speculation if a currency is significantly overvalued – thus it is not a panacea for all the ills of the financial system. Achieving greater foreign exchange market stability also requires changes in the policies that lead to overvaluation in the first place, and complementary national and international controls and regulation on capital flows. It should be remembered that much potentially volatile capital in 'emerging markets' is invested in shares, bonds, short-term lending and bank deposit accounts; it is thus not primarily concerned with profiting from exchange rate fluctuations, though it may well flee if it anticipates a devaluation.

Where governments are

The main challenge for the Tobin tax idea is political. As a technical instrument, it was proposed by a renowned economist and many economists recognise its potential to help reduce volatility. The proposal is unusually clear and relatively well researched. It is also likely to be acceptable to the public since, in US political jargon, it is a tax on Wall Street, not Main Street.

Nevertheless, the idea is opposed or ignored by the leading American policy makers and by the international financial establishment.

(a) How would a Tobin tax work to reduce currency speculation and is it feasible?
(b) How could such a tax be used to support economic development in developing countries?
(c) Summarise the potential strengths and weaknesses of the Tobin tax.
(d) Given the above, which case do you think is the stronger and why?

The article below by Gavyn Davies, taken from *The Independent* of 16 November 1998, explores the role of the IMF and the manner in which it attempts to deal with problems in international capital markets.

The real cost of IMF rescue deals

The role of the International Monetary Fund (IMF) in the world economy has never been more crucial than now – or more vulnerable to attack. In the past few weeks the IMF has been central in stitching together a package of international financial assistance for Brazil – an effort which culminated with the $41bn (£25bn) loan announced on Friday. By avoiding a disorderly series of devaluations in Latin America (for a while at least), this breakthrough reduces the recession risks facing the world economy in 1999.

But at the very same moment that the IMF has been critical to the health of the world system in this regard, a powerful political and intellectual assault on the institution is being mounted, especially in the United States. This raises huge question marks about the future role of the organisation, and indeed whether it has any real future at all.

The present structure of the IMF is a relic of the reconstruction of the world financial system which immediately followed the Second World War. Learning the lessons of the 1930s, the great Western powers decided that free trade should be made central to the new world economic order and, because of the risk of competitive devaluations, they decided that this would not be compatible with an era of floating exchange rates. Under the Bretton Woods system, the major exchange rates were therefore fixed, both against gold and against each other, subject only to infrequent adjustments when 'fundamentals' changed irrevocably.

The key role of the IMF in this system was to provide a multilateral source of temporary liquidity for countries which ran into balance of payments difficulties. By providing such liquidity, the IMF could give troubled countries more time in which to adjust their domestic economic policies in response to international trade problems, thus maintaining political support for the free trade/fixed exchange-rate system.

With the break-up of the fixed exchange-rate system in the early 1970s, the Fund increasingly focused its attention on the emerging world. Initially, the bulk of this work related to traditional balance of payments financing for countries which hit problems on their trade balances. But, by the 1990s, the massive increase in the scale of private sector capital flows into the emerging world meant that the IMF inevitably became enmeshed in problems on the capital account of the balance of payments, rather than on the trade account.

This soon entailed a wide range of new dangers and pitfalls. In the 1994/95 Mexico crisis, and in the 1997/98 Asian and Latin American crises, IMF lending to troubled economies has had little to do with the traditional task of smoothing the process of trade adjustment, but instead has been intended to prevent widespread defaults in the financial system. The provision of liquidity to help countries with trade problems had been transformed into a form of bridge lending for countries with insolvent financial systems.

In the rare instance that the IMF has bungled in this new role – notably, Russia 1998 – the consequences for the world's financial system have been extremely disturbing. However, according to many economists, the deeper long-term consequences of the IMF packages themselves, even where successful, have been equally disturbing. For example, it is clear in retrospect that the allocation of IMF funds to Korea last year had the effect – whether intended or not – of bailing out the Western banking system. International money sent to Korea was immediately used to pay down foreign bank debt which would otherwise have been subject to a high risk of default.

Up to a point, this result was to be highly welcomed. The Russian example shows that the alternative to IMF action – major defaults on bank debt, leading to a much greater risk of recession in the world economy – would have been much worse in the short term. But the IMF programmes inevitably involve major disadvantages, and it is disingenuous to deny this.

First, the money has to come from somewhere – in point of fact, either from taxpayers in Western economies or from the central banks which they ultimately own. Typically, though, these taxpayers have no idea that their money is being spent in this manner.

Admittedly, the vast majority of IMF lending is repaid in full, and at attractive rates of interest for the lending country. But sometimes (for example, in the recent case of Russia), these loans are not repaid, disappearing instead into Swiss bank accounts. And, in all cases, IMF programmes imply that taxpayers are assuming risks that the private sector is not willing to assume. This means that there is an implicit transfer of wealth away from the taxpayers of the lending countries.

Who are the beneficiaries of this implicit transfer? Obviously, the most direct beneficiaries are the shareholders of Western banks, who would otherwise suffer much larger write-offs on their emerging market loan books. This transfer from the general taxpayer to the bank shareholder almost certainly implies gains by the rich at the expense of the poor. It is not difficult to imagine what would happen if a political party openly proposed such a programme to its electorate, which is perhaps why governments are generally at pains to disguise these effects of IMF programmes.

This is not all. Within the emerging nations themselves, the arrival of the IMF is typically used as the excuse needed by governments to raise taxation in order to 'recapitalise' their domestic banking industries. Once again, this involves taxing the general population to bail out bank owners, who are usually mega-rich industrial oligarchs. These transfers within the emerging nations have recently been of truly herculean scale, amounting to 25 per cent of GDP or more.

Many economists would argue that these latter transfers have little to do with the IMF, since they would be necessary anyway in order to rescue the banking systems in countries like Mexico or Thailand. But there is a genuine issue here. Why have these bank losses recently become so extraordinarily large? When bank failures were common in the industrial countries during the last century, the losses rarely amounted to more than a few per cent of GDP. Even the widespread bank failures in the US in the 1930s cost no more than 4 per cent of GDP. So what has suddenly happened to produce a position in which bank losses have increased almost tenfold?

It is hard to avoid the conclusion that the massive growth in international bank lending from the OECD economies to the emerging world has been central to this process. After all, in the Asian crisis economies, foreign bank debt had grown to 25 to 45 per cent of GDP just before the storm broke. And it is hard also to escape the suspicion that Western banks were willing to take on such huge exposures partly because they expected IMF help to be available in case of problems. The 1995 Mexican bailout certainly encouraged this belief.

If Western governments subsidise risk-taking activities, they can hardly be surprised when levels of risk rise to intolerable levels. This is a problem that needs to be addressed as soon as the present crisis subsides.

(a) When the IMF was set up at the end of World War Two, what was its principal role?
(b) How was the IMF's role to change, following the demise of the Bretton Woods system in the early 1970s?
(c) What concerns does Davies have about the IMF's approach to financial bail-outs, such as those of south-east Asian countries in 1997/98?

In the following article, taken from *BusinessWeek* of 17 June 2002, Jeffrey E. Garten examines the implications and consequences for the global economy of the growth in the Chinese economy and its rising share of world production.

When everything is made in China

The world economy is getting more reliant on Chinese factories. But having one giant supplier could mean a giant disruption.

During the past few months, Intel Corp. announced a $100 million investment in Shanghai to assemble Pentium 4 microprocessors. Dell Computer Corp. moved its giant PC-making facility from Kuala Lumpur to Xiamen. The provincial government of Shenzhen said it would provide $5 billion to boost its integrated-circuit industry. It's not hard to connect the dots. 'China is becoming a manufacturing superpower,' Kenneth Courtis, Goldman, Sachs & Co.'s vice-chairman for Asia, says, 'and the momentum seems unstoppable.'

The big question is whether the world economy is becoming so dependent on China as an industrial lifeline that it will soon be dangerously vulnerable to a major supply disruption caused by war, terrorism, social unrest, or a natural disaster. In other words, will China's importance to global manufacturing soon resemble Saudi Arabia's position in world oil markets?

Among developing nations, China has been the largest recipient of foreign investment, averaging about $40 billion per year during the late 1990s. Membership in the World Trade Organization will result in even higher levels. US companies are shifting manufacturing from Malaysia, Thailand, Indonesia, and even Mexico to China. Toshiba Corp. is making its TVs on the mainland, and Sony Corp. is manufacturing its PlayStations there. Taiwan's companies produce half of all their information-technology products in the country.

China's advantages are numerous. Its wage rates are a third of Mexico's and Hungary's, and 5% of those in the US or Japan. China's investments in education and training are attracting research facilities from companies such as IBM, Motorola, and Microsoft. The critical mass of factories, subcontractors, and specialized vendors has created a manufacturing environment with which few can compete. China is not just an export platform, either; its large and expanding domestic market is another attraction.

The mushrooming investment also reflects the obsession among global CEOs to lower production costs by outsourcing whatever they can to large-scale specialists. According to Bear, Sterns & Co., 50% of all manufacturing could be outsourced by 2010. Flextronics International Ltd, the world's largest manufacturing subcontractor, is illustrative. It operates in 28 countries on behalf of companies selling everything from cell phones to washing machines. Its revenues have grown from $100 million in 1993 to an estimated $14 billion today. Its business in China is projected to double this year over 2001 and could reach 40% of its worldwide production in two years, up from 24% in 1998.

How worried should the US be? To be sure, in the 1980s, one heard false alarms about Japanese dominance of high-tech industries. But China is far more open to foreign investment, along with greater cost advantages and more rigorous higher education.

No one would say China dominates manufacturing – yet. But in April, Congress' General Accounting Office criticized the Clinton and Bush Administrations for failing to analyze China's growing sophistication in semi-conductor technology. In the June issue of *Harper's*, investigative journalist Barry Lynn underscores the vulnerability of the US economy to global supply lines that originate in China and Taiwan and are designed for just-in-time delivery to our critical industries. Michael Marks, chairman and CEO of Flextronics, has concerns, too. 'I worry that CEOs are overreacting to short-term cost considerations,' he told me. 'Too much concentration in China could lead to serious supply disruptions. It would be better if their manufacturing facilities were more geographically dispersed.'

Unfortunately, it is no one's job to analyze the aggregate risks. Chief executives are rightfully seeking profits in a hypercompetitive world. China is admirably opening its economy to foreign investment. The national-security community is understandably focused on terrorism and weapons of mass destruction. Threats to highly complex global supply chains seem not to be the subject of any national or international group.

There isn't an easy answer for every problem, of course. But it is not too much to ask the Bush Administration to create a joint government–business task force to examine key questions. Is the approximately 90% of all foreign investment that is geographically located in China's coastal provinces a dangerous concentration? Should Washington take another look at tax and tariff incentives to make the entire Caribbean Basin – Mexico, Central America, and the islands – more attractive to foreign manufacturers? Should multinational companies be encouraged to hold larger inventories closer to home? Does China need to beef up its security around its vast industrial parks?

For a quarter of a century, Washington and Wall Street have wanted China to become an integral part of the world economy. Their wish has been granted, and now it's time to come to grips with the implications.

(a) Why is China attracting so much foreign direct investment?

(b) What are the implications for the global economy of China's increasing domination of markets such as that for semi-conductors?

(c) How should developed economies, like the USA, deal with the increasing competition from countries such as China?

E ANSWERS

Q1. *an expansion of output in other countries.* This will occur via the following process. A rise in US national income will lead to a rise in US expenditure on imports. These increased US imports represent an increase in exports for other countries, and hence an injection into their economies. These increased injections lead to an expansion in output of these other countries.

Q2. E.

Q3. *(a)* *False.* The higher interest rate will attract an *inflow* of finance.

(b) *True.* The inflow of finance will drive up the exchange rate.

(c) *True.* The higher exchange rate will cause exports to be less competitive.

(d) *True.* The higher interest rate will cause lower investment. This, combined with lower exports, will cause national income to be lower than it would otherwise have been.

(e) *Uncertain.* A higher exchange rate will make imports relatively cheaper and hence increase them, but a lower national income will tend to reduce expenditure on imports.

(f) *True.* Lower US exports (and possibly higher imports) will mean lower imports (and possibly higher exports) for the USA's trading partners.

(g) *False.* A rise in US interest rates will tend to drive up interest rates in the rest of the world (albeit by probably not so much as in the USA).

(h) *Uncertain* (although probably *False*). Higher interest rates in other countries will cause their investment to fall and lead to a fall in confidence. It is possible, however, that higher exports to the USA (injections) combined with lower imports from the USA (withdrawals) could lead to *higher* national income, and, via the accelerator, to *higher* investment. It is likely, however, that the first effect would be the dominant one.

(i) *Uncertain* (although probably *False*). There are two effects here: (i) the fall in their imports (and possible rise in their exports) will cause their national income to rise; (ii) the rise in their interest rates and probable fall in investment will cause their national income to fall. Probably the interest rate effect will be the dominant one, leading to a net fall in national income.

Q4. *similar.*

Q5. *international financial flows.*

Q6. *more.*

Q7. C. In the case of (i), an expansionary fiscal policy in the USA will lead, via the international trade multiplier, to higher national incomes in other countries. This effect will be amplified by lower interest rates, transmitted to them from the USA via international financial flows. In the case of (iv), the contractionary international trade multiplier effects of a contractionary fiscal policy will be amplified by higher interest rates, again transmitted via international financial flows.

Q8. (a) and (e) will help to stimulate other countries too, via the international trade multiplier. They thus *benefit* other countries.

(b), (c) and (d) reduce other countries' exports and/or increase their imports and thus *hinder* their recovery.

Q9. *Yes*. All of them. In the case of (c), with monetary policy determined by central banks, it makes it impossible for G7 politicians to use changes in interest rates as a means of achieving harmonisation. In the case of (d), with different rates of productivity growth, different underlying inflation rates, different propensities to import, and different sizes of budget deficits and national debts as a proportion of GDP, achieving similar growth rates may involve considerable interest rate differences and currency instability.

Q10. *(a)* With different underlying rates of inflation (e.g. different cost-push pressures), to achieve similar rates of inflation between countries may require quite different rates of interest.

(b) Budget deficits differ substantially from one country to another as does the balance between saving and investment. To achieve similar budget deficits will entail considerable fiscal policy changes between countries and different rates of economic growth.

(c) To achieve similar rates of inflation between countries will involve changing interest rates for this purpose. These changes in interest rates can cause considerable exchange rate volatility.

Q11. E. Each one would cause a different rate of growth of imports and exports (the last one because it would affect the rate of inflation) and thus a change in the equilibrium rate of exchange over time.

Q12. D. From August 1993 to the start of the euro in 1999, the band was fixed at a ±15 per cent divergence from any other ERM currency (the exception being the German mark and the Dutch guilder, where the band was ±2¼ per cent). Previous to that the band was ±2¼ per cent for all currencies other than those of Spain and Portugal (and the UK before it left the system in 1992), where the band was ±6 per cent.

Q13. D. Interest rates could not be raised because this would put further upward pressure on the exchange rate.

Q14. D. Speculators did not generally doubt the commitment of Italy and the UK to maintaining their exchange rates within their ERM bands: it was their ability to do so that was in doubt. (Note in the case of (iii) that low US interest rates led to speculative flows of finance to Germany, thus further strengthening the mark and weakening the relative position of the lira and the pound.)

Q15. *True.* There was divergence not only between economic indicators such as growth and government finances, but also between the different economic objectives of the member states.

Q16. *True.*

Q17. *Yes*: (c), (d), (f), (g), (h) and (j).
No: (a), (b), (e) and (i).
Note that when the euro has fully replaced the previous currencies (by 1 July 2002) there will be no 'exchange rates' between member countries – any more than there is between England and Wales. Note also that, although types of tax must be harmonised and rates of indirect taxes should be similar, direct taxes could differ: they would be like different local taxes within a country.

Q18. Advantages include: elimination of the costs of converting currencies; elimination of uncertainties associated with possible exchange rate realignments and fluctuations within the permitted band; a lower average rate of inflation (provided that the European Central Bank is truly independent from short-term political considerations); greater macroeconomic stability which will promote higher levels of investment.

Q19. Disadvantages include: problems of domestic adjustment if the economy is not in harmony with other members (e.g. if it has higher cost-push inflationary pressures), with the country maybe becoming a depressed 'region' of the union; adjustment to asymmetric shocks (shocks that have different effects on the various member countries); loss of political sovereignty (some see this as an advantage).

Q20. E. The benefits (or costs) of a single currency are not confined to one indicator (such as inflation or trade or economic growth). An optimal currency area is one which maximises the *overall* benefit to the members. If the current area is the optimal size, then altering the size (either increasing it or decreasing it) will lead to a decrease in the overall benefit from having the currency area.

Q21. *True* (50 per cent of 20 per cent).

Q22. *False.* 10 per cent per week compounded over a year is equivalent to over 14 000 per cent per annum.

Q23. *Yes*: (a) and (d). With a free-floating exchange rate, there is no need for exchange rate intervention at all. With a common currency, you give up monetary policy, but there can be no speculation as there is no possibility of a currency depreciating against itself! With anything other than these extremes, as soon as the pegged or fixed rate ceases to be the perceived equilibrium rate, speculation is likely to force an exchange rate adjustment.

Q24. They may discourage international investment; they may discourage international trade; they are disliked as 'anti-market'.

Q25. *True.* Such a tax would help to discourage speculation by making it more expensive.

Q26. Because speculation, if dampened, is likely to be stabilising and may help force countries to move towards an equilibrium exchange rate, rather than maintaining one which does not reflect underlying economic fundamentals, such as purchasing power parities.

Q27. (a) *True*; (b) *False* (bands would be wide: e.g. ±10%); (c) *True*; (d) *False* (the central parity may have to be adjusted very frequently, if the country's rate of inflation diverges from the weighted average of its trading partners); (e) *True* (the closer the rate approached these buffers, the greater would be the scale of exchange market intervention).

Q28. It removes pressure on high-inflation countries to bring their inflation under control; monetary policy may have to be geared to keeping the exchange rate within the bands, rather than being used for domestic purposes (though this problem is not as great as it would be with a more rigid exchange rate system).

Chapter Twenty-six
26
Economic Problems of Developing Countries

A REVIEW

In this last chapter we look at some of the economic problems of the poorer countries of the world, problems beside which those of the affluent North pale into insignificance. We start by examining the nature and extent of poverty in developing countries. This poverty cannot be examined in isolation from these countries' relationships with the rest of the world and thus we turn to this topic next. We continue by looking at some specific internal problems such the neglect of agriculture and the huge scale of unemployment. Finally we examine the massive international debts that many poor countries have incurred and the difficulties in overcoming them.

26.1 The problem of underdevelopment

(Pages 733–4) One way of defining the level of development is the extent to which a country provides the basic needs of life.

◐ **Q1.** Which of the following would you include as basic needs?
(a) Adequate food. Yes/No
(b) Free education for all children up to 12. Yes/No
(c) Sufficient time free from work to be able to rest and enjoy social interaction. Yes/No
(d) Adequate clothing, warmth and shelter. Yes/No
(e) Freedom to choose where to work and live. Yes/No
(f) Adequate health care. Yes/No
(g) Adequate care for the elderly and those without work. Yes/No
(h) Fulfilment at work. Yes/No
(i) Proper sanitation. Yes/No
(j) Self-esteem. Yes/No

? **Q2.** Give three problems in defining development in terms of basic needs.

1. ....
2. ....
3. ....

(Pages 734–7) The single most commonly used measure of economic development is GNY per head, measured in some international currency such as the US dollar.

◐ **Q3.** Which of the following are advantages of using GNY as an indicator of the level of a country's economic development?
(a) GNY statistics are available for all countries. Yes/No
(b) A sustained rise in GNY is generally considered to be a necessary condition for a sustained increase in economic welfare. Yes/No
(c) A sustained rise in GNY is generally considered as a sufficient condition for a sustained increase in economic welfare. Yes/No
(d) Exchange rates accurately reflect domestic purchasing power. Yes/No

≡ Multiple choice   ? Written answer   ◐ Delete wrong word   ⊖ Diagram/table manipulation   ✕ Calculation   ♟ Matching/ordering

(e) Virtually all goods and services that are produced are included in GNY. *Yes/No*

(f) Prices, although not exactly equal to marginal costs, do roughly reflect the opportunity costs of production. *Yes/No*

(g) The rules for measurement of GNY are generally agreed. *Yes/No*

(h) GNY takes externalities into account. *Yes/No*

(i) There is a fairly close correlation between the ranking of countries by GNY per head and by other indicators of development (taken as a whole). *Yes/No*

As a country's economy grows, it is likely that there will be movement from subsistence agriculture to cash crops and industrial production. This structure of production means that GNY statistics for developing countries will tend to **Q4.** *overstate/understate* the level of production and **Q5.** *overstate/understate* the rate of growth of production.

Q6. GNY is based on market prices, but market prices are often distorted. Which of the following are typical market distortions in developing countries?

(a) Rates of interest in the towns are below the opportunity cost of capital. *Yes/No*

(b) Producers of manufactured goods often have considerable market power. *Yes/No*

(c) Wage rates in the modern sector are typically below the market-clearing level. *Yes/No*

(d) Exchange rates are typically overvalued. *Yes/No*

(e) Protection (in the form of tariffs or quotas) is given unevenly to different industries. *Yes/No*

(f) Rates of interest in the countryside are often much higher than those in the towns. *Yes/No*

(g) Prices of foodstuffs are kept artificially high. *Yes/No*

(h) Mine and plantation owners often have considerable monopsony power to drive down wages. *Yes/No*

26.2 International trade and development

(Pages 737–40) Trade is of vital importance for most developing countries, and yet most suffer from chronic balance of trade deficits. It is therefore of vital importance for countries to adopt the most appropriate trade policies.

Traditionally, developing countries have been **Q7.** *primary/secondary* exporters and **Q8.** *primary/secondary* importers.

Q9. There are various arguments why developing countries should export food and raw materials. These include:
 (i) the vent for surplus theory;
 (ii) the Heckscher–Ohlin theory;
 (iii) the engine for growth argument;
 (iv) differences in technology and labour skills.

Match each of the following arguments to the above.
(a) As industrial expansion takes place in advanced countries, so their demand for developing countries' primary products will increase.
....

(b) Advanced countries can produce industrial goods with comparatively fewer resources than primary products when compared with developing countries.
....

(c) Developing countries have a relative abundance of labour and a relative scarcity of capital when compared with advanced countries.
....

(d) Trade allows developing countries to exploit resources that would not otherwise be used.
....

Q10. According to the Heckscher–Ohlin theory, international trade will lead to an increase in income inequalities. *True/False*

Q11. Which of the following are problems that might arise from a policy of specialising in the production of primaries for export?

(a) Technological progress is less rapid in the production of primaries than in manufactures. *Yes/No*

(b) The benefits from the trade may only accrue in small part to the nationals of the country. *Yes/No*

(c) Primary products have a high income elasticity of demand. *Yes/No*

(d) The price elasticity of demand for primary products from an *individual* country is very low. *Yes/No*

(e) Relying on primary exports may lead to long-term balance of payments deficits. *Yes/No*

(f) Relying on primary exports may lead to long-term increases in the terms of trade. *Yes/No*

(g) The income elasticity of demand for manufactured imports is high. *Yes/No*

(h) The price elasticity of demand for manufactured imports is high. *Yes/No*

(i) The world price of primaries is subject to sharper price fluctuations than the world price of manufactures. *Yes/No*

(j) Exporting primary products may involve substantial external costs. *Yes/No*

(Pages 740–3) A second approach to trade is that of *import-substituting industrialisation* (ISI).

Q12. Define *import-substituting industrialisation*.

....

....

ISI has typically involved a process of *tariff escalation*.

Q13. Tariff escalation is where the government imposes larger and larger tariffs on products:

A. the closer they are to the finished stage.
B. over time.
C. the greater the monopolistic power of the foreign importers.
D. the more established the domestic producer becomes.
E. the higher the rate of domestic inflation.

◐ **Q14.** Import substitution through protectionism is likely to encourage multinational investment in a country.
True/False

Despite its popularity with developing country governments, ISI has involved some serious disadvantages.

◐ **Q15.** Which of the following have tended to result from ISI?
(a) It has encouraged the establishment of monopolies and oligopolies. *Yes/No*
(b) It has involved artificially high real interest rates. *Yes/No*
(c) It has led to an overvaluation of the exchange rate. *Yes/No*
(d) It has led to urban wages being kept down relative to rural wages. *Yes/No*
(e) It has led to a bias against the agricultural sector. *Yes/No*
(f) Effective protective rates have differed widely from one product to another. *Yes/No*
(g) Effective protective rates have generally been below nominal protective rates. *Yes/No*

(?) **Q16.** Give three other problems with import-substituting industrialisation.

1. ....
2. ....
3. ....

(Pages 743–5) A third approach, and one that many countries have turned to after their experiences with the limitations of ISI, is export-orientated manufacturing.

◐ **Q17.** The developing countries which have experienced the most rapid rates of economic growth have tended to be export-orientated manufacturing countries.
True/False

(?) **Q18.** What does the Heckscher–Ohlin theory suggest about the type of manufactured goods in which developing countries should specialise?

....

▤ **Q19.** Which of the following will help promote the development of export-orientated industries?

(i) Devaluation.
(ii) Removal of tariff barriers.
(iii) Reduction in taxes on employing labour.

A. (i).
B. (ii).
C. (i) and (ii).
D. (i) and (iii).
E. (i), (ii) and (iii).

The gains from an export-orientated manufacturing policy will tend to be greatest for **Q20.** *small/large* countries and when there are **Q21.** *minimal/substantial* internal economies of scale in the potential export industries.

(?) **Q22.** Give three possible drawbacks of pursuing a policy of export-orientated manufacturing.

1. ....
2. ....
3. ....

26.3 Structural problems within developing countries

(Page 746) The neglect of agriculture
Policies of import-substituting industrialisation have tended to involve an urban bias.

◐ **Q23.** Examples of urban bias include:
(a) *High/Low* food prices.
(b) *High/Low* rural rates of interest.
(c) *Overvalued/Undervalued* exchange rates.
(d) *High/Low* manufactured prices.
(e) *High/Low* tariffs on imported manufactures.
(f) *High/Low* tariffs on imported foodstuffs.

(?) **Q24.** Give three examples of policies that can help to develop the agricultural sector.

1. ....
2. ....
3. ....

(Pages 747–8) Inappropriate technology
In the urban sector of developing countries, the wage/interest rate ratio has typically been **Q25.** *above/below* the market-clearing level. The effect has been to create a **Q26.** *capital/labour* intensity bias in the choice of techniques. This **Q27.** *is in accordance with/contradicts* the implications of the Heckscher–Ohlin theory.

Nevertheless, capital-intensive techniques may bring some advantages.

366 CHAPTER 26 ECONOMIC PROBLEMS OF DEVELOPING COUNTRIES

Q28. Which of the following are possible advantages for developing countries of capital-intensive techniques?
 (i) They are in accordance with the law of comparative advantage.
 (ii) They typically yield a higher rate of profit, which can be used for reinvestment.
 (iii) They may have a lower capital/output ratio despite having a higher capital/labour ratio.

A. (i).
B. (ii).
C. (iii).
D. (i) and (ii).
E. (ii) and (iii).

Q29. Give three possible disadvantages of capital-intensive technologies.

1. ....

2. ....

3. ....

(Pages 748–9) Unemployment
In addition to high rates of open unemployment, developing countries may suffer from considerable disguised unemployment and underemployment.

Q30. Which of the following two definitions is of disguised unemployment and which of underemployment?
(a) Where people are unable to find sufficient work to occupy them full time.
  disguised unemployment/underemployment
(b) Where the same work could be done by fewer people.
  disguised unemployment/underemployment

Q31. A cause of disguised unemployment in the countryside is the level of overcrowding on the land and the resulting low marginal productivity of labour. *True/False*

Q32. How may the creation of jobs in towns also create more open unemployment in the towns?

....

....

Q33. Rural–urban migration will be greater:
(a) The greater the income differential between the towns and the countryside. *True/False*
(b) The higher the level of unemployment in the towns. *True/False*
(c) The greater the level of disguised unemployment in the countryside. *True/False*
(d) The higher the cost of living in the towns. *True/False*
(e) The lower the costs of migration. *True/False*
(f) The more risk averse a potential migrant is. *True/False*
(g) The more attractive the potential migrant believes city life to be. *True/False*

Q34. Of the following, which will help to reduce urban unemployment?
 (i) Concentrating investment in the towns.
 (ii) The adoption of more capital-intensive techniques.
 (iii) Increasing food prices.
 (iv) Labour-intensive rural infrastructure projects.

A. (i) and (iv).
B. (ii) and (iii).
C. (iii) and (iv).
D. (i), (iii) and (iv).
E. (i), (ii), (iii) and (iv).

(Pages 749–51) Inflation
Inflation rates are generally higher in developing countries than in advanced countries.

Q35. Structuralists blame inflation on:
A. excessive growth in the money supply.
B. the adoption of labour-intensive technology.
C. adaptive expectations.
D. rational expectations.
E. supply bottlenecks.

Q36. High rates of inflation in developing countries are generally accompanied by rapid rates of increase in the money supply. *True/False*

Q37. What problems arise from attempting to control inflation by reducing the rate of growth of the money supply?

....

....

26.4 The problem of debt
(Pages 752–3) After the 1973 oil crisis, many developing countries borrowed heavily in order to finance their balance of trade deficits and maintain a programme of investment. After the 1979 oil price rises, however, the problem became much more serious.

Q38. In the world economy after 1979, when compared with the period after 1973:
(a) real interest rates were *higher/lower*.
(b) nominal interest rates were *higher/lower*.
(c) monetary policy was generally *tighter/more relaxed*.

(d) the resulting recession was *deeper/shallower*.
(e) the resulting recession was *shorter/longer lasting*.
(f) a greater proportion of debt was at *variable/fixed* interest rates.
(g) a greater proportion of debt was in the form of *official government/commercial bank* loans.
(h) the effect on developing countries was *more/less* severe.

(Pages 753–5) To cope with the debt crisis and the difficulties of servicing these debts, many countries' debts have been *rescheduled*.

Q39. Give three ways in which debts could be rescheduled.

1. ....
2. ....
3. ....

Official loans are renegotiated through the **Q40.** *London/Paris/Houston/Toronto* Club, whereas commercial bank loans are often rescheduled by collective action of banks which form a Bank Advisory Committee. Such arrangements are referred to as the **Q41.** *London/Paris/Houston/Toronto* Club.

Q42. One of the difficulties in solving the debt problem has been the phenomenon of 'capital flight'. This is defined as:
A. loans made to developing countries that are then merely put on deposit back in rich countries.
B. investors in developing countries pulling out of their investments and reinvesting their money in rich countries.
C. a reduction in new investment in developing countries by investors in rich countries.
D. profits made by multinationals from their activities in developing countries being used for investment in rich countries.
E. illegal repatriating of profits from developing countries to rich countries in order to evade taxes.

Q43. The following are various types of swap arrangement for reducing countries' debt burden:
(i) Debt-for-cash swaps.
(ii) Debt-for-equity swaps.
(iii) Debt-for-development swaps.
(iv) Debt-for-bonds swaps.
(v) Debt-for-nature swaps.
(vi) Debt-for-export swaps.
(vii) Debt-to-local-debt swaps.

Match each of the above to the following definitions:

(a) Where banks help developing countries sell their products in rich countries on the condition that the revenues gained are used to pay off the debt.
(b) Where banks allow developing countries to buy back their own debt (i.e. repay it) at a discount.
(c) Where banks agree to convert debt into low-interest-rate securities.
(d) Where debt is sold to companies exporting to or investing in the debtor country. These companies then sell the debt to the central bank for local currency at a discount. This provides these companies with a cheap source of local currency.
(e) Where banks sell debt. The purchasers can then exchange this debt with the central bank of the debtor country for local currency to use for purchasing shares in companies in the debtor country.
(f) Where debts are sold to an international environmental agency. This agency then swaps this debt with the central bank of the debtor country for a local bond which pays interest. The interest is then used to finance environmental projects.
(g) As (f) except that the interest is used to finance a range of projects in such fields as education, health, transport infrastructure and agriculture.

(Pages 756–9) A long-term solution to the debt problem will involve a restructuring of the economies of developing countries and their relationships with the advanced countries.

Q44. Which of the following policies for highly indebted developing countries are recommended by the IMF?
(a) Tight monetary policies.   *Yes/No*
(b) Tight fiscal policies.   *Yes/No*
(c) Greater economic planning to direct resources into investment.   *Yes/No*
(d) Import controls in order to reduce balance of payments deficits.   *Yes/No*
(e) Policies to promote greater national economic self-sufficiency.   *Yes/No*
(f) Privatisation.   *Yes/No*
(g) Devaluation.   *Yes/No*
(h) Market-orientated supply-side policies.   *Yes/No*
(i) A more open trade policy.   *Yes/No*
(j) The abolition of price controls.   *Yes/No*

Q45. Give three disadvantages of the policies recommended by the IMF.

1. ....
2. ....
3. ....

Another requirement for a long-term solution to the debt problem is the cancellation of some of the debts of the most heavily indebted poor countries. Under the HIPC initiative of 1996, and revised in 1999, some of these countries would have a proportion of their debts cancelled.

Q46. Give three criticisms of the HIPC arrangements:

1. ....
2. ....
3. ....

B PROBLEMS, EXERCISES AND PROJECTS

Q47. Either individually or in small groups, you should select two of the most highly indebted developing countries and write a report that analyses their economic situation.

The report should: (a) identify the level and nature of their international debt using appropriate debt indicators; (b) paint an economic profile of each of the two countries; (c) explain why they have reached a position of severe indebtedness; (d) identify similarities and differences in the causes of their current situation; (e) consider whether the complete cancellation of all their international debts would be the best alternative for them (if such were on offer!).

References include the World Bank Web site (http://www.worldbank.org) and the One World portal site (http://www.oneworld.net). Other sources of information on your chosen countries can be found by using a search engine, such as Google (http://www.google.com).

C DISCUSSION TOPICS AND ESSAYS

Q48. Is GNY a suitable measure of the level of a country's development?

Q49. Why do developing countries tend to suffer from chronic balance of payments problems?

Q50. Developing countries generally have a comparative advantage in primary products. Why should this be so? Does this imply that investment should be focused in the primary sector?

Q51. What are the problems of using protectionism as a means of encouraging industrialisation?

Q52. Does import-substituting industrialisation inevitably involve a bias against agriculture?

Q53. Is increased inward investment by multinational companies the best means of improving economic growth rates in developing economies?

Q54. Should labour-abundant countries always adopt labour-intensive techniques?

Q55. Do all farmers gain equally from the Green Revolution? In what ways could the government help to ensure that the poorest farmers benefit from new agricultural technologies?

Q56. To what extent has unemployment in developing countries been caused by an 'urban bias' in development policy?

Q57. If high inflation in developing countries is generally accompanied by rapid increases in the money supply, does this mean that such countries should adopt monetarist policies?

Q58. To what extent is developing countries' debt problem the direct result of mistaken development policies of the 1960s and 1970s?

Q59. How would you advise a developing country seeking a long-term solution to its massive international debts?

Q60. Would it be desirable to cancel *all* the debts of developing countries? Why might there be a problem of 'moral hazard' if this occurred?

Q61. Debate
The problems of the developing countries have generally been exacerbated by trade and other economic relationships with the developed world.

Q62. Debate
Making debt relief for developing countries conditional on their making 'structural adjustments' to their economies is the best way of ensuring their long-term development.

D ARTICLES

The issue of agricultural policy is not just a debate between the USA and EU as the media may lead you to believe. In fact, the struggle between these two regional giants is having an enormous effect on agricultural markets in the developing world. The article below, taken from the *Oxfam* Web site on 23 June 1998, discusses the implications of the US/EU agricultural war and the role the WTO should be adopting to support farmers in the developing world.

Farmers, food and the WTO

Governments in Europe and the US may profess faith in free-trade principles, but when it comes to agriculture there is a wide gulf between principle and practice. For decades the US and European Union (EU) have been restricting agricultural imports, subsidising their agricultural producers and dumping highly subsidised surpluses on world markets at prices which undermine other producers – all in defiance of the principle of a 'level playing field'.

The US and EU each spend tens of billions of dollars per year on large and costly systems of protection and subsidy for their farmers – including guaranteed minimum prices, subsidised farm inputs, export subsidies and in the case of the US direct 'deficiency payments' to producers. In 1995 the OECD (Organisation for Economic Co-operation and Development) countries together spent about $182 billion ($112 billion) subsidising their agricultural production, equivalent to about 40 per cent of the total value of farm output (and about four times what they spend on overseas aid). For the EU agricultural support remains the largest single item in its budget, accounting for nearly half of total spending in 1996. The cost to governments of the support schemes has soared in recent years.

While the US and EU may wish to reduce these costs, the intense competition between them means they are not willing to do so at the expense of losing markets to the other. Also, of course, they are under pressure from their domestic farm lobbies to retain them.

These schemes provide support for virtually unlimited production by US and EU farmers, and the result has been that output has far outstripped domestic demand and large surpluses created. To get rid of these surpluses, the US and EU have resorted to selling them at subsidised rates on export markets. In 1992 for example, the EU was selling wheat on the world market for around $80 per ton, for which it was paying producers around $180 a ton.

Inevitably, developing countries are seen as a useful place to dispose of farm surpluses, and concerted efforts are being made to open up these markets.

For countries which export agricultural products, this dumping of subsidised exports onto world markets means depressed prices and the loss of markets to unfair competition. This in turn translates into lower household incomes for producers. For those who produce for the domestic food market, it has a similar effect of reducing prices and incentives to agricultural production. According to one study of the maize market in Kenya, competition from subsidised imports resulted in losses to maize farmers of around $439 million in 1994–95.

It is true that these cheap imports mean cheaper food for some – for those who have to buy it, which means mainly urban dwellers. But for those who grow it or sell it, it means serious loss of income. In developing countries, farmers are being exposed not to a mythical 'level playing field', but to unfair competition from these surpluses. It is competition which, left unregulated, will destroy livelihoods on a vast scale and leave countries increasingly dependent on food imports.

The inequity in this is immense. Currently each farmer in the US receives over $14 000 in subsidies per year – equivalent to around 30 times the average income in the Philippines for example. This unequal competition between the treasuries of the industrial countries and peasant farmers has led to a fall in rural incomes in developing countries, reduced rural employment, falling investment in agriculture, and migration from the land to the cities.

In theory, countries receiving cheap food imports are supposed to turn from food production to higher-value cash crops or other exports which they then sell on international markets to earn hopefully enough to buy the food they need, plus more. However, for many poor countries this is a very risky and problematic strategy.

For a start, not all developing countries have particularly marketable exports for sale. For example, for the Sub-Saharan African countries which are dependent on primary commodity exports, generating foreign exchange can sometimes be a real problem. Many are heavily indebted and foreign creditors usually have first call on export earnings. Also foreign exchange spent on buying food is then not available for more productive investments needed for long-term economic development. In some circumstances, buying 'cheap' food can be an expensive option.

Unfortunately this is the way things are going. Food imports into Sub-Saharan Africa for example, which were insignificant in the 1960s, now account for almost 20 per cent of the region's total foreign exchange earnings. In West Africa, cereal and livestock imports now account for around half of the region's current account deficit. The group of countries classified as 'low-income food deficit' are now spending about half their foreign exchange earnings on food imports, which is double the proportion they spent 30 years ago.

Another problem is that the farmers who are pushed out of domestic food production are not the ones who will take up the more lucrative cash cropping. If it was as simple as that, they would have all changed years ago. The fact is that it takes capital to get into cash crops like tropical fruit or out-of-season vegetables for export, and peasant farmers just don't have such capital. Their poverty prevents them from changing. It is those with capital who will make the money while the peasant becomes destitute or, if he or she is lucky, a seasonal labourer on a plantation.

The other option for people forced off the land is to move into 'more productive' industrial jobs in factories; but in most cases these jobs are not being created fast enough to soak up the vast numbers who are or will be seeking them. In Mexico for example, now starting to feel the effects of unrestricted cheap agricultural exports from the US, the number estimated to leave the land over the next 15 years ranges from a few hundred thousand to two million. However, the rate of creation of new industrial jobs has levelled off.

A third problem is that this approach leaves developing countries vulnerable. They become dependent for the most basic of all needs, the food to stay alive, on economic factors beyond their control – the depressed and unpredictable market for their commodity exports, or the volatile markets for their manufactured exports, the ups and downs of world food prices – not to mention the vagaries of varying exchange rates. In addition when the level of food self-sufficiency is very low, countries can become politically vulnerable to pressure from those on whom they rely for food.

For decades the US has utilised quotas, subsidies and other distortions of free trade at variance with the rules of the GATT (General Agreement on Tariffs and Trade), under waivers and exemptions granted to it by GATT in the 1950s. Likewise the EU took advantage of this and refused to subordinate its agricultural support schemes (the 'Common Agricultural Policy') to GATT principles, using quotas, export subsidies and other devices in violation of the GATT.

The recent round of international trade negotiations under GATT, the Uruguay Round, was supposed to be the beginning of the end for this. The agreement on trade in agriculture reached during that Round included a commitment by developed countries to cut spending on agricultural export subsidies by 36 per cent and to reduce the volume of subsidised exports by 21 per cent over a six-year period. Subsidies to producers which are defined as 'trade distorting' also have to be reduced by 20 per cent. Also, all import restrictions have to be converted into tariffs which must then be reduced on average by 36 per cent over six years.

Developing countries also have to reduce such restrictions and supports, but to a lesser extent, and various concessions and exemptions were made for 'least developed' countries. Nevertheless this imposed a constraint on the ability of developing countries to promote increased food security through the use of import restrictions and guaranteed price supports for farmers.

The net result is that the Uruguay Round agreement will have little if any effect on the level of US and EU subsidisation, nor on the dumping of agricultural products in developing countries. So with food exports continuing to be dumped and developing countries' ability to protect themselves against this, or to support increased domestic production being restricted, the threat to food security is very real.

Another outcome of the Uruguay Round was the decision to establish the World Trade Organisation (WTO) to take over from the GATT and administer its agreements. The first ever Ministerial Conference of the WTO is about to take place in Singapore in early December. There will be no negotiations at Singapore on the further liberalisation of trade in agricultural goods. This is not scheduled to happen until 1999. Even so, the opportunity should be taken to highlight the inequities of the current situation and its negative effects and to suggest what should happen when negotiations on agriculture are reopened. Oxfam believes this should include the following:

1. WTO rules should be amended to include a food security clause which allows developing countries to protect their food production systems for social, environmental or poverty protection and be exempt from some liberalisation measures.
2. The WTO's anti-dumping rules should be extended to include agriculture. Agricultural trade remains the only area of world trade in which dumping is not only accepted but actively sanctioned by multilateral rules. The export of any agricultural commodity at prices which do not reflect the real cost of production and marketing should be outlawed under anti-dumping provisions, just as it is for television sets or cars.
3. Any further liberalisation of agriculture by developing countries or opening of their markets should be conditional on the 'agricultural superpowers' doing likewise; that is liberalising their markets and reducing their levels of subsidisation.

(a) What do you understand by the term 'dumping'?

(b) What impact is the dumping of US/EU food surpluses on world markets having on farmers in developing countries?

(c) Why is the author sceptical that agricultural agreements made under the Uruguay Round will have any effect on improving the plight of farmers in developing countries?

(d) What policy initiatives do Oxfam argue are necessary, if the WTO is to help farmers in developing countries?

In the following article, taken from *The Guardian* of 19 June 2002, Charlotte Denny and Larry Elliott explain how globalisation is intensifying poverty around the world rather than alleviating it.

100m more must survive on $1 a day

More than 100m people in the world's poorest countries will be dragged below the basic subsistence level of a dollar a day by 2015 as they become ensnared in globalisation's poverty trap, the UN warned yesterday.

An in-depth study into the world's 49 least developed countries rejects claims that globalisation is good for the poor, arguing that the international trade and economic system is part of the problem, not the solution.

'The current form of globalisation is tightening rather than loosening the international poverty trap,' the study warns.

As markets become more entwined, the UN says the world economy is becoming increasingly polarised and the least developed countries are being left behind.

Shut out of more lucrative markets by western trade barriers, they depend on cash crops for survival, but the prices of their main export goods have crashed over the last two decades. Living standards in the least developed countries, which depend on basic commodities, are lower now than they were 30 years ago.

'International policy needs to give more attention to breaking the link between primary commodity dependence, pervasive extreme poverty and unsustainable external debt,' the UN says.

Simplistic calls for poor countries to open their markets will not help them escape the poverty trap, according to the study.

Trade's poverty trap

'Contrary to conventional wisdom, persistent poverty in poor countries is not due to insufficient trade liberalisation,' the study says. In fact in the poorest countries, trade accounts for just over 40% of GDP – higher than the average for rich countries.

'The problem for the least developed countries is not the level of integration with the world economy but rather the form of the integration,' the report says. 'For many LDCs external trade and finance relationships are an integral part of the poverty trap.'

Despite efforts by western donors to tackle the third world's loans burden, the poorest countries are still lumbered with unpayable debts. The 23 least developed countries have a debt burden which is unsustainable, according to the World Bank.

The UN says that servicing the debt overhang is swallowing official aid budgets. 'Aid disbursements have increasingly been allocated to ensure that official debts are serviced,' the study says.

'In this aid/debt service system, the development impact of aid is being undermined.'

Widespread poverty is itself contributing to economic stagnation. With most households earning barely enough to survive, there is no spare cash for the investment that might help countries break out of the poverty trap.

'Low income leads to low savings, low savings lead to low investment and low investment leads to low productivity and low income.'

The UN says the number of people living in extreme poverty in the least developed countries is greater than had previously been thought. The study calculates that 307 million people live on less than a dollar a day, a number which is set to rise to 420 million over the next decade and a half.

The study underlines the scale of the challenge global leaders set themselves two years ago when they promised at the UN's millennium summit to halve the number of the world's population that live on less than a dollar a day by 2015.

None of the 49 least developed countries is on track to meet the poverty reduction target.

Although it warns that the extent of poverty has been underestimated, the study manages to strike an upbeat note, insisting that with better policies, rapid gains in living standards could be achieved. Poor countries should be allowed to abandon the economic adjustment programmes they were forced to adopt in the 1990s by the IMF and the World Bank.

Countries must 'shift from adjustment-orientated poverty reduction strategies to development-oriented poverty reduction strategies,' the study says.

It adds that widespread poverty in the least developed countries could be cut by two-thirds over the next 15 years, if the right policies were adopted.

(a) How, in theory, should the process of globalisation improve living standards of all, both rich and poor?

(b) What, according to the article, is happening in practice as a result of globalisation?

(c) What arguments, based on the article, could we put forward to encourage a process of debt forgiveness for the world's most indebted economies?

Is the giving of aid a good thing? Most would argue that it clearly is, so long as it is not wasted. A book published by the World Bank, however, suggests that a lot of aid is indeed wasted and calls for aid to be targeted on those countries which are pursuing the right economic policies and which can therefore use aid effectively. The article below, taken from *The Economist* of 14 November 1998, looks at the findings of this World Bank study.

Making aid work

This week the World Bank published a new book which will henceforth be *the* book on foreign aid: *Assessing Aid: What Works, What Doesn't, and Why*. The authors, David Dollar and Lant Pritchett, are to be congratulated: by any standards, but especially by Bank standards, they have produced a forthright and lucid piece of work. Too forthright and too lucid for some, one imagines.

Joseph Stiglitz, the Bank's chief economist and overall supervisor of research, deserves credit for letting the report see the light of day; his tepid and convoluted foreword suggests he had his doubts. Mr Stiglitz draws readers' attention to two 'key themes': 'effective aid requires the right timing and . . . the right mix of money and ideas.' Platitudes such as this may be what Mr Stiglitz had hoped to find in the report; or maybe his comments were intended for some other book, and were printed at the front of this one in error. In any event, the true key themes of *Assessing Aid* come through loud and clear: (a) aid works only if it is spent on the right countries and (b) rich-country governments and multilateral agencies (including the Bank) spend a lot of it on the wrong countries.

Reviewing earlier research and drawing on new work for this book, Messrs Dollar and Pritchett establish, first, that the raw correlation between aid and growth is near zero: more aid does not mean more growth. Perhaps other factors mask an underlying link, they concede; perhaps aid is deliberately given to countries growing very slowly (creating a misleading negative correlation between aid and growth, and biasing the numbers). On closer study of such complications, however, the result holds. No correlation: aid does not promote growth.

What transforms the picture is dividing countries according to the quality of their economic policies. Do this and you find that in countries with good economic policies (low inflation, small budget deficits, openness to trade, strong rule of law, competent bureaucracy), aid does indeed spur growth. Aid equivalent to 1 per cent of the recipient's GDP leads, on average, to a sustained increase of 0.5 percentage points in the country's annual rate of growth. In countries with bad policies, on the other hand, the data say that aid actually retards growth – although in this case the estimated multiplier (1 per cent of GDP in aid slows growth by 0.3 percentage points a year) is statistically less robust.

The next question is whether growth reduces poverty – since rich-country governments all say that reducing poverty is what their aid is for. The answer is yes. Recent evidence shows 'conclusively' that growth reduces poverty; its benefits are not undone, as used to be feared, by growing inequality. The converse is also true: in countries with slow or no growth, poverty declines slowly if at all, and in the worst cases it increases. To sum up, in good-policy countries, aid reduces poverty; in bad-policy countries, it doesn't.

A new map

The authors then ask how aid should be spent if the only consideration were (as governments say) to reduce poverty. If that were so, the money would go to countries that combine two things: good policies and lots of poor people. Plenty of countries, many of them recent reformers, meet both tests. Out of the authors' sample of 113 countries, 32 lie in this 'high-impact quadrant', with poverty rates of more than 50 per cent and better-than-average policies. Some of the poorest countries in the world (such as India, Ethiopia and Uganda) are among them.

Now suppose, the authors say, that donors increased the global aid budget by $10 billion. If this were spent across the board, in proportion to existing allocations, an extra 7m people a year would be lifted out of poverty. If it were concentrated instead on the good-policy, lots-of-poverty countries, the corresponding reduction would be 25m people.

This is an indirect way of saying that present allocations are hugely wasteful. The paper on which that calculation is based shows that if the present aid budget were switched entirely to an efficient poverty-reducing allocation, 80m people a year would be lifted out of poverty at a cost of $450 per person, compared with the present 30m a year at a cost of $1,200 per person. (Most of the 80m would in fact be Indians. Their country has vast numbers in poverty and since the early 1990s has had reasonably good policies. Its capacity to absorb aid and use it well is therefore enormous.)

The waste revealed by these figures is the result of a pattern of aid that is almost exactly the opposite of what effective reduction of poverty requires. Countries with good policies should get more aid than countries with bad policies. Actually they get less. This would be justified if aid encouraged countries to improve their policies, but on the whole it does not. For every case where aid has promoted reform there is a case where it has retarded it. Aid can keep bad governments in business; and promises to improve policy, made when the aid is first offered, are often forgotten once it has been delivered. The effort to encourage policy reform – if that is what today's pattern of aid describes – has been made at an enormous cost in terms of unrelieved poverty.

Should countries with bad policies simply be left to their fate? By no means, the authors argue: donors can still help by spreading knowledge of a technological or institutional sort. This is one rationale for (small-scale) project aid. But what donors should not be spreading in these cases is large quantities of cash. That policy not only wastes money; it also undermines political support for every kind of aid, including those that work. While it remains true – as this study makes crystal clear – that the key to development is good economic policy, and that this is something which only the governments concerned can put into effect, aid can playa useful role. It is up to donor governments to see that it does.

© *The Economist*, London (14.11.98)

(a) What is the aim of giving foreign aid?
(b) What recommendations does the World Bank report make for improving the effectiveness of aid giving?
(c) Should aid go only to countries with good economic policies? Should countries be made to change their economic policies as a condition for receiving aid?

Of all the regions of the world, Africa is the poorest and in need of the greatest help. In the article below, taken from *The Guardian* of 1 June 1998, Larry Elliot considers the plight of Africa and why it is in desperate need of help with its crippling debt burden.

Why the poor are picking up the tab

It is just before dawn in Kinshasa on October 30, 1974. In a boxing ring in the middle of a football stadium lies the prostrate body of George Foreman, knocked out by Muhammad Ali in one of the biggest sporting upsets of the century. As the lightning crackles overhead, 60 000 Zairians cheer Ali, world champion again after seven years.

It took 10 seconds for the referee to count Foreman out and end the Rumble in the Jungle. It has taken 24 years for the West to face up to the enormity of the debt crisis in the developing world.

After years of foot-dragging, the need to relieve the poorest nations of their unpayable debts has moved to the top of the agenda for the meeting of the Group of 8 leaders in Birmingham this weekend. Backed by a coalition of churches and charities, Tony Blair will be urging the West to make deep cuts in the debt burden an urgent priority for the summit.

Chancellor Gordon Brown said at the end of the G8 foreign and finance ministers meeting on Saturday that he was confident that the scene was set for a major debt breakthrough.

Officials will spend the week piecing together a deal to provide speedier relief for seven African countries grappling with mountainous debts in the aftermath of military conflicts – Rwanda, Burundi, Liberia, the two Congos, Sierra Leone and Somalia.

And Britain is attempting to bring all eligible countries under the umbrella of the joint World Bank–International Monetary Fund Highly Indebted Poor Countries (HIPC) initiative by the millennium.

'The millennium objective is . . . now part of the G8 process,' Mr Brown said.

The Prime Minister was still at Oxford when Ali and Foreman left the ring to collect their purses, more than $5 million (£3 million) each for 24 minutes work, provided by Zaire's tyrannical president, Mobutu Sese Seko, to spread his name and the name of his country across the globe. The fight did that all right. But at what a cost – $10 million was money Zaire could ill afford 24 years ago, and the torrential tropical thunderstorm that flooded the Stade du 20 Mai within minutes of the fight's end was symbolic of the economic torrent that was to engulf Africa from the mid-1970s onwards. When the bills started to come in for the continent's collective Rumble in the Jungle, they could not be paid. One poster for the fight, 'From the Slave ship to the championship', had to be withdrawn after it offended Zairians. It has a hollow, ironic ring to it now, because for many African nations the crushing burden of debt has indeed returned them to a new form of slavery.

How so? A few, simple statistics illustrate the horrific cost of the crisis affecting the poorest nations.

According to the United Nations Human Development Report, about a quarter of the world's population – some 1.3 billion people – are living on incomes of less than 50p a day. Nearly a billion are illiterate, some 840 million go hungry or are living from hand to mouth. And whereas those lucky enough to live in the developed West can expect to live until they are almost 80, nearly one third of the people in the least developed countries are not expected to survive to 40.

The epicentre of the problem is Sub-Saharan Africa, which accounts for 33 of the 42 low-income countries which the World Bank rates as highly indebted. In 1962, Sub-Saharan Africa owed $3 billion. By the early 1980s their debts had mounted to $142 billion. Today the debt mountain stands at about $225 billion, which is $379 for every man, woman and child in the continent. It is getting bigger all the time, because countries are falling behind with repayments.

What's more, the gulf between rich and poor is getting wider. The share of the poorest 20 per cent of the world's people in global income stands at a paltry 1.1 per cent, down from 1.4 per cent in 1991 and 2.3 per cent in 1960. The income of the top 20 per cent was 30 times higher than the poorest 20 per cent in 1960. By 1991 it was 61 times higher. The UN says the latest figures put it at 78 times as high.

But it is not just in per capita income that the disparities show up. The UN's annual Human Development Index is effectively a league table for standards of life across the world, looking at a whole range of social indicators including illiteracy, child mortality, numbers without access to health services, and life expectancy.

For the richest 20 countries, the index reveals few, if any serious social problems. In Britain, ranked 15th, nobody lacks access to health care or water, there is no adult illiteracy, 10 000 children die before the age of one, and every child is in primary school.

Now take Ethiopia, 170th out of 175 in the table. There, 54 per cent are without access to health services and 75 per cent lack access to safe water. The adult illiteracy rate is 64.5 per cent, 625 000 children died in 1995 before the age of one. There are no figures for children not in school.

Aid agencies say that a concerted attack on poverty must start with a grassroots expansion of basic social services, particularly health and education. The problem, however, is that the poorest developing nations have precious little to spare on schools and hospitals once they have serviced their enormous debts.

In Britain there would be an outcry if the Government were to introduce charges for education, leave children without desks and roofs on their classrooms, or let hospitals and clinics run out of basic drugs. In the developing world, it happens every day of every year, as money is siphoned off to pay debts.

According to Oxfam, more than 100 000 Ethiopian children die each year from easily preventable diseases, but debt payments are four times more than health spending.

In Africa as a whole, one out of every two children does not go to school, but governments spend four times more in debt payments to northern creditors than they spend on health and education.

Why did this happen? One school of thought says the West is to blame for encouraging developing nations to borrow recklessly recycled petro-dollars from oil-rich Opec nations for inappropriate projects.

Another school of thought says the blame lies squarely with corrupt post-colonial elites, who either squandered the money from loans on grandiose projects or else salted it away in numbered Swiss bank accounts.

There is an element of truth in both arguments, but the real explanation goes deeper. As David Landes puts it in his book, the *Wealth and Poverty of Nations*: 'The continent's problems go much deeper than bad policies, and bad policies are not an accident. Good government is not to be had for the asking. It took Europe centuries to get it, so why should Africa do so in mere decades, especially after the distortions of colonialism?' Many of the nations that gained independence in the 1950s and 1960s were artificial constructs of the colonial era, built around commodities and with borders often cutting across racial and tribal lines. On top of this was overlaid a centralised state, with power concentrated in a party, a ruling elite and ultimately an all-powerful leader. This quasi-Soviet system of government was a disaster, particularly when the economic climate turned nasty in the mid-1970s.

In the 1950s and 1960s rising commodity prices fed through into higher per capita incomes and more money for health, education and infrastructure, and still left something to be creamed off into Swiss bank accounts. But in the 1970s and 1980s commodity prices fell sharply, so that they are now lower in real terms than during the Great Depression almost 70 years ago.

The problem of falling commodity prices was intensified by higher oil prices, and the debts run up to pay for the imported machinery designed to enhance the prospects of industrialisation. Africa was caught in the jaws of a vice; to make matters worse most of the borrowed money went on projects utterly inappropriate for the needs of developing countries.

To crown it all, the West then imposed economic policies on the indebted countries that made matters a lot worse. The idea behind structural adjustment was that countries would export their way out of trouble, but since they were often one- or two-commodity economies, attempting to increase exports involved increasing supply, which drove down prices.

Aid agencies argue that action to help the poorest countries is long overdue. Addressing Chase Manhattan shareholders on the eve of the Ali–Foreman showdown, Nelson Rockefeller said: 'I hope you enjoy the fight, because you're paying for it.' Rockefeller was wrong. The banks were bailed out by the IMF, who lent money to poor nations so they could pay off their commercial creditors. Zaire has not been so lucky. The people there are still picking up the tab.

(a) How did Africa's debt originate? How far were the development strategies adopted by the countries themselves to blame?

(b) What facts does the article identify to illustrate the poor economic and social position of the African countries?

(c) What are the most appropriate policies for African countries to adopt in order to tackle the problem of extreme poverty? What should the rich countries' role in this process be?

E ANSWERS

Q1. Deciding on what constitutes a *basic need* is to some extent a normative judgement. Clearly, adequate food, shelter, clothing, warmth, health care, sanitation, care for the elderly and those without work, etc. can be regarded as basic needs, but there is still the problem of deciding what constitutes 'adequate'. The other items in the list could *all* be regarded as basic needs: it depends on people's value judgements. This is clearly a problem for defining development.

Q2. Problems are: what items to include, how to measure them, how to weight them (given that they are expressed in different units), how to take distribution into account.

Q3. *Yes*: (a), (b), (f), (g) and (i).
No: (c), (d), (e) and (h).

Q4. understate. Many subsistence items will not be included.

Q5. overstate. As people now begin to purchase items (which thus get included in GNY statistics) that they would previously have produced themselves (and which would not have been included in GNY statistics), so it appears that production is growing faster than it really is.

Q6. *(a)* Yes. Real rates of interest are often kept deliberately low by governments in order to encourage investment. This has the effect, however, of worsening the shortage of saving.

(b) Yes. The market is often too small to allow effective competition.

(c) No. Although wage rates are very low, they are typically *above* the market-clearing level

(perhaps because of minimum wage legislation). There is often high unemployment as a result.

(d) Yes. This is often the result of import restrictions, which thus improve the balance of trade. Foodstuffs and raw materials thus come cheaply into the country, while exporters find it difficult to export profitably.

(e) Yes. There is often huge variation in protection rates.

(f) Yes. The only source of loans is often the local moneylender, who may charge exorbitant interest rates.

(g) No. Typically they are kept artificially low by price controls. This makes farming less profitable.

(h) Yes.

Q7. *primary* (food and minerals).

Q8. *secondary* (manufactures).

Q9. (a) (iii), (b) (iv), (c) (ii), (d) (i).

Q10. *False*. By countries specialising in goods which are intensive in the abundant (and hence relatively low-priced) factors of production, this will result in an increase in the demand for these factors, an increase in their relative price, and hence an erosion of inequalities.

Q11. *(a)* Yes: the rate of growth in GNY may thus be correspondingly less for primary producers.

(b) Yes: especially if mines and plantations are foreign *owned* and if they have monopsony power in employing local labour.

(c) No: they have a low income elasticity of demand. The demand for primaries therefore grows only slowly as the world economy grows.

(d) No: developing countries tend to be price takers (facing a virtually infinitely elastic demand curve).

(e) Yes: the demand for developing countries' primary exports is likely to grow less rapidly than the demand by developing countries for manufactured imports.

(f) No: the terms of trade are likely to decline: the price of manufactured imports is likely to grow more rapidly than the price of primary exports.

(g) Yes: and hence their demand grows rapidly over time.

(h) No: there are few if any domestic substitutes.

(i) Yes: their world demand and supply is less price elastic and the supply curve is subject to shifts.

(j) Yes: mining can lead to the despoiling of the countryside, damage to the health of miners and the breaking up of communities. Plantations can also lead to undesirable ecological, social and cultural effects.

Q12. A strategy of building up domestic manufacturing industries by protecting them from competing imports.

Q13. A. Thus a finished product would have higher tariff protection than component parts. This therefore allows a firm setting up in assembly to import the components at a lower tariff than that protecting it from imports of the finished good.

Q14. *True*. By setting up plants in the developing country, the multinationals will receive the protection themselves. If, however, they were to attempt to export to the country from plants abroad, they would be faced by the trade barriers.

Q15. *(a)* Yes: firms are protected from foreign competition.

(b) No: often governments have kept interest rates low in order to encourage investment. Also with less pressure on the current account of the balance of payments, there is less need for a surplus on the short-term financial account.

(c) Yes: the improvement in the balance of payments from the protectionism pushes up the exchange rate.

(d) No: it has led to relatively higher urban wages compared with rural wages.

(e) Yes: the overvalued exchange rate has made it less profitable to export primaries. The higher prices of manufactured goods, combined with low food prices, have worsened the rural–urban terms of trade (a unit of agricultural produce buys fewer manufactured products than before).

(f) Yes: enormous differences in effective rates occur from one product to another, thus causing huge market distortions.

(g) No: given tariff escalation, effective protective rates have generally been above nominal rates.

Q16. Other problems include: social/cultural problems of urban living, often in appalling conditions; environmental costs of industrialisation; increased inequality (between the urban and rural sectors, between the employed and unemployed, between relatively high-paid jobs in some industries and pittance wages in others); increased dependence on specific imports (raw materials, capital equipment and component parts) often from monopoly suppliers; inefficiency due to lack of competition.

Q17. *True*. Export-orientated countries such as South Korea and Singapore have had exceptionally high growth rates (except during the Asian crisis of 1997–8).

Q18. They should be labour-intensive goods (or at least be produced using relatively labour-intensive techniques).

Q19. E. Devaluation increases the profits from exports; removal of tariff barriers helps to reduce the exchange rate and also reverse the bias towards the home market; reductions in employment taxes reduce the costs of producing (labour-intensive) exports.

Q20. *small*: such countries are likely to have a much more limited home market.

Q21. *substantial*: the domestic market under such circumstances is likely to be too small for production at minimum costs.

Q22. Drawbacks include: possible continuing neglect of agricultural sector; trade barriers to developing countries' manufactured exports erected by advanced countries; difficulties in competing against other developing country exporters already established in various markets; risks of shifts in world trading conditions and a rise in protectionism.

Q23. (a) *Low*, (b) *High*, (c) *Overvalued*, (d) *High*, (e) *High*, (f) *Low*.

Q24. Examples include: increasing food prices; provision of rural infrastructure (roads, irrigation schemes, distribution agencies, etc.); provision of low-interest finance to the rural sector; education and training in new techniques; land reform; the encouragement of rural co-operatives.

Q25. *above*.

Q26. *capital*.

Q27. *contradicts*. The Heckscher–Ohlin theory suggests that a labour-abundant country ought to choose labour-intensive techniques.

Q28. E. (i) is incorrect (see answer to Q33). In the case of (iii), if the techniques are more sophisticated they may economise not only on labour, but also (to a lesser extent) on capital costs and thus have a lower capital/output ratio as well as a lower labour/capital and labour/output ratio.

Q29. Possible disadvantages include: capital-intensive techniques may require more maintenance; they may require more imported raw materials, equipment and components; they may involve more pollution; they may provide only very limited employment.

Q30. *(a) underemployment.*
(b) disguised unemployment.

Q31. *True*. This 'surplus' labour is supported because they are either the owners of the land themselves or are part of a family which owns the land and is therefore prepared to support its relatives.

Q32. Because the extra jobs encourage people to migrate from the countryside to the towns, but more than one person migrates for each extra job created.

Q33. *True*: (a), (c), (e) and (g).
False: (b), (d) and (f).

Q34. C. Higher food prices will discourage migration, as will rural infrastructure projects. Investment in the towns may create more urban jobs, but it is likely to encourage more migration and thereby increase urban unemployment.

Q35. E. The economy has various structural rigidities that prevent aggregate supply expanding to meet increases in aggregate demand despite large-scale unemployed resources.

Q36. *True*.

Q37. Just because inflation is accompanied by increases in the money supply, this does not necessarily mean that the cure for inflation is a simple one of controlling the money supply. Money supply may be endogenously determined, and even if governments could control the money supply, they may choose not to, finding it to their advantage to finance government expenditure through the 'printing presses' rather than through higher taxes. Even when governments do attempt to reduce the growth of the money supply (perhaps because of pressure from the IMF) this may involve large-scale cuts in government expenditure or tax increases, and huge problems of hardship for the poor.

Q38. (a) *higher*, (b) *lower* (inflation was generally lower), (c) *tighter*, (d) *deeper*, (e) *longer lasting*, (f) *variable*, (g) *commercial bank*, (h) *more*.

Q39. The length of loan could be extended; a temporary delay could be granted in repaying loans due to mature; countries could be allowed to pay interest only (rather than capital as well) for a period of time; countries could acquire new loans on more favourable terms and use them to pay off the old debts.

Q40. *Paris*. (Note that the Toronto and Houston terms were new Paris Club agreements negotiated at these two places. These new terms allowed greater concessions to be made to low-income debtor countries and lower-middle-income debtor countries respectively.)

Q41. *London*.

Q42. A. Loans are granted to developing countries to help finance their debt, but instead of it being used to pay previous debts or to restructure the economy, it is simply put on deposit by private individuals or firms in foreign banks, or used for the purchase of foreign property or stocks and shares.

Q43. (a) (vi), (b) (i), (c) (iv), (d) (vii), (e) (ii), (f) (v), (g) (iii).

Q44. The IMF generally favours market-based solutions combined with tight demand-side policies. These include (a), (b), (f), (g), (h), (i) and (j).

Q45. Disadvantages include: economic recession while inflation is being squeezed out of the economy – this may take a long time; higher initial inflation as price controls are removed; greater inequality; increased structural unemployment; more vulnerability of the economy to world economic fluctuations.

Q46. The debt thresholds have been set too high, with the resulting reduction in debt being too low; countries have to have adhered to two three-year IMF structural adjustment programmes (reduced to one three-year programme in 1999) before they can receive debt reduction – but debt relief is needed more quickly than that; countries have to pay any arrears to multilateral agencies, such as the IMF or World Bank, before they can receive debt reduction; the IMF structural adjustment programmes are very harsh and can cause great hardship for the very poor.